The European Economy Since 1914

The fifth edition of *The European Economy* provides a succinct and lucid account of the development and problems of the European economy since the first world war. It covers the whole of Europe including Russia and Turkey. The text divides into several clearly defined sub-periods: the impact and aftermath of the First World War and recovery and reconstruction during the 1920s; the depression and the recovery of the 1930s; the impact of the Second World War and the new political division in Europe; the post-war boom of the 1950s and 1960s and then into the growth slowdown of the 1970s and the persistent problems of inflation and unemployment. It then analyses the demise of the centrally planned economies of eastern Europe and the move to a more united Europe and then discusses the financial and economic problems that have emerged in the early twenty-first century.

This new edition has been extensively revised, new chapters have been added and the reading lists updated.

Though the volume is designed as a basic introductory text the authors elicit some of the lessons that can be learnt from a study of past development, one of which is the limited power of governments to influence the course of events and to combat the operation of market forces.

Derek H. Aldcroft is University Fellow in the School of Historical Studies in the University of Leicester.

Steven Morewood is Senior Lecturer in International History in the University of Birmingham.

The European Economy Since 1914

5th Edition

Derek H. Aldcroft and
Steven Morewood

 Routledge
Taylor & Francis Group

LONDON AND NEW YORK

First published 1978
Fifth edition published 2013
by Routledge
2 Park Square, Milton Park, Abingdon, Oxon OX14 4RN

Simultaneously published in the USA and Canada
by Routledge
711 Third Avenue, New York, NY 10017

Routledge is an imprint of the Taylor & Francis Group, an informa business

British Library Cataloguing in Publication Data
A catalogue record for this book is available from the British Library.

Library of Congress Cataloging in Publication Data
A catalog record for this book has been requested.

ISBN: 978-0-415-43889-6 (hbk)
ISBN: 978-0-415-43890-2 (pbk)
ISBN: 978-0-203-09476-1 (ebk)

Typeset in Times New Roman
by RefineCatch Limited, Bungay, Suffolk

MIX
Paper from
responsible sources
FSC
www.fsc.org   FSC® C004839

Printed and bound in Great Britain by the MPG Books Group

Contents

Figures and tables

Figures

Tables

Maps

Preface

For this fifth edition, the opportunity has been taken to carry out a major overhaul of the text. Several chapters have been rewritten, some have been split into two, additional material has been incorporated to take account of recent research and the bibliography has been revised and extended. Two new chapters have been written to bring the account up to date and several maps have been inserted. Given the significant contribution made by Dr Steven Morewood, it seemed appropriate at this stage to make this a joint-authored volume.

Grateful thanks are extended to Dr Richard Jones of the School of Historical Studies at Leicester University for very helpful assistance with computing technicalities and map scanning. Due acknowledgement is also accorded to John Mitchell CPA, Financial Controller, Southside Mitsubishi, for providing invaluable secretarial support while Derek Aldcroft was in Perth and to Dr Elizabeth Stephens, political risk analyst at JLT Group, for reviewing the new chapters.

Derek H. Aldcroft
University of Leicester

Steven Morewood
University of Birmingham

Abbreviations

CAP Common Agricultural Policy
CMEA or Comecon Council for Mutual Economic Assistance
EBRD European Bank for Reconstruction and Development
EC European Community
ECA Economic Cooperation Administration
ECB European Central Bank
EEC European Economic Community
EFSB European Financial Stability Fund
EPU European Payments Union
EFSF European Financial Stability Facility
EFTA European Free Trade Association
EIB European Investment Bank
EMI European Monetary Institute
EMU Economic and Monetary Union
ERM Exchange Rate Mechanism
ERP European Recovery Programme
EU European Union
FDI foreign direct investment
GATT General Agreement on Tariffs and Trade
GDP gross domestic product
GDR German Democratic Republic
GNP gross national product
IBRD International Bank for Reconstruction and Development
IMF International Monetary Fund
IT information technology
ITO International Trade Organization
NAIRU non-accelerating inflation rate of unemployment
OEEC Organization for European Economic Cooperation
PASOK Panhellenic Socialist Movement
PHARE Poland and Hungary Assistance for Restructuring the Economy
PIIG Portugal, Ireland, Italy and Greece
SDR Special Drawing Rights

SEM single European market
UNRRA United Nations Relief and Rehabilitation Administration
WTO World Trade Organisation
WWW World Wide Web

Introduction

Both politically and economically, the twentieth century was more turbulent than the nineteenth. Two world wars and a great depression are sufficient to substantiate this claim. And if the 1950s and 1960s seem by comparison relatively stable, the history of Europe since then suggests that this may not necessarily be the natural order of things.

The liberal and fairly stable order of the first decade or so of the twentieth century was rudely shattered by the outbreak of the First World War. Up to that time, international development and political relations, though subject to strains of a minor nature from time to time, had never been seriously exposed to an external shock of such violent magnitude. Unfortunately, at the time, few people realized what a lengthy war it was going to be, and even fewer appreciated what an enormous impact it was going to have on economic and social relationships. Moreover, there was a general belief, accepted readily in establishment circles, that after the period of hostilities it would be possible to resume where one had left off – in other words to recreate the *belle époque* of the Edwardian era.

This was not to be, however, though for nearly a decade statesmen strove to get back to what they regarded as 'normalcy'. In itself, this was one of the profound mistakes of the first post-war decade, because it should have been clear that the war and post-war clearing-up operations had shattered Europe's former equipoise and had sapped her strength to a point at which the economic system had become vulnerable to external shocks. Moreover, it was not only in the economic field that her strength had been eroded; both politically and socially, Europe was weakened and many countries in the early post-war years were on the verge of social upheaval.

For the most part, Europe's economic and political fragility was ignored in the 1920s, out of ignorance rather than intent. In trying to resurrect the pre-war system, statesmen believed that they were providing a solution, and the fact that Europe shared in the prosperity of the later 1920s seemed to indicate that their judgement had not been misplaced. But as soon as the bubble of prosperity burst in 1929, the vulnerability of the European economy became apparent. The structural supports were too weak to withstand violent shock and so the edifice came tumbling down.

It is not surprising therefore that the years 1929–32 saw one of the worst depressions in history. Nor given the state of economic science at the time is it surprising that governments adopted policies that served only to worsen the crisis. Moreover, the policies adopted tended to be of a protective nature designed to insulate domestic economies from the influence of external events. When recovery came in 1933, it owed relatively little to policy considerations, though subsequently some governments did attempt more ambitious programmes of stimulation. But recovery, at least in terms of employment generation, was slow and patchy, so that even by 1937 many countries were still operating well below their resource capacity. The gap was subsequently closed by rearmament and the outbreak of the Second World War.

Europe entered this second major conflict in a relatively weaker state than in it had in 1914, and subsequently emerged from it in 1945 in a more prostrate condition than in 1918. Certainly, in terms of the loss of life, physical destruction and decline in living standards, Europe's position was much worse than after the First World War. On the other hand, both during the war and in the post-war reconstruction phase of the late 1940s, some of the mistakes and blunders of the earlier experience were avoided. Inflation was contained more readily between 1939 and 1945 and the violent inflations of the early 1920s were not for the most part repeated in the aftermath of the Second World War (Hungary and Greece excepted). The map of Europe was divided more clearly and neatly (with the exception of Berlin) than had been the case after 1918, even though it resulted in two major power blocs, the east and the west. The vanquished were not burdened by unreasonable exactions, which had been the cause of so much bitterness and squabbling in the 1920s, though the Soviet Union did impose harsh retribution on some of its satellites. Finally, governments no longer looked backwards to the halcyon pre-war days; this time, it was planning for the future that occupied their attention. This line of thought was reflected in the commitment to maintain a high level of employment and all that this entailed in terms of growth and stability. On a wider plane, it also found positive expression in the readiness to cooperate internationally to further reconstruction, and the liberal American aid programme of the later 1940s was a concrete manifestation of the new approach.

Thus by the early 1950s, Europe had recovered sufficiently to be in a position to look to the future with confidence. During the next two decades, her record of economic advancement was better than anything previously recorded, and this is true of both western and eastern Europe. The latter forged ahead under a planned regime, while the western democracies achieved their success under a mixed enterprise system, with varying degrees of market freedom. In both cases, however, the state played a more important role than hitherto, and neither system was free of problems. The planning mechanism in eastern Europe functioned less smoothly than its proponents anticipated, with the result that it had to be modified in due course. The market system of the west also seemingly failed to register the right results on occasions so that governments were forced to interfere to an increasing extent. The biggest problem was trying to achieve a series of objectives (full employment, price stability, growth, stability and external equilibrium) simultaneously. In practice it proved impossible given the policy weapons available to governments.

Despite what seemed to be incompatible objectives, there was little cause for serious alarm throughout the period. It is true that there were minor lapses from full employment and fluctuations still occurred, but these were moderate and took the form of growth cycles; some countries experienced balance-of-payments problems, while prices rose continuously, though at moderate annual rates. But such lapses could be accommodated within an economic system that was growing rapidly. By the late 1960s, it seemed that Europe had entered a phase of perpetual prosperity akin to what the Americans had conceived in the 1920s. However, it was not long before that particular illusion was shattered. By 1974, the growth trend had been reversed, the business cycle had reappeared and most western governments were experiencing inflation at a rate higher than at any time in the last half century. Henceforward and through to the 1990s, growth was less robust and governments faced an uphill struggle to stabilize their economies against a background of competing demands. With the collapse of the Soviet bloc and the more vigorous efforts to forge a united Europe, a new chapter in the history of Europe was in the process of unfolding at the turn of the millennium.

The chapters that follow examine Europe's development since 1914 along the lines indicated above. They aim to show the main trends in that development and the forces that have determined it. Though the volume is designed primarily as an introductory text, it is hoped that readers will be able to draw some lessons from the study of European economic development over the past century and beyond. Perhaps one of the most important is that governments have not become more adept at dealing with economic and financial problems despite the greater degree of policy intervention over time. When confronted by serious problems such as inflation, depression, fiscal deficits and unemployment, they have often been unable to respond in a positive and constructive way. What is especially note-worthy is that they have been powerless to combat market forces and often their policies have exacerbated rather than alleviated the problems. For example, take the case of inflation in the 1920s and the 1970s: initially policies were generally too accommodating and hence intensified the inflationary pressures, while cos-metic measures such as the control of prices, incomes and profits were no substi-tute for monetary restraint to eliminate the main underlying source of inflation. Hence the eventual policy to bring inflation under control had to be more severe, with serious consequences for the real economy. Another example is the efforts to combat recessionary forces, which often proved counterproductive, because when real growth forces were weak anyway, there was little governments could do to revive the economy. The recent experience from 2008 onwards is an excellent case in point. Ironically, probably the best practice was in the much-maligned crisis of the 1930s, when Schumpeterian creative capacity destruction was allowed to run its course and then an easing of monetary policy provided the conditions for real growth forces to re-emerge naturally. Fiscal policy was kept under tight rein (a lesson for today!), which raised confidence in financial markets, while the international currency crisis was gradually rectified by the formation of defined currency blocs, the chief one of which was the sterling area. The sterling area currency was stronger and more stable than the current euro.

In more recent times, financial problems and fiscal deficits have dominated the scene. The two are of course interrelated. In the first years of the present century, governments were bent on forcing growth along an unsustainable trajectory, partly by increasing public spending at a faster rate than the growth of the real economy. This was a fatal mistake because it caused a massive jump in budgetary deficits and public debt levels in many countries, especially Greece, Italy, Spain, Portugal, and Ireland, and even Britain and France were not immune. This also stimulated a large rise in consumer indebtedness, which in turn was aggravated by the irresponsible lending and credit policies of banking and financial institutions. Inevitably, this put pressure on currencies, especially the euro, which was at the centre of the crisis. Until fiscal deficits are reduced and the terms of the Maastricht treaty are adhered to strictly, the threat to financial and monetary systems remains.

Technically, many of the economic problems encountered during the past century are not especially difficult to solve. The real issue is that politics gets in the way of straightforward solutions. Governments and policy-makers are terrified of the political and social consequences of taking firm action. Rostow (1979) has neatly summarized the political and social constraints involved in this context: 'Taxes, public expenditure, interest rates, and the supply of money are not determined antiseptically by men free to move economies along a Phillips curve to an optimum trade-off between the rate of unemployment and the rate of inflation. Fiscal and monetary policy are, inevitably, living parts of the democratic political process.'

There are many lessons to be gleaned from a study of European development over time and readers should bear in mind that this is perhaps the most interesting and useful exercise of historical study. Had governments, and for that matter many financial institutions, taken more heed of the past, they might have improved their policy performance over time. Sadly, this has not been the case, and we can but hope that this volume helps to improve knowledge and lessons of the past.

Finally, and most important of all in view of the current economic climate, the sooner governments and policymakers recognise that the euro standard, like the gold exchange standard before it, is constraining economies and policy formation, the better. The constraint can only be relieved by abandoning the euro standard.

Because the study is designed primarily as an introductory overview, it of necessity deals in fairly broad aggregates. Readers who wish to inquire further into specific areas and topics should consult the chapter reading lists at the end of this book.

Map 1 The impact of the First World War

Source: J. Lee, *The European Dictatorships*, London: Methuen, 1987.

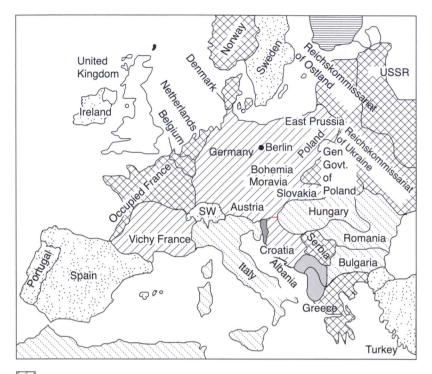

Extent of the Third Reich

States under German occupation or administration

Puppet regimes under German influence

Germany's allies, including Italy

Italian acquisitions

Neutral states

States at war with Germany and her allies

Map 2 Germany at war 1939–45

Source: J. Lee, *The European Dictatorships*, London: Methuen, 1987.

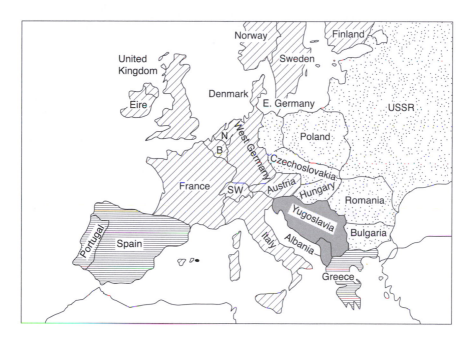

Communist states under the influence of the USSR

Communist states eventually outside the Soviet bloc

States experiencing right-wing regimes but eventually establishing parliamentary democracies

Parliamentary democracies

Map 3 The political division of Europe after 1945

Source: J. Lee, *The European Dictatorships*, London: Methuen, 1987.

Map 4 Eastern Europe in 1993

Source: D. Johnson and L. Miles, *Eastern Europe: Economic Challenges and Business Opportunities*, Hull: Hidcote Press, 1994.

Political Map of Europe

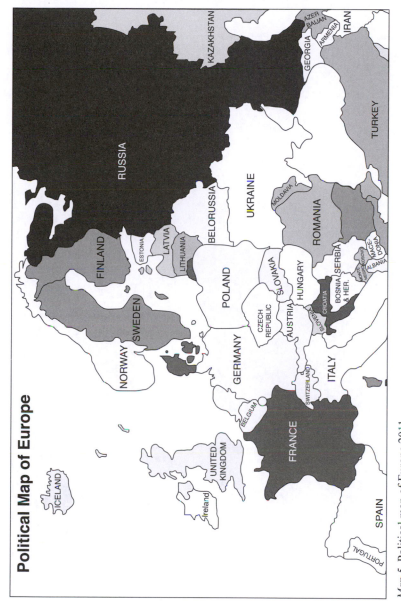

Map 5 Political map of Europe 2011

Source: Current History, Inc.

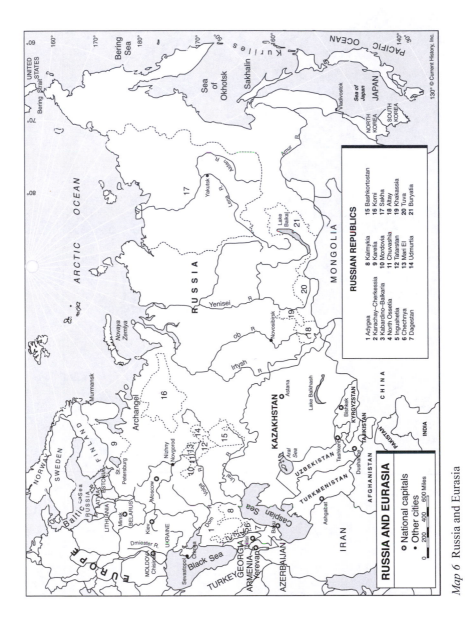

Map 6 Russia and Eurasia

Source: Current History, Inc.

1 The end of the old order, 1914–21

Introduction

During the nineteenth century, the European continent (taken here to include Britain at one extreme in the west to Russia in the east) had experienced substantial economic development. Few countries had failed to be affected in some way by the forces of modern economic growth, which had had their origins in the northwest corner of the continent. As Pollard rightly points out, the development process may be seen as a general European phenomenon transcending national frontiers rather than as something confined to the geographic boundaries of a few states. On the other hand, economic growth was very uneven in its incidence, although in comparison with more recent times rates of economic growth were modest. The centre of progress was undoubtedly in northwest Europe (Britain, France, Germany, Belgium, Holland), whence it spread south and east through the rest of the continent, getting weaker the further it moved from the point of origin. It is true that in the later nineteenth century and through to 1914 the pace of economic change was rapid in some of the lesser developed countries, notably Italy, Austria and Russia. Even so, by the eve of the First World War most of the countries of east and southeast Europe remained backward compared with the northwest. Incomes per head on average in southern and eastern Europe were one-half or less those in the northwest, and in some cases (for example, Bulgaria, Romania, Spain and Greece), they were but a fraction of those prevailing in the most developed sector of the continent. In fact, an income contour map for Europe would show (with minor exceptions) income contour lines of steadily diminishing strength as one moved south and east from the 'high pressure' zone of advanced development.

Though eastern and southern Europe undoubtedly benefited from the transmission of growth forces from the point of origin, modern capitalism found more fertile ground in some overseas territories, particularly in North America and Oceania, than it did elsewhere in Europe. These regions were more receptive to the flows of European capital, labour and technology, so much so that by 1913, incomes per head were already above those in northwest Europe. What is more, these three areas (northwest Europe, North America and Oceania, more especially the first two) monopolized modern economic development. They accounted for the bulk of the world's manufacturing production, and though containing only

18 per cent of the world's population, they accounted for nearly 62 per cent of global income.

To a certain extent, Europe's position was already being challenged by developments overseas, more especially by the rapid rise in the economic strength of the United States. But the threat to European supremacy was not at this stage serious, because in many respects developments in both continents were partly complementary. Moreover, the world order of the pre-war period was such as to ensure the survival of both parties. The strength of pre-war capitalist development rested on the freedom with which resources could be transferred between nations, the ease with which the industrial nations of the centre, especially northwest Europe, could draw upon the primary resources (food and raw materials) of the periphery (mainly but not exclusively the less developed nations) and the fact that there was no serious disparity in the rate of economic progress among the major industrial countries. The latter point is important because it was this rather than the commonly alleged virtues of the international gold standard that gave the pre-war system a measure of stability, a stability that was regarded with some nostalgia in the years of disequilibrium after the First World War.

What would have happened to this set-up had the 1914–18 war not intervened is a debatable counterfactual proposition, which will no doubt be put to the test in the course of time. However, one can say with certainty that the war affected Europe's economic position adversely. Europe emerged from the war in a seriously weakened state and with a residue of problems that were to plague it and the international economy for much of the inter-war period. But whether the war can be blamed for all the difficulties of that period or whether it can be regarded as a direct cause of the slump of 1929–32 are matters that will be taken up at a later point in this study. Some of the more immediate consequences of the war must be considered first.

Given the scale of the European war, it is hardly surprising that the consequences were far-reaching. Resource mobilization exceeded anything previously known. Altogether more than 60 million men were drafted into the armed services during the four years or so of hostilities, and in all belligerent countries there was extensive control of economic activity, especially in the latter half of the period. The details of wartime operations and resource mobilization need not concern us here because the primary interest is to determine the main consequences of war, and more especially those that have a bearing on subsequent events in the 1920s and early 1930s.

However, it is important to distinguish between the direct economic consequences of war and the policy actions of the Allied governments in the immediate aftermath. The war itself gave rise to workforce losses, physical destruction, financial disorganization, a contraction in output and unstable social and political conditions. Given the weakened state of many countries, especially in central and eastern Europe, the process of reconstruction and recovery required the assistance of the Allied powers, the United States in particular. In fact, as we shall see, not only was the amount of direct assistance forthcoming minimal, but the process of reconstruction was hindered by the peace treaty settlements and the policies adopted to deal with the boom of 1919–20.

Population losses

It is difficult to make an exact count of the population losses arising from the war. This is partly because the data for the period are far from perfect but also because military casualties were but a small proportion of the total number of deaths recorded in the period. Many more people died of starvation and disease, or as a result of civil war, than on the battlefield. In addition, some estimate must be made of the population deficit caused by the shortfall in births as a result of wartime conditions. The Russian statistics are notoriously difficult to interpret.

Military casualties were small in relative terms. During the period of hostilities some 8.5 million men (including tentative guesses for Russia) lost their lives in active service, that is, about 15 per cent of those mobilized for duty. This was equivalent to less than 2 per cent of the total European population and about 8 per cent of all male workers. In addition, some 7 million men were permanently disabled and a further 15 million more or less seriously wounded.

The incidence of fatalities varied considerably, although obviously the belligerents were the main sufferers. The largest absolute losses were in Germany and Russia, with 2 and 1.7 million, respectively; France lost 1.4 million, Austria-Hungary 1.2 million and the UK and Italy almost three-quarters of a million each. Some of the smaller countries such as Romania (250,000) and Serbia and Montenegro (325,000) also suffered badly. However, in most cases, the proportionate impact in terms of population was small. Of the major powers, France was the chief loser, with 3.3 per cent of the population killed through military action; Germany was not far behind, with 3 per cent; in most other cases the proportion was 2 per cent or less. In fact, in relative terms, the smaller countries came off worst generally; Serbia and Montenegro, for example, lost 10 per cent of their population.

Of course, the impact was greater than the absolute figures indicate because most of the persons killed were in the prime of their life and therefore constituted the most productive part of the labour force. In the case of Germany, 40 per cent of the casualties fell within the age group 20–24 and 63 per cent were between 20 and 30 years old. Both France and Germany lost about 10 per cent of their male workers, Italy 6 per cent and Britain 5 per cent. On the other hand, callous as it may sound, the losses may have been something of a blessing in disguise given the limited employment opportunities that were to eventuate in the inter-war period.

Civilian losses are more difficult to determine; these arose from several causes, including disease, famine, and privation as well as military conflict, the assumption being that they would not have occurred but for the war. War-induced deaths of civilians probably amounted to about 5 million in Europe excluding Russia, with Austria-Hungary, Germany and Italy bearing the brunt of the burden in absolute terms, though once again Serbia and Montenegro experienced the greatest relative impact.

Adding together military and civilian deaths gives a combined death toll for Europe excluding Russia in the region of 12 million, of which just over 6.5 million were due to military causes. This amounted to some 3.5 per cent of Europe's pre-war population. Germany and Austria-Hungary had the largest absolute losses, while in relative terms mortality ranged from about one per cent in Scandinavia to as much as 20 per cent in Serbia. France, Italy, Germany and Austria-Hungary lost about 4 per cent of their populations, and the UK and Belgium under 2.5 per cent.

Account must also be taken of the birth deficits or numbers of unborn arising from wartime conditions. Some of the belligerents recorded very high birth deficits: Austria-Hungary, 3.6 million; Germany, 3 million; France and Italy had deficits of about 1.5 million; Britain, 700,000; and Romania, just over 500,000. Altogether the population loss from this cause was similar to the combined figure for military and civilian deaths.

The combined tally of the European population deficit therefore amounts to between 22 and 24 million people. This was equivalent to 7 per cent of Europe's pre-war population, or the whole of her natural increase between 1914 and 1919. Thus, at the beginning of 1920, Europe's population was about the same as it was at the start of the war. The largest absolute losses were incurred by Germany and Austria-Hungary, with over 5 million apiece, but in relative terms, Serbia and Montenegro were by far the worst sufferers, with deficits approaching one-third of their pre-war population. The neutral powers fared best, with losses of two per cent or less. Of the Allied powers, France and Italy bore the brunt of the burden. France's population deficit amounted to just over 3 million, or 7.7 per cent of her pre-war population. This includes a shortfall of some 1.4 million in births as a result of a dramatic decline in her birth rate. The net result was that by the middle of 1919 France's population, at 38.7 million, was some 1.1 million lower than in 1914, even with the inclusion of Alsace-Lorraine, which she had recovered from Germany.

The figures for Russia are less reliable, though it is probable that losses in this country exceeded the combined total for the rest of Europe. Military casualties in the Great War itself were relatively small, but millions died in the subsequent revolution and civil war. The total toll was not far short of 16 million. Add to this some 10 million for birth deficits and one gets a figure of 26 million, and even this takes no account of the losses in the territories ceded by Russia as a result of the peace treaty concluded with Germany in 1918.

Europe therefore suffered a serious depletion and deterioration in quality of population during the war period. Moreover, the figures cited are not strictly complete because further losses, arising from causes associated with the war, occurred in the post-armistice period. The influenza epidemic of 1918–19 claimed many victims, and substantial numbers of people died in eastern Europe and the Balkans as a result of famine. Post-war border conflicts and massacres between 1919 and 1921, especially in southeastern Europe, added further to the toll.

In sum, therefore, the final casualty list for the whole war period and post-war period (1914–21), runs into many millions. An approximate figure would be between 50 and 60 million, with Russia accounting for around one-half. Direct military deaths in the war proper formed only a small proportion of the total population loss in this period.

In human terms, the disaster can be regarded as nothing short of tragic. But it is doubtful whether the loss had a severe or lasting impact on the countries concerned. Of course, most countries lost some of their best workforce, often highly skilled, but few, apart from France, suffered from labour shortages in the decade following the war. Indeed, as it turned out, the post-war period was marked by high unemployment in many European countries and so it could be argued that the check to population growth was something of a mixed blessing.

Physical destruction and capital losses

Capital losses are even less easy to estimate with accuracy than those of population. The value of Europe's capital stock undoubtedly deteriorated during the war as a result of physical damage, the sale of foreign assets, the check to investment and the neglect of maintenance. Stamp calculated that the war destroyed some three to four years' normal growth of income-yielding property in Europe (excluding Russia), or one part in thirty of its original value, and to this must be added an unknown quantity for the deterioration of the existing capital stock as a result of neglect or lack of maintenance. Europe also lost about one-thirtieth of her fixed assets as a result of destruction and physical damage, and some countries, notably France and Germany, relinquished most of their foreign investments. In addition, of course, some countries sacrificed territory and property under the peace treaty settlements. This aspect is discussed separately in a later section.

The incidence of the destructive impact varied considerably from country to country. The neutral countries (Scandinavia, the Netherlands, Switzerland and Spain) escaped unscathed and in some cases were in better physical shape in 1919 than at the beginning of the war. Most of the belligerent countries, on the other hand, experienced substantial cuts in investment, with the result that their capital stocks were lower at the end of hostilities. Physical damage was greatest in the main theatres of war, especially in France and Belgium, though Italy, Russia and some eastern European countries also fared badly. By comparison, Britain, Austria and Germany, though major belligerents, got off fairly lightly. Bulgaria too did much better than her neighbours on the Balkan peninsula, because the country never became a war zone and so avoided severe destruction or despoliation of property.

The occupied territories undoubtedly fared the worst because they shared the privations of the central empires while at the same time they were exploited to the utmost for the good of their temporary masters. It was inevitable that Belgium and France should bear the main burden given that much of the fighting occurred on their land. Destruction of farms, factories and houses was widespread and substantial in both cases, though in France most of the physical damage tended to be concentrated in the north of the country. Belgium was less fortunate. Practically the whole of the country was invaded and the list of damage makes dismal reading; about 6 per cent of the housing stock, half the steel mills and three-quarters of the railway rolling stock were destroyed or smashed beyond repair; thousands of acres of land were rendered unfit for cultivation; the animal population was destroyed.

Though geographically concentrated, France's losses were severe and they occurred in the richest and most advanced part of the country.

In absolute terms, these two countries accounted for the bulk of the wartime property losses. Yet in relative terms some of the smaller countries further east probably emerged from the war in an even more devastated condition. The value of property lost by Poland was only a little less than that of Germany, but the impact was very much greater. The occupying powers literally devastated the country by destruction and looting. Large tracts of good agricultural land were laid waste; 60 per cent of the cattle stock disappeared; much of the railway rolling stock was taken; many factories were either destroyed or denuded of equipment; and 1.8 million buildings were lost by fire. The same story could be told of Serbia, parts of Austria and also of Russia, though in the last case much of the damage occurred as a result of the civil war. In fact, in some areas, the scale of destruction was so great that the question of repair could scarcely be considered; rather it was a matter of clearing the land and rebuilding from scratch.

Elsewhere the physical damage was far lighter, though most countries had a substantial backlog of investment to work off. Germany lost few domestic assets, but most of her foreign assets were either sold or seized, and she was to pay a heavy price in reparations for her transgression. Most of Britain's physical losses consisted of shipping, though she did sell a small portion of her overseas investments to pay for the war. France lost about two-thirds of her pre-war foreign assets by sale, default (as in the case of Russian investments) or through inflation.

The task of reconstruction was certainly a substantial one and in some countries it could be accomplished only by a resort to inflationary financing. However, the process of European recovery as a whole was made more difficult because the peace treaty settlements imposed heavy penalties on the vanquished and proceeded to carve up the map of Europe in a manner detrimental to the economic well-being of the continent.

Financial legacies of war

The financial implications of the First World War were more serious than those of the second European conflict. Essentially, this was because the method of financial control was laxer in the first case, and not because the scale of military operations was greater; in fact, it was the reverse. The total direct cost was of course large (some 260 billion dollars if all the belligerents are included), though the absolute figures do not have a great deal of meaning. The largest expenditures were incurred by Britain, the United States, Germany, France, Austria-Hungary and Italy, in that order. An idea of the magnitude of the total outlay can be gained from the fact that it represented about six and a half times the sum of all the national debt accumulated in the world from the end of the eighteenth century up to the eve of the First World War.

The size of the war-expenditure programme is not particularly significant, though one could naturally point to the more fruitful and constructive ways in which the money might have been spent. What matters is the way the spending was financed. Almost overnight, governments hastily abandoned the sound financial orthodoxy of the nineteenth century, which meant abandonment of the discipline of the gold standard and a resort to deficit financing. Credit operations of one sort or another rather than taxation were the main source of war finance. For example, Germany and France relied almost entirely on borrowing, while even in the United States only just over 23 per cent of war expenditures was derived from revenue sources. On average, some 80 per cent or more of the total war expenditure of the belligerents was financed by borrowing. This method of financing the war need not have been unduly inflationary had the loans been derived from genuine savings, but in fact much of the finance was raised through bank credit. Banks either granted loans to governments by the creation of new money or else received 'promises to pay' from the governments and then proceeded to increase the supply of money using the promises as reserves. The details of the mechanism varied from one country to another, but the result was much the same. Public debts rose rapidly, with the proportion of short-term debt rising as time went on, the money supply was increased considerably, and the metallic reserves of the banks in relation to liabilities fell sharply. By the end of 1918, the German money supply had risen ninefold, the budget deficit six times, and the ratio of metallic reserves to bank notes and deposits had declined from 57 to 10 per cent. The situation was even worse in the case of the Austro-Hungarian Empire, and France and Belgium also fared badly. In general, the deterioration in financial conditions was most acute in central European countries, least acute in the neutral countries, and of moderate extent elsewhere.

Such conditions automatically gave rise to price inflation and currency depreciation, because nearly all countries abandoned the fixed parities of the gold standard either during the war or shortly thereafter. Inflation was more rapid than during the tighter financial regime of the Second World War. Most countries experienced a doubling or trebling of prices and, in some cases, much more, depending upon the degree of monetary inflation. For example, wholesale prices in Germany at the end of hostilities were five times the pre-war level, whereas the mark had declined to 50 per cent of its former value. Austria and Hungary experienced even greater inflation, with currency values falling to between 30 and 40 per cent of the original parity. Other countries whose currencies had begun to depreciate significantly were Finland, France, Italy, Belgium and Portugal. On the other hand, most of the neutrals managed to retain or improve the value of their currencies despite significant degrees of inflation. The loss in value of European currencies during and after the war can be seen from the data in Table 1.1.

The implications of the wartime financial arrangements are important and will be taken up in greater detail later. At the end of the war, the inflationary problems were not for the most part unmanageable, with the possible exceptions of those of Germany and Austria-Hungary. However, they were made worse in the first year or so of peace by continued lax monetary and fiscal policies. The policy turning-point came in 1920, when several countries (the United States, Britain and Sweden in particular) imposed savage retrenchment policies, which adversely affected

Table 1.1 Exchange rate values of European currencies (December averages, par value = 100)

	1918	1920	1923
Austria	31.3	3.2	0.01
Belgium	71.2	49.8	23.8
Bulgaria	–	13.7	4.2
Czechoslovakia	–	10.0	14.4
Denmark	101.0	70.1	66.4
Finland	62.6	15.9	12.9
France	95.2	47.9	27.2
Germany	50.8	8.8	(1)
Greece	100.0	84.9	9.8
Hungary	40.7	15.5	0.03
Italy	81.5	39.6	22.5
Netherlands	106.2	94.2	94.5
Norway	103.7	76.9	55.6
Poland	–	6.3	(2)
Portugal	61.5	30.9	3.3
Romania	–	18.2	2.7
Spain	106.8	101.1	67.4
Sweden	108.6	80.6	98.1
Switzerland	106.9	95.5	90.7
UK	97.8	78.3	89.6
Yugoslavia	–	25.7	5.9

(1) 0.000,000,000,084; (2) 0.000,034

Source: League of Nations 1943, 42.

their domestic economies and made recovery in the rest of Europe more difficult. However, most European countries continued to inflate, with disastrous consequences for some (notably Germany, Austria, Poland and Hungary). Second, currency instability hindered the process of long-term recovery, while the failure of governments to accept the decline in currency values and the abandonment of gold as anything but temporary eventually led to a disorganized attempt to try to restore the pre-war monetary system in different conditions. Third, reference may be made to the complex series of intergovernmental debts contracted among the Allies and the reparations burdens imposed on the vanquished, which not only proved a source of international friction throughout the 1920s but also hampered the process of financial reconstruction.

Europe's economic decline

Perhaps more serious than war losses and destruction from the long-term point of view was the severe check to European income and output growth during the war, and the fact that from this point, Europe's position in the world economy began to decline. Nearly all countries experienced a decline in output despite the exertions on the war front, and at the end of hostilities the stock of productive assets was in poor shape. At the same time, many European countries became dependent on external sources of supply and finance, while some were forced to sell both domestic and foreign assets. In a global context, the United States of course was the main beneficiary of war, and she in turn helped to finance the Allied cause and later became a source for European loans. However, the United States was not the only country to gain from the ordeal. Many countries on the periphery of the international economy received a stimulus from wartime demand for food and raw materials, while the shortage of manufactured goods in Europe accelerated the process of industrial development in overseas countries.

By the end of the war, the world as a whole was certainly worse off than in 1913–14, even though some countries, such as the United States and Japan, had considerably surpassed their pre-war levels of production. But in terms of output and income, the brunt of the burden fell on Europe. Svennilson has calculated that if there had been no war and the 1881–1913 European rate of industrial output growth had been maintained (3.25 per cent per annum), then the 1929 level of production would have been achieved in 1921. Thus, on a crude basis, it can be said that the war caused an eight-year setback to the growth of production.

Most countries suffered a reversal in the level of economic activity, especially during the latter part of the war, and given the run-down condition of fixed assets together with the dislocation after the war, levels of economic activity in 1919 and 1920 were still some way below those of 1913. The extent of the short-fall varied from country to country. By far the worst performance was recorded by Russia, where industrial output in 1920 was down to about 13 per cent of the 1913 figure. Here there were special circumstances to account for the disastrous performance, in particular the continuing border conflicts, the repercussions of the civil war through 1920, and the general chaos and mismanagement of the new Soviet regime. Indeed, the economy was in a state of complete collapse in 1920, and with justification Nove has referred to this period as one of 'nightmare conditions'.

No other country could match this dismal record, but many did experience a severe check to growth in the later years of war. Even by 1920, industrial output in Germany, France, Belgium, Bulgaria, Poland, Czechoslovakia, Austria, Hungary, Romania and Latvia was at least 30 per cent lower than in 1913. Yet even this was an improvement from the position prevailing immediately after the war, when in central and eastern Europe industrial production was about 50 to 60 per cent less than pre-war. Agricultural activity held up better, though even here there was a serious shortfall. Production was about one-third below normal in continental Europe, though in some of the devastated regions in France, Belgium and eastern Europe, the decline was considerably greater.

Most of the neutrals and one or two other countries fared better. Both Britain and Italy managed to regain their 1913 levels of output in 1920. However, Sweden, Norway and Switzerland did much better, and easily surpassed their previous peak levels of activity. The neutral countries, and Sweden in particular, benefited considerably from wartime demands, which caused a rapid expansion in heavy manufacturing and which gave rise to a number of innovations and new methods of production. For example, the metal shortage gave a boost to new methods of ore prospecting, and the kerosene shortage accelerated the process of electrification, while the rapid breakthrough in lightweight metals can be attributed to the same cause. However, there were losses as well as gains in the neutral countries. Apparent prosperity was purchased at the expense of a sharp rise in the cost of living, a shortage of essential commodities and a stagnation or decline of certain trades and classes of exports.

Europe's output loss would not have mattered so much had countries overseas not gained at her expense. The two chief beneficiaries were the United States and Japan. American production was boosted sharply by Allied requirements and demand from countries formerly supplied by Europe. America therefore ended the war with a large excess balance in commodity trade. Furthermore, largely as a result of loans floated on behalf of the European Allies and the liquidation of foreign holdings in the United States, America was transformed from net debtor status and became a large-scale creditor, a position that she strengthened during the course of the 1920s. Japan also emerged from the war in a stronger position. Her participation in the war was only marginal and she was therefore able to benefit from the opportunities opened up by the indisposition of the major belligerents. She became more industrialized and technically mature and, with a large increase in output to her credit, a creditor instead of a debtor nation. As a result, Japan became a serious competitor in many markets formerly supplied by European countries.

Japanese competition was not the only source of worry for European industrial countries. In many lesser-developed countries, wartime shortages and suspension of competition had provided the opportunity to expand the industrial sector. Wherever one looks, the story is the same: in the Far East, in Asia, in Latin America, in the White Dominions and even in parts of Africa, especially South Africa, acceleration in industrial activity can be discerned. Of course, some of it was little more than hot-house growth that withered away when trading conditions returned to normal and foreign supply was resumed. Even so, there is little doubt that many formerly dependent countries had become industrially more self-sufficient by the end of the war to the detriment of the European exporting nations. To add to Europe's difficulties, at least later in the 1920s when agricultural output recovered, the war gave a big stimulus to primary production, both food and raw materials, in overseas countries. The expansion of cereal output in particular was to pose a serious problem for high-cost European producers later in the 1920s, when overcapacity became endemic.

Thus the overall effect of the wartime check to activity was a shift in the balance of economic power away from Europe towards the Americas and to a lesser extent the Pacific. In the inter-war years, Europe never recovered her former economic power status. Much of the gain accrued to North America and Japan, though the war fostered sufficient interest in industrial activity in the lesser-developed areas to ensure that import substitution and subsequently export competition would increase rather than diminish in the decades following, to the detriment of Europe. The extent of the shift in power can be appreciated from the figures for the distribution of world trade: by 1920 the Americas accounted for 32.1 per cent of world trade as against 22.4 per cent in 1913, whereas Asia's share rose from 12.1 to 13.4 per cent. By contrast, the share of Europe and the USSR fell from 58.4 to 49.2 per cent over the same period. As it turned out, it was to be many years before Europe began to regain some of its former economic glory.

Structural problems

Svennilson has suggested that the European economy suffered a prolonged structural transformation crisis during the inter-war period; growth was slowed down because of formidable structural problems that the war had thrown into relief. Only countries that adapted rapidly to new conditions could hope to achieve a satisfactory performance; Sweden might be cited as one of the few examples. But even the most enterprising countries were not wholly immune to the more pervasive maladjustments arising out of the war, maladjustments in the international economic mechanism rather than simply problems of industrial structure with which Svennilson was most concerned.

In fact, it could be argued that the dislocation of economic relationships caused by the war was far more serious than actual physical destruction. It disrupted former economic systems and partially destroyed the elaborate and often delicate trading connections of the nineteenth century. For example, the whole system of banking, credit and organization of money markets was suspended, controlled or modified during the war and had to be reestablished or adjusted to new conditions. The delicate mechanism of the gold standard was abandoned and most currencies lost much of their former value and stability; indeed, the problem of currency stabilization became one of the crucial issues in the post-war years. New problems in the form of large internal debts, war debts among the Allied powers and massive reparations imposed on the vanquished made the problem of currency stabilization an even more difficult one. Severe capital shortages in central and eastern Europe hampered the process of reconstruction, which in turn accentuated the problem of currency stabilization. Furthermore, as we shall see, the redrawing of many boundaries in Europe entailed the recasting of trading connections and lines of transport and communication, the adoption of new currencies and, in some cases, the entire replanning of economic systems.

During the war the productive effort of belligerent countries, and to a certain extent that of the neutrals, was directed to new purposes; new trading links were often hastily improvised; and relations with former customers had to be severed. Many of the former trading links were lost for ever; others had to be painfully rekindled during the course of the 1920s at a time when import substitution and increasing production made the going more difficult. Thus the trading operations of the Baltic ports (Riga, Revel and Narva), as suppliers of products to the Russian Empire and as entrepôt centres in the trade between Russia and western Europe, were shattered beyond repair by 1918. Russia herself, the main source of some materials and an important supplier of timber and wheat, was cut off from the west after the civil war, only to reemerge again late in the 1920s as an exporter at a time when her products were least required. The break-up of the Austro-Hungarian Empire dealt a serious blow to the economic relationships established within central Europe during the latter half of the nineteenth century and necessitated the creation of altogether new patterns of trade and exchange among the successor countries. Similar problems, as noted earlier, were encountered by European countries in their trading connections overseas.

One of the most serious and intractable problems of the inter-war period was that of excess capacity. Even before 1914 there were signs that some industrial countries in Europe were beginning to experience excess capacity in certain sectors, and that a process of structural transformation associated with new technologies was imminent. The war accelerated this process and at the same time brought several new factors into play. In the process of servicing the war machine, certain sectors of activity became seriously overexpanded in relation to peacetime requirements, and, unfortunately, they were often the very sectors whose long-term growth potential was limited. Thus shipbuilding, iron and steel, some branches of engineering and coal were considerably expanded in the war, with the result that excess capacity developed in the 1920s. For example, world shipbuilding capacity almost doubled during the war, and by the time the post-war boom was complete, there was enough shipping space in existence to last a decade or more without further building. Iron and steel capacity of continental Europe and Britain was some 50 per cent higher by the mid-1920s than before the war, yet for much of the inter-war period output remained below the pre-war level. The coal industry was also affected adversely by a sharp deceleration in the growth of demand and the opening up of new seams on the continent. Moreover, the problem was by no means confined to Europe. Many countries overseas expanded their primary and industrial base in response to war demands, and inevitably this posed a threat to European producers once their production recovered. The situation was perhaps most serious with respect to primary products. The vast expansion of wheat production in North America and Australia and sugar in Cuba would have spelt utter ruin for high-cost European producers but for tariff protection.

Of course, the problem was aggravated because the war stimulated import substitution and economic nationalism. One of the most notable sufferers in this respect was the Lancashire cotton industry, with India and Japan contributing significantly to the decline in its fortunes. But it was only one of many. The major industrial nations faced the same process over a wide range of manufactured commodities, and they were also participants in the game. The manufacture of dyestuffs provides a good illustration of this point. Before the war, Germany produced over 80 per cent of the world output of dyes. When this source of supply was cut off during hostilities, several countries, including Britain, France, Italy and Japan, were forced to increase their own output. Important dye industries were created and subsequently protected, with the result that Germany's share of world production had fallen to 46 per cent by 1924.

Finally, new technical developments and the speeding up of the application of existing ones added to the structural problem and inevitably gave rise to redundant capacity in competing industries. The boost given to electricity and oil, the internal combustion engine and rayon are some of the more obvious examples, all of which had serious implications for the future prosperity of older staple industries. In a longer-term context, civil aviation might also be mentioned, the feasibility of which became clearly apparent as a result of wartime aerial activities, but which did not present a real threat to surface and ocean transport until after the Second World War. The way in which the simultaneous emergence of a series of innovations and new methods together with a more rapid application of existing methods created tensions between new and old sectors of activity, thereby forcing a rapid and painful liquidation of the latter, is well illustrated by the Swedish case. Fortunately, Sweden accomplished the transformation process fairly quickly and hence avoided some of the more severe structural problems that were to confront the older capitalist countries during the inter-war period.

Political and social changes

Though the immediate concern of this book is with economic matters, it is important to stress that the war had important political and social consequences, which were subsequently to influence, if not determine, the course of development in many European countries. Indeed, it could scarcely be expected that political and social life would remain immune after a war of such magnitude. The great mixing of the social classes within the military ranks, the influx of women into industrial occupations, the strengthening of trade unionism and workers' participation in industry and the levelling effect of high taxation could scarcely fail to have some impact on society.

In particular, these changes found expression in the demand for more democratic government and greater equality. Inevitably, the response fell short of the ideal but there can be little doubt that heightened social consciousness paved the way for improvements in the conditions of the less fortunate classes of society. Progress may at times have seemed slow, but the lower classes stood to benefit in the long term from the increasing participation of the state in economic and social affairs. In turn, this participation can be ascribed in part to the influence of war. It gave governments considerable experience in the management of economic affairs, and though most of the wartime control apparatus was hastily abandoned, the precedent for greater state participation had been set and partially accepted. Second, the war itself exposed some of the inequalities and social injustices present in most societies. Third, and perhaps most important, it raised the tolerance level of taxation. Although the high levels of wartime taxation were reduced, taxation rates never returned to their former peacetime levels; the displacement effect worked in favour of permanently higher levels of taxation. This gave governments much greater leverage in economic matters and provided a basis for more extensive social reform than could have been achieved under the narrow and constrained pre-war fiscal systems.

In this respect, therefore, the war might be regarded as beneficial to society. However, in a wider context, it can be argued that it had an adverse effect in that it seriously weakened the stability of existing social structures. For some people, of course, this was undoubtedly a gain, because it accorded greater power to the lower orders, whose long-standing discontent was expressed forcibly once their position was strengthened. Where representation was granted and class divisions eased in some way, it no doubt helped to counter incipient social upheaval or revolution. If not, then the way was paved for much unrest and turmoil in society as the lower classes clashed with the once entrenched ruling establishment. Russia provides the best example in the sense that the political coup was a complete success, though economically it was disastrous in the short term. In this case, the seeds of change had been sown long before 1914, though whether they would have borne fruit so early, if at all, had it not been for the war is a debatable point. Elsewhere events were much less dramatic, though some countries were close to social revolution in the immediate post-war period. The degree of success was generally limited and short-lived. Hungary spawned a temporary communist dictatorship in 1919, whereas the existing regimes in Germany, Austria, Bulgaria and Turkey were deposed, though the replacements could scarcely be regarded as revolutionary or particularly stable. In Italy, there was a wave of strikes, with workers occupying factories and farm estates, but again little was gained from the exercise. Strikes of course were commonplace within the western world and beyond in the aftermath of war. The growth in the size and importance of labour organizations during the war strengthened the power of the workers and gave rise to severe industrial unrest in most countries. France, Britain and the United States in particular were hit by massive strikes, some of them inspired by political motives, but for the most part the concrete achievements were either very limited or lost in the subsequent depression.

At the same time as new regimes emerged in central and eastern Europe, there were widespread demands for land reform, which envisaged the break-up of large estates and the redistribution of land to small impoverished farmers (the possible exception being Russia, because the ultimate aim there was to liquidate the independent farmer). Altogether twelve European countries carried out agrarian reform, and some 60 million acres or 11 per cent of the total territory was redistributed. More than half the acreage was allotted to former tenants, landless labourers and owners of small plots, one-quarter was acquired by the state and the remainder was retained by the former landlords. The area redistributed was greatest in Latvia and Romania, (approximately 42 per cent and 30 per cent, respectively) and least in Finland and Bulgaria (about 2 per cent).

Few countries escaped social and political disturbance in these years. The important point is not the degree of success achieved, which was generally small, but the fact that the social fabric of society was weakened by such events. It gave rise to weak governments and inevitably to policies that impeded reconstruction and economic progress. For example, the movement against the forces of reaction in Germany led to a series of weak governments under the Weimar Republic that were powerless to stem the tide of inflation; in fact, it could be argued that they helped to propagate it. Similarly, the political upheavals in Bulgaria resulted in policies (notably victimization of owners of wealth and capital) that penalized economic initiative and thereby paralysed the forces of economic recovery. Nor did the land ownership reforms in the east bring immediate economic benefits. Indeed, because of the fragmentation of holdings, the marketable surpluses of agricultural products often fell after the completion of reform. Thus, however desirable in practice, it would probably be true to say that on balance the move towards greater political and social equality was not in the best interests of the immediate task of economic recovery.

Post-war policy reversals

There can be little doubt that the war left Europe in a seriously weakened state. Few countries escaped unscathed from its influence, and for many countries, the task of reconstruction and recovery was substantial. At the time of the armistice, few statesmen of the world appreciated fully the enormity of the economic problems that the war had left behind. Moreover, it was generally believed that such problems as there were would soon disappear once things got back to normal; and getting back to normal meant recreating the world that had been lost. Thus in contrast to the position after 1945, when economic conditions were far worse but when the motto was 'looking to the future, not hankering after the past', governments vainly sought to move back into the past to what they deemed to be the *belle époque*, without realizing that there could be no viable return given the substantially changed conditions. Only by the time it was too late, when a new set of problems emerged in the form of a world slump and gathering political tensions internationally, was it realized that the past held no special attractions. Some may say that this judgement is too harsh. It could be argued that statesmen were overtaken by a series of events as a result of which they had little time and energy to spare for more fundamental problems. Certainly, in the early years after the war, there was much to occupy the policy-makers, though some of their decisions suggest that the previous comments are not far wide of the mark. The immediate post-war years especially were not marked by wise decisions.

Initially, it is true that there were signs that governments were about to plan a better future. Grandiose reconstruction schemes were being planned in the later stages of the war, when there was much talk of creating a land fit for heroes to live in, the relief of Europe was under consideration, and it seemed possible that the beneficial experience of international cooperation in wartime might bear fruit in peacetime. President Wilson's Fourteen Points and the launching of the League of Nations seemed to herald a new spirit of international harmony and goodwill. Yet within less than three years, little was left of these high ideals. By a series of policy reversals, the Allied powers left Europe in a more precarious state than at the time of the armistice. In particular, the provisions of the peace treaties, the abandonment of European relief and the measures taken to control the boom of 1919–20 adversely affected the recovery of Europe. Even the much-vaunted League of Nations failed to acquire American sanction and remained a sickly child from the onset of its creation.

The peace treaty settlements

Separate peace treaties were made with each of the enemy powers, the most important of which were those with Germany, Austria and Hungary.[1] They not only imposed heavy penalties on the enemies but also made provision for extensive territorial changes in central and eastern Europe. In fact, the post-war geographic changes constituted the biggest exercise in reshaping the boundaries of Europe ever undertaken. The process involved the greater part of the continent and the only countries not affected were Holland, Luxembourg, Switzerland, Spain and Portugal. The number of separate customs units in Europe was increased from 20 to 27, and political frontiers were lengthened by 12,500 miles. The newly created or reconstituted independent states comprised Poland, Czechoslovakia, Yugoslavia, Finland, Estonia, Latvia and Lithuania. These states were created out of the ruins of the German, Austrian and Russian Empires.

The German losses were considerable. Under the terms of the Treaty of Versailles, she lost all her colonies, Alsace-Lorraine and the Saar, which went to France,[2] North Schleswig to Denmark, West Prussia and Upper Silesia to Poland, Eupen and Malmédy to Belgium, as well as a number of smaller territories. In total, she was deprived of about 13.5 per cent of her pre-war territory and 10 per cent of the population of 1910. However, these figures tend to underestimate the extent of the damage, because the areas ceded contained some of the richest agricultural and industrial resources. In addition, the Allies confiscated nearly the entire German mercantile marine, almost all her foreign investments, while payments in kind were demanded in the transitional period before the heavy reparations bill was presented in 1921. The Treaty also provided for the disarmament of Germany; she was forbidden to have an air force, the army and navy were reduced to insignificant proportions and conscription was abolished, while provision was also made for an Allied occupation force in the Rhineland.

The loss of resources was bad enough, but perhaps even worse was the dislocation caused by the partition of industrial regions that had once formed single integrated units, such as Upper Silesia, and the breaking of the link between Ruhr coal and the iron of Lorraine. But this sort of partitioning was not confined to Germany, because the peace-makers were to repeat the exercise again and again in the course of treaty formulation for the European continent.

An even worse fate awaited the Austro-Hungarian Empire, which was already on the point of disintegration in the latter stages of the war. The old empire was destroyed, with the result that in territorial terms, Austria and Hungary were but a quarter of their former size and only marginally larger in terms of population. Economic criteria were scarcely taken into account when the partitioning took place. Hungary was dismembered largely on the grounds of racial diversity, yet the resulting territorial formations proved no more racially homogeneous and made even less economic sense. Slabs of the empire were distributed among no fewer than seven states, including the remnants of the old regime, Austria and Hungary. Romania alone secured an area larger than that left to Hungary herself. Austria did little better; she ceded major territories to Italy, Romania, Yugoslavia and Czechoslovakia, including some of her best industrial areas. In effect, therefore, both Austria and Hungary became landlocked areas smaller than some of their surrounding neighbours.

Other countries to suffer territorial losses were Bulgaria, Turkey and Russia. In the case of the first two, the concessions were relatively small, but Russia gave up much territory. She lost Bessarabia to Romania, four peripheral territories (which became the independent states of Finland, Estonia, Latvia and Lithuania), and subsequently a large slice of her western frontier after the Polish defeat of the drive on Warsaw in 1920.

The main beneficiaries from the carve-up of Europe were Poland, Yugoslavia, Czechoslovakia and Romania. Poland, back on the map after more than a century, secured substantial chunks of territory from Germany, Austria and Russia, the original partitioning powers in the late eighteenth century. The newly created states of Czechoslovakia and Yugoslavia also did well from the break-up of the Habsburg Empire, and Romania more than doubled its former size as a result of gains from neighbouring countries. Czechoslovakia was the main beneficiary of some of the best industrial regions of the Austro-Hungarian Empire, which made her one of the economically strongest of the newer states; though Yugoslavia, the main component of which was Serbia, was less fortunate in her inheritance (see below). Greece, which joined the allied side late in the conflict, was also a significant beneficiary, though her gains fell well short of the extravagant claims she tabled at the peace conference. She secured Western Thrace from Bulgaria and was allowed to occupy Smyrna (Izmir), from which she launched the ill-fated campaign against Turkey in 1920. Nevertheless, she was able to unite most Greeks under one roof, and her territory and population had doubled in size since 1912. Finally, little Albania just managed to squeak onto the map of Europe after confirmation of her newly won independence, much to the chagrin of both Italy and Greece.

It is worth taking a closer look at the new state of Yugoslavia, because it illustrates vividly the anomalies that can arise from cosmetic creations. Never was there a better recipe for national disaster. In fact, one can say that it was the most extraordinary concoction to emerge out of the peace settlement. Formally proclaimed as the Kingdom of the Serbs, Croats and Slovenes on 1 December 1918 (officially renamed Yugoslavia in 1929), it consisted of a motley collection of territories and an even more motley collection of peoples of diverse ethnic and religious origins inherited from the ruins of the Austro-Hungarian Empire. It acquired a completely bogus national identity, which in view of its diverse population composition it could never aspire to and which came to haunt the country throughout the twentieth century. Much of it had been put together in the unseemly grab for territory in the closing stages of the war, subsequently sanctioned, albeit somewhat reluctantly, by the Paris peace-makers and formally confirmed in the peace treaties with Austria, Hungary and Bulgaria. Its components included the former independent kingdoms of Serbia and Montenegro and incorporated respectively Croatia-Slavonia, part of the Banat and other small pieces of territory from Hungary; the province of Dalmatia, Carniola and the mainly Slavic-speaking areas of Styria and Carinthia as well as part of Istria from Austria; Bosnia and Herzegovina from Austro-Hungary; and small bits of territory from Albania and Bulgaria. The final result was a country nearly three times the size of the original Serbia whose peoples 'had little in common except language' and who could never agree 'on a common interpretation of what the country meant' (MacMillan 2003, 133). As was to be expected, scarcely a single frontier of the new country went undisputed in the inter-war years, and Yugoslavia had perpetual border squabbles over peoples and territory with all her neighbours (Austria, Hungary, Italy, Romania, Bulgaria and Albania).

Yugoslavia had in fact more nationalities and religions than any other country in Europe. She was even more diverse ethnically than the Czech Republic. Taking the Serbs as the main contingent, and even they constituted less than half the population, then some 57 per cent of the population could be classed as minorities. It is true that the bulk of the population could claim Slavic origins, but this meant very little in practice, because harmony among the different Slavic groups was conspicuous by its absence. There was a long history of bitter rivalry between the Serbs (the largest component, who came to dominate the government of the country) and the Croats, Slovenes, Macedonians and other Slavic groups, and the latter in turn were hostile to one another. The country also contained sizable numbers of non-Slavic peoples, including Germans, Magyars, Albanians, Turks, Vlachs, Italians, Romanians, Jews and Gypsies, most of whom were hostile to each other. The ethnic composition ran as follows: Serbs, 43 per cent; Croats, 23 per cent; Slovenes, 8.5 per cent; Bosnian Muslims, 6 per cent; Macedonian Slavs, 5 per cent; Albanians, 3.6 per cent; Germans, 3.6 per cent; Magyars, 3.4 per cent; with the remaining 3.9 per cent made up of Romanians, Italians, Turks, Jews, Gypsies and Vlachs. None of these peoples regarded themselves as belonging to one nation, and so a distinct Yugoslav identity failed to materialize. From the inception of the new state, the Serbs, who were weaker than their Czech brethren and economically inferior to the Croats and Slovenes, sought to dominate the regime by imposing centralized control and for the most part disregarding the interests of many of the smaller minority groups. The Croats and other large minority groups sought to resist the rule of the Serbs and struggled to gain greater autonomy and power. The problem was accentuated because Serbia sincerely believed she ought to own or at least dominate the whole of the Balkans and that other folk of alien persuasion living there should clear out and leave the Serbs in control. Thus inevitably, ethnic conflict was a serious source of weakness for the new state, and at times the rivalry between the two largest groups (the Serbs and Croats) virtually paralysed the country and left it vulnerable to external predators.

Overall, the gains and losses as they affected central–east Europe can be seen from the data on population and territorial changes in Table 1.2.

The post-war territorial realignments cannot be regarded as satisfactory from any point of view, and least of all from an economic one. In truth, they created more problems than they solved. The reorganization brought into being several new states, with a consequent increase in the number of separate tariff units; it left many national minorities under alien rule; and it created enormous problems of

Table 1.2 Territorial and population changes in central-east Europe 1914–21

	Area (km²)		Population (000s)	
	1914	*1921*	*1914*	*1921*
Austro-Hungarian Monarchy	676,443		51,390*	
Austria		85,533		6536
Hungary		92,607		7600
Czechoslovakia		140,394		13,613
Bulgaria	111,800	103,146	4753	4910
Poland		388,279		27,184
Romania	137,903	304,244	7516	17,594
Serbia	87,300		4548	
Yugoslavia		248,987		12,017

*Includes Bosnia and Herzegovina.

Source: Berend and Ranki 1969, 170.

economic integration. Possibly, these difficulties were the inevitable outcome of an attempt to satisfy several objectives simultaneously, namely ethnic delineation, national self-determination, the reconstruction of historic frontiers and economic requirements, because to satisfy one often meant the modification of another.

If economic factors were not completely ignored, it is clear that they were given very short shrift when defining the boundaries of the newly created and reconstituted states. Each country received whatever resources and equipment happened to be located in the territory assigned to it or in what land it had been able to lay claim to in the grab for territory that transpired in 1918–19. This often meant the complete break-up of former trading patterns and lines of communication and the separation of mutually dependent branches of industry. Such problems were particularly acute in central and eastern Europe. Yugoslavia, for example, inherited five railway systems with four different gauges; each of the systems served different centres so that they were practically unconnected with each other, and the task of unifying these disparate parts took most of a decade. The textile industry of Austria was split apart; the spindles were located in Bohemia and Moravia, which became part of Czechoslovakia, whereas the weaving looms were mainly in and around Vienna. Hungary, a country that before 1914 had been making reasonable industrial progress, was shorn of some important raw materials needed to service her developing industries. She retained about half her industrial undertakings but lost the bulk of her timber, iron ore, salt, copper and other non-ferrous metals and water power. Such changes were bound to hinder economic recovery, and in the long term, they created resentment and frustration, which were partly reflected in the growing tide of nationalism throughout the inter-war period.

Apart from the normal job of reconstruction, therefore, the new states had the additional task of building new economic organizations out of the multiple segments of territories they inherited. This usually involved the creation of new administrative units, new currencies, new lines of communication and the forging of fresh economic and trading links to replace those that had been destroyed. Inevitably, it led to the increased role of the state in economic affairs and a drive towards greater self-sufficiency. The gainers as well as the losers faced equally difficult problems. Romania and Yugoslavia, with their domains greatly enlarged, had the task of integrating the diverse parts, with their ethnic contrasts, into unified states. In terms of industrial equipment, Czechoslovakia did very well, but she was left with a host of racial minorities to consolidate. Poland faced the most difficult task, that of welding together three separate segments of territory formerly under different alien rule, with no natural frontiers and little in the way of developed industry. The three parts did not constitute a single economic unit because they had different systems of civil, commercial and fiscal legislation, they belonged to different customs units and they had different money and credit systems.

In contrast, Austria and Hungary had the reverse problem of creating viable economic units out of remnants of the old empire. Not that the former monarchy had been a very efficient economic organization, but at least it had a greater degree of economic coherence than what was to follow. The best portions of the empire were sliced off and Austria and Hungary were left with the rump. Austria ended up with a head larger than its body in that Vienna, the once glittering capital city of Europe but now utterly destitute, and which now harboured an overgrown bureaucracy, tended to dwarf the rest of the country. With a population of under 6.5 million, nearly one-third of whom lived in Vienna, Austria had become a top-heavy and economically precarious state. Hungary secured a larger population, but because she lost many valuable resources to neighbouring countries, her economic system was considerably weakened and disrupted.

Apart from the dislocation caused by geographic changes in Europe, a second impediment to recovery arose out of the failure to devise a satisfactory solution to the problem of war debts and reparations. Except in the case of Hungary and Bulgaria, the peace treaties did not deal with these matters specifically. Allied war debts were negotiated among the interested parties, while the burden imposed on Germany was finally determined by the Reparations Commission in only 1921. The sums were large in both cases, and initially no attempt was made to scale them down, or to link the two. The reasons for this were simple: the United States insisted on recouping the loans it had made to the Allies, whereas the latter, France in particular, maintained that these could be paid only if reparations from the enemy were forthcoming (hence the large reparations bill of $33 billion imposed on Germany in 1921). Because France and Britain were the largest debtors of the United States and at the same time the chief recipients of reparations from Germany, their debits and credits could have been offset, with Germany settling direct with the United States. However, America opposed the mixing of claims on the grounds that there was a greater likelihood of Germany defaulting on her obligations than the Allies, in which case America would have been left with a larger balance of bad debts than if one of the Allies had ceased payment.

The post-war debt problem created a great deal of bitter feeling among the nations concerned; it involved complex difficulties with respect to the transfer of payments and imposed severe burdens on the debtor countries. Subsequent events in Germany, in particular the great inflation of 1922–23, were not unrelated to this issue. Eventually, some scaling down of debts was achieved in the 1920s, but not before damage had been done.

The peace treaty settlements of the post-war years have been one of the most maligned in history. They have received a remarkably bad press and the reverberations have continued to affect Europe to this day. In all fairness to the treaty-makers, it was undoubtedly an extremely difficult exercise given the many conflicting demands, the political and social turmoil of the time and the fact that the major figures at the peace conference were in a state of perpetual disagreement. The wrangling negotiations and deal-making that went on at the Paris Peace Conference in the first half of 1919 have been vividly illustrated by Margaret MacMillan in her fascinating and entertaining volume *Peacemakers*. It should also be noted that their hands were often tied by the fact that emerging national groups were already laying claim to lands even before the guns had ceased to fire. Hence the statesmen responsible for the final settlement were often forced to endorse *de facto* claims, whether justified or not.

Having said that, there is no gainsaying the fact that the settlement was largely flawed. Few, if any, European states were happy with the outcome, and from the very onset, most states sought revisions to the settlement. However well-intentioned the peace-makers may or may not have been, there was no possibility that the final settlement could ensure the integrity of Europe either politically or economically, or that it would secure a lasting peace.

The longer-term international implications of the peace settlement are worth examining in a little more detail in the light of subsequent events that led up the Second World War. Whether the statesmen at Versailles really believed that they could provide the conditions for long-term peace and stability in Europe is a moot point. That issue apart, however, it soon became apparent that the stage had been set for later conflict, and not simply conflict through rivalry and tension among the smaller states themselves, though that was bad enough whenever territories and populations were in dispute. But more important from a longer-term perspective and taking Europe as a whole was the very integrity of the continent given the power vacuum that emerged in central-east Europe with the creation of new states that were weak in every sense of the word, politically, economically and militarily. Many of them also suffered from acute political and social tensions, partly because of linguistic, ethnic and cultural diversity of their populations, and rivalry among them was fostered by territorial and nationality issues, fanned in turn by a growing sense of national identity.

The new geographical configuration of Europe did not really solve the ethnic problem because many national minorities were left under alien rule. Though the peace settlement reduced minority status compared with before the war, it still left many citizens stateless in the sense that that they constituted national minorities. This was especially the case in eastern Europe, where up to a third of the population of some countries lived outside their national borders. For example, some one-third of Hungarians were located outwith the new state of Hungary. The fact that nations were defined largely in ethnic terms served to heighten national perceptions of ethnic perfection, giving rise to demands for ridding nations of 'alien' elements, who had once lived and worked fairly peaceably together, while at the same time fostering claims for the reconciliation of expatriates. The fiercest protagonists on the latter issue were Hungary and Germany, both of which had many nationals living outside their state boundaries. In fact, Versailles had made Germans one of the largest minority populations in Europe. Out of a total minority population in east-central Europe of some 36 million, Germany probably accounted for 8–9 million. The largest contingents were in Czechoslovakia (3.5 million) and Poland (1.2 million), along with significant numbers in Hungary, Italy, Romania, Yugoslavia, Russia and the Baltic states, as well as scatterings in nearly every state in Europe. Given these large minority groups throughout Europe, it is not surprising therefore that irredentist movements gathered strength in the inter-war years. In fact, ethnic nationalism was to become an important element in the rise of fascist movements in many central and east European countries during this period. Some 13 per cent of the German population were now marooned outwith the borders of the former German Reich, which provided strong grist for the nationalist cause.

Thus, far from providing a bulwark against the incursion of a more powerful neighbour, as the Austro-Hungarian Empire had once done, though albeit decreasingly over time, the new or reconstituted states were destined to become the prey of a predator power, and Germany was the obvious candidate in this respect. The vacuum left in central-east Europe by the demise of the Austro-Hungarian Empire in a very real sense therefore set the stage for later conflict. Newman (1968) repeatedly stresses the crucial role of this region in determining the subsequent distribution of power within Europe, and ultimately the fate of the continent as a whole. Power vacuums do not generally remain unfilled for long, because an ambitious predator nation soon takes advantage of the situation. The central-east European region provides a classic example, because the states in question were, as Newman describes it, 'extremely weak reeds to place in the path of Germany, and they possessed few features that could lead to any hope of their being anything but satellites . . . of Germany, Hitler or no Hitler.' Whether they could have survived had there been greater mutual cooperation and trust in the region is a debatable point, but in isolation there was little hope once European security fragmented in the 1930s.

On this interpretation, therefore, one scarcely needs a figurehead in the guise of Adolf Hitler to explain the eventual political disintegration of Europe because the seeds of its destruction were already sown and taking root long before he came to power. In Overy's words (1995), 'Hitler played a part already written for him'. The question is why Germany played out the role. There are a number of sound reasons. First, there was no other obvious candidate. The other possibilities were Britain, France, Italy and Russia but each in turn was ruled out for various reasons. Britain for the most part took a rather arms-length and at times ambivalent attitude to European events and in any case she was more preoccupied with her imperial interests. France was not powerful enough, and Italy even less so, the latter having more interest in the Mediterranean and the Middle East. Russia (or the USSR) was embroiled with her own domestic problems. Second, Germany emerged from the war as the strongest political and economic power on the continent. This may seem strange given her defeat in war and the losses and exactions imposed by the treaty settlement. But in fact Germany was far from crippled by these events and despite her losses and continual complaints about the harsh penalties of the settlement, her potential strength given stable conditions and a fair wind far outmatched that of any other country. Third, Germany had always coveted designs on the east, a fact borne out by the wartime plan to colonize the region by setting up a chain of puppet monarchies in the conquered states from the Baltic to the Black Sea. Such objectives did not evaporate with the defeat in war; if anything they were strengthened since the terms of the peace settlement fired resentment in Germany giving her greater cause to seek revenge.

Whatever the rights and wrongs of the peace settlement as polemicized by Keynes in 1919–20 and Mantoux in 1946, the fact is that Germany regarded the peace terms as harsh and iniquitous. But it was not only the loss of territory, assets, population, financial penalties, restraints on rearmament and the occupation of key frontier zones, all of which it was hoped would contain German ambitions in the future, that were at stake. The crowning insult, and one that impugned Germany's honour, was the famous (infamous?) war guilt clause, Article 231 of the Treaty. Further, Germany was excluded at the onset from the League of Nations, which fostered the belief among the German population that it was a victors' club designed to impose the terms of the peace settlement. In fact, the new legal order in the form of the League of Nations was seen as a device whereby the victors could 'bank their gains'. With the mandates conferred by the League on Britain and France, imperial control by the metropolitan powers was at its zenith, and the British Empire and the United States together controlled nearly three-quarters of the world's mineral resources (Mazower 2009, 576). Little wonder that the defeated powers believed that they had been left out in the cold and that they would need to compete for more living space and control over resources.[3]

Thus, Germany believed that she had every right to be aggrieved and France had every justification to fear her close neighbour. Far from hobbling Germany, the peace terms gave rise to resentment and a determination to whittle them away bit by bit while keeping a close eye on the eastern situation. This was done during the course of the 1920s and early 1930s and subsequently accelerated by Hitler, who added a new dimension: fanatical racial hatred. Thus one can argue that the flawed peace settlement and the failure of the victors to uphold its provisions, especially those relating to security, left Europe vulnerable to a new conflict with the Germans, who in the ensuing years exploited the weaknesses of the settlement.

On balance, then, the European peace settlement was not a striking success. The settlement was a patchwork of compromises cobbled together by the great powers, who had very different views about what kind of post-war world they wanted. It was, as the title of Dockrill and Gould's book suggests, a *Peace without Promise*.

It left too many problems unresolved and its implementation was left largely in the hands of Britain and France, who could never agree about its enforcement or its revision. Not surprisingly, therefore, once Germany and Russia recovered, central and eastern Europe became vulnerable to the economic and political ambitions of these two powers.

Reconstruction issues

Perhaps the most serious criticism of the peace-making arrangements was the lack of a solid post-war plan for the relief and reconstruction of Europe. Keynes, in his vitriolic denunciation of the peace settlement, noted with dismay that no provision had been made for the reconstruction and rehabilitation of stricken Europe (Keynes 1919, 211). Once the peace-makers had redrawn the boundaries and punished the vanquished, they concluded their deliberations in the belief that Europe could look after itself. But this was a forlorn hope, because by the end of hostilities, much of Europe was literally destitute. There were severe shortages of almost everything: food, raw materials and equipment, and also a lack of hard currency with which to purchase supplies from the United States. Economic activity and trade had sunk to very low levels in many countries; in 1919, industrial production on average was running at about half pre-war levels, while agricultural output was down by about one-third. Many parts of Europe were desperately in need of external aid for the immediate task of dealing with starving populations, let alone addressing the longer-term issue of tackling the process of reconstruction in badly devastated areas. In one of its later reports, the League of Nations graphically captured the plight of Europe in the immediate aftermath of the conflict:

> All countries in Europe were suffering from a lack of working capital and from a loss through wear and tear or physical destruction of fixed capital . . . stocks (of food, raw materials and manufactured goods) had been exhausted during the war . . . Durable consumers' goods were likewise largely worn out, destroyed or in need of repair. Housebuilding and repair in particular had been practically at a standstill during the war, and in war zones whole areas and villages had been devastated . . . much of the machinery had not been replaced and in certain areas machinery had been deliberately destroyed by retreating armies . . . The mechanism of transportation was particularly affected. Railway rolling stock was in a deplorable condition all over Central and Eastern Europe . . . The state of roadbeds was often inadequate for rapid traffic, and many bridges were in a dangerous state (League of Nations 1943b, 7–9).

The scale of the operations is difficult to comprehend fully because the ramifications of more than four years of bitter hostilities had been so far-reaching. It was not simply a matter of making good physical damage and restoring former levels of output, though both were essential. The war had affected every conceivable aspect of the economic and social life in every European country, even the neutrals, though obviously to a lesser extent. Apart from the setback to economic activity and the severe shortage of essential commodities, there was widespread physical damage to property and landscape, significant losses in population, a loss of former markets and trading connections, while government finances and currency systems were in disarray and transport systems were in a chaotic state. Added to these problems, there were the longer-term tasks of assimilating the new territorial arrangements, setting up new constitutions and parliamentary systems, and unifying economic, legal and administrative institutions. All this at a time when resources were short, people were starving, social and revolutionary ferment was widespread, and border conflicts and disputes over territory and populations were common.

The peripheral countries, apart from Spain and Portugal, were in a far worse position than the major powers. In general, they were the poorer countries in Europe, and many had suffered disproportionately from the ravages of war and the post-war geographical realignments. The Baltic states had lost their main Russian market and were engaged in border disputes with Germany and the Soviet Union. Greece was in confrontation with Turkey, while Albania was fearful of losing its newly confirmed independence. Hungary was trying to get to grips with a much reduced size and reclaiming lost populations, while in Romania the reverse was the case. For Poland and Yugoslavia, the two most severely devastated countries, there was the task of welding together disparate economic and social systems. Eastern Europe as a whole was in a very bad way and at the close of the war, its economic and social system was on the point of collapse.

The failure of relief

Despite the manifold problems, in the immediate aftermath of war, the paramount issue in Europe was the need for short-term relief. The greater part of the continent was impoverished in nearly every conceivable respect. Output was low, famine was imminent, capital and raw materials were in desperately short supply, transport systems were completely disorganized and currency and financial mechanisms were running out of control. Social and political ferment led to weak governments with limited capacity to deal with the situation. Conditions were worst in central and eastern Europe; indeed, the position in some countries was little short of chaotic, with economic and social systems bordering on collapse. Russian society had already disintegrated and economic activity there was virtually at a standstill. Prospects of recovery were slim indeed without external assistance because inexperienced governments battled against almost insuperable odds. The failure to organize a comprehensive programme of reconstruction and assistance was partly responsible for the collapse of some economic systems.

In one respect, the Allied governments were forced to take action, namely the relief of poverty and hunger. By the end of 1918 the spectre of famine prevailed over a wide area of central and eastern Europe. Food was in short supply because output of agricultural products was one-third or more below pre-war levels, while countries in this region had limited means of paying for imports of food.

The bulk of the relief provided was effected by or through American organizations, principally the American Relief Administration created early in 1919 as the executive agency of the Allied Supreme Council responsible for relief. Under arrangements made by this body a steady stream of food deliveries began to take place, and by August 1919, food to the value of $1,250 million had been delivered to Europe. Some 20 countries were recipients of supplies, most of which was provided on a cash or credit basis, and less than 10 per cent consisted of outright gifts. The Allied and liberated countries generally got their provisions on credit, most of which was never repaid, whereas enemy countries had to pay in cash.

After the middle of 1919, official relief programmes were sharply curtailed, and subsequently relief activities were confined mainly to private and semi-official organizations. These managed to distribute some $500 million worth of foodstuffs over a period of two to three years, mostly in the form of gifts. Basically, however, the task of providing sufficient food for the people of Europe was left to the respective governments.

Useful though the relief programme was, it fell short of real needs. Except for deliveries to Belgium and northern France, supplies on any scale never really got under way until the beginning of February 1919, and then they came to an abrupt halt in the summer of that year, long before the problems of hunger and poverty had been solved. On average, every child in central and eastern Europe was fed for one month only by US relief organizations. Child poverty alone, therefore, remained critical in many countries; a League of Nations medical inquiry carried out in Czechoslovakia in March 1921 showed that 60 per cent of the country's children remained undernourished or lacking in vitality. The real extent of the problem was never adequately surveyed; the whole exercise of relief was hastily improvised and there were innumerable difficulties encountered in coordinating the relief efforts of the United States and the Allies. Though the United States was the main participant, it should be borne in mind that she had large food stocks at the end of the war and this was obviously an important consideration in drawing up the relief programme. Furthermore, the fact that the enemy states were expected to pay their way where possible only made the task of reconstruction that much more difficult.

Relief of famine was of course only the first step in the process of reconstruction. Europe was short of raw materials, capital and consumer goods, and supplies of the first two were especially important for purposes of recovery. But no overall plan of reconstruction relief was ever conceived and international efforts outside that of meeting food requirements were limited. Consequently, Europe had to fend as best she could, and in the scramble for materials in the boom of 1919–20, many central and eastern countries were left with a minimal supply. Raw material and capital equipment imports were only a fraction of pre-war levels, and food imports fell off sharply later in 1919 when the relief programme expired. Data on the level of import volumes demonstrate the gravity of the situation for some countries: Germany and eastern Europe obtained only about one-third of their 1913 level of imports, the neutral countries fell short by some 20 per cent, while the Western Allies slightly exceeded their peacetime import volumes. The most serious shortfall was in the import of raw materials and semi-finished goods. (Orde 1990, 111). High prices were paid for what was imported and the large deficit in the trade accounts that resulted had to be covered by borrowings. In monetary terms, the total import surplus of continental Europe on trade account in 1919 and 1920 was $12.5 billion, of which less than one-half was covered by invisible receipts and the export of gold, leaving $6.7 billion to be financed by the import of capital.

Clearly, then, international efforts to promote reconstruction in Europe were woefully inadequate after the First World War, a lesson that was appreciated by the planners responsible for the same task after 1945. A coordinated plan for the relief and reconstruction of Europe was never conceived at any stage, let alone implemented, and the relief that was handed out was inadequate. Moreover, it tended to be regarded more as a form of charity that should be extended to some countries but not to others. Political considerations rather than need or capacity to pay determined the type and amount of relief given, which is why Western countries did better than their counterparts in central and eastern Europe.

The consequences of inadequate action had a direct bearing on later events. Because many countries were unable to obtain sufficient supplies, recovery was delayed, factories remained idle and unemployment high. As a result, unemployment benefits, relief programmes and continued military spending kept government expenditure at a high level, which, coupled with the low taxable capacity of the population, meant that balanced budgets were out of the question. In Austria, for example, over one-half of public spending in 1921 went on food subsidies alone. Furthermore, inadequate foreign credits to finance imports meant pressure on the demand for foreign exchange, with a consequent depreciation of currency values. It is true that for a time each depreciation of the exchange helped to promote exports and create employment. But the final consequences were disastrous. The price paid for temporary relief was increasing inflation, declining real incomes, loss of confidence and eventually the flight of capital from productive activity. Ultimately, it led to the disintegration of several economies. For several years, the whole economic and social organization of many countries was allowed to rot away. and as the League of Nations observed in one of its later reports, 'when it was finally faced, it had ceased to be a general problem of transition and reconstruction and had become a problem of cutting the gangrene out of the most affected areas one by one'. Ironically, this observation was made by the League of Nations, an organization of which so much had been expected but from which so little transpired.

Thus the breakdown in several European countries in the early 1920s can be attributed partly to the failure to take effective action to check the disease before it got too severe. This required adequate provision for the most stricken areas to permit rehabilitation and hence obviate exchange depreciation; the immediate support of currencies weakened by inflationary policies rather than waiting until the collapse was under way. And, finally, if the boom of 1919–20 had been controlled more sensibly, the European burden would have been eased. It is to this aspect we now turn.

What is perhaps most disheartening about this whole episode is that the Allied powers, having devised a new geographical configuration for Europe and accorded self-determination to many peoples and created new states, then decided that it was time to withdraw from the scene and leave the stricken countries to fend for themselves, which they patently were not in a position to do.

The post-war boom and slump, 1919–21

While much of Europe was struggling to cope with famine, poverty and reconstruction, the Western Allies and not a few other countries (especially the neutrals) were enjoying one of the most spectacular booms in history, only to be followed by an equally spectacular slump. The causes of the boom and of the subsequent collapse are important, and even more so are the consequences in terms of European recovery.

Initially, it was expected that the war would be followed by a recession as military orders were cancelled, soldiers were demobilized and the process of converting to peacetime operations took place. For a few months after the armistice, there was a mild recession, but this soon gave way in the spring of 1919 to 'a boom of astonishing dimensions'. It was one of the shortest and sharpest upswings on record. It lasted for about a year, with the peak occurring in the spring and summer of 1920. One of its most notable features was the sharp rise in prices as pent-up demand for commodities was unleashed at a time when production was still recovering from the effects of war. Factories were swamped with orders, and the consequent demand for labour assisted the process of demobilization. Within just over a year from the armistice, Britain had demobilized some 4 million men and had abandoned most wartime controls. The process of conversion was even more rapid in the United States.

The boom was most marked in the United States, Britain and Japan and in some of the neutral countries, because their economies were in better shape to meet the sudden upsurge in demand. Much of continental Europe and Russia were in no fit state to participate properly, though inflationary conditions continued unchecked in many European countries. Primary producers also benefited from the sharp rise in commodity prices, while everywhere there was a great deal of speculative activity.

One of the main forces behind the boom was undoubtedly that of war. A large pent-up demand for goods had been created, which was backed by financial assets accumulated during the period of hostilities. This demand was released at a time when stocks were low and productive capacity was still recovering so that initially it was simply translated into soaring prices. The price inflation was aggravated by several other factors. Shortages of shipping space and dislocation of internal transport systems in the immediate post-war period tended to create artificial shortages, because in some cases there were considerable accumulations of primary commodities overseas waiting to be moved. There was also a considerable amount of speculative stock buying in anticipation of rapid upward price movements, because the gains to be made from cornering markets were large.

Government policies must also share part of the blame. Controls over economic activity were abandoned rapidly after the war as businessmen pressed for a return to 'normalcy' as soon as possible. Thus despite the fact that commodities were in short supply, many wartime controls were dismantled during the first half of 1919. Relaxation of control was followed in nearly every instance by a sharp price increase, and had control been retained longer, it is almost certain that the severity of the price rise would have been lessened. In addition, lax fiscal and monetary policies pumped funds into the economy and expanded credit. For much of 1919, government spending continued at a high level and credit conditions remained easy. In fact, all over the world, partly by force of circumstances, governments tended to pursue fiscal and monetary policies that accentuated the upswing. The inflationary process went further in central and eastern Europe, where financial and currency conditions were already in a chaotic state before the end of the war. The needs of reconstruction, limited tax potential and weak administrations meant a continuation of inflationary fiscal and monetary policies. Here little attempt was made to check the process. Indeed, in most cases, it was aggravated by policy measures, with the result that the inflationary spiral got worse and eventually ended in disaster.

Elsewhere the boom ended almost as dramatically as it had begun. The first sign of a break came early in 1920, when business activity began to slacken in the United States. During the spring of that year, a number of countries including Britain recorded turning-points in economic activity, and by the autumn there was little doubt that the bubble had burst. During the remainder of the year, production, exports and prices fell far and fast, while unemployment rose sharply. As a result the year 1921 proved to be one of the worst on record.

Few countries escaped the severe check to activity between 1920 and 1921 (and in some cases it ran on until 1922) except those in central and eastern Europe, whose currencies had so depreciated that they were enjoying a temporary boost to exports. Thus Germany, Austria, Czechoslovakia and Poland actually recorded increases in industrial production in 1921. Here, inflation gave an artificial stimulus to activity, though still well down on pre-war levels, but the consequences were soon to follow. Elsewhere the picture was grim and for some the downturn proved to be more severe, though of shorter duration, than that of 1929–32. Production and incomes in Sweden and Britain fell much more sharply in 1920–21 than they were to do in the downswing following 1929. On a monthly basis, the decline was also more severe in the United States. The main blessing was that the post-war depression was shorter than the later one, and by 1922 most countries had begun to show signs of revival.

Several reasons can be put forward to explain this sudden and sharp contraction. One simple and commonly quoted reason is that it was the inevitable reaction to the violent boom; as output began to catch up with demand and supplies of commodities began to arrive from overseas, the basis of the boom disintegrated. A second possibility is that price inflation produced its own cure, in that rapidly rising prices and lagging wages checked the growth of real incomes and led to consumer resistance. There is certainly evidence to suggest that consumer demand began to tail off in the first few months of 1920 in Britain. Furthermore, the rapid rise in industrial costs produced business uncertainty, while in some cases, notably the United States, supply inelasticities became operative in the winter of 1919–20. These aggravated the pace of inflation and thereby increased consumer resistance, though supply constraints were probably not the chief cause of the turning-point.

Many writers place considerable emphasis on the role of government policy in checking the boom. Restrictive fiscal and monetary policies, especially in the United States and Britain, served to curb expansion and reduce the flow of credits abroad, which in turn curtailed the demand for exports. Certainly, the timing of policy measures in the United States is not inconsistent with the belief that the downswing was induced by government action. Government spending declined after the middle of 1919, and tax revenues rose, while monetary policy was tightened severely late in the year. Severe retrenchment measures were also implemented in other countries, notably Britain, Sweden and Japan, at roughly the same point in time. Though it is not always easy to determine just how crucial government policy was in breaking the boom, there can be little doubt that the sharp monetary contraction and fiscal retrenchment of this period exacerbated the downswing once it was under way. Such action certainly put paid to inflation but, given the magnitude of the subsequent slump, it must be condemned for being too severe and too late.

In the circumstances, it is not surprising that severe corrective action was taken to control the boom. It did appear to be getting out of hand during the course of 1919, and the rapid rise in prices in particular was bound to give grounds for alarm given the prevailing conditions in much of Europe, where lax financial policies were seen as being a powerful force in the inflationary spiral. If the boom did not break through natural forces, then the danger of continuing inflation was real, given no change in government policy. In any case, there was almost bound to be a reaction against wartime financial practices because belief in the virtue of sound finance was still widely held in some countries. This along with other adjustments in policy, including abandonment of controls, reductions in government spending and taxes, removal of trade barriers and a speedy return to gold as the basis for national currencies, were regarded as vital prerequisites for a return to 'normalcy' in economic affairs. Thus it is not so much that the policies were wrong in the conditions then obtaining, but rather that they were pursued too vigorously and for too long. Unfortunately, the lessons of this episode went unheeded in 1929.

However, the consequences were not as disastrous as those that followed from the great inflations in central and eastern Europe. Nevertheless, they should not be minimized. The prospects of a smooth and speedy transition to peacetime conditions were shattered. In 1921, many factories lay idle, millions of men and women were without work, and industrial unrest was widespread as wages were forced down sharply under sliding-scale agreements. Inevitably, this delayed the process of reconstruction. Moreover, the boom itself was not an unmixed blessing. In many respects, it was an artificial one created by paper shortages and supply bottlenecks arising out of the dislocation caused by war. Though production expanded, in the short term it could not keep pace with rising demand, and hence inflationary conditions dominated the upswing. Under these conditions, it developed into a speculative ramp. In fact, the outstanding feature of the boom was the extent of speculative buying in commodities, financial securities, real estate and shipping space, and the very large number of industrial transactions at inflated prices. The financial orgy was made possible by the extremely liquid state of firms as a result of high wartime profits, the relatively easy money conditions and the large-scale creation of bank credit. Activity in the new issue market reached phenomenal proportions. New issues on the London market increased by a factor of more than six between 1918 and 1920 to reach a total of £384 million, a level that was not surpassed until the 1960s. Most of the increase in new issues represented flotations for domestic purposes.

The worst excesses occurred in some of the older industries (coal, cotton, shipping and shipbuilding and steel and the metal trades), the future growth prospects of which were limited. The flotation of new companies, the sale of old ones and the issue of new shares became almost a daily event in 1919. Expectations of high profits attracted speculators, and many companies were bought up and refloated at inflated capital values, often with the assistance of the banks. Such transactions had disastrous consequences for the industries concerned. Their wartime profits were dissipated in a frivolous manner, and once the bottom fell out of the market, they were left with virtually worthless assets together with a heavy burden of debt as a result of increased interest liabilities, the issue of bonus shares and the watering of capital stock. The cost of overcapitalization in the boom was to remain a heavy burden to some industries throughout the interwar period. Finally, the boom fostered the growth of capacity often in sectors in which future prospects were least promising. The most notable example is in the maritime trades, in which enough shipping capacity came on stream to last a decade or more.

The boom and slump of the Western hemisphere had important implications for European debtor countries, comprising most of central and eastern Europe. It impeded their reconstruction and forced them to adopt dangerous expedients. During the boom, these countries found difficulty in securing essential supplies, and for what they did obtain they were forced to pay high prices, thereby incurring further debt. Moreover, when commodity prices collapsed in the latter half of 1920, the burden of debt increased, especially in east European countries with heavy dependence on primary exports. Second, retrenchment in the United States had serious repercussions for Europe as a whole. The drop of more than 40 per cent in the general level of dollar prices imposed a heavy burden on all European countries that had contracted debt at inflated prices. The transfer problem was aggravated because it was difficult to service debt at lower prices, and the result was that European primary producers strove to increase their output, which only made matters worse. The price decline in the United States also accentuated the deflationary difficulties of countries attempting to restore their currencies to prewar parity. This is particularly true of Britain, because sterling prices had risen more than dollar prices during the war.

Furthermore, the downturn in the United States led to a sharp curtailment of imports into that country and a check to overseas lending, with the result that the volume of dollars supplied to foreigners was reduced by no less than 50 per cent between 1919 and 1921. By late 1920, the dollar shortage in Europe had become so acute as to require an increasingly large outflow of gold. In the face of their difficulties, therefore, the European debtors abandoned any attempt at financial reform and currency stabilization; instead, they allowed their exchanges to slide further, thus aggravating the problem of inflation.

In short, therefore, American economic policy in the post-war period exacerbated Europe's problems. The United States failed to take account fully of its changed status during the war: to a large creditor nation with a strategic role in the international economy. Adjustment to a positive trade balance required that it continue to enlarge its imports and lend abroad. The cutback in both respects in 1920–21 was a vital blow to European countries struggling to recover from the war. Had the American authorities stimulated demand in the spring of 1920 instead of deflating, the process of European reconstruction would have been eased and some of the worst excesses of inflationary policies might have been avoided. The sad thing is that America repeated the exercise again in the years 1928–30.

Conclusion

The decade of the 1920s did not open on a very auspicious note. Several major economies were sliding into recession, while others were continuing on an inflationary course. Reconstruction and recovery from the war were far from complete, and the policies of the Allied governments in the post-armistice period had done as much to hinder as to promote the economic revival of Europe. In particular, the failure to organize a satisfactory programme of international assistance to enable war-stricken countries to get on their feet again may be regarded as one of the chief mistakes of this period. It contrasts sharply with the position after the Second World War when both America and the United Nations came to the rescue of Europe in a big way. The failure in the earlier instance can be readily explained. The League of Nations was a relatively weak and ineffective organization, which for the most part took action to assist individual countries only when they were on the verge of collapse. The weakness of the League partly reflected the fact that the spirit of international cooperation was still in its infancy; hence, some member countries accorded the League only token support, whereas the United States refused even that. Of course, the United States was the one country that was in a position to render assistance to Europe, but because she was anxious to disengage herself from this area as rapidly as possible it is not surprising that the relief programme was short-lived.

In the event, therefore, Europe was forced to work out her own salvation. The process of recovery for some countries proved a long and painful one, punctuated by crises and reversals. In certain cases, notably Austria, Poland, and even Germany, complete recovery had scarcely been achieved before the slump of 1929–32 struck a further blow to their prospects. For others, however, the decade of the 1920s was one of significant economic progress although, as the next chapter shows, it was a period of unstable equilibrium, which eventually terminated with one of the severest depressions on record.

Questions for discussion

1   Why did the post-war peace settlement lead to the Balkanization of Europe?
2   How significant was a) the death toll and b) the physical damage, caused by the First World War?
3   Why were the financial legacies of war so severe?
4   Did the failure of the post-war relief programme retard Europe's economic recovery?
5   What were the main political and social consequences for Europe of the First World War?

2 Post-war reconstruction and instability problems in the 1920s

Although in terms of economic growth the 1920s were far from being an unrespectable decade, any broad generalizations about the performance and achievements of Europe as a whole during this period are not particularly illuminating given the widely differing experience among countries within the region and the difficulties of choosing a satisfactory base year for comparison. Nearly all countries registered some economic progress in the 1920s and most of them managed to regain or surpass their pre-war income and production levels by the end of the decade. But there was a world of difference between the rapid output growth in the Netherlands, Norway, Sweden, Switzerland and Greece and the near stagnation recorded by Austria, Russia (USSR) and Poland and the sluggish UK performance compared with the pre-war base. Clearly, any comparison of relative performance depends on the time span chosen. Thus although Austria and Poland struggled to regain their 1913 output levels, they did record rapid growth from the early post-war years through to 1929 simply because recovery was taking place from a very low base. Moreover, for the decade as a whole, it is important to distinguish between the first and second halves. Up to 1925, most countries were in the process of recovering from the war; growth rates were often very high, though a number of countries, especially in central-east Europe, still had not regained their pre-war output levels by the middle of the decade. The second half of the 1920s was one of consolidation and further growth, with boom conditions in some cases, albeit against an unstable international background, with obvious implications for the cyclical downturn that began in 1929. In these later years, eastern Europe probably performed slightly better than the west, though one should note that the region still remained extremely backward compared with the major industrial countries.

Whatever the record of individual countries, it should be stressed that European development of the 1920s took place against an unstable political and economic background. Even by the middle of the decade, by which time a greater degree of political and economic stability and a substantial measure of recovery had been achieved, the international economy was still in a fragile state and it continued to remain vulnerable to shocks throughout the later 1920s despite the semblance of equilibrium achieved in that period. Perhaps this is not so surprising, because the war had given rise to many problems, most of which were only partially solved, if at all, during the course of the decade. Apart from the question of physical reconstruction, some of the most important included war debts and reparations, currency disorganization, inflation, and structural problems reflected in excess capacity and higher unemployment compared with the pre-war period. Furthermore, the fact that Europe, and especially central and eastern Europe, emerged from the war in a weakened state meant that the area as a whole became more dependent on outside assistance, which again served to expose the vulnerability of the European economy.

Given the magnitude of the problems, what is perhaps surprising is that Europe's performance in the 1920s was as good as it was. No doubt but for these difficulties the overall performance would have been better, though quite by how much it is impossible to tell. But clearly also, despite the complications, there were forces making for growth, notably war-induced recovery forces, new technological opportunities and even, especially in eastern Europe, a greater degree of autarchy with respect to economic matters. However, possibly of greater relevance than the growth-retarding effects of the specific problems listed above is the way in which their existence and the solutions adopted served to limit the achievement of a stable equilibrium, which meant that the European economy was less able to withstand the pressure of external events as they developed from 1928 onwards.

The reconstruction phase

Seven years elapsed before Europe as a whole gained her former levels of activity, and even by 1925 the process of recovery was not really complete. Some countries had still not managed to reach their pre-war output levels, while many of those that did continued to suffer from excess capacity and heavy unemployment; at the end of 1925, there were more than 2.5 million unemployed workers in Britain, Germany, Belgium, Italy and Poland, not to mention the large number of under-employed workers, especially in agriculture. Second, Europe's trade still fell short of the pre-war volume. Third, the fact that production had barely surpassed the 1913 level at a time when population was increasing suggests that income per head was still below the pre-war peak.

The rate of recovery was very uneven not only between regions but also among countries in the same area. Central and eastern Europe, which had suffered the most from the war and its aftermath, lagged seriously behind the west. The fact that some countries in this region escaped the post-war slump because of inflation was little consolation because once it got out of hand and stabilization measures had to be implemented, economic activity was checked more sharply than in countries that had adopted deflationary policies in the first place. The result was that by 1925, industrial production in this area was still 13 per cent below that of 1913, whereas the western Allies and neutral countries were recording gains of a similar magnitude. The difference in performance between east and west can be seen from the data on industrial production given in Table 2.1. Within these major groupings some countries did very much better than others. Italy, for example, far surpassed the performance of any of her allies; Denmark and the Netherlands did

Table 2.1 Industrial production and mining in Europe, 1920–25 (1913 = 100)

	1920	1921	1922	1923	1924	1925
Western Allies*	70.3	66.2	85.1	94.6	112.2	114.9
Neutrals+	98.7>	87.3	92.4	98.7	105.1	111.4
Central and eastern Europe^	57.6	69.5	76.0	58.6	77.2	87.0
Total continental Europe	66.7	70.2	81.0	75.0	91.7	98.8

*Includes Portugal.
+Denmark, Netherlands, Norway, Spain, Sweden, and Switzerland.
^Germany, Czechoslovakia, Austria, Bulgaria, Estonia, Finland, Greece, Hungary, Latvia, Poland, Romania, and Yugoslavia.
>Excludes Netherlands and Norway.

Source: League of Nations, *Europe's Overseas Needs 1919–1920 and How They Were Met,* 1943, 9.

better than the other neutrals, whereas Finland outpaced the Scandinavian countries. France and Belgium, though subject to similar amounts of destruction, registered different rates of recovery, whereas France did better on balance than Britain. As far as central and eastern Europe is concerned it is a case of selecting the best out of a bad lot, though Czechoslovakia stands out, with an increase in manufacturing output of more than one-third above the pre-war level.

Most countries, of course, had special problems to contend with in this period, but several general factors can be presented to explain the relatively slow rate of European recovery as a whole. For one thing, the task of reconstruction was a large one. It was not simply a question of restoring physical damage, although this in itself was a considerable item in some cases. The absolute amount of physical destruction of land and property may not in total seem large, but for some countries it constituted a severe burden at a time when resources were in short supply. In addition, for many countries in central and eastern Europe, there was the problem of literally creating viable economic systems out of territories that had been sliced up and reformulated by the peace treaty provisions.

At the same time, economic and political conditions were scarcely conducive to rapid recovery in the first few years after the war. Hardly a year passed without some event or crisis occurring that served to hamper progress. Between 1919 and 1922, strikes, political upheavals and border hostilities abounded throughout Europe. The sharp contraction in economic activity in 1920–21 in some west European countries, aggravated by deflationary policies, abruptly cut short recovery, and for some it spelt the beginning of an intermittent policy of deflation in preparation for the return to the gold standard. Meanwhile, inflationary pressures were building up in the rest of Europe, and 1922–23 saw the unleashing of these forces on a grand scale in Austria, Hungary, Poland and Germany, accompanied in the latter case by the abortive occupation of the Ruhr by France and Belgium. After 1923, things quietened down, and by the middle of 1924, the outlook was generally more favourable to sustained progress than at any time since the armistice. Even so, there were still events that gave cause for alarm; Germany and

Poland in 1924 experienced partial stabilization crises, while in the following year, the French and Belgian currencies weakened seriously at a time when other countries, notably Britain, Switzerland and Norway, were experiencing deflationary pressures in connection with the return to gold. Finally, in 1926, Britain experienced the worst strike in history.

Some of these events affected particular countries more than others, though by no means all the problems were of a local nature. Currency difficulties were widespread throughout this period and currency instability was certainly an important impediment to general recovery, even although some countries gained, at least initially, from depreciated currencies and inflationary financing of reconstruction. But against this have to be set certain adverse effects. Several countries failed to bring inflation under control and their currencies eventually collapsed under the strain, which left them in a much weaker state than at any time since the end of the war. Second, the uncertainty created by extremely volatile exchanges hindered the revival of foreign trade and made it difficult to plan for the future. Much energy was spent in speculative currency deals rather than in cultivating real trade transactions, and the very slow recovery in European trade must in part be attributed to the uncertainty engendered by currency instability. Third, whereas certain countries, notably France, did derive benefit from inflation and depreciated exchanges, many in central and eastern Europe did not. For these countries, a depreciated currency often brought little real gain because supply inelasticities precluded them from taking advantage of their more competitive position, while imports of equipment on which their future development depended were made more expensive. Furthermore, the artificial protection that currency depreciation provided tended to lead to the establishment of inefficient enterprises or industries that subsequently had to be given state assistance to keep them in business.

A further important barrier to recovery was shortage of resources. This was undoubtedly a major problem in central and eastern Europe in the immediate post-war years and even beyond. Nor was it simply a question of a physical shortage of equipment and raw materials, though this was certainly an acute problem in the early years after the armistice. However, there was the added problem of a serious shortage of capital, both long and short term. Central and eastern European countries were incapable of raising sufficient capital internally, nor were they able to earn sufficient foreign exchange to pay for imports of materials and equipment essential for the development of their economies. The only solution to this problem was recourse to foreign borrowing, but this failed to materialize on anywhere near the scale required. Once the post-armistice assistance for famine and relief dried up, the import of capital into continental Europe was limited. Unsettled political and economic conditions made investors reluctant to grant long-term loans to these countries, and hence they had to struggle on as best they could, relying on short-term credits and limited assistance from the League of Nations under its *ad hoc* rescue operations. Not until the middle of the 1920s, when economic conditions became more stable, did the flow of lending increase markedly, but by this time the damage had already been done. Later it will be noted how increasing external indebtedness posed a problem for some countries in the later 1920s.

Undoubtedly, the task of reconstruction and recovery in the territories of central and eastern Europe was on a scale quite different from that in western Europe.[1] Virtually all the countries of this region were faced with a whole series of almost insuperable problems, and with resources very much inferior to those of the west European powers. The list of problems makes depressing reading: physical devastation; territorial adjustments and all that this entailed in terms of economic reorganization; financial chaos, including unbalanced budgets, inflation and currency instability; balance of payments problems, unemployment, rapidly rising population and agrarian reform; political instability and weak administrative organizations; lack of balanced economic structures and shortages of almost everything. Not every country suffered from all these problems simultaneously, though it is difficult to find any that did not face at least a large proportion of them. Thus for the most part, it was scarcely a case of getting back to normal as quickly as possible; rather it was a question of trying to avoid economic disintegration. Indeed, many of these countries barely managed to regain pre-war levels of activity by the middle of the decade, and some failed to do even that.

The region as a whole had of course been economically backward before the war. The extent of industrial development, even in the Czech lands and in western Russia, was relatively limited and the population was still heavily dependent on agriculture; in Bulgaria, Romania and Yugoslavia, up to 80 per cent of the population earned a livelihood from the land. Productivity and income per capita were low, which meant limited savings for purposes of investment outside the primary sector. Yet though economically very backward, there was a degree of economic cohesion and stability within the region before the outbreak of the war, especially within those lands encompassed within the Austro-Hungarian Empire. However, the impact of war and its aftermath shattered any semblance of unity and stability that central and eastern Europe might once have had. The economic, political and social life of virtually all the countries in the region was left in complete chaos. Famine was rife, destruction and pillage by invading armies had damaged much of the productive facilities, trade was almost non-existent, while financial and currency systems were in ruins. The peace treaty settlements made things worse because the new territorial arrangements, by splitting up viable economic units and destroying former patterns of communication and trading links, merely served to impede economic development. Moreover, the new states inherited various fragments of territory that required welding into viable and cohesive political and economic units. In other words, not only had these countries to tackle the ordinary problem of physical reconstruction but they literally had to create new administrations and national economies out of the motley collection of territories they inherited. Moreover, they were left to accomplish these tasks almost unaided at a time when resources were desperately short, and with financial and administrative systems far from commensurate with the needs at hand.

Population pressures added to these problems. In many countries, population was rising much faster than in the west, and at a time when the traditional safety-valve of emigration was closing down. This meant even further pressure on already densely populated farmlands, and the attempt to solve this problem by extensive land reforms led to a fragmentation of holdings and a significant increase in small-scale subsistence farming. The effect of the land reforms is difficult to assess precisely because the extent of reform and its impact varied a great deal from one country to another. But initially it probably had a perverse effect on production and yields by reducing the scope for mechanization and improved efficiency and by perpetuating all the defects of individualistic farming. In Romania, for example, where large estates were confiscated and some 30 per cent of the land redistributed, the reforms definitely had a harmful effect and delayed recovery. The cultivated area declined sharply and the output of cereals fell likewise. But land reform was only one of many factors that retarded the recovery of the primary sector. Others included the widespread wartime devastation, increased tax burdens, shortage of capital, the fall in primary product prices in the early 1920s, and again at the end of the decade, and the closing of west European markets to the agricultural produce of the east.

In any case, recovery of agricultural production could not really offer a viable long-term solution to the basic problem, namely increasing pressure on land resources. The obvious alternative was industrial development, but conditions were far from conducive. Shortages of plant, raw materials and capital were widespread, while currency depreciation and financial instability of the new states left little prospect of much assistance from abroad. Moreover, several countries, for example Hungary and Austria, had lost parts of their industrial sectors as a result of the peace treaty terms. The disorganization of the infrastructure, particularly communications, the generally chaotic economic conditions after the war and the poverty of the mass of the people were scarcely conducive to rapid industrialization. Export outlets were also limited because of the loss of many markets and the inefficient nature of production. Furthermore, the state could provide little direct assistance, at least initially, given the inefficient tax systems and the large burden of public debts.

Under such circumstances the only solution lay in short-term expedients. Thus inflation, currency depreciation and tariff protection became the means by which these countries sought to adjust their economies by artificially fostering industrial development. The first two are normally regarded as detrimental to economic systems, and so they are once they get out of control. On the other hand, both inflation and exchange depreciation did initially provide a stimulus to investment and exports and also to employment. Nearly all the countries concerned solved their low capacity problem temporarily by the inflationary financing of investment. Thus in Austria, there was a big expansion of capacity between 1919 and 1923, with the result that industrial equipment was some 20 per cent greater than pre-war. The same was true in Hungary, where virtually every industry except clothing recorded additions to industrial capacity. Physical reconstruction also proceeded rapidly in Poland, while currency depreciation allowed the country to exploit the markets of countries with more stable currencies. At the same time, currency depreciation and liberal tariff protection helped to protect the domestic market from competing imports. Most of the countries in the region had higher tariffs than before the war, a reflection of what was to become a more sustained drive towards economic autarchy in later years. When completed in 1925–26, the Czech tariff structure was almost double that of the old Austro-Hungarian tariff, representing 36.4 per cent of the total value of imports.

It is doubtful whether the expedients used offered a real and lasting solution to the problems of this area. Certainly, inflation and currency depreciation did for a time serve to boost activity in these countries, but once they got out of control, as in the case of Austria, Hungary and Poland, they probably did more harm than good. The German example is instructive in this respect, as we shall see later. Once stabilization and financial control were effected there was a temporary set-back to industrial growth. Forced industrialization gave rise to inefficient under-takings and much excess capacity. In fact, development was reflected more in the expansion of capacity than in output. For example, though Austria and Hungary expanded their industrial capacity considerably in the early 1920s, by the middle of the decade industrial output was running at about 75–80 per cent of pre-war, or about two-thirds the capacity available. Over the region as a whole, capacity was probably expanded in excess of requirements, once the artificial conditions of inflation and currency depreciation had ceased to exist.

In other words, the measures resorted to in the early 1920s gave an artificial boost to the economies but they produced few real and lasting benefits. For the region as a whole, industrial and agricultural output by 1925 still fell short of the 1913 level. There were one or two notable bright spots. Czechoslovakia, which inherited important industrial interests from Austro-Hungary and had reformed her financial and currency systems at an early date, experienced rapid growth, with an increase in manufacturing output of 36 per cent above the 1913 level. But for the majority, it was a struggle for survival, with little hope at this stage of working off the 'gigantic backlog of backwardness'. Inflation and currency depreciation could provide only temporary alleviation of the fundamental problems of this region, and they in turn became problems that ultimately necessitated remedial action. Once some sort of financial stability was restored, capital imports provided a source of relief, but again these proved to be transient because at the crucial moment, in the late 1920s, they were hastily curtailed.

Russia presents a different case and therefore merits a few separate comments. Under the new regime the country was virtually cut off from the west, and in the years 1919 to 1921 the economy ground almost to a halt under the impact of civil war and external border hostilities, inflation and communization. The process of recovery from this chaos was long and arduous, but the groundwork was laid in the years 1922–24, with a partial return to private enterprise under the New Economic Policy (NEP), the stabilization of the currency, the restoration of budg-etary equilibrium and the end of civil violence and external conflict. In the first year of what might be regarded as normality (1922–23), output of large-scale industry rose by 50 per cent, but this still left it some 60 per cent down on the 1913 level. Not until 1926 did industrial and agricultural output exceed the pre-war base, and then only by a small margin. A multiplicity of factors impeded recovery, including the famous shortages of skilled labour, fuel, materials and spare parts, a disorganized transport system and the lack of competent managerial personnel.

Compared with the east, the problems facing western Europe were less severe, though one or two countries, notably France and Belgium, were in a poor state at the end of the war. France emerged almost bankrupt, with large debts and some 10 per cent of her territory devastated. Industrial and agricultural output was some 40 per cent down on 1913, with exports a fraction of their pre-war level. In fact, France's industry and agriculture were probably more severely crippled than those of her neighbours, with the possible exception of Belgium. The franc had lost 50 per cent of its former purchasing power and worse was still to follow in this respect.

Despite these setbacks, France made a fairly rapid recovery. By the middle of the 1920s, most major indices had regained or surpassed pre-war levels, though agriculture lagged behind. Several factors were responsible for the success. Physical reconstruction went ahead rapidly, assisted by generous governmental aid on the assumption that the Germans would foot the bill through reparations. In the process, France gained a more modernized industrial structure, with heavy investment in new equipment and modern technology that made French industry more competitive than previously. The sharp decline in the value of the franc encouraged industrialists to borrow for investment purposes, while the same factor also boosted the tourist trade and exports. The latter increased rapidly after 1922, and by 1926 they had risen by 56 per cent, at which point they were some one-third higher than in 1913. The economy still suffered from weak spots, and France nearly paid the price of inflationary financing in a collapse of the currency, but she was probably one of the few countries to gain on balance from inflation and currency depreciation. Belgium had a similar experience, though here the recovery effort was not so impressive.

Of the belligerent powers, Italy's post-war performance was probably the most spectacular. This country was less severely affected by the war and post-war slump than either France or Belgium, although according to some accounts, Italy's economic machinery was badly disorganized, almost to the point of breakdown in the post-armistice period. If this is correct, then Italy certainly staged a remarkable recovery, because by 1922 industrial production and domestic output had regained their pre-war levels. From 1922 onwards, Mussolini's industrialization and efficiency drive did much to hasten expansion. Aided by generous government assistance and a liberal credit policy, Italy enjoyed continuous industrial expansion through to 1926. By that date, manufacturing output was more than 60 per cent above the pre-war level, with domestic output one-fifth higher. Exports too rose strongly because they received a boost from currency depreciation and the occupation of the Ruhr, which allowed Italy to re-enter eastern markets. Good harvests in 1923 and 1925 and a flow of surplus labour to neighbouring countries assisted the process of development. But then the expansion came almost to a halt as the favourable factors disappeared one by one. Credit facilities were tightened, emigration outlets declined, and bad harvests followed good. Above all, Mussolini's promise to defend the lira resulted in an overvalued currency after stabilization in 1927.

The country least affected by wartime dislocation, Britain, had a rather chequered performance in the first half of the 1920s. A fairly strong recovery to

1920 was followed by one of the most severe depressions in history, when all indices of activity fell sharply. Recovery set in during late 1921 and 1922 and was sustained through to 1925 when income and production levels had cleared those of 1920 or 1913 by a reasonable margin. However, the recovery was by no means complete. Exports were still 25 per cent down on 1913, while unemployment, even at its lowest, was still around one million, or 9.2 per cent of the insured labour force. The intermittent policy of deflation in connection with the return to the gold standard in April 1925 helped to depress activity below potential, though the main problem was a structural one. A large proportion of resources was tied up in the old basic industries such as textiles, shipbuilding, coal, iron and steel, the demand for products of which, both at home and abroad, was either declining or stagnant.

Though the main neutral countries (Norway, Sweden, Denmark and the Netherlands) were not directly involved in the war effort, their economies did not escape unscathed. One of the biggest setbacks was the loss of export markets, especially in Europe, so that by 1920 export volumes were some 30–50 per cent lower than pre-war. These countries also made the effort to return to the gold standard at pre-war parity, which meant they experienced a bout of deflation during the course of the 1920s. After the post-war boom, they experienced a sharp contraction in activity (with the exception of the Netherlands), which was partly occasioned by severe retrenchment policies, to check the boom and in preparation for the return to gold. Nevertheless, compared with Britain, the neutrals recorded a far better performance in the first half of the 1920s.

Initially, recovery from the wartime setback in activity was rapid, so that by 1920, levels of output were already above the pre-war base. The collapse of the boom coupled with deflationary policies brought a violent contraction in 1921 in all countries apart from the Netherlands. It was most severe and prolonged in Sweden, largely as a result of the government's severe retrenchment policy in anticipation of the return to gold in 1924, after which renewed progress set in. On the other hand, Norway and Denmark recovered more rapidly from the 1921 depression because deflationary policies were not forced to such extremes as in Sweden. Both achieved rapid rates of expansion through to 1925, when levels of activity were far higher than in 1913. The Netherlands avoided the severe post-war deflationary crisis and experienced sustained growth throughout the decade, assisted by a strong upswing in exports.

The boom of the later 1920s

By the middle of the 1920s, economic and political conditions in Europe were more stable than they had been in the early 1920s. The evacuation of the Ruhr in 1923, the revised reparations settlement with Germany in 1924, the signing of the Locarno Pact in the following year[2] and the negotiated agreements relating to Allied war debts did much to boost international confidence and reduce political tensions and suspicions of war. Most of the great inflations had run their course, and Britain's return to the gold standard in 1925 paved the way for the completion

of currency stabilization elsewhere. Primary commodity prices had firmed considerably after the disastrous drop following the post-war boom. Above all, the European reconstruction process was almost complete and it seemed that Europe could look forward to a period of real and sustained progress. The tensions and underlying weaknesses of the international economic system were all but forgotten in the boom of the later 1920s.

The expansion in activity was a fairly worldwide phenomenon, although the most dramatic manifestations of the boom occurred in America, where excessive stock market speculation attracted much attention. However, the upswing of the later 1920s differed in several respects from those of the past. For one thing, there was no significant pressure on real resources at the peak of the cycle; indeed, if anything, there was still a considerable amount of slack to be taken up in most economies. Unemployment rates remained high, and there was still a margin of underutilized capacity. Prices were trending downward slowly, while wages were subject to only marginal upward adjustments. The main point of similarity was the significant rise in output, together with the upsurge in business profits in industrial countries. But these were by no means spectacular compared with those occurring in similar phases of past cycles. What marked the boom out from previous ones was the intense stock market speculation that occurred in the United States, and to a lesser extent in some European countries, and for this reason, together with the dramatic collapse that followed, the boom has attracted more interest than it would otherwise deserve.

Europe as a whole progressed more rapidly than most of the major regions of the world in this period. Industrial production kept pace with the average, while the output of crude products advanced at a considerably faster rate. Hence by 1929, Europe had recovered part of the ground lost earlier, though the League of Nations' comment to the effect that the pre-war equilibrium between Europe and the rest of the world had largely been restored now seems wide of the mark. If there was an equilibrium, it was more apparent than real. Below the surface there were plenty of signs of maladjustment, notably large areas of underemployed resources in certain sectors, the rise in primary inventories, the dependence of some countries on foreign capital and the patched-up nature of the international currency system. But despite these difficulties, Europe enjoyed some real progress, and by 1929, income per capita was greater on average than in 1925 or 1913, even though it still remained unevenly distributed.

Though most countries experienced an increase in economic activity in the years 1925–29, the pace of expansion varied considerably from country to country and it was rarely free from interruptions. It ranged from the dramatic, with Russia surging ahead in the last year or two under the impetus of the first Five-Year Plan, to partial stagnation in the case of Denmark and Norway, both of which were suffering from gold parity deflation. Italy, the UK and Austria performed modestly, and in the west the best achievements were recorded by Sweden, Germany, Belgium, France and Luxembourg. On balance, eastern Europe probably did marginally better than the west (Hungary, Romania and Czechoslovakia in particular had impressive rates of industrial growth together with a good recovery

Table 2.2 Indices of industrial production for selected regions, 1926–29 (1925 = 100)

	1926	1927	1928	1929
Industrial Europe*	95.6	113.2	116.5	123.1
Agricultural Europe+	105.6	112.2	113.3	122.2
USSR	143.8	168.4	205.3	256.1
United States	106.0	105.0	110.0	123.0
World Total^	102.2	108.7	113.0	120.7

*Austria, Belgium, UK, Czechoslovakia, Denmark, France, Germany, Luxemburg, Netherlands, Sweden, Switzerland and the Saar.
+Bulgaria, Estonia, Finland, Greece, Hungary, Italy, Latvia, Poland, Portugal, Romania, Spain and Yugoslavia.
^The world indices are probably on the low side since the League of Nations' estimates for the United States require some upward revision.

Sources: League of Nations, *World Production and Prices, 1925–1932* 1933, 45, 49; OEEC, *Industrial Statistics, 1900–1959* 1960, 9

in primary production), though one should bear in mind that the east was only recovering most of the ground lost during the war and through to 1925. Cyclical experience also varied a great deal, especially at the upper turning-point. Several countries experienced minor interruptions to growth (for example, Britain in 1926 and again in 1928, Germany in 1926, France, Italy and Denmark in 1927), while the spread at the turning-point was wide. Poland hit the peak as early as February 1929, followed by Belgium in March and Germany in April. The Swedish downturn came in the second quarter of the year, then the British in July 1929, but France hung on until March 1930. This suggests some evidence of independent recessionary tendencies within Europe before the US downturn in the summer of 1929, though in some cases these could have been prompted by the prior decline in American lending.

Several countries suffered the adverse effects of currency policy in this period. The classic case frequently cited is that of Britain, where the return to the gold standard at the pre-war parity in 1925 is estimated to have overvalued sterling by some 10 per cent. This certainly made exporting more difficult for Britain, but the dampened nature of the boom during this period cannot be attributed solely to the lag in exports, while it is debatable whether a lower parity for the pound would have made that much difference to exports. The main problem with the export trade was a structural one, namely specialization in a range of products for which the demand was declining, and which could not readily be cured by an undervaluation of the currency. Unfortunately, the domestic market did not compensate for the weakness of exports. In the United States, for example, the boom of the 1920s was powered by domestically based industries, construction, services, transport and the new consumer durable trades, some of which experienced rapid technical progress, leading to a sharp fall in unit costs. These sectors were less buoyant in Britain. The rise in investment was very modest, especially after 1927, while many of the potential growth industries exerted only a moderate impact on the economy.

Building, for example, collapsed in 1927–28 after the cutback in subsidies, and over the years 1926–29 there was a negative rate of growth in construction. Most of the service industries recorded modest rates of expansion, while the rates of growth in some of the newer industries, electricity, electrical engineering and vehicles in particular, were no greater than the average for all industry and considerably lower than in the first half of the 1920s.

Currency policy had a far more drastic impact in the case of Italy. The deliberate appreciation of the lira by Mussolini in 1927 was clearly a mistake, because it involved severe domestic deflation and high unemployment. Unemployment nearly tripled between 1926 and 1929, industrial production stagnated and the growth of exports was checked. The Italian economy made limited headway compared with the first half of the 1920s, though some slowing down was probably inevitable given the overvigorous expansion through to 1926 and the fact that many factors favourable to growth were beginning to disappear by the middle of the decade. Norway and Denmark also had a similar experience, though it was less severe in its effects than in the case of Italy. Here, the objective of monetary policy was to increase the exchange value of their currencies before stabilization (1926–28) at the pre-war parities. The example of Finland, a country that achieved rapid economic progress throughout the 1920s, suggests that Denmark and Norway could have avoided severe compression and disequilibrium had they allowed their currencies to depreciate. Sweden went through a similar experience earlier, but managed to adjust more rapidly partly thanks to sustained industrial transformation and a buoyant demand for exports. Thus in the later 1920s, Sweden's economy was expanding vigorously despite a return to parity in 1924, though one should bear in mind that much of the domestic adjustment required to carry through the stabilization had been accomplished in the violent contraction of 1920–22.

Two countries that did better in the later 1920s were France and Belgium, partly by dint of different policies from those followed by the countries previously discussed. Both countries had faced a big reconstruction task at the end of the war, but they had made the most of government reconstruction payments, inflationary financing and disrupted exchanges to recoup lost ground. Nor did currency stabilization in the mid-1920s halt the process of expansion, because neither country made the mistake of restoring the former parity, much though it was desired. In fact, both currencies were somewhat undervalued in the later 1920s, though the gains on this account were probably less marked than in the first half of the decade. France's achievements were impressive. Industrial production rose by a quarter between 1925 and 1929, while income per head increased by nearly 17 per cent. By the end of the decade, industrial production was some 35–40 per cent greater than pre-war, income per head was higher by one-quarter or more, while the volume of exports was nearly 50 per cent larger. Such gains were partly the result of a considerable increase in industrial capacity, especially in sectors such as chemicals, engineering and metallurgy, and fairly rapid technical advances in new industries such as rayon, electricity and motor-car manufacturing. France did much to modernize her industrial structure in these years.

While both France and Belgium were consolidating on the reconstruction gains of the early 1920s, Germany by contrast had to start the reconstruction phase again because the explosive inflation of 1923 wreaked havoc with the economy. True, it did not destroy fixed assets (indeed, it brought into being much new plant and equipment, albeit that a considerable part of the new capacity was not suitable for future needs), but the process of stabilization did severely check the expansion of the early 1920s, so much so that the level of activity was little better than it had been at the end of the war. Most fixed debts were wiped out, but this was offset by a severe loss of working capital. For a short time, stabilization itself exerted a deflationary impact and led to the collapse of a number of cumbersome industrial empires that had been formed during the inflationary period. Doubts about whether stabilization would hold led to a minor crisis in 1926, with further deflationary implications.

The tasks ahead were formidable. Apart from the critical liquidity problem, much industrial plant and equipment required renovating to make it more efficient. Productivity had sunk to a low level in 1923, and the large amount of capacity brought on stream did little to improve the situation. Moreover, given the reparations bill, Germany needed a large boost to exports and this could be attained only by improving her competitive position.

Despite the difficult situation, Germany achieved a remarkable rejuvenation of her economy in the later 1920s. Heavy reliance was placed on foreign borrowing, the consequences of which are discussed elsewhere. It is doubtful whether much of this found its way directly into 'productive' or foreign-exchange-earning enterprises, but the inflow of funds certainly eased the capital shortage and released domestic resources for internal development. Whatever the precise direction of the capital flow, the record is impressive. Progress was especially marked in the heavy capital goods sector and the newer science-based industries, but less apparent in the consumer goods trades. Large additions to capacity were accompanied by extensive programmes of mechanization and rationalization in many of the key sectors such as coal, iron and steel, chemical and electrical industries. The loss of hard coal reserves in Silesia and the Saar was offset by rapid exploitation of lignite, the production of which doubled. Mining operations in general were extensively mechanized, and, by 1928, 75 per cent of the Ruhr coal output was cut mechanically. This was an impressive achievement when set against the British record.

By dint of these efforts, German industry was placed on a more secure footing by the end of the decade. But though considerable expansion was achieved between 1925 and 1929, much of it only made up for ground lost earlier. It was only in the last couple of years that levels of economic activity and real income regained or surpassed pre-war dimensions, and by then there were signs that the economic prosperity was coming to an end as the inflow of foreign capital diminished. There were, too, several weak spots. Certain sectors remained depressed, notably agriculture despite substantial protection, and unemployment was still too high. Exports barely managed to regain their pre-war level, a performance hardly in keeping with Germany's heavy external commitments. Indeed, given the weaknesses in the latter respects, one cannot but conclude that Germany's prosperity was precariously based and that the economy was kept in motion by the influx of foreign funds.

It is more difficult to make firm generalizations about the rest of Europe and the Baltic countries owing to the paucity of information on some of the countries. But it does appear that eastern Europe as a whole did slightly better than the west in terms of absolute growth in the later 1920s. Certainly, primary production increased more rapidly and there were some impressive gains in industrial production, particularly in Hungary, Romania, Latvia, Czechoslovakia and Poland. As noted earlier, Russia also experienced a sharp burst of expansion under the first Five-Year Plan. After the lean years of reconstruction, the whole area registered an expansion of capital formation and a diversification of output with notable gains in coal, iron and steel, cement and oil production. The process of adaptation was assisted by the influx of foreign capital and systematic encouragement of industry by state subsidies, tax reliefs, import controls and high tariffs. The drive towards greater self-sufficiency was also accompanied by an extension of state enterprise. Even so, the gains in per capita income were often very modest, partly because of rapid population growth in some of the countries, notably in Romania, Bulgaria and Poland. Income levels generally throughout the region were very much lower than in western Europe, and in the case of Romania and Poland, income per capita had barely changed since 1913 by the end of the decade.

For virtually all the countries in what may be termed the agrarian sector of Europe (the population dependent on agriculture was 50 per cent or more in all central and eastern European countries apart from Austria and Czechoslovakia), the 1920s as a whole was a period of reconstruction and fundamental adjustment to new conditions both internally and outwith these countries. New economic systems had to be established, new markets sought, new products developed, agricultural methods were in urgent need of improvement, while expansion in the industrial sector was required to cater for the growing population and the resources released from the land. Most countries managed to make some progress in all respects, albeit slowly. Given the high agricultural content of their economies and their dependence on imported supplies to further the process of industrial diversification, probably the first and most essential step was to reform agriculture and improve its efficiency so as to permit an increase in exports to provide much-needed foreign exchange. This in itself was no easy task in this period, because the outlets for primary products, especially in western Europe, which had been the traditional market, were drying up. Moreover, some of the land reforms of the post-war period served only to impede progress in this respect, because they led to a greater fragmentation of holdings, which was inimical to innovation and enhanced efficiency. Nevertheless, several countries did make considerable progress, which helped to strengthen their economic position. An enlightened agricultural policy in Czechoslovakia did much to support the prosperity of industry. Land reform was accompanied by technical and financial assistance to farmers, which enabled them to improve their methods of production and concentrate on the more profitable crops such as sugar beet. The break-up of large estates in

Lithuania was replaced by a progressive cooperative movement, the leaders of which recognized that unless old practices were changed, the peasantry would be condemned to subsistence farming. Within the matter of a decade, Lithuania, like Denmark, had shifted from cereals to dairy and livestock products, which fetched good prices abroad. The other Baltic states also proved highly successful in adapting their primary sectors by exploiting their forest resources and, in the case of Estonia and Latvia, developing foreign markets for butter and bacon.

Evidence of progress is not difficult to find, but it hardly amounted to a revolution. By the end of the 1920s, eastern Europe for the most part still remained a backward and economically vulnerable area. Standards of living were low and both agriculture and industry were highly inefficient compared with western standards. A policy of economic nationalism, although it had visible effects, tended to foster inefficiency and high-cost enterprises. The area remained sensitive to tendencies in the outside world because of its heavy dependence on the export of primary products, especially agricultural commodities, at favourable prices and reliance on imported capital. Only so long as these conditions held could this shaky equilibrium be maintained.

On balance, therefore, the economic performance of Europe during the 1920s as a whole was respectable. After a shaky start in the immediate reconstruction period, many countries managed to achieve high rates of growth, though inevitably the rates are inflated by the low base prevailing at the end of the war. However, even considering the transwar period as a whole (1913–29), the average rate of growth of domestic output for western Europe was about 2 per cent per annum and slightly less for eastern Europe. This compares favourably with the period following (1929–38), when average growth rates were about half this figure. The most successful countries were the Netherlands, Finland, Norway, Sweden, Switzerland and Denmark, with growth above average, whereas Austria, Germany and the UK had a below-average performance. In eastern Europe, Czechoslovakia and Yugoslavia did better than the average for this area. The Baltic states also performed well, as did Spain and Greece.

Despite the creditable growth performance the foundations of prosperity, at least in Europe and probably elsewhere, remained 'fragile and precarious'. There were certainly signs of underlying weaknesses within particular countries and also with the working of the international economy as a whole. These, of course, became all too apparent once the basis of prosperity was undermined. But for the time being, the expansion of these years was sufficient to conceal the sources of instability, which in turn reduced the urgency for making the necessary adjustments. We must now turn to examine some of the major international problems that affected European stability.

War debts and reparations

War debts and reparations proved to be one of the most controversial and intractable issues of the post-war decade. Negotiations as to the amounts involved and methods of payment dragged on endlessly and to little avail, because most of them were never paid. Apart from causing considerable international bitterness, the process of debt collection impeded the smooth functioning of the international economy and seriously weakened Germany, the main debtor.

Altogether some twenty-eight countries were involved in one way or another with war debts and reparations. But for many countries the amounts involved were small; by far the most important participants were Germany, the United States, Britain, France, Italy and Belgium. Germany was of course the chief debtor, with eleven creditors to her name, whereas the United States had sixteen debtors, Britain seventeen and France ten. The sums involved were enormous; inter-Allied debts alone amounted to $26.5 billion, most of which was due to the United States and Britain, with France the principal debtor. The burden imposed on Germany, as eventually fixed by the Reparations Commission in 1921, was $33 billion, the greater part of which was to be paid to France and Britain. These amounts were scaled down during the course of the 1920s, though the sums, together with accrued interest, still remained large: too large, in fact, to be met in full, with the inevitable result that they were declared moribund in the depression of the early 1930s.

Whether sums on this scale should have been imposed and whether in practice they could have been paid are still matters of debate. What is certain is that in the political context of the time there was little prospect of them either being cancelled altogether or of the two, that is reparations and war debts, being linked together. France insisted on exactions from the enemy, whereas the United States expected payment for services rendered to the Allies. Allied payment of war debts was dependent upon reparations flowing from Germany. The possibility of offsetting reparations and inter-Allied claims so that Germany could have settled directly with the United States was thwarted by America's opposition to the mixing of claims, partly no doubt on the grounds that there was a greater likelihood of Germany defaulting on her obligations than the Allied powers.

Most of the reparations bill fell to Germany. Interim payments had been made before the final bill of $33 billion was presented that provided for fixed payments on a quarterly basis beginning in January 1922. The Germans, although accepting the imposition with reluctance, regarded the claims as excessive, and argued that on both budgetary and exchange transfer grounds, it was not within the country's capacity to pay. Certainly there was some justification for these views at the time because Germany's financial and economic situation deteriorated markedly during the course of 1922 as inflation and currency depreciation rapidly accelerated. Repeated requests for a moratorium were met with refusal. By the end of 1922, Germany's capacity to meet its obligations was virtually exhausted and the prospects of further payments looked bleak. Fearing the worst, French and Belgian troops were marched into the Ruhr on 11 January 1923.

The invasion completed the collapse of Germany's financial system. The objective was to enforce payment by direct control of the Ruhr industrial system, but passive German resistance thwarted French efforts, the financing of which sent the mark up to 'stellar magnitudes'.[3] Neither side gained, but the struggle continued until the mark was rendered worthless. Whether the German government deliberately provoked the inflationary crisis to prove to the world that she could not pay reparations is a moot point, but the effect was certainly spectacular. By September 1923, the currency was in such a state that Germany called off the resistance and proposed the introduction of a new currency, the *Rentenmark*.

The upshot of this débâcle was a reconsideration of the reparations issue by the Reparations Commission. A committee under General Dawes proposed an extension of the payment period and a reduction in annual payments to more manageable proportions, though no reduction in the total reparations debt was contemplated. The Dawes Plan came into force in September 1924, and on the surface it worked well. Annuities were paid regularly and transferred without much apparent difficulty. But the underlying weaknesses in Germany's payments situation were masked by an entirely new factor, namely massive foreign borrowing mainly from America. Because of budgetary and balance of payments difficulties, Germany borrowed 28 billion marks abroad in the period 1924–30, out of which she paid reparations amounting to 10.3 billion. In other words, her reparation payments were covered at least two and a half times by the import of capital. So long as foreign capital poured into the country, the settlement of reparations ran smoothly, but once funds dried up, then the basic weakness of the position was exposed. The crunch came in the late 1920s, when American lending was sharply curtailed; this set off a chain reaction among foreign banks demanding the withdrawal of loans from Germany. The position was extremely tricky because not only had Germany piled up large foreign liabilities, but many of these were in the form of short-term debts liable to immediate recall.

Recognition of Germany's precarious financial position led to one last attempt to solve the reparations issue. A committee of experts set up in 1929 under Owen D. Young proposed a reduction in the capital sum and a scaling down of the annuities. By the time the new arrangements came into effect, in April 1930, the impact of depression was making it difficult to comply with even these modified terms. Within a year Germany was engulfed in financial crisis, and in June 1931, President Hoover proposed a moratorium on reparations.

Altogether Germany paid only a fraction of the original reparations bill of $33 billion; estimates vary, but the highest suggest no more than one-third. Clearly, it was a futile exercise to attempt to recover such large debts. Whether Germany could have discharged her obligations more satisfactorily had she made the effort is a debatable point, though most writers have tended to argue that they were beyond her means. Whatever the true position the fact remains that the reparations burden had unfortunate consequences for Germany, especially in 1923 and again in 1929–31 and, in turn, for the economic and financial tranquility of Europe. The other point to bear in mind is that Germany was embittered by the severity of the peace terms and the burden of the war guilt clause, which proved to be grist to the mill of Hitler's fascist party.

The first mistake of the Allied powers when dealing with the problem was not so much that they accepted an unrealistically large reparations bill but that initially the annuities were set at too high a level. These could easily have been set at a more reasonable level in the early years when Germany was in the process of recovery from war and the shock of 1923, and then adjusted in time in accordance with improvements in her economic position. By fixing them as they did, they left Germany with what seemed an impossible task, and hence little real effort was made to try to meet either the budgetary or transfer objectives. The second mistake was for the Allies to continue to bale out Germany with loans. Foreign borrowing on the scale indulged in during the later 1920s had several adverse consequences. For one thing, large capital imports tended to aggravate the transfer problems in so far as they raised Germany's propensity to import, and at the same time reduced the buying power of lending countries and hence their import of German products. In addition, the rise in German purchasing power occasioned by capital inflows meant a diversion of resources towards production for the home market rather than for exports. Capital imports all too frequently were channelled into non-export-earning activities. In a wider context, massive foreign borrowing only stored up trouble for the future: Germany simply incurred one debt to pay another and the real problem of redemption was never squarely faced. As it was, Germany was able to meet her payments without great hardship to herself and with the minimum of disturbance to creditor nations in the form of unwanted German goods. Borrowing merely concealed the payments problem for the time being, but it could not do so indefinitely. Once foreign lending dried up, Germany, and other European countries with large external debts, were unable to stand the strain; financial collapse was therefore inevitable.

The settlement of debts among the Allied powers proved no more satisfactory. The final tally amounted to $23 billion (excluding Russian debts, which became worthless after the Bolshevik revolution). The United States was the largest creditor, accounting for about one-half of the total, most of it having been lent to Britain, France and Italy. Britain was the next largest creditor, with claims on other countries far exceeding her debts to America. The main net debtors were France, Italy and Belgium.

Several early attempts to find a workable solution to the war debts issue all ran foul of the United States, who insisted on being paid in full. This meant that the other Allied powers had no alternative but to insist on collecting their own debts, including reparations. Subsequently, the United States relaxed its hard attitude and concluded agreements with countries individually, by which the terms of payment were liberalized and the capital sums scaled down considerably. Even these concessions did not solve the problem. As with reparations, the payment of war debts raised budgetary and transfer difficulties. Easily transferable commodities were in short supply and creditors were reluctant to accept payment in competing goods. Clearing claims with the United States proved the most difficult task because increasing protection in that country and her demand for payment in gold and dollars made it difficult for the debtors to raise the requisite funds, especially because nearly all of them had unfavourable payment balances with the United States. In fact, payments were made but the process was farcical, and indirectly it involved a link with reparations, which the Americans were never prepared to accept in practice. The United States, and to a lesser extent other creditors, made capital loans to Germany, who then paid her creditors, while the latter in turn passed on the money to the United States in settlement of their own war debts. This process went on until the flow of funds from America dried up, and when, in the early 1930s, the Allies were forced to relinquish their claims on Germany, war debts soon died a natural death. The final accounting shows that America received $2.6 billion from the European Allies, a small amount compared with the original $12 billion and less than half that under the revised settlements of the 1920s. Four countries (Britain, France, Italy and Belgium) were responsible for the bulk of the payments to America and collected most of the reparations, which more than covered their combined external payment obligations.

Thus after a decade of political wrangling, relatively little was paid, either in reparations or war debts, against the original claims presented. The process of negotiation involved valuable time and energy, and the continued existence of the problems served as a source of international friction throughout the 1920s. The manner in which the payments were eventually effected concealed the real issues and gave rise to basic disequilibrium in the international payments mechanism, which was bound to be exposed sooner or later.

Inflation and currency stabilization

Few countries emerged from the war with their monetary and currency systems unscathed. Nearly all currencies lost their stability and depreciated in value once the tie with gold was broken or the artificial pegging practised in wartime was released. By the end of 1920, most European currencies were well below their pre-war par values in relation to the dollar and in some cases the depreciation had much further to go. The loss in value was not surprising because the war had seriously weakened the productive mechanism of economies; it had also created balance of payments problems, and inflationary methods of financing had been widespread.

The restoration of monetary stability was regarded as a matter of some urgency after the war. It was considered highly desirable that each nation should return to a fixed gold parity as soon as possible. But the stabilization process proved to be a long drawn-out affair that lasted most of the decade. No systematic plan was drawn up to deal with the problem, although the United States, which had little difficulty in readopting the full gold standard in 1919, served as a rough benchmark for the realignment of all other currencies. Each country stabilized and returned to the gold standard as soon as conditions were deemed to be suitable, and this depended very much on how quickly countries got their financial affairs under control.

The manner in which stabilization was carried out and the characteristics of the new standard varied considerably. At one extreme, there was a select band of countries that managed to regain their pre-war parities: these were Britain, Switzerland, the Netherlands, Denmark, Sweden and Norway. Rigorous retrenchment at an early stage enabled these countries to avoid the inflationary problems of much of Europe. At the other extreme, there were five countries (Austria, Hungary, Poland, Germany and Russia) who were forced to introduce new monetary units, because violent bouts of inflation wrecked their currencies completely.

Table 2.3 Dates and levels at which currencies stabilized in the 1920s

Country	Stabilisation date*	% of Pre-war Value
Austria	1922	new currency
Belgium	1926	14.3
Bulgaria	1924(1928)	3.7
Czechoslovakia	1923	14.3
Denmark	1926	pre-war parity
Estonia	1924(1927)	1.1
France	1926(1928)	20.0
Finland	1926	12.5
Germany	1923(1924)	new currency
Greece	1928	6.7
Hungary	1924	new currency
Italy	1927	25.0
Japan	1930	pre-war parity
Latvia	1921	0.8
Netherlands	1924	pre-war parity
Norway	1928	pre-war parity
Poland	1926(1927)‡	new currency
Portugal	1929(1931)	4.6
Romania	1927(1929)	3.0
Sweden	1922	pre-war parity
Switzerland	1924	pre-war parity
United Kingdom	1925	pre-war parity
Yugoslavia	1925(1931)	9.1

* Dates of _de jure_ stabilization where different from those of _de facto_ stabilization are shown in brackets.
‡ Poland initially stabilized the gold value of its currency in 1924 but was forced to abandon it the following year.

Source: League of Nations 1946, 92–3.

The remaining countries stabilized between these two extremes at values well below pre-war, as, for example, France at 20.0 per cent of the former dollar value, Belgium (14.3 per cent), Italy (25.0 per cent), Romania (3.7 per cent), Bulgaria (3.7 per cent), Yugoslavia (9.1 per cent), Czechoslovakia (14.3 per cent) and Finland (12.5 per cent). Dates and levels at which currencies were stabilized are given in Table 2.3.

The full gold standard, or specie standard, in which gold coins circulate internally and all other money is readily convertible into gold, was abandoned almost universally. Instead, a watered-down version of the gold standard (the gold exchange standard) was generally adopted, which meant that restrictions were placed on the convertibility of non-commodity money into gold and on the export of gold. Even in the case of the few countries that went on to the gold bullion standard (e.g., Britain, Denmark, Norway), notes could not readily be converted into gold on demand except for export purposes and then only at a fixed price and in large minimum amounts. However, the majority of countries opted for a gold exchange standard whereby the monetary authority of a country tied its currency to gold indirectly by maintaining a fixed exchange rate with a foreign currency that was on either a gold coin or gold bullion standard. In other words, the central bank had the obligation to maintain the value of a national currency at par with other gold currency countries by buying and selling foreign exchange at the gold parity.

For most European countries, currency stabilization could be achieved only when inflation had been brought under control. Much of Europe suffered from inflationary forces of varying degrees of intensity in the early 1920s. The methods of financing the war had started the inflationary process, and the fiscal demands of governments after 1918 ensured that it would continue. The burden of reconstruction was heavy in many parts of Europe and this was one of the main factors making for large budgetary deficits. Government expenditures were also boosted by continued heavy military outlays, rising social security spending, and, in the case of Germany, reparation payments that accounted for one-half of the budgetary deficit in the early 1920s. The pressures came at a time when savings were low and the administration of tax systems was inefficient and hence inadequate for the tasks in hand. In any case, a squeeze on consumption through increased taxation would probably have been politically unacceptable at the time, given that consumption levels were already low in many countries. The easiest way out was therefore to resort to inflationary spending, which imposed the sacrifices in a roundabout way. This form of enforced taxation was relatively easy to administer and therefore held attractions for governments that were weak, inexperienced and disorganized. The whole process was ultimately dependent on one factor, namely ignorance about inflation and what it implied, because Europe had not experienced severe inflation for more than a century.

But in several cases it moved into the runaway stage of hyperinflation. The process by which this develops is complex and dependent partly on the psychological reaction of the people. Once they realize what is happening, they begin to take steps to protect themselves against inflation and by so doing complicate the fiscal process and throw the monetary mechanism into disorder. First, the lag between money incomes and prices is eliminated by adopting systems of indexation for wages and salaries. Second, the savings propensity drops rapidly as money loses its value and ultimately dis-saving takes place, which forces up the velocity of circulation of money. Finally, capital flight occurs as the market loses confidence and anticipates further currency depreciation, which in turn speeds up exchange depreciation and the rise in prices. As a result the fiscal needs of government are in jeopardy, because of the fall in the real value of tax receipts, and reaction to this aggravates the inflationary conditions. This process played an important part in all cases of hyperinflation in the early 1920s. By 1923, the depreciation of tax revenues in Germany had reached a point at which taxes cost more to collect than they brought in.

It has been argued that hyperinflation could never have occurred but for the continued increase in the money supply and that the process could have been checked at any time had the authorities tapered off the issue of new money, which finally they did. This argument, although not incorrect, tends to overlook the *raison d'être* behind the growth of the money supply, namely fiscal needs. That the money supply was pumped up so vigorously can be explained because printing money provided a convenient way of providing governments with real resources and, second, because the effectiveness of the process declined over time as ever larger issues were required. The size of the problem was compounded in the case of Germany because of the financing of passive resistance to the Ruhr invasion in 1923. The issue of money provided governments with a means of revenue by a special kind of tax on cash balances held by people, and the rate of tax was equivalent to the depreciation of the value of money. Not until tax rates exploded (that is, prices), causing wholesale disruption to the economic system as normal economic transactions became virtually impossible to perform, did the authorities substitute a traditional tax programme for a policy of printing money.

The consequences of inflation are difficult to assess precisely. The first phase of relatively moderate inflation probably did make some contribution to the resources needed for reconstruction. Countries that experienced inflation escaped the worst effects of the depression of 1921 (in Germany, output actually rose quite strongly) and benefited from the encouragement given to capital investment. France and Belgium, who managed to contain inflation within reasonable bounds, probably did well out of it. But once inflation was allowed to run out of control, the story was different. Germany, for example, gained initially from inflation, in that production and employment were higher than in countries that followed a policy of retrenchment. But she reaped the costs in 1923, when activity rates fell sharply. By the end of that year, real income was barely one-half of that in 1913 and industrial production was below even the level of 1920. Unemployment rose to very high levels towards the end of 1923. In fact, it took some time for Germany to recover from the shock, and it was not until the later 1920s that production and real incomes were restored to pre-war levels. Moreover, because most liquid capital and savings were destroyed in the inflation, the propensity to save was low after 1923; this meant that capital was short and interest rates high, forcing Germany to borrow heavily, with unfortunate consequences from the point of view of economic stability.

The way in which inflation was brought under control and stabilization was effected varied a great deal from one country to another, though usually severe financial and monetary measures were required to ensure success. One of the first countries to achieve success was Latvia, who, without foreign aid, put a definite stop to inflation in the summer of 1921. State recourse to the printing press for budgetary purposes ceased in July 1921, and the national currency was abandoned for fiscal accounting purposes, with taxes being 'valorized' in terms of gold, a practice adopted by Germany in 1923. Czechoslovakia also dealt with the infla-tionary problem promptly by instituting severe fiscal measures. All the countries that experienced hyperinflation were forced to bring in new currency units. In the case of Austria and Hungary, both of which secured League assistance, the cur-rency was stabilized by means other than fiscal policy so as to achieve a monetary unit on the basis of which fiscal policy could be made effective. Though attempts were made to increase taxes in both cases, there was no systematic effort to adjust them to the depreciation of the currency through tax 'valorization' schemes. The initial stabilization was achieved by a return of confidence as a result of the League of Nations' financial reconstruction schemes. The League arranged international loans for Austria in 1922 and Hungary in 1924, and the League's staff took over the supervision of the finances of both countries until 1926. Once confidence in the new currencies was secured fiscal policy rapidly became effective, and budgetary equilibrium was achieved in a short time.

Germany, on the other hand, managed her preliminary stabilization without external assistance, though subsequently an international loan was arranged to ensure its success. Two important measures preceded the stabilization of the mark in November 1923. The passive resistance expenditure in the Ruhr was stopped in September and taxes were assessed in terms of gold. Almost simultaneously with preparations for restoring budgetary equilibrium, it was announced that a new currency, the *Rentenmark*, would be introduced to replace the worthless currency then in existence. Its success was ensured by two factors: the issue was strictly limited and it was backed by the security of an internal loan on the basis of real assets (land and buildings). In the final analysis, much depended on the public's confidence in the experiment. Once there appeared to be a reasonable prospect that the *Rentenmark* would retain its value, the public's demand for cash recovered quickly, though it is doubtful whether the new currency would have lasted long had the government failed to complete its fiscal reforms quickly.

Attempts at currency reform were sometimes prolonged and often involved an initial stabilization of the currency and then a return to the gold standard. This was true in the case of France, Belgium and Italy, as well as a number of other countries. Though inflation was not excessive in these cases, the early and half-hearted attempts at reform ensured its continuation. The French franc, for example, was almost on the point of collapse before firm action was taken. Fortunately, the right-wing Poincaré government of July 1926 restored confidence quickly by a series of rigorous measures, including increased taxes, reduced public spending and the funding of a large part of the floating debt. By the end of the year *de facto* stabilization of the franc was achieved, and in June 1928, France completed her currency reform by returning to the gold standard at the existing exchange rate, which effectively undervalued the franc. Being closely tied to the French currency, the Belgian reform followed a similar pattern, but Italy provides something of a contrast in that political authority assumed a greater role. Mussolini, intent on demonstrating his absolute authority and enhancing his prestige, pledged support for the currency 'to the last drop of blood'. He pushed through a hefty deflationary package of measures and then proceeded to stabilize the lira (December 1927) at an overvalued rate, which adversely affected the Italian economy in the later 1920s.

By the end of the decade, nearly all European countries had brought inflation under control, stabilized their currencies and adopted some form of the gold standard. In fact, the dominant issue in economic policy throughout the period was the currency question: first, the effort involved in stabilizing exchange rates and returning to gold, and then the struggle to maintain the new standard. The monetary ideal took predominance over all other matters of economic policy simply because the authorities believed that by restoring the pre-war monetary mechanism the post-war economic maladjustments would be corrected. However, these illusions were soon shattered. Far from correcting the underlying maladjustments, the restored gold standard itself was subject to serious strains from the start, and it disintegrated soon after it had been reestablished. To understand why the system failed to function in the expected manner, it is important to examine some of the weaknesses of the post-war gold standard.

The gold standard under pressure

The gold standard of the 1920s differed considerably from what might be termed the classical system of the pre-war period. It was not a full gold standard, because gold coins disappeared from circulation almost everywhere; nor could it be regarded as a proper bullion standard by which currencies were directly convertible into gold, because few countries adopted this form. Most countries, through lack of gold reserves and other factors, were forced onto a gold exchange standard under which they held their legally required reserves partly or wholly in the form of foreign exchange. This system was not unknown before 1914, but it became more widespread during the 1920s. The effect was to increase considerably the foreign exchange component of central bank reserves; by 1927, foreign exchange accounted for 42 per cent of the total reserves (gold and foreign exchange) of twenty-four European central banks compared with only about 12 per cent in 1913.

The gold exchange standard may have eased the pressure on gold supplies, but it only transferred the problem by one remove. Indeed, it was a source of weakness rather than one of strength. It led to a 'pyramiding' of claims on gold centres, so that in the event of a crisis in one country, a whole series of currencies might be affected, with serious consequences for the reserve currency. Gold exchange standard countries built up their exchange reserve holdings by short-term claims on key currencies, chiefly sterling and the dollar, the accommodation of which put severe strain on the central money markets because the funds proved highly volatile and moved from centre to centre in response to shifts in interest rates and changes in confidence. The fact that there was now more than one international financial market of importance (New York as well as London, and later Paris) provided ample opportunity for fund switching, whereas before the war the unchallenged supremacy and strength of sterling provided less incentive for such activity. And there was always the possibility that such funds might be withdrawn in the form of gold at short notice. Nor was the danger of conversion contingent solely upon a crisis of confidence. The gold exchange standard was regarded by many as a temporary expedient or transitional phase before the adoption of the real thing. France in particular was loath to sacrifice national prestige by remaining on an exchange standard. After the *de facto* stabilization of the franc in 1926, the Bank of France acquired the largest stock of foreign exchange (mainly in sterling and dollars) in the world. This was partly to prevent unnecessary appreciation of the French currency, but at the same time, there was the ever-present threat, which in the later 1920s became a reality, that these holdings would be liquidated and converted into gold in order to realize French dreams. Germany also followed a similar policy soon after the stabilization of the mark.

Inevitably, therefore, the gold exchange standard put greater pressure on the key centres (London and New York). This meant that they needed to hold larger gold stocks than those required to meet normal trading transactions in order to guard against the possibility of the sudden conversion of foreign claims into gold. In this respect, New York, with its large gold stocks, faced no real problem. It was London that was the weak link, because this centre had large claims against it but little with which to meet them because gold stocks were low. Had sterling been a strong currency with no competitors, as before the war, there would probably have been little difficulty in operating with a low gold reserve. But in fact sterling was continually under strain in the 1920s, and the gold exchange standard merely served to increase the pressure. Indeed, Britain's inability to exercise control over the international monetary system in the way she had formerly done was an important factor contributing to the collapse of the gold standard in the early 1930s.

A further source of weakness arose out of the stabilization process itself. The piecemeal and uncoordinated manner in which it was accomplished meant that little attention was paid to the crucial question of correct parity values. The haphazard choice of exchange rates, often under the influence of speculation and political motives, invariably meant that countries ended up with the wrong parities. Some were overvalued, others undervalued, and it was a stroke of luck if a country made the right selection. Thus the system started off from a point of disequilibrium, and once the pattern was set, there was little chance of adjustment. The rates chosen came to be regarded as sacrosanct so that the authorities were reluctant to adjust them even when they were seen to be incorrect. Countries that had undervalued their currencies were unwilling to forgo the benefits derived from a depreciated exchange; France in particular did her best to neutralize the impact of the flow of funds into the country immediately after stabilization by acquiring large amounts of foreign exchange. Those countries with overvalued currencies faced a more difficult problem. To devalue soon after stabilization was out of the question, because this would have involved a serious loss of prestige. In any case, the currency most out of alignment was the British, and a devaluation of sterling might well have set off a chain reaction and undermined the whole process of stabilization. The alternative was therefore to adjust the domestic economy to accord with the exchange rate, which involved compressing domestic cost and price levels. One or two countries, notably Sweden, managed to do this fairly well, but Britain was unable to deflate to the necessary extent given the already high unemployment. Sterling could not therefore regain its former strength.

Given the initial disequilibrium in exchange rates, it is not surprising that the gold standard functioned less smoothly than before 1914. The choice of the wrong exchange rates magnified balance of payments problems, and, consequently, the system was called upon to make adjustments on a scale far greater than previously and for which it was never designed, and at a time when the adjustment mechanism was less easy to operate. Few countries were prepared to sacrifice the stability of their domestic economies completely for the sake of external equilibrium. Thus, countries with overvalued exchanges were reluctant to carry through the necessary adjustment to their domestic economies, whereas surplus countries were equally unwilling to meet the former halfway. This is shown clearly by the frequency with which central banks neutralized the domestic monetary effects of gold flows, which had formerly been the traditional mechanism for dealing with balance of payments disequilibrium. Gold surplus countries in particular were active in this respect: the United States throughout the 1920s and France in the later 1920s, when she experienced a 'golden avalanche'.

Such stabilization procedures may have been justified in terms of insulating domestic economies from monetary movements but they were not compatible with the maintenance of the gold standard. In particular, neutralization of gold flows by the major surplus countries placed a severe strain on the system and threw much of the burden of adjustment onto those countries experiencing gold outflows. This was an especially serious problem for Britain, with her persistent tendency to lose gold, and one she was not fully prepared to accept given the weak state of her domestic economy. The Bank of England therefore attempted to minimize the impact of gold losses as far as possible.

The failure of surplus and deficit countries to meet each other halfway meant that the pre-war adjustment mechanism was rendered largely inoperative, a situation all the more serious given the initial disequilibrium arising from the fixing of exchange rates. Inevitably, this accentuated the maldistribution of the world's monetary reserves that had been in process since 1914. The United States, France and the European neutrals absorbed an increasing share of the world's gold reserves so that by the end of the 1920s they accounted for nearly 65 per cent of the total as against 54 per cent in 1913. For the most part, gold went to those countries that did not need it, either because their currencies were not used for reserve purposes (e.g. those of the neutrals) or because they had more than enough gold in relation to current liabilities. American gold stocks, for example, amounted to over $4 billion in the later 1920s against dollar liabilities (central bank holdings of dollar exchange) of only $0.6 billion. By contrast, Britain's sterling liabilities to central banks were nearly four times the Bank of England's gold reserves. It is true that Britain had short-term assets on which she could theoretically call in an emergency, but even allowing for these, her liabilities still amounted to some three times the Bank's free reserve. In practice, however, short-term assets became 'locked-in' during a crisis, as in 1931. Clearly, then, Britain was the weak link in the system. She had the largest liabilities and the smallest gold reserves of any major country, while her balance of payments was far from strong. Any deterioration in the latter or loss of confidence in sterling was bound to bring pressure to bear on the reserves, which could not be met. It is true that Britain operated with a very small gold reserve before the war but then her liabilities were smaller, her quick assets could easily be recalled, the balance of payments was stronger and confidence in sterling remained firm.

Given the manner in which it was restored and the way in which it was subsequently operated, it was inconceivable that the gold standard of the 1920s could have provided any solution to the fundamental problems of the period. Indeed, it was only a matter of time before the new system itself disintegrated, because once exposed to pressures, countries were not prepared to sacrifice their domestic economies on the altar of the exchanges. Although the depression of 1929–32 cannot be attributed directly to the defects of the gold standard, the latter did make it more difficult for adjustment to take place between creditor and debtor nations and, as we shall see, the existence of a system of fixed exchange rates tended to exacerbate the downswing once it got under way.

It is possible that the new system might have been able to hobble along for several years in the absence of severe strains and as long as American lending continued to paper over the fundamental maladjustment between creditor and debtor countries. Once the United States relinquished its stabilization role, then the pressures on the system were too great to withstand. To complete the story, therefore, we must look briefly at the position of the debtor countries and the role of foreign lending in this period.

International lending and the debtor nations

The war had a dramatic effect on the pattern and character of international debts and international lending. For one thing, it created a whole series of new international debts in the form of reparations and war loans. Second, western Europe's status as a creditor changed substantially. Most European countries were forced to relinquish sizeable portions of their foreign assets either to help pay for the war or because of default on the part of debtors. Germany lost most of her overseas holdings, France over one-half and Britain about 15 per cent. At the same time, these countries contracted heavy debts as a result of the war. By contrast, the United States emerged as a strong net creditor; excluding intergovernmental debts, America's net position on long-term account was $3.3 billion compared with a net debtor status of a similar amount before the war.

During the 1920s, international lending was resumed on a scale comparable with that before 1914, and by 1929 the total volume of foreign-owned assets was considerably larger than in 1913. The United States replaced Europe as the major investor. Between 1919 and 1929, her long-term investments abroad rose by nearly $9 billion, accounting for two-thirds of the global total increase and raising her stake to nearly one-third of the world total. No other country came anywhere near to matching the scale of America's lending. Britain resumed lending on a diminished scale, while France failed to recoup all her wartime losses. These three countries accounted for over three-quarters of all foreign investments in 1929.

Though the volume of foreign lending was substantial after the war, it by no means follows that it was utilized or disbursed in an optimal way. Indeed, it can be argued that the manner in which it was invested did more to destabilize the international economy than to maintain equilibrium. Low-income underdeveloped countries came off badly, because the bulk of long-term lending went to developed or semi-developed countries not all of which were equally deserving. In the first instance, funds tended to flow to the richer credit-worthy countries rather than to areas most in need of assistance. This reflected a lack of coherent policy on the part of the creditor nations as to what factors should determine the flow of funds to particular areas and the continued dominance of the profit motive in selecting areas for investment. Even so, extravagant and imprudent lending was common in the 1920s, no doubt a product of uncertain conditions and speculation. The United States, with her lack of experience in this matter, failed to exercise a discriminating policy, with the result that unwise investments were often made, particularly in European and Latin American countries. Loans were often used unproductively, in the sense that they failed to guarantee sufficient exchange proceeds to service the debt. In effect, borrowers were allowed to overextend themselves, the debt burden mounted and the only way out was to keep on borrowing.

The flow of funds was far from steady from year to year and such instability gave rise to difficulties in the borrowing countries. Large swings in the volume of investment were quite common partly as a consequence of changes in domestic conditions in the creditor countries. Thus in 1921, 1923 and again in 1926, the net capital outflow from the main creditors fell sharply only to rise equally sharply in subsequent years. The contraction in the immediate post-war period was particularly serious because it delayed the European recovery effort. The really critical period came in the years 1928–30, when overseas lending collapsed at a time when many borrowers were showing signs of strain. The position was made worse by the increasing pressure on short-term funds, many of which had been used unwisely in central Europe. After 1925 especially, there was a growing volume of short-term lending, part of which was used to finance long-term projects. In addition, short-term capital movements in and out of the major financial centres added a further destabilizing influence.

Most countries in central and eastern Europe depended heavily on foreign capital throughout the 1920s, first for reconstruction and stabilization purposes and second for furthering the diversification of their economies. After the war, all these countries were desperately short of resources, especially capital. The immediate problems were the financing of relief and reconstruction and the stabilization of currency and financial systems that had been severely weakened by current economic conditions. Because conditions were not propitious for large-scale private lending in the immediate post-war years, it was left to governmental agencies to fill the gap. Unfortunately, the US government aid programme for relief and reconstruction in Europe was curtailed sharply in 1920–21, and by 1923 the supply of overseas finance generally had dwindled to insignificant proportions. Moreover, the amounts involved were generally insufficient and much of the aid went to countries who needed it least. First-aid loans, organized under the aegis of the League of Nations, provided a second source of assistance. These were designed to provide borrowers with exchange reserves, to assist with currency stabilization, to establish central banks and supply them with capital, and to fund short-term debts at home and abroad. For the most part imported capital in this reconstruction phase did not go directly into productive enterprise, though it would be a mistake to level too much criticism on this score. Stabilization and relief loans were necessary and foreign capital played a positive role in stabilizing monetary systems and preventing total collapse of economic systems. That they were not represented by income-producing assets should not be allowed to obscure that they were an essential condition for obtaining further capital that could be invested in self-liquidating assets. On the other hand, it is clear that the relief offered by foreign capital in this period was insufficient for the tasks in hand.

Foreign lending on a large scale was resumed again in 1924. The improvement in economic and political conditions generally, and particularly the progress achieved in currency stabilization in central and eastern Europe, encouraged the movement of private funds. But it was borrowing in the post-stabilization phase that was the primary cause of the subsequent difficulties in many European countries. The need for imported capital was not in dispute, yet reliance on foreign investment served to create more problems than it solved. One of the main problems was that insufficient attention was given to ensure that the increase in debts was self-liquidating. Only a small proportion of government loans (between 30 and 50 per cent) was used for increasing the productive capacity of the borrowing countries. Nor was private capital always in the best interests of the debtors. Its flow was unstable and it did not automatically find its way into foreign-exchange-earning activities. Moreover, in so far as capital imports were used as safeguards to plug up balance of payments disequilibria, they simply served to increase the debt service burden without contributing to the process of development in a way that would have rectified fundamental imbalances. Also part of the capital receipts was used to stimulate agricultural development in an effort to boost exports, a process that led to a deterioration in agricultural prices that provided the basis for foreign-exchange earnings.

For most of the period, the cost of borrowing was high and inflexible. Most of the foreign capital absorbed by central and eastern Europe went into fixed interest securities at nominal interest rates of between 6 and 9 per cent, and often more when allowance is made for the discount price of many issues. This meant that a large proportion of the debt service burden remained fixed when incomes and activity declined. An additional complication was that high interest rates tended to attract short-term capital, which, up to 1929 at least, often served to offset temporary declines in long-term capital inflows, and the internal credit systems tended to convert external short-term loans into long-term domestic ones. This proved a serious source of weakness once the going got sticky, as in 1930–31, because then it was impossible to attract short-term accommodation to offset the decline in long-term borrowing. Hungary was particularly affected in this respect, although in most central and east European countries, foreign liabilities constituted between 20 and 40 per cent of commercial bank deposits.

Thus by the end of the 1920s the debt burdens of central and east European countries had reached alarming proportions. Throughout the years 1924–29 all countries, with the exception of Czechoslovakia, borrowed heavily, and on average foreign capital equalled or exceeded the rate of domestic accumulation. Because much of the foreign capital was not self-liquidating in terms of foreign exchange

Table 2.4 Debt servicing as a percentage of export earnings in eastern Europe

	1928/29	*1931/32*
Bulgaria	12.3	22.0
Greece	32.0	44.0
Hungary	17.9	48.0
Poland	11.3	27.0
Romania	14.6	36.0
Yugoslavia	18.1	36.0

Source: Aldcroft 2001, 127.

earnings, former debts could be serviced only by raising new loans. In most countries, the sums required for amortization purposes annually were larger than the amount of new loans; for example, in the case of Hungary, the total interest and amortization due in 1929 exceeded the amount of new loans by 16 per cent, and half of the new credits were used to pay off old debts. In many cases, debt service payments constituted one-quarter or more of the value of current exports, though given that servicing of the foreign loans called for 'strong currencies' obtainable from a limited range of exports, the actual strain on the balance of payments was heavier than these figures suggest. In view of the initial strain, it could be argued that the insolvency of these countries was simply aggravated rather than created by the depression of the 1930s. The weight of the burden was of course increased by the large decline in capital inflows and primary product prices after 1928, and, with limited reserves, the burden of adjustment was bound to fall with a vengeance on the domestic economic structure. The rising debt service burden in eastern Europe can be seen from the data in Table 2.4.

Germany's problem was different in that the magnitudes involved were greater and her position was complicated by reparations. Furthermore, she was not dependent on primary products for exchange earnings as was the case with her eastern neighbours. Nevertheless, she too resorted to borrowing on a massive scale to patch up a temporary stability at the expense of the future. Large-scale borrowing began effectively with currency stabilization and the floating of the Dawes Loan in 1924. The main attraction for investors was the high rates of interest consequent upon the scarcity of capital and the degree of risk. Lenders poured capital into Germany without much thought as to how the loans were to be serviced. At the peak of indebtedness in the summer of 1930, Germany's external liabilities were of the order of 28 billion marks, some 16 billion of which were in the form of short-term credits. The bulk of this sum came from the United States, Britain and the Netherlands.

It would be a mistake to infer that most of this capital was squandered on frivolous activities such as pleasure gardens and planetaria, so much lamented by Dr Schacht in 1927. Some of it certainly was, but even so capital imports did assist German recovery after the great inflation, when two-fifths of Germany's investment funds came from abroad. Nearly three-quarters of the total capital imports found their way into private industry, and this facilitated re-equipment and expansion. Nevertheless, borrowing did seriously increase the vulnerability of the German economy. Most of the foreign investment proved unproductive in the sense that it did relatively little to boost exchange earnings, while part of it financed an import surplus, which raised the standard of living. More serious was the use to which short-term funds were put. A large part of these consisted of loans to German banks by foreign bankers, which were then invested in long-term projects. Because such funds were liable to sudden withdrawal in times of difficulty, this left the German banking system in a potentially vulnerable state. The first indication of what lay in store came in the spring of 1929, when pressure on Germany's foreign exchange position resulting from reparation payments caused a temporary financial crisis. Foreign banks withdrew their support and called in some of their short-term loans, and the difficulties were aggravated by the decline in American short-term lending as a result of the stock market boom. This crisis was soon overcome, but it was merely the tip of the iceberg. Far greater disasters were to hit the German banking system in the liquidity crisis of 1931.

In effect, therefore, Germany, like her neighbours, was living on borrowed time in the later 1920s. Foreign debts were allowed to pile up to an extent that could never be justified by reference to her actual or potential export earnings. How Germany was supposed to meet her obligations once capital imports ceased was something her creditors never seem to have considered seriously. Even had there been no economic crisis or check to lending at the end of the decade, it was inconceivable that Germany could have gone on absorbing capital imports on such a scale for much longer. The alternatives were no doubt limited, because any attempt to secure an improved external balance would have required severe domestic deflation. It is possible that the Germans shrank from more positive action in an attempt to demonstrate their aversion to the obligations imposed by the Allies. Be that as it may, that the latter should have attempted to conceal the impossibility of the burden, at least in the short term, by pouring capital into Germany speaks volumes for their lack of economic wisdom.

In short, therefore, the international lending of the 1920s created an illusion of soundness and stability that did not in fact exist. So long as the flow of capital to debtor countries continued, the cracks in the international economic structure remained concealed. Yet at the same time, the process of lending served to widen the cracks, so that once the flow was cut off, the superficial stability of the system was undermined completely.

The post-war decade of the 1920s is perhaps one of the most fascinating of the twentieth century. It could never be described as dull, nor could it be regarded as stable or in equilibrium. The first half of the decade was noted for its turbulence and instability; the second half was more tranquil and the economic performance was creditable but the structure of that prosperity was based on very insecure foundations. At best, it was a period of fragile equilibrium, aptly summed up by Sally Marks (1976, 108) as 'a period of surface harmony and apparent economic prosperity'. There were certainly many signs of underlying weaknesses within particular economies, and the same may be said for the working of the international economy. Zara Steiner believes that the international order was too weak to shoulder the burdens of national adjustment and that there was no one hegemonic power able to maintain the status quo (Steiner 2005, 631). Her remarks are addressed more to the political scene, but they could equally apply to the economic side of the equation.[4] Once the basis of the fragile prosperity was undermined by the contraction in international lending and the downturn in the American economy at the close of the decade, the fundamental weaknesses of the international economic system became all too apparent.

Questions for discussion

1   What factors most impeded the reconstruction of Europe?
2   Why did it prove so difficult to resolve the problem of war debts and reparations?
3   What caused the major inflations in Europe?
4   What were the defects of the gold exchange standard?
5   How stable were the European economies by the end of the 1920s?

3 Economic crisis and recovery, 1929–39

Europe in depression

Throughout 1929 and even some way into the following year, few people appreciated that the world was on the point of experiencing one of the worst depressions in history. Even after the dramatic collapse of the American stock market in October 1929 and the sharp check to economic activity in many countries in the latter half of that year, there were still many people, especially in America, who were prepared to believe that these events represented merely a temporary and modest break in the rate of expansion, a view that gathered some force in the first half of 1930, when the US economy showed some signs of revival. Two years later, all such illusions had been well and truly shattered. After nearly three years of precipitous decline and severe financial crises in Europe and America, no one could be in any doubt about the gravity of the situation. At that point, the burning question was 'When was recovery going to take place?' It was not long before this question was answered.

Some idea of the magnitude of the depression can be gleaned from the data in Table 3.1 showing the fluctuations in domestic output and manufacturing production through successive phases of the inter-war years for most European countries. The figures are best used for indicating broad dimensions of change because not all the estimates are equally reliable. For the depression period itself, 1929–32/33, one can see that most countries experienced substantial falls in both output and manufacturing activity, the major exceptions being Bulgaria, Portugal and the USSR, with the latter largely insulated from the ravages of the capitalist system and steaming ahead under the first Five-Year Plan. Outside the United States, the most severe declines in economic activity occurred in Austria, Germany, France, Czechoslovakia and Poland. By contrast, Britain, the Netherlands, Spain, Switzerland, Romania and the Scandinavian countries were less seriously affected, at least in terms of total output, though some suffered sharp setbacks in industrial activity. Denmark and Greece were exceptional, in that they experienced a mild recession. Taking into account financial and debt problems partly as a result of the large decline in commodity prices, east European countries (excluding the USSR) probably fared worse than their western counterparts, even though physical output indicators appear to tell a similar story in many cases.

Table 3.1 Percentage changes in gross domestic product and manufacturing production 1913–38

Country	Gross Domestic Product				Manufacturing Production			
	1913–29	1929–1931/33	1931/32–1937/38	1929–1937/38	1913–29	1929–1931/33	1931/32–1937/38	1929–1937/38
Austria	5.1	−22.5	25.8	−2.5	−18.0	−34.3	53.9	1.0
Belgium	25.5	−7.1	9.8	2.0	39.9	−27.1	42.3	3.7
Denmark	53.0	4.3	16.9	21.9	48.7	−5.6	47.1	38.9
Finland	45.6	−4.0	46.9	41.1	97.6	−15.0	89.4	60.9
France	34.4	−14.7	13.5	−3.1	42.7	−25.6	20.0	−10.7
Germany	21.3	−23.5	63.7	25.2	17.3	−40.8	122.2	31.6
Greece	70.2	−6.5	40.5	31.4	–	0.9	60.0	61.5
Italy	31.1	−5.5	21.7	15.0	81.0	−22.7	48.5	14.8
Netherlands	77.4	−7.8	14.4	5.5	87.3	−9.8	35.1	22.0
Norway	58.6	−1.0	32.5	31.2	31.2	−18.2	58.7	29.9
Portugal	27.2	13.3	14.4	29.7	–	33.0	9.8	46.0
Spain *	49.7	−5.3	−9.4	−14.2	–	−15.7	−19.7	−32.3
Sweden	35.9	−4.3	31.4	25.8	50.8	−10.8	72.4	53.8
Switzerland	54.5	−8.0	14.4	5.2	17.5	−20.8	29.8	2.8
UK	11.9	−5.8	25.7	18.4	22.0	−10.8	49.0	32.9
Bulgaria	−2.2	27.3	17.2	−49.1	79.0	8.9	25.6	36.9
Czechoslovakia	52.2	−14.1	14.6	−1.6	71.8	−39.8	60.0	−3.7
Hungary	29.2	−9.4	26.4	14.6	13.9	−19.8	64.2	31.7
Poland	–	−20.7	44.9	14.9	−14.1	−38.6	99.6	22.5
Romania	–	−1.2	16.3	15.0	36.9	−18.2	63.4	33.6
Yugoslavia	–	−11.9	28.0	12.8	40.0	−17.1	63.8	35.7
USSR	2.6	6.7	59.3	70.0	–	66.7	146.7	311.1
USA	63.0	−28.5	38.1	−1.3	–	−44.7	86.8	3.3

*Spain cols. 3–4 1931–40 and 1929–40; cols. 7–8 1931–40 and 1929–40.

Source: see list of sources in D. H. Aldcroft and M. J. Oliver, *Exchange Rate Regimes in the Twentieth Century* 1998, 86–87.

Other indicators of economic activity confirm the severity of the depression. Commodity prices, share prices, exports and imports all fell sharply, while unemployment rose to alarming levels. Wholesale prices and share values fell by one-half or more, while the value of European trade declined from $58 billion in 1928 to $20.8 billion in 1935, and even by 1938 it had recovered to only 41.5 per cent of its former peak in value terms. Socially perhaps, the worst aspect of the depression was the high levels of unemployment experienced by most countries, because for those who remained in work there was some compensation in so far as prices tended to fall faster than wages and salaries. In this respect, Germany had one of the worst records; between 1929 and the end of 1930, unemployment more than doubled to reach a figure of 4.5 million; two years later, it had crept up to 6 million. Britain's worst figure was just over 3 million, which though bad in percentage terms appears modest compared with Germany's total. For Europe as a whole, it is likely that unemployment exceeded 15 million at the trough of depression, though the true figure may be much higher if one allows for statistical underrecording, disguised unemployment and part-time working. During the course of the downswing, many firms, banks and financial institutions went out of business altogether. In one year alone (1931), about 17,000 enterprises in Germany closed down.

Bald statistics do not do full justice to the dramatic course of events, but they do show clearly the scale of the cataclysm. Yet as Landes has observed, it is difficult to give a coherent analysis of the crisis 'that does justice to the rush of disasters, tumbling one upon another; or to give a narrative account that illuminates the confusion of events'. Moreover, it is doubtful whether a detailed blow-by-blow account of the crisis would serve a useful purpose in this context when there are so many pressing questions to be posed. In particular, therefore, we should attempt first to determine the origins of the downturn and explain why the depression was so long and so intense.

Origins of the 1929 downturn

It has been argued that apart from its unusual severity, the depression of 1929–32 was no exception to the long-run historical sequence of cyclical activity and hence requires nothing more in the way of explanation than a general theory of the cycle. Although perhaps a little overdrawn, this point of view merits consideration. The depression did occur at a logical sequence in time on the basis of past business-cycle history, and some of its characteristics had been reflected in previous downturns. The war did not break the pre-war pattern of business-cycle periodicity. In 1914, most industrial countries were about to move into recession, but the outbreak of hostilities postponed the working out of normal forces and in effect produced a distorted or muted continuation of the upswing, which eventually peaked in 1919–20. The reaction came in the sharp slump of 1920–21, which was then followed, with minor interruptions, by another major upswing to a peak at the end of the decade. Thus the nineteenth-century Juglar pattern of cycles of about seven to ten years' duration was preserved and a depression could have been expected in 1929–30. Moreover, the amplitude of the 1929–32 slump was no greater in some countries than that of the immediate post-war depression, while its duration had been matched in crises of the nineteenth century though not simultaneously with the same intensity. Even the worldwide scope of the depression was not especially unique; the immediate post-war depression fell not far short in this respect, while international recessions were not unknown in the nineteenth century. The question is therefore whether we should simply regard it as another contraction in the business-cycle sequence or whether it was unique in itself and needs to be explained in terms of special circumstances, for example by the maladjustments in the economic system arising from the shock administered by the war.

On balance, given the combination of duration, intensity and worldwide scope, the crisis of 1929–32 may be regarded as a rather special case worthy of particular attention. It may also be regarded, if we ignore the rather minor recession of 1937–38, as marking the grand culmination to trade-cycle history for, soon after the Second World War, the growth cycle became the established norm. However, this does not mean that the downturn of 1929 can be explained specifically in terms of unique circumstances. For instance, it would be difficult to argue that the First World War and its aftermath was the prime causal factor of the crisis that began at the end of the 1920s. Certainly, the repercussions of war created maladjustments and elements of instability within the world economy, which thereby made it more vulnerable to shocks of one sort or another, but the turning point of the cycle cannot be attributed directly to the war itself. Indeed, though the war imparted a severe shock to the economic mechanism, it did not, as we have noted, upset the former cyclical pattern. It distorted the economic system in several ways and made it more unstable, while it also probably aggravated the amplitude of subsequent cyclical movements, but it did little, if anything, to destroy the traditional periodicity of cyclical activity.

The real origins of the slump must be located in the United States. This is not to say that there were not cyclical weaknesses elsewhere; indeed, it is quite possible that several European countries would have experienced at least a moderate recession in the early 1930s even had conditions not deteriorated in America. But events in the United States, together with that country's influence over the world economy, determined to a large extent the timing, the severity and the duration of the depression. In brief, the United States administered two severe shocks to the world economic system at a time when it was most vulnerable and therefore least able to withstand them. The initial shock came with the curtailment of foreign lending in 1928–29, and the second with the peaking of the American boom in the summer of 1929.

The first of these had serious implications for debtor countries. There can be little doubt that many debtor countries, both in central and eastern Europe and elsewhere (Latin America especially), were in a precarious financial position in the latter half of the 1920s. They had borrowed freely and accumulated massive obligations, which for the most part were not self-liquidating. Consequently, they depended on continued capital imports to maintain external equilibrium. These fulfilled the purpose in the short term, but inevitably they aggravated the debt burden and served to conceal the basic disequilibrium between creditors and debtors. This process could not continue indefinitely and any reaction on the part of the creditors was bound to throw the burden of adjustment onto the debtors. Unfortunately, the creditors reacted rather too sharply in applying the brake to foreign lending.

The United States and France were largely responsible for the initial check to foreign lending because total British lending held up fairly well until 1930. French lending was in fact the first to decline (1927–28), though in sheer magnitude it was swamped by the American cutback in the following year. French capital exports were halved in 1928 and wiped out altogether in 1929. A good part of this movement represented the withdrawal of French short-term balances abroad (especially from Britain and Germany) and the import of gold after the legal stabilization of the franc in June 1928. Because French investors could not be persuaded to place their funds abroad on a long-term basis, it was inevitable that a large part of them should have been repatriated because, apart from increasing fears as to their safety, especially in the case of Germany, the balances could not be attracted to any great extent by short-term rates in London or, after the autumn of 1929, by those in New York. French action put strain on the major centres of credit and also on Germany, but for the most part it left the debtors on the periphery unscathed.

The major destabilizing influence came with the collapse in American lending. This began in the summer of 1928 and was prompted by the domestic boom and the action of the Federal Reserve to check it by raising interest rates, both of which had the effect of attracting funds into the home market. US capital issues on foreign account fell by over 50 per cent between the first and second halves of 1928; there was then a slight revival in the first half of 1929, followed by a further sharp fall in the second part of that year, giving a total for 1929 of $790 million as against $1,250 million in 1928 and $1,336 million in 1927. Altogether, the net outward capital flow (both long-term and short-term) from the major creditors fell from $2,214 million in 1928 to $1,414 million in 1929, while an even greater fall to $363 million occurred in the following year.

This dramatic curtailment of lending exercised a powerful deflationary impact on the world economy. Of course, it did not affect all countries simultaneously, but it was sufficiently widespread to undermine the fragile stability of the international economy. The position of the debtor countries deteriorated sharply between 1928 and 1929 as they experienced a hefty drop in their net capital inflow. Net capital imports into Germany, the largest borrower, fell from $967 million in 1928 to $482 million in 1929 and to $129 million in 1930. Other European borrowers (Hungary, Poland, Yugoslavia, Finland and Italy) suffered similar sharp reversals to their capital inflows. The cessation in the flow of capital affected these countries directly in that it led to a tailing off in domestic investment and economic activity. It also in turn reduced Europe's import demand for products outside the region. However, it was through the balance of payments that the impact was first felt, because most debtor countries depended on capital imports to close the gap in their balance of payments. Hence once capital imports declined the only way of adjusting their external accounts was to draw upon their limited reserves of gold and foreign exchange to cushion the impact. When these were exhausted more drastic measures became necessary, involving domestic deflation and protective restrictions.

The initial shock to the system might have been overcome had it not been for subsequent adverse events. For a time, debtor countries could meet temporary difficulties by drawing on their reserves and by taking measures to ease the strain on their external accounts. But this process of adjustment could not cope indefinitely with a prolonged strain following from reduced lending at a time when primary product prices were giving way. Nor could it cope with further pressures. The second shock came in the summer of 1929, when the American boom petered out. The reasons for the reversal in US activity are still the subject of debate, though it seems likely that it was partly a reaction to the over-hectic expansion of the 1920s. Certainly, there were signs of a temporary exhaustion of investment opportunities especially in those sectors (construction and consumer durable products) that had led the upswing, and this, together with a restraint on the growth of incomes and consumer expenditure towards the end of the decade, led to a deterioration in business confidence. A tightening in monetary policy at this time may also have contributed, though monetary factors probably played a relatively minor part in the initial breaking of the boom. However, once the downswing was under way, it was aggravated and prolonged by the severe monetary contraction initiated by the Federal Reserve System. The rapidity with which the American economy slid into depression was aggravated by the sharp decline in business confidence following the Stock Market crash of October 1929.

The American downturn in economic activity was accompanied by a further reduction in foreign lending and a sharp contraction in import demand, the consequences of which were a severely reduced flow of dollars to Europe and the rest of the world. Given America's preponderating influence in the world economy, the impact on the rest of the world was bound to be severe. The process of attrition in debtor primary producing countries was completed as commodity prices fell dramatically. These countries faced a severe deterioration in their trade balances as export values fell faster than import values, while external interest obligations, which were fixed in terms of gold, rose sharply as a proportion of export receipts. Attempts to make up the deficiency by releasing stocks of commodities, which were costly to maintain, on to the market only made matters worse, because it aggravated the fall in prices. Thus with dwindling reserves and an inability to borrow further, debtor countries in Europe and overseas were forced to take drastic measures to staunch the outflow of funds. The way out of the impasse was sought through deflation, devaluation, restrictive trade measures and default on debts. The initial deflation was quickly transmitted through the links forged by the fixed exchange rates of the gold standard, but deflation could never be more than a temporary expedient because to meet external obligations would have required politically intolerable doses of deflation. Consequently, the easiest solution was to break the links by abandoning the gold standard. This was done by several Latin American countries and Australia and New Zealand late in 1929 and early in 1930.

Inevitably, this imposed a greater burden on the countries still on gold and hence intensified the deflationary spiral either automatically or through deliberate government action. Industrialized countries in Europe felt the impact directly from America and indirectly via the periphery as demand for industrial imports declined, and in turn declining demand for raw materials and foodstuffs on the part of the industrial powers fed back to the periphery. Once started, therefore, the deflationary process became cumulative and eventually led to the general collapse of the gold standard and the adoption of restrictive policies to protect domestic economies. These events are taken up in the next section.

Though the role of the United States is seen as crucial in determining the world-wide slide into severe recession, it should be stressed that the sequence of events in that country came at a weak time as far as the international economy was concerned. For one thing, cyclical forces were reaching their peak in a number of countries (for example, Britain, Germany and Poland) in the later 1920s, and in some cases independently of the United States. Britain, for instance, experienced sagging demand for her exports to primary producing countries a year or so before the peak in economic activity in the United States. At the same time, the incomes of the primary producers in eastern Europe and elsewhere were being squeezed as a result of the weakness of world commodity prices stemming from oversupply problems in some cases. Second, the cyclical developments of the period must be set against the background of an unstable international economy arising partly from the legacies left by the war. Thus the cyclical downturn came at a time when many countries were still struggling with post-war distortions to their economies that left them inherently unstable. Structural or sectoral deflationary tendencies were common, and these were reflected in excess capacity problems, in both industrialized and primary producing countries, and in external account imbalances, arising from reparations and war debts, tariff policies, and the distortions produced by the ill-conceived currency stabilization process among other things. The position was also aggravated by the transformation of economic power relationships because of the war and the lack of strong and enlightened economic leadership on the part of the new creditor powers that might have helped to stabilize the international economic system. These disequilibrating forces were not crucial to the initial downturn, but they were sufficient to ensure that the system exploded once the initial shocks had been imparted, thereby producing a depression of unusual severity.

That the depression was so intense and widespread and of long duration is not altogether surprising. Given the severity of the American depression and the repercussions this had on foreign lending and US import demand, the multiplier effects were bound to be large. Moreover, the fact that the cyclical downturn occurred against a backdrop of structural deflation and international disequilibrium was bound to intensify the process. Misguided government policies also helped to aggravate the deflationary spiral. Monetary and fiscal retrenchment, tariffs and other protective measures simply made things worse. The spread of depression was also encouraged by the close economic relationships between nations; in particular, the complex but precarious monetary relationships and the fixed exchange rates of the gold standard system facilitated the transmission of recessionary forces from one country to another.

Finally, we should ask what could have been done to avert or alleviate the crisis. With the benefit of hindsight it is easy to argue that enlightened government policies applied rapidly by the major powers might have eased the situation. But in the conditions then prevailing, it is difficult to conceive that this could or would have been done, and even less likely that the depression could have been avoided altogether. At the minimum, it would have required appropriate policy action to have been taken a few months before the peak in economic activity because of the lag effects involved. Of course, this is assuming that governments had the foresight, skill and aptitude to do so, which clearly they did not at that time. In fact, it is doubtful even today whether they are any better at forecasting turning points in the cycle and timing their policy actions correctly. However, the question of expertise apart, it is doubtful in the conditions then obtaining whether such action would have been forthcoming. Initially, the main burden of adjustment lay with the United States, because the other two major creditors (France and Britain) were unable and also unwilling to stabilize the system. Two courses of action would have been required of the United States: first, reversing the contraction in foreign lending and, second, taking measures to refuel the boom. Neither of these courses would have appeared logical to the US authorities at the time in question. By the late 1920s, it was apparent that debtor countries had borrowed too much and that their capacity to repay was being severely strained. To have kept up the rate of lending, let alone to have increased it, would have made things worse and at best would only have postponed the date at which adjustment had to be made. The mistake in the 1920s was that creditor nations had been too generous with their funds: debtors had been allowed to overborrow, and as a consequence, they had made little attempt to adjust their economies so that they developed within their means. That the crunch came in 1928–29 as a result of the US boom was unfortunate, but it was bound to occur sooner or later because creditors were hardly likely to maintain lending indefinitely to insolvent borrowers. The difficulties of European debtors could have been alleviated by the scrapping of war debts and reparations and a more liberal commercial policy on the part of the United States, but such adjustments would have by no means solved the fundamental problem. But the United States was in no mood anyway to alleviate world problems as evidenced by her more restrictive commercial policy in the Hawley–Smoot tariff of 1930.

As to the second course of action, the last thing the authorities were likely to do in 1929 was to take action to revitalize the boom. After all, with memories of the inflation of 1919–20 and the subsequent European inflations still close at hand, the authorities were more concerned with bringing it under control, and more particularly with curbing the excessive stock market speculation. In any case, heavy government spending would not have gone down well with the American public because of the tax implications that it would have entailed. Moreover, for most of 1929, many Americans were still convinced that the country had entered a period of perpetual prosperity and there seemed little indication to them of the dire events that were soon to follow. In these circumstances, therefore, it is very unlikely that any government would have acted differently. It was not until after the stock market crash in October that Americans began to realize that the halcyon days were over, and by then it was too late. Economic activity and business confidence drained away so rapidly, both in America and elsewhere, that it is unlikely that any policy action could have done much to save the situation in the short term. This should not be construed as an apology for inaction on the part of the government. Clearly, had they made a concerted effort to combat the depression in 1929, and early in 1930, the duration and severity of the downswing and the accompanying financial crisis could have been modified. Indeed, determined action on the part of the major powers might even have saved the gold standard. What we would stress, therefore, is that some degree of recession was inevitable in 1929–30; that it developed into a global crisis of such magnitude can be attributed not only to the convergence of a combination of unfavourable circumstances but also to the fact that governments, instead of cooperating to rescue the situation, simply resorted to policies that made things worse rather than better.

Deepening depression and financial crisis

By the middle of 1930, most countries were engulfed in depression. Despite the sharpness of the initial downturn, the decline in activity through 1929 and 1930 was considered to be little more than an ordinary downward phase in the business cycle. Indeed in the first half of 1930, there were some signs, especially in the United States, that the decline was levelling off and there was also some revival in international lending. But this proved to be nothing more than a temporary respite from depressing forces that soon became overwhelming and that were to be accompanied by financial crisis and monetary disorders on a scale never before experienced in peacetime. The events spelt the end of the gold standard and the liberal economic regimes that had prevailed hitherto.

Throughout the latter half of 1930 and 1931, economic conditions steadily deteriorated everywhere. As incomes fell, domestic budgets and external accounts became unbalanced and the first reaction of governments was to introduce deflationary policies, which only made things worse. Little assistance was forthcoming from the creditor countries. The main surplus countries (the United States and France) failed to make sufficient funds available to the debtor nations on either a long-term or a short-term basis. This is perhaps not altogether surprising because the creditworthiness of the borrowers was weak and hence the creditors were reluctant to grant further accommodation. France in particular, despite her large reserves, was unwilling to bale out debtor countries and Germany especially, given France's hostility towards that country. In any case, the creditor nations themselves were experiencing financial difficulties and monetary disorders during 1930–31.

Thus the European financial crisis that culminated in the summer of 1931 can be seen as a general failure on the part of creditor countries to provide accommodating finance to overcome the effects of depression. The subsequent collapse of confidence was reflected in a virtual cessation of lending and an attempt on the part of creditors to demand repayment of previous loans. Under these pressures, debtor countries were forced to pursue deflationary policies or repudiate their international obligations, which, being denominated in gold terms, had become vastly more burdensome by 1930–31.

Of course, the antecedents of the financial crisis of 1931 can be traced back to the late 1920s, when overseas lending first contracted and international liquidity became tighter. The financial pressures on debtor countries were increased after the breaking of the American boom, which further reduced the flow of dollars to Europe. Despite temporary alleviation in the early months of 1930, by the middle of that year, conditions were such that debtor countries could expect little assistance from the creditor nations. During the course of that year, the chief creditors began to experience severe monetary problems. The United States suffered a wave of bank failures after the stock market crash; no fewer than 1,345 banks collapsed in 1930 and another 687 went under in the first half of 1931, the vast majority of them being linked to the fortunes of agriculture. This banking crisis together with a further deterioration in economic conditions forced the United States to reduce its international commitments even further, and by 1931 the former outflow of capital was being transformed into a net inward movement. France also suffered monetary disturbances in the latter half of 1930 that weakened confidence and led to increasing demands for liquidity. This was reflected in a repatriation of commercial bank balances held abroad, especially from Germany and Austria, which put further strain on an already weak financial position in central Europe.

The increasing demand for liquidity in 1930 and 1931 on the part of foreign creditors at a time when European financial institutions were overstretched in their commitments to depressed industries led to a crop of bank failures throughout Europe. In many European countries, some one-quarter or more of bank liabilities were foreign owned, and this complex interlocking of balances served only to propagate the spread of the crisis. Attempts to meet demands for liquidity led to forced realization of assets and deflationary monetary policies, and this weakened the structure of financial institutions and reduced foreign confidence even more. The final phase of the European crisis was played out in the summer of 1931. It began in May with the crash of the Austrian Credit Anstalt, which accounted for over two-thirds of the total deposits of the Austrian banking system. The illiquid state of this bank created panic in European banking circles. Within weeks, the banking crisis had spread to Germany and eastern Europe, and by July, the German banking system was on the point of collapse. The crisis enormously increased the demand for liquidity and much of the strain was now transferred to London as one of the few places still prepared to grant accommodation. The outflow of funds from Britain reached panic proportions in July and August, when some £200 million left the country. The rapid rate of withdrawal from London was largely occasioned by the European financial crisis; but the situation was undoubtedly aggravated by the loss of confidence in Britain's ability to maintain solvency in the light of her deteriorating balance of payments position and her unfavourable short-term liquidity account. Britain's position was rendered the more difficult by her heavy financial commitments in Europe (the assets being frozen in the crisis) as well as the weak and passive policy of the Bank of England and political instability in 1931. Attempts by New York and Paris to come to the rescue were too little and too late. In the circumstances, the authorities could think of little else to do but release the parity of sterling, and on 21 September 1931, Britain officially went off gold.

In retrospect, the financial panic of 1931 can be seen as a typical crisis of confidence, which had deep-seated causes. The contraction of foreign lending and the impact of depression started the chain of causation, in that pressure was put on debtor countries. But it was exacerbated by the widespread foreign ownership of national bank deposits, a large volume of liquid and mobile balances and the misuse of these funds by recipient countries. Once confidence in the monetary institutions of the debtor countries collapsed, the demand for liquidity rose sharply, and the only prospect of salvation lay in a concerted rescue operation by the creditor countries. When this failed to materialize, the disintegration of the international monetary system was a forgone conclusion.

Aftermath of the crisis

The financial panic of 1931 left its mark on the world economy in many ways. Any prospect of an early end to the depression (there had again been some signs of improvement in the first few months of 1931) was shattered completely because the crisis shook even the strongest countries. As the panic swept from one country to another, hurried measures of national economic defence were taken, and these inevitably resulted in further damage to economic activity and international economic relations. Thus output, already at a low level in most countries in the summer of 1931, declined further during the course of the next twelve months. Production in most cases reached its lowest point in the summer and autumn of 1932, at levels ranging between 20 and 55 per cent below previous peaks. Primary producing countries both in eastern Europe and elsewhere did not suffer so much from decreased production but were more severely hit by the fall in primary product prices, the effect of which was to reduce incomes by up to 50 per cent or more. Probably the worst-hit sector of the world economy was international trade. Both the volume and value of trade, already seriously diminished before the financial crisis, declined even more as countries resorted to restrictive measures to insulate their domestic economies from the impact of depression. By the third quarter of 1932, the value of world trade was less than 35 per cent of that in the corresponding quarter of 1929; this decline was made up of a fall in average prices of about 50 per cent and a reduction of some 25 per cent in the quantum of goods traded. The decline was not evenly distributed; primary producing countries fared the worst because prices of commodities fell more sharply than those of industrial products that they imported. Thus at the low point in the third quarter of 1932, the trade of European countries fell for the first time below 40 per cent of the 1929 reference level, whereas for the rest of the world it had dropped below 30 per cent.

Perhaps even more serious than the collapse in economic activity was the disorganization and partial destruction of the delicate machinery of international economic and financial cooperation. Indeed, the depression and financial crisis more or less destroyed the former international economic mechanism. Most countries eventually abandoned the gold standard and devalued their currencies. Then in order to shield domestic economies from external influences, a battery of protective restrictions was employed, including tariffs, import quotas, exchange controls and special devices to iron out fluctuations in the exchanges. This spelt the end of the pre-1914 system of multilateral trade and payments and the free flow of commodities, capital and labour across national borders. Instead, nationalistic economic policies and managed currencies became the order of the day. The finishing touch to the previous system came with the breakdown of the World Economic Conference in 1933, which effectively 'signalized the end of any general attempts at international action in the economic field during the inter-war period'.

The most notable manifestation of the decline of the old order was the general abandonment of the gold standard. Several countries had already gone off gold before September 1931, when Britain broke its links with the gold standard. Almost simultaneously with Britain's departure, many countries abandoned the standard and devalued their currencies. By the end of 1932, more than one-half of the countries of the world had formally abandoned gold and most others maintained it or its semblance only by virtue of rigid exchange controls. When in 1933 the United States gave up the standard, only a handful of countries (France, Switzerland, the Netherlands, Belgium, Italy, Poland) continued to adhere to it, and these countries formed a gold bloc for settlement of balances among themselves.

The benefits arising from general abandonment of the gold standard were mixed. It is true that adherence to the system of fixed exchange rates had helped to propagate the spread of the depression, because for countries faced with balance of payments problems it meant a resort to deflationary measures, which simply aggravated the depression. Thus for any individual country, departure from the gold standard and depreciation of the currency released that country from deflationary constraints and gave a boost to exports. On the other hand, once the same line of action was adopted by many countries, then the benefits formerly reaped by the leaders soon disappeared. The gold bloc countries found themselves in an invidious trading position simply because they retained the former fixed exchange values at a time when most other currencies had depreciated. A second possible benefit flowed from the fact that some countries found the burden of external indebtedness reduced in so far as their debt was held in terms of currencies that had depreciated. Conversely, of course, those countries that subsequently went on to depreciate their own currencies below the level of the currencies in which their debts were due found the external burden of their debt was greater than before.

In other words, individual countries, depending on the timing of their departure from the gold standard, the extent of the ensuing currency depreciation and the structure of their debt burden, stood to benefit. Some also gained from a boost given to their exports. Whether the economic situation in 1932 would have been better or worse if the gold standard had not been widely abandoned is more debatable. It is probable that trade would have continued to decline during that year, with investment remaining paralysed, even had it been possible to retain the stand-ard, because the trends were already firmly operational before the breakdown and in fact were among the causes of that breakdown. Moreover, there is little evi-dence that countries adopted reflationary fiscal policies of any substance once they were released from the straitjacket of the gold standard, despite some easing of monetary policy. On the other hand, it is also clear that the widespread exchange instability that arose during 1932 following the general abandonment of gold greatly complicated the economic situation. Fluctuating exchange rates aggra-vated by speculative and non-economic capital movements, the prospect of com-petitive depreciation of currencies and restrictive measures of defence thrown up by the threat, together with renewed deflationary pressure, banking crises and rigid exchange controls to protect weaker currencies, created a thoroughly unstable situation. These uncertainties were not only a serious impediment to economic recovery but presented a constant threat of further deterioration. While the coun-tries already off gold experienced temporary relief in their domestic situation, they were confronted by an accelerated fall in gold prices and a further reduction in international trade. Moreover, efforts to maintain the external values of their cur-rencies were threatened by flights of capital as confidence in the security of vari-ous financial centres waxed and waned. Thus, on balance, the relief arising from abandonment of the gold standard both for individual countries and for the world as a whole was limited in the short term. Prices did not rise and trade continued to dwindle, while exchange instability and various controls imposed fresh obstacles to capital movements and trade recovery.

However, one should not exaggerate the adverse impact of exchange volatility in the 1930s. In the short term, the turmoil in foreign exchange markets certainly was an impediment to economic recovery, but 1932–33 marked the nadir of the turbulence. From thereon, exchange markets began to settle down, and what is remarkable is the speed with which the volatility in exchange markets calmed down once the main devaluations had taken place and the way in which the tradi-tional currency relationships were restored. From 1933, there was a steady trend towards greater exchange stability as the majority of trading currencies moved into alignment with the major currencies (sterling, the dollar and the franc). As early as March 1934, *The Economist* could report on the comparative stability of the exchange markets, and by the end of that year the movements of currencies had become modest and continued to decline in subsequent years. By the middle of the decade the daily and weekly fluctuations of the key currencies was almost back to the range of the old gold parity points, with significant movements occurring only at times of major policy changes, the main one being the devaluation of the French franc in September 1936, which marked the final demise of the gold bloc.

One factor that assisted in the stabilization of currencies in the 1930s was the emergence of several distinct currency areas or blocs. The most important were the sterling area, the gold bloc and the exchange control or Reichsmark bloc. It is also possible to identify a dollar zone incorporating primarily the Latin American countries, and possibly a yen bloc covering a significant part of East Asia. These regimes were also roughly coterminous with recognised trading blocs among whose members trade increased during the 1930s. Most of the currency groupings were loosely drawn and none of them had any formal organization with executive power over currency activities and valuations. Nevertheless, a measure of informal leadership was undoubtedly exercised by the dominant country in each group, which encouraged members to link their currencies to and track the currency of the leader. The largest and most successful of these currency zones was the sterling area. Paul Einzig, a notable contemporary guru in international finance, believed that as a result of these new arrangements 'There was *de facto* stability practically all over the civilized world' by the end of 1936 (Einzig 1937, 309).

The circulation of both long-term and short-term capital had been impaired at an early stage in the depression, but by the middle of 1932 the financial panic had led to almost a complete paralysis of capital movements and had done much to restrict the servicing of existing debt. Problems arising from overborrowing had forced many countries to repudiate debts, to suspend interest payments on them or to impose rigid exchange controls in an effort to achieve currency stability and safeguard the external account. The steady decline in international trade was mainly responsible for this and for the freezing of short-term debts, because amounts of short-term indebtedness adequate to finance trade at its 1929 volume became unnecessary but difficult to repudiate when trade fell to 1932 levels. The stoppage of capital movements, freezing of short-term debts and assets and the use of exchange controls were not confined solely to European countries. By the middle of 1932, there were moratoria on the foreign service of the public debt in seventeen countries and on private debt in seven others. Many other countries, especially among agricultural producers, faced with a crushing burden of external debt payments as export values plunged and their currencies depreciated below those in which the debts were held, were forced to take emergency action to deal with the problem, either by severe domestic deflation or by restrictions on trade and payments or both.

By virtue of increasing restrictions on trade and capital flows, there was an obvious danger that the international trading machinery would be smashed as completely as the international monetary system. Of course, increasing resort to restrictive policies had been evident before the financial panic, but after September 1931, the use made of such measures became more widespread and severe. It is difficult to summarize briefly the multiplicity and variety of emergency restrictions promulgated to deal with the crisis of 1931. Most countries, as already noted, eventually abandoned gold soon after Britain did and devalued; by the end of 1932, thirty-five countries were already off gold and twenty-seven, including nine still nominally on the gold standard, were officially exercising exchange control, while yet others were exercising unofficial controls or import prohibitions tantamount to exchange control. General tariff increases had been imposed in twenty-three countries, while customs duties had been increased on individual items or groups of commodities by fifty countries. Import quotas, prohibitions, licensing systems and other quantitative restrictions had been applied in thirty-two countries. Import monopolies, mostly for grains, were in existence in twelve countries; milling or mixing regulations in sixteen others. Export premiums were being paid in nine, while export duties or prohibitions had been imposed in seventeen.

By the summer of 1932, therefore, the economic situation in Europe and the wider world appeared very grim. True, the immediate panic had subsided, but the international economy was badly shattered after three years of depression and crisis. Economic activity almost everywhere was at a low ebb. Capital and labour were seriously underemployed, investment was negligible and international trade had received a serious battering. The international economic and financial system had been seriously weakened and in some parts destroyed in its original form, and fears were expressed at the time that a general collapse or total breakdown of the economic mechanism would ensue. Yet within a few months, despite continued depression, there were signs that the turning-point was close at hand. Confidence began to revive, albeit slowly, and during the autumn of 1932, the US economy showed signs of life. Though this proved to be something of a false dawn (a final wave of bank failures in 1932–33 stifled the first signs of revival), the undercurrent of cautious optimism continued and was rewarded early in the New Year, when it became apparent that the corner had been turned and most countries had seen the trough in economic activity.

The extent of recovery

Though the beginnings of recovery can be detected in some countries late in 1932, it was not until the following year that it took firm hold. Even then the process was by no means rapid and widespread. Some countries, notably France and Czechoslovakia, continued to experience further declines in economic activity, while in the United States, the pace of revival was slow and faltering. But during the next two or three years, the recovery gathered momentum, so that by the middle of the 1930s nearly all countries were registering at least modest gains in activity over the levels reached in the trough of the depression. Recovery was interrupted temporarily in 1937–38, when several countries experienced a mild recession, after which it was resumed once more largely under the influence of rearmament for the Second World War.

Despite several years of growth, by the end of the decade, recovery from the slump was only partially complete. Most countries still had high unemployment levels, while the agrarian sector acted as a drag on the countries of eastern Europe. Some of the more industrialized countries (France, Austria and Czechoslovakia, for example) failed to regain their predepression levels of activity, while even the United States barely reached her previous peak of 1929 (see Table 3.1). One of the most successful countries was Germany; she virtually eradicated unemployment and achieved substantial gains in output by dint of policies that were unacceptable to most other countries. Sweden too recorded an impressive performance, largely on the back of strong export growth and continued structural adaptation assisted by sensible government policies, while Finland was another export beneficiary. Britain's achievements were also impressive, though she still had a large pool of unemployment by the end of the decade. However, the presence of high unemployment does not necessarily denote an abortive recovery because, at least in the case of Britain, much of the unemployment at the end of the 1930s was structural rather than cyclical in character. The most spectacular performance was undoubtedly that of the USSR, where industrial output surged ahead under the Five-Year Plans. However, the social costs of this forced industrialization were more dreadful than those experienced in fascist Germany.

As the scale of recovery varied from one country to another so too did the forces promoting it. Indeed, the diversity of factors involved makes it difficult to generalize about the initiating forces, though it is possible to make some broad observations. The first thing that can be said is that recovery owed virtually nothing to international action. International attempts to provide a solution were rare and unsuccessful. Though the League of Nations had played a useful and constructive role in the 1920s, its impact in the following decade was negligible. It produced many valuable reports and masses of useful statistical data, but as far as policy was concerned, it had virtually no worthwhile effect. Attempts at international cooperation to sort out the monetary and trade situation foundered after the failure of the World Economic Conference in London in 1933, and only sporadic and half-hearted efforts were made in the later 1930s, principally by the United States, to ease the restrictions on trade. Indeed, for the most part, the restrictions on trade and capital movements tended to increase rather than diminish. Consequently, international lending never revived to any extent, trade volumes remained well below their former peak levels and the ratio of trade to national income therefore declined. Not surprisingly, exports did not for the most part play a significant part in the recovery process, though there were important exceptions (for example, Finland and Sweden). Of course, most countries did experience a revival in exports from the low levels reached in the trough, and devaluation frequently gave a temporary boost to exports, but more often than not pre-depression levels of exports proved unobtainable.

One factor common to all countries was the increase in government participation in the economy. Given the severity of the depression, it was almost inevitable that this would be the case. Again, the methods used varied a great deal, as did their impact, which generally was not very significant. As we have seen, the early 1930s were characterized by a wave of currency devaluations followed by the imposition of severe restrictions on trade, payments and capital movements. These were primarily defensive measures designed to insulate domestic economies from unfavourable external influences. In some countries, especially Germany and in eastern Europe, the 'planning' of foreign trade came to be more widely accepted as a normal function of the state, and the weapons originally forged as an emergency defence of prices, production or currency were not discarded but tended to be pressed into service as permanent elements of trade regulation, dovetailed into programmes of national economic development.

Such policies have been regarded as reactionary and restrictive and in many respects they were because they were implemented with little regard as to their effects on other countries. As restrictions increased, trade was diverted more and more into bilateral channels, and hence the scope for expansion in foreign intercourse became limited. Ultimately, the policies were self-defeating because the gains initially derived from devaluation and restrictive controls or whatever soon disappeared as other countries adopted similar procedures. Of course, it is easy to be critical of past events; one should bear in mind that, though many policy measures were restrictive and reactionary and tended to be income destructive, at the time in question, governments had little choice but to safeguard the external side of the balance sheet as a prelude to the introduction of domestic recovery measures. What can be fairly criticized is the reluctance of governments to relax such restrictions once recovery got under way and the limited and half-hearted efforts made to stimulate recovery in the first place. Many countries adopted easier monetary policies after abandoning gold, but thereafter constructive policy action was limited and inadequate. Attention was concentrated on bolstering up and protecting established producers and declining staple industries, while expansionary fiscal measures were notable for their absence. Fear of inflation (surprising though it may seem), adherence to the time-honoured principle of balanced budgets, coupled with a general ignorance as to the role of state spending in a depression, inhibited many governments from pursuing a policy of deficit financing to stimulate recovery. There were of course some notable exceptions, for example the United States and Sweden, though even in these two cases the policies pursued left something to be desired.

Given the narrow scope of government policies in the 1930s, it is not surprising to find that their impact in terms of recovery was often limited. With the exception of Germany, to a lesser extent Sweden and possibly one or two east European countries that attempted to force industrialization by autarchic planning measures, national economic policies contributed little to recovery from the depression. Even in Sweden, with its enlightened budgetary policy, the impact was too late to start the initial upturn, whereas in France and Belgium (both countries clinging to the gold standard until 1935–36), government policy was positively detrimental. The same applies to the remaining gold bloc countries. One can go further and argue that recovery took place in most countries despite domestic policy measures that, if not actually harmful, were too little and too late to have much bearing on the recovery effort. Again, there are exceptions to the rule; one should not totally underestimate the impact that cheap money had on stimulating investment in residential construction in say Britain and Sweden, though generally the favourable influence tends to be exaggerated.

By and large, therefore, it was real forces rather than policy measures that were instrumental in bringing about recovery. And to a large extent that recovery was based on home rather than export markets. The outstanding case in the latter respect was Britain, where the demand for products of the newer industries and the upsurge in building activity provided important stimulants. In part, this process reflected a structural transformation that many European countries were experiencing to a greater or lesser degree in the inter-war years and that was by no means complete at the end of the period. Svennilson has stressed the severe structural transformation problem in Europe, which in the industrialized countries was characterized by a shift of resources from old staple industries to newer lines of development, whereas in the east, it was largely a question of effecting the transition from predominately agrarian structures to economies based more solidly on manufacturing activity.

Despite the common features outlined above, the diverse nature of the recovery process and the forces responsible therein can be appreciated properly only by looking more closely at the experience of individual countries or regions. In the remainder of this chapter, therefore, we examine the record of five industrialized countries (Britain, France, Sweden, Germany and Austria), all of which had one-third or more of their active population engaged in industry by the end of the 1930s. Eastern Europe and the European periphery are discussed in the next chapter.

Recovery in industrialized countries

The five countries selected for treatment in this section all displayed different features: Britain experienced vigorous growth based largely on the domestic market, with government policy contributing very little to recovery; France had an abortive recovery largely because of misguided policy measures; Sweden forged ahead under the influence of exports, a housing boom and enlightened government policies; Germany achieved great success, but at a price, both politically and socially; whereas Austria had a chequered recovery as a result of conflicting forces and policies. The one common feature to all, at least towards the end of the period, was the increasing influence of rearmament in sustaining recovery, which showed signs of flagging in 1937–38.

Britain's internal recovery policy was remarkably orthodox. The economic crisis did not give rise to any great programme of public works nor did it produce any marked increase in state interference in, or control of, the economic system. For the most part, the government confined itself to providing what it thought were favourable conditions for the recovery of private enterprise. Reliance was therefore placed on indirect measures such as cheap money, protection and other trade controls, and industrial reconstruction schemes aimed at propping up the old staple industries. External policy was perhaps more notable for its departure from traditional liberalism than for its effect on recovery, because the initial gains stemming from devaluation, tariffs, etc. were soon whittled away as other countries followed suit.

Government policy has traditionally been seen as having had a marginal influence on Britain's recovery, though recent research accords greater weight to the beneficial effects of devaluation and tariff protection. Industrial assistance measures, on the other hand, were of limited value because they merely helped to prop up ex-growth industries. The stimulus from cheap money was greater, but it was certainly not the chief agent of recovery. Cheap money probably imparted a greater stimulus to the housing market than to industrial investment, yet it cannot be regarded as the major causal factor responsible for the housing boom of the 1930s. There were several important stimulants to housing, including falling construction costs, rising real incomes partly as a result of the favourable shift in the terms of trade, and a shift in consumer tastes. Nor did fiscal policy make any notable contribution to recovery. Here, government action was extremely orthodox, differing little from practice in the 1920s. Deficit financing was avoided, the size of the budget was not materially increased, and the component most crucial from the stabilization point of view (capital spending) was cut substantially. On balance, therefore, fiscal policy was at best neutral, though the favourable psychological impact of balanced budgets in an age still conditioned by orthodox finance should not be overlooked. Even the Labour Party was an advocate of fiscal prudence in those days. Apart from a small increase in public expenditure between 1929 and 1931, government spending (both at central and local levels) remained remarkably stable until the late 1930s, when rearmament began to take effect, and in practically every year the central government's accounts showed a surplus.

Despite the relative ineffectiveness of government policy, recovery in Britain was more pronounced and sustained than in many other countries. Apart from exports, most indices of economic activity rose sharply after 1932, and over the decade as a whole, Britain's rate of growth compared favourably with that of other industrial countries. Admittedly, unemployment still remained a problem in the later 1930s, but to a large extent this was a structural matter rather than a cyclical one. The domestic market provided the main basis of recovery; important real forces were at work, notably rising effective demand, which led to vigorous growth in housing and consumer durable industries. These sectors were certainly important to the recovery, though their role should not be exaggerated. In time, it became more broadly based, with exports and some of the staple industries staging a revival, especially in the later 1930s, when rearmament assumed importance.

If British policy had limited influence on the recovery effort, France's economic policy was little short of disastrous, and it goes far to explaining why the French economy stagnated in this period. Initially, France was in a strong position, because growth had been vigorous in the 1920s, the downturn in economic activity came late and was less severe than in some countries, and the balance of payments was strong. However, the large gold stocks accumulated in the late 1920s and early 1930s allowed France to pursue an independent policy. Thus, even when the defensive policies of other countries began to affect the economy adversely, France was in a strong enough position to maintain the gold standard, and her fear of the inflationary consequences meant that she was unlikely to abandon it willingly. This line of action had unfortunate implications, because in order to get French costs and prices in line with world levels (given the general devaluation of currencies), it was necessary to resort to severe deflation. Between 1931 and 1936, deflationary policies were pursued relentlessly; money wages were reduced by more than 12 per cent, prices fell and government expenditures were cut sharply. At the same time, various trade restrictions were imposed to protect the external account. These policies had the opposite effect to what was desired, because until 1936 production and employment continued to decline.

It is not difficult to see why French policy failed to revive the economy. The maintenance of the gold standard at a time of general devaluation inevitably meant that the burden of adjustment was thrown onto the domestic economy.

This entailed high interest rates, which did little to restore business confidence. Second, economy measures and sharp cuts in government spending only served to aggravate the depression. Third, the efforts made to reduce costs and prices were partly self-defeating, because wage cuts reduced effective demand in the short term until prices had adjusted. Moreover, the expectation that costs and prices would fall further coupled with high interest rates induced business people to postpone investment.

The adverse consequences of the deflationary package were partly responsible for the sweeping victory of a left-wing coalition in 1936. Between June 1936 and March 1937, the new Blum Government introduced what might be described as a miniature New Deal experiment. It was an expansionist programme that reversed the policies followed in the first half of the 1930s. It entailed the abandonment of the gold standard and devaluation of the franc, a moderate programme of public works, increased money wages and a reduction in hours of work. For a time, the French economy experienced a temporary fillip, but growing labour shortages, continued distrust of the franc and the ensuing international recession (1937–38) led to renewed stagnation in the latter half of 1937. Subsequently, the Blum policies were modified, but a reversal in the trend of economic activity awaited the rapid increase in military expenditures in 1938–39.

French experience demonstrates clearly how disastrous government policy can be. Even by the late 1930s, output and production were still below pre-depression levels, and unemployment had been reduced only by the artificial manipulation of working hours. Because the French economy was in a relatively strong position at the onset of depression, one might have expected a reasonably firm recovery in the 1930s. The absence of any marked revival can be attributed chiefly to the severe deflationary policy of the first half of the decade, the effects of which were not easily reversed.

The other gold bloc countries (Belgium, Holland, Italy, Luxembourg, Poland and Switzerland) had a similar experience to France. Adherence to the former gold standard parity rate made it difficult to adopt any sort of reflationary action to combat the depression, because in order to maintain the old parities in the face of depreciation in other countries, deflationary policies were unavoidable because of the pressure on the balance of payments and the exchange rate. Adjustment had to be made, albeit not always very successfully, by compressing the internal price level and stringent import controls. In the final analysis, such policies eventually proved intolerable because of the disastrous effects on domestic economies and unemployment, quite apart from the fact that they proved somewhat ineffective in restoring external equilibrium. They experienced much the same fate as Britain when it restored the gold standard at the pre-war parity in 1925. Thus, eventually, the gold bloc began to crumble; in 1935, Belgium and Luxembourg resorted to devaluation, and in the same year, Italy was forced to withdraw from the gold bloc because of surreptitious devaluation of the lira and the introduction of exchange control. The following year saw the final demise of the gold bloc as France, the Netherlands and Switzerland capitulated in the face of pressure on their exchange rates and capital flight. On balance the gold bloc countries paid a high price for their faithful attachment to the gold standard. Industrial production declined on average by some 14 per cent between 1929 and 1935, and by the end of the decade output and production levels were little advanced on those of the cyclical peak of 1929. Their record was in marked contrast to the strong economic recovery recorded by countries that had left the gold standard and depreciated their currencies, especially those belonging to the sterling bloc.

Sweden offers a sharp contrast with the two countries so far considered, not only in respect of the strength of her recovery but also on account of the enlightened policies adopted. Sweden avoided the mistakes of many other countries in that she did not resort to extreme measures of protection nor did she follow the deflationary course of the gold bloc countries. Even better, the government attempted to phase its public expenditure to offset fluctuations in business activity. The country was fortunate, too, in having experienced strong growth and rapid structural change in the 1920s, with plenty of potential still left, and because the depression was later and weaker than in some countries.

Initially, it is true that Sweden, like so many countries, imposed some deflationary measures, for example wage cuts; but public spending continued to rise throughout the depression years, and by 1932–33 nearly one-quarter of unemployed people were being given relief work. Meanwhile, the deflationary tendencies were being reversed. During 1931–32, the krona was devalued and cheap money was adopted. In the following year, it was announced that budgetary policy was to be made an important instrument of recovery. The Finance Minister's speech of January 1933 is notable not only for its open declaration of an unorthodox budgetary policy but also because it formally acknowledged the state's responsibility for promoting recovery. Accordingly, a large programme of public works was implemented and the resulting budgetary deficit was to be financed by loans amortized over a period of four years. By 1934–35, the proportion of budgetary expenditure, when public works absorbed some 15 to 20 per cent of the total, met by borrowing amounted to one-quarter as against one-twentieth in the four fiscal years between 1928–29 and 1931–32. After 1935, when recovery was well under way, expenditure on public works was sharply reduced and the loans previously incurred were amortized.

By contrast with most other countries, Swedish economic policy in the 1930s was impressive and exemplary, but one should be wary about overemphasizing its contribution to the recovery. Currency devaluation certainly gave an initial boost to exports, which showed vigorous growth from the middle of 1933, though the main stimulus eventually arose from the demand abroad for Sweden's industrial materials as industrial recovery took place elsewhere, and later because of rearmament. Cheap money also gave a boost to the housing market and industrial investment, which surged forward after 1933. However, the public works programme was a carrier of recovery rather than an initial stimulator, because it did not really get under way until 1934, by which time economic activity was moving ahead strongly. Moreover, there were strong real or autonomous forces at work as in Britain, notably housing, consumer durables and new industries and exports, the recovery of which owed little to policy action. Thus, though policy measures were certainly favourable to Sweden's economy, it is probable that the main agents of recovery lay elsewhere. And it should be noted that though Sweden put up an impressive record in this period, the recovery was by no means complete, for even by 1937 unemployment still amounted to 11.6 per cent, though some of this was structural. Nevertheless, such facts should not be allowed to detract from the importance of Swedish policy; Sweden was the first country to acknowledge and use a countercyclical fiscal policy, and in the later 1930s preparations were made to continue the procedure in any future slump.

The German economy had two unique features in the 1930s: the strength of its recovery and the degree of state involvement in economic affairs. Though Germany suffered more than most from the slump, she also staged one of the strongest recoveries after 1932. Output rose by more than one-third between 1929 and 1939, while unemployment was abolished, being reduced progressively from a peak of 44 per cent in 1932 to 14.1 per cent in 1934 and to less than one per cent in 1938. Few other nations could match such a record and probably few wished to do so, given the high political and social price entailed in the process. Following the Nazi seizure of power in 1933, the economy was steadily transformed into a prototype of rigid control, and it became, in the latter part of the period, dominated by war motives.

Though the degree of state interference in economic affairs was eventually more extensive than in any other country outside Russia, the system of production, distribution and consumption that the Nazis erected defies classification in any of the usual categories of economic systems. It was neither capitalism, socialism or communism in the traditional sense of these terms; rather the Nazi system was a combination of some of the characteristics of capitalism and a highly planned economy. A comprehensive planning mechanism, which was by no means highly efficient, was imposed on an economy in which private property was not expropriated, in which the distribution of national income remained largely unchanged and in which private entrepreneurs retained some of the prerogatives and responsibilities of traditional capitalism. Moreover, by extensive control over trade and payments, the German economy came to exercise considerable influence over the economies of central and southeast Europe.

Initially, however, the economy of the Third Reich was peace-orientated, as Nazi economic policy concentrated its attack on the unemployment problem. The deflationary policies of the previous governments (of Brüning and von Papen) had done more to aggravate than alleviate the crisis, though in the middle of 1932, a moderate programme of public works had been instituted. Immediately the Nazis assumed power, they extended the relief policy by launching a massive programme of public works involving an outlay of some 6 billion Reichsmarks. The employment-creating effects of this expenditure soon set recovery in motion and mopped up a good deal of the unemployment, though before the sum had been fully spent the basis of economic policy shifted dramatically. From November 1934 onwards, priority was given to rearmament and preparations for war, and as early as 1936, military spending was beginning to dominate certain sectors of the economy, though the really big peacetime build-up in the defence sector did not occur until 1937–38. The shift in policy gave rise to a large increase in government spending, selective economic planning and extensive regulation of many sectors of the economy, including wages and prices, foreign trade and exchange and the money and capital markets. It also entailed higher taxes, selective depreciation of the mark and controls designed to shift resources from consumer to producer goods industries.

A policy geared to rearmament inevitably led to the increased importance of public as opposed to private spending and consumption. Between 1933 and 1939, the Reich government claimed that it had spent roughly 90 billion Reichsmarks on preparing for war, which was equivalent to one year's income on the standard of 1938. Modern authorities tend to downgrade the sum, but it still remains large. Military spending as a proportion of national income rose from 3 per cent in 1933 to 23 per cent in 1939, much of the increase occurring in the last two years, when it accounted for over one-third of total government spending (Britain's share, it may be noted, was almost as high in 1939 following a massive armament drive in that year). Of course, the state's influence was larger than this, because these figures refer specifically to military expenditure. By 1938, the public sector accounted for 57 per cent of Germany's gross investment as against 35.2 per cent in 1929, while total state spending as a proportion of national income increased from 11 per cent to over one-half between 1929 and the end of the 1930s. In effect, therefore, the government by the latter date had become the largest investor and consumer in the German economy.

The vast expansion in the size of the military machine and the public sector would not have been possible without extensive controls on private spending designed to shift resources away from this sector. To achieve this, the government maintained tight control over private investment, especially that in consumer goods industries. Effective demand for consumer goods was kept in check by controls over wages and prices, increased taxes and forced savings. Money wages remained more or less stable after 1933 at a level below those of 1929, and given the moderate rise in prices, real wages therefore fell slightly. In other words, the general consumer failed to benefit from the increase in aggregate national income. The real per capita income of the average worker was little different from that in 1929, while private consumption as a proportion of national income fell from 72 to 54 per cent between 1929 and 1939. The main beneficiaries were those now in work who had previously been unemployed and the business community who thrived on munitions orders. Much of the increased public spending was financed by higher taxation and borrowing, though the latter rarely accounted for more than one-quarter of total government receipts.

The network of controls was completed by extensive regulations on trade, payments and exchange. The chief aim of these was to restrict inessential imports and where possible boost exports and secure the benefits of favourable trade terms. The results in terms of exports were disappointing, despite the fact that eventually some 60 per cent of Germany's exports received a subsidy in one form or another. The import policy was more successful, with essential raw materials comprising an increasing share of the bill. At the same time, Germany's foreign trade was increasingly directed towards those countries with whom she had concluded bilateral clearing agreements, thereby avoiding the need to release free exchange currency for the payment of imports from such countries. By 1938, some 40 clearing agreements had been negotiated, covering about 80 per cent of Germany's imports. This involved a striking shift in the geographical direction of Germany's trade away from western Europe and towards southeastern Europe and countries overseas, notably Latin American, which were favourably disposed to Germany. Eventually, as we shall see, German economic influence over eastern Europe became very strong, and it paved the way for subsequent political control. On balance, the net cost of German imports (including allowances for quality differences in raw materials) probably rose as a result of her regulated trade policy.

Whatever the social costs of the German system, and they were substantial, there can be little doubt that it was successful in terms of recovery from the depression. Germany was the only country to eliminate unemployment and her record in aggregate output was impressive. It is very probable that some degree of recovery would have taken place without such extensive government intervention, but it would not have been anywhere near as strong or as sustained. On the other hand, it should be noted that the state's increasing participation in the economy was motivated, especially after 1934, largely by political considerations rather than by dictates of modern business-cycle theory. Nor should policy action be accorded all the bouquets in the matter of recovery. By the time the first large injection of expenditure in the 1933–34 relief programme had taken place, recovery in economic activity had already begun, though the process was markedly speeded up as a result of the new spending. There were too some real forces at work that were largely outside the government's domain. In particular, the 'motorization' of the German economy, namely the widespread use of motor vehicles and the road-building programme, was important in this period and played a significant part in sustaining if not initiating the upswing in the German economy. However, in so far as Hitler gave it his blessing and active encouragement, one might be inclined to argue that it represented yet another arm of the state's influence.

The final case to be considered is rather a sad story. Austria fared badly in the 1920s and little better in the 1930s, so that by 1938 her domestic output was no greater than in 1913. During the 1920s, the country had had many problems to contend with, including war exhaustion and the task of reconstruction, structural deficiencies in the economy, the loss of industrial areas to Czechoslovakia, the loss of a large customs-free market for her products and a bout of hyperinflation. Before she had time to recover properly, Austria was engulfed in depression; this was accompanied by the collapse of the Credit Anstalt and the financial crisis of the summer of 1931. It left the country almost as prostrate as it had been after the war. The subsequent flight of capital from Austria and the consequent drain on her foreign exchange reserves forced the government to take drastic action in the latter half of 1931. This entailed the adoption of exchange control, import and other trade controls and a deflationary package. Devaluation was ruled out for fear of its inflationary consequences, the memory of the great inflation of the early 1920s still being strong. But such policies were bound to aggravate the depression.

By July 1932, industrial production was 43 per cent below the 1929 level and unemployment was in the region of one-quarter. There was also a big trade deficit because of the collapse of exports and a continued high volume of imports because of the overvalued exchange. Foreign capital was not now available to cover the deficits, and in the summer of 1932, transfer on foreign debts had to be suspended.

Austria's economic position was therefore extremely serious in 1932. The monetary system had disintegrated as a result of the wave of bank failures, the government had a serious fiscal problem because of the collapse in tax receipts, the foreign exchange position was acute, while entry to traditional markets had been closed by protection. Though signs of an upturn in business activity were apparent in 1933, the recovery was weak and hesitant and the government was precluded from following an expansionary policy, even had it had the inclination to do so, by financial pressures. Fiscal and monetary policy therefore remained deflationary, and the accompanying high interest rates deterred business investment. However, some alleviation was provided by *de facto* devaluation through the use of private 'clearing', whereby certain exporters could sell their foreign exchange directly to importers at a negotiated rate, while in 1933, financial reconstruction measures were taken to prop up the banking system and the public finances with the help of a foreign loan. In addition, the devaluation of the dollar eased the budgetary problem by reducing overseas indebtedness. This enabled a moderate programme of public works to be instituted, but in 1936, public investment had to be cut back sharply because of financial constraints, and it revived again only when rearmament expenditures came into focus.

Austria therefore had little scope for manouevre in the 1930s because of her serious financial and monetary problems. It was never possible for the government to carry through a large programme of state spending to boost the economy, and real forces were far from strong. Consequently, the recovery was weak and erratic, being determined largely by the vagaries of export demand, the impact of the limited public works programme and later by rearmament. Even in 1937–38, the volume of output was barely the same as in 1929, though exports did slightly better. Unemployment remained high at about 17 per cent. Given Austria's weak position, it is not surprising that she succumbed to political and economic domination by Germany.

Questions for discussion

1   How did America contribute to the depression of the early 1930s?
2   Why was the depression in Europe so severe and so deep?
3   Why did most countries abandon the gold standard in the early 1930s?
4   Compare and contrast the recoveries in Germany and Britain.
5   Explain why the economic recovery was so diverse within Europe.

4 Eastern Europe and the periphery in the 1930s

For the most part the countries of eastern Europe and the periphery contrasted sharply with those of the industrial west that were discussed in Chapter 3. They had low incomes, and were predominantly agrarian, with poor infrastructure facilities. Rates of illiteracy were high and population growth often rapid. As a working concept, we may define the impoverished peripherals as those countries that in the early twentieth century still had around one-half or more of their populations directly dependent on agriculture for a livelihood and with per capita incomes of 50 per cent or less of the advanced nations of western Europe. On this basis, therefore, we encompass much of eastern Europe (Poland, Hungary, Romania, Yugoslavia and Bulgaria), Spain, Portugal, Greece and Turkey in southern Europe, along with the Baltic states of Estonia, Latvia and Lithuania and ending up with Albania. Some idea of the low level of development in most of the peripheral countries can be gleaned from the selection of indicators in Table 4.1. Most of these countries can be classed as peripheral in a geographic as well as an economic sense. The main exceptions were the four Nordic countries of Finland, Denmark, Norway and Sweden, which though geographically peripheral were certainly not peripheral in economic terms. In fact, these four countries had a robust economic performance in the inter-war period in contrast to the chequered economic record of many other countries along the periphery.

Stagnation in Eastern Europe

Apart from Russia, which, cut off from the western world, forged ahead economically in the 1930s under the stimulus of the Five-Year Plans, the east European countries had a rather chequered performance and achieved little in the way of bridging the gap in income levels compared with the west. Indeed, for the most part, per capita income levels stagnated in this period. The severity of the great depression almost wrecked the sickly economics of this area, and in the struggle for survival, most of the countries were forced to adopt strongly nationalistic policies. Even more pernicious, they were, for want of an alternative escape route, drawn into the German economic sphere.

That the depression should have proved to be a calamity for eastern Europe is not altogether surprising. As noted previously, apart from Czechoslovakia, none of

Table 4.1 Development indicators for European peripheral countries

	% of population dependent on agriculture circa 1930–34	Per capita GNP in 1938 in 1960 US dollars	Growth rate of population 1920–39	Illiteracy rate: % of 7–10-year-olds 1930–34	Infrastructure scores based on five components, circa 1937+	Productivity in calorie units per male employed in agriculture (average 1931–35, Europe = 100)
Albania	80	179	1.50	80	8.0	25
Bulgaria	75	420	1.30	31.4	13.9	55
Estonia	56	501*	0.10	4.0		103
Greece	46	590	1.93	40.8	18.3	48
Hungary	51	451	0.76	8.8	21.4	75
Latvia	55	501*	1.00	13.5		103
Lithuania	70	501*	1.10	37.0		74
Poland	60	372	1.44	23.1	18.8	56
Portugal	46	351	1.50	59.0	13.1	53
Romania	72	343	1.27	42.0	13.5	53
Spain	50	337	0.90	31.0	17.0	94
Turkey	81	220	2.10	90.0	9.3	39
Yugoslavia	76	339	1.43	45.2	14.3	43
England and Wales/UK	5	1181	0.49	0.0	70.3	240

+Transport, communications, housing supply, health care and educational and cultural services.

*Average of the three Baltic states.

Sources: see the references in Aldcroft, *Europe's Third World*, 5, 6, 14, 173.

the countries had what might be called a structurally sound economy. They were heavily dependent on agriculture, which in itself was badly organized and inefficient compared with that of the west: too many small farms, limited capital and low productivity. In three countries (Yugoslavia, Bulgaria and Romania), some three-quarters or more of the population was dependent on agriculture, whereas in Poland and Hungary the proportion was well over one-half; even in Czechoslovakia, it accounted for one-third, but this country did have a strong industrial base. Agriculture therefore provided the main source of exports, accounting for one-third or more of all exports, while foodstuffs, raw materials and semi-manufactures were responsible for three-quarters or more of all exports. By contrast, finished goods accounted for over 70 per cent of Czechoslovakia's exports.

The vulnerability of eastern Europe to changing fortunes in agriculture can be readily appreciated. During the economic crisis, primary product prices collapsed, falling by one-half to two-thirds between 1929 and 1934, the decline being partly accentuated in the early stages by increasing production as farmers sought to maintain their incomes through increased sales. As a result, agrarian incomes declined by up to one-half in Romania, Bulgaria, Poland and Yugoslavia and by about one-third in Hungary. This collapse in incomes was little short of disastrous given the already heavy indebtedness of the farming sector; the debt burden increased proportionately to income and the distress was aggravated by the fact that agricultural prices fell faster than those of industrial products purchased by the peasant. Thus by 1932, many peasants were on the verge of bankruptcy. In Yugoslavia, for example, more than one-third of all rural households were seriously in debt (many more being too poor even to obtain credit), and the sum of the indebtedness amounted to 80–90 per cent of their total cash incomes. Many farms collapsed altogether and rural communities were put under severe social strain, though the problem was subsequently alleviated to some extent by government relief in the form of credits, debt moratoria and other measures of assistance.

The position was equally serious on the export front. Agricultural exports were hit by falling prices, severe competition and increasing self-sufficiency and protection in former markets. The volume of both cattle and cereal exports fell sharply, but the shortfall in revenue was even greater because of the dramatic price decline. For example, in Romania, the volume of cereal exports fell by 42 per cent between 1929 and 1934, but export receipts fell by no less than 73 per cent, whereas for Hungary, the percentage changes were 27 and 60 per cent. For the area as a whole, export incomes fell to about 40 per cent of the pre-crisis level. The collapse in export receipts inevitably affected the ability of these countries to import and resulted in a sharp deterioration in their external accounts. Between 1930 and 1933, Hungary was able to buy on average 15–20 per cent fewer foreign goods for the value of equal quantities of her export articles than in the period 1925–27.

Moreover, it was little consolation that the industrial sector suffered less acutely from the crisis, because for most of the countries in this region, industry accounted for such a small proportion of total economic activity. Experience here varied more widely than in the case of agriculture, depending in part on the structure of each particular economy. In the Balkan countries, for example, industrial overproduction was not particularly pronounced, partly because of the relative insignificance of this sector, and in any case reduced consumption was usually counterbalanced in many fields by import restrictions. Thus production declined only moderately in Romania thanks to a large increase in oil output, while Bulgaria experienced a significant advance in manufacturing between 1929 and 1932. The setback was severe in Yugoslavia, but the most serious industrial consequences occurred in Czechoslovakia, which had the most advanced industrial sector, and to a lesser extent in the mixed agrarian-industrial economies of Hungary and Poland. Even so, for all countries except Czechoslovakia, it was the agrarian sector that determined the scale and severity of the crisis.

A further major problem was of course the region's international indebtedness. Most of the countries (again excepting Czechoslovakia) had relied heavily on foreign credit of one sort or another in the 1920s. The drying up of foreign lending between 1928 and 1931 caused acute problems, because the servicing of previous debts was dependent on the ability to raise new loans; even by the late 1920s the amount of yearly amortization was usually in excess of new loans. By the time of the European financial crisis in 1931, the situation had become desperate; all external sources of finance had disappeared, incomes and export receipts had plummeted and as gold and foreign exchange reserves drained away the countries faced the threat of complete financial collapse. With the rapid fall in export receipts the interest payments on former debts accounted for one-third or more of these revenues. Only Czechoslovakia, never a large debtor, escaped financial ruin.

The consequences of the crisis in terms of later events and policy may be summarized as follows: (1) emergency measures to deal with the immediate situation; (2) the rise of dictatorships or semi-dictatorial regimes bent on fostering development along autarchic lines; and (3) the increasing stranglehold exercised by Germany over the region's economic and political future.

The problem initially in the early 1930s was not so much one of recovery as of economic salvation. Drastic measures were required to shore up the tottering economies and these were soon forthcoming: they included not only severe deflationary policies but also a battery of restrictions typical of siege economies, which were designed primarily to deal with the external account. Among them were temporary closure of banking institutions, rigorous exchange control, limitation on debt payments and tariffs, quotas and import prohibitions. Thus, for example, by early 1933, the import of almost all finished products into Hungary was prohibited except under special permit. At the same time, attempts were made to boost exports by subsidies, special and advantageous exchange facilities in favour of exporters often in place of devaluation, and the widespread use of clearing agreements in foreign trade relations, because the acute shortage of foreign exchange rendered previous methods of foreign trade impossible. Clearing agreements proliferated in the 1930s (by which foreign trade turnover was based on reciprocal exchange of products of approximately equal value wherever possible, with the use of foreign exchange being restricted to the payment of balances where liabilities arose, especially with countries outside such agreements), and by the end of the decade much of the trade of east European countries was settled through bilateral clearing arrangements.

If bilateral trade and barter offered some alleviation to the external problems of these countries, they also presented Germany with an opportunity to increase her economic, and subsequently political, influence in this area. In September 1934, Dr Hjalmar Schacht had launched a plan designed to regulate Germany's trade and payments and to import from countries that did not demand payment in foreign exchange. This was clearly well suited to strengthening economic relations with an area heavily dependent on exporting primary products and importing finished goods, especially producer goods, and which was still facing severe economic difficulties. At first, only Hungary was really sympathetic to Germany's new economic foreign policy, but in time other countries succumbed to the temptation and signed trade agreements with Germany. By offering a ready market for primary products in exchange for imports of equipment, Germany came to exercise increasing dominance over the trade and development of eastern Europe. By 1937, total German trade amounted to only 40 per cent of the 1929 value but that with southeast Europe (Bulgaria, Romania, Yugoslavia and Hungary) had attained the previous peak level; these four countries accounted for about 10 per cent of Germany's trade as against 4 per cent in 1929. Their dependence on Germany as an outlet for their exports rose sharply; exports to Germany as a percentage of the total between 1933 and 1939 increased from 36 to 71 per cent in the case of Bulgaria, 11 to 52 per cent for Hungary, 17 to 43 per cent for Romania and 14 to 46 per cent for Yugoslavia.

Though Germany's economic penetration into the area was not wholly exploitive, in that it provided the eastern countries with a market for their commodities and at the same time allowed them to secure imports of much-needed capital equipment, the balance of advantage lay with Germany. For one thing, Germany was able to dictate the prices to be paid for the region's primary products and at the same time she piled up large import surpluses with the countries in question, which were not matched by German exports. The accumulating arrears in the German supply of goods meant in effect that Germany was financing part of her rearmament interest-free at the expense of her suppliers in the east. And though the eastern countries did secure some capital equipment from Germany, it was too little and too late to do much in the way of transforming the structure of their economies. Finally, economic penetration paved the way for ultimate military and political conquest of Germany's eastern neighbours.

There is still some controversy as to the division of benefits from the system. Conventional wisdom asserts that Germany exploited the region for her own purposes to gain access to food and raw materials on favourable terms, and in so doing she piled up large import surpluses with the countries, the Reichsmark balances from which could be used to purchase only German goods. Indirectly, therefore, one could argue that Germany was rearming at the expense of weaker nations. In turn, Germany was accused of dumping large quantities of unwanted goods such as aspirins and cuckoo-clocks on eastern Europe. Contemporary reports maintain that Yugoslavia received enough aspirins from Germany to last a decade, whereas Romania did even better with aspirin supplies sufficient to relieve 500 years of headaches.

Apocryphal or not, there was a credit side to the relationship. One has to remember that these countries had few other secure outlets for their products, and evidence suggests that they did receive more than ephemeral goods in return. They acquired a large part of their machinery and arms supplies from Germany as well as a variety of consumer goods. Moreover, Germany's monopsonist power was by no means as exploitive as some contemporary writers would make out. German purchases helped to raise the export prices and incomes of the countries in question and they generally paid above world prices, while Germany did not take undue advantage to turn the terms of trade in her favour. Possibly increasing dependence on the stronger economy slowed down structural diversification and reintegration into the world economy, but such observations are largely academic given the conditions of the time and Germany's long-term plans for the region.

On the other hand, trade relationships with Germany could be unpredictable, and the large unrequited balances, though reduced in time, left the countries highly vulnerable to political and economic pressures when market conditions deteriorated as they did later in the decade. An illustration is provided by the German decision in September 1939 to refuse purchase of Yugoslavia's bumper plum crop despite previously having negotiated a guaranteed contract. The incident had a happy ending, however. Undaunted by the reversal, the plums were turned into brandy, the Bosnians got drunk and so they were able to use some of the aspirins dumped on Yugoslavia by the Germans through clearing agreements. On a more serious note, Germany undoubtedly used her trade connections with southeast Europe to infiltrate Nazi agents and spread political propaganda. Political agents were widely employed, ostensibly under cover of commercial disguise, throughout the region. In one case, the Germans established a soya-bean company in Romania employing no fewer than 3000 commercial agents to spread the Nazi gospel, while in Bulgaria, German military experts dominated the army. In fact, Nazi 'commercial' agents were thick on the ground in southeast Europe by the end of the decade, and the countries in question realized only too late in the day that economic dependence was but a prelude to political control.

Elsewhere, Germany had less success on the economic front in the conquest of territories, though economic factors were not entirely absent in the eventual domination of Poland, Austria and Czechoslovakia. The scope for economic penetration by purchasing agricultural and raw material surpluses was much less in the case of the latter two countries, given their more advanced economic structures, while Poland managed to do without German economic assistance. Hitler therefore adopted alternative methods, which included overt pressure and military blackmail, economic blockade, prohibition of German tourists from visiting these countries, limitations on foreign trade and conquests of markets supplied by these countries. This policy culminated in the crushing of Austria and Czechoslovakia and their annexation in 1938–39, with Poland following soon after. Thus, by the outbreak of war, Germany's economic and political domination of central and eastern Europe was almost complete, because all the states in the area had succumbed to her offensives, though German ambitions for the area as a whole were fully realized only during the course of the war itself.

Germany's domination of eastern Europe is not particularly surprising given her grandiose military ambitions and the weakness of the states concerned. The fact that the economic crisis subsequently gave rise to dictatorships or quasi-dictatorships in these countries was not necessarily a barrier to these ambitions, because the new regimes tended to be more favourably disposed towards German interests and more responsive to pressures than their democratic counterparts of the 1920s. Moreover, despite efforts to foster industrialization, their economies remained weak and structurally unsound.

The depression undoubtedly strengthened nationalist sentiments within eastern Europe and gave rise to the increasing involvement of the state in economic affairs. The drift towards étatism took different forms, but basically the common aim was to improve the economic performance of the countries in question. Accordingly, attempts were made to promote exports and industry in an effort to cause a shift in the structural format of the economies away from the predominant base of agriculture. Apart from specific measures of protection and subsidy and the like, this policy involved an increase in the state-owned sector of economic activity. The prime example in this respect was Poland. Here, the focus of attention was concentrated on the industrialization of the central industrial region within the triangle bounded by Warsaw, Krakow and Lwow. As a result of steady acquisition of undertakings, the Polish state owned about 100 industrial enterprises by the end of the 1930s; they included all the armament factories, 80 per cent of the chemical industry, 40 per cent of the iron industry and 50 per cent of other metal industries, and 20 per cent of the oil refineries. The state also held the majority of stock in some fifty companies. The state's direct role was not quite so important in other countries, though it certainly increased in this period. In Hungary, it accounted for only about 5 per cent of industrial investments in the later 1930s. A notable feature in some eastern countries was the experiments made in medium-term planning of economic development. Hungary, for example, launched a Five-Year Plan early in 1938 that included a big programme to develop the armament industries and build up a modern army.

On balance, the efforts made to foster industrial development were not an unqualified success. Certainly, industry proved to be the most dynamic sector in the 1930s, and in most cases, the share of this sector increased in importance, albeit rather marginally in most cases. Moreover, industrial expansion was probably faster on average in eastern Europe than in the west, though the most industrialized country (Czechoslovakia) scarcely made up the losses incurred in the depression partly because of the closing of western markets to her industrial products. But the advance generally on the industrial front was not spectacular when it is recalled how small the industrial sector was in the economies of eastern Europe. More to the point, however, is that certain aspects of the pattern of development gave cause for concern. For one thing, state policy tended to foster unproductive or non-economic investments. Second, the state's financial resources were limited; it could not replace the role of the foreign capitalist when overseas loans dried up in the early 1930s, and the 'nostrification' policy designed to discourage the influx of foreign funds and ownership did not help matters. Third, efforts to mobilize domestic resources were frequently offset by restrictive monetary and fiscal policies, including higher taxation. Fourth, the direction of investment was not especially conducive to promoting rapid development. It was frequently channelled into textiles, food-processing and light industries, where the growth potential was low, to the comparative neglect of modern science-based industries such as chemicals, the electrical trades, telecommunications and the motor industry. One of the most obvious deficiencies in the investment strategy is shown by the failure in eastern Europe to shift from the railway to the motor age. The motor vehicle did not replace the railways as a growth force in the inter-war period. An index of motorization based on the number of cars in use in relation to territory and population gives values of between 0.3 and 0.5 for Poland, Hungary, Yugoslavia and Romania, as against 5.7 for Europe as a whole in 1938. Moreover, the infrastructure of eastern Europe was probably more backward compared with that of the west than it had been in 1913.

Apart from its rather lop-sided industrial structure, eastern Europe also retained its traditional dual structure, namely many small-scale inefficient firms competing with a few modern large-scale corporations. During the inter-war period, small-scale business was as viable as ever partly because of the weakness of large-scale concerns, the abundant labour supply and the predominance of those industrial activities in which small-scale firms tended to thrive. Furthermore, the large-scale corporation failed to make much progress in production and management methods, which were a feature of those in the west. Modern mass-production methods made little headway, and for the most part, the largest companies remained little more than 'general stores' supplying a multiplicity of products in small batches to limited markets within a rigid protectionist framework.

In this period too, agriculture acted as a drag on economic progress. Before the war, the agrarian sector, though still far behind western standards, had made significant advances partly as a result of the gradual spread of capitalist farming; hence it provided something of a stimulus to the economy in general. During the inter-war years, this sector lost its dynamic role and therefore it could not perform its previous function of capital accumulation. Throughout the 1920s, agriculture struggled to recoup its wartime losses only to be dealt another shattering blow in 1929–32. In the 1930s, recovery was slow, though output did manage to surpass 1913 levels in some products by the end of the decade. Even so, it remained an extremely weak sector: there was no radical transformation in the structure and methods of farming partly because of the shortage of capital and the existence of too many small farming units. Even in countries where large estates still remained important, for example Poland and Hungary, small farms still predominated, while in Yugoslavia over 75 per cent and in Bulgaria over 60 per cent of the farms were under 5 hectares in size. In Poland, 47 per cent of the peasant farms consisted of narrow strips. Small-scale peasant holders, often overburdened with debt, were not in a position to farm land profitably and economically, and they lacked the capital and incentive to shift to larger and more efficient units of production.

Consequently, new techniques, mechanization and the use of fertilizers made relatively little progress, and productivity stagnated. In some cases, crop productivity levels were little better than those before 1914 and generally they were well below those of western Europe. High rates of population growth in some countries also exerted pressure on the land and helped to press down productivity levels.

Low productivity, capital shortages, low incomes and agrarian overpopulation formed a vicious circle that could be broken only by radical changes in market conditions. But there was little prospect of these occurring because overpopulation, low incomes and a weak industrial sector meant a limited domestic market. Moreover, former export markets for agrarian products disappeared because of protection and reduced cereal consumption in the west – hence the attraction of trade links with Germany. In the 1930s, agricultural exports of most eastern countries were still about 20–25 per cent below pre-war levels. Market prospects were better for certain vegetables, fruits and animal products, and some countries adopted intensive market farming to cater for new demands, as for example chickens and fruit in Hungary, tobacco and garden produce in Bulgaria, and oilseeds in Romania, together with a more general shift towards livestock farming. But such changes were insufficient to offset the setback in cereals, nor did they produce a radical transformation in the structure of agriculture. Yet despite its inherent backwardness, agriculture remained, except in Czechoslovakia, the most important single factor determining the economic position of eastern countries in every year until the Second World War.

The progress achieved in industry during the 1930s was insufficient to counterbalance the stagnation in agriculture and population growth, with the result that, with the exception of Bulgaria, real incomes per head remained fairly static between 1929 and 1938, and in the case of Czechoslovakia, they probably fell slightly. Over the period as a whole (1913–38), income growth per head of population was fairly modest, with the main exception of Bulgaria, less than that in western countries and weaker than before 1914. Agriculture stagnated for most of the period, while only modest gains were made on the industrial front. The progress in the latter did not produce any significant change in the structural format of the eastern economies. By the end of the 1930s, about 75–80 per cent of the active population in the Balkan countries (Romania, Bulgaria and Yugoslavia) was still engaged on the land, a proportion similar to that in 1910. There was a shift away from agriculture in Hungary and Poland, albeit modest, the proportions engaged in this sector falling from 72 to 65 per cent and from 56 to 51 per cent, respectively, over the years 1920–40. In terms of the generation of national income, the shift from agriculture to industry was a little more pronounced, but in the Balkan countries the proportion of income derived from industry remained less than one-quarter, and only in Czechoslovakia did it surpass one-half.

In short, therefore, up to 1939, eastern Europe remained a backward and predominantly agrarian-based region, and by every conceivable indicator it was less productive, less literate and less healthy than western Europe or even west-central Europe (Austria and Czechoslovakia). It was potentially a rich region stocked with a poor people in which the maldistribution of poverty was the central feature and whose development had been stunted by the vicissitudes of war and the unfavourable economic climate that followed. The depression and its aftermath finally set the seal on any further substantial development. The dynamism apparent at the turn of the century all but petered out in the 1930s, and there were no radical changes in the economic structure of the region of a type propitious to rapid economic growth. With the exception of Czechoslovakia, the countries of eastern Europe remained suppliers of food and raw materials and buyers of industrial goods. Politically, economically and socially, they were backward and weak, struggling with inner tensions and contradictions, and with little prospect, as war loomed near, of solving their fundamental problems.

Along the European periphery in the inter-war years

We now turn to the remaining countries on the European periphery, mostly very backward and poor societies, which languished well behind the industrial countries of the west and sometimes behind the east European countries. They include Greece, Turkey and Albania, Spain and Portugal and the three Baltic states of Estonia, Latvia and Lithuania. Their economic performance between the wars was mixed.

Let us begin with Albania, the smallest and poorest country in Europe, with powerful enemies and few friends. Before the war, there had been little in the way of modern development and a largely illiterate population scratched a precarious living from the land. The country was occupied and partitioned during the First World War, and only by the fortuitous intervention of Britain and the United States did it manage to retain its recently won independence after the conflict. Even then, the post-war settlement left 44 per cent of Albanians outwith the new state, most of whom were in Greece and Yugoslavia.

Political stability proved illusive in the immediate post-war years because of clan and tribal feuding, but in 1922, along came the powerful leader of the Mati tribe, Ahmed Zogolli (later known as King Zog), who, when he became prime minister at the end of the year, set about restoring order and stability in the country; from 1928, when he proclaimed himself monarch of the Albanians, he ruled Albania with almost unlimited powers until the country was invaded by the Italians in 1939.

Nevertheless, he did make some attempt to reform and modernize the country. He set up a National Bank and introduced a national currency, new civil, penal and commercial codes were enacted and an attempt was made to reduce the forces of tradition and tribal custom. In addition, there was a measure of land reform and educational policies designed to reduce the high rate of illiteracy. The reforms had mixed results, and they did little to drag Albania into the twentieth century. The country remained a primitive land-based society with unchanged medieval techniques. Of all the Balkan states, Albania changed the least structurally. It failed to enter the initial stages of industrialization and there were few signs of sustained progress and modernisation. The statistical data for Albania are patchy, but what we have suggests that there was virtually no improvement in the standard of life during the inter-war years. When account is taken of the 25 per cent increase in population, then by the end of the period per capita income had probably fallen, so that the Albanians were worse off than at the time of their liberation. Compared with her Balkan neighbours, Albania was very poor indeed.

Turkey emerged from the ruins of the Ottoman Empire following the post-war peace settlement. It was therefore predominantly a non-European Muslim country with now only a toehold in Europe. However, in view of its past history in Europe and its current aspirations, it seems apposite to comment briefly on its history.

Though a very backward country, Turkey had more going for it than Albania. It is true that before 1914 the Ottoman Empire was in a state of terminal decline despite some signs of modernization and progress and the emergence of a small manufacturing sector. The interlude of war and the protracted peace negotiations caused a setback, but the country's integrity was saved by Mustafa Kemal (popularly known as Atatürk), who defeated the Greeks in the Asia Minor campaign and secured better peace terms than might have been expected. In October 1923, he set up the Turkish Republic under his own presidency and remained in power until his death in 1938.

He inherited a country whose economy was in a parlous state after some ten years of almost continuous warfare. It had been drained of resources, left with a legacy of inflation, a weak currency, budgetary and trade deficits and a loss of many productive and skilled workers as Armenians, Greeks and other unwanted nationals fled the country. Yet a decade later, writers were highlighting significant transformation. As with King Zog in Albania, though to greater effect, Atatürk set about reforming and modernizing the country by promulgating civil and economic reforms, including religious reformation, educational measures and the modernization of basic infrastructures. Industry was left largely in private hands, but with the provision of various financial incentives and state initiatives. During the 1930s, there was a move to a more state interventionist approach, as was the case in many other countries during the period. The reasons for the shift in strategy are not difficult to discern. Turkey was badly affected by the great depression, and especially by the large fall in primary commodity prices. The desire for greater self-sufficiency in industry and defence motives also prompted a change of direction. The examples of Soviet Russia and Nazi Germany in planning and state control also had some influence, and the former country in fact sent a delegation to Turkey to advise on industrial development backed up by a loan. A further motive for intervention was the alleged shortage of indigenous enterprise with the requisite capital to undertake large-scale industrial development.

The principles and objectives of the new policy were enshrined in the first Five-Year Plan implemented at the start of 1934. This was revised in 1936 by a second Five-Year Plan and then reduced to four years in 1938. The chief aims were to be greater emphasis on the use of domestic raw materials and to produce goods that would reduce the country's dependence on imported manufactures. The main target areas for development were textiles, ceramics, chemicals, iron and steel, paper and cellulose, sulphur and copper mining, glass, cement and the sponge industry. Defence operations also became increasingly important in the later 1930s, when budgetary expenditure devoted to the military sector rose by 44 per cent. The state itself directly controlled a large range of activities, especially in key areas such as infrastructure facilities, transport and postal and telecommunications services.

The results of the exercise appear impressive. Industrial growth was rapid in the 1930s, probably only surpassed by that of Japan, the Soviet Union and Greece, and most of the main targets were achieved. Though private enterprise still accounted for one-half or more of industrial output and investment, much large-scale modern development was conducted by the state. However, the planning exercise was not free from imperfections. There was a distinct lack of coherence in the planning structure, and it was certainly never as detailed or embracing as that in Soviet Russia. Although industrial expansion was impressive, it tended to be high cost and inefficient, using cheap, untrained labour but with stagnant productivity so that unit costs were high. Costs were high because of a combination of factors: lack of skilled labour, difficulties in organizing a modern industrial labour force, low wages and salaries encouraged corruption and inefficient management, expensive transport facilities and the poor planning and location of plants. Furthermore, the drive for industrial expansion came at the expense of the agrarian sector, which was heavily taxed to provide resources for industry, and in the process agriculture itself was neglected and starved of investment.

The aggregate data on Turkey are still fragile, but most estimates suggest that there was solid progress in all sectors during the inter-war years. Income per head rose by 7.3 per cent per annum between 1923 and 1930 and 4.0 per cent between 1930 and 1939, whereas industrial production increased by 8.6 and 11.1 per cent a year, respectively. The figures are impressive but one should bear in mind that they stem from a low base. If we take the immediate pre-war years as a base, then it is possible that real wages and real per capita incomes did not progress all that much beyond that reference point. Moreover, even with the burst of expansion in the inter-war years and the shoots of modern development, Turkey still remained mired in backwardness at the end of the period. Structurally, there had not been a dramatic change. The bulk of the population was still based on the land, deriving a meagre livelihood from antiquated agrarian practices, culturally backward and poverty-stricken. One author has stated that there were effectively two Turkeys: 'That of the aeroplane and that of the oxen-cart. The latter represented the actual living Turkey, while the former implied the potentialities' (Hershlag 1954, 337). The institutions of the country may have been given a face-lift, but the new industrial developments were little more than islands of capitalism in a sea or primitivism, while the society around remained in abject poverty.

Turkey's arch-foe, Greece, represents a more promising picture, and indeed it was the star performer in the inter-war period, with an advance in per capita income higher than any other country. Yet at first sight one would not have expected this to be the case. Though culturally and economically a little more advanced than the Ottoman Empire before 1914, her development profile before the First World War did not give great grounds for optimism. Industrial development and modern communications were still limited, agriculture was painfully antiquated and inefficient (so much so that one-third of grains consumed along with other foodstuffs had to be imported), while the state finances were in such a mess by the end of the nineteenth century that the country was declared bankrupt by the western powers, who instituted international control down to 1913.

The war and its aftermath did not help matters, of course. It led to strong inflationary pressures and further debt problems. Politically, the country was split in two by the conflict, and the ensuing peace settlement, although favourable to Greece, ultimately led her into the disastrous Asia Minor conflict with Turkey. However, one important benefit emerged in that Greece united most of her nationals under one roof, so to speak, with the country's size doubling in both population and territory. In the process, she absorbed a large contingent of Greek nationals from Turkey, many of whom proved to be beneficial to the economy. At long last Greece had a fairly cohesive national identity even if her original ambitions of a Greater Greece were not fully realised.

In many ways, the 1920s were a challenging time, with the task of assimilating a large immigrant population, the need to check inflation and stabilize the currency and also to deal with public debt problems and institute land reform measures. Remarkably, despite these difficulties, Greece had one of the fastest rates of growth in Europe, especially in industry, which surged ahead at 7.2 per cent a year between 1921 and 1927, though growth in the economy as a whole was slower because of the heavy weighting of agriculture. The gains in the industrial sector can be attributed to several factors, including the short-term stimulus imparted by inflation and currency depreciation, heavy tariff protection, policy incentives to stimulate industry and the sharp fall in real wages after 1921, the wage level being depressed by the increase in the labour force caused by immigration.

No sooner had Greece secured a sounder economic and financial basis and a more stable political environment than the world economic crisis broke out and upset the situation. The main impact was on the financial side rather than on the real economy, because Greece was one of the few countries to record a positive expansion in output through the course of the depression. The main difficulty again proved to be one of debt, because Greece was heavily dependent on foreign finance to meet her budgetary requirements and for closing the balance of payments account. The country had one of the highest per capita foreign debts in eastern Europe, and debt servicing absorbed around one-third of export earnings in the years 1928–30. Budgetary revenues were declining and there was a large fall in export earnings together with a deficit on capital account. Fortunately, Greece avoided taking extreme deflationary measures as was so common in many other countries at this time. Instead, the currency was devalued, exchange control imposed and the servicing of foreign debt suspended.

These external policy operations proved beneficial for Greece. With one of the largest currency devaluations (60 per cent by the end of 1933), she secured a competitive advantage in export markets, while the debt servicing moratorium was an immediate relief to the balance of payments. Henceforward, the economy became more inward-looking and state directed, though never systematically planned as in some neighbouring countries. High tariffs, quantitative trade restrictions and the use of bilateral clearing agreements were extensively employed and policy was directed towards achieving greater self-sufficiency based on the use of domestic resources wherever possible.

The strategy seems to have paid off, judging by the growth record. Greece had a 'spectacular recovery', with one of the highest growth rates in Europe. Depreciation of the currency, trade restrictions and a fall in real wages were the main forces at work. Import volumes fell sharply and by the end of the decade were no greater than they had been in the late 1920s, whereas exports doubled between 1928 and 1938. A large part of Greece's trade was conducted under bilateral clearing, with Germany becoming the major trading partner. In fact, by the end of the decade, the League of Nations even classified Greece as being part of the German economic bloc.

Despite the impressive growth and the visible trend towards greater self-sufficiency, the structure of the economy did not change significantly. In 1938, four main sectors (textiles, chemicals, food processing and tanning) accounted for nearly three-quarters of industrial output; on the external side, tobacco still accounted for nearly one-half of all exports, while a handful of commodities (tobacco, currants, sultanas, olive oil, wine and skins) made up some 70 per cent of total exports. In fact, the structural composition of agriculture may have changed a little more, with tobacco, wheat and cotton production all rising sharply, whereas the output of currants remained stable. Wheat production was one of the great success stories in the government's policy of greater self-sufficiency in grain; wheat production trebled in the 1930s after being fairly stable in the previous decade.

Though estimates of output and industrial production vary, all point to a significant increase during the inter-war years, while income per capita rose by over three-quarters between 1913 and 1938. Despite this impressive record, it is doubtful whether the economy was based on secure foundations. In fact, the governor of the Bank of Greece admitted in 1936 that the expansion of industry was built on sand and heavily dependent on stiff protection and depreciation of the drakma. Manufacturing industry was deemed to be backward, with a proliferation of many small, inefficient, high-cost producers. Employment in handicraft trades far outweighed that in modern factory operations. The relatively static structure of the economy and foreign trade pattern still reflected that of an underdeveloped economy. The export trade was dominated by a handful of primary commodities (mainly agrarian), while manufacturing output was concentrated on a limited range of products serving mainly the domestic market and uncompetitive in international markets. Agriculture too was backward in methods and equipment and dreadfully inefficient. Labour productivity on the land was only about one-fifth that in England and Wales. As for infrastructure facilities, these were reckoned to be the worst in Europe, with the exception of Turkey and Albania. Overall, therefore, the Greek economy had by 1939 probably reached the limits of development under a regime of high protection and unchanging production functions. In other words, the economy was close to its production ceiling under existing techniques, and there were few signs of a radical transformation to effect an outward shift in the supply curve.

The Iberian countries (Spain and Portugal) differed from the other backward European peripheral countries in that they were not seriously damaged by the 1914–18 conflict. Spain remained neutral and Portugal did not join the allied cause until March 1916 and then played a rather minor role. Nor did they experience territorial or population shifts as a consequence of the post-war peace settlement. Ostensibly, therefore, they should have been in a stronger position to develop their economies in the aftermath of war. On the other hand, they had much in common with the other lagging countries in Europe. Agriculture was the mainstay of their economies, and needless to say it was extremely backward by western standards, while illiteracy was high, especially in Portugal. By most measures of development, they could be classed as extremely backward countries, with levels of income per capita less than one-half of those in the industrialized west.

Once a world power with a glittering future, Spain lost its way from the seventeenth century onwards, and despite some signs of modern development in the latter half of the nineteenth century, by 1914, the country was overwhelmingly agrarian and backward. However, as a neutral country, Spain was able to take advantage of the dislocation in the belligerent countries in the Great War. Exports were stimulated, as was import substitution. A wide range of industrial activities were given a boost, including iron and steel, metal and engineering, coal, shipbuilding and electrical goods. These benefits were reflected in Spain's external account: before the war, the balance of trade was permanently in the red, but through the years 1915–19, a substantial surplus was recorded. Agriculture too benefited as supplies of foodstuffs from traditional suppliers were curtailed. However, there was also a downside. Not all sectors flourished: construction and services languished, while some of the wartime developments could be classed as hot-house growth, which became stunted or withered on the vine once conditions returned to normal and foreign supplies resumed. In fact, reversal was rapid and Spain was hit hard in the international recession of 1921–22.

The other unfortunate thing is that Spanish enterprise did not capitalize on its wartime bonanza. Both industry and agriculture made substantial profits during the war, yet little was ploughed back to modernize Spain's archaic industrial and agrarian structures to provide a firm platform for future development. Instead, many of the wartime gains were dissipated by their recipients in conspicuous consumption, property development and financial dealings. Moreover, the immediate aftermath of war had left Spain with many of the same problems that affected other countries: rising budgetary deficits, inflation, currency instability, rising unemployment, a string of bank failures and political and social unrest, including a wave of strikes. Not a very pleasant cocktail for a country that had done so well out of the war.

The deepening economic and financial crisis proved too much for the weak parties and administrations of the restoration monarchy. A *coup d'état* was launched by the army in September 1923 under General Miguel Primo de Rivera, which was the prelude to a dictatorship lasting until January 1930. When Primo was ousted from power, a civil directorate took over before the emergence of the Second Republic in April 1931.

The main aims of Primo's administration were to restore order and stability and stimulate the economy, while at the same time preserving established institutions and traditional values. It was not a fascist-type regime based on the mobilization of the masses but one of land-owning and small gentry dedicated to conservative policies.

There have been mixed views on the economic achievements of the new regime, but the latest data do suggest a fairly healthy performance, with per capita income rising by some 22 per cent between 1921 and 1929 and industrial production expanding at over five per cent a year. Factors favourable to expansion included a strong housing boom and considerable urban development, especially in the major cities, an ambitious infrastructure programme that included roads, railways, reservoirs and electricity supply, a certain degree of technological catch-up in a range of industries, some modernization in agriculture and the trading advantages flowing from protection of the home market and a floating currency. Spain, as with Turkey, did not return to the gold standard but retained a floating currency, which meant that the economy was not constrained by the straitjacket of an overvalued fixed exchange rate regime as was the case in some countries during the latter half of the 1920s.

In fact, it has been argued that the floating exchange rate insulated Spain from the worst ravages of the depression of the early 1930s. However, this is only part of the story. In fact, industrial output and exports fell sharply, but this was offset by the stability in agriculture as a result of good harvests and the buoyancy of the service sector. In any case, the currency advantage proved short-lived. After 1931, it disappeared as many countries left gold and devalued, while Spain imposed exchange control in May 1931, which effectively tied her to those countries with overvalued exchange rates.

Recovery from the depression had only just begun when it was abruptly cut short by the protracted civil war (July 1936 to April 1939), with the subsequent emergence of the Franco regime. The conflict effectively wrecked the Spanish economy for the time being. A full economic analysis of the civil war's impact has yet to be written, but there is little doubt that it was cataclysmic. There was severe damage to property, physical assets and infrastructure and considerable loss of life. The worst affected sector was probably agriculture, with significant reductions in livestock numbers, the wrecking of much farm machinery, damage to the land itself, which resulted in a 30 per cent drop in land under cultivation, leading to severe food shortages. Overall, agricultural production fell by 21 per cent between 1935 and 1939, industrial production by 30 per cent, and gross domestic product per head by around one-quarter. In fact, by the end of the decade, Spain's income per head was probably slightly lower than it had been in 1913, so that all the gains made in the 1920s had effectively been lost. It was not until the 1950s that 1929 levels of output were regained. This was one of the worst performances along the periphery and compares unfavourably with her Iberian neighbour Portugal.

Portugal's economy and society were more backward than those of Spain before 1913, yet by the end of the inter-war period, she finished in a relatively stronger position. The majority of the population was illiterate and dependent on the land for a living. The land tenure system was regarded as one of the worst in Europe, with a proliferation of many small and inefficient farms, very low productivity and many landless labourers. Exports consisted mainly of primary products and industry was sparser than in Spain, consisting mainly of textiles. Economic progress in the nineteenth century was slower than in Spain, being held back by the unyielding nature of the agrarian sector and the low level of human capital formation.

The post-war situation was devastating despite the lack of material damage. Siding with the Allies had cost the country dearly, leaving in its wake a large public debt, including war debt to Britain. Portugal also had one of the highest inflations in Europe, barring the hyperinflationary countries, because of the large increase in currency circulation during the conflict so that the escudo had depreciated to 31 per cent of its pre-war value by 1920 and then to 3.3 per cent in 1923. As a consequence, there was a large drop in living standards; by 1921, real income per capita was less than 60 per cent of pre-war, and in 1925, it was still 25 per cent lower and not until 1928 did it surpass the pre-war level. This resulted in waves of strikes and labour unrest between 1919 and 1925 because the government's diminished revenue base meant that it had little scope to alleviate the situation. By 1923, public spending was running at only about half the pre-war level.

The other main problem was the extreme political instability in Portugal at this time. Coalition or one-party governments came and went with indecent frequency. Between January 1919 and May 1926, there were no fewer than 28 different administrations and nearly half the cabinets were presided over by the military. Because ministers revolved in rapid succession, many had little experience and this made for weak and incompetent administrations, while political fragmentation was exacerbated by the multiplicity of parties. In time, however, conservative and military forces came to exert their power after much political violence, assassinations and rebellions. In May 1926, there emerged the figure of Antonio de Oliveira Salazar (a professor of economics at the University of Coimbra), who became minister of finance in 1928 and effectively dictator of Portugal from the early 1930s.

In fact, economic and social conditions had begun to improve before the political coup. From the early 1920s, living standards were slowly improving, the public debt was being reduced and inflation and currency depreciation were being brought under control. During the subsequent international crisis, Portugal fared reasonably well, being one of the few countries to record positive movements in both output and industrial production. The subsequent progress in economic activity was erratic, but nevertheless latest estimates suggests the country registered a 21 per cent gain in real per capita output through the cycle 1929–39, despite a strong rise in population.

It is not immediately obvious why Portugal fared so well in this period, especially as she did feel the backwash of the Spanish civil war. Some authors cast an explanation in terms of the country's general economic backwardness and its scope for catch-up, together with its relatively low exposure to international trade. However, industrial production was still limited, and much of what there was consisted of small units of production serving local or regional markets and uncompetitive internationally. The agrarian sector was probably less vulnerable than many because it was not heavily dependent on grain products. There were some good harvests in the 1930s, and government assistance through price support schemes and credits were helpful to the sector. External trade, though mainly in primary products, was in less price-sensitive commodities such as wines, fruits and fish, and it was assisted by the special commercial relationship with Britain. Portugal left the gold standard soon after Britain abandoned it in September 1931 and became a member of the sterling area and therefore was not constrained by an overvalued exchange rate. Increasing confidence in the currency encouraged the repatriation of capital and along with growing receipts from tourism led to balance of payments surpluses in the 1930s and the accumulation of gold and foreign exchange reserves.

The state also assumed a more interventionist role in the economy during these years. Salazar's regime was not an unduly harsh one, as was the case in Germany and Soviet Russia. It was more benign and low profile, but nationalistic, and the aim was to strengthen Portugal from within. The main objectives were to maintain financial stability and a sound currency, foster industrialization through import substitution and to improve the country's infrastructure, all of which necessitated increasing regulation of economic activity by controls imposed by a bureaucracy under a corporatist structure. Some writers have seen the state-dominated corporatist structure as an adverse influence, in that it stifled enterprise and competitive forces and retarded modernisation and technological improvement, while doing little to deal with the inefficient agrarian structure. However, one should not take too negative a view of the new strategy. Some stimulus was given to industry through import substitution and government assistance, while infrastructure developments were promoted by public spending, though in the later 1930s, this was slanted more towards defence needs. Fiscal prudence and sound money were also good for confidence, while monetary policy was more relaxed in the 1930s, with the money supply rising steadily and interest rates falling.

Though estimates vary, it seems that Portugal's overall economic performance was better than Spain's over the transwar period (1913–38), which effectively reversed their previous positions in terms of the absolute levels of per capita output. But by the end of the period, both countries still remained woefully backward and both had failed to transform their agrarian sectors. In the medium term, there was little prospect of either country moving forward to sustained growth and structural transformation because the foundations of modernization had still to be put in place. In the event, war intervened again to obfuscate the situation.

The Nordic countries (Denmark, Finland, Norway, and Sweden) proved to be one of the strongest growth areas in the inter-war period, especially in the 1930s. Annual GDP growth for the years 1919–39 was 2.7 per cent in Denmark, 3 per cent in Norway, 3.3 per cent in Sweden and 5.3 per cent in Finland. In the 1930s, Finland recorded a remarkable 7 per cent per annum and went from being a poor agrarian country to a relatively modern industrialized state. There was a fairly mild depression, in fact one of the mildest in Europe, with GDP per capita declining by 5.2 per cent in the Nordic countries, with the shallowest in Denmark (the next best being the UK, Switzerland and Italy).

The relative mildness of the depression and the strong recovery can be attributed to the early abandonment of the gold standard and the adoption of a more inflationary monetary policy as a consequence. Tariff and trade policies also helped, whereas fiscal policy was fairly neutral despite the much vaunted Swedish countercyclical budgetary pronouncements. In fact, latest research suggests that it is difficult to trace a persistent deficit budgetary action during the 1930s in any of the Nordic countries. These countries were also helped by the significant structural transformation taking place through the period, which involved a shift from lower-margin to higher-margin activities. It is true that unemployment remained high during the 1930s, but this was mainly because of a rapid growth in the labour supply, the check to emigration to the United States and the process of labour saving accompanying depression.

Overall, the performance of the Nordic countries was even more remarkable when one recalls their rather stodgy performance in the previous decade as a result of *paripolitik* deflation, except in Finland. The Scandinavian countries had a more severe downturn in 1920–22 and the struggle to get back to the gold standard at the pre-war parity left their economies in limbo for part of the decade. Finland avoided this legacy by refraining from defending the pre-war currency value.

The three Baltic states of Estonia, Latvia and Lithuania also did remarkably well considering their chequered history. Much of their past culture and development had been influenced by larger countries (Sweden, Germany, Poland and Russia), the latter acquiring these provinces in the eighteenth century under whose domain they remained until acquiring their independence after the First World War.

Though still fairly backward by western standards, they were more highly developed both culturally and economically than either the Russian empire or the other peripheral countries. They also had a strong sense of national identity compared with the Slavic countries, and in many respects their frame of reference was closer to Scandinavia and Finland. Educational and infrastructure facilities were also better, and before 1914, there had been some worthwhile industrial developments, especially in Estonia and Latvia, even though these were heavily dependent on the Russian market. The demographic structure was also fairly benign. Minority groups accounted for a relatively small proportion of their populations, while population growth was not excessive. Literacy levels were also high compared with the other peripheral countries. Another factor to their advantage was the more favourable man/land ratio than in many other countries, so that the surplus agrarian population was not excessive. Agriculture was more efficient than in most other low-income peripherals.

However, the post-war aftermath was not an easy time. The Baltic countries were cut off from the large Russian market for industrial products and there were many pressing internal problems such as political instability and the need to establish viable parliamentary regimes, sorting out currency and financial issues, the reestablishment of national life after being vassals of the Russian empire and the need for further land reform.

It is remarkable how expediently the newly independent Baltic nations grappled with the tasks that confronted them post war. Latvia, for example, was one of the first countries in Europe to stabilize her currency, which was a model procedure. Land reform made steady progress in all three countries during the 1920s. New parliamentary regimes were established, though political instability was never far from the surface. Industrial production recovered from the setbacks of 1914–18 as firms sought to adapt to the loss of the Russian market. Agriculture too responded to new opportunities by moving towards more intensive farming in high-value products such as bacon, butter, eggs and meat products to supply foreign markets. Estonia and Latvia were especially advanced in this respect, and the process was facilitated by the spread of the cooperative movement.

By the end of the inter-war period, the Baltic states were in a stronger position than many of the other peripheral countries. One main reason for this was that they were able to obviate being locked into traditional, low-productivity agriculture. The lower man/land ratios, more efficient land reforms and enlightened government policies towards the agrarian sector contributed to this transformation. Agriculture became noticeably more efficient, and it did not act as a drag on the economy as in so many other peripheral countries. In the matter of land reform, the Baltic states appear to have been more creative than many of their neighbours. They addressed the issues of viability and land shortage by creating middle-sized holdings (over 90 per cent were in this category by 1930) rather than excessive fragmentation, even though it left some peasants landless. The governments of these countries also actively encouraged export-orientated farming together with the spread of cooperatives, which were important factors in their success in exporting meat and dairy products and for the steady rise in farm productivity.

Though the industrial sector was still small, there were some important advances, especially in Estonia and Latvia, which were all the more striking given the setbacks incurred during the war years. A major effort was made to find replacement markets in Britain and Germany for the loss of the Russian outlet, and trade with these two countries eventually accounted for one-half or more of the total. Major advances in education and training and provision of infrastructure facilities were also contributing factors to the success of industry.

Though aggregate income data for the Baltic states is not extensive, what we do have suggests that income per capita levels were higher than in eastern Europe by the end of the period and that there was a steady advance throughout the inter-war years. More important, the Baltic countries were better adapted structurally for sustained growth given a favourable international climate than most of the other European countries along the periphery.

Europe on the eve of the Second World War

Taking Europe as a whole, the inter-war period was one of chequered growth, financial crises, political tensions and latterly the growing threat of war. Some economic advances were made during the period, but progress was uneven and not nearly so robust as before 1914. Not only was economic growth interrupted by the slump of 1929–32, but throughout the period, most countries faced important structural problems and adjustments as new technologies, changes in tastes and patterns of demand, shifts in market structures and political boundaries created both new opportunities and difficulties for established producers. Recovery from the depression was often slow and patchy, and even towards the end of the 1930s, many economies were still not operating at full capacity. Generally speaking, those countries, especially the sterling area ones, that left the gold standard and depreciated substantially experienced the strongest recoveries, whereas those countries that clung to gold until the mid-1930s or artificially maintained their exchange rates by controls of one sort or another fared less well.

Through the period 1914 to 1939, Europe's position in the world economy steadily declined. Not only did the war seriously weaken the European economy, but it provided the opportunity for countries outside Europe, notably the United States and Japan, to strengthen their economic power, and subsequent events did little to redress the balance. Western Europe in particular was no longer strong enough to continue to dictate the pattern of world development as she had done to a large extent in the previous century. America now assumed this role, but with fateful consequences, especially during the depression. Politically too, Europe was seriously weakened by war and its aftermath. It had lost its nineteenth-century balance of power cohesiveness; in east-central Europe a multiplicity of autonomous but weak and struggling states emerged from the ruins of the Austro-Hungarian, Germanic and Romanov empires, while bitter political tensions and weak democracies left the west in a disunited state. Ultimately, neither the west nor the east was capable of resisting the designs of the new German regime, while after 1945, the eastern countries became the prey of a new world power, the USSR.

Within Europe itself, the balance of economic power did not change significantly during this period. The richest industrial centre remained firmly anchored in the west, and as one moved south and east so the strength of the income and industrial contour lines steadily diminished. On the eve of the Second World War, about two-thirds of Europe's industrial output was produced by the UK, Germany and France, and the share of the first two countries in industrial production was more than twice their share of Europe's population. There were also several smaller industrially advanced countries, for example the Netherlands, Belgium and Switzerland, with larger proportionate shares in production than population, but their absolute contribution to Europe's total industrial production remained small. Moving into central Europe, one finds two relatively advanced countries (Austria and Czechoslovakia), with industry and population shares about equal. Then, shifting further east, one reaches Hungary, with a 60 per cent gap between industry and population shares, and then Poland and the Balkans, where the discrepancy was even greater.

Income levels tell a similar story. Though many of the estimates of national income no doubt contain margins of error and are continually being revised, they do provide a basis for making broad comparisons between countries and across regions. By the end of the period, per capita national income was highest in Britain, Belgium, Denmark, Germany, Sweden, France and the Netherlands and lowest in the Balkans and Poland, with central Europe (Austria and Czechoslovakia) occupying an intermediate position. The average per capita income of the seven western countries (in constant 1960 US dollars) was $1046 in 1938, that is nearly three times greater than the average for the four poorest countries (Poland, Bulgaria, Romania and Yugoslavia) at $368. Austria and Czechoslovakia were better placed than their eastern neighbours, even though their income per capita was only about half that of the west. Although such comparisons cannot provide a precise guide to the standard of living within individual countries, they do illustrate the large disparity in income levels between west and east, a disparity that was of more or less the same order of magnitude as it was in 1913. In other words, eastern Europe still remained desperately poor by comparison with the west, and the fact that incomes were probably more unevenly distributed in the former region must have meant that many people were living close to the subsistence level. A similar situation was to be found in southern Europe (Spain, Portugal, Italy and Greece). It is this contrast between poverty and wealth between countries and within regions that has given rise to the term Europe's Third World.

Questions for discussion

1. Explain the strong economic performance of the Nordic countries during the inter-war period.
2. Discuss the economic problems of Poland in the 1930s.
3. How did the Balkan countries cope with the Great Depression?
4. How did the Baltic states adapt their economies during the inter-war period?
5. Why did many European peripheral countries remain so poor?

5   The battle for Europe 1939–45

Hitler's conquest of Europe

From the middle of the 1930s, international tension had been mounting steadily, a fact reflected in the frequent and often frantic attempts among the European countries to forge agreements, uneasy alliances and pacts to improve security. It was also mirrored in the increased defence budgets of nearly all European countries in response to the military build-up in Nazi Germany and the Soviet Union and to a lesser extent in Japan. By any peacetime standard, the defence procurements of the first two countries were exceptional. Between 1933 and 1938, both countries spent on defence more than three times the amount disbursed in Britain, France and the United States, and by the end of the 1930s, Britain and the United States produced about 13 per cent of the weapons turned out in Germany. Germany's total military spending increased by no less than 23 times between 1933–4 and 1938–9, and by the latter date, Germany's outlay on the military sector accounted for around 29 per cent of total national product and 17 per cent in the case of the Soviet Union. The vast scale of the provision is apparent if we look at figures for defence expenditure on the eve of the First World War, when Russia's military spending was less than 5 per cent of national product and Germany's a mere 3 per cent. In the 1960s, at the height of the Cold War, the western powers were allocating around six per cent of their national income for military purposes (see Overy 2004, 422–23, 452–53).

Undoubtedly, the major danger was the growing threat from Nazi Germany under Adolf Hitler, though the situation remained fluid until the summer of 1939, because there was always the hope that Hitler's bellicose posturing could be appeased by negotiation and some territorial concessions in Europe. It is doubtful whether at this juncture Hitler was really prepared for a full-scale European war. A later date would have suited him better, by which time he would no doubt have hoped to have wrung further concessions from the appeasing nations while attaining an invincible position over Britain and France in military capability. Despite the pace of rearmament in the 1930s, Germany was not prepared for the type of war that finally emerged, and it is doubtful if Hitler himself was ever psychologically attuned for a long war of attrition. Indeed, he wished to avert a rerun of the Great War, when the British naval blockade helped lead to an implosion on the home front.[1] Unfortunately for him, the attack on Poland went one step too far, because it brought him into conflict with the western powers (Britain and France) on 3 September 1939.

It is tempting to argue that had it not been for Britain and France's guarantee of support to Poland in the event of her independence being threatened, which was announced by the British Prime Minister, Neville Chamberlain, in the House of Commons on 31 March 1939, the scope and contours of the conflict might have been different. As it turned out, the Polish guarantee proved worthless because Britain and France were powerless to uphold it and they simply watched helplessly as the German onslaught smashed the country in a matter of weeks and then proceeded to partition it with the Soviet Union following the terms of the secret accord of the Nazi–Soviet Non-Aggression Pact. To add to the ignominy, Britain and France had to witness, within less than a year, German forces taking over Norway, Denmark, Holland, Belgium, Luxemburg and France as well as driving the British Expeditionary Force unceremoniously back to its homeland. In other words, Britain and France could do nothing to check Hitler's onslaught on the west. One can speculate, therefore, that had Britain turned a blind eye to Poland's fate, as she had done in the case of Austria and Czechoslovakia,[2] the European conflagration might have been contained and Britain could have avoided getting involved in a European war, because Hitler's main interest lay in eastern Europe and Russia, where he sought *Lebensraum* for the German population. In fact, for some time, even up to the point of the invasion of Russia in June 1941, Hitler cherished hopes of reaching a settlement with Britain on a basis of a division of the world space and a promise to guarantee the integrity of the British Empire in return for a free hand on the continent. At that point, he had not contemplated a full-scale European war, but the intervention of Britain and France provided him with an opportunity to capture western Europe quickly and cheaply. The east of Europe, and especially Russia, was what really mattered to Hitler and the Nazis. In fact, the eastern policy was crucial to the Nazi objective of ensuring German supremacy over the Slavic races and this meant that European Russia had to be exterminated because its very existence was anathema to Nazi ideals. The defeat of the west, therefore, can be seen as a preliminary step to the main task of invading and conquering the eastern lands. Whether in the long run Hitler would have confined his sights to the east and exactly how he would have dealt with the conquered western countries are moot points, of course, but the fact is that once Britain and France intervened, the war rapidly moved on to a global scale.

Speculation apart, the two years following the outbreak of war were to bring a remarkable transformation to the map of Europe as it was steadily engulfed by the Nazi regime. Hitler's march across Europe, which had started in a preliminary way before September 1939 with the annexation of Austria and Czechoslovakia, proceeded virtually unchecked, and by 1942, the new German Empire was practically synonymous with that of continental Europe. It stretched from the Channel Islands and Brittany in the west to the mountains of the Caucasus in the east, and from the arctic tip of Norway to the shores of the Mediterranean. At the peak, the German empire covered about one-third of the European land area and embraced around half the population. Independent states and territories disappeared almost over-night under Hitler's onward drive, and only a few nations managed to retain their autonomy, and even then it was not always secure. These nations comprised the neutral countries of Portugal, Spain, Eire, Switzerland, Sweden and Turkey, none of which could be said to be wholly unsympathetic to the Nazi regime. In addition, Romania, Bulgaria and Hungary, and possibly Finland, which slipped from neu-trality to quasi-alliance with Germany, retained a semblance of sovereignty by joining Hitler as military allies, though in practice they became very much satellite dependencies of the German Reich. Italy, ostensibly an equal partner in the exer-cise of European domination, soon became more akin to a satellite country, or jackal, because her economic and political structure and her military capability were no match for those of Germany. Thus, in time, Italy became something of a liability, as did a number of other countries that ostensibly supported the Axis powers. In fact, Mussolini's efforts to wage a parallel war devoid of German sup-port brought only military disasters.

Control of the new empire

How was this vast empire controlled and administered? The new Nazi empire consisted of a motley collection of territories at different stages of development and with a bewildering array of ethnic and religious affiliations, most of which were alien to the Nazi creed. They were acquired in an unsystematic manner and ruled in different ways. 'The Third Reich covered the New Europe with a patch-work of more or less provisional regimes' (Mazower 1999, 149). In practice, as each piece of territory was acquired, Hitler assigned to it, in an *ad hoc* manner, the type of governance that seemed least likely to pose a threat to the Reich's military security. Moreover, Hitler had no intention of establishing uniform systems of governance in the occupied territories that might serve as a basis for the creation of power bases to rival his own. There was also probably some attempt, at least initially, to allot a form of administration suitable to its final place in the Nazi conception of the New Order for Europe. This envisaged the formation of a single economic community for the whole of the continent, working under German direction and with the Reich as the industrial hub of the system (see below). The restructuring was both political and economic and one might add a social dimen-sion to take account of the regime's harsh racial policies.

The 'patchwork of jurisdictions' imposed on Nazi-dominated Europe makes it difficult to slot control systems into neat classifications. The type of administrative control varied a great deal and the system remained highly fluid depending on the course of events. Initially, occupied territories were administered by the military occupation authorities, but these were usually replaced in due course by civilian administrations, which in turn relied heavily on the local civil bureaucracy to keep things running and to economize on the use of German labour. The extent of German supervision varied a great deal: it tended to be relatively lighter in the west, especially in countries such as Denmark and the Channel Islands, but much tighter and rigorous in the territories of the east. Of course, this was consistent with Nazi racial beliefs, which recognized certain affinities with civilized western countries but not with the populations of eastern territories, who were classed as subhuman and uncivilized. To facilitate the reader's path, an attempt is made to bring order out of chaos with the identification of the following groupings:

1. Countries or territories incorporated, or annexed all but in name, to form part of the Greater German Reich. These included Austria, Alsace-Lorraine, Luxemburg, the Sudetenland, Memel, Danzig, Bohemia-Moravia (under a special Protectorate), northern Slovenia, parts of northern Belgium and France and the provinces recovered from Poland including Upper Silesia. Some of these countries or regions, such as Luxemburg and Alsace-Lorraine, along with the Baltic states, were to be prepared for formal annexation at some future date, but to all intents and purposes they were well integrated into the German economic system by the middle of the war. These areas along with Germany proper were to form the core of the country's industrial belt and were to be assimilated into the economy of the Greater Reich. They were the regions of primarily heavy industry essential to the German war effort and to the fulfilment of the longer-term objective of making Germany the industrial heartland of Europe. For the most part, their populations conformed to the German Nordic ideal, and where this was not the case they could be Germanized if necessary.

2. The western countries, that is occupied northern France, Belgium, Norway, Denmark and Holland. These were usually converted to civilian administration after initial military control and administered with varying degrees of severity. Norway had the distinction of having a native fascist leader installed. They occupied a more favoured position than the eastern territories, though they were exploited ruthlessly to service the German war machine. The level and extent of control varied a great deal. For example, France was closely controlled, with 40–50 per cent of its industrial output being acquired for German purposes by the autumn of 1943, though the ratio of Germans to local officials was modest compared with Norway and the Protectorate of Bohemia-Moravia. Norway too was exploited intensively. By contrast, Denmark was lightly controlled, with fewer than one or two hundred German staff present in the country.[3] In fact, Denmark retained its own government operating under the former constitution, a pseudo-democracy. Later on in the war, however, the Danes were subject to more rigorous control by the German authorities. The same was largely true for the Channel Islands, which has been described as the model occupation, though it is doubtful whether many of the inhabitants and even less so the foreign workers would have considered it in those terms. For many German troops stationed in the Islands, it was like being on an extended holiday. Given the limited strategic value of the Islands, there were an enormous number of German troops stationed there.[4]

3. Occupied eastern Europe including Poland, Yugoslavia, northern Greece, Russia and the Baltic states. This grouping consisted of what were termed the 'colonial' territories inhabited by what the Nazis regarded as the inferior races

or *Untermenschen*; they comprised the General Government of Poland, the Baltic States,[5] and the occupied parts of Soviet Russia and southeastern Europe. The lesser races were to be economically and socially subordinated to the master race of Nordic-Germans. Direct control of economic activity in these regions was imposed by Germany to ensure that the best possible use was made of their resources and that they produced what the Reich required. They were to be exploited ruthlessly, with no concern for the welfare of the citizens because most of them, especially the Slavic races, were regarded as subhuman.

4. A fourth category included the puppet governments or client states of Croatia, Slovakia and Vichy France, semi-autonomous administrations that were dependent on or at the service of Germany's pleasure. Vichy France was something of an anomaly, enjoying a largely independent and non-belligerent status until occupied by the Germans in November 1942 after the Allied invasion of Tunisia.

5. Finally, there were the satellite or allied countries of Germany, namely Italy, Hungary, Romania and Bulgaria. These countries were nominally independent but supported the Nazi cause with varying degrees of intensity. The last three countries became subsidiary members of the Tripartite Pact, originally formed in September 1940 by Germany, Italy and Japan to support each other in the event of an attack by an external power.

The complexity of the control system is well illustrated in the case of central-east Europe. It is true that in one way or another most of the region came within the German orbit and that a large part was designated as colonial territories. But the format of the control system varied a great deal and there was some transfer of territories. Hungary, Romania and Bulgaria, countries with pro-German leanings, slipped from initial neutrality into quasi-alliance with Germany. They retained a semblance of sovereignty by joining Hitler ostensibly as military allies, but in practice they became satellite dependencies of the Third Reich. At the other end of the spectrum, the fate of those countries with strong pro-western sympathies (Czechoslovakia, Poland and Yugoslavia), was less favourable. All three were invaded and dismembered between 1938 and 1941. Czechoslovakia was first on the list when in October 1938 she lost the Sudeten lands, which were occupied by Germany. In the following March, Germany invaded the rest of the country and proceeded to dissect it as follows: southern Slovakia, western Ruthenia and the sub-Carpathian Ukraine went to Hungary; Bohemia/Moravia became a protectorate of the Reich; while the rest of Slovakia was set up as a nominally independent state. Poland's turn came in September 1939. Western Poland, including the free city of Danzig, was incorporated into Germany, while central Poland became a protectorate under the General Government of Poland. Most of the rest of Poland was absorbed by the Soviet Union under the terms of the Nazi–Soviet Pact of August 1939. Supplementary economic or trade agreements concluded between the two countries in October 1939, February 1940 and January 1941 made provision for supplies of food and raw materials for Germany from the Soviet

Union.[6] However, following the invasion of the latter in the summer of 1941, the Russian Polish territories were then occupied by Germany. As for the occupied parts of western Russia behind the areas under military administration,[7] that is Byelorussia (or White Ruthenia, which had been acquired by the Soviet Union under the Nazi–Soviet Pact) and the Ukraine, these were placed under two Reichcommissariats (Ostland and the Ukraine, respectively), within the Reich ministry for occupied eastern territories run by the Baltic German, Alfred Rosenberg. The Baltic states were also included in Ostland, while the Ukraine comprised all lands inhabited by Ukrainian nationals, including a large area that had been part of Poland before 1939.[8]

Finally, in April 1941, came the fate of Yugoslavia and Greece. The former country, consisting of a myriad of ethnic and religious groups and with no real national identity, was ripe for dissecting. Northern Slovenia and the major part of Serbia were absorbed by Germany as colonial territories; southern Slovenia and much of the Dalmatian coast went to Italy, which also acquired Montenegro as a protectorate. Other parts of Yugoslavia were distributed among Hungary, Bulgaria and Italian Albania, while Croatia, along with Bosnia and Herzegovina, became nominally independent states under German and Italian military influence. In addition, Romania, one of the main beneficiaries of the peace settlement following the First World War, lost a large proportion of territory to Russia (Bessarabia and northern Bukovina), to Hungary (the northern part of Transylvania) and to Bulgaria (southern Dobrudja). The defeat of Yugoslavia made it all the easier to take Greece along with Crete, which the Germans proceeded to occupy in the spring of 1941. Greece had in fact entered the war in October 1940, when it refused to allow the Italians access to the country for its troops. It repulsed the Italians into Albania and it was left to the Germans to invade the country through Yugoslavia and install a puppet government in conjunction with the Italians and Bulgarians, who had captured parts of Macedonia and Thrace.

These territorial and governmental arrangements, with some modest adjustments and changes from time to time, remained more or less intact until the latter half of the war, when Germany's hegemony was on the wane and the German empire in Europe began to crumble.

The New Order for Europe

It is difficult to discern any consistent and coherent plan in the patterns of control and administration of the conquered territories. In fact, no systematic plan was ever drawn up for their administration. Structures of control were imposed on a trial-and-error basis, with considerable variations in the format of control. So, what happened to the much vaunted idea of a New Order for Europe? At the beginning of the war, the prospects of a New Order for Europe emerging out of the ruins of the Versailles settlement seemed a distinct possibility – and one that was initially greeted with a degree of approval even by some non-fascists. The concept was much debated in establishment circles in the early years of war, though it is doubtful if any detailed and coherent plan was ever formulated.

The nearest to an official statement on the issue was that released on 25 July 1940 by Walther Funk, Reich Minister of Economics, who was entrusted by Göring to formulate arrangements for the New Order. The wider political and international aspects were given more concrete substance by the signing of the Tripartite Pact on 27 September 1940 between Germany, Italy and Japan, which delineated spheres of influence in the Euro-Afro-Asian hemispheres. From these and other official statements made by Reich ministers and also by Hitler himself, it is possible to piece together the main outlines of the Nazi plans for Europe.

The idea of the New Order has parallels elsewhere. It has been seen as having a passing resemblance to the Austro-Hungarian Empire and to the European Common Market and it harks back to an earlier age when Germanic influence in Europe was extensive. Parallels can also be drawn with the Roman Empire. An alternative inspiration, and one that Hitler absorbed, was the imperialist exploits of the western powers in the nineteenth century, especially the British, with their large territories and populations in Asia and Africa. Thus Hitler's vision of the conquered colonial territories in the east was partly modelled on the west's imperial past. He especially admired the British administration of India, where around 200,000 civil servants and military personnel administered a continent of many millions. He referred to European Russia as 'our India'. For much of western Europe, a tariff-free zone was planned, together with the integration of manufacturing interests with those of the central zone of manufacturing located in the Reich itself. For the less developed regions to the east, partial deindustrialization was prescribed so that they could concentrate on supplying the Reich with foodstuffs and raw materials. Funk himself acknowledged that he was essentially interested in the economic exploitation of Europe, while Reich Commissar Erich Koch declared that he would pump everything out of the Ukraine.

In essence, the New Order envisaged a single economic community for Europe, a largely tariff-free zone and the cross-border movement of resources. A working group in the Economics Ministry early on in the war had a vision of a unified economic community in Europe with free capital flows, common tariffs on imports, a unified currency and transportation system under German leadership. But it was not to be a community of equality. The degree of freedom allowed was limited. Production, trade and exchange were to be vigorously controlled, the main aim being to make Europe self-sufficient *vis-à-vis* the rest of the world. Extensive state control and state ownership of economic activity were also contemplated. Industry throughout Europe was to be extensively restructured and plans for the post-war rationalization and integration of various industries, including textiles, iron and steel, chemicals and oil, were being prepared by Göring's staff between 1940 and 1942. It is also clear that the scheme was not to involve an equal partnership of nations. Indeed, Hitler's ultimate aim was to transform Europe into a German empire, a unified Europe but one dominated by Germany in which the outlier territories would service the needs of the German people. In fact, it had more affinity with nineteenth century imperialism than modern economic unions. The New Order could be seen as a synonym for imperialist exploitation. As one historian has written: 'What was afoot was an old-fashioned economic imperialism, with an industrially developed core surrounded by a periphery producing food and raw materials, along the lines of the relationship Britain was said to have with her empire' (Burleigh 2001, 424).

Though the long-term plans for the restructuring of Europe, however vaguely conceived, were never actually abandoned, the New Order failed to take concrete shape during the course of the war. Some aspects of the conceived New Order did in fact emerge in the course of time, such as all international dealings being denominated in Reichsmarks, but for the most part Hitler was not prepared to commit himself in any detail far in advance of events, and it was said that he was more interested in his grandiose building and architectural schemes for the Reich than in what he regarded as mundane matters such as tariffs and currency issues. In any case, more pressing problems eventually took precedence, though in part some of these, such as the exploitation of non-German territories, might be seen in terms of their eventual place in the new Europe. In practice, therefore, apart from this and the centralization of financial dealings in Berlin (with the use of the Reichsmark as the main unit of settlement within the German dominated territories), little further progress was made with the New Order despite considerable propaganda on the topic in 1940. It retained a shadowy existence but discussion on the subject steadily diminished as the prospect of victory receded, and by the winter of 1942–43, the German media had lapsed into silence on it, by which stage the new German Empire was far from being a coherent and efficient economic structure. There was no coherent planning for the future structure of the European economy. The new empire effectively consisted of a motley collection of territories acquired in a haphazard manner and ruled or controlled in a variety of different ways. Why therefore did Germany fail to consolidate the hegemony so rapidly achieved between 1938 and 1941 to realize the ambition of a more united, streamlined and integrated Europe?

The reasons for failure on this score are not difficult to discern. For one thing, the Nazis never had a clear idea of what was involved in setting up the New Order. No complete and comprehensive plan for the restructuring of Europe was ever published, so the concept remained vague and confused, being based largely on the conflicting statements made by Reich ministers from time to time. It is doubtful whether Hitler himself had a clear notion of what was involved in creating a new structure for Europe, though he did have ambitions regarding the eastern territories (see below), and it is even more doubtful that he could be considered as a European idealist in today's terminology. While he envisaged a more self-sufficient Europe after the war, it is doubtful whether his concept got beyond the stage of German domination and ethnic cleansing, that is ridding Europe of the Jews and *Untermenschen* which, as far as he was concerned, was the number one priority. By the end of 1941, with Russia still undefeated, America entering the war and Britain holding out, he felt that the matter should be left in abeyance until the domination of Europe had been completed.

Second, in the first two years of hostilities, the speed of military conquest outran the regime's plan for a new empire. The success of Hitler's campaigns exceeded even the most optimistic expectations and as a result of the rapid acquisition of new territories, the Nazi rulers became increasingly preoccupied with the urgent task of administering them. Then, just at the time when the Reich might have been in a position to give more attention to the idea of a new Europe, that is, when it was master of most of Europe, things began to go wrong on the battlefront and the conglomerate empire showed signs of strain. In particular, the Russian giant proved more resilient than anticipated, while the entry of the United States into the war at the end of 1941 considerably altered the balance of forces. Hitler was now faced with the long war of attrition that he had sought to avoid, requiring total mobilization and full exploitation of all resources under German control. This could mean only one thing: a struggle for survival involving a shift to immediate and pressing military objectives and the abeyance of any detailed work on the new Europe. By the final year of the war, when everything was going wrong, the Nazi regime was more concerned about boosting arms production in any way possible than planning the future structure of the European economy.

Thus, once the war turned against Hitler and Germany was faced with a long and costly war, the focus of attention inevitably turned towards making the most of her conquests to service the war machine. The urgency of the situation was all the more acute because Germany's domestic economy had not been performing particularly well under Göring. The lack of coordinated planning, the multiplicity of controlling agencies, and the frequent quarrels and boundary disputes between different agencies and ministries and between party and state officials were some of the factors explaining why the economy did not produce in greater quantity during the years 1939–42. Hitler, of course, had not envisaged a long or full-scale war, at least not so soon, so that the economy was not fully geared for this eventuality. It could cope with short, lightning campaigns that brought quick victories, but not with a long war of attrition against the likes of Britain and Soviet Russia. The Blitzkrieg strategy had delivered an unbroken run of stunning victories over Poland, the Low Countries, France, Yugoslavia and Greece but it then ran into the mud and snow of Soviet Russia and the envisaged six weeks' campaign became paralysed. Thus Hitler's reluctance to contemplate a drastic cut in domestic consumption and his prevarication over sanctioning total mobilization, at least until the winter of 1942–43, added further pressure to complement domestic resources from outwith Germany. By then Germany was beginning to suffer the effects of Allied bombing (the United States attacked Germany by day and the UK Royal Air Force [RAF] bomber command by night) and so there was even greater urgency for relocating industrial activity and extracting as much as possible from the colonial territories. They were in fact plundered mercilessly but rather inefficiently. There was no systematic plan for extraction; it was more like a 'gigantic looting operation' with little that was orderly in the process.

Even had the occupied territories been exploited more efficiently and humanely, it is doubtful whether this could have saved Germany from defeat. The crux of the matter was that Germany was at a serious disadvantage compared with the Allies when it came to energy and strategic raw materials and for that matter resources overall. The really critical factor was energy, and here it was the oil deficiency that became the stumbling block rather than coal resources, which were fairly abundant.

In fact, given the country's slender oil margin at the start of the war, it is doubtful whether a long war was really feasible. The 1942 campaign in Soviet Russia was designed to seize the oilfields of the Caucasus to sustain the German war effort and immobilize Soviet forces, but it foundered at Stalingrad. Even with the development of synthetic fuels and access to Romanian oil until mid-1944, when American bombers obliterated all the refineries at Ploesti, the oil fuel position was always going to be weak. By the autumn of 1944, the fuel reserves for the *Luftwaffe* were down to a minimal level, one reason why Germany's air defence became so weak in the latter stages of the war.[9] That Germany was able to carry on so long was because of the absence of another major front after the collapse of the Soviet Union in 1941 and the incompetence of the Allied retaliation. The latter delayed a major strike until 1944, and then instead of concentrating on Germany's energy bases such as oil plants and power stations, they launched mass bombing attacks on industrial and urban centres, which did little to incapacitate Germany's ability to continue the war, while at the same time strengthening the resolve of the population to continue the resistance. As Jensen points out, the Allies were slow to grasp the fact that 'with the supremacy of energy in war, it was not manpower but the power of the fuel-consuming engines which was the decisive weapon of war' (Jensen 1968, 554).

In raw materials and minerals, the Allies also had the upper hand. At the peak of wartime activity, the British Empire and the United States had control or access to approaching 60–70 per cent of the value of the world's mineral production, whereas Germany could at best muster about 14 per cent. Britain's vast imperial connections came into their own at this time. The African continent yielded a rich harvest in strategic minerals. At the peak of wartime production, Africa accounted for the following percentages of world output: gold, 50 per cent; manganese, 19 per cent; chromite, 30 per cent; vanadium, 24 per cent; copper, 17 per cent; tin, 22 per cent; platinum, 13 per cent; cobalt, 90 per cent; nearly all of the uranium and industrial diamonds, as well as smaller amounts of other materials (Dumett 1985, 382). Even more crucial given that modern warfare was heavily dependent on oil fuel was the fact that the United States and the USSR accounted for about 77 per cent of the world's oil production, whereas Germany's access to oil was limited. At best, Germany had access to 2–3 per cent of world oil, most of which was in Romania. Thus, as Mazower observes, Germany was in no real position to fight a long modern war that was dependent on mechanized transport and oil fuel as opposed to coal and horses (Mazower 2009, 291).

Thus, taking everything into account (that is, labour, energy, raw materials and productive capacity), the Allies had, by the second half of the war, an overwhelming superiority over the Axis powers.

Finally, of course, racial issues intervened to cloud the issue. Racial ideology often prevailed over economic rationality, and though the New Order failed to take clear shape, it may have provided a useful smokescreen for legitimizing the more extreme ideological beliefs of the Nazi hierarchy, possibly to the regime's ultimate detriment, simply because it alienated so many peoples in the occupied territories. As Rothschild notes:

Had Hitler's 'new order' not been such a blatantly transparent screen for racial imperialism, exploitation, and genocide, had he instead offered a dignified status and role to the East Central European peoples under his hegemony, he might have averted their resistance movements, harnessed sustained local support, and possibly consolidated East Central European conquests as a rampart against the Soviet Union (Rothschild 1989, 26).

That apart, much time and energy went into running the gigantic ethnic cleansing operation involving the movement, resettlement, and extermination of millions of people, together with the construction of a vast network of concentration and extermination centres, work camps and other ghettoes of one sort or another throughout Europe.

The Nazi regime scarcely provided an integrated or unified Europe. In fact, in some respects, the Europe the Germans controlled was more fragmented than before. There were few unifying ideas or institutions and some of the conquered territories, for example Czechoslovakia, Poland, Yugoslavia and France, were broken up into smaller governmental or administrative units while at the same time losing some of their territory to neighbouring countries. Furthermore, in those countries not annexed or incorporated into the Greater German Reich, different forms of administrative control were imposed. One of the few unifying elements in the vast administrative complex was the authority of Hitler himself, who effectively was the fulcrum of power on all policy decisions. Possibly the other consistent feature of the New Order was the ideological racial issue, primarily, though not exclusively, the task of dealing with the Jews, who had been targeted from the inception of the regime. Rich believes that the basis on which the New Order was established was inimical to its success: 'The manner in which the New Order was established unquestionably contributed to the weakening of Hitler's empire; it may even have been the decisive factor in his defeat.' (Rich 1973, 249).

One thing is certain, however: had the Third Reich survived, it is doubtful whether the contemplated post-war New Order for Europe would have produced an integrated continent on the basis of an equality of nations. From the statements made by various Nazi leaders, all the signs point to a Europe in which Germany would exercise hegemonic power and subordinate much of the continent in the process to a colonial or semi-colonial status. This would have been especially so in the eastern sector of the continent because it was here that Hitler's attention was primarily focused to provide the *Lebensraum* for Germany, a convenient base for dealing with the *Untermenschen* and the source of food products and raw materials. The colonization of the east (and here Hitler was mainly interested in the vast Russian lands) would provide an excellent opportunity for dealing with the inferior peoples: not only the Jews, but the Poles, Czechs, and Slavic races. Hitler envisaged a future greater Germany where farmer soldiers would settle in the east and help to provide resources for the Reich while containing the indigenous population, which would be relegated to the role of slaves. The colonization would require dealing with the native population in different ways: Germanization, enslavement or extermination, and it called for the destruction of cities. Clearly, it was a long-term plan, which could be fully implemented only once victory was achieved. In fact, after the middle of the war, planning for the future of Europe in peacetime had more or less ground to a halt.

However, Heinrich Himmler, leader of the SS, never lost sight of the long-term strategy of colonizing Europe and ridding the continent of Jews. His Nordic ideology probably surpassed even that of Hitler; he believed that the German *Volk* should reign supreme in Europe by relegating the *Untermenschen* to subject races. The Russians in particular would eventually be pushed beyond the Urals and into Asia, and thereupon a Chinese Wall would be erected by Slavic labour to prevent them seeping back westwards. The peoples of the east were deemed to be fit only for slave labour and therefore were to be mobilized to build German cities, villages and farms, where ethnic Germans would be settled and offered a higher standard of living than the indigenous population. What happened to the latter was of no consequence but it was vitally important that they were not allowed to breed with true Germanic stock because this would weaken and dilute the master race. 'This is the task [Himmler announced in June 1942]: to exploit them for Germany, to keep them weak so that they can never defeat or harm us, and so that we may at a given time drive them out and settle Germans in their place.'

In May 1942, Himmler's SS Planning Office produced a report entitled *A General Plan East,* which received Hitler's approval. This envisaged a wholesale clearance and resettlement programme in western Russia, Poland and the Baltic states involving the forcible removal of most of the indigenous peoples to the east as far as Siberia to make room for the settlement of ethnic Germans. During the course of the war, the resettlement programme did not progress far; some 400,000 ethnic Germans were resettled in the annexed provinces of Poland such as the Warthegau, but an even larger number who had been uprooted and transferred from their homes in Hungary, Slovakia, Romania and parts of Yugoslavia remained footloose refugees. The few who got as far as the Ukraine and Byelorussia were obliged to return westwards in 1943–44 after the retreat of German forces, while the same fate awaited the ethnic Germans settled in the Black Sea coastal region who had been liberated by German troops. Although the resettlement programme was a long-term one to be carried out in full after the successful conclusion of the war, Himmler found ironically that it was difficult to entice native Germans to participate in the colonization scheme; Reich Germans in particular were not keen to move to the outlier regions of the new empire. The main contingent of Reich Germans of perhaps half a million in total, who did migrate to provinces in Poland and a few to western Russia, were not the farmer-soldiers so idealized by the Nazi regime, but urban dwellers who certainly were not prepared to defend the regime from Euro-Asiatic hordes of the east. They too had a short transition because they were forced back into the Reich when the Red Army marched westwards (Bullock 1993, 871, 897–98).

Two quotations from speeches by Hitler and Göring make it clear that the Aryan German was to be the supreme being in the new set-up. Hitler's main objective was to exploit the advantages of continental hegemony for the benefit of the 'master' race:

The German colonist [Hitler stated in late September 1941] ought to live on handsome spacious farms. The German services will be lodged in marvellous buildings, the governors in palaces. . . . Around the city, to a depth of thirty to forty kilometres, we shall have a belt of handsome villages connected by the best roads. What exists beyond that will be another world in which we mean to let the Russians live as they like. It is merely necessary that we should rule them (quoted in Bullock 1962, 657).

Göring was even more dismissive about the fate of the indigenous peoples in the occupied territories. In a conversation with Count Ciano, Italian foreign minister and son-in-law of Mussolini, towards the end of the same year (1941) he was brutally indifferent to what happened to the *Untermenschen*:

We cannot worry unduly about the hunger of the Greeks. It is a misfortune which will strike many other peoples besides them. In the camps for Russian prisoners they have begun to eat each other. This year between twenty and thirty million persons will die of hunger in Russia. Perhaps it is well that it should be so, for certain nations must be decimated. But even if it were not, nothing can be done about it. It is obvious that if humanity is condemned to die of hunger, the last to die will be our two peoples (quoted in Bullock 1962, 657, 659–60).

Germany's treatment of conquered peoples was an expensive mistake and one that possibly lost Hitler the war. Racial doctrine came before strategic interests in Hitler's view. The alienation and extermination of so many peoples meant that Germany squandered valuable labour. After all, in some regions, for example the Ukraine, the population actually welcomed German troops initially, only to turn against them when the SS and the *Wehrmacht* engaged in atrocities inspired by Hitler's edict that this was a war of annihilation. The mass elimination of the Jews, an obsession of Hitler's, deprived Germany of some of the most creative and qualified people, scientists and engineers, some of whom were of great benefit to the Allies.

Such issues are now academic because the New Order never came to pass. Instead of creating a new Europe, Hitler left the old one in ruins, weaker than in 1918 and at the mercy of two superpowers. Before turning to these topics we must first look at several other wartime issues.

Because the events and battles of the Second World War have been recounted all too frequently and in great detail in the voluminous literature on the subject, it would be pointless to repeat the exercise here. However, there are some less well-known economic aspects of the war effort and one or two general questions that are worth considering in more detail: (1) How was it that one country, Germany, was able to overrun the European continent in so short a space of time? (2) Why, given the extent of Hitler's power and control by 1942, did his regime eventually collapse? and (3) Why, in view of the far greater resources of the Allied powers, was victory for the Allied cause so long delayed?

The Speed of Conquest

The first of these questions cannot be answered simply in terms of the greater military and economic potential of Germany before the war, though, as we shall see, this was by no means an irrelevant factor. It must be recognized first of all that the peace treaty exercise after the First World War had left a power vacuum in east-central Europe. It had created several independent states, all of which were relatively small and weak, both politically and economically, compared with their neighbours to the east and west. They therefore became an obvious target for large predator nations, notably Germany and Russia, once the latter powers had recuperated from the impact of the First World War. By the later 1930s, both these countries were conceivably in a position to extend their spheres of influence in Europe, and the fact that Germany got there first can be attributed to that country's superior strength and political ambitions under Hitler coupled with the fact that the Soviet Union was still in the throes of sorting out its own development process, with Stalin espousing 'socialism in one country'. But the important point is that the post-war structure of Europe left the successor states vulnerable to attack from any larger power in the 1930s, the two most obvious candidates being Germany and Russia. Moreover, there was no effective bulwark to prevent this taking place. France was weak economically, politically unstable and defeatist and, despite the Maginot Line,[10] she was open to invasion, a point borne out by her precipitous collapse in 1940.[11] Britain, by virtue of her equivocal attitude towards Germany in the 1930s and for that matter towards the European continent as a whole, dithered between appeasement and rearmament and finally ended the decade in no position to prevent the German onslaught. The only power that might conceivably have been able to do justice to the situation, the United States, had retreated into isolation after 1920, and by the time war broke out again, her military potential was far from ready to counter the German attack.

Hitler's initial successes derived largely from the strategy employed to conquer Europe. The Blitzkrieg strategy eschewed any commitment to a long drawn-out war involving armament in depth. Rather it entailed swift attack on specified but limited objectives, a procedure that took its adversaries by surprise and left them debating whether each new conquest would be the last. The key to Germany's sweeping victories lay in her ability to back up threats with force, the superior skill of her fighting forces and the absence of serious opposition, together with her greater military build-up before the war. The expenditure of the Axis powers (Germany, Italy and Japan) on armaments in the period 1934–38 increased twice as fast as that of the UK, the Soviet Union and France combined, and it accounted for 52 per cent of all war expenditure of thirty nations in 1938 as against 35 per cent in 1934. The countries that faced Germany in September 1939 (France, Poland, Britain, India and the belligerent Dominions) had budgeted in the previous year for a total armament expenditure little more than a third as great as that of Germany. Poland and France, of course, fell quickly, while Russia, though she had armed rapidly before the war, was on the Axis side at the start of the war and did not join the Allied cause until 1941. The United States, on the other hand, preserved her neutrality at the onset, and in any case her military expenditure was little greater than that of France. Thus, given the weakness of the Allied position together with the geographical dispersion of the countries that faced the Axis powers, it is scarcely surprising that Hitler swept all before him in the first phase of the war.

Though attempts have been made to downgrade the extent of Germany's military preparations before the war, there seems little doubt that Germany did hold an initial superiority in terms of military and economic potential. However, the important point to bear in mind is that her military preparedness was designed primarily for a series of short wars with certainty of victory. One must stress again that Hitler had never any intention of engaging in long drawn-out battles for which the country was definitely not prepared, and this point is borne out by the fact that the onset of war did not produce any significant change in Germany's economic and military priorities. For the most part, sufficient preparation had already been made to carry out the type of war contemplated by the Nazi administration. Only when Germany was forced to abandon her 'smash-and-grab' tactics and switch to fighting defensive and rearguard campaigns of indeterminate length did the limitations of her military preparations become apparent. It was unfortunate, at least as far as the Allied cause was concerned, that Britain in particular mistook the nature of the German war plans. Britain had assumed that Germany had been arming heavily and in some depth for many years in order to wage a massive and prolonged attack and it was therefore concluded that little could be done in the short term except defend against invasion until such time as her own military potential had been built up. Priority was therefore given to long-term armament in depth, the consequence of which was to allow Germany a relatively free hand in Europe in the first two years of war.

It was also anticipated that the *Luftwaffe* would attempt to deliver a knockout blow to Britain from the air. Accordingly, priority was given to the Air Defence of Great Britain Scheme, which proved its worth in the Battle of Britain when monoplane fighters (Spitfires and Hurricanes) allied with a radar early warning system, prevailed over a German air force that had in fact been developed primarily as a support arm for the *Wehrmacht* rather than as a strategic bombing force. But this meant leaving Britain with a miniscule expeditionary force and deprived it of an effective deterrent or interventionist capability. Conscription had not been introduced until April 1939, reflecting the greater priority accorded to the Royal Navy and the Royal Air Force. This knowledge influenced Hitler to go for broke in September 1939.

The elapse of these two years left Germany in what seemed to be an invincible position. Yet during the course of the following year, the tide was turning distinctly against the Reich, and by the winter of 1942–43, Germany's empire was on the wane. Although it was to be another two years or more before the country was defeated, the seeds of decay were sown by the halfway stage.

The collapse of the Third Reich

Several factors can be adduced to explain the demise of the Reich despite its seemingly insuperable position at the height of conquest. One of Hitler's early and chief mistakes was to launch an attack on Russia (June 1941).[12] This was at a time when he was still engaged on the western front with Britain, an exercise that was proving costly and unsuccessful. Britain was always going to prove difficult to attack and defeat given the RAF's supremacy over southern England and the Royal Navy's dominance of the Channel, because it would have rendered any attempted invasion by sea precarious given the need to ferry troops and equipment across in slow barges and other craft. The motive for attacking Russia was Hitler's dissatisfaction with what he regarded as an uncooperative and untrustworthy ally, which left him with the conviction that she should be dealt with promptly before she grew any stronger. The conquest of the Soviet Union was also part of Hitler's longer-term plan to provide living space in the east as part of his grandiose plans for remodelling Europe and which would provide Germany with foodstuffs and raw materials and also act as a convenient repository for *Untermenschen* or racially inferior peoples. He also feared a Soviet swoop on Romania, Germany's main oil supplier, while his concern to acquire Soviet oil supplies in the Ukraine subsequently led to a diversion of Army Group Centre from its drive on Moscow, which was to prove fatal.

It was not only physical living space or *Lebensraum* that dominated Hitler's mind when contemplating the conquest of Russia. There was also the question of strategic raw materials supply. Though conquests in the west and in eastern Europe had improved Germany's economic position, the country was still seriously short of critical raw materials and liquid fuel. The significance of Russia in this context is not only that the country supplied Germany with the bulk of the raw materials drawn from abroad, but that the Soviet Union also controlled access to many of the supply routes, which they could cut off at any time. Thus Hitler reasoned logically that knocking out the Russian giant would not only provide Germany with free access to that country's rich resource base, but it would also eliminate the threat to Germany's foreign economic lifelines, one of the most important of which was the Romanian oilfields. A further plus factor was that it would put paid to the threat of Bolshevism. He was also convinced that the Soviet Union was the reason why Britain would not make peace.

At the same time, Hitler mistakenly believed that the war in the west was virtually won, and even at this late stage he had not quite abandoned the notion of the possibility of enticing Britain over to the Axis side. Moreover, it never occurred to him that Russia would pose much of a problem. The purges of the High Command in the 1930s had left the Red Army in a shambles, an image that the struggle to overcome Finland in the 'Winter War' of 1939–40 appeared to confirm. And, indeed, to begin with, the Russian campaign went well and once again it appeared that Hitler's strategy was sound. Within five months, an area some five times greater than that of Germany proper had been conquered, and it seemed only a matter of time before the Russian giant was subdued. Unfortunately, Russia simply refused to 'collapse on schedule'; Russian forces put up a stubborn resistance, and from the autumn of 1942, the German forces were confronted with the mud and snow of the worst winter for fifty years. The fierce resistance of the Russian troops made it clear that the *Blitzkrieg* phase was finally over. Hitler had been staggered by the resilience of the Russian forces and his enemy's capacity to throw more divisions into the fray. What neither Hitler nor the German Intelligence, the *Abwehr*, fully realized was that Russia, far from being reduced to a vassal state, still had great reserves on which to fall back. She was not short of manpower, and the region round the Urals and beyond contained sufficient raw materials and resources to make feasible a reconstitution of the Russian war effort so that even had Moscow fallen (as it did to Napoleon in 1812), Soviet Russia's ability to retaliate would still have prevailed, especially given Stalin's willingness to sustain huge losses and his totalitarian regime's capacity to sustain them. Hitler's main miscalculation, partly because of poor German intelligence information on the state of Russia, was in believing that the Soviet Union could be taken early and quickly. Consequently, the whole exercise was badly planned, resulting in short-ages of food, clothing, equipment and ammunition for the advancing troops, while a third of the operating divisions were still engaged in the west. The Russian cam-paign was probably Hitler's biggest blunder.

Meanwhile, the United States had been drawn into the war by the Japanese attack on Pearl Harbor (December 1941). Hitler then committed another gross blunder by declaring war on the United States in support of his Japanese ally. This at the onset proved a useful diversionary move from Hitler's point of view, but it was only a matter of time before the United States turned its focus on Europe. Hitler mistakenly believed that the Americans would be preoccupied with Japan and did not anticipate a serious threat from this quarter until much later. In point of fact, America adopted a 'Germany first' policy strategy and geared up its civil-ian economy to produce armaments. Virtually all the capacity of the automobile industry was converted to war production and the Ford Motor Company was even-tually producing more armaments than the whole of Italy.

The decision to invade the Soviet Union can be seen in retrospect as Hitler's biggest blunder, and it ultimately led to Germany's downfall. The Russian campaign eventually absorbed a disproportionate amount of the nation's resources at the expense of all other theatres of war.[13] The decision to attack Russia was in the short term motivated by distrust of his ally and an innate suspicion that she might attack first, and also by the fear that Britain might try to seek an alliance with the Soviet Union. But more importantly, the conquest to the east fitted in with his consistently declared strategy for the future of the German Reich in that it should have living space in the rich lands in Poland and the Ukraine and that the Euro-Asiatic lands could be used as a dumping ground for Slavic and other populations who failed to meet Hitler's exacting tests of racial quality.

Unfortunately, Hitler failed to appreciate the magnitude of the task of slaying the Russian giant, but once committed, there was for him no turning back. The early victories over the Red Army forces lulled Hitler into a false sense of security as to the prospects of a speedy victory. But once Germany's forces got bogged down in the vast and inhospitable terrain, he failed to sanction an orderly retreat and regrouping, insisting instead that resolute defence *in situ* should be main-tained. This gave the Soviet Union valuable breathing space to reorganize her forces and battle techniques and to recuperate economically after the devastation of the economy by the invading German forces. Hitler entirely misjudged the Soviet Union's capacity to retaliate, believing that the country was close to collapse by the end of 1941. Two main factors were responsible for the turnaround in fortunes. First, the Red Army, through improved organization and more efficient and effective battle techniques, succeeded in keeping the Germans at bay, with the result that they failed to capture key cities such as Moscow and Stalingrad and were locked in an endless struggle in Leningrad, which endured the longest siege in history. Second, despite severely depleted resources and the loss of much productive capacity as a result of the German occupation, the Soviet economy was able to stage a remarkable recovery in the later years of war by transferring production facilities eastwards, centralizing production methods and producing military hardware on a mass production basis. Some 10–12 million industrial workers, many hundreds of enterprises and a great deal of machinery and equipment were transferred to the eastern regions of the Soviet Union in what can only be described as an outstanding feat of industrial relocation in such a short space of time. This transformation was crucial for the eventual success of the Red Army, because in the latter part of the war, the Soviet Union was producing more battlefront weapons than Germany. German weapons may have been technically superior but they were often produced in small batches to satisfy the technical requirements of the army; for instance, there were no less than 151 types of lorry in production at one stage. Russia, to some extent following American practice, eschewed quality for quantity production, which eventually paid off. Had Germany done the same and had she also exploited her vast resources in the Greater Reich, in the occupied territories and in the Axis allied countries more efficiently and humanely, then the outcome of the war on the eastern front might have been different.

The start of 1942 therefore marked a crucial turning point in the Second World War. It was by then becoming apparent that the regime had taken on too much: German forces were involved in the Balkans, in North Africa, against the British at sea and in the air and against the Soviet Union. Such massive and extensive operations outstripped the supply capability of the economy, which in turn reflected the failure to mobilize fully. Göring also admitted that the economy was riddled with muddle and waste, though he himself had contributed in this respect and yet did little to rectify the situation. It spelt the end of the *Blitzkrieg* strategy on which Germany's whole plan of campaign decisively turned, which meant that the regime was forced to commit itself to a long drawn-out struggle for which it was neither militarily prepared nor temperamentally suited. In effect, the war now turned into a struggle between opposing economic potentials, which weighted the odds heavily in the Allies' favour. The United States, UK and USSR alone had accounted for some 60 per cent of world manufacturing production in 1936–38, as against about 17 per cent for the main Axis powers. It is true that the latter could also draw upon the resources of the conquered territories, but so in turn could the major Allies tap the resources of an even wider area beyond Europe. Germany had been brought down by a coalition of three great powers in the First World War and would suffer the same fate again at the hands of the Grand Alliance.

The commitment to total war on the Allied side prompted a massive build-up of armament strength and extensive mobilization of manpower and economic resources. It also led to a more extensive system of planning and controls than had been the case in the First World War. Thus from early 1942, arms production in Allied countries rose rapidly to reach a peak in 1944. On the Axis side, a similar trend was apparent, but the commitment to an all-out effort came later and was less energetically pursued. In fact, as late as September 1941, Hitler had made the fatal mistake of cutting back war production schedules on the assumption that the war was virtually won, an order that was to prove costly in terms of military supplies for a time in 1942. Even then, Hitler remained reluctant to agree to anything like a general mobilization of personnel and resources because he still laboured under the delusion that the war could be won by his favoured strategies. Thus although arms production did increase in 1942, thanks largely to Albert Speer's efforts in improving resource utilization, it remained inadequate, and the failure to mobilize fully meant a continuing shortage of labour for both defence and production purposes. Instead, the regime was content to alleviate the labour shortage in some degree by drafting workers from occupied territories. Of course, slave labour was far from ideal, lacking the training and patriotic spirit of native workers.

However, the Stalingrad disaster, marking the failure of the final *Blitzkrieg* campaign, at the close of 1942, when the Sixth Army surrendered, made it clear that fundamental changes were required in the conduct of the German war economy. Before this event, in February 1942, Albert Speer had been appointed Minister of Armaments and Munitions and during the course of that year he had achieved some notable results in boosting production under conditions that were far from propitious. But it was not until September 1943 that a single authority to direct the whole German war economy was realized, when Speer was made Minister of Armaments and War Production with powers over both the military and civilian sectors of the economy. Though Speer accomplished spectacular feats against great odds, because Hitler remained unwilling to let the output of civilian goods fall appreciably, the main opportunities for restructuring the economy had been missed. Because of Germany's initial delay in mobilizing fully, the Allies were given a head start in arming in depth, apart from the fact that their combined strength was infinitely greater (see Table 5.1).

Thus, by the time it was fully appreciated that a change of direction was required, it was too late for Germany to attempt a radical overhaul of her war economy with a view to broadening the industrial base. By 1944, German war production was triple that of 1941 but this resurgence came three years too late. Germany was now on the defensive and therefore immediate needs were paramount; labour and materials could no longer be spared for projects which did not yield quick returns. In other words, Germany was now forced to concentrate her energy on boosting arms production as best she could, drawing as far as possible on supplies of labour and materials from occupied Europe. In time, these supplies began to dry up, and by 1944, growing personnel and raw material shortages were seriously hampering the war effort. By the autumn of the same year, it was becoming increasingly clear that Germany had insufficient resources to carry on the war

Table 5.1 Allies/Axis economic strengths (ratios)

	1938	1939	1940	1941	1942	1943	1944	1945
GDP	2.4	2.3	2.1	2.0	2.1	2.5	3.3	5.1
Armed Forces:								
Eastern sector	–	–	–	1.1	1.5	1.4	1.9	2.3
Western and Pacific fronts	–	1.2	0.8	0.9	1.1	1.9	1.9	1.6
War Production 1942–44								
Rifles, carbines	2.7							
Machine pistols	15.6							
Machine guns	3.2							
Guns	3.1							
Mortars	5.3							
Tanks	4.7							
Combat aircraft	2.6							
Major naval vessels	5.5							

Source: Harrison 1998, 10, 14, 17.

much longer. However, even at this late stage, Germany had not fully tapped all her own reserves: the mobilization of women, for example, could have been intensified, while slave labour could have been utilized more humanely and more productively. In the spring of 1942, Hitler had rejected the outright conscription of women to work in war production, and by September 1944, there were only 271,000 more women in employment than there had been in May 1939. Even so, as a result of the drift of males to the forces, the male component was shrinking and so the share of women in the total German labour force increased from 37 to 51 per cent, a higher proportion than in either Britain or the United States. Farming was heavily dependent on female labour, which constituted over one-half the total employment in agriculture. Likewise, the culling of men from civilian work for service in the armed forces was not as rigorous as it might have been. This neglect can again be attributed to Hitler's original conception of war, which made him reluctant to sanction an all-out effort as far as mobilization was concerned. Furthermore, a large proportion of those serving in the German army were not actually engaged on the battlefront but in occupation duties and in an administrative capacity. Another wasted opportunity to exploit labour resources was the policy of mass extermination of the Jews and prisoners of war. In the winter of 1941, for example, nearly three million prisoners of war were liquidated, which meant that a frantic conscription drive had to be launched throughout the continent in 1942. Germany had a large reservoir of labour on which to draw in the Greater Reich, in the occupied territories and in allied countries such as Finland, Hungary, Romania and Slovakia.

Table 5.2 provides a snapshot of the overall position with regard to German labour supply. As a result of the drain to the armed forces, 11.2 million by 1943, the domestic German labour force declined dramatically and it was not fully

Table 5.2 German labour force 1939–44 (million)

	Male	Female	Total	Foreign labour	Total labour force, German and foreign
1939	24.5	14.6	39.1	0.3	39.4
1942	16.9	14.4	31.3	4.2	35.5
1944	14.2	14.8	29.0	7.1	36.1

Source: Braun 1990, 122.

supplemented by foreign labour, so that by 1944 there were over three million fewer workers engaged in the home economy. Furthermore, there was no dramatic increase in productivity to compensate for the shortfall. In fact, in some sectors, productivity actually declined because of long hours, insufficient nourishment and problems of acquiring the basic necessities of life, while the efficiency of foreign workers was lower than German labour.

The policy adopted towards the conquered territories was also unsatisfactory in terms of securing the maximum potential for war purposes. The Nazi regime never sought to persuade any one of the nominally allied or conquered countries that their interests were identical to those of the German people. For the most part, Hitler treated all non-German countries in Europe alike, that is, as territories to be exploited to serve German needs. This policy had two unfortunate consequences as far as Germany was concerned. It precluded the possibility of securing the voluntary support of non-Germans for Hitler's war effort. How extensive this might have been is a moot point, but certainly the inferior treatment of non-Germans did little to encourage such support and it often bred latent hostility. Second, the outright exploitation of occupied territories as opposed to the building up of their productive potential was eventually self-defeating. It is true that Germany acquired considerable resources from the domains she ruled (rough estimates suggest that the foreign contribution to Germany's wartime gross national product was of the order of 20 per cent), but it is more than likely that the contribution would have been even greater had a more humane and constructive attitude been adopted towards these territories. In particular, had they not been seriously weakened by the policy of exploitation, their contribution in the later stages of the war could have been crucial to Germany's final effort.

On other grounds too, it could be argued that Germany made a serious mistake in not securing the full cooperation of the occupied countries, because by the middle stage of the war, her main allies (Italy and Japan) were proving something of an incubus. Italy was a weak country, despite Mussolini's vainglorious attempts to ape the Führer, and the country provided little effective support for the German war effort. Italy had few minerals and raw materials to offer, and her fighting prowess certainly did not match that of the Germans. To make matters worse, Mussolini had independent ambitions, especially in Africa and the Balkans, while the disastrous war record of the Italian economy meant that Germany was virtually forced to prop up the country until the Fascist experiment collapsed. Japan's record initially was better, and Japan proved a useful ally in the effort to deflect the United States from Europe. But Japan failed to attack the Soviet Union in the Far East or to check the United States, and when she subsequently developed wider ambitions within the Pacific area, her strategic usefulness to Hitler diminished. Indeed, the decision to support his Japanese ally and declare war on the United States came back to haunt him. The Japanese made no attempt to prevent American Lend-Lease supplies reaching Russia through Vladivostok, fearing it might provoke the Soviets. Nor was there proper coordination within the Tripartite Pact. For example, Hitler invaded Romania and Russia without consulting Mussolini, while in turn the latter sent his forces into Greece in defiance of German wishes not to disturb the Balkans because they provided important raw materials and minerals. Similarly, Japan concluded a non-aggression pact with the Soviet Union in April 1941, electing to turn south against British and American interests in Southeast Asia rather than north against Asiatic Russia. By averting a two-front war for Stalin, this allowed him to transfer divisions from Siberia to defend Moscow. Again the Japanese attack on Pearl Harbor was as much a surprise to Hitler as it was to the US President.

Finally, one should note that the German regime itself was far from united. Bitter inter-Nazi feuds and struggles for power went on throughout the war and served to weaken the administrative and organizational effort of the Third Reich. The effects were seen in the relatively inefficient organization of the conquered territories, where there was 'a bewildering overlap of authority among the various German administrative agencies and a vicious competition for power' (Rich 1974, 203). There was an incredible maze of overlapping administrative offices and agencies of party, state and private organizations, described in the case of France as 'an inpenetrable chaos of competencies', such that it is amazing that anything was ever achieved out of the confusion. There were also the frequent disputes about the conduct of the German war economy itself. At one time or another, every prominent member of Hitler's entourage indulged in feuding with his immediate adversaries, a practice that Hitler chose largely to ignore for personal reasons. His divide-and-rule policy protected his own power base, but the resulting fragmentation of command rendered effective military leadership almost impossible, especially because Hitler himself made all the decisions, many of which were wrong because he was never prepared to listen to advice. Thus Germany's failure was partly the result of an absence of efficient leadership. As one historian has observed: 'Four years after the Blitzkrieg victory over France, the German command system was in a shambolic state' (Roberts 2003, 142). This internecine warfare among Hitler's subordinates can have done little to assist the efficient planning and organization of the war effort and it may well have given Germany's opponents an opportunity to break the German hegemony. According to Höhne, the hallmark of the Nazi regime was the absence of system and structured hierarchy: 'nonsensical, chaotic and structureless was the jungle which served as a system of government in the Führer state' (Höhne 1969, 340). Bullock (1962, 676) is equally critical of the shortcomings of the Nazi machine:

The boasted totalitarian organization of the National Socialist State was in practice riddled with corruption and inefficiency under the patronage of the Nazi bosses, from men like Göring and Himmler down to the Gauleiters and petty local racketeers of every town in Germany. At every level there were conflicts of authority, a fight for power and loot, and the familiar accompaniments of gangster rule, 'protection', graft, and the 'rake-off'. The Nazis did not change their nature when they came to power, and they remained what they had always been, gangsters, spivs, and bullies – only now in control of the resources of a great state.

That Germany was not totally ruined by Nazi control Bullock attributes to the organizing ability of the permanent officials of the civil service and local government and leaders of industry, who continued to function as best they could in the hostile environment.

The above comments provide some of the reasons why the Axis eventually succumbed to defeat. The counterfactual is: could Germany have won the war? Unfortunately, this speculative exercise cannot be entered into here, but enthusiastic scholars are directed to Andrew Roberts's book *The Storm of War*, which has some interesting views on this matter.

The Allied delay

By the start of 1944, Germany should have been virtually finished given the disasters in the east and North Africa, the collapse of Italy, the aerial warfare over Germany and the preparations for the western landings. Taking into account also the weaknesses and mistakes of the Nazi regime and its inferior economic potential compared with its adversaries, it may seem surprising that it took the Allied powers so long to secure victory. The general provision of goods and services for war of Britain and the United States alone probably exceeded those available to Germany in 1944 by some 75 per cent, while in various types of munitions production the advantage in favour of the Allies was substantial (Table 5.1). Also, by early 1944, Allied air superiority was clearly evident and was later to be demonstrated on the western front.

There are several reasons to explain the delay. For one thing, after the entry of the United States into the war, the Allies were faced for a time with the task of maintaining a holding operation until such time as they were able to build up their military strength to a point at which they could launch a full-scale attack on Germany. In the summer of 1940, the United States was in no position to enter a major war because it could field only one-third the number of divisions that Belgium could draw upon. Allied defence capability therefore took some time to accomplish, especially the tooling-up operations required for American mass production methods, while heavy shipping losses as a result of German submarine activity played havoc with the movement of supplies. The divisive issue of when to establish a second front against Germany in western Europe was also a factor. In 1942–43, Churchill persuaded the Americans to back a Mediterranean strategy, which culminated in the defeat of fascist Italy but in the process delayed the build-up of forces in southern England to invade France. Stalin had been pressing his allies to organize a western landing from 1942 onwards but, much to his annoy-ance, this did not materialize until 1944. In addition, war on the eastern front subsequently absorbed a large proportion of resources, especially American, thereby reducing the European effort. For a time too, the Red Army's striking force was seriously weakened as a result of Hitler's initial victories. The Soviet Union had also lost a large part of its industrial resources to Germany, and it was not until a new industrial base had been created in the Urals and beyond the Volga that Russia was in a position to launch an effective attack from the east. It is also pos-sible that the Allies underestimated the war production potential of Germany after the *Blitzkrieg*. Despite increasing difficulties, German production of munitions did increase rapidly, and in the first half of 1944 (by which time the Allied superiority was clearly apparent), Germany was able to make one last effort and in the process managed to increase the output of certain vital armaments faster than the Allies.

Some of the blame for the allied delay can certainly be attributed to the wasteful and inefficient allied bombing campaign. This was especially the case with RAF Bomber Command in 1943, when it unleashed heavy and indiscriminate night-time bombing on German cities instead of concentrating more closely on key industrial sites. True, there had been repeated raids on the Ruhr during the course of 1943 by RAF Bomber Command, but the periodic sorties had made only a modest impact on the industrial capacity of the region. Many civilians were killed or wounded in what has been called a 'tragic operational error' and the failure to clinch victory gave Germany the chance to launch one last effort. The Americans enjoyed little more success with their daylight raids from English air bases and suffered proportionately heavier losses. Far from turning the civilian population against the Nazi regime, the Allied bombing sorties rallied support. And even when the Allied bombing campaign became more focused on key military and industrial installations, it had only a limited impact on Germany's capacity to produce, partly because of a relocation of strategic military production facilities. However, there was at least one beneficial effect from the Allied point of view. The intensive air attack forced Germany to divert a large proportion of its air resources from the east to cover the western approaches. By the spring of 1943, 70 per cent of German fighters were engaged in the western theatre of war, thereby exposing German ground forces on the Russian front to enemy air attack.

That the Germans were able to hold out for so long can partly be explained by the superior fighting capabilities of their forces. The Allies could not match the fighting prowess of either the German or Japanese troops, nor could they make better equipment. However, they could make much more of it, and in the end it was quantity not quality that finally clinched victory for the Allied side. As was the case in the First World War, it took the efforts of three great powers to subdue Germany. After the middle of 1944, however, the defeat of Germany was only a matter of time. Until then Germany's war production had not been too seriously hampered by a shortage of resources. Thereafter the position deteriorated rapidly. The Normandy landings in the summer of 1944 together with intensive bombing put Germany in a state of siege. During the last year of war, the Allies had the upper hand in the air on all fronts. The supply of raw materials became increasingly tight as the area under German control diminished, while heavy Allied bombing reduced the productive capacity of the Axis powers and their occupied territories. For example, the sustained aerial attacks from May 1944 on German oil resources were extremely successful; they reduced the amount of fuel available by 90 per cent, thereby rendering Germany's new tanks and jet planes inoperative. Fuel shortages put paid to much flying time by new jet fighters that could have been potentially devastating on Allied bombers. The increasing shortage of resources had a serious impact on production in the latter half of the year. Thus, with rapidly dwindling reserves and declining production, Germany faced the combined onslaught of the Allied nations on all fronts. Their superior economic and military strength was telling. By the spring of 1945, the position had become desperate, and on 7 May, Germany surrendered. 'The hard facts of economic power, expressed in the form of military equipment and the men to operate it, in the end overwhelmed both [Hitler] and Germany' (Wright 1968).

Economic aspects of the war effort

By the winter of 1943–44, the world economy was far more mobilized for war than at any time in the past, including the period of the First World War. The planning and control of economic resources was more extensive and detailed than it had been in 1914–18, while the proportion of output devoted to war purposes was also greater. At the peak of activity, well over one-third of the world's net output was being devoted to war. Of course, military spending was heavily concentrated on a small number of countries. The major belligerents including the British Dominions were spending about £36,000 million to £38,000 million a year on war or defence, while the rest of the world had an annual budget of £1500 million at the most for such purposes. At the same time, the main combat powers were drawing some £3,000 million to £3,500 million from the rest of the world in the form of levies, exactions and loans.

The distribution of war expenditures among the major participants varied considerably. Reckoning on the basis of budgetary responsibility for the war goods and services provided, the United States easily topped the list, her share accounting for 30 per cent of the world total. The next largest spender was Greater Germany, with 25 per cent, which includes exactions and levies imposed on occupied territories. The Soviet Union and the UK accounted for one-seventh and one-eighth, respectively, while Japan's share was about one-fourteenth. These five countries accounted for some eleven-twelfths of total world expenditure on war, though their combined share of world output in 1943–44 was just under 70 per cent. The proportions vary if based on the countries to whose governments the goods and services were finally made available.

As well as being the largest spender, the United States also provided invaluable assistance to the allied combatants. Under the Lend-Lease programme approved by Congress in March 1941, America was able to supply allied countries with war materials, equipment and provisions. In total, throughout the entire period of hostilities, some $50 billion was dispensed under Lend-Lease to no fewer than 38 countries, with the bulk of it going to Britain and the USSR. The war effort in both these countries was literally kept going by western aid, which in 1943 and 1944 contributed as much as 10 per cent to the Soviet campaign.

The war effort was sustained by three main factors: increasing output, a fall in consumption and capital depletion. During the course of the war, net world output probably rose by between 15 and 25 per cent, though the output record of countries varied enormously, with the biggest gains occurring in North America. The extent of the depletion in capital resources is more difficult to estimate with any precision, but at a rough approximation, it may be put at about two per cent of total output annually. Global consumption also probably fell but there are no reliable figures on the magnitudes involved. However, the impact of each of these factors varied considerably from one country to another. Most of the main belligerents managed to increase output to some extent, at least for part of the time, though this was often at the expense of consumption. The most impressive performances occurred in the United States and, to a lesser extent, in the Dominion countries. The former was undoubtedly the major beneficiary of war because the American economy was much stronger in 1945 than it had been at the time of its entry into the war. Industrial production rose at an annual rate of some 15 per cent, while new investment increased the capacity of the economy by about 50 per cent. War production, which accounted for a negligible proportion of total output in 1939, rose to 40 per cent in 1943. A rise in gross domestic output of some 70 per cent between 1939 and 1945 was sufficient to cover this outlay and leave something over for an improvement in living standards. At the same time the United States became the lifeline for the Allied powers, providing some $50 billion of Lend-Lease goods between 1941 and 1945 (about 5 per cent of US national income in this period), the bulk of which went to Britain and the Soviet Union. This largesse was critical in keeping Britain afloat in the war and rectifying equipment deficiencies in the Red Army (such as wireless sets, jeeps, trucks and clothing), which ultimately allowed it to pursue successfully its own form of *Blitzkrieg* to drive the *Wehrmacht* all the way back to Berlin. Having said that, one must not underestimate the spectacular relocation and regeneration of the Soviet industrial base after the setback following the German invasion.

In other words, the war stimulated growth and led to an improvement in living standards in the United States, and the same may be said for some of the Dominion countries. Elsewhere this was not the case. Though many of the belligerents managed to increase their output, it was usually insufficient to meet the demands of war and so something else had to suffer. Net output in the UK, for example, rose by 22 per cent between 1938 and 1944, but this fell far short of the war effort requirements, which absorbed some 50 per cent of total income at the peak. The leeway had therefore to be made up by the disposal of foreign assets, debt accumulation, capital depletion and a fall of 22 per cent in personal consumption. Japan too suffered a cut in consumption despite a considerable rise in net output and an extension of capital equipment.

The Axis performance could not match that of the United States, one reason why the Allies eventually predominated. On the continent of Europe it was Germany, ironically enough, which probably fared the best, at least until the closing stages of the war. In large part, this can be explained by the fact that Germany was able to maintain herself by exacting large contributions from occupied territories, and as a consequence the population suffered only moderate inconvenience. The national product of Germany as constituted at the outbreak of war rose modestly (14 per cent between 1939 and 1944), though there had been a sharp increase just before the war. However, the total resources available to the Reich were greater than this figure indicates, because foreign contributions and levies accounted for about 14 per cent of Germany's domestic product between 1940 and 1944, while if the contribution of foreign labour is included the total addition to domestic resources was of the order of one-quarter. Foreign workers certainly made a substantial contribution to Germany's overall stock of labour resources. In 1944, there were nearly 8 million foreign workers in the Third Reich, that is more than 20 per cent of the German workforce (at its peak, it may have approached one quarter), though this barely compensated for the drop in the domestic workforce caused by losses to the armed forces. In agriculture, 46 per cent of the workforce was foreign and similarly over one-third of armament workers and about one-third in construction and mining, while in some plants the proportions were much higher. Much of the foreign labour was recruited by force through regular man-hunts in the territories administered by Germany and only a small proportion came voluntarily. The main source was the Soviet Union and Poland with around one-half the foreign workers recruited from these two countries. Speer claimed, in July 1944, that up to that date some 25–30 per cent of Germany's war production had been furnished by the occupied western territories and Italy, though he probably exaggerated the latter's contribution. In fact, after 1939, much of the increase in the product available to Germany came from foreign contributions, including slave labour in Germany, which accounted for over a fifth of the civilian labour force in the later stages of war. 'Like a gigantic pump, the German Reich sucked in Europe's resources and working population' (Kulischer 1948). Thus despite the fact that the state's share of total output was as high as 63 per cent at the peak, consumption levels were maintained well until near the end of hostilities. Drafts on capital equipment were substantial, though the extent of the depletion has usually been overstated.

Italy, on the other hand, proved a great disappointment to Hitler, and in more ways than one. From the economic viewpoint, the war was a disaster for Italy. Even during the period of German victories, Italy's output increased only marginally over 1938, while after 1942 it fell sharply, bringing it back by 1945 to a level close to that of the first decade of the century. Consumption was sharply reduced, while inflation reached serious dimensions. An interesting contrast is provided by Russia, which for a poor country devoted a high proportion of resources to military activities. She was badly devastated by the German invasion, losing about half her industrial capacity; as a consequence, production slumped to a low point in 1942 and living standards declined seriously from levels already low by western standards. However, the Russians proved incredibly resilient and resourceful; they undertook a massive relocation of industry and workers in the Urals and beyond, putting them well beyond the bombing range of the *Luftwaffe*. In what can only be described as an astonishing feat of relocation, some 10 to 12 million industrial workers, hundreds of enterprises and large amounts of plant, machinery and equipment were shifted to the eastern regions of Russian, with the result that by 1944, total output was running at 38 per cent above the 1938 level, though it fell back sharply in the following year.

The impact of the war elsewhere in Europe varied a good deal depending upon the extent of fighting and the degree of exploitation carried out by the Germans. Countries allied with Germany and nominally independent such as Finland, Hungary, Romania and Bulgaria did not do too badly, though their living standards fell as they became increasingly dependent on servicing the German war machine. The main brunt fell upon the occupied countries, the consequences of which were often little short of disastrous. The chief objective of German policy was to extract the maximum benefit from the occupied territories without consideration of the interests of the countries in question. Thus the imposition of heavy levies, looting, the removal of plant and labour, together with general devastation after military operations, led to a fall in output and a general decline in living standards over a large area of Europe. Germany assigned to herself an ever-increasing proportion of the total output of the countries concerned, and the financial practices of the Reich vastly increased the means of payment, thereby creating a highly inflationary situation. A large increase in the supply of occupation currency together with a decrease in the supply of goods led to a flight of money and widespread blackmarket operations, though only in a few countries (notably Greece) did a complete financial breakdown occur. The practices pursued not only increased the resources available to the Reich but also helped to damp down the inflationary potential in Germany. In 1942–43, occupied Europe was supplying Germany with more than a fifth of its grain, one-quarter of its fats and nearly 30 per cent of its meat requirements, as well as making a significant contribution to industrial and labour resources (especially coal and steel deliveries). Greater success was achieved in the west than in the eastern sector. France, for example, provided Germany with as much food as the USSR, while the industrial contributions from France, Belgium, the Netherlands, Norway and Bohemia-Moravia were substantial. In fact, France alone was responsible for some 42 per cent of the total foreign contributions to Germany's war economy. Even so, exploitation often fell short of true potential because of inefficient management, competing agencies and alienation of the local workforce as a result of German control methods. A good case in point is the French aircraft industry, which in 1940 had the capacity to produce around 5000 aircraft per annum. Over the whole of the war period 1940–45, the Germans realized a total of 2516 machines, mostly trainers, that is only one tenth of the capacity of the industry. It would be interesting to know how far the Germans failed to exploit the full potential in the occupied territories overall and what difference this made to their total war effort.

Occupation and financial costs became a heavy burden for France, the Low Countries and Norway. All the occupied countries were forced to pay levies to meet the costs of occupation as well as making deliveries of food, raw materials and manufactured goods to the Reich. The levies were often unduly inflated, while prices and exchange rates were fixed in favour of Germany. Payment for goods received was made in blocked credits that were to be settled at some future date, if ever. By the third quarter of 1944, the German debt outstanding on trade account amounted to some 42 billion Reichmarks, around one-half of which was on account of France, the Netherlands, Belgium and Luxemburg. In proportionate terms, France probably bore the largest burden. In all, French payments to Germany accounted for about one-half of all French public expenditure in 1940–42 and as much as 60 per cent in 1943, when Germany was estimated to be using some 40 per cent of French resources. By 1943, around one-half the French workforce was contributing, either directly or indirectly, to the German war effort, while as much as one-third of the French national income was being drained off for Germany's benefit (see Mazower 2009, 261–62). The extraction process was not so successful in eastern Europe, and the Ukraine in particular did not turn out to be the El Dorado anticipated. This was largely because much of the food was consumed on the spot by the occupation forces so that it never reached Germany. Ironically, the Germans did better under the delivery system of the Nazi–Soviet Pact.

The overall contribution of the occupied territories, both east and west, to the German economy throughout the war was probably of the order of 20–25 per cent of the total. This was undoubtedly a significant contribution, though it could have been higher had a more efficient and humane extraction policy been implemented. From an economic point of view, the German war machine was more successful in the west than in the east, partly because of a certain degree of capitalist cooperation between German and foreign companies and in some cases a relatively tolerant administrative regime. In the east, it was more a case of brutal exploitation regardless of the human cost, which did nothing to endear the indigenous population to the Nazi cause. Nevertheless, however efficient the extraction process, Germany's total resource base was never going to be able to match the combined resources of the United States, the Soviet Union and the British Empire.

The worst effects of the occupation were felt in Greece, Poland, France, Belgium, the Netherlands and the occupied parts of the Soviet Union. In all these countries, output fell sharply, capital was seriously depleted or damaged, labour resources were exploited and living standards declined, in some cases to subsistence levels. Extensive general damage also occurred in those countries where heavy fighting took place. France especially was badly affected by the occupation, the levies from which absorbed some one-third of total output and 40–50 per cent of industrial production; by 1944, output had fallen to only one-half that of pre-war and personal consumption was even lower. In Belgium and the Netherlands, the experience was similar, though not so severe. Further east, the position was even worse; output declined to very low levels and many consumers struggled along on subsistence rations or less, some dying of starvation and malnutrition.

In Poland in the last year of war, many urban dwellers were getting only half the quantities of food received by their German counterparts, while in the Athens-Piraeus region the daily food intake of the majority of the population was down to 600–800 calories in 1941 and 1942. By contrast, Norway and Denmark did rather better. Denmark suffered little serious privation, while in Norway the fall in output was slight but the cost of troop occupation absorbed a large share of income, thereby reducing the living standards of the indigenous population. One high estimate, but surely incorrect, suggests that the German occupation cost in Norway amounted to some three-quarters of the country's national income. Taking continental Europe as a whole, it appears that every second consumer obtained only about two-thirds to three-quarters of his or her pre-war food intake in most years; many received less, and as a consequence substantial numbers died of starvation.

Though German policy in the occupied territories created strong inflationary pressures, price inflation was less severe generally than was the case in the First World War. Despite enormous war expenditures, which involved heavy borrowing and large increases in the money supply, the rate of inflation in most western countries, apart from Belgium, France and Italy, was modest in the circumstances. Improvements in monetary and fiscal control, with a larger share of war expenditure being financed by taxation than in 1914–18, were partly responsible for the better out-turn. But the main reason was the extensive use of price controls and rationing, which were more effectively applied than in the previous experience. Only in countries with weak governments or under enemy occupation (for example, France, Hungary, Portugal, Greece and China), did inflation assume alarming proportions. In the Second World War, it was left to the Balkan and Middle East countries to suffer inflation comparable with that experienced by some of the major belligerents in 1914–18, and only Greece and China had by the end of the war suffered a fate similar to that that overtook the defeated countries after 1919. On the other hand, the greater success in restraining inflation by controls did create difficulties for peacetime, because it meant the build-up of a large suppressed inflationary potential. Fortunately, government policies in the early post-war period kept this potential within bounds and only in one or two countries (Hungary and Germany, for example), did inflation and currency problems pose a really serious threat.

One final issue should be mentioned: the loss of life because of the war and Nazi brutality. This was on a far greater scale than during the First World War. The estimated loss of life, including civilians, during the Second World War was around 40 million, with Poland, the Soviet Union, Yugoslavia and Germany the worst sufferers. By comparison, less than eight million perished in the First World War. Racially driven Nazi brutality alone probably accounted for some 18 million deaths, including nearly six million Jews and several million prisoners of war, many of which occurred in former Polish territories and the Soviet Union. In fact, the first half of the twentieth century was probably one of the most brutal in the history of Europe. If added to the losses in the two great wars the deaths arising in the Russian and Spanish Civil Wars and those associated with the various purges occurring in Stalin's Russia, then the total number of people who perished unnecessarily amounts to some 75 million upwards.

Questions for discussion

1   How did Hitler achieve the domination of the European continent?
2   Why did Hitler prefer short military campaigns to a long drawn-out struggle for supremacy?
3   What contribution did economic factors make to the eventual Nazi defeat?
4   Analyse the concept of the New Order for Europe and assess how effectively it worked in practice.
5   Given the greater resource potential of the Allied countries, why did they take so long to defeat the Axis powers?

6   Europe's reconstruction

The devastation of Europe

At the end of the war, Europe was in a shambles, and little short of destitute. From Stalingrad to Saint-Nazaire and from Murmansk to Bengazi, there was a trail of devastation and destruction, with the worst ravages occurring in central and eastern regions. The extent of the damage and loss of production was even more serious than it had been in the First World War. Manufacturing was paralysed, commerce was almost at a standstill, agricultural production was well down and communications were badly disrupted. Shortages of almost everything prevailed over a wide area of the continent. Financially, Europe was in an extremely weak state, with huge budgetary deficits, swollen money supplies, a severe shortage of foreign exchange reserves and strong inflationary pressures. Of course, conditions varied from country to country, but there were few, apart from Sweden and Switzerland, that had not suffered severely from the impact of several years of hostilities. Europe's position stood out in sharp contrast to that of the United States and it soon became apparent that the task of rebuilding Europe would depend on the policies adopted by that country, because without external assistance the prospects of an early European revival looked grim. Fortunately, the post-war policies of America were more conducive to recovery than those pursued after the First World War. Despite some initial hesitation, the United States did not, as after 1920, retreat into isolation, but instead became, partly because of political factors, the universal provider of western Europe. As a result the reconstruction and recovery of Europe proved to be more rapid and sustained than anything conceived possible in 1945.

As far as the chief productive assets (labour and capital) are concerned, European losses and damage as a direct result of war were greater than in 1914–18, but the extent of the net depletion of resources is easily exaggerated. However, the problem in both cases is one of obtaining reliable data. For example, there are several different estimates of population losses. The most acceptable figure for the whole of Europe is one of 40 million, which covers military and civilian casualties sustained in the war. Civilian deaths far outnumbered military ones because of the mass extermination policies of the Nazis. Some two-thirds of the Jews on the continent were victims of the Holocaust. Loss of life through disease, epidemics and civil war was modest, while the wartime birth deficit appears to have been low. These factors probably account for another 5 million to 7 million persons, excluding the Soviet Union, where the birth deficit was high. Thus, though direct slaughter was far more severe than in the previous war, the toll of life from other factors was very much less. However, apart from actual deaths, some 35 million people were wounded, while millions suffered from malnutrition.

The distribution of the losses varied enormously. On the whole, northern and western Europe (excluding Germany) escaped lightly, whereas central and eastern Europe suffered badly. Over half the total, about 25 million persons, was accounted for by Russia, while large absolute losses occurred in Poland, Germany and Yugoslavia. Nearly one-fifth of Poland's population was killed during the war, while Germany's loss may have exceeded 6 million, though estimates vary widely. Casualties in some of the smaller eastern countries, though small in absolute numbers, were often significant relative to their total populations. Thus on average about 5 per cent of the population of Hungary, Romania, Czechoslovakia, Yugoslavia and Greece perished.

However, few countries, apart from France, Poland and the Soviet Union, emerged from the war with seriously depleted populations. The overall losses were offset by a remarkable excess of births over deaths, the major boost coming from the sharp rise in fertility in northwest Europe (France excepted), so that the total non-Russian European population in 1945–46 was similar to what it had been just before the war. In other words, the war had simply served to wipe out the natural increase in population. Perhaps more important from the economic point of view was the effect on the composition of populations. In countries with large losses such as Germany and Russia, there was a serious deficiency of population in the most productive age groups, together with a marked sex imbalance. In West Germany, for example, females outnumbered males in the 25–45 age group in the ratio 100:77 in 1950, while over the whole population the excess of females numbered 3 million. Another problem, particularly in some of the badly devastated and poorer countries of the east, was the shortage of skilled workers and people with managerial and professional training. The mass extermination of the Jewish population deprived several countries of valuable financial and business talent.

The war also caused an enormous upheaval in population, resulting in the displacement of many nationals from their country of origin. Altogether, upwards of 30 million people were transplanted, deported or dispersed. Many of these persons subsequently disappeared from the scene altogether, but by the end of the war more than 15 million people were awaiting transfer from one country to another. Thus in the immediate post-war period, dispersal and resettlement affected most European countries to some degree, with Germany, Poland and Czechoslovakia bearing the brunt of the burden. The biggest single transfer consisted of German nationals living outside post-war German territory, who were obliged by the Potsdam Agreement of 1945 to return within the new German boundaries. By October 1946, nearly 10 million Germans had been transferred; over two-thirds of the total migrated to the western zones, which were later to receive a continuous stream of people from East Germany when the Cold War broke out. Initially, this influx posed serious economic and social problems for West Germany, but eventually the expellees provided a valuable addition to the workforce. In relative terms, transfers of Polish nationals were even more significant; large numbers of Poles returned from Germany and Russia, while the cession of territory to the Soviet Union and territorial gains from Germany led to further movements. The net result was that Poland acquired a more homogeneous population but a much smaller one (24.8 million in 1950 as against 32.1 million in 1939).

The loss and destruction of capital assets are even more difficult to quantify precisely. Extensive fighting together with heavy bombing and deliberate devastation meant that the damage to land, property and industrial equipment was more severe than it had been in the First World War. A trail of devastation stretched from west to east across the European continent, with some of the worst damage taking place in the occupied countries. In the invaded areas of the Soviet Union, for example, some 17,000 cities and towns and 70,000 villages were devastated, as were 70 per cent of industrial installations and 60 per cent of transportation facilities. Some of the worst damage was to social capital. Cities were particularly vulnerable to aerial bombardment and many large cities, especially in Germany, were virtually obliterated. In most countries including the UK, the damage to city structures and property was considerable. The destruction of dwellings as a percentage of pre-war stock was as high as 20 per cent in Germany, Poland and Greece, 6–9 per cent in Austria, Belgium, France, Britain and the Netherlands, 5 per cent in Italy and 3–4 per cent in Czechoslovakia, Norway and Hungary. The range of magnitudes is similar for non-residential properties. The backlog of housing to be made good at the end of the war was enormous because new construction was virtually at a standstill during the war except in neutral countries. To the 10 million houses destroyed or badly damaged in Europe, one must add at least 6 million to make up the deficiency from the cessation of building. Buildings generally, both public and private, had also suffered badly through neglect of repair and maintenance.

Transportation facilities were also badly damaged and disrupted. In several countries, especially in eastern Europe, over one-half of the railway bridges, junctions, marshalling yards, signalling systems, stations, permanent way and other installations were destroyed or in need of major capital repairs. Rolling stock was also seriously depleted and damaged and much of what was left was scattered throughout Europe. In fact, rail transport had almost broken down completely in many areas, and for some time after the end of the war, there was little regular overland traffic in large parts of Europe apart from military convoys. The position was little better in other forms of transport. Many ports were blocked or destroyed, waterways were out of action, while the use of road transport was limited, partly of course because of the shortage of fuel. In addition, Europe's merchant fleet was only about 61 per cent of that of pre-war. The west as well as the east was severely affected in transport. In France, the Low Countries and Germany, most waterways and harbours were out of action, many bridges were destroyed and a large part of the rail system was temporarily suspended.

The catalogue of disasters was similar in industry and agriculture. Industry's working capital was seriously depleted and almost non-existent in former occupied areas, apart from the scattered stocks left by the Germans. Industrial equipment and factory buildings suffered severe damage as well as deterioration through continuous working and neglect of maintenance. But in this sector, the impact was less severe than in transport and housing. The incidence of outright loss was patchy, being most extensive in major basic sectors such as coal, steel and power. Moreover, there was an imbalance between consumer and producer goods industries, many of the latter having been expanded at the expense of the former during the war. Against the losses must be set the additions made to capacity during the war, which, though not always directly suitable to peacetime needs, were substantial. It is possible therefore that there was little diminution of the capital stock. In fact, the United Nations, in a report published in 1953, even maintained that Europe's industrial capacity at the end of the war was larger than before and more suited to its new needs. While this report may have sounded a rather optimistic note and almost certainly did not refer to the USSR, nevertheless it does seem that many countries were able to maintain and even increase in some cases their industrial capacity. In Britain, France and the neutral countries, manufacturing capacity expanded modestly, while Roskamp (1965) suggests that West Germany actually had a greater industrial capacity in 1946 than a decade earlier, a position that was not fundamentally changed by the dismantling for reparations. Even in eastern countries, where the damage was on balance greater, the aggregate losses often did not exceed the additions to industrial capacity since 1936. Though prolonged fighting and civil war brought great destruction to Yugoslavia and Greece, in Austria, Romania, Bulgaria and Czechoslovakia there were significant additions to capacity, which more than offset the losses. And in the case of Czechoslovakia, the reduction in population as a result of the expulsion of the Germans led to a large increase in the amount of capital per worker. Even in Poland, where capital losses were heavy, amounting to perhaps a third of the pre-war stock, subsequent additions to capacity plus gains of assets from former German territories together with population losses left Polish industry with a much higher capital/labour ratio than previously. And even Russia, with her enormous losses in the invaded areas, was able to make good much of the deficit by the time the war ended, largely as a result of a shift of industrial activity beyond the Urals.

The situation in agriculture is more difficult to assess. Agricultural potential was severely disrupted by the war through damage to the land, the destruction and looting of equipment and the loss of livestock. The extent of the total damage is unknown but it was probably worst in Poland and Russia. Polish estimates suggest that 60 per cent of the livestock was lost, 25 per cent of the forests and 15 per cent of the agricultural buildings. Damage to the land itself entailed a serious loss of fertility often through lack of fertilization. Perhaps most important in the short term was the loss of working capital and livestock. In east and southeast Europe, over half the pre-war livestock was lost, while the damage and destruction to farm equipment and buildings was also heavy.

On balance, therefore, the net loss of productive assets during the war was much less serious than often imagined. Certainly the amount of loss and damage was considerable but its incidence was patchy, being more severe in eastern countries than in the west. More often than not the losses were quickly made good so that soon after the end of the war Europe's population and productive capital were back to the pre-war levels, even though they were differently distributed between countries and economic activities. There was of course a large amount of restoration and repair work to be undertaken, especially in construction and transport equipment, but the main deficiencies were confined to a few countries.

The setback to current output was substantial and will require explanation in view of what has already been said about the position with regard to capital assets. Almost everywhere on the continent, industrial and agricultural output was well down on pre-war levels by the end of hostilities. Industry was almost at a standstill in several countries. In the summer of 1945, industrial production was less than half that of pre-war in all countries except Britain, Switzerland, Bulgaria and the Scandinavian countries. It was only about one-third in Belgium, the Netherlands, Greece and Yugoslavia, while in Italy, Austria and Germany, it was less than one-quarter. Even by the spring of 1946, the general level of production was still only about two-thirds or so that of pre-war, with serious lagging in Greece, Finland, Germany, Italy and Austria, as against an approximation to former levels in the UK and Scandinavia. The shortfall in agriculture was not quite so sharp but it was far from modest. Only one or two countries, notably Denmark and Britain, managed to increase agricultural output during the war. In Europe as a whole, the production of bread and coarse grains was running at about 60 per cent of pre-war, with the largest declines in occupied countries: for example, Poland had a 60 per cent drop in grain production. Potato output suffered similar declines, while the shortage of fats was even more acute. In some countries, the domestic production of fats was only a fraction of peacetime levels because of low yields and losses of livestock: 13 per cent of pre-war in Poland, 25 per cent in Yugoslavia, 33 per cent in Belgium and somewhat less than 50 per cent in France, Austria and Czechoslovakia; only Sweden recorded an increase. Meat and livestock products were also well down. The overall decline in meat production was about one-third, but in Poland it was only 14 per cent of pre-war, in the Netherlands one-third and in Belgium, Austria and Yugoslavia two-fifths.

Rough estimates for total national output in real terms suggest a considerable fall in most countries between 1938 and 1946, even though some recovery had taken place in the latter year from the low point reached in 1944–45. The decline was about 50 per cent in Poland and Austria, 40 per cent in Greece, Hungary, Italy and Yugoslavia, 25 per cent in Czechoslovakia, 10–20 per cent in France, the Netherlands and Belgium, whereas in the UK, Switzerland, Denmark, Norway and Sweden, output levels were similar to or somewhat better than those of pre-war.

The general reduction in productive activity was far greater than that which outright physical loss of assets and population would appear to indicate. However, the discrepancy can be readily explained in terms of the conditions obtaining at the end of the war. Destruction of capital was the least of the worries in 1945. Far more important were the general dislocation and disruption to productive activity as a result of the war: in particular, the winding down of armaments production and the problems involved in converting to peacetime operations; the severe shortage of essential raw materials, components and repair facilities; the scarcity of technical skills and the bottlenecks in communications; and, perhaps most important of all, the sheer exhaustion of a generally undernourished population. The conclusion of the war marked the climax of six years of struggle and privation, at the end of which workers were in no fit condition to exert themselves. Serious food shortages meant that per capita food consumption in most countries in 1945– 46 was well below peacetime levels, with the shortfall bearing most heavily on urban industrial populations. In Germany and Austria, it was less than 60 per cent of normal, in Italy 68 per cent, in Belgium, France, the Netherlands, Finland and Czechoslovakia about three-quarters of the pre-war levels; elsewhere it was higher but still below normal. Under such conditions, it is scarcely surprising that production and productivity levels were low.

The shortage of food, raw materials and consumer goods in general was acute in Europe but it was part of a wider problem. In the immediate post-war period, there was a world shortage of materials and foodstuffs. Even by 1947–48, world food production was some 7 per cent below the pre-war level and in the interven- ing period there had been an increase in global population. In addition, shortages of shipping space and dislocation in inland transport facilities impeded the move- ment of supplies. But these problems apart, Europe's position was made worse because she had little means to pay for imports of essential commodities, espe- cially from the dollar area, which was the main source of supply. When hostilities ceased, the export trade of many European countries was almost non-existent, and even by the end of 1945, the volume of exports was below 20 per cent of pre-war in all countries except the UK, Switzerland and Scandinavia. Furthermore, the invisible export earnings of many countries, especially Britain, France and the Netherlands, had been seriously impaired by the decline in trade, the loss of shipping and the liquidation of foreign assets, while new debt burdens had been incurred. The loss of income on foreign assets alone was serious enough; in 1938, the income earned by western Europe as a whole on foreign holdings was equivalent to 32 per cent of its exports, whereas by 1950–51, it amounted to only 9 per cent of what she sold to the rest of the world. As a result of these factors, the volume of imports into Europe in the post-liberation period rarely exceeded 50 per cent of the 1937 level; in many countries, it was less than one-quarter and in some eastern countries almost negligible. Thus while physical shortages and transporta- tion bottlenecks presented the immediate problems, it soon became apparent that the overriding difficulty was going to be one of earning sufficient foreign exchange. Europe desperately needed imports but her capacity to export was limited; conse- quently, the ability to carry out reconstruction would depend on the amount of assistance derived from the United States, the only country in a position to supply both goods and financial aid on a large scale.

Low production and widespread shortages of goods also exacerbated the inflationary and monetary problems of Europe, and these in turn impeded the task of reconstruction. Inflationary pressures rarely reached the serious dimensions of the early 1920s, but all European countries suffered from inflation and monetary disorders to a greater or lesser extent in the post-war period. The situation was worst in some of the occupied countries and in the east, and several countries were forced to undertake monetary reform. It was less severe in western Europe and Scandinavia, where it was suppressed in many cases by physical controls.

Thus in the latter half of 1945, the economic outlook in Europe was far from bright. The immediate problem was not one of a shortage of assets, despite the heavy destruction, but a severe scarcity of essential supplies including food and a weakened and undernourished population. Imports were urgently needed to bring about a recovery in production, but because of a low export potential, Europe had not the means to pay for them. Europe's position was aggravated by many other factors, including large public debts, new waves of inflation, the loss of markets and unfavourable terms of trade and by social and political upheavals. It soon became apparent that Europe would not be able to undertake the task of reconstruction unaided. Fortunately, the policies of the Allied governments and of the American government in particular proved to be more constructive than was the case after the First World War.

The politics of reconstruction

Europe's immediate need was aid, which she got on a temporary basis at first and then more permanently under the Marshall Plan. Beyond the short term, the strength of European recovery would also depend upon the international economic environment, and in particular upon the institutions devised for improving economic relationships. There were also the questions of boundary changes to be settled and the amount of reparations to be exacted from the vanquished. In all these matters, politics determined the final format of the arrangements made. Although these were not always ideal, some of the most glaring mistakes of the post-1918 period were avoided and as a result a more solid foundation for European recovery was secured.

Though there were some important territorial changes following the Second World War, these did not involve the extensive carve-up of Europe that had taken place after 1918. In fact, the victors in 1945 did not rush into formal peace treaty negotiations but instead arranged informally among themselves what boundary adjustments should be made. Because of strong political differences between the Allies and the Soviet Union, this inevitably resulted in the marking out of spheres of influence in Europe leading to the east–west split. The onset of the Cold War meant that the *de facto* boundaries that emerged were not formally accepted until 1975.

Nowhere was this more apparent than in the case of Germany. Decisions regarding the future structure of the country were reached piecemeal well before the end of the war. Spheres of influence were worked out by the European Consultative Commission, set up following a conference in Moscow in October 1943 of the Foreign Ministers of the United States, UK and the Soviet Union, the Big Three powers of the Grand Alliance. This Commission fixed the limits of the zones of occupation in Germany (the three western zones that became the German Federal Republic and the Soviet zone, later to become the German Democratic Republic) and in effect created the east–west split. Russia was placed in a strong position to control the region east of the western line of her occupation zone, and her hand was considerably strengthened after the Yalta and Potsdam conferences of February and July 1945. Russia was allowed to increase her territory considerably, mainly at the expense of Poland, while the western boundary of the Soviet Union was fixed by a line running from the Bay of Danzig north to Braunsberg to a meeting place on the frontiers of Lithuania and Poland. This gave Russia an additional 274,000 square miles and added 25 million to her population.

The rivalry between the west and the Soviet Union was reflected in subsequent peace negotiations with Italy, Romania, Bulgaria, Hungary and Finland. Each side attempted to gain as much as possible, with the Soviet Union further strengthening her position in the east. Romania had to give up Bessarabia and Bukovina to Russia, while Finland ceded one-tenth of her agricultural area and one-eighth of her industrial capacity to that country. Hungary was reduced approximately to its post-First World War size, losing southern Slovakia to Czechoslovakia and northern Transylvania to Romania. Bulgaria surrendered land formerly acquired from Yugoslavia with Nazi support, while the latter gave up Fiume and a large part of the Istrian Peninsula. Italy released its colonies and the Dodecanese islands to Greece. Finally, Trieste was placed under international control but later returned to Italy, while the Saar was incorporated into France until 1957, when it was given back to Germany.

Although the territorial changes were not enormous, they were significant in terms of later political events. They also involved considerable movements in population. The major losers were Germany and Poland, while the Soviet Union was the main beneficiary not only in terms of territory and population, but also because she was left in a stronger position to exert control over eastern Europe. However, in some respects, this can be seen as a benefit from the point of view of western Europe, because the rivalry between east and west meant a greater readiness on the part of the United States to assist and strengthen the west European economies, which served to accentuate the divergence in the economic performance of the two sides of the continent.

One big improvement compared with the First World War was that the fiasco over reparations and international war debts was largely avoided, at least as far as western Europe was concerned. As regards German reparations, the major disagreement arose between the Soviet Union and the west over the amount to be levied. The Russians wanted substantial reparations on the grounds that they had suffered badly at the hands of the Germans, whereas the Allies (the United States in particular) were less ambitious in their demands, realizing that to penalise Germany heavily would hinder the latter's recovery and thereby weaken the position of western Europe. Both sides were agreed, however, that Germany should lose her foreign assets and much of her shipping, that she should bear the costs of occupation and the indemnification of injured parties including minority groups, and that her future war potential should be held in check by prohibiting the production of military equipment. Subsequent negotiations established a formula whereby reparations would be paid not from current output but from Germany's existing stock of capital, mainly by dismantling industrial equipment. This procedure had the advantage of avoiding the financial difficulties after the First World War, when payments out of current output had involved the transfer of scarce foreign exchange. However, the original dismantling schedules were fixed at a relatively high level and would probably have crippled German industry for a time. Fortunately, they were later reduced substantially, and the total value of reparations equipment finally made over was quite modest. On the other hand, the total costs borne by Germany on account of reparations, occupation and indemnification costs and other miscellaneous costs were greater than the Allied aid she received initially, but they did not cripple the country and for the most part they did not involve a serious loss of foreign exchange. Other enemy countries including East Germany were treated less favourably. The Russians, incensed by the lenient treatment of West Germany, insisted on exacting large payments from the smaller enemy countries including East Germany (see below).

War debts proved much less of a problem after the Second World War for most countries, with the exception of Britain. America's Lend-Lease policy meant that no charge would be made for the aid and goods sent to the Allies (principally Britain and the Soviet Union) during the war and for the most part other members of the Allied coalition adopted a similar procedure. When hostilities ceased, the Lend-Lease arrangements were terminated, but it soon became clear that the United States would be forced to provide for the relief of poverty-stricken Europe. In fact, long before the war ended it had been recognized that relief aid would be required in European liberated regions, and in November 1943 the United Nations Relief and Rehabilitation Administration (UNRRA) was set up, principally at the behest of the United States, to organize aid and distribute supplies in liberated countries. It was financed largely by American (72 per cent) and British (18 per cent) contributions, and by the end of June 1947, it had spent $3.5 billion worldwide, most of which (80 per cent) had gone to Europe. By far the largest part of the European aid went to east-central and southern Europe (86 per cent), the main recipients being Austria, Czechoslovakia, Greece, Italy, Poland, Russia and Yugoslavia, and some countries received as much in per capita terms as western countries were to receive subsequently under the Marshall Plan. A large part of the relief under UNRRA consisted of food and clothing, but there was also an important element consisting of supplies and materials for industrial and agricultural rehabilitation and vital materials for infrastructure repairs.

The contribution of UNRRA was probably of critical importance to many parts of eastern and southern Europe in the interim period and especially as the former would not be included in Marshall Aid. The aid proved a vital lifeline to devastated areas and it helped to provide a considerable part of the imports of the countries in question. Not only were the supplies critical in terms of alleviating hunger and privation but UNRRA also provided some supplies essential for a start on rehabilitation of their economies.

Apart from the relief dispensed by UNRRA, there was also a very much larger funding in the form of grants and loans to European countries totaling nearly $15 billion in the period from May 1945 through to the autumn of 1947. Almost one-half of this total consisted of grants and loans made to the UK by the United States and Canada, but several other countries received important contributions, including France, Germany, Greece, the Netherlands, Italy, Poland and Czechoslovakia. These credits, together with the UNRRA relief, covered a large part of the import bill of several countries in the transition period, especially for Germany, Greece, Austria, Czechoslovakia, France and Poland.

It is important to note therefore that the volume of aid of one sort or another to assist stricken Europe was already considerable before the launching of the much vaunted Marshall Plan. The reasons for the emergence of this new initiative were both economic and political. The interim aid programmes were not free from criticism. The funding was soon depleted and in terms of recovery it appeared to have only a limited effect, at least initially. This was not altogether surprising. For one thing, much of the aid was disbursed rather indiscriminately with scant regard, either by lending or borrowing nations, as to the most profitable uses to which it could be put. Second, in the conditions then prevailing, a good part of the aid was used simply to keep people alive, especially in eastern Europe. Third, much of the aid was on a loan basis, thereby creating debt problems for the borrowing countries; in some cases, strings were attached, as with the British loan of 1946/47, which involved acceptance of currency convertibility and non-discrimination at a specified date (see below). Finally, national policies were not always conducive to immediate recovery; in the early post-war period, radical new policies, including extensive nationalization in Britain and France and socialization in eastern Europe, the stultifying effects of the German occupation, as well as financial and monetary disorders generally, meant that many economies were not receptive initially to foreign aid. Finally, the United States felt that it did not have enough control over the disbursement of the relief funds.

Recognition of the relative ineffectiveness of the relief programme was one factor prompting a change in policy in 1947. But the shift was probably conditioned more by the turn of political events, in particular the expansionist policy of the Soviet Union, including its hardening line over Germany, which eventually culminated in the blockade of West Berlin. Fear of social and political disturbances and the threat of communist regimes in the west played no small part in the formation of the new aid programme. When the new offer was first announced in June 1947, by Secretary of State George Marshall, it became clear, for political reasons, that it would be confined mainly to western Europe. Moreover, it was made conditional on self-help by the recipient nations, that they cooperate for purposes of ensuring that the aid was used in the most effective way possible. The funds were to be administered on the US side through the Economic Cooperation Administration (ECA), while on the European side sixteen nations joined together to form the Organization for European Economic Cooperation (OEEC), which had the tasks of estimating national requirements and dividing the aid among members, while acting as a clearing-house for national economic plans so as to avoid countries working at cross-purposes.

The Marshall Plan came into effect in April 1948 and was designed to last for four years, though in actual fact it was merged into the Mutual Defense Assistance

Programme in 1951, after which the emphasis shifted to military rather than economic aid. The European Recovery Programme (ERP) was based on the principle of helping those who were willing to help themselves. It provided aid to pay dollars for commodities and services required by Europe; it required recipients to pay for what they received in their own money, with outright grants being confined to emergency cases, while the accumulated funds of local currencies were to be used to promote recovery of national economies. To estimate individual needs, the OEEC used deficits in trade and payments, especially dollar deficits, as the main criterion.

Most of the Marshall Aid (90 per cent) was provided as outright gifts, with the remainder in the form of loans at low rates of interest. The funds came in the form of dollar credits, and the major recipients were Britain ($3176 million), France ($2706 million), Italy ($1474 million), West Germany ($3176 million), the Netherlands ($1079 million), Greece ($700 million) and Austria ($700 million). European governments were the purchasers of imported goods under the programme, which they resold to consumers in their countries. The latter paid for the products in national currencies, and governments thereby acquired large non-dollar balances known as the counterpart funds, which could be used for a variety of purposes subject to ECA approval.

On the whole, the funds of the programme were well administered; they were not squandered by political mismanagement as much previous aid had been. Although in the first year or so, a considerable part of the aid was required for food purchases, later on the funds were used for raw materials and rebuilding productive capacity. Altogether the United States paid out $13,365 million for commodities required by the sixteen nations of the ERP, of which $5,539 million went on food and agricultural products, $6,167 million for industrial commodities and the rest for services of one sort or another. To this must be added the total counterpart deposits of $10,509 million, 95 per cent of which was available to member countries.

Its difficult to estimate the impact of the programme with any precision, and scholars are still divided on the issue, but it is clear that without aid recovery in western Europe would not have been so strong. The Marshall planners budgeted for a 30 per cent advance in industrial production by the end of the ERP programme. This was easily achieved. Industrial production rose by some 45 per cent above the 1938 level excluding Germany and 35 per cent including Germany. By 1951, all countries barring Germany and Greece had well surpassed the target level. Of course, one cannot attribute this solely to the implementation of the Marshall Plan. Overall, Marshall Aid was equivalent to about 2–3 per cent of the combined gross domestic product of the recipient countries during the period 1948–51, with much of it being concentrated in the first year. However, the incidence of aid varied a great deal from country to country. Though the data in Table 6.1 are not complete, it can be seen that the contribution of external aid to national income was not insignificant in several countries, notably France, the Netherlands, Italy, West Germany and Greece, even though it varied from year to year. However, it should also be noted that for several countries, earlier flows of aid were as important as those under the Marshall programme. In terms of capital formation, external aid

Table 6.1 External aid as a percentage of national income 1946–51

	1946	1947	1948	1948/49	1949	1950	1951
Austria				14.0			
Belgium				0.6			
Britain	2.8	7.8	2.1	2.4	2.8	1.9	0.5
Denmark				3.3			
France	7.7	11.3	10.4	6.5	7.5	1.8	4.3
West Germany		4.2	5.3	2.9	4.1	2.3	1.6
Greece			2.9		10.9	14.9	11.5
Netherlands	5.7	4.9	6.8	10.8	4.9	6.9	2.3
Ireland				7.8			
Italy	6.8	3.1	3.4	5.3	2.4	1.7	1.4
Norway	1.0	1.2	3.1	5.8	5.2	6.3	2.2
Sweden				0.3			

Sources: Milward 1984, 95–96; Killick 1997, 97.

was significant in a number of countries: 10–12 per cent in the UK and France between 1948–50 and between one quarter and a third in Italy and West Germany in 1948 and 1949.

Moreover, it should also be stressed that recovery was well under way in many countries before Marshall Aid began to have a significant impact. Despite these caveats, Marshall Aid did have an important part to play in the reconstruction process. What it did do was to ensure that the recovery would be sustained rather than halted in its tracks through lack of resources and essential supplies. The crucial problem for western Europe was the acute shortage of foreign exchange, primarily dollars, with which to procure much-needed imports, not only food and raw materials but also equipment and investment goods for essential reconstruction work, and in this respect, the aid was important in enabling these countries to square their external accounts. In Germany's case, for example, 57 per cent of that country's imports between 1947 and 1949 were financed by foreign aid. It is true that in most years total foreign aid deliveries amounted to less than 5 per cent of Germany's national income, while counterpart investment was equivalent to 9 per cent of gross investment (1950). But as a contribution to total resources over and above minimum requirements, the amounts involved are impressive, and at a critical time, they provided resources of a kind that Germany would have been hard pressed to obtain. Moreover, the qualitative impact of these additional increments was important, especially in terms of the reconstruction of the basic industries.

The counterpart funds, that is the currency receipts from the sale of Marshall Aid supplies, also made an important contribution to western Europe's reconstruction. The ECA tried to encourage governments to use these funds for investment in industry and infrastructure facilities. Most countries, apart from Britain and Norway, who used the bulk of the proceeds to reduce their public debts, used the counterpart proceeds on a range of productive activities in industry, mining, agriculture and infrastructure projects. Thus, in Germany, new electrical generating capacity was financed in this way; in Italy, the funds were spent on a variety of projects including agriculture, railroads and public works; and France put the sums toward financing the Monnet Plan.

In more indirect and discreet ways, the Marshall Plan also influenced the configuration of Europe's reconstruction and recovery. Its role in financial stabilization and monetary reform has been recognized, even though most of the monetary and stabilization measures, apart from the German, had been promulgated well before the launching of the Plan. Reichlin argues that it may have been important in cementing macroeconomic stability, especially in countries vulnerable to distributional conflicts over the division of the national income. It helped to ease the burden by increasing the size of that income and encouraging a more cooperative spirit among the labour force (Reichlin 1995, 64). At the same time, it tried to change European attitudes to production and work methods in an effort to foster the implementation of American practices of scientific management, mass production techniques and more cooperative labour relations through the technical assistance programme designed to boost productivity and reform outdated European work practices. Although the overall effect in this direction was limited and American ideas received a mixed reception in many European countries, probably in the longer term, it encouraged business leaders to examine seriously their work practices and production modes with a view to raising the level of productivity towards the American level.

In sum, therefore, it would be more correct to say that the Marshall Plan facilitated the continuation of Europe's reconstruction and recovery but it did not initiate it. In most cases, recovery was well under way before Marshall Aid was implemented. What it did was to ensure that the recovery would be sustained rather than halted in its tracks through lack of funds. But it did not solve all Europe's problems overnight. Contrary to original expectations, western Europe continued to remain in deficit on external account, in some cases seriously so, until well into the 1950s. In fact, the aid programme may well have retarded progress in this respect, because some countries were inclined to view the elimination of external account deficits as less than pressing given that the larger their deficits, the greater would be their share of American aid. Perhaps the best overall assessment is the sobering conclusion of Lucrezia Reichlin: '. . . the Marshall Plan was important not just for helping to restore the domestic political and economic stability but in promoting the reconstruction of Europe's trade and encouraging European integration, factors which combined to stimulate European growth over the post-war decades' (Reichlin 1995, 53).

Apart from the immediate reconstruction issues, efforts were being made well before the end of the war to secure a greater measure of international economic cooperation among nations on a wider and more permanent scale than anything that had been tried in the past. From the negotiations at Bretton Woods in 1944, two important institutions emerged: the International Monetary Fund (IMF) and the International Bank for Reconstruction and Development (World Bank), while in 1947, after a meeting of twenty-three nations at Geneva, the General Agreement on Tariffs and Trade (GATT) was signed.

The World Bank may be dealt with briefly because it had little significance in terms of reconstruction. The original intention was that this institution should assist the recovery process by providing loans for productive purposes. In practice, its role in this respect was negligible partly because of its limited funds and terms of reference, and because by the time it began operations, the task of aiding Europe had already begun under other auspices in a big way. Thus so far as reconstruction and economic cooperation were concerned, the World Bank contributed little, though subsequently it did become an important source of long-term loans for projects the world over.

By contrast, the IMF and GATT were more concerned with improving international relations within the field of trade and payments. In both cases, the general philosophy was one of freedom for trade and payments, the elimination of discrimination between nations and the restoration of currency convertibility. While GATT was primarily concerned with tariff matters, the IMF's main focus of attention was on monetary questions. The Agreement procedure specifically provided for the restoration of exchange stability, with exchange rate adjustment taking place only in cases of fundamental disequilibrium in the balance of payments of member countries. Members were to desist from imposing restrictions on current transactions and engaging in discriminatory currency practices without the approval of the Fund. The most important provision was the creation of an international pool of reserves derived from members' quotas, which could be drawn upon by individual countries to meet temporary imbalances in their external accounts (see Chapter 7).

Early attempts to restore non-discriminatory multilateral trade proved disappointing. The major initiative in this direction was made by the United States, who proposed the creation of an International Trade Organization (ITO), which would embody the objective of moving quickly towards the goal of free trade. This was a premature move simply because most countries were scarcely in a position to abandon controls over trade, given their weak external positions. Not surprisingly, therefore, the proposal did not gain a particularly sympathetic hearing outside the United States. In an effort to force the issue, the United States laid onerous conditions on the loan agreement concluded with Britain in 1946, which required, among other things, British support for the ITO and the restoration of sterling convertibility. The terms proved disastrous; during the first half of 1947, Britain made a progressive move towards convertibility, and by early July, full convertibility on all current transactions had been restored. In the process, the US loan was quickly dissipated and the reserves fell sharply so that within five weeks the experiment had to be abandoned.

This experience was proof enough that it was too soon to expect much progress in restoring freedom to trade and payments. In the event, therefore, the ITO was not ratified by a sufficient number of countries but out of subsequent discussions emerged GATT. This agreement was more limited than the original ITO charter, being confined mainly to tariff policy, with emphasis on multilateralism and non-discrimination. In later years, it came to play a key role in negotiating worldwide tariff reductions.

In short, therefore, the reconstruction period following the Second World War was marked by a more constructive attempt to foster international economic cooperation and establish conditions under which European recovery could thrive and remain sustained than had been the case after 1918. As far as the immediate task was concerned, the most important contribution was the stream of American aid that flowed into Europe. It is true that most of the institutions established, apart from the OEEC, did not have a crucial part to play in the reconstruction process because they were not designed specifically to cope with immediate difficulties, or alternatively they had objectives, for example the removal of restrictions on trade and payments, which in the conditions of the early post-war years could never be achieved. Nevertheless, one should not underestimate their importance, because they provided a basic framework for post-war international cooperation, and in a later period, they were to achieve considerable success in promoting the liberalization of trade and payments and also in ensuring a reasonable degree of stability in international monetary relationships. Moreover, they provided the precedent for later cooperative efforts, especially in western Europe in the 1950s, with the establishment of the European Payments Union (1950), the European Coal and Steel Community (1952), the European Economic Community (1957) and the European Free Trade Association (1959).

It is important to stress these points because there have been attempts to deride the importance of these experiments in international cooperation and to see the new institutions as being essentially tools of American foreign policy. The facts of the situation cannot be disputed, but the realities should be faced squarely. The American approach in Europe was conditioned by the intransigence of the Soviet Union and its satellites, which eventually meant a confrontation between two great military and economic powers with designated spheres of influence. Europe needed American aid and assistance and it was natural enough that this should be made contingent upon policies and institutions that would satisfy America's overriding objective of defending the west against the Soviet bloc. The major mistake of American policy was the attempt to force western Europe into adopting policies that were clearly not practical in the difficult years after the war. Nor should the split between the east and the west be regarded as a disaster. Certainly, a more harmonious relationship between the two sides would have been preferable, but failing that (a failing that owed as much to American as to Soviet attitudes), it was better to have two equally powerful and self-contained blocs within Europe rather than the power vacuum that existed after the First World War and that paved the way for the Holocaust of less than a generation later.

The road to recovery in the west

Despite the extensive damage and the substantial check to productive activity, the rate of recovery in Europe in the five years or so after the war was impressive. Within two years of the termination of hostilities, many countries had already achieved considerable increases in output, albeit from a low base, while by the late 1940s most countries, both in the east and west, had surpassed pre-war levels of activity, in some cases by a substantial margin. However, experience varied considerably both in terms of the progress achieved and in the policies pursued. Until 1948, western Europe did rather better than the east, which had suffered more severely in the war and was disrupted in the immediate post-war years by radical changes in political and economic structures. Conversely, between 1948 and the early 1950s, it was eastern Europe that set the pace in terms of industrial expansion, though agricultural output lagged behind that of the west. Germany, on the other hand, had much the slowest rate of recovery, and it was not until 1951 that industrial production surpassed pre-war, while in Berlin the level of activity still remained seriously depressed.

As far as western Europe (including Scandinavia) is concerned, the period between the end of the war and 1950–51 was one of fairly continuous expansion, though there were minor interruptions. Positive government policies probably contributed less to this expansion than the successive waves of external stimuli that enabled it to continue each time it was threatened from either the demand or the supply side. Until 1949, there were few signs of serious demand deficiencies because of the large pent-up demand for goods, excess liquidity and inflationary pressures in one form or another in most countries. The main difficulty was that of obtaining adequate supplies of food, raw materials and fuel, because of supply shortages and exchange problems. Fortunately, the supply difficulties were considerably alleviated by the stream of American aid that provided the most important external stimulus. At the same time, inflationary pressures were gradually damped by various means, including controls of one sort or another, counterinflationary policies, an improvement in the supply of goods and a reduction in excess liquidity through large import surpluses and improved budgetary positions. During the first half of 1949, inflationary forces were further checked by the backwash of the temporary recession in America, though by the second half of that year a new push to business activity and prices was being felt as a result of the currency devaluations of September 1949. Less than a year later, another external stimulant, the Korean War, produced a violent outburst of speculative demand in the latter half of 1950, to be followed by increasing production and further price increases in 1951 as a result of the demand for military goods.

Western Europe as a whole staged a rapid recovery in the first two years after 1945 so that by 1947 industrial production had surpassed pre-war levels in most countries except Austria, Italy, France and the Netherlands. However, agriculture lagged behind, being adversely affected by poor crops as a result of bad weather, especially in 1946–47. The hard winter of 1947 also checked industrial output for a time. Moreover, serious shortages, especially of food and raw materials, continued to prevail throughout 1947 and into 1948. Nevertheless, progress continued, and by 1950–51, nearly all countries had increased their industrial output by a third or more above pre-war, with the largest gains taking place in some of the smaller countries, for example Sweden and Denmark (see Table 6.2). One should bear in mind, of course, that some countries (notably France, Belgium and Austria) had levels of output in 1938 that were the same or slightly lower than in 1929, so that their progress through to 1950 was not so striking when compared with Britain

Table 6.2 Western Europe: indices of industrial production (1937–38 = 100) and
agricultural production (1934–38 = 100)

	Industrial production 1947	*Agricultural production 1946–47*	*Industrial production 1949*	*Agricultural production 1948–49*	*Industrial production 1951*	*Agricultural production 1950–51*
Austria	56	70	123	74	166	98
Belgium	106	84	122	93	143	111
Denmark	123	97	142	97	162	126
Finland	117	75	142	106	177	115
France	92	82	118	95	134	108
Ireland	122	100	151	96	176	106
Italy	86	85	101	97	138	109
Luxemburg	109	–	138	–	175	–
Netherlands	95	87	126	104	145	123
Norway	115	98	140	101	158	118
Portugal	112	99	112	95	125	102
Spain	127	88	130	80	147	86
Sweden	141	104	157	109	171	113
Switzerland	–	107	–	112	–	120
UK	115	117	137	122	155	130

Sources: United Nations, *Economic Survey of Europe in 1950*, 43; *Economic Survey of Europe in 1951*, 179.

Note: The industrial production series exclude building but include electricity, gas and water and mining.

and Sweden, for example, where pre-war performance had been rather better. Agriculture still continued to lag behind. Indeed, it was not until the turn of the decade that most countries regained or exceeded their pre-war levels, and even by 1951–52, the gross agricultural output of western Europe was not much more than 10 per cent above the peacetime level.

Income gains, especially on a per capita basis, were lower than the rise in industrial output partly because of the slower growth in agriculture and the service sectors of the economy. In addition, there was a loss of income on overseas investment equivalent to about 1 per cent of the aggregate product of the main countries; this loss bore most heavily on Britain, France and the Netherlands, though in no country did it exceed 3 per cent of the national product. Furthermore, deterioration in trade terms involved a loss of some 3 per cent of the product of western Europe, the most seriously affected countries being Britain, the Netherlands and Denmark. When these factors are taken into account together with the increase in population, the gains in real per capita income up to 1951 turn out to be modest in many cases. The rise over the period 1938–51 was less than 10 per cent in the Netherlands, between 10 and 15 per cent in Britain, France and Denmark, 20 per cent in Switzerland and over 30 per cent in Sweden, while for Italy it was about the same as pre-war and in Germany well below the former level.

Because of the weak external position of western Europe in these years (see below), the recovery effort was dependent on the flow of overseas aid. At the same time, however, national policies did have an important contribution to make. The big task of reconstruction together with new government commitments in terms of social welfare, full employment and greater income equality, among other things, meant that governments generally intervened more extensively in economic matters than before the war. The need to allocate scarce investment resources also involved close control over economic variables, while problems of inflation and external imbalances required attention.

The range of policies adopted varied considerably and it is only possible to outline some of the most important of these. One of the major tasks was to raise the level of investment, especially in the basic industries, in order to ensure rapid growth in output and exports and improve productivity performance. All countries gave priority to investment at the expense of consumption. Private consumption was restrained by controls, while every effort was made to boost investment. Incentives included cheap and easy credit, favourable tax provisions and measures to stimulate savings. The government itself became the largest single investor either directly in its own public enterprises (France and Britain especially where a substantial part of industry was nationalized soon after the war) or through intermediary channels. Thus, in France between 1947 and 1951, some 30 per cent of all investments came from government sources, and in some countries the proportion was as high as one-half. Overall, investment spending as a proportion of income rose substantially above the pre-war levels, though government policies were not the sole reason for this. A high level of demand, rising prices and an investment backlog were conducive to capital spending, and in the event investment demand was so high that it had to be controlled in order to steer resources into priority areas. Some of the policies proved conflicting: for example, incentives to boost savings and investment but heavy taxes on high income earners and corporations. Controls over resource allocation were often piecemeal and too rigid so that the final allocation was not always the most optimal. Generally speaking, however, the investment policies were successful; they encouraged a high level of investment and resources were not seriously misallocated.

The control of inflation was a more difficult task. Given the pressure on scarce resources as a result of heavy reconstruction programmes, the commitment to full employment and social welfare policies, together with excess demand in the economy generally, the authorities could do no more than keep inflation within bounds. Indeed, the problem was aggravated by wartime policies of control, including subsidization of key commodities, which meant the build-up of a latent inflationary potential, while strong pressures came from the import side after the war because of a world shortage of commodities at a time of rising demand. Policy action varied, though in no case was it wholly successful. A number of countries (Denmark, the Netherlands, Norway, Sweden and Britain) used a combination of fiscal and physical controls to restrain prices and demand, though in time, as physical controls were gradually dismantled, the emphasis was shifted towards the control of aggregate demand by fiscal measures. Intermittent attempts were also made to control profits and restrain wages. But such controls could only suppress inflation; they could not stop it. Moreover, lax monetary policies worked in the opposite direction. In time, as demand and supply conditions became more normal, inflationary pressures abated, only to be revived by the devaluations of 1949 and the Korean War. Some countries, notably France and Italy, found it more expedient politically to let prices rise and therefore did relatively little to restrain inflation.

Undoubtedly, the priority in the post-war years was the need to improve the external account. In the first three years after the war, western Europe's trade deficit exceeded $5 billion as against $2 billion in the years before the war. The current account as a whole, which had been roughly in balance in 1938, showed a large though gradually diminishing deficit, from $7.4 billion in 1947 to $2.5 billion in 1950. It was principally a dollar imbalance because nearly three-quarters of Europe's cumulative deficit in the period 1946–50 was with the United States. Given the area's inability to earn sufficient dollars, it was forced to draw upon reserves and rely on large credits to make up the difference.

Reasons for the large deficits are not difficult to find. The war had shattered Europe's export trade, resulting in markets being lost for good, either to local or to North American suppliers. War damage and shortage of resources meant that imports were urgently required in the post-war years when exports were less readily available. The result was that export volumes fell more than imports over the period 1938–47, while unfavourable price trends had the effect of raising the total monetary deficit. In addition, there had been a large drop in invisible earnings through the liquidation of foreign assets, the loss of shipping and tourist trade, and a contraction in financial services, while new debt-servicing burdens had been incurred, notably by the United Kingdom. Finally, Europe's external position was affected adversely in the post-war years by a deterioration in the terms of trade and currency overvaluation, at least until 1949.

Adjustments to this new situation could be made in several ways, although in practice there were certain difficulties. The opportunities for adjustment in the invisible account were limited given the loss of foreign assets and shipping together with the growth of world fleets. This meant that the burden of adjustment would have to fall on commodity trade and principally exports, because a large part of Europe's imports consisted of food and raw materials and these were bound to rise in the early post-war years given the urgent need for commodities. Thus if the entire adjustment were to take place on the export side, the volume of exports on average would need to be about 80 per cent greater than in 1938 to pay for the same amount of imports, or 60 per cent if there were a 10 per cent saving on 1938 import volumes.

However, the position was slightly more complicated than this, because a large part of the deficit was with the dollar area. Unfortunately, this area was the main source of supply for food and raw materials and also for essential equipment, while Europe's ability to earn dollars to pay for these imports was, for one reason or another, limited. Apart from domestic supply problems, it was difficult for Europe to earn dollars directly in the North American market largely because of the relative self-sufficiency of the United States, while indirect dollar earnings from third countries, on which Europe had relied before the war to clear her accounts with the dollar area, were no longer available simply because these countries themselves were now in need of dollars. In other words, the restoration of external equilibrium was not simply a matter of a large increase in exports and a restraint on imports; it required in the main a vast improvement in Europe's dollar trading relationships.

In an effort to deal with the problem, most governments took active steps to increase exports and restrain imports. Resources were channelled into export activities, consumption was held down to release as many resources as possible for exports, while vigorous export promotion campaigns were launched. Imports were held in check by tight physical controls, the restraint on consumption and by import substitution wherever possible. The results, although superficially impressive, were not entirely satisfactory. The volume of west European imports remained consistently below the already low level of 1938: 15 per cent less in 1950 and 10 per cent less in 1951. However, the shifts in the sources of supply were the exact opposite of what was required. The fall in imports reflected the low level of supplies obtained from non-dollar sources (especially eastern Europe), whereas dollar imports were consistently above pre-war, by as much as 31 per cent in 1951. Likewise, export achievements were substantial but inadequate. The total volume of west European exports rose by 40 per cent between 1938 and 1951, but this was insufficient to cover the loss in invisible earnings and the effects of the deterioration in trade terms. Moreover, performance in the dollar area was not satisfactory. Though exports to the United States between 1949 and 1951 were well above pre-war, they remained below the level of 1925–29, while the share of western Europe's exports going to the dollar area rose only moderately. Thus, by the turn of the decade, the dollar scarcity still remained an intractable problem. Contemporary estimates suggested that Europe required additional dollar earnings of some $4 billion annually to make a full and effective adjustment in the external accounts. This figure takes into account the removal of restrictions against dollar imports, the elimination of American aid and the need to build up reasonable gold and dollar reserves. At the time, this seemed an almost impossible task, but during the course of the 1950s, Europe's balance of payments position was radically transformed for the better (see Chapter 7).

On balance, therefore, western Europe staged a remarkable recovery in the period 1945–50, though her external position continued to remain weak. The performance contrasts sharply with the unhappy experience after the First World War. Economic progress rested on the achievement and maintenance of high levels of employment and investment, a large influx of foreign aid and strong demand pressures, which were never allowed to get out of hand. However, the high level of demand did give rise to inflationary pressures that aggravated the exchange difficulties, hence the need to retain tight controls on imports and consumption and the resort to devaluation in 1949. In this period, the authorities became acutely aware of a problem that incidentally was to remain beyond the reconstruction years: this was their inability to pursue successfully a series of incompatible objectives, namely rapid expansion, full employment, price stability and external equilibrium. At the time, many governments were forced to rely on a fairly wide range of direct controls and sharp fiscal measures to suppress inflation, shore up the balance of payments and allocate resources to priority needs. These measures proved unpopular and in time they outlived their usefulness; they produced irrational effects on investment, trade and payments and they could not eliminate inflation when there were strong external forces pushing up prices. Under these conditions, it became increasingly difficult to maintain controls and the whole system was seriously weakened by onslaught from the demand side in 1950–51 arising from the 1949 devaluations and the Korean War. Henceforward, greater reliance was to be placed on more general methods of controlling inflation and achieving macroeconomic objectives (see Chapter 7).

The German situation

Germany deserves separate and more detailed treatment because its recovery experience was different from that of any other country in Europe. This in large part stemmed from the Allied and Soviet occupation policies, which until 1948 effectively checked any real progress. In 1947, industrial output, in both the western and eastern zones, was not much above what it had been at the end of the war, at 47 per cent and 33 per cent of the 1938 levels, respectively. During 1948, a radical policy change took place that encouraged a rapid recovery, so that by 1950–51 pre-war output levels were finally attained. Berlin, for obvious reasons, did not participate in this leap forward.

The plan to divide Germany had been formulated well before the end of the war. Spheres of influence were drawn up by the European Consultative Commission set up in November 1943 after a meeting in Moscow of the foreign ministers of the United States, the Soviet Union and the United Kingdom. The Soviet Union was particularly anxious to dissect Germany in the interest of its own security and to further its policy of hegemonic control in the eastern sector of Europe. The Commission therefore fixed the boundary line limits for the zones of occupation in Germany: three in the west and one in the east, with the division centering on Berlin, which effectively became the dividing line of the east–west split in Europe.

Initially, when the occupation forces took control, they were not only directed to hold down Germany but they were also precluded from undertaking rehabilitation schemes. In practice, these directions could not be carried out to the letter, apart from which the orders had an air of unreality at a time when the United States was providing relief aid to prevent starvation. In order to maintain themselves, the occupation authorities were obliged to carry out a certain amount of repair and reconstruction work, while they probably felt under some moral obligation to ensure that sufficient supplies of necessities were made available to the indigenous population. Thus a certain amount of restoration work was undertaken in this period, more especially in the US zone. However, such relief measures were relatively insignificant against the generally repressive impact of the occupation administrations. The occupation forces ran the zones on military lines, imposing detailed and rigid orders together with stringent controls to suppress inflationary forces. The result was that the economies were almost paralysed.

From the middle of 1947, this hardline attitude was gradually modified. It began to dawn on the Allied powers at last that a prosperous Europe would depend in large part on the reconstruction of the German economy. Furthermore, the increasing friction between the east and the west lent greater urgency to the need to strengthen Germany so as to provide a bulwark against the Soviet Union. Accordingly, the policy of repression was steadily abandoned in favour of constructive measures. These comprised the inclusion of Germany in the ERP programme, a sharp reduction in the dismantling schedules, currency reform and the removal of controls, more positive reconstruction measures by the forces of occupation and attempts to fuse the western zones into one. The latter efforts culminated in the formation of the German Federal Republic in September 1949, after which the Allies surrendered a substantial share of their power in Germany.

By far the most urgent task was that of currency reform. The war had left Germany's financial system in chaos, with an enormous oversupply of money in relation to the availability of goods, which meant strong inflationary pressures. These were suppressed for a time by the rationing and price control systems of the occupation authorities, but at the expense of strangling economic activity. Moreover, a significant black-market sector developed, in which average prices were some fifty times higher than the legal prices. The desirability of reforming the currency was not in dispute, but its implementation was delayed by the large number of different plans put forward, and also by political factors. The Potsdam Agreement of 1945 had specified that Germany should be treated as one unit in economic matters, including currency reform. However, disagreement among the Allied powers themselves did little to further this objective in the early years, while the clash between east and west over reparations and the control of German industry held up progress with currency reform. Russian intransigence on this issue ultimately led to separate currency reforms being undertaken in the two sectors, a move that merely served to strengthen the division of the country into two parts. The split involved some short-term losses for West Germany, for example food imports from the east, but it did not have a serious or lasting impact on the economy of West Germany.

When the currency reform was finally enacted in the summer of 1948, it proved extremely rigorous and inequitable. It reduced the money supply from the 122.4 billion Reichsmarks presented for conversion to 10.5 billion new Deutschmarks, though this was increased to 13.2 billion Deutschmarks by the end of the year. It heavily penalized people with liquid assets but greatly improved the position of those with non-monetary assets. However, it did markedly increase incentives for business, and with the subsequent removal of controls the way was left open for a sharp rise in profits. Thus after two or three years of stagnation, industrial output shot forward in the latter half of 1948, and thenceforward Germany's recovery proceeded unchecked. It was assisted by a large influx of foreign aid (which provided foreign currency and investment funds), a strong revival in exports and an elastic labour supply, together with policies designed to stimulate investment and profits, hold down wages and ensure monetary stability. However, it was not until 1951 that industrial production exceeded the pre-war level, while agriculture and services lagged behind. Net per capita income still fell short of the pre-war level because of the large influx of population from the east. Nevertheless, the economy was in a healthier state than it had been a few years earlier.

East Germany fared less well under Soviet domination, though even here there was a marked recovery after 1948. Berlin, however, was another matter. The city was badly damaged by the war, with the result that its economic and financial activities were seriously impaired. But worse was yet to come. A partial dismantling of industry soon after the war followed by a curtailment of foreign aid and the Russian blockade left Berlin almost prostrate. Industrial production, already at a low level in 1946 and 1947, declined even further, to just under 20 per cent of pre-war in 1949. Though conditions eased subsequently with the renewal of aid to the western sector, it was not until the middle of the 1950s that the city got within striking distance of former levels of economic activity.

Socialist transformation in Eastern Europe

Reconstruction and recovery in eastern Europe were at first slower than in the west, though later the east made up some of the ground lost. The initial lag was not surprising, given the fact that eastern Europe had been more severely devastated than the west. Whatever temporary gains may have arisen from servicing the German war machine, ultimately the region bore a heavy cost. The scale of losses and destruction was probably greater than during the First World War. Millions of people had been killed, murdered, tortured, wounded, displaced or simply gone missing. There was extensive destruction of property and equipment, severe despoliation of agricultural land and total disorganization of transport and financial systems and the means of distribution. When hostilities ceased, industrial production in most countries, apart from the Soviet Union, was one-half or less that of pre-war, while agricultural output was extremely depressed. In fact normal economic life had almost ground to a halt in many areas and many people were on the brink of starvation.

The two worst affected countries were Yugoslavia and Poland. The bitter partisan and inter-ethnic fighting in the former country resulted in massive losses of assets and lives. About one-tenth of the population perished, around one-half of the country's transport equipment, including roads, was destroyed, as was a similar proportion of the livestock, one-fifth of the housing stock and one-third or more of industrial capacity, including 70 per cent of iron-making facilities. Yugoslavia suffered one of the worst falls in the standard of living in Europe, and by the end of the war a large part of the population was bordering on starvation. Poland did not fare much better either. Bitter resistance fighting took its toll on the population: six million perished, half of them Jewish. Again there was extensive damage to property and capital stock: one-third of the housing, two-thirds of industrial premises, one-third of the railway track and 80 per cent of the rolling stock were destroyed. In agriculture, around 60 per cent of the livestock, 25 per cent of the forests and 15 per cent of agricultural buildings were lost or destroyed. Damage to land resources through wanton laying of waste by the armies of occupation and subsequently the liberating forces and the lack of fertilization and general neglect of upkeep meant that much of the land was rendered infertile for the time being.

The losses suffered by Hungary were also substantial, though she possibly fared a little better than either Yugoslavia and Poland. More than one-half the industrial capacity and two-thirds of the transport equipment were destroyed or rendered useless, the livestock population was reduced by nearly one-half and about one-fifth of the housing stock was destroyed. War damage and destruction were also serious elsewhere in eastern Europe, but generally less extensive. Bulgaria, Romania and Czechoslovakia managed to escape the worst of the direct conflict, and so they emerged from the war with their productive structures in better shape. Their capital losses were less extensive than in the other three countries and output levels were also less seriously affected. Thus, income and output in Yugoslavia and Poland fell by 50 per cent or more between 1938 and 1944/45 and 40 per cent in Hungary, but in Czechoslovakia the drop was only around one-quarter.

The overall reduction in productive activity was greater in some cases than the actual loss or destruction of physical assets seems to indicate. This can be explained by the chaotic conditions prevailing in most of these countries at the end of the conflict. More telling in the short term than the loss of capital assets was the sheer scale of dislocation and disruption to economic systems and normal economic life arising from six years or so of mobilization and warfare, reflected in the severe shortage of working capital, of essential raw materials, components and repair facilities, the scarcity of technical skills, bottlenecks in communications, the problems of converting to peacetime production, and above all the utter exhaustion of undernourished populations. After several years of struggle and severe privation, few people had the strength and will to exert themselves unduly, especially because food shortages reduced their calorific intake. The general shortage of foodstuffs, especially filler foods such as grains and potatoes, was a real problem in the immediate aftermath of war. For example, Poland suffered a fall of 60 per cent in bread and coarse grains output, while meat production was only about 14 per cent of pre-war. The shortage of fats and animal products was particularly acute as a result of the loss of livestock and the lack of fodder. In some countries, the production of fats was only a fraction of normal: 13 per cent in Poland, 25 per cent in Yugoslavia and less than 50 per cent in Czechoslovakia.

Food shortages were certainly the most pressing problem in the short term in view of the imminence of starvation. The food problem was a global one and it was exacerbated by distributional difficulties worldwide because of shipping losses and the breakdown of inland transport facilities. Eastern Europe's position was also aggravated by the limited means to pay for imports from the dollar area, which was virtually the only ready source of supply in the short term. Thus apart from anything else, it soon became apparent that without some external assistance many people would soon die of starvation. In fact, but for temporary relief under the UNRRA programme, this would certainly have been the case. These relief supplies were of vital importance to Poland, Czechoslovakia, Hungary and Albania in the immediate post-war years; for example, they amounted to about 11 per cent of Polish national income in 1946. However, they declined rapidly after 1946, and eastern Europe, for obvious reasons, was not included in the Marshall Plan. Thus eastern Europe had to struggle along with limited external assistance; the Soviet Union provided little aid and indeed exacted reparations from East Germany and her former allies Hungary and Romania (see below).

Amid the many difficulties facing these countries, they also had to contend with radical regime transformation soon after the war. Though by the end of 1945 the Soviet Union had become the dominating influence in eastern Europe, only Yugoslavia had in fact succumbed to the socialist challenge, with the establishment in November 1945 of the Socialist Federal Republic of Yugoslavia. Here, the work of Tito and the partisan cause was instrumental in creating new political institutions and mobilizing the disparate ethnic elements under the banner of nationalism. Elsewhere in eastern Europe interim coalition governments, with the communists as just one component, were the general rule in the early post-war period.

Yet within the span of some three years, all the countries of this region had acquired full socialist regimes, adopting the Soviet model as the benchmark. This sudden transformation may at first sight appear puzzling, because the majority of the populations in these countries did not have strong communist leanings. For example, in Poland barely 5 per cent of the population was said to be committed to the communist cause, and the same was true of other countries. It is of course tempting to see the role of the Soviet Union as the moving force behind the regime transformation in view of its powerful influence in the region, even before the war, when agents were infiltrating to spread the communist gospel. Nevertheless, although communist support did gain some ground, it was far from being a dominating force at the point in time.

The conundrum can perhaps be best explained in terms of what Rothschild (1989) sees as the element of continuity between German conquest and control and the shift to communist rule, which provided a break with what went before. The Great Depression and the Second World War had seriously weakened the power of the old political guard at a time when there was a growing demand among the population for change. The communists exploited these opportunities to the full, and in many respects their methods of gaining control bore a striking resemblance to those of the former National Socialists in Germany. Within the large multiparty coalitions of the early post-war years the communists, with assistance from the Soviet Union, were able to subvert the normal political processes and emerge as the dominant political force by means of fraudulent electoral practices and terrorist tactics. Non-communist elements were steadily ousted from the scene of power by various malpractices such as beatings, jailings and death threats. As the element of terror increased, many victims either capitulated or fled abroad, leaving the communists to assume control. By the end of 1948, communist administrations were in full control in all the countries under rulers who owed their allegiance and power to the Soviet Union. Once in command these dictators then set about preventing any reversal by intensive campaigns of Russification, adopting the Soviet model of the one party state and centralized control of all political activity. In the course of time, this led to the abuse of their position and the subjugation of the populations to the whims of authoritarian dictators.

Thus for all the east European countries, the later 1940s was a time of violent political and social upheaval involving a complete change in the system of property relationships and the emergence of the state as the main agent of economic activity. Accordingly, in the reconstruction years, all countries moved rapidly from capitalism to socialism. In most cases, a start had been made by the interim coalition governments, but it was greatly speeded up and extended under the new regimes. Land reform was the first item on the agenda, followed by the expropriation of industry, finance, banking, trade and finally distribution. By 1949 most major branches of economic activity were owned and operated by the state. Foreign trade also became a state monopoly and the countries of the Eastern Bloc were encouraged by the Soviet Union to draw closer together economically to the exclusion of contacts with western countries. Early in 1949, the Council for Mutual Economic Assistance (CMEA or Comecon) was established for the purpose of fostering closer economic relations and more integrated development among member countries of the socialist camp.

However, progress in respect of the socialization of agriculture was more protracted. The first main task had been that of land reform in order to satisfy the strong demand of the peasantry for greater equality in land ownership. The land reforms of the inter-war years had not fully solved the problem because there were still many large estates and many peasants without land. Thus, apart from Bulgaria, where the land ownership system was equitable, extensive land reforms were promulgated in all countries. At this juncture, the land was not nationalized but redistributed to smallholders and landless peasants, and in the process large-scale land ownership was phased out. But it was not until the early 1950s, with the decision to collectivize agriculture against former promises to the contrary by the communist leaders, that the transition to a socialist agriculture was finally made.

In practice, the land reforms may have been a mixed blessing, though assessment is difficult because they were soon overtaken by the collectivization programme. No doubt the reforms satisfied many peasants, because smallholders and landless peasants received plots of land, which provided a means of livelihood, albeit a poor one, and helped to erase the concept of land hunger. But commercially, it was less of a benefit, because it fragmented many large commercial farms into tiny plots, not all of which could be farmed efficiently. As a consequence, the changeover probably helped to retard the recovery of agricultural output at a time when it was most required. Nor could land reform fully solve the basic problem of overpopulation on the land, which in the long term could be alleviated only by industrialization and structural change.

The full development of socialist planning took longer to implement. because until private enterprise was fully eliminated from the scene, it was difficult to introduce rigorous planning exercises. There was fairly widespread support for some form of planning given the underdeveloped state of the economies and the urgent need to industrialize. In fact. the interim coalition governments had taken tentative steps in this direction because short-term reconstruction plans were launched soon after the war which focused attention on large-scale industry and set targets for the main sectors of the economy. Towards the end of the decade, when the reconstruction phase was drawing to a close and the policy of nationalization was nearing completion, attention was turned to longer-term and more comprehensive planning under the socialist model.

Yugoslavia, the first country to set up a socialist state, was also the first to introduce long-term planning, with the inauguration of a Five-Year Plan in 1947. However, Yugoslavia also adopted a more independent line from Moscow, and consequently it was expelled in the summer of 1948 from the Communist Information Bureau (Cominform), which had been set up late the previous year to facilitate Moscow's control over international communism. Other countries followed suit, though they did not depart from the Soviet line. In 1949, Bulgaria and Czechoslovakia launched Five-Year Plans, Hungary did likewise in 1950, as did Poland but with a Six-Year Plan, while Romania brought up the rear with a Five-Year Plan in 1951.

The main objectives behind these new planning strategies was to build up powerful economies by means of central planning and detailed direction and control of all economic activity to the almost complete exclusion of private enterprise and market forces. Inevitably, therefore, this involved the final offensive against the remnants of the private sector, especially in the retail trades, together with a start on socializing agriculture. By the early 1950s, therefore, few traces of private sector activity were left other than in agriculture. The chief feature of the exercise was the centrally drawn-up plan setting out in some detail the targets to be met in different sectors of the economy. Norms for labour productivity were prescribed and conversion ratios between inputs and final outputs specified. Wage rates and material allocations were to be related to these norms. The plans also emphasized the need to maximize growth by boosting investment, with priority being given to heavy capital goods sectors and military equipment at the expense of consumer products. In other words, it was to be extensive growth at all costs rather than intensive development. As we shall see in later chapters, for a time the planning strategy worked, in that it delivered large absolute growth rates, but in the longer term, extensive growth proved to be inefficient and technologically backward and was a factor behind the collapse of the socialist regimes at the end of the century.

To return to the immediate issue of reconstruction and recovery in the post-war era, eastern Europe was a slow starter compared with the west, but given the daunting problems facing the countries, this is scarcely surprising. In the latter part of the period, there was some catching up and the overall performance was creditable. The situation in the immediate aftermath of war appeared hopeless, because many people were on the brink of starvation. In fact, had it not been for the early emergency relief efforts principally under the aegis of the UNRRA, the loss of life through outright destitution would have been serious. Relief supplies from this agency were especially crucial to the former allied sympathizers (Czechoslovakia, Poland and Yugoslavia) in the early years. Much of the aid came in the form of food, clothing and medical supplies, though there was also some preliminary assistance specifically to foster the rehabilitation of agriculture and industry. The chief beneficiary of UNRRA supplies in the first eighteen months to the end of 1946 was Poland, with 10 per cent of that country's total supply of goods and services coming from that source, with a peak in the second quarter of 1946 of 16 per cent.

The short-term assistance was a welcome lifeline to these countries, especially because most of the aid came free of charge, though western experience with Marshall Aid was to demonstrate that more was required. The major part of UNRRA relief was designed to satisfy the most urgent short-term needs, and it was heavily concentrated in the years 1945 and 1946. Moreover, the assistance was made available only to allied partisans, so that Bulgaria, Hungary and Romania were automatically excluded. The same was true of commercial credits, the bulk of which went to Czechoslovakia, Poland and Yugoslavia. Nor was there any fol-low-up for mainstream reconstruction as in the west because the outbreak of the Cold War precluded Eastern Europe from participating in Marshall Aid.

Nor surprisingly did the Soviet Union do much to help its socialist brethren. In fact, rather the reverse in the case of the ex-enemy countries, because it demanded substantial reparations from them, with only Bulgaria escaping relatively lightly. Thus eastern Europe was denuded of much of its productive assets, which were shipped to the Soviet Union to assist the reconstruction of that country's devastated economy. In 1945–46, Hungary's reparation deliveries to the USSR amounted to no less than 17 per cent of an already depressed national income, and even in subsequent years the proportion ranged between 7–10 per cent. In the case of Romania, the proportion of income surrendered amounted to 14–15 per cent in 1947–48, about half the deliveries consisting of oil. But East Germany probably bore the worst brunt of the reparation policy as well as having to meet the cost of Soviet troops stationed in the German Democratic Republic (GDR). At the peak in 1950–51, Soviet exactions were over 17 per cent of the GDR's national income and the impositions continued at a declining rate for another two or three years until riots in 1953 forced the Soviet Union to modify its policy.

In general, therefore, eastern Europe was treated more harshly than after the First World War. But this, of course, was not the only factor delaying the recovery. Frontier changes and population movements posed considerable problems for Czechoslovakia, Poland and East Germany, especially the movement of German nationals to the west. Inflation and currency disorders were also common features, especially in the former occupied countries, and extensive fiscal, monetary and currency reforms were required to deal with the situation. The worst cases were in Romania and Hungary, where prices moved into the hyperinflationary phase (in Hungary's case, a historical record), while Poland's inflation was strong in the first two years following hostilities. By 1948, however, when the German currency was reformed, most countries had brought their financial systems under control. Finally, one should stress again the inevitable dislocation caused by regime changes and the concomitant transition from capitalism to socialism.

In the event, the strength of the recovery in eastern Europe was remarkable. By 1949, the general level of activity had exceeded that of pre-war in all but Romania and East Germany, largely because of the strong rise in industrial production, which was given priority in the planning process. Apart from the special case of

East Germany, where Soviet policy undoubtedly hampered recovery, all countries had exceeded their pre-war industrial production levels, in some cases such as Bulgaria and Poland by a large margin, whereas two years earlier the shortfall had still been substantial. However, agriculture did less well. By 1948–49, agricultural output in the seven countries was still only about 80 per cent of the pre-war 1934–38 base. This was partly because of the low priority accorded to the sector in the planning mechanism and the uncertain future status of the industry. Indeed, it was to be a few more years before agriculture recovered fully from the ravages of war.

The slower recovery in agriculture and also in the service sectors of the economy had the effect of moderating the overall gains in national income, while per capita changes varied considerably from country to country because of differing population experiences. Thus, in East Germany and Romania per capita income levels remained below those of pre-war because of population movements and lower rates of recovery. Poland and Czechoslovakia, on the other hand, recorded significant increases in income per head because of strong recovery and population losses. However, the consumer benefited little from any improvement. While the distribution of income may have been more equitable under the socialist regimes from what had gone before, the amount consumed by the population was deliberately kept down by the planning authorities in the interests of pushing up the rate of investment and the priority accorded to producer durables. Consumption was also depressed by the slow recovery of food production, while the per capita consumption of non-food goods fell short of former levels. East Germany was easily the worst affected in this respect. Consumers bore the brunt of the harsh reparations policy of the Soviet Union, so that consumption remained depressed for several years. Even after 1950, the share of income going to personal consumption was only around 50 per cent, compared with more than 60 per cent pre-war. Moreover, the quality and variety of consumer goods on offer left much to be desired.

All things considered eastern Europe's recovery from the war was commendable, though at a cost to the consumer. After a slow start, the overall performance bears comparison with that of western Europe. Given the manifold problems facing these countries, the transition to new regimes and the limited assistance from external sources, it was no mean achievement. It speaks volumes for the grit and determination of the populace and the achievements of the planners in driving these countries forward and placing their economies on a firm footing. By the start of the new decade, all the countries of the region had institutionalized their planning mechanisms, the transition from capitalism to socialism was more or less complete except for agriculture, while the links with the international economy had largely been severed. Planning by the state had become a new way of life for these countries. Whether the New Order was capable in the years to come of delivering the needs of society is another matter, and one that will be discussed in later chapters.

*

The Soviet Union's recovery was even more impressive given the fact that the country had suffered enormous damage during the war. Apart from large industrial losses in the occupied areas, there had been serious damage in the agrarian sector, including substantial livestock losses. However, industry proved more resilient, and, as already noted, Soviet industrial production staged a marked recovery after the low point in 1942 largely as a result of the creation of a new industrial base in the east. Thus, by the end of the war, industrial output in Russia was closer to the pre-war level than in any of the eastern countries. The Fourth Five-Year Plan (the third had been started in the late 1930s, but was interrupted by the war) was to cover the period 1946–50 and gave priority to the reconstruction of devastated areas and the continued build-up of heavy industry, especially in the newer regions not damaged by war. The results were impressive in the industrial sector, though agriculture failed to meet its targets. By 1950, industrial production was higher than before the war, with the main expansion taking place in producer goods. However, agriculture barely managed to attain its former peacetime level of production. There was also a large rise in national income, but the bulk of this increase was devoted to investment and defence and little went to raising the levels of consumption, which remained close to or slightly below those of pre-war.

Questions for discussion

1   Compare and contrast the post-war settlement with that after the First World War.
2   What contribution did Marshall Aid make to the post-war recovery of Europe?
3   Why did eastern Europe become a socialist bloc after the war?
4   Why was recovery in Germany delayed?
5   What part did political factors play in the post-war configuration of Europe?

7 The golden age of post-war economic growth

Post-war growth in historical perspective

Without a shadow of doubt, the two decades of the 1950s and 1960s were, from an economic point of view, by far the best in the whole of the twentieth century. Not only in Europe, but also globally, economic growth was by historical standards exceptionally strong. Even in Africa, many countries experienced robust growth at the end of the colonial period. These were in truth the boom years or golden era of the century. What was so remarkable was not only the high rates of growth recorded but also that there were few serious interruptions to economic activity of the type so characteristic of the inter-war years. In fact. depressions of the traditional type were conspicuous by their absence, the worst being a slowing down of the rate of growth. Nor were there any serious financial and monetary crises similar to those in the inter-war years and those after the end of the golden years of expansion.

Considering how Europe had suffered during the 1940s, the subsequent economic performance seems little short of spectacular. After the initial post-war recovery, which by 1949–50 had brought most countries back to, or beyond, their pre-war output levels, a sustained rise in output and industrial production occurred in all regions: industrial western Europe, southern Europe (Greece, Portugal, Spain and Turkey), and the eastern sector. In fact, there were few significant interruptions to progress and Europe's advance was more rapid than that of the rest of the world. Between 1950 and 1970, European gross domestic product (GDP) grew on average at about 5.5 per cent per annum and 4.4 per cent on a per capita basis, as against world average rates of 5.0 per cent and 3.0 per cent respectively. Industrial production rose even faster, at 7.1 per cent a year compared with a world rate of 5.9 per cent. Thus, by the later date, output per head in Europe was almost two and one-half times greater than in 1950. The pace of advance contrasts sharply with the long-term rate of growth before 1950. According to Bairoch's calculations, European income per capita growth barely reached 1 per cent per annum from 1800 through to 1950 as against 4.5 per cent since. In other words, in the generation from the late 1940s, per capita income had made greater progress than in all of the 150 years or so before 1950. The European growth record also compares favourably with the post-war record of the United States, a country that emerged stronger from the two world wars; after 1950, American per-capita output growth was only one-half that of Europe at 2.2 per cent per annum. Only Japan of the major countries outperformed Europe in the 1950s and 1960s.

The net result of this striking performance was a considerable strengthening of Europe's economic position in the world economy. Whereas during the inter-war years and through to 1950, Europe's economic influence was declining as a result of the effects of two world wars and a great depression, after 1950 or thereabouts, her share of global economic activity increased noticeably. During the period 1950–70, her share of world output of goods and services (GDP) rose from 37 per cent to 41 per cent, while in the case of industrial production the increase was even greater, from 39 per cent to 48 per cent. By contrast, Europe's population grew at only about one-half the world rate (1.1 per cent as against 2 per cent per annum) so that by 1970, she accounted for some 26 per cent of the world's population compared with 31 per cent in 1950.

An important feature of the post-war period was the widespread diffusion of growth throughout Europe generally. Virtually all countries experienced continuous growth and at a higher level than anything achieved in the previous half century. Though differences in national income accounting practices and data discrepancies make precise comparisons hazardous, it seems that on balance eastern and southern Europe did slightly better than the industrial west. The growth of output in the eastern communist countries (including the USSR) averaged 7.0 per cent per annum in the 1950s and 1960s, that in southern Europe was between 5 and 6 per cent, while in the industrial west it was of the order of 4.5 per cent. However, in per capita terms, the differences are less on account of the faster rate of population increase in southern and eastern Europe. Nevertheless, differences in output growth of the order of magnitude shown here were not sufficient to close the gap in income levels between the rich industrial west and the rest of Europe. This chapter is concerned primarily with the dozen or so countries in the former area, while the next chapter examines the experience of the east European countries, which operated within a different political and economic institutional framework.

Table 7.1 provides some key data on the countries of the industrial west. It can be readily seen that the growth in output was fairly uniform between the 1950s and 1960s, though a slight acceleration is apparent from the late 1950s. The fastest-growing countries were Austria, West Germany, France, Italy and the Netherlands, though there were some contrasts between the two decades. France, for example, stepped up her growth rate appreciably in the 1960s, whereas Austria and Germany both recorded a deceleration in output expansion. At the other extreme, Britain and Ireland, though improving on past performance, did badly compared with all other countries in western Europe, with growth rates less than half those of the most successful nations. The remaining countries expanded at close to the average for the region as a whole or slightly below. On balance, there was some tendency over time for output growth rates to converge towards the average of around 4.5 per cent.

The growth of output per capita was also fairly rapid, partly as a result of the modest increases in population. Apart from Switzerland, most countries had

Table 7.1 Industrial western Europe: total output, employment, labour productivity and population, 1950–69 (annual percentage compound rates of growth)

	Output (GDP at 1963 f.c.)			Employment			Output per person employed			Population 1950–70
	1950/2–1967/9	1950/2–1958/60	1958/60–1967/9	1950/2–1967/9	1950/2–1958/60	1958/60–1967/9	1950/2–1967/9	1950/2–1958/60	1958/60–1967/9	
Austria	5.0	5.7	4.5	0.1	0.4	-0.2	5.0	5.3	4.7	0.3
Belgium	3.5	2.5	4.5	0.4	0.2	0.6	3.1	2.4	3.8	0.6
Denmark	4.0	3.2	4.7	1.1	1.0	1.2	2.8	2.2	3.4	0.7
West Germany	6.2	7.5	5.1	1.2	2.2	0.3	5.0	5.2	4.8	0.9
Finland	4.4	4.3	4.6	0.9	1.0	0.9	3.5	3.3	3.7	0.7
France	5.0	4.3	5.5	0.4	0.0	0.7	4.6	4.4	4.8	0.9
Ireland	2.5	0.8	4.0	-0.7	-1.6	0.1	3.2	2.5	3.9	0.0
Italy	5.4	5.3	5.5	0.4	0.7	0.2	5.0	4.6	5.3	0.7
Netherlands	5.0	4.5	5.5	1.1	1.1	1.2	3.9	3.4	4.3	1.3
Norway	4.1	3.0	4.9	0.3	0.0	0.6	3.7	3.1	4.3	0.9
Sweden	4.1	3.6	4.5	0.3	0.2	0.4	3.8	3.4	4.1	0.7
Switzerland	4.2	4.0	4.4	1.6	1.4	1.8	2.5	2.6	2.5	1.5
UK	2.7	2.4	2.9	0.5	0.5	0.4	2.2	1.8	2.5	0.5
Average	4.6	4.5	4.7	0.6	0.8	0.5	3.9	3.6	4.2	0.8

Source: United Nations (Economic Commission for Europe), *Economic Survey of Europe in 1971*, Part 1, *The European Economy from the 1950s to the 1970s*, New York, 1972, 6, Table 1.2

population growth rates of less than 1 per cent per annum. The overall average for the region was just under 0.8 per cent per annum, giving a per-capita output growth of around 4 per cent. Though slightly less than the average for all Europe, this was still high by historical standards and it implied a considerable advance in real living standards for the majority of the population. Low population growth also meant that the annual additions to the labour force were modest (about 0.6 per cent per annum), though a few countries (Germany, Switzerland and the Netherlands) had labour inputs above 1 per cent per annum. From this, it follows that the main output gains were derived from increased labour productivity (see Table 7.1 and below).

As one might expect with such rapid growth, there were significant broad structural changes within the economies in question. Agriculture almost everywhere declined in importance in terms of both output and employment shares. The increase in agricultural output was only about one-third to one-half of the rate recorded for domestic output as a whole, at approximately 2 per cent per annum for industrial western Europe (though faster in the east), ranging from a fall in Norway to 2.5 per cent in the UK and Sweden. Employment in agriculture fell rapidly in most countries, averaging about 3.5 per cent a year, with the result that the share of employment of agriculture declined faster than its output share. For some countries, notably Britain and Belgium, the change was not significant because agriculture accounted for only a small proportion of both output and employment at the beginning of the period. But in the case of Finland, Ireland, Italy and to a lesser extent France, the shift from agriculture was of some significance because of the greater weight of this sector initially. By 1980, few industrial countries in western Europe had an agrarian sector that accounted for a large share of income and employment.

The most rapidly growing sector of the economy was industry, though mainly in terms of output rather than employment. This sector gained most of the loss of output share by agriculture, but its share of employment remained fairly constant, except in Italy and Ireland, where it rose rapidly. In few countries, apart from Britain and Germany, did it account for more than 40 per cent of total employment by the end of the 1960s. By contrast, the service trades (construction, transport and communications and other services) absorbed an increasing share of employment while maintaining a fairly stable output share, a reflection in part of the low rate of productivity growth in this sector. Thus, its overall share of employment in the industrial west rose from 45 per cent to 54 per cent and in most cases big declines in the share of employment of agriculture were accompanied by a corresponding rise in the service sector's share of this factor. Investment patterns were characterized by a shift towards services at the expense of industry.

Apart from high growth and structural change, there are several features of western Europe's development since 1950 that contrast sharply with experience in the inter-war period. As already noted, there were few interruptions to the growth process. Rarely did countries in the post-war period experience absolute contractions in output in any one year, and the old trade cycle of the past, which involved severe declines in economic activity in the depressed phases of 1921,

1929–32 and 1937–38, disappeared. Of course, this does not mean that economies were perfectly stable throughout the period; fluctuations in activity occurred frequently, but these were usually against the backdrop of continually rising output. Thus, recessions were characterized by decelerations in output growth rather than by absolute contractions, while boom periods were those when output was advancing more rapidly than the secular trend. This has prompted some commentators to suggest that the former trade cycle had been replaced by a growth cycle for which the peaks and troughs can be determined by the rates of acceleration or deceleration in aggregate growth. The notion that the business cycle (or what was formally referred to as the trade cycle) was becoming obsolete was soon to be shattered by the events of the 1970s and beyond.

The concept of the growth cycle has also been linked with the policy reactions to changes in growth rates, giving rise to what has been termed a political growth cycle or policy-induced instability, as politicians manipulated the economy to suit their electoral interests. Although many would not be happy with the latter interpretation, there are also some writers who have challenged the very concept of the growth cycle itself. Tests of the growth cycle hypothesis for the period 1950–69 for sixteen OECD countries proved to be statistically insignificant (Licari and Gilbert 1974). In other words, the fluctuations observed in practice were found to be not statistically distinguishable from those generated by a random process. There was no systematic regularity akin to the pre-war cycle or nineteenth century cycles, and exogenous influences, particularly policy-dominated ones, may have been responsible for producing these random fluctuations, in which case the growth cycle may be, as Licari and Gilbert note, more of an interpretative myth than an empirical reality.

Even if this interpretation is correct, it does not alter the fact that there were fluctuations in economic activity in all countries in the post-war period that are readily distinguishable. On average, they occurred every four to five years, and while there was a certain degree of divergence in timing among countries, it is also possible to discern some pattern of synchronization in the movements of various countries. The first major boom after the immediate post-war recovery phase culminated in 1950–51 with the Korean War. It was dominated, as might be expected, by reconstruction and the final recovery from the impact of the war, assisted by American aid and later by rearmament. Reaction after the Korean War brought a recession in 1952, when rates of growth fell sharply. In the following year, expansionary forces set in again and these reached a peak in the middle of the 1950s, after which the rate of expansion tailed off through to 1958. The recession of that year was severe by post-war standards; GDP grew by less than 2 per cent in western Europe and in one or two countries (Belgium, Norway and Ireland) it actually fell. During 1959, a strong recovery set in and this ushered in a longish period of steady expansion, though with minor peaks in 1960 and 1964 and troughs in 1963 and 1967. The expansion was fed by a massive movement of workers from Mediterranean regions to the industrial areas of Europe, involving the migration of about 5 million workers between 1959 and 1965. Late in 1967, a new cycle of expansion began, culminating in a peak two years later and then followed by two years of slow growth. An important feature of these years was the almost universal pressure of inflationary forces; inflation followed output expansion more rapidly than in earlier cycles, it was stronger, and it persisted and even accelerated when rates of growth declined and unemployment increased in the early 1970s. It not only delayed re-expansionary policies to deal with the recession but it also marked a new and alarming pattern of relationships between output, employment and prices for the future.

The inflationary pressures provide another marked contrast with the pre-war period. Whereas for much of the inter-war period, prices (apart from during the strong European inflations of the early 1920s) were trending downward on balance, during the 1950s and 1960s, there was a persistent tendency for prices to increase, with some acceleration in the rate of increase towards the end of the 1960s. On average, prices in western Europe rose by 3–4 per cent per annum through to the end of the period, with low rates of increase being recorded in Germany and Belgium and high rates in France, Denmark and the Netherlands. However, actual rates of inflation were nowhere near as large as they were to become in the first half of the 1970s. At the same time, there was a continuous upward drift in wages and inflexibility in a downward direction, which helped to set a floor to consumption levels in recessionary periods.

The level of unemployment was also lower than in the inter-war years. It is true that in the first half of the 1950s, some countries, notably Austria, Denmark, Belgium, Germany and Italy, were still experiencing high rates of unemployment, but in most other countries, unemployment was less than 2 per cent of the labour force during the 1950s, and throughout the decade unemployment was declining everywhere. The average unemployment rate in western Europe during the 1950s was 2.9 per cent and this dropped to 1.5 per cent in the following decade, with only Italy and Belgium recording rates above 2 per cent. Precise comparisons with the earlier period are difficult to make because of changes in the basis of compiling unemployment data in the post-war period. But there is no doubt of the marked improvement compared with the inter-war years, when unemployment rates on average were double or treble those of the post-1950 period. Concomitant with the shift to full employment, there was greater utilization of capacity and less drag exerted by declining basic sector industries than was the case before 1939.

The volume of commodity trade grew rapidly in the post-war years, in contrast with the near-stagnation in the period 1913–50. After 1948, the volume of imports and exports of western Europe rose about twice as fast as GDP, with exports rising by between 8 per cent and 9 per cent per annum during the 1950s and 1960s. The exchange of manufactures or semi-manufactures among high-income countries was the most buoyant sector of international trade. This expansion was facilitated by a more favourable international environment, in particular the greater degree of international economic cooperation on trade and payments matters, which, among other things, ensured the requisite amount of international liquidity to finance the growing trade volumes. This is not to say that the international financial machinery always worked smoothly, because some countries experienced periodic payment problems, but until the 1970s there was nothing akin to the severe monetary and financial disorders of the inter-war period. For example, there was an absence of severe deflationary shocks to the international system, either government-induced or otherwise, of the type imparted, say, by the collapse of American lending in the late 1920s.

Perhaps most important of all, the government's role in the economy changed dramatically in the post-war period. Not only did the state absorb a greater, and increasing, share of national resources, which in some cases involved an extension of public ownership of economic activities, but it also accepted responsibility for maintaining a high and stable level of employment, achieving faster growth and greater stability, among other things. Such policy objectives were not regarded as falling within the province of governments during the inter-war years. Then the basic aims of policy were of a kind that would now be regarded as of a second order of magnitude, namely the restoration of currency stability, maintenance of the gold standard and balancing budgets. The tools of economic policy and the statistical information on economies were also more limited in the earlier period; the main weapon of economic management, at least until it became discredited in the early 1930s, was monetary policy, whereas an important new dimension in the form of fiscal policy was added in the post-war period, as well as a number of smaller, more specific measures such as incomes policies, which previously would have been considered inappropriate. Some countries, notably France, also went in for economic planning in a big way. In effect, therefore, governments in the post-war period accepted a wider range of responsibilities, including overall management of economic activity, and they used a greater variety of policy measures to achieve their objectives than their counterparts before 1939. The extent to which the greater degree of state involvement was responsible for the more satisfactory economic out-turn in the 1950s and 1960s remains to be seen.

Some of the above points are taken up later in this chapter, when the forces affecting the process of development are examined. First, however, we propose to pursue a more formal analysis of the role of factor inputs in the growth process to see what contribution labour, capital and technical progress made to the growth of output.

Sources of growth: factor inputs and technology

In recent years, the debate about the sources of growth has reached gigantic proportions. Various writers have stressed the importance of different factors in trying to explain Europe's post-war growth; for example, Kindleberger has espoused the role of abundant labour supplies, Maddison emphasizes the importance of investment, while Denison allocates a large part to technical progress. If from a theoretical point of view it may seem relatively easy to state the determinants of growth, in practice it is a complex task to allocate to particular factors their specific contribution to total output growth. To complicate matters further, there are now so many different estimates of growth accounting for the period that students of the ongoing debate may be more confused than enlightened.

In the account that follows, we have simplified the exposition to render it intelligible to the non-specialist.

Basically, the direct sources of growth may be divided into two broad categories. First, there are changes in the volume of resources used to produce the national product: these include inputs of labour, capital and land, the last of which is normally excluded on the grounds that its contribution to growth is small. Second, growth may occur as a result of increases in output per unit of input. This is commonly described as the residual element: that part of the growth of output that cannot be attributed directly to changes in factor inputs. This category covers a wide range of variables that influence productivity, the most important of which are advances in knowledge and new techniques, the improved allocation of resources, economies of scale and the foreign trade effect. Growth may therefore be achieved either by increasing the inputs of capital and labour or by changes in the residual items, which improve the productivity performance of the factor inputs (total factor productivity growth). In practice, growth occurs as a result of simultaneous movements in all the variables, though obviously not in equally proportionate changes.

Any attempt to explain differences in rates of economic growth must in part be based on an examination of the interrelation between increases in output and additional inputs of capital and labour. As a preliminary to such an exercise, some key data on output, employment and investment have been assembled in Table 7.2.

As far as employment is concerned, this input over the longer term will be determined primarily by the natural increase in population. However, over shorter periods of time, a number of factors serve to cause a divergence in the rates of change between the two; these include migration, the age distribution of the population, the rate of participation in the labour force of those of working age and the level of unemployment. The impact of these factors varied from country to country. In some countries (Austria, France, Ireland, Italy, Norway, Portugal and Spain), employment grew at a rate at least 50 per cent less than the native population, whereas in Denmark, West Germany and Switzerland, the reverse was the case. However, because for most of the period, agriculture was losing labour as the workforce shifted into other activities, a more useful series is that for non-agricultural employment. This shows a more rapid growth than that for total employment, and on average it was more than twice the latter for western Europe as a whole. Only in Britain, where there was little surplus labour in agriculture, were the rates of growth the same. The labour flowing from agriculture went into both the industrial and service sectors, principally the latter. The shift into services was especially marked in France, Belgium and Denmark.

One explanation of the better growth performance post-war compared with the period 1913–50 can be found in the employment data. Because of the better utilization of labour through reduced unemployment, the drift out of agriculture and the shift of surplus labour from southern Europe (Italy, Spain, Greece and Turkey) to northern Europe (especially Germany), non-agricultural employment between 1950 and 1970 grew faster than hitherto; the average for western Europe was 1.6 per cent per annum as against only 1 per cent in the years 1913–50. Only

Table 7.2 Industrial western Europe: output, employment and investment, 1950–70

	Output growth		Employment growth			Investment ratios		
	GDP	Manufacturing	Total	Manufacturing	Non-agricultural employment	Total economy	Excluding dwellings	Manufacturing
Austria	5.0	5.6	0.1	0.6	0.5	26.2	21.1	15.9[a]
Belgium	3.5	5.3	0.4	0.2	1.0	22.4	16.2	18.1
Denmark	4.0	4.6	1.1	1.2	2.0	21.0	17.1	8.5
Finland	4.4	5.7	0.9	1.5	3.2	27.3	21.2	19.6
France	5.0	5.8	0.4	0.5	1.6	23.7	17.8	21.1[b]
Germany	6.2	8.0	1.2	2.1	2.4	27.0	20.2	18.3[b]
Greece	6.0	8.1	0.9	1.5	2.3	23.1	19.4	20.3
Ireland	2.5	4.7	-0.7	1.0	0.4	21.9[c]	18.2[c]	19.8[c]
Italy	5.4	7.9	0.4	1.7	2.3	22.1	15.6	19.6
Netherlands	5.0	6.3	1.1	1.0	1.4	26.0	20.8	20.3
Norway	4.1	4.7	0.3	0.7	1.4	32.0	26.7	18.5
Portugal	5.1	8.6	0.2	1.9	1.1	18.8	14.8	15.1
Spain	6.1	8.4	0.8	2.9	2.5	22.6	16.7	n.a.
Sweden	4.1	5.1	0.3	0.3	1.2	24.4	18.4	16.4
Switzerland	4.2	4.6	1.6	1.8	1.8	23.9	18.3	n.a.
UK	2.7	3.3	0.5	0.4	0.5	17.5	14.0	12.6

Source: United Nations, Economic Survey of Europe in 1971, Part 1, The European Economy from the 1950s to the 1970s, New York, 1972, pp. 12–14; A. Maddison, Economic Policy and Performance in Europe 1913–1970, London: Collins/Fontana, 1973, 51.

Notes: [a] 1960–69; includes mining and construction.
[b] Includes construction.
[c] 1960–69; investment ratio for manufacturing includes construction.

Austria, the Netherlands, Sweden and the UK went against the trend. Several countries were major beneficiaries: France, West Germany, Italy and Switzerland in particular, where non-agricultural employment grew faster than in the earlier period.

When we turn to an examination of the relationship between output and employment growth, the position is less clear-cut. There is a positive association between the two; that is, high rates of output growth tend to be accompanied by high rates of employment growth and vice versa, but it is by no means perfect. The association was stronger in the 1950s than the 1960s, which may partly reflect the reduction in unemployment in the earlier period. Moreover, relatively high rates of growth in the labour force tended to be associated with high labour productivity growth rates as well as with GDP, which suggests the importance of demand forces; that is, rapid expansion of demand encourages the fuller use of resources than would obtain in conditions of slow expansion.

Closer inspection reveals several discrepancies that make it impossible to state categorically that labour inputs were always of crucial significance in explaining growth performance. Thus, while Germany at one end of the spectrum obviously secured substantial gains through rapid employment growth, and the UK at the other end experienced slow growth in both output and employment, several countries ran counter to the trend. Thus, Austria's employment record was no better than that of Britain, yet her output performance was considerably superior. Both France and Belgium experienced higher growth rates of output and non-agricultural employment than before 1950, though most of the increase in the latter went into the service sector so that manufacturing employment grew slowly, at about the British rate. Sweden, with growth rates comparable with those of Switzerland for total output and manufacturing activity, had a lower rate of employment growth, especially in manufacturing. Clearly, therefore, employment growth, while not unassociated with output performance, cannot fully explain inter-country differences in output growth. Moreover, recent growth accounting calculations generally suggest that augmented labour inputs (even allowing for the inclusion of human capital improvement) contributed less to growth than did capital inputs and total factor productivity improvement. Thus Kindleberger's notion, invoking the Lewis growth model of unlimited supplies of labour, that the European boom was based mainly on large infusions of labour, is patently misleading.

To what extent therefore can these differences be explained by varying rates of capital accumulation? Investment may contribute to grow in various ways: it provides increasing employment opportunities; by providing more equipment per worker, it raises the productivity of labour; and it is an important vehicle by which new techniques and processes become embodied in the production process. Although the general character of the relationships are well established, there are serious problems regarding the measurement of their relative importance. Furthermore, there are practical difficulties relating to the definition and measurement of the capital stock. Capital stock accounting procedures are still far from perfect, and consequently, a sufficiently reliable series of data for all countries for the period 1950–70 that would allow a meaningful cross-country comparison to be made is not readily available. For want of a better indicator, the shares of gross investment in gross domestic output and in manufacturing were used as proxies in order to determine the relationship between capital accumulation and the growth of output. The method is not ideal because investment ratios among nations may vary for reasons other than the requirements of growth, but it should allow a first approximation of the importance of the variable.

One thing is certain: investment ratios in all countries were higher than in the inter-war period. They rose between the 1950s and 1960s almost everywhere and averaged 15–20 per cent (excluding dwellings) as against about 10 per cent between 1920 and 1938. As with employment growth, therefore, the higher rates of investment compared with the inter-war years helped to improve the growth performance in the post-war period. The net effect of generally higher investment ratios and fairly stable rates of output growth between the 1950s and 1960s was that in most countries the marginal capital output ratios rose, suggesting lower returns to investment, although productivity growth rates improved because of greater capital intensity per worker.

What is noticeable from the data in Table 7.2 is the wide spread of investment ratios among western nations, ranging from a high of 32 per cent in Norway to 17.5 per cent in the case of the UK. The range is almost as great if investment in dwellings is excluded or if manufacturing investment ratios alone are considered. The main conclusion to be drawn from the data is that there is a positive association between investment and growth but that it is not as strong or as uniform as one might expect. Countries with high investment ratios tended to grow rapidly (Germany and the Netherlands), whereas those with low ratios grew slowly (the UK). But that is probably about all one can say with certainty because there are so many cases that do not conform closely to the pattern. Thus Norway had the highest overall investment ratio but was in the bottom half of the growth league table, whereas Portugal was first in terms of manufacturing growth but twelfth in terms of the respective investment ratio. Italy's total investment ratio was low compared with her high ranking in output growth, though the correspondence was closer in the case of manufacturing, whereas France's excellent investment record in manufacturing was not matched by her placing in the growth stakes. Of course, there is no special reason why investment ratios and growth rates should correspond exactly because so much depends on the composition of investment, the way in which it is utilized and the structure and pattern of development of the countries in question. Thus, for example, Norway's high investment ratio is explained by the large proportion of capital formation in shipping, while Portugal's good growth record with a relatively low investment ratio may partly reflect the early stage of development of that country, where large output gains were derived from the more efficient utilization of existing stock of resources (the Kuznets phenomenon). The same could also be said of Italy. Clearly, the less developed of the west European countries gained much from the catch-up and the reallocation of resources to more productive uses.

So far, therefore, we may conclude that in general, high rates of employment and investment were conducive to rapid growth, whereas low rates tended to produce the reverse, but that the relationship between growth and factor inputs is not consistently and uniformly strong over a broad cross-section of countries. Nor does such an analysis tell us much about the respective contributions of capital and labour inputs to the growth of output, and, of course, it provides no indication of the relative importance of factor productivity growth as opposed to augmented factor inputs.

To estimate more precisely the contributions of capital and labour to economic growth in western countries, the relevant data are tested for consistency with a production function incorporating predetermined estimates of the 'true' marginal productivities of labour and capital. The residual increments of output in individual countries not explained by the production function can then be regarded as indicative of the contribution to output growth of all influences other than those two inputs, though at the same time also reflecting any failure to estimate correctly the true contribution to growth of increases in labour and capital (the error component). Many growth accounting studies are now available for western countries, but one of the first and still the most elaborate and detailed is that carried out by Denison for northwestern Europe for the period 1950–62. Table 7.3 presents a summary of the key figures for eight countries, which show the estimated contributions to growth from capital and labour inputs, together with estimates of the main sources of changes in output per unit of input.

The main conclusion to emerge from these figures is that factor productivity improvements were the most important source of growth in all countries, accounting in some cases for two-thirds to three-quarters of the rise in national income. The UK is the major exception, with only around one-half coming from this source. The productivity improvements were derived mainly from advances in knowledge, reallocation of labour resources and economies of scale. What should be stressed is that although fast-growing countries such as Germany, Italy, France and the Netherlands had high contributions from these factors and from productivity improvements in general, it was also true that the contribution from the increase in factor inputs was larger in absolute percentage point terms than was the case in slow-growing countries, for example the UK and Belgium. This seems to imply that countries with high rates of labour and capital input were in a better position to exploit productivity gains than were countries with low factor input growth.

Several points of reservation may be made with respect to this type of analysis. First, Denison assumes that advances in knowledge and techniques made a uniform contribution to growth in all countries. Although one would not disagree with the relatively high value accorded to this factor because rapid technical progress was a marked feature of the period, as countries sought to catch up to the best practice techniques in America, it is doubtful whether all countries benefited to the same extent. True, the diffusion of new technologies and ideas was more rapid than before 1939, but the advances among the countries are unlikely to have been as uniform as Denison suggests.

A more substantial point concerns the validity of the mode of analysis itself. The results suggest a downgrading of the role of factor inputs in the growth process, but the question remains whether the findings are particularly meaningful.

Table 7.3 Sources of growth of total national income, 1950–62 (contributions to growth in percentage points)

	Belgium	Denmark	France	Germany	Italy	Netherlands	Norway	UK	North-west Europe
National income	3.20	3.51	4.92	7.26	5.96	4.73	3.45	2.29	4.78
Total factor input	1.17	1.55	1.24	2.78	1.66	1.91	1.04	1.11	1.69
Labour	0.76	0.59	0.45	1.37	0.96	0.87	0.15	0.60	0.83
Capital	0.41	0.96	0.79	1.41	0.70	1.04	0.89	0.51	0.86
Output per unit of input	2.03	1.96	3.68	4.48	4.30	2.82	2.41	1.18	3.07
Advances in knowledge	0.76	0.76	0.76	0.76	0.76	0.76	0.76	0.76	0.76
Reallocation of labour	0.35	0.59	0.88	0.91	1.26	0.47	0.77	0.10	0.60
Gains from trade	0.16	0.09	0.07	0.10	0.16	0.16	0.15	0.02	0.08
Scale economies and income elasticities	0.51	0.65	1.00	1.61	1.22	0.78	0.57	0.36	0.93
Residual items	0.25	−0.13	0.97	1.10	0.90	0.65	0.16	−0.06	0.70

Source: E. F. Denison, *Why Growth Rates Differ*, Washington, DC: Brookings Institution, 1967, 300–318.

Measurement of the contribution of factor inputs requires calculation of the quality of inputs, which may involve a degree of circularity. Furthermore, attempts to measure the contribution of separate factor inputs have usually rested on the assumption that factor income shares reflect the marginal productivity of those factors. The validity of this procedure, given the extent of non-competitive and institutional factors in the process of income determination, has frequently been questioned and is still the subject of serious controversy. But the main area of debate and uncertainty, both in theory and measurement, really centres on the question whether it is possible to allocate growth precisely to particular factors given the degree of overlap and interrelationship among the factors concerned.

What this amounts to is that the technique of apportioning growth to factor inputs and productivity improvements may well understate the role of capital, in particular if, as is often the case, technical advances are embodied in investment, part of which comprises the replacement of assets. This implies, therefore, that gross investment, rather than simply net additions to the capital stock, is of greater significance. It is probable that improvements in many of the residual items are dependent on capital accumulation to some degree. For example, the enhancement of the quality of the labour force, by such means as better education, vocational training, and improved health services and housing standards, is likely to be dependent on a certain minimum rate of capital formation. In so far as this is the case, there is an inherent danger of underestimating the role of capital in any attempts at measuring the sources of growth using the production function method. In reality, therefore, the residual item, or that part of growth not attributable to factor inputs, must be interpreted, as noted earlier, not only as an indication of the influence of technical and organizational progress but also as an indication of the errors embodied in the allocation process itself.

The possibilities of reinterpretation are illustrated by Maddison's (1972) reworking of Denison's basic data for the same countries. The main difference is the larger weight assigned to capital by making allowances for the input of government capital and the effects of education and by assuming that technical progress (advances in knowledge in Denison's case) is all embodied in either capital or labour, in which case it disappears as a separate item. On this basis, Maddison concludes that factor inputs played a larger role, explaining on average about three-quarters of the growth in west European countries as against less than half in Denison's calculations. The debate on the relative importance of both labour and capital inputs and total factor productivity has been a continuing one, which remains far from resolved as each new set of computations puts a different gloss on the outcomes. Readers may follow the debate in the edited volumes by Van Ark and Crafts (1996) and Crafts and Toniolo (1996), which also present detailed quantitative estimates on the sources of growth.

Clearly, therefore, the dispute over the weights to be attached to particular factors leaves the growth problem unresolved. That factor contributions to growth differed considerably among the several countries is stating the obvious, but at least there is one point of significance, namely that high income growth countries such as Germany, Italy and the Netherlands tended to secure larger absolute contributions from all factors than slow-growing countries such as Britain. Perhaps of greater relevance at this stage, then, than the proximate causes of growth is to determine what forces influenced changes in the growth factors; that is, what determined the rate of technical progress and organizational change, the high levels of investment and variations in the labour supply?

Several favourable influences were bearing on supply factors in the post-war period. These were both general and specific in nature and the strength of their impact varied from one country to another. In the first half of the 1950s, for example, some countries, notably Germany and Italy, were still under the influence of reconstruction from the war. These countries had only just surpassed their pre-war levels of output by 1950 and there was still considerable slack to be taken up. Unemployment was still high in both Germany and Italy, but it was declining steadily, with the result that employment growth was rapid. Moreover, extensive reconstruction of productive facilities, especially in Germany, had to be carried out, which meant rapid capital accumulation and a more efficient and up-to-date capital stock than in countries less seriously damaged by the war. However, it should be noted that Germany's capital stock was not nearly so badly damaged as is often supposed. Despite the destruction caused by heavy Allied bombing in the later stages of the war, German industry and its asset base were by no means decimated. New capacity created during the period of hostilities more than made up for the losses, so that the country's capital stock at the start of the post-war era was about one-tenth higher than before the war, which left the country in a better position than France, Italy or the UK. However, by the mid-1950s, the special circumstances associated with the aftermath of war ceased to be important and therefore they cannot be used as an explanatory factor for high growth countries in the later 1950s and 1960s.

Several countries experienced high rates of employment growth in both the 1950s and 1960s. These included advanced industrial countries such as Germany, the Netherlands and Switzerland as well as some of the smaller and poorer countries (Portugal, Greece, Spain). In part, this can be accounted for by the reduction in unemployment especially in the 1950s, and the removal of disguised unemployment, in particular in agriculture, which in turn was associated with a reallocation of labour resources, that is a shift of labour from agriculture to industry and services. Some countries also benefited considerably from increased immigration in both the 1950s and 1960s, together with an improvement in the quality of the labour force. In France, Germany and Switzerland, total population grew at a rate at least 50 per cent higher than the native population as a consequence of a continual stream of immigrants into these countries. They were the chief host nations to migrating workers from the European south, and by the end of the 1960s, foreign workers constituted between 5 and 7 per cent of their respective work forces. Sweden too absorbed foreign workers on a considerable scale. West Germany was probably the major beneficiary, with a large influx of refugees and expellees from eastern Europe in the 1950s followed by the migration of workers from southern Europe in the 1960s. By 1961, West Germany had absorbed some 12 million refugees and expellees, 7 million of whom had become active participants in the labour force. By contrast, employment growth in the Netherlands was boosted by the natural increase in population, which was one of the highest in Europe. In all these countries, the demand for labour remained high, but the supply was elastic so that pressure on the labour market never acted as a serious brake on the economy and on wage levels. Kindleberger invokes the Lewis model of unlimited supplies of labour in this context. This in turn kept demand buoyant and increased the need for new investment in both productive facilities and social overhead capital.

Several European countries (Italy and to a lesser extent France and of course the southern European countries) were less highly developed than Britain and Sweden at the beginning of the period. Their levels of income per head were lower and structurally they still had a relatively large proportion of resources tied up in low productivity sectors such as agriculture. In the process of catching up, they were bound to reap substantial gains from the reallocation of resources and economies of scale associated with large-scale industrial development. There was also greater scope for the adoption of best practice techniques and general improvements in efficiency. Both France and Italy gained substantially from these influences. According to Denison's calculations, 2.48 percentage points (42 per cent of the total) of Italy's income growth between 1950 and 1962 came from resource reallocation and scale economies, whereas a further 0.9 was derived from changes in the lag in the application of knowledge and general efficiency. During the 1950s, the industrial sector in Italy absorbed some 2 million additional workers, most of them coming from agriculture. In the same way, France gained about 1.90 percentage points (39 per cent of the total income growth) from the first two factors, 0.65 of which came from the reduction in agricultural inputs. In fact, most European countries stood to gain more from resource reallocation than countries such as Britain and Belgium, where the opportunities for shifting labour out of agriculture were virtually exhausted. Even in the 1960s, the reallocation of labour from the primary sector to industry and the service trades continued strongly in some of the major countries. In Germany, farm employment dropped by more than 1.2 million between 1960 and 1970, whereas non-agricultural employment rose by 2 million; in France, the figures were 1.3 and 3.0 million and in Italy 2.9 and 1.7 million, respectively. The importance of this shift in employment structure tended to diminish after the early 1970s.

The post-war period was characterized by a high level of technological innovation, especially in science-based industries such as chemicals, pharmaceuticals and electronics, and a rapid diffusion of technical developments among the major industrial countries. Several strong forces were at work to explain the accelerated rate in the application of new inventions and the diffusion of techniques. These include the high rate of capital formation, the larger proportion of resources devoted to research and development and the continuing growth of education at all levels, to all of which governments contributed considerably. Human capital development was becoming more crucial as skill-intensive activities replaced labour-intensive ones. Furthermore, the transmission of ideas and techniques and their rapid spread and diffusion throughout western countries were facilitated by the removal of trade barriers and the growth of trade, especially that in manufactured products, the general improvement in communications, the expansion of international investment and the exploitation of new products by multinational companies. The high level of demand also helped to encourage the adoption of new products, especially in the consumer durable goods field.

More generally, it can be argued that the greater internal stability within Europe compared with the pre-war period was favourable to growth. This is a difficult factor to measure, but both in a political and economic sense the climate was more favourable to international economic progress. The political situation, despite the east–west split and the Cold War, was more stable than in the inter-war years and this in turn encouraged a greater degree of international economic cooperation among western nations. This assisted the removal of many restrictions on trade and payments (see below). The east–west split itself probably encouraged a greater degree of cooperation and at the same time prompted America to give as much assistance to western Europe as possible. Perhaps even more important was the fact that economic fluctuations and crises were milder than previously, possibly because of the more active participation of government in economic affairs (see below). These more stable conditions provided a climate conducive to high investment and sustained growth.

However, the major reason for western Europe's good showing in the 1950s and 1960s was the high and sustained level of demand. Nearly all countries experienced both a rapid increase in exports and an increasing volume of domestic consumption. The importance of demand, and especially export demand, has been stressed frequently by economists and it is difficult to deny that a high level of demand is a necessary condition of growth. Buoyant markets raised businessmen's expectations about future profits and this in turn encouraged investment. Continuous incremental growth is important because it is the marginal additions to output that make such a difference to the bottom line in company profits. The reverse side of the coin (falling output) tends to have an even more dramatic impact on company profitability, as was evident in the downturns in the inter-war years, and later to be experienced after the early 1970s. Whether demand is the autonomous element that induces changes in supply or whether it is autonomous changes in the latter that govern the rate at which demand increases is still a matter for debate. Nevertheless, the fact remains that demand was sustained throughout the period. It is therefore important to analyse the determinants of export demand and its impact on growth and also to examine the influence of government operations on the level and pattern of domestic consumption.

The role of exports

The unprecedented growth in western Europe in the 1950s and 1960s was accompanied by an even better performance in the trading sphere. This was also true of the world in general. The volume of west European exports rose by between 8 and 9 per cent in the two decades, with a slight acceleration in the 1960s. All countries except the UK achieved rates of export growth in excess of 5 per cent per annum, and in the case of Germany and Italy, the rates ran into double figures. In fact, western Europe's trade performance was better than that of the world as a whole and very much better than the stagnation in trade in the period 1913–50. Trade grew considerably faster than output and it was most buoyant in manufactured goods. The effect of this was to raise the trade/output ratio above unity, whereas in the past it had been close to unity, except in the 1930s. Europe's trade with outside regions grew only slightly more than output in Europe. The main part of the trade expansion was concentrated on intra-European exchange and was dominated by the exchange of manufactured products among countries having not very dissimilar levels of income per head. The growth of trade volumes was also accompanied by an increasing flow of international capital, both short term and long term. This was dominated in the first decade by American lending and investment in Europe, but in the 1960s the flow of portfolio investment from Europe to the United States assumed increasing importance, as did short-term capital movements once freed from administrative regulations. Direct investment by international corporations also increased in importance, which was advantageous from the point of view of trade growth and for the diffusion of technical advances.

There are several reasons why trade expanded so rapidly in the post-war period. As noted in the previous chapter, western Europe's trade was sharply reduced during the war, and even in the immediate post-war years, it remained well below the pre-war level, largely because of supply difficulties. Intra-European trade in fact regained the 1913 level only in 1950. Yet because of severe payment imbalances, especially with the dollar area, it was vitally important that Europe should increase her exports substantially. Hence it is not surprising that priority was given to exporting because, given Europe's dependence on dollar supplies in particular, this was the only way of clearing the accounts once American post-war aid ceased to flow. In fact, by 1950, as a result of increased production, the control of inflation and the correction of currency overvaluation in 1949, the European current account deficit had been cut by two-thirds to $2.5 billion. However, the balance of payments problem still remained acute, and it worsened during 1951 on account of the Korean War, which caused a sharp rise in the price of commodities. If Europe were to dispense with external aid and liberalize her trade, as well as compensate for a deterioration in terms of trade and loss of invisible earnings, the requirement in terms of increased exports still remained large. Fortunately, continued US aid and rising American military expenditure in Europe contributed to Europe's dollar receipts, and these together with rapidly rising exports meant that some countries achieved a surplus on their current accounts by the middle of the 1950s. At the end of 1955, eleven OEEC countries felt strong enough to restore currency convertibility for non-residents, and in 1958, a general move to full currency convertibility was made by most countries. By that time, though certain payment problems remained, the dollar scarcity was all but over, and rather sooner than most people would have believed possible at the beginning of the decade. During the 1960s, the position was reversed; America incurred large deficits on current account, and western European countries recorded an aggregate surplus on current account of about $2.5 billion dollars.

Meanwhile, other influences were beginning to have a favourable impact on trade, especially within Europe, where the prospects for the exchange of manufactures became increasingly apparent. These prospects were enhanced by the improving payments position, the liberalization of trade and payments and the creation of new trading blocs. Among the more important developments affecting international trading relations in the period were the removal of trade restrictions by the OEEC liberalization programme of the 1950s, the general reduction in tariffs through GATT, and the formation of new trading communities (the European Economic Community [EEC] and the European Free Trade Association [EFTA]) in the later 1950s.

In the early post-war years, not only was the volume of intra-European trade at a low level but the trade and payments between western European countries tended to be along bilateral channels and backed up by rigorous quantitative restrictions. In an attempt to break down these obstacles to trade, the United States made its aid conditional upon the removal of trade and payments restrictions by fostering economic cooperation among western nations. Thus in July 1950, the European Payments Union (EPU) was established, which, by providing effective means for clearing intra-European payments, paved the way for the termination of bilateral trade agreements and trade restrictions. The latter became the province of the OEEC, and its Code of Liberalization set out a programme for the progressive removal of trade restrictions. Progress was rapid and, by 1955, 84 per cent of the quantitative restrictions had been removed. Subsequently, the easing of tariff policies was taken in hand by GATT, and in the later 1950s and 1960s, several rounds of general tariff reductions were made.

The late 1950s saw the development of closer and more intricate cooperation among the western nations. In 1958, after the signing of the Rome Treaty in the previous year, the EEC was established. Its founder members consisted of France, West Germany, Italy, the Netherlands, Belgium and Luxemburg. The Community's long-term objectives were ambitious and wide-ranging, but it is as a customs unit that it was of most significance in the post-war period. By 1968, intra-community trade in non-agricultural products had been freed of duties and a common external tariff had been established. On the other hand, agricultural products enjoyed considerable protection especially from outside competition. The following year also saw the creation of EFTA: its members included Austria, Denmark, Norway, Portugal, Sweden, Switzerland and the UK, with Finland becoming an associate member in 1961 (in the early 1970s, the UK and Denmark withdrew on joining the EEC). The aims of the Association were more limited than those of the EEC, being largely confined to trade matters. The abolition of restrictions on trade between member countries proceeded rapidly and by the mid-1960s quantitative restrictions and customs duties had all but disappeared.

Thus substantial and rapid progress was made in the 1950s and 1960s in abolishing barriers to foreign trade. The impact of the liberalization policy is difficult to estimate precisely but there seems little doubt that it created greater trade opportunities. The progressive relaxation of quantitative restrictions in the 1950s and early 1960s was an important factor encouraging the growth of exports, while the establishment of the two trading communities in the late 1950s produced both trade creation and trade diversion effects. Trade of the member countries grew more rapidly than the world average until the early 1970s. Among the countries of the EEC, it rose by nearly 13 per cent per annum between 1955 and 1969, with manufactures recording a higher rate and agricultural products about 10 per cent a year. The most dynamic sector was intra-EEC trade, which by 1969 accounted for one-third of the total intra-European trade, compared with one-quarter in 1955. The performance of the EFTA countries was not so strong but this was principally because of the sluggish growth of UK exports. If the latter are excluded, intra-EFTA trade rose by 11.5 per cent per annum over the same period, with the Nordic countries showing the most spectacular gains.

The trade diversion effects are less easy to demonstrate but the general consensus seems to be that the diversion of trade in manufactures from third countries as a result of enhanced intra-European trade was roughly balanced by the creation of new trade with non-members. But in the case of agrarian products, the agricultural policy of the EEC probably entailed a net loss in trade for outside members. Apart from the specific trade effects, an important by-product of the EEC was its negotiating strength *vis-à-vis* non-members. The importance of the Community as a trading partner, for example, was recognized by the United States in the 1960s, when unilateral tariff cuts of about one-third were agreed in the Kennedy Round of GATT negotiations.

It is important to recognize that the international economic environment as a whole was distinctly more favourable to the growth of trade than it was in the inter-war years. In this respect, the strong and sustained economic cooperation between nations since the end of the war, which contrasts sharply with the breakdown in international economic relations in the 1930s, must be accorded an important role. This was manifested in several ways. Initially, the United States was instrumental in fostering European reconstruction and recovery with its enormous aid programmes, amounting to some \$43 billion net. Subsequently, there were big payments both on military and private accounts to Europe, including the large US payments deficit in the 1960s, which facilitated European expansion. Second, western European cooperation was fostered by several organizations, including the EPU, GATT, OEEC and later the EEC and EFTA, the main impact of which, as already noted, was the progressive elimination of trade barriers. Finally, international monetary cooperation was more in evidence and more effective than before the war. Even before the war had ended, an international governmental conference at Bretton Woods had drafted the Articles of Agreement of the IMF, which was to become the main institution responsible for international financial and monetary matters. Three main provisions emerged from the complex negotiations at Bretton Woods. Fixed exchange rates were to be introduced and currency parities altered only to correct fundamental dis-equilibrium in external accounts; a pool of international credit derived from members' quotas to the IMF was available to finance temporary balance-of-payments difficulties, including those caused by speculative raids; and, third, there was provision for currency convertibility on current transactions and prohibition of discriminatory currency practices, the payments equivalent to non-discrimination in trade.

It would be wrong of course to assume that the existence of the IMF provided a solution to all international monetary problems. Indeed, in the early years and through the 1950s, the IMF pursued a passive policy, partly because its reserves were never large enough to offer more than token support to countries in difficulties. During the following decade, its lending activities became more pronounced, partly as a consequence of the increase in members' quotas in 1958 and 1962 and the institution of Special Drawing Rights (SDRs) in 1969. Moreover, the work of the IMF was greatly assisted in this decade by arrangements for short-term support and swap facilities among the central bankers of the major countries, while the international liquidity position was boosted by the recycling of dollars arising from the large US payments deficit in what became known as the Eurodollar market.

Even with these arrangements, periodic strains in the international financial mechanism did occur. The most important sources of disequilibrium were the ever-increasing surplus of some continental European countries, Germany in particular, and the intractable deficit of the UK, and later the United States. Eventually, such disequilibria reached the scale at which no amount of liquidity would obviate adjusting exchange rates. But even before the upheavals of the early 1970s, when rate adjustments and floating rates became commonplace, there had been several disturbances caused by payment imbalances, which involved major realignments of exchange rates in several cases, including the French devaluations of 1957–58 and 1969, the British devaluation of 1967 and the German and Dutch revaluations in the early 1960s.

Despite these upsets, it is fair to say that in the post-war period through to the end of the 1960s, the international financial machinery conferred net benefits to the economic system. Certainly, it was a vast improvement on anything that had gone before. Its inherent weaknesses were masked by a regime of relatively stable exchange rates, moderate inflation and a reasonable supply of international liquidity. The international monetary climate was generally favourable to growth and the expansion of trade and with notable exceptions, the UK in particular, governments did not feel the need to check output severely because of a lack of liquidity. International financial cooperation among the major powers meant a continuous expansion in the supply of liquidity, which in turn bolstered confidence among businessmen and traders. The strains in the international mechanism that did occur from time to time were not severe enough to cause permanent damage or were repaired before they could do so. It was not until the early 1970s that the foundations of successful post-war monetary and financial cooperation were undermined, but that is part of another story.

If international cooperation in its many forms was conducive to trade expansion, so too was the growth process itself within the major economies. Rapid growth brought scale economies and considerable output diversification. This in turn encouraged the increasing exchange of industrial products among the wealthier nations, a process no doubt facilitated in some fields, for example consumer durables, by demonstration effects. Rapidly expanding domestic markets, especially in Germany and Italy, enabled these countries to benefit considerably from scale economies in the production of consumer durables, thereby reducing unit costs and providing a strong launching-pad for export penetration into overseas markets. In addition, high technology investment, notably in Germany, provided a medium for expanding the exports of producer goods to other advanced nations.

This of course more or less brings us back to the original point of departure in this section, namely, are exports good for growth or does the causal link flow in the reverse direction? In this context, one frequently encounters the phrase export-led growth, and some economists have assigned an independent role to the export component in the growth process. The main crux of the argument rests on the following premises: that export growth stimulates industries with significant scale economies and, second, that by inducing strong external accounts it encourages investment. However. the evidence is conflicting; although most analyses confirm a general positive association between exports and growth, the direction of the causal mechanism is frequently disputed. Statistical tests on data for eleven leading manufacturing exporters for the period 1950–69 (Lubitz 1973) do cast doubt on the alleged export-led mechanisms. Rates of economic growth were found to be correlated more strongly with total export growth than with manufacturing export growth, thereby raising doubt as to the strength of the scale economies effect in manufacturing. Moreover, when the investment ratio was used alongside export growth as a second independent variable in the regression equations, it turned out to be statistically significant, implying that exports did not stimulate growth through their effects on investment. In other words, the results are more consistent with a theory of growth-induced exports rather than with one that ascribes an independent and dynamic role to the export component. This would be quite a plausible interpretation; high growth countries gained competitive strength through rapid domestic investment, whereas slow growth countries, Britain in particular, ran up against supply constraints because of low investment, which in turn reduced their competitive edge.

Policy variables

Any survey of economic development in modern industrial economics cannot be complete without a discussion of the role of government in economic affairs. This is not simply because the goals and instruments of economic policy are now much greater than before 1939 but also on account of the sheer scale of government economic operations in the post-war period. The war of 1939–45, even more so than that of 1914–18, led to a vast increase in the size of public sector activities. Only part of this increase was reversed afterwards because the shift upwards during the war in what were regarded as tolerable levels of taxation allowed governments to retain part of the increase in peacetime, while in more recent years the public sector's share of resources has been increasing again by a stealthy incremental approach. Thus since 1945, the government sector has been a major component in every western economy. The ratio of public sector outlays (including transfer payments) to gross national income ranged between 30 and 40 per cent in the 1950s, rising steadily to exceed 50 per cent by the early 1970s in Scandinavia, the Netherlands and Britain, most of the later increase being accounted for by transfer payments. These high rates, which on average are more than twice those attained pre-war, have given governments enormous leverage over their economies.

Not only has the increase in government operations itself inevitably resulted in the state's greater involvement in economic affairs, but changes in attitudes as to the state's responsibilities with regard to economic matters also played an important part. In some cases, for instance, ideological commitments led to a significant increase in the public ownership of economic enterprise, notably in France and Britain, where several important sectors of the economy were nationalized shortly after the war. Perhaps of more general importance was the natural unwillingness of societies to contemplate a return to pre-war conditions as they had been disposed to do after the First World War. This is not surprising, given the high unemployment and poor performance of most economies during the 1930s. Thus instead of opting for a return to 'normalcy' as after the first war, governments in the mid-1940s were inclined towards planning for the future, a shift of opinion well illustrated by the British Labour Party's 1945 election manifesto entitled *Let Us Face The Future*. In effect, therefore, what this implied was that governments would have to accept greater responsibility for achieving full employment and faster growth among other things than had been the case before the war. Not that policy aims had been entirely absent before 1939, but for the most part they were of a kind that came to be regarded as secondary, if not irrelevant, in the different climate of the post-1945 period.

Changes in economic thinking and statistical reporting also gave governments greater scope for manoeuvre. Whereas inter-war governments, at least until the 1930s, had relied primarily on monetary policy as a policy weapon, post-war governments, partly as a result of the revolution in economic thinking wrought by Keynes, were able to add fiscal policy to their armoury of weapons. Not that fiscal action was absent in the pre-war period, but for the most part, it involved passive and often perverse adjustments of expenditures and taxes often for purposes of balancing budgets, with little contemplation of using the fiscal device as a means to influence changes in broad economic aggregates; in fact, at the time, there were few references to aggregate demand or total investment as factors determining or influencing employment or to the overall level of economic activity. Thus, although the inter-war years saw substantial stabilization action on the part of governments, it was generally of a restrictive type that had an adverse influence on the economy. As Lundberg rightly observed: 'The measures taken were more inappropriate, more badly timed, or more obviously wrong than most measures of similar importance adopted in the post-war period' (Lundberg 1968).

Apart from improvements in theoretical analysis and practical policy application, there was also a concomitant improvement in the gathering and processing of economic data and their evaluation. The policy debate before 1939 had to make do with a limited range of imperfect statistics, and for this reason, the debate was limited in scope because the data available did not allow a proper evaluation of aggregate magnitudes. During and after the Second World War, the quality and range of statistical reporting, both official and otherwise, improved enormously, most notably in the field of national income accounting. In addition, technical expertise in the assessment of the material became better, allowing the construction and testing of increasingly complex models of the economy. Whether this was always as beneficial in terms of policy application as we should like to believe is another matter, but at least it provided a basis for a more positive and realistic assessment of how economies worked in practice.

These, then, are some of the main reasons why governments since the war have become such active agents in the economic sphere, and indeed increasingly so, until nowadays their electoral prestige depends on how well they can manage the economy. In the context of the post-war decades, they were concerned with two basic issues: the growth and the stability of economic systems, the ideal aimed for being sustained growth with relative stability. These two broad dimensions may be expanded into four main responsibilities or objectives: fast growth, full employment, price stability and external equilibrium. To these may be added others such as the more equitable distribution of income, the modification of structural or regional imbalances and the development and improvement of specific welfare objectives, for example social security systems, as well as a host of smaller issues, such as environmental betterment. But, generally speaking, the latter tended to be regarded as matters of secondary importance given the commitment to the first four objectives, though experience in this matter varied from one country to another. In any case, fulfilment of the basic aims may assist in realizing the second-order priorities; for example, rapid economic growth will make it easier to improve social security services and reduce income inequalities (a fact that the zero growth enthusiasts would do well to bear in mind).

In practice, however, things did not always work out quite so neatly, because for all but a few countries, the range of objectives proved to be incompatible. Few countries were able to achieve fast growth combined with price stability, whereas others found that growth and balance of payments equilibrium did not make happy marriage partners. One possible problem, apart from inherent structural weaknesses in particular economies such as the British, was that the number of objectives was generally larger than the number of major policy weapons, the assumption being that there must be a one-for-one relationship between aims and policies, or as many control measures or policy levers as there are objectives. This is probably true up to a point, but more so for basically weak economies like the British than for strong and vigorous economies such as the German. The one-for-one relationship also poses something of a prescription problem because of the difficulty in defining what constitutes a major policy control weapon. Is fiscal policy to be counted merely as one lever or does it consist of a series of instruments, for example tax changes, investment incentives, aggregate spending volumes, etc., which in total form an omnibus holding labelled fiscal policy?

In fact, some countries neatly sidestepped some of the above difficulties by ordering their priorities in terms of both objectives and instruments of control. For instance, not all countries gave priority to full employment and growth.

The German neoliberals argued, and for the most part the authorities accepted their basic premise, that these two goals would be achieved by ensuring internal and external stability, or price stability and balance of payments equilibrium, which in the German case was usually interpreted to mean a surplus on the external account. Accordingly, economic management was geared primarily to achieving the latter objectives even if at times it might run counter to full employment and growth. The German authorities were very active in monetary policy, whereas fiscal policy was used mainly to encourage savings and investment. In the event, this type of policy direction proved to be correct because Germany was blessed with success on all fronts. The containment of prices through firm monetary policy meant that Germany became very competitive, and with strong export growth, there were few constraints from the external side. Germany was not plagued by periodic balance-of-payments crises so familiar to Britain, and so fast growth and a high level of employment were ensured. Possibly the one area in which there was some lagging was in social matters and particularly the achievement of a more equitable distribution of income, but then Germany never regarded these as being high on its list of priorities, at least not in the early years; given the rapid overall growth, it could afford such a deferment.

On the other hand, France, encouraged by faith in her planning ventures, hedged her bets on growth for most of the period, but sometimes at the expense of monetary and price stability. The final out-turn was good but not as favourable as the German because France's rapid growth led to more severe inflationary pressures and at times a precarious balance-of-payments situation, which resulted in recourse to the devaluation of the currency. Planning became a way of life in France and it seemed to take precedence over everything else. Doubts have been expressed, especially for the later years, whether it was effective in terms of growth. It is true that the French economy performed strongly throughout the period, but so did the German economy in the absence of formal planning, and it was basically stronger than the French, which at times suffered from inflationary pressures and balance-of-payments problems.

The British experience provides a sharp contrast with that of Germany or France. In fact, it is a good example of poor policy direction. The British authorities never seem to have been able to decide upon any scale of priorities among the main objectives listed, in addition to which they flirted, and very seriously at times, with a fifth: social progress and equality. This proved an ambitious cocktail for a country whose economy was basically weaker than those of most other west European countries. They tried something that few other countries dared to contemplate, namely to march along on four or five fronts simultaneously with an inadequate armoury of weapons, primarily fiscal policy, a weak and negative monetary policy and a dead-set against using external regulators (though eventually they were forced to devalue in 1967), together with an almost deliberate refusal to recognise that under such conditions the objectives were bound to be incompatible. Not surprisingly, the results were poor: slow growth, inflationary pressures, a precarious balance of payments and (one bright spot) fairly full employment. But the last of these was achieved more by accident than design as a result of a very slow growth in the labour force and a bad track record in productivity. It is true that policy mistakes cannot be held solely responsible for the sad failings of the British economy, but it is difficult to resist the conclusion that the out-turn might have been better had the authorities launched a frontal attack on one or two objectives rather than spreading their efforts so widely. Pollard's trenchant criticism of policy direction in Britain, in *The Wasting of the British Economy*, is a serious indictment, though he may place too much blame on the dereliction of Treasury officials. Perhaps the British authorities heeded too closely the warning about placing 'all one's eggs in one basket'.

As hinted above, the methods used to manage economic systems varied from one country to another. Though most countries at one time or another tended to use a variety of policy measures, in practice there was a specific predilection for one particular set of policy instruments. Thus, for example, Germany, Belgium and Italy generally placed their faith in monetary controls of one sort or another, whereas the UK gave first preference to fiscal regulators, though backed up by credit and discount controls from time to time. Indeed, contrary to general impressions, Britain was exceptional in her emphasis on fiscal policy because many continental countries were less ready initially to use fiscal weapons specifically for purposes of countercyclical manipulation. As might be expected, Sweden, as a pioneer in this field of policy, continued to be in the forefront in the development of Keynesian methods of economic management, though perhaps her most distinctive and well-known contribution was her labour market policy. Norway's policies were similar. Some countries were strong on planning in one form or another. The best known is France, with her heavy emphasis on government investment planning and active sponsorship of investment projects by subsidies and licensing systems, together with the periodic use of import controls and devaluations. The Dutch followed a similar path, but they used a more sophisticated econometric model for forecasting and planning purposes, and until the mid-1960s, they also had the bonus of a remarkable wages policy. By contrast, planning was inconsequential in Italy, though here the state institutions provided a major force in the economy, controlling the key sectors and accounting for nearly one-third of gross investment in industry. However, planning as such cannot act as a substitute for policy control; it provides only the basis on which action may be taken, so that ultimately the French and Dutch had to use the main weapons of control to achieve the aims or targets outlined in their plans.

Other policy instruments were used less frequently. Direct physical controls were used extensively during the war and the immediate post-war years, but most of the detailed system of controls of these years had been abandoned by the early 1950s. Price and income controls of one sort or another were used from time to time, but apart from the Dutch case, they rarely formed part of the permanent policy package of governments. The major policy gap was probably on the external side, that is, the absence of a specific policy weapon for dealing with balance-of-payments disequilibrium. Of course, exchange rate adjustments were made on occasions and the French probably made more use of external regulators than most other countries; but by and large, until the early 1970s, currency realignment was regarded as a policy of last resort. For much of the period, exchange rate adjustment was out of favour as a policy instrument (and indeed it did not accord with the IMF rules), so that it was used only in cases of fundamental disequilibrium. The same goes for trade controls of one sort or another because these conflicted with the general movement towards trade liberalization. However, one should add that until general currency convertibility in 1958, many countries employed protective devices to safeguard their external accounts, while in the 1960s special measures to control the movement of short-term capital were widespread.

Although individual countries tended to pursue one type of policy in preference to others, this was not to the complete exclusion of the other alternatives. Indeed, in the 1960s, there was some tendency towards policy convergence among the European countries. One reason why some continental countries preferred to give priority to monetary weapons is that their budgetary systems were less centralized and therefore less efficient for purposes of fiscal regulation than was the case in Britain or France. The complex political and administrative procedures involved often hampered the speedy introduction of tax and spending changes. For example, the German public financial system was highly decentralized; in 1959, the central government accounted for only 20 per cent of total public expenditure (current and capital) as against 59 per cent in France and Britain, while local authorities and social security agencies controlled 41 per cent and 39 per cent respectively. Clearly, this gave the central government less scope for pursuing an active fiscal policy, and even if it did so, there was always the danger that, as in America in the 1930s, its actions would be offset by reverse spending patterns on the part of the financially autonomous *Länder* governments. In the case of Italy, the reluctance to resort to fiscal policy arose from the inherent weakness of the whole budgetary system, including the structure of the tax system and its general inefficiency, the defective procedural, institutional and administrative framework within which budgetary policy was formulated and implemented, and the antiquated and overcautious attitudes towards deliberately using budgetary deficits as a policy measure to induce expansion. Yet in both countries, there was a move away from too heavy reliance on monetary policy in the later 1960s. After 1965, Italy used budgetary policy more strenuously than hitherto, though not always to good effect, while in 1967, under the Stabilisation Law of that year, Germany acknowledged some responsibility for demand management and deliberately adopted an expansionary fiscal policy, in combination with monetary policy, to prevent the then current recession, severe by post-war standards, from developing into a full-blown depression. Up to that time, Germany had never taken major fiscal policy measures to stimulate the economy, because the post-war slowdowns were regarded as useful cooling-off periods and they had normally been reversed by an upswing in exports before becoming really serious. However, as it turned out, the measures taken proved too strong because the ensuing upswing coincided with yet another burst of export demand.

Similar shifts in policy direction were evident in other countries. Britain in the later 1960s began to pay more attention to monetary policy than had previously been the case. Not that reliance on fiscal policy had ever meant the complete exclusion of monetary controls, but in this case the authorities had had some difficulty in sorting out their attitudes towards monetary policy, partly because of influences stemming from historical experience with monetary policy (for example, in the 1920s) and partly because of the uncertainty as to the role and impact of monetary controls, not helped on this score by the ambivalent attitude of the Radcliffe Committee of 1959, which by emphasizing the 'general liquidity position' above all else tended to send the authorities along interest rate and credit control channels at the expense of monetary aggregates. Thus the change when it came was not simply a shift from fiscal to monetary controls. It also involved a shift of emphasis within the monetary spectrum, that is, away from credit and interest rate weapons *per se* towards broad monetary aggregates: first, domestic credit expansion, and later, the growth of the money stock, equivalent to domestic credit expansion but inclusive of the monetary counterpart of any overall surplus or deficit on the balance of payments. This redirection of emphasis, which was partly conditioned by academic arguments and analyses of various monetary authorities, most notably the IMF, was consummated in the credit reforms of the early 1970s.

The process of policy convergence was apparent in other respects in the 1960s. Whereas the French began from the mid-1960s to place decreasing emphasis on the detailed design of their investment plans and at the same time gave greater weight to monetary and fiscal controls, Britain became more planning conscious, as did Germany and Italy in the later 1960s, though few concrete results emerged from these forays into uncharted waters. Similarly, the Dutch attachment to complex and sophisticated model-building for purposes of prediction, which had yielded mixed results, softened, and they began to pay more attention to surveys of business expectations of the type used in Sweden. Ironically, at the very same time, the Swedes were beginning to make increasing use of the techniques of econometric analysis. The Dutch centralized wage-bargaining system also broke down in the middle of the 1960s, when other countries (for example, Britain) were starting to think seriously about the expediency of wages and incomes policies. The process of policy convergence became even stronger in the early 1970s, when the system of fixed exchange rates partly disintegrated and the upheavals of these years prompted the adoption of rather similar emergency measures in many countries.

Shifts in policy emphasis in part reflected the dissatisfaction of individual countries with prevailing policies; in part, they were determined by changes in the order of priorities and by the changing fortunes of economic events. Few countries were able to retain throughout the period unrelenting reliance on one particular set of policies, because there was a continuing need to adapt them to changing circumstances. The next step is to determine how effective these policies were in achieving the main macroeconomic aims and here we pay particular attention to the questions of growth and stability. Of course, it should be borne in mind that the two are closely interrelated: measures to achieve greater stability say in investment or consumer spending or the balance of payments may also contribute to the long-term growth of the economy. Conversely, a too rapid promotion of investment for growth purposes may create greater instability. A distinction should also be made between longer-term policies designed to promote growth, especially those relating to the supply side, and the essentially short-term policies of demand management for purposes of achieving a greater measure of stability. In practice, of course, the distinction is sometimes difficult to make, though it would be true to say that successful long-term growth depends on effective demand management policies.

Impact of policy measures

The high and sustained level of demand in the post-war period is generally regarded as an important component in the rapid growth of most European countries. There were strong autonomous forces at work that promoted consumption, for example the widespread desire to accumulate consumer durables. At the same time, real growth forces were strong because European countries had a large back-log to catch up to American standards of productivity and technical application. Nevertheless, government budgetary operations contributed to the continued high level of demand. Not only was government spending itself on goods and services higher than before the war but the level and pattern of private consumption were partly determined by the fiscal process. In particular, the enlarged importance of taxes and transfer payments created a built-in stabilizing mechanism or compensatory device that led to greater stability in consumption and set a floor to consumption in times of recession. Thus disposable incomes and hence consumption tended to fall less than national income in recessionary periods compared with the inter-war period because of higher marginal tax rates and compensatory welfare payments, whereas conversely they rose less than total income during boom periods because of rising tax rates and reduced transfer payments. At the same time, the long-term tendency towards greater income equality through taxation meant a shift in the distribution of income towards those people with a high marginal propensity to consume, which in turn helped to maintain consumption levels. Also the greater security involved under the post-war welfare society probably meant a stronger inclination to maintain consumer spending in difficult times.

The impact of compensatory budgetary forces varied between nations. It was strongest in those countries with rigorous fiscal policies and in which direct taxes and social security systems were well developed. In this category are included Sweden, Norway and the UK, at least. It has been estimated that in Sweden, over 50 per cent of a 'primary' gross national product (GNP) recession impulse could be neutralized by built-in budgetary responses, though this is taking a broad definition of the stabilizing properties including the starting of relief works. However, a strong compensatory fiscal mechanism did not automatically lead to a high rate of growth in consumption in the long term, as the British case shows. Here the problem was that, despite the high floor to consumption in recessions through the working of the fiscal adjustment mechanism, the expansion of consumption in the upswing phases of the cycle had to be squeezed prematurely by restrictive action in order to deal with balance-of-payments problems. These were usually caused by the overheating of the economy because of supply bottlenecks.

In many continental countries, the compensatory mechanism was not so strong. This was because of the greater reliance on indirect taxes and also on account of the structure of social security payments. Though welfare schemes were well developed, they were generally less compensatory than those of the UK or Sweden. Many of the social transfer payments were fixed and they were financed by fixed charges that were insensitive to income fluctuations. Similarly, a large proportion of European tax receipts were insensitive to cyclical changes and many taxes were collected in arrears.

It seems probable therefore that consumption as a whole was maintained at a higher and more stable level by compensatory adjustment and the higher level of government spending on goods and services. In turn, this helped to make conditions more favourable for investment. But governments were also active in this regard. After 1945, most European governments took steps to encourage savings and productive investment for purposes of reconstruction, and such policies were continued during the 1950s. For example, German fiscal policy was designed mainly to encourage savings and investment. In the 1960s, however, less importance was attached to increasing aggregate investment ratios, which were already high, and so few new measures were taken to that effect, though attempts were made to influence investment for countercyclical purposes.

The methods used to influence the course of investment varied a great deal and often they were designed to achieve greater stability rather than expressly for the purpose of raising the long-term rate of investment. Moreover, the state's own capital outlays were large, especially in those countries in which public ownership was significant, while the housing sector was influenced strongly by government policy. There was a wide range of measures to encourage investment by private enterprise, including loans and grants, subsidies and various types of tax incentives. In addition, most countries created schemes for mobilizing savings, especially those of the lower income groups.

The most readily identifiable attempt to influence seriously the course of investment over the long term was made by France. Perhaps more than any other country, France was concerned with the question of long-term growth and investment, to the neglect at times of short-term disturbances in the economic system. Since 1946, the authorities regularly instituted a series of major investment plans, which, among other things, defined targets for private and public investment and for housing. The state was not only an important investor in its own right but it also did much to foster private investment by way of loans, subsidies and guarantees. The investment programme needs to be seen within the wider context of the planning mechanism, which cemented relationships within the mixed economy by involving the active participation of the main corporate interests in the economy: business, trade unions and government departments. In fact, planning became a way of life in France and it gave valuable guidance and direction to an economy that had previously suffered from years of stagnation. The active investment strategy provided business with the much-needed assurance of the long-term future. Judged by the record, the experiment paid off: France enjoyed rapid growth and a high investment ratio (especially in manufacturing), even if these were achieved at the expense of price and monetary stability. Nevertheless, some writers have sought to downgrade the contribution of planning to French economic growth, given the strong expansive forces at work globally.

While most other countries provided various incentives for investment, few had the same overriding long-term aims in view as the French. Indeed, many of the measures, though ostensibly designed to stimulate private investment, tended to fall foul of short-term stabilization policies. Thus, Britain in the 1950s and early 1960s provided several investment incentives, including investment allowances, investment grants and changes in tax rates, but their impact was mixed and often slow to materialize, partly no doubt because there were frequent switches in policy, which often counteracted their beneficial effect. In fact, at times, the complexity of the incentives, especially those related to regional development, were such that business people chose not to factor them into to their strategic plans, regarding them instead as an added bonus if their investment decisions coincided with a regional incentive. Monetary policy was also used for the same purpose from time to time, though its influence on investment tended to be weak and indirect and certainly less than in some continental countries, for instance Germany, where institutional (bank and government) financing was more important. Moreover, until 1958, Britain still operated a negative control over investment through the Capital Issues Committee. In Germany, direct state investment was relatively less important than in Britain, but the government made loans to private industries operating in key areas and fiscal policy was used for purposes of encouraging a high level of investment. On the other hand, monetary policy was employed mainly for countercyclical purposes, but it sometimes had a considerable impact on investment because of the wide range of monetary weapons used, the illiquidity of German business after the currency reform of 1948 and the important part played by the banks in the supply of long-term capital.

Both Sweden and the Netherlands employed a variety of fiscal devices to encourage investment, and budgetary policies were formulated with a view to satisfying savings needs, especially of the public sector, which was large. Here again, however, the devices seem to have been used more for short-term stabilization purposes than as a long-term stimulus to investment. The Swedes, for example, employed an investment reserves fund scheme by which taxes levied on investment in boom periods were released when the economy was moving into recession.

The measures used to stimulate investment in west European countries were varied and it is difficult to assess their impact precisely. One of the main problems is the difficulty of distinguishing between long-term incentives and short-term stabilization measures, though it seems that much of the policy action was designed to achieve the latter rather than the former. Certainly, public investment was at a higher level than pre-war, and in some cases, loans and tax incentives played an important part in boosting investment in certain sectors, and probably the general level of investment as well. In the Netherlands, for example, investment was increased by tax rules favouring the use of retained business earnings for reinvestment and allowing unrestricted compensation for initial losses. But it is difficult to believe that policy measures were instrumental in securing the high investment ratios recorded in the post-war period, except possibly in the case of France. Throughout the period, these ratios remained fairly stable, and if anything they increased slightly in the 1960s, when deliberate investment stimulation became less pronounced. One might also at this point take the contrast between Italy and the UK as a reflection of the weakness of the impact of policies on investment. Italy achieved a high rate of growth and a relatively high investment ratio despite a fiscal policy that was basically unfriendly towards growth and investment, though to some extent large public sector investment offset this. In the case of the UK, however, investment incentives, especially in the 1950s, were high by international standards, yet her investment ratio and rate of growth were low compared with those of other major countries. That investment ratios were high generally during this period can be attributed to the basically favourable economic climate, in which real growth forces were strong, rather than to active stimulation on the part of governments.

Finally, we turn to the general question of economic stability; it is in this area that governments were most active, that is, in short-term demand management rather than in the longer-term field of raising supply potential. One of the central issues in economic policy since the war was that of demand management, the aim being to secure a reasonable degree of economic stability within the context of the desired objectives. The dilemma facing governments was that they were committed, in a greater or lesser degree, to achieving a series of basically incompatible objectives, namely growth, full employment, price stability and external equilibrium, and possibly greater social equality. Thus it was found in practice that full employment could be achieved only at the cost of creeping inflation, or conversely price stability was possible only with a degree of unemployment that was politically unacceptable. Alternatively, in some cases, rapid growth proved incompatible with balance-of-payments equilibrium. Of course, some countries opted for one or two objectives, notably Germany, with her concentration on monetary (price) stability and external equilibrium, and in so doing managed to achieve a fair degree of success on all fronts. Nevertheless, even these countries had from time to time to face an alternate tightening and slackening of pressure on resources, and as a consequence, were forced to take action to stabilize the level of activity. In practice, therefore, it became a question of trading one objective off against another (price stability versus employment, growth versus the balance of payments) in order to maintain a reasonable degree of overall stability in the level of economic activity.

The task of economic stabilization involved the use of a wide range of fiscal and monetary instruments, and sometimes more direct controls, in order to influence both consumption and investment. As far as fiscal policy is concerned, the general practice, especially in continental Europe, was to use budgetary policy selectively to effect particular types of demand rather than to rely on budgetary surpluses or deficits as a macro regulator. Selective measures were therefore used to influence the level of activity in the private sector, though at times governments also varied their own spending programmes. The fiscal instruments used were varied and included investment allowances, subsidies, variations in tax rates on distributed and undistributed profits, changes in consumer taxes, tax rebates for exports, etc. As already noted, some countries placed greater emphasis on monetary policy. This proved to be an easier and more flexible instrument, especially in those countries where the fiscal process did not make it easy to achieve rapid changes in the policy mix. The range of monetary instruments was also wide, including variations in discount rates, open market operations, selective credit controls, reserve ratios, the imposition of ceilings on advances and rediscounts of commercial banks and moral suasion. The first two were the most popular, though not in every country. Sweden had little faith in the efficacy of discount rates, while the absence of an adequate and efficient bond market in Italy meant that that country made little use of open market operations. A few countries also at times limited the borrowing of local authorities and restricted the flow of capital issues. Special measures to control the movement of short-term capital were widespread. From the middle of the 1960s onwards, nearly all countries began to pay greater attention to the question of the aggregate money supply as opposed to the question of liquidity and credit facilities, in which the task of control became increasingly complex as a result of the growth of non-bank financial institutions.

Given that fluctuations in economic activity were less pronounced in the post-war years compared with previous experience, one might argue that government policies had a beneficial impact. The larger share of government purchases of goods and services and public investment could have led to greater stability of incomes and resistance of GNP to fluctuations in private investment, while the enlarged importance of taxes and transfer payments promoted greater income stability via the stabilization of consumer incomes. This is in accordance with the hypothesis of policy-induced stability expounded by Lundberg. On the other hand, Maddison has suggested an alternative interpretation: that economic systems had become more stable than previously as a result of endogenous influences but that policy factors caused the minor oscillations around the trend. However, these two views are not necessarily incompatible. It could be that the post-war cycle was modified by the greater impact of government operations within the economy, which ensured that fluctuations occurred at a higher level of output and employment than was previously the case, but that at the same time, policy factors were the cause of fluctuations within a limited range of deviations.

Evidence suggests that on balance governments were not adept at what has been termed 'fine-tuning' their economies. Frequently, policy action was often both badly timed and of the wrong order of magnitude, so that it turned out to be destabilizing. The classic example is that of Britain, where periodic balance of payments crises in 1947, 1949, 1951, 1955, 1957, 1960–61, 1964–65 and 1967–68, which were partly caused by allowing the economy to overheat in the first place, forced the authorities to adopt restrictive policies. But the timing of the policy action was usually mismanaged and often the authorities exerted too much pressure in both the upswing and in the recessionary phases of the cycle. For the most part, therefore, policies tended to have a destabilizing effect in both the 1950s and the 1960s. The situation was not helped by the fact that the authorities lacked effective instruments with which to act directly on the balance of payments and hence they were forced to aim at a level of economic activity that was more compatible with external equilibrium. Denmark also faced a similar situation until the late 1950s, with frequent exchange difficulties giving rise to restrictive policies, which in turn damped down the growth of the economy. On the other hand, France, who suffered from similar problems in the 1950s, did not resort to the restriction of internal demand in the way Britain and Denmark did but used import controls and devaluation to deal with the external problem. Between 1949 and 1958, France devalued her currency no fewer than seven times. Consequently, French economic policy did not act as a serious brake on the domestic economy. On the other hand, French policy probably caused greater instability in the economy and higher inflation than would otherwise been the case.

Countries without serious balance-of-payments problems did not necessarily have a better record with their stabilization policies. In Sweden, the main concern was with demand pressures and inflationary developments. Generally speaking, the government had greater difficulty in preventing expansions from developing into inflationary boom conditions than in counteracting recessionary tendencies. Thus, the strong expansions that got under way in 1954, 1959 and 1963 were badly controlled, with the result that drastic action had to be taken, which caused disruption and jerkiness in the process of expansion. Despite some degree of success with the more even phasing of investment through the investment reserves fund scheme, budgetary policy was badly coordinated with the cycle. In years of rapid expansion, there was no significant tendency for rising surpluses or reduced deficits in the total budget, and in some cases, for example the mid-1950s, large budgetary deficits created surplus liquidity that had to be mopped up by credit restrictions. Countercyclical measures to deal with recessionary phases were more successful, though in part these may have been favoured by the inherent strength of the Swedish economy and the lack of a serious balance of payments constraint. Not that the Dutch, with the aid of their sophisticated econometric forecasting model, were any more successful in stabilization policy. The model was used partly for the purpose of inferring short-term disturbances in the economy, but unfortunately it did not provide a reliable guide for policy decisions. Tensions within the Dutch economy were revealed by the model only when there were already clear indications of disequilibrium, by which time it was too late for the authorities to take the appropriate policy action.

The German record was also mixed. The authorities relied heavily on monetary policy to curb expansionary and inflationary tendencies in the later stages of the upswing, as for example in 1956 and 1965–66, because budgetary policy was not actively used for countercyclical purposes. On the whole, monetary restriction was effective in damping boom conditions, though usually it went too far, thereby aggravating the recessionary downturn. But the subsequent revivals owed little to policy stimulus; they were initiated primarily by an upsurge in the demand for exports. In the more severe recession of 1967, the government did for the first time adopt an expansionary fiscal policy to back up its monetary measures. The slowness of the economy to respond to the measures also prompted the authorities to contemplate an incursion into medium-term growth planning.

Italy's experience in demand management in the 1950s and 1960s was not dissimilar to that of other countries. Action was usually hesitant and belated, with the measures being taken in an *ad hoc* manner in response to predictions of economic events that often reflected past rather than current trends. As with other countries relying primarily on monetary weapons, these tended to invoke a strong response in periods of restraint but a weak and slow response in times of recessions. The increasing inadequacy of monetary control, in the 1963–64 recession in particular, forced the authorities to turn increasingly to fiscal policy, though the record of achievement on this score in the later 1960s was not promising. The timing of reversals in policy was such that their impact came when the opposite influence would have been more appropriate.

The mixed success of governments in dealing with short-term fluctuations in economic activity is not altogether surprising. Though state control over national resources was large and the automatic stabilizing element within the fiscal process may have been significant, nevertheless the macroeconomic policies of governments were often perversely destabilizing. Even though not all countries used fiscal spending deliberately as a countercyclical device, many items of budgetary expenditure were volatile and they frequently moved in a destabilizing manner. This is particularly true of defence expenditure and investment, which fluctuated sharply and often in the wrong direction, most notably in 1950–51. Up to a point, the same is also true of public spending on goods and services. Of course, it should be recognized that government spending, and especially investment expenditure on public utilities, is difficult to regulate sharply in response to sudden changes in activity, and for this reason, governments often thrust the burden of adjustment onto the private sector under the curious assumption that it is easier for this sector to respond in the way required. Of course, the task of regulating state spending was greater in countries where financial control was fragmented, for example in Germany, where local authorities and social security agencies accounted for a large part of public spending, and in countries such as Italy, where administrative and constitutional difficulties posed a restraint, one reason no doubt why these countries preferred monetary controls.

A further difficulty may have been that some governments had too few control levers for the tasks in hand. This is particularly relevant to countries with serious balance-of-payments problems such as Britain, because it involved juggling with a series of objectives and trying to maintain a semblance of stability with an inadequate armoury of weapons. The main problem was the want of an effective external regulator, and it is interesting to contrast this with France's readiness in the 1950s to use external controls to deal with the balance of payments. It is also important to note that in the 1960s, both Italy and Germany became aware of the need to broaden the range of their policy weapons.

Perhaps the major problem in economic management is the inherent time-lags involved in the process of formulating and applying stabilization policies. The initial perception of the need for policy action may be delayed because of the difficulty of obtaining the requisite statistics promptly. Another delay is incurred in the time taken to interpret the data once collected because it is often difficult to distinguish, on the basis of weekly or monthly data, whether, for example, there is a basic underlying change in the trend of economic activity. Then when a policy change is eventually decided upon, there can be a severe time-lag before it begins to take effect. All these lags can involve a considerable period, which may result in policies that are the reverse of what are required because of an intervening change in circumstances, or alternatively it may lead to policy action that is either too severe or too moderate. It is difficult to know how this problem can be readily overcome, although a solution is essential if short-term stabilization management is to be successful. Unfortunately, the task has not been made any easier in more recent years by the welter of contradictory forecasts of short-term trends in economic activity.

Conclusion

Western Europe's successful economic performance in the post-war period contrasts sharply with that of the inter-war period. The marked acceleration in growth in the 1950s and 1960s can be attributed to a number of factors, including higher rates of input of capital and labour, rapid technical progress, factor productivity improvement and a high level of demand. The greater degree of international economic cooperation and better macroeconomic policies also had a favourable impact on growth generally, and especially on demand, though there were strong autonomous forces stimulating the latter. Differences in growth rates among nations can only be partly explained by differing rates in the growth of factor inputs, because much depended on the way in which resources were utilized. However, it is important to note that countries with high rates of factor input also tended to reap large productivity gains and they also did well in exports. It is unlikely that variations in growth rates can be attributed in any significant degree to differences in government policies, though again it should be stressed that countries that concentrated on one or two objectives were more successful than those that attempted to do too much.

The record of governments with regard to stabilization was mixed but the greater stability of the post-war decades compared with pre-war can be set on the credit side. As Lundberg has noted, compared with the inter-war years, policy strategy certainly saw a vast improvement. However, it could be argued that given the strong real growth forces obtaining in the post-war period, government policies did not make much difference to the growth process overall. They were a benign influence that provided a favourable backdrop to the post-war expansion. If one looks ahead to the later twentieth century and beyond when the economic climate became less favourable and economic and financial instability increased, governments proved little more adept at dealing with the problems thrown up by a more hostile climate than they had shown in the inter-war years. This reinforces a point made throughout this volume, namely that government policies can have only a limited impact on economic performance. When real forces are naturally strong they can assist and encourage the process of expansion, but when real forces are weak and instability increases they are largely powerless to do much to ameliorate the situation.

Questions for discussion

1   Why was western Europe's economic growth in the period 1950–70 so much better than that in the inter-war years?
2   What contribution did government policy make to the post-war boom in Europe?
3   What developments led to the concept of the growth cycle?
4   Why did trade grow faster than output in western Europe?
5   Evaluate the usefulness of growth accounting analysis.

8 The socialist economies of Eastern Europe, 1950–70

Eastern Europe (comprising the eight socialist countries of Bulgaria, Czechoslovakia, East Germany [German Democratic Republic], Hungary, Poland, Romania, the Soviet Union and Yugoslavia) achieved an even better economic performance than the west in the 1950s and 1960s. But this was accomplished under a different political and economic institutional framework. Whereas in the west, the mixed social market economy prevailed, in the eastern bloc the means of production were owned and operated by the state. After the war, the eastern countries followed the Soviet model, though with some variations, of economic and political control, and by the early 1950s, they had emerged as fully fledged socialist states, firmly embraced within the Soviet sphere of influence. The partial exception was Yugoslavia, which after 1948 distanced herself from the Soviet line.

Socialism in more than one country

For a second time war shattered the economic and social life of central and eastern Europe, including the Soviet Union (see Chapter 6). The unification of a considerable part of central-east Europe within the Third Reich collapsed on the expiry of Hitler's regime, and the result was another redefining of national frontiers, together with the migration of millions of people. But the geographical carve-up of territory was less extensive and less damaging than that after the First World War, and the region did not return to the fragmented state that prevailed after 1918. Instead, the countries drew inspiration from their larger eastern neighbour (the USSR) and quickly established themselves as socialist states using the Soviet model as a benchmark. The main objectives were seen to be industrialization and the transformation of the social structure, tasks that could best be carried out by the abolition of private ownership of the means of production and the creation of a centrally administered and planned economic system.

Consequently, during the immediate post-war years, when these countries were engaged in fostering economic recovery, the state was steadily acquiring ownership of the means of production. The focus of attention initially was on the nationalization of industry. This proceeded more slowly than had been the case in the Soviet Union after the 1917 Revolution, partly because it took time to eliminate non-communist interests from power, but at least there was no policy reversal as in the USSR in the early 1920s. Nationalization occurred more rapidly in the former allied countries (Czechoslovakia, Poland and Yugoslavia) than in the ex-enemy territories (Bulgaria, Hungary and Romania). The former, having suffered German occupation, emerged from the war in a devastated condition and this left the way open for the state to extend its influence through the appropriation of ex-enemy property. By 1948, however, the socialization of the industrial sector was almost complete in all countries except East Germany (the Soviet zone of occupation). Here, the transition was effected rapidly when the German Democratic Republic was formally established in 1949. By this time, considerable progress had been made in the takeover of other sectors of the economy, including banking and finance, the distributive trades and other services. Thus, by the early 1950s, nationalization had been extended to most of the main branches of economic activity apart from agriculture.

The agrarian sector posed a more difficult problem. Though early attempts were made to nationalize the land, especially in Bulgaria, for the most part, this had not got far by the end of the 1940s. In fact, it was soon recognized that outright state ownership was impractical on account of the peasants' strong attachment to the soil. They regarded the land as rightfully theirs and expected one thing only: expropriation of the land and its redistribution among themselves. The obvious solution was therefore to allow the peasants to retain ownership but to organize their activities into collective enterprises, which in some ways would be a logical follow-up to the partial reforms of the inter-war years. Thus land, in varying amounts, was confiscated from the former owners without compensation and redistributed free among the peasantry, with the state retaining a part for its own purposes. This inevitably led to an extreme fragmentation of holdings, and hence the next step was to group holdings into larger units. Accordingly, the cooperative pooling of farm units became the dominant form, though the process of reorganization was slower and less brutally administered than had been the case in the Soviet Union before the war. It was accomplished steadily during the course of the 1950s, and by the beginning of the following decade, the bulk of agricultural production was under collectivized methods. State farms, on the other hand, accounted for only between 5 and 10 per cent of the land; however, in two countries (Poland and Yugoslavia), where opposition to agricultural socialism was strong, little progress was achieved. By the end of the 1960s, only about 15 per cent of the land in these two countries was run by collectives or state farms. Yugoslavia, it should be noted, had since 1948 deviated from the Soviet camp and followed a nonconformist brand of socialism.

Taking the countries as a whole, therefore, little was left of private enterprise by the early 1960s except in some small-scale minor activities such as handicrafts and catering. Virtually all mining, industry, transport, trading and financial activities were socially owned and operated. Some 95 per cent of the total national income of the eastern countries was derived from the socialized sector and an even higher proportion of industrial output and retail turnover. Only in agriculture was the socialized component less prominent, though even here it accounted for a large proportion (some 90 per cent) of the land. The deviations from the average were small, except in Poland and Yugoslavia, where the income derived from the state sector was about 75 per cent, and this was largely because in these two countries agriculture was mostly outwith the socialized sector of control.

Apart from state ownership and control, the second major feature of the socialist countries was the emphasis on central planning. In contrast to the situation in most west European countries, all decisions affecting the economic process were planned and determined centrally, the functions being carried out in each case by the State Planning Commission or Office. Of course, the methods of planning did vary from country to country and, as noted above, Yugoslavia deviated from the other socialist countries in her mode of operation at an early stage. Moreover, significant changes in the planning mechanism, especially the radical economic reforms enacted in the 1960s, were introduced from time to time. Nevertheless, throughout the period to 1970, the major economic variables strategic to the process of economic development continued to be determined by the central planning authorities. These included the determination of the proportions of income to be devoted to consumption and savings and between productive and non-productive investment and the allocation of investment among the major sectors and branches of the economy. In practice, the planning process went deeper than this because detailed targets were set for each sector and branch of activity in the central plans, which were drawn up periodically, on the basis of which allocations of factor inputs were made. Although this type of planning may not always have been efficient, it was possible to implement it in practice simply because of the absence of a significant private sector within the economy.

By virtue of their ideological commitments as well as recognition of their relative backwardness compared with the west, the socialist countries were conscious of the need to achieve a fast rate of development. To further this aim, priorities were accorded to capital formation and industrialization, and in the case of the latter, emphasis was placed on the heavy producer goods industries, especially iron and steel, machinery, chemicals and electronics. Inevitably, this meant some neglect of other sectors, notably agriculture, consumer goods industries and certain services, while it also entailed a slower rate of improvement in personal consumption and general welfare than in western countries. In addition, the strong emphasis placed on boosting growth by raising factor inputs, capital especially, particularly in the 1950s and early 1960s, probably led to a wasteful and inefficient use of resources. Later, however, some attempt was made to reduce this deficiency by focusing on ways to improve both the quality and productivity of factor inputs.

The planning process and the reforms of the 1960s are discussed at greater length later in this chapter. First, we must take a look at the socialist record in terms of growth and structural change.

Growth and structural change

Although the growth of output was rapid in eastern Europe in the post-war period (and on balance better than in the west), it does not appear at first glance that centralized planning made much difference to the performance of the socialist countries compared with their free market counterparts in the west. This could in part be explained by the fact that, though growth was a central objective, it entailed too great a priority being accorded to some sectors of the economy, for example heavy industry, whereas too little attention was paid to improving the efficiency with which resources were used. Furthermore, given the backward state of these countries and the slower recovery from the war compared with western Europe, one might have expected a strong performance in subsequent years. In 1950, most western economies had well exceeded their pre-war output levels, whereas eastern Europe as a whole had only just about managed to regain the pre-war position. Apart from the Soviet Union, only Czechoslovakia and Bulgaria had surpassed the pre-war benchmark in 1950, though Poland also showed significant advance as a result of boundary changes. But in East Germany (GDR), Hungary and Romania, output fell short of the former level by amounts varying between 2 and 15 per cent. In other words, the differences in income levels between east and west in 1950 were even greater than they had been in 1938, so that socialist countries had a big task in hand if they were to approach the living standards of their capitalist neighbours.

Any discussion of growth performance is a hazardous exercise given the reliance one is forced to place on aggregate statistics, which may contain substantial errors. Even in the west, the methods of calculating income generated by the service sectors are far from perfect. In the case of the socialist countries, the difficulties encountered are greater because national income accounting procedures differed substantially from those used in western countries. One of the main differences is that socialist countries recorded only material production in their national income accounts, thereby excluding most of the income generated by the service sectors, while they valued the product at realized sale prices (that is, inclusive of turnover taxes) as against the western practice of valuation 'at factor cost'. This means that official socialist income data are not directly comparable with those of western countries unless adjustments are made. Unfortunately, scholars themselves disagree as to the adjustments required, though most take the view that the official figures on material production tend to overstate the growth performance of the communist countries, because if services were included the effect would be to lower the overall rates of growth.

For our purposes, we use the estimates of GDP compiled by the United Nations, which as far as possible conform to a standardized system of national accounting. Because of the obvious difficulties involved in adjusting the accounts, the data are subject to margins of error so that too much reliance should not be placed on the precise accuracy of individual figures. Nevertheless, the magnitudes involved are broadly comparable with other estimates of income and output for these countries, and they do correspond approximately to the data on western Europe used in the previous chapter.

Data on output, employment, productivity and population growth are given in Table 8.1 for the eight countries. In eastern Europe as a whole, domestic output grew at 7 per cent per annum through the 1950s and 1960s, a rate considerably in excess of that in the west (4.6 per cent). However, population rose more rapidly in

Table 8.1 Eastern Europe: output, employment and labour productivity growth, 1950–69 (annual percentage compound rates of growth)

	Output (GDP at 1963 f.c.)			Employment			Output per person employed			Population, 1950–70
	1950/2–1967/9	1950/2–1958/60	1958/60–1967/9	1950/2–1967/9	1950/2–1958/60	1958/60–1967/9	1950/2–1967/9	1950/2–1958/60	1958/60–1967/9	
Bulgaria	6.9	6.4	7.4	0.5	0.7	0.4	6.4	5.7	7.0	0.8
Czechoslovakia	5.2	5.7	4.8	1.2	1.0	1.3	4.0	4.7	3.5	0.8
German Democratic Republic	5.7	7.1	4.5	0.4	0.7	0.1	5.3	6.4	4.4	–0.2
Hungary	4.8	4.1	5.5	1.0	1.2	0.7	3.8	2.9	4.8	0.8
Poland	6.1	6.2	6.0	1.8	1.7	1.9	4.2	4.4	4.0	1.4
Romania	7.2	6.3	8.0	0.9	1.4	0.4	6.2	4.8	7.6	1.1
Soviet Union	7.6	8.3	6.9	2.0	1.9	2.1	5.5	6.3	4.7	1.5
Yugoslavia	6.2	6.4	6.1	0.8	0.5	1.1	5.4	5.9	5.0	1.1
Eastern Europe	7.0	7.6	6.5	1.7	1.7	1.7	5.2	5.8	4.7	1.3

Source: United Nations (Economic Commission for Europe), *Economic Survey of Europe in 1971*, Part 1, *The European Economy from the 1950s to the 1970s*, New York, 1972, 6, Table 1.2.

the east, especially in the Soviet Union and Poland, so that the differential in per capita output growth rates was narrower: 5.7 per cent per annum as against nearly 4 per cent in the west. The higher rates of population growth (the main exception being the GDR) also led to a more rapid growth in the labour force, while the productivity record was also superior to that of the west.

In general, there was not a wide spread between countries in growth performance. It was fastest in the Soviet Union and in the least developed countries (Romania and Bulgaria), while Hungary's performance was relatively poor by the standards of the east. Between the two decades there was a tendency for rates of expansion to decline, especially in the more advanced economies of the USSR, Czechoslovakia and East Germany, whereas Hungary and the two least developed countries (Romania and Bulgaria) achieved some acceleration. In fact, during the early 1960s, there were signs of a slowing down in growth in most of the socialist countries except Romania, a feature that prompted the introduction of economic reforms in the planning and management of these economies (see below).

As one might expect given the ideological commitment of these countries, there was a substantial sectoral imbalance in rates of expansion. Priority was given to industry and especially the heavy sector, including producer durables, with the result that there was a more marked disparity than in the west between the rates of growth of different sectors of the economy. Thus in eastern Europe as a whole industrial output over the period 1950–70 rose by just under 10 per cent per annum, with Bulgaria, Romania and the Soviet Union recording double figure increases. By contrast, agriculture, with a low priority, expanded by only 3 per cent a year, with Czechoslovakia actually recording a slight fall in the output of this sector. Indeed, the agrarian sector generally proved to be a persistent weak spot in what otherwise was a splendid record of achievement, though in part the authorities had only themselves to blame through their neglect of this branch of activity. It was a decade or more before agricultural production in the east surpassed the pre-war levels, as against a 50 per cent rise in the west, while even by the early 1960s, the more developed countries of East Germany and Czechoslovakia still fell short of the pre-war targets. The remaining sectors of the economy (transport, trade, construction and personal and government services) grew in aggregate slightly less rapidly than the economy as a whole, though there were considerable variations between different branches. Government services, for example, expanded faster than direct personal services and housing, and in some cases the output of personal services actually declined. Transport also expanded more rapidly than most of the other activities in this group.

These differences in performance reflected the order of priorities accorded to particular sectors. Industry, for example, received a large part (sometimes one-half or more) of the available investment resources, whereas agriculture was starved of capital. Moreover, within the broad sectors certain branches were singled out for top priority treatment. This was particularly the case with the industrial sector, in which the emphasis was placed on producer durables to the neglect of consumer goods. Consequently, industries such as chemicals, metals and machine-building grew twice as rapidly as food-processing and consumer durables and considerably faster than industry as a whole, while three branches (electric power, mechanical engineering and chemicals) accounted on average for about one-third of industrial production in the mid-1960s. The share of capital goods as a whole in gross industrial production had risen to over 60 per cent in most countries by the 1960s compared with 40 per cent or less in the immediate pre-war years (1938–39). The increasing orientation towards the heavy industrial sector is reflected in the capital formation figures. From a relatively low level at the beginning of the period, investment ratios rose steadily to reach around 30 per cent by 1970 in most cases. It has also been noted that if socialist income figures were put on a comparable western basis the proportion of saving in national income would range between 20 and 40 per cent as against 10–25 per cent in capitalist economies at a similar stage of development (Wilczynski 1972).

Not surprisingly, rapid growth brought about significant structural changes in the socialist economies, which were more pronounced and diverse than those in western Europe during the same period. The data in Table 8.2, showing the composition of national income and employment by main sectors of the economy, provide a broad idea of the main trends. The figures purport to be no more than approximate measures, but those for the composition of the national product have been adjusted to correspond more closely than the official estimates with those used in western countries. They are based on independent estimates of GNP at factor cost, and unlike the official figures, they include the service sectors. Unfortunately, comparable estimates for the Soviet Union are not available.

The most significant change was in the shares of industry and agriculture in income and employment. All countries experienced a shift from agriculture to industry, and in some cases, this was substantial, more particularly in the Balkan countries (Yugoslavia, Romania and Bulgaria), where industry eventually accounted for one-third or more of total income, whereas agriculture's share declined to one-quarter or less. The same trends are illustrated by the employment data, though in the less developed countries some 40 per cent or more of total employment was still located in the agrarian sector. However, this was a substantial improvement on the pre-war period, when between 75 and 80 per cent of all employment in Yugoslavia, Bulgaria and Romania was to be found in the primary sector. In fact, these countries were fast losing their predominantly agrarian base against which they had struggled for so long. The trend away from agriculture was also significant in the more advanced economies of East Germany, Czechoslovakia and the Soviet Union, and in the case of the first two countries their economic structures were then similar to the west European pattern. One should also note the marked difference between the income and employment shares in agriculture. The higher share of the latter reflects the substantial difference in productivity levels between industry and agriculture. As for construction and trade, there were no marked trends in these two sectors, but transport and communications tended to increase in importance in terms of both income and employment, except in the GDR. The last category in the table, which includes government and personal and miscellaneous services, displayed contrary tendencies. The income share of this sector declined in all countries, reflecting no doubt the low priority accorded to the

Table 8.2 Composition of gross national product and structure of employment (in percentages of total)

		Industry/handicrafts		Agriculture/forestry		Construction		Transport/communications		Trade		Other services	
		GNP	Employment	GNP	Employment	GNP	Employment	GNP	Employment	GNP	Employment	GNP	Employment
Bulgaria	1939	9.5		55.1		3.0		2.5		6.9		23.0	
	1950	18.1	7.9[a]	39.4	82.1	5.6	2.0	5.9	1.5	4.8	2.2	26.2	4.3
	1967	42.7	28.2	15.6	41.8	9.3	7.5	10.4	5.3	7.2	5.4	14.8	11.8
Czechoslovakia	1937	30.6		28.9		7.5		4.4		7.4		21.2	
	1950	34.8	27.9	23.9	36.9	6.7	6.0	7.3	4.9	7.1	8.0	20.2	16.3
	1967	45.0	38.0	12.4	19.1	7.7	8.0	12.8	6.2	7.7	8.0	14.5	20.7
East Germany	1950	36.8	39.7[b]	11.3	22.9	4.7	5.8	10.4	7.0	7.3	10.7	29.5	13.8
	1967	50.8	41.1	8.7	15.6	7.8	5.8	9.2	7.1	8.5	11.5	14.8	18.9
Hungary	1938	20.7		37.3		4.3		5.0		6.7		26.0	
	1950	25.3	19.7	29.7	49.8	6.2	5.3	9.5	4.2	6.2	4.8	23.1	16.2
	1967	36.0	33.5	20.6	30.0	7.1	6.3	13.2	6.3	8.1	7.2	15.0	16.6
Poland	1937	18.9		36.6		4.0		3.4		12.3		24.8	
	1950	22.0	20.7	36.9	53.5	4.5	5.1	5.7	4.7	6.2	6.0	24.7	10.0
	1967	36.0	27.3	24.2	39.9	6.2	6.9	8.7	6.1	7.1	5.9	17.8	14.0
Romania	1939		9.1		80.0								8.0[c]
	1950	19.2	12.0	31.3	74.3	4.1	2.2	6.5	2.2	7.4	2.5	31.5	6.8
	1967	32.9	20.0	22.0	53.8	11.1	7.1	8.8	4.0	5.4	4.2	19.8	10.9
Yugoslavia	1939		10.0		76.3						4.2		9.5[c]
	1950	22.7	9.3[b]	27.6	78.3	5.9	3.2	8.6	2.0	5.2	2.3	30.0	4.9
	1967	37.2	19.6	22.6	56.7	3.4	5.4	10.2	3.3	7.9	4.9	18.7	10.0
USSR	1950		22.0		46.0		4.0		7.0				21.0[d]
	1967		29.0		30.0		7.0		8.0				26.0[d]

Sources: T. P. Alton, 'Economic structure and growth in eastern Europe', in Joint Economic Committee, US Congress, *Economic Developments in Countries of Eastern Europe*, Washington, DC: US Government Printing Office, 1970, 54, 58; J. C. Wilczynski, *Socialist Economic Development and Reforms*, London: Macmillan, 1972, 190.

Notes: [a] 1948. [b] 1952. [c] Includes construction and transport and communications. [d] Includes trade.

provision of personal and private services, but in most cases, the employment share rose, suggesting a poor productivity performance in these activities.

In sum, therefore, though some of the socialist countries still had some way to go before the structural format of their economies resembled closely that of the advanced capitalist economies, it is clear that the rapid development of the post-war period had already brought about a considerable transformation of economies that not many years previously had been basically agrarian.

Consumption and income levels

Despite rapid growth and structural change the consumer in eastern Europe did not benefit commensurately. Moreover, income levels still remained far below those of the western world. It is true that the standard of living of most people in the socialist countries improved substantially between 1950 and 1970 and in some cases by appreciable amounts. In the GDR, for example, real wages more than tripled in this period, whereas in Bulgaria, Yugoslavia and Romania they rose by over 150 per cent. By contrast, the real income gains of the workers in Poland, Hungary and Czechoslovakia were considerably less. However, real wages did not keep pace with the growth in national output, while personal consumption was held back to an even greater extent through the emphasis on savings and investment and the limited range of choice as regards consumer products. Whereas in the west personal consumption advanced almost in step with national income, in the east this was far from being the case. On average, the increase in per capita consumption in eastern countries was probably only about one-half that of the west, though there were considerable variations between countries. Czechoslovakia recorded one of the lowest increases, whereas in Bulgaria and Romania consumption advanced rapidly. Political factors in part determined the speed with which consumer welfare was satisfied. For example, the Hungarian revolt of 1956 led to a sharp increase in living standards, which had been held back severely before that event. Conversely, the closing of the German border between east and west led to a restriction on the growth of consumption in East Germany because there was no longer any pressure to try to maintain the standards of the west. Similarly, fluctuations in Polish living standards were partly dependent on political circumstances.

Of course, the compression of personal consumption levels reflects the socialist order of priorities, particularly the emphasis on building up investment at the expense of consumption. In effect, therefore, it meant that socialist consumers benefited less than their western counterpart from the rapid growth in economic activity. Moreover, for some countries, it meant a widening gap in consumption levels compared with western countries, where formerly there had been fairly close parity. For instance, before the war, East German consumption levels were not far removed from those of the western half of the country, while Czechoslovakia was not far behind. By the middle of the 1960s, per capita consumption in East Germany and Czechoslovakia was only about 60 per cent of the West German level, and it also trailed Austrian per capita consumption by a large margin, whereas there had been a clear lead before the war. Or again, whereas Hungary and Austria had similar levels of consumption before the war, in the mid-1960s, there was a 40 per cent gap between the two, with Hungary's consumption not much above the Polish.

Of course, the bare statistics of consumption do not fully reflect consumer welfare in the socialist countries because there are a number of other relevant factors that need to be taken into account. These affect both sides of the balance sheet. Adverse features include the limited range of product choice (especially in consumer durables), the poor design and quality of consumer products, the frequent shortages of goods and in some cases the need for rationing or queuing. On the other hand, the population did benefit from a big increase in the supply of free or nearly free social services, probably at least equal to those in the west. Lower paid and less skilled workers gained through a narrowing of pay differentials, while the peasants, despite an initial squeeze on their incomes, were major beneficiaries as a result of the shortage of agricultural products. Agricultural wages generally were brought more closely in line with industrial earnings during the period. Furthermore, lower paid workers in general benefited substantially from the low prices of necessities, the letting of housing at nominal rents and the greater security of employment compared with before the war. By contrast, skilled and white-collar workers suffered a relative decline in their living standards, while middle-class professional and managerial groups fared worst of all.

If the consumer did not benefit fully from the impressive growth record of the socialist countries, at least some consolation may be derived from the fact that in this period the income gap on a per capita basis between the east European countries and the advanced countries of the west began to decline for the first time. This of course was only to be expected given the higher rate of income growth in eastern Europe compared with most other countries except Japan. Even so, the leeway to be made up still remained large by the end of the 1960s. Although levels of national income per capita in the east European countries taken together were nearly double those of all capitalist countries and the world in general, they fell short of American and west European income levels. They ranged from about one-quarter to less than one-half those in the United States, with the highest being recorded in Czechoslovakia, East Germany and the USSR and the lowest in Bulgaria, Romania and Yugoslavia. Moreover, many westerners would have found life drab in the eastern sector, given the limited range and poor quality of consumer products, the dreary urban morphology and the limited range of modern entertainment.

Growth factors

For much of the period, at least until the economic reforms of the 1960s, the countries of eastern Europe concentrated their attention on what has been termed extensive growth, that is, boosting output by raising the inputs of labour and capital. This probably involved some loss of efficiency and was one of the reasons for the move for economic reform in management, but it did mean that these countries achieved faster rates of input growth than was the case in western Europe. For example, employment grew at an annual rate of 1.7 per cent in the area as a whole compared with 0.6 per cent in the west (1950–70), and apart from East Germany all the socialist countries experienced high rates of labour input. This can partly be explained by the more rapid rate of increase in population in the east (the major exception being the GDR), but policy factors were also instrumental in securing the maximum use of the available labour reserves. Thus there was a determined effort to eliminate unemployment and increase the participation rates, especially among women, who now provided a larger proportion of the labour force than in western Europe. At the same time, the effective labour force was augmented by long hours of work, the shift of labour out of agriculture and the squeeze on the growth of the service sectors, which were labour-intensive activities. Despite these measures, labour shortages did occur from time to time because of the high growth targets set, capital shortages or bottlenecks and the emphasis on output rather than efficiency.

Capital inputs also rose sharply in the post-war period. Though Marxist theory may hold that the only source of growth is labour, the socialist authorities were never under any delusion as to the indirect contribution of capital growth in terms of raising output and labour productivity. Consequently, a determined effort was made to raise investment ratios at the expense of consumption, and investment resources were directed to what the socialists regarded as the productive sector (namely industry and especially producer durables), to the neglect of services and agriculture. Thus, the fixed capital stock in industry in the eight socialist countries rose on average by 8.3 per cent per annum over the years 1950–70, with the Soviet Union and Bulgaria recording double-figure increases. By contrast, in the service sector and agriculture, fixed capital stock rose by only just over 5 per cent a year. Yet, despite the strong emphasis given to capital accumulation, the stock of fixed assets in the economy as a whole rose at a slightly slower rate than national output, at 6.1 per cent per annum, though there were times, especially in the 1950s, when it expanded more rapidly than output. Taken in conjunction with employment growth of 1.7 per cent a year, this suggests that of the combined growth rate in output of 7 per cent for the east, some 3 percentage points can be accounted for by the increase in factor inputs, while the remainder was a result of increases in output per unit of input. In other words, factor productivity accounted for some 57 per cent of the growth achieved, a share less than that for west European countries.

However, in terms of major sectors and countries, there were some marked differences in the relative contribution to growth of the various factors. Table 8.3 gives details of the growth attributable to employment, capital and productivity in percentage terms in the three main sectors of the economy for the several countries in question. The first thing to notice is the sharp contrast between the different sectors in terms of the sources of growth. In the case of industry, total factor inputs and factor productivity were roughly equally responsible for the overall growth in output during the 1950s and 1960s. But in agriculture, less than one-third of the growth in output was derived from increases in inputs, and in some cases (notably Czechoslovakia, Hungary and the GDR), this source produced

Table 8.3 Eastern Europe: contribution of factor inputs and factor productivity to growth in output of major sectors

| | Output growth (annual rate) | | | Percentage contribution to output growth of | | | | | | | | | | | | |
| | | | | Employment | | | Capital | | | Total factor input | | | Output per unit of input | | |
	A	B	C	A	B	C	A	B	C	A	B	C	A	B	C
Industry															
Bulgaria	13.5	15.5	11.5	31.6	33.4	29.2	30.9	25.9	36.5	62.5	59.3	65.7	37.5	40.7	34.3
Czechoslovakia	6.7	8.0	5.5	24.0	23.6	25.5	21.5	17.3	27.8	45.5	40.9	53.3	54.5	59.1	46.7
German Democratic Republic	7.5	10.1	5.2	5.6	9.0	-1.4	18.8	10.7	32.9	24.4	19.7	31.5	75.6	80.3	68.5
Hungary	7.9	7.1	8.7	33.7	47.3	24.1	30.7	35.9	26.9	64.6	83.2	51.0	35.6	16.8	49.0
Poland	8.9	9.4	8.3	29.1	29.8	29.5	17.2	9.9	25.3	46.3	39.7	54.8	53.7	60.3	45.2
Romania	12.6	11.9	13.2	23.9	22.3	25.5	22.9	21.2	24.3	46.8	43.5	49.8	53.2	56.5	50.2
Soviet Union	10.3	11.2	9.4	21.7	17.5	26.1	31.5	31.6	31.9	53.2	49.1	58.0	46.8	50.9	42.0
Eastern Europe	9.6	10.6	8.8	22.6	19.2	25.5	25.9	22.4	29.3	48.5	41.5	54.8	51.5	58.5	45.2
Agriculture															
Bulgaria	1.6	1.3	1.8	-131.3	-102.3	-151.7	129.4	117.7	143.3	-1.9	15.4	-8.4	101.9	84.6	108.4
Czechoslovakia	-0.4	-0.5	-0.3	-455.0	-294.0	-700.0	375.0	258.0	560.0	-80.0	-36.0	-140.0	-20.0	-64.0	40.0
German Democratic Republic	2.0	2.3	1.7	-84.0	-79.1	-94.7	73.5	41.7	112.9	-10.5	-37.4	18.2	110.5	137.4	81.8
Hungary	1.1	2.0	0.5	-120.9	-28.0	-392.0	120.0	66.0	270.0	-0.9	38.0	-122.0	100.9	62.0	222.0
Poland	1.9	2.2	1.6	0.0	-3.2	0.0	37.9	24.5	56.3	37.9	21.4	56.3	62.1	78.6	43.7
Romania	2.8	3.3	2.2	-27.5	8.5	-73.2	39.6	21.8	65.5	12.1	30.0	-7.7	87.9	69.7	107.7
Soviet Union	3.8	5.7	2.1	-16.6	-2.5	-53.3	58.4	42.1	98.5	41.8	39.6	45.2	58.1	60.4	54.8
Eastern Europe	3.1	4.4	1.9	-22.6	-4.8	-62.6	54.2	36.1	93.2	31.6	31.3	30.6	68.4	68.7	69.4

Construction and services

Bulgaria	6.8	6.4	7.2	45.3	48.1	42.8	20.3	17.8	22.1	65.6	65.9	64.9	34.4	34.1	35.1
Czechoslovakia	5.7	6.1	5.4	34.4	28.7	41.5	14.7	12.8	17.2	49.1	41.5	58.7	50.9	58.5	41.3
German Democratic Republic	4.5	5.1	4.0	24.9	26.1	22.8	11.3	6.5	16.5	36.2	32.5	39.3	63.8	67.5	60.7
Hungary	3.3	2.6	3.9	42.4	40.4	43.1	26.4	26.5	26.9	68.8	66.9	70.0	31.2	33.1	30.0
Poland	6.1	6.4	5.8	36.7	33.9	39.8	14.8	13.1	16.6	51.5	47.0	56.4	48.5	53.0	43.6
Romania	6.2	5.5	6.8	49.7	49.6	50.4	24.2	23.5	24.7	73.9	73.1	75.1	26.1	26.9	24.9
Soviet Union	6.9	7.5	6.3	43.6	39.2	50.0	36.1	34.4	38.1	79.7	73.6	88.1	20.3	26.4	11.9
Eastern Europe	6.4	6.8	6.0	42.7	38.1	47.8	25.3	22.1	29.0	68.0	60.2	76.8	32.0	39.8	23.2

Source: Calculations based on data in United Nations (Economic Commission for Europe) *Economic Survey of Europe in 1971*, Part 1, *The European Economy from the 1950s to the 1970s*, New York, 1972, 6, Table 1.2.

Notes: A, 1950/2–1967/9; B, 1950/2–1958/60; C, 1958/60–1967/9.

a negative contribution. Of course, the reason in this case is the large negative contribution from employment as a result of the substantial shift of labour out of the sector. Though agricultural expansion was relatively modest in most countries, the loss of labour resources was often beneficial to productivity because it relieved the land of low or zero marginal productivity workers. The third sector (construction and services) also shows some interesting features. Here, factor inputs were more important than productivity as a growth source. This is perhaps not altogether surprising given the traditionally low productivity growth in many of the branches of this sector. However, what is noteworthy is the high rates of employment and capital growth in the sector as a whole. In fact, employment expanded more rapidly in services than in industry, which implies that the socialist authorities were not as successful as often imagined in containing the movement of resources into what they regarded as the non-productive areas of the economy.

Country differences within the major sectors were also significant. Bulgaria and Hungary, for example, derived about two-thirds of their industrial growth from factor input expansion, with labour and capital contributing roughly equal proportions, whereas in East Germany it was productivity change that accounted for most of the growth recorded. East Germany also had a similar experience in construction and services. However, for most other countries, the major contribution to growth in the latter sector was employment, with productivity accounting for one-third or less in Bulgaria, Romania and the Soviet Union. The biggest inter-country variations occurred in agriculture, and these were partly occasioned by the sharp and general contraction in labour inputs. As a result, the contribution of total factor inputs to growth was negative in several cases, and only Poland and the USSR secured a substantial positive contribution from resource expansion. Inevitably, therefore, productivity accounted for most of the output growth in agriculture, ranging from over 100 per cent in the case of Bulgaria, Hungary and East Germany to about one-half or more in the USSR, whereas in the case of Czechoslovakia, it was a negative quantity, a reflection of the disastrous record of Czech agriculture.

Though for the economy at large the relative contributions to growth of factor inputs and productivity were not markedly different from those of western industrial countries, it should be stressed that eastern countries did experience faster rates of expansion in the inputs of capital and labour. Moreover, if anything, the input intensity of total output tended to increase between the 1950s and 1960s as a result of an acceleration in capital growth. In fact, in all countries apart from the Soviet Union, fixed capital per person employed increased in all three sectors during the period. This led to declining efficiency; with the major exception of Hungary, most countries experienced a deceleration in the growth of labour productivity and output per unit of input, a trend that is reflected in the declining contribution of factor productivity to overall growth (see Table 8.3). This adverse movement in productivity was mainly responsible for the fairly general decline in rates of output growth in several countries during the 1960s, a matter of some concern to the authorities and one that prompted an overhaul of the basis of economic management.

The costs of economic growth

In view of the extremely backward state of eastern Europe generally, both before the war under capitalist regimes and in the immediate transitional post-war years, the socialist countries of this area achieved little short of a miracle in the generation or so after 1945. Their record of achievement was certainly more impressive than anything the west had achieved at a similar stage of development given the initial starting disparities. Formerly low-income, agrarian-based economies with limited growth potential had been transformed into relatively modern and dynamic structures with a solid industrial foundation. Rapid economic growth, high by virtually any standard, led to a more than fourfold increase in national income and a sevenfold increase in industrial output within the space of two decades. By 1970, the eight socialist countries accounted for some 30 per cent of world industrial output as against 18 per cent in the early 1950s.

The development strategy adopted to achieve this result inevitably entailed considerable costs. Whether such results could have been achieved without them or whether the benefits outweighed the costs are matters that have given rise to endless debate. However, it is important to recognize that the growth strategy imposed several costs on the populations of these countries.

In the first place, as noted earlier, the consumer did not reap the full benefits of the economic advance. The investment and growth strategy of the authorities dictated a restriction on the expansion of consumer spending and a low priority for consumer goods and service industries. This meant that not only did consumption rise by considerably less than national income but that the range and quality of goods and services available were inferior to those in western countries. Shortages of goods were also common, and this led to queuing, rationing and black-market activities. The market situation for many consumer products resembled that in western democracies in the war and immediate post-war years, when rationing, shortages and low quality products were common features. On the other hand, one must bear in mind that under socialism the economic position of the masses did improve to a certain degree, and that an alternative growth strategy, with a lower growth profile, might not have brought any greater benefits to the individual consumer.

Perhaps more serious is the way in which the socialist development strategy led to an extravagant use of resources. Labour, capital and natural resources were used in a profligate manner. In part, this was the inevitable result of the original socialist conception that quantity not quality provided the key to faster growth. Thus, under the extensive growth phase, the emphasis was directed towards increasing the inputs of labour and capital, especially the latter, at the expense of productivity or the efficiency of input use. This may have led in some cases to the injection of labour inputs to the point of zero marginal productivity, while with increasing capital intensity per worker and rising capital/output ratios, the marginal productivity of capital declined. These trends are reflected in the deceleration of factor productivity growth in the 1960s. Moreover, by western standards, resources were inefficiently utilized in the socialist economies. Ernst (1966) reckoned that investment costs (that is, the ratio of gross fixed investment to increments in output) were higher than in western Europe by an average of 25 per cent for the total economy, and up to 40 per cent in industry. Productivity levels were also lower than in the advanced capitalist economies. Wilczynski (1972) maintains that productivity in the USSR in the early 1960s was only 40 per cent of the American level despite the fact that the rate of capital accumulation was three times the US rate.

Apart from the overriding belief of the socialist authorities in the importance of the quantity of resources, the planning mechanism itself, at least until the reforms of the 1960s, tended to encourage the wasteful use of resources. The high and often increasing targets set by the plans provided an incentive for managers of plants and factories to secure as large an allocation of resource inputs as possible, even though they sometimes remained underutilized. The hoarding of labour by enterprises was a common occurrence, a result partly of the general excess demand for labour. Moreover, slack labour discipline, increasing absenteeism and high labour turnover led to poor utilization of the available labour resources.

Capital resources were also hoarded and used inefficiently. This partly stemmed from the fact that, until the mid-1960s, capital was allocated to enterprises without charge except for depreciation rates, which were kept low. But it was also a product of the planning and management process. Investment planning was highly centralized and largely divorced from current production activities. The absence of a market mechanism and the inherent socialist antipathy to the concept of cost and scarcity as criteria for allocation purposes meant that investment resources were allocated in an arbitrary and bureaucratic manner, often without reference to real needs. In the absence of a rational price structure, prices did not reflect opportunity costs, so that production costs and demand factors were imperfectly incorporated into the planning mechanism. Inevitably, therefore, this led to a misallocation of investment and, as a consequence, the underutilization of capital. For example, on grounds of prestige and propaganda, the planners often made extravagant provisions for space per worker. The insistence on high rates of investment sometimes strained the capacity of the construction and machinery industries, which in turn entailed long gestation periods and the accumulation of half-finished projects. New plant facilities often ran well below capacity because of poor planning of locations and the lack of complementary and back-up supplies and facilities. In the industrial sector, for example, a substantial part of the investment was earmarked for new plants in previously undeveloped sites. This involved an excessive amount of capital for infrastructure and complementary facilities, which sometimes meant that there were insufficient resources for modernizing or maintaining plants in already established industrial areas. Finally, there is the possibility that the investment requirements of the least developed heavy sectors (chemicals, metallurgy and fuel) were accorded too great a priority to the neglect of light industry and industries producing materials, which often provided supplies of intermediate products for the heavy sector.

It is possibly inevitable that a centralized planning system divorced from the market will give rise to discontinuities and a suboptimal allocation of resources.

Furthermore, the socialist emphasis, at least in the earlier part of the period, on growth at any cost also had adverse implications for technological progress. Generally speaking, a growth policy based on raising the quantity of inputs was not conducive to rapid technical progress. In theory, the relative backwardness of eastern Europe should have provided opportunities for more rapid technical transformation than in the west. And the possibilities for taking advantage of such opportunities were good, given the high levels of investment and the scope this provided for technical change and scale economies. Yet eastern Europe remained behind the west in the application of new technology, and there is some evidence that the gap was increasing up to the 1960s. Wilczynski (1972) suggests that the Soviet lag in civilian technology behind the United States was greater in 1962 than in 1940, whereas Poland was some forty years or more behind Britain and nine behind France. The proportions of national income spent on science and technology were generally lower than in the west, while the growth derived from technological improvement was also lower. In time, the technological weakness was to become a more serious issue (see Chapter 11).

In the lesser developed economies of eastern Europe, one would expect that the level and intensity of technological development would be less strong than in the more mature countries, though the opportunities for catch-up with best western techniques were correspondingly greater. However, one should also bear in mind that the socialist countries had limited access to the best western technology simply by virtue of their restricted trade and cultural contacts with the west. Yet the lag was also serious in the most industrialized of the eastern countries, namely Czechoslovakia and East Germany, which suggests that there may have been other factors at work. Certainly, under the extensive phase of socialist growth, technology was not accorded a high priority, while poor planning and management of investment resources did little to offset the emphasis on quantity rather than quality. The high proportion of investment resources earmarked for buildings and construction (up to one-half of productive investment at times in the period before the reforms) as opposed to investment in plant and machinery (which provide the source of new technology) did not help matters either. It is true that the large share of investment devoted to construction can be partly explained by climatic conditions and the need for extensive infrastructure facilities in economies at an early stage of development. But there is evidence to suggest that an excessive amount of investment was devoted to buildings and other construction works to the detriment of alternative types of investment.

Finally, and on a different matter, one might expect that in centrally planned economies, fluctuations in economic activity would be less evident than in the market-oriented economies of the west. It is true that employment remained at a continuously high level and that unemployment was rarely a serious problem, except in one or two cases such as Yugoslavia. The high employment situation was partly at the expense of efficiency, because labour hoarding was not uncommon and effective labour utilization was poor. On the other hand, there were some large variations in rates of growth from year to year (as in the west, absolute contractions in output were rare), though there were no clearly defined cycles akin to the policy-influenced ones in western Europe. But on balance, the socialist economies appear to have been no more stable than those of the west. In a study of eight planned economies and eighteen free market ones for the period 1950–60, Staller (1964) found that the planned economies of the eastern communist bloc were subject to fluctuations in economic activity equal to or greater than those experienced by the market economies of the OECD. No consistent pattern was apparent between fluctuations and rates of growth, though the lesser developed countries of Bulgaria, Yugoslavia and Romania did tend to be subject to greater instability. Thus central planning and control were not able to eliminate fluctuations in economic activity, though, as with management policies in western countries, they probably did help to modify their severity.

Economic reform

During the 1950s, several attempts, notably in Yugoslavia, Hungary, Czechoslovakia and the German Democratic Republic, were made to reform the economic planning mechanism. However, many of the more ambitious reforms were blocked by the opposition from Stalinist hardliners. Except in Yugoslavia, where considerable progress was made in decentralizing the planning mechanism, the reforms made only minor modifications to the economic systems of socialist countries. For the most part, they remained, as in the original conception on the Soviet model, command economies with highly centralized planning and management. But during the 1960s, a new wave of reforms achieved greater success and led to a more radical overhaul of the planning mechanism.

One of the main forces behind these reforms was the realization that fast rates of growth could not be obtained indefinitely under the original policy of extensive growth, with its emphasis on boosting factor inputs. Indeed, by the early 1960s, there were already signs, especially in the more advanced countries of East Germany and Czechoslovakia, that resources, particularly labour, were becoming scarce and that efforts would have to be made to tap intensive sources of growth (productivity) if high rates of growth were to be maintained. The gradual decline in rates of growth in the late 1950s and early 1960s (except in Romania), together with a deceleration in productivity performance, gave additional weight to pressures for reform. In addition, the desultory performance of agriculture, the crises in which never ceased to surprise the socialist authorities despite the fact that the problems of this sector stemmed largely from resource neglect and the inhibiting effects of socialization, gave further impetus to the reform movement. It seems to be a persistent feature of backward countries that they tend to neglect or squeeze their agrarian sectors, with detrimental effects for the rest of the economy. This was certainly true in eastern Europe in the later nineteenth century and beyond and even more so in African countries since the Second World War.

At the same time, several enlightened economists in the socialist countries pressed the need for reform on the grounds that the rigid and centralized planning system led to waste, inefficiency and the misallocation of resources. Czech economists in particular argued that the policy of extensive growth tended to retard technical progress and created disequilibrium between different sectors of the economy. Furthermore, it may be noted that political disturbances, for example in Hungary and Poland in the 1950s, and increasing consumer dissatisfaction also played a part in the growing pressure for reform.

Such factors eventually convinced the authorities of the basic deficiencies of the Soviet-type economic management, which, with minor modifications, had been followed by the satellite countries of eastern Europe, with the main exception of Yugoslavia. Basically there was a threefold problem: (1) the planning mechanism was not based sufficiently on rational economic considerations; (2) management was not flexible enough to adapt to changing needs and circumstances; and (3) central planning was too rigid, inflexible and bureaucratically unwieldy. In short, the system lacked flexibility. If, therefore, these countries were to move to a more intensive phase of growth and thereby secure the gains of more efficient production, it was essential to decentralize the planning mechanism to make it more flexible, and at the same time adapt the structure of production to demand conditions by strengthening incentives through competitive forces and the market mechanism.

Thus the economic reforms, which began in the early 1960s and continued for much of the decade, were designed to loosen up the system and make it more flexible in the manner indicated above. The changes were first applied to industrial enterprise and then gradually extended to trade, transport and agriculture. The pace and timing of the reforms varied from country to country and there were considerable differences in detail. Nevertheless, it is possible to summarize some of the chief features of the reforms that were common to most of the eastern countries.

The first major change occurred in the planning and management of economic activity. Detailed planning directives were replaced by broad indicative plans, with the number of compulsory targets being considerably reduced. The planned targets were now expressed partly in value terms rather than solely in physical ones as previously and a greater role was accorded to branch associations and enterprises in the planning process. The plan was no longer simply a blueprint formulated and handed down by the central authorities without participation of the executive agents. At the same time, individual enterprises and branch associations were given a greater degree of independence in the management process. Instead of the detailed system of commands and directives handed down by the central planners to the local units of industry, the central authorities concentrated their attention on overall coordination of economic resources, leaving the individual enterprise greater latitude and initiative in managing its activities.

Former detailed directives, which were often unrelated to economic considerations, were replaced by a series of incentives of the market variety. Profits became the criterion of success and flexible price systems allowed prices to be determined to a greater degree than hitherto by market conditions. It was now in the interests of enterprises to minimize costs of operation and maximize output for which there was a demand, because profits were calculated on output sold, not that produced. Similar incentives were introduced for workers. Differentials in pay were increased to reflect variations in levels of skill and responsibility, while in some cases profit bonuses were paid.

The third main revision related to investment and financial facilities. The former practice of allocating capital to enterprises free of charge was drastically reduced and even abolished in some cases. Enterprises were encouraged to finance a larger share of investment out of their cash flows, while capital charges were introduced to secure an optimal allocation of investment resources. Depreciation charges were raised from their previously low levels, and the cost of credit facilities was varied according to the credit rating of the borrower.

The reforms were also accompanied by some relaxation in the activities of private enterprise. Greater freedom was accorded to individual initiative in some areas, including certain branches of retailing, catering, laundering, house construction and transport. The private sector of the economy still remained small of course, though its contribution to national income was greater than the official figures suggest simply because most of the private enterprise activity took place in services that were not included in the national income accounts of socialist countries. Private enterprise was also given a new lease of life in agriculture. As noted earlier, in some countries (Poland and Yugoslavia particularly), socialized agriculture had never been strong, and during the 1950s, a process of decollectivization occurred. Elsewhere, socialized agriculture (state farms and collectives) remained predominant, but more scope was allowed to private initiative. In all countries, the restriction on private plots was lifted and compulsory state deliveries were reduced or even abolished. Agriculture generally participated in the reforms. Agricultural prices, which for many years had been artificially depressed, were adjusted to reflect market conditions more closely, and even in some cases in line with world prices. As with industrial enterprises, detailed central control of agrarian activities was reduced and was replaced by market incentives and new accounting procedures.

Finally, control over foreign trade was eased. The state monopoly on trading activities was relaxed and greater freedom was allowed to individual trading enterprises to negotiate directly in foreign markets. These changes were accompanied by an attempt to improve trading connections, not only with the western world but also through greater economic cooperation within the eastern bloc as a whole. These aspects are dealt with more fully in the next section of this chapter.

These reforms represented a radical departure from the centralized and bureaucratic planning and management methods that prevailed throughout the 1950s and that were similar in each country, with the exception of Yugoslavia, where the strict orthodox line had been abandoned at an early stage. The extent of reform varied from country to country: it was most radical in Hungary and Czechoslovakia, but less extensive in the USSR, East Germany and Romania, though in some cases it was still not complete by the end of the decade. In place of the former rather identical versions of economic planning and control in each country, there emerged almost as many variants as countries in the socialist bloc. However, although there were now no longer any examples of extreme centralized command economies, neither were there any market economies of the western type. The changes wrought by the reforms might be seen to represent a synthesis of what is regarded as the best of socialism and capitalism. In effect, an attempt was made to use the market mechanism to varying degrees in order to enhance the efficiency of economic operations, while leaving the long-term planning of the main macro goals and targets to the central authorities. In the process, planning lost some of its rigidity and inflexibility, and the combination of broad central planning of the main aggregates combined with decentralized operations geared more to the market may have provided a better reflection of consumer needs, while at the same time ensuring a more efficient allocation of resources and improved efficiency.

At first sight, the post-reform economies of eastern Europe might appear to have moved to a position similar to those of western Europe. In fact, however, though there had been some convergence between the two, there was no evidence that any of the socialist countries, even Yugoslavia, the most liberalized and westernized of them all, was approaching a capitalist state. Indeed, though the reforms brought into being many facets of the capitalist market system, it should not be forgotten that the bulk of productive activity was still owned and operated by the state, while the central planning authorities retained a firm control over the broad objectives of policy and over the main aggregate variables in the economic system. The aim of these countries was still that of moving towards pure communism, and the liberal phase was seen as a transitional interlude in some ways similar to that of the New Economic Policy in the USSR in the 1920s.

In fact, debate on further reform continued, because ironically the reforms of the 1960s did not have the favourable impact anticipated by the authorities, at least not initially. Indeed, at first they often had a depressing effect on growth performance, though this could no doubt be partly explained by the rather lengthy process involved in completing the reforms and the attendant disruption that they caused, and partly it was a reflection of the degree of opposition to the new policies. In fact, embedded cultural traditions were to become a persistent feature in these countries in later years, which hampered the transition to capitalism. The growth record generally improved in the later 1960s, though it was not as strong as in the 1950s, and possibly this could be attributed partly to the revisions in economic management. There is also some evidence to suggest that a slightly larger share of that growth was a result of improvements in factor productivity, a trend in keeping with the new intensive growth policy. The changes in planning and management procedure and the new financial incentives also appear to have provided greater stimulus to technological improvement. For example, it is noticeable that the central plans of the early 1970s laid greater stress on the scientific and technical aspects of development. During the 1960s as a whole, the indications point to a greater interest generally, both at central and local level, in technological and scientific progress, and in most countries, the number of expert personnel and amounts spent on science and technological research increased considerably. Thus, the USSR could boast as many research workers as the United States by the end of the decade, while some countries (notably Czechoslovakia, East Germany and also the Soviet Union) were spending as much on scientific and technological research as a proportion of national income as some western countries. But again, in their effort to match the west, there was an overriding obsession with quantity that tended to be at the expense of quality. Not surprisingly, therefore, the technology gap in these countries did not diminish and in fact tended to widen in later decades (see Chapter 11).

Foreign trade and international cooperation

So far, little has been said about the external aspects of socialist development. It is true that foreign trade and intercourse with other nations in a wider sense featured less prominently than was the case with western Europe. Nevertheless, the external activities of the eastern countries increased considerably in the post-war period, especially after the middle of the 1950s, while there were some important developments in international cooperation among the socialist countries themselves.

In the immediate post-war years, and in fact well into the 1950s, conditions were not particularly favourable for the development of international relations, at least as far as the eastern countries were concerned. Political differences tended to isolate the eastern bloc from the western capitalist nations and thereby effectively limited access to foreign goods and western technology. What trade there was between east and west was conducted on a bilateral basis and even this was subject to the dictates of the political climate. Relations among the socialist countries were also far from cordial. The main problem here was the Soviet Union's exaction of payments from her satellites in the early post-war years. Unlike western countries, which received substantial aid from the United States, the eastern bloc countries were forced to make large net payments to the USSR to cover reparations, dismantlings and occupation costs. Altogether, the Soviet takings on these counts amounted to between $15 and $20 billion at post-war prices, some two-thirds of which were derived from East Germany. Hungary and Romania also suffered considerably from the appropriation of fixed assets and current production by the Soviet Union, while Poland delivered large quantities of coal to her neighbour at nominal prices. Most of the reparation payments were made in the period between the end of the war and the early 1950s, and the burden declined over time. During the same period Soviet aid to eastern Europe (mainly in the form of credits) was small (probably just over $1 billion).

The absence of close trading relationships also reflected the prevailing ideology regarding development. Foreign trade did not have a significant part to play in the extensive growth phase of socialist development. It was regarded at best as a necessary evil to be dispensed with as much as possible because each country was bent on achieving self-sufficiency. Hence, imports were rigidly controlled, while exports were looked upon as a sacrifice to pay for those imports, especially producer goods, which could not be supplied indigenously.

Thus for a decade or more after the war, external forces were scarcely conducive to socialist growth. Indeed, for some countries they were positively harmful. Soviet exactions certainly retarded recovery in Hungary, Romania and East

Germany, especially East Germany. That the GDR lagged seriously behind West Germany can be attributed, among other things, to the heavy payments she was forced to make to the USSR, which, at the peak, amounted to some 10–15 per cent of her GNP. Investment was stifled and it was not until the later 1950s, when reparations ceased, that East Germany was able to undertake a substantial investment programme. The burden on Hungary and Romania was rather less but it still impeded their development in the early years.

More generally, the drive towards self-sufficiency meant that socialist countries could not readily draw upon the expertise and technology of the west. This was particularly unfortunate at the time because these developing countries were urgently in need of supplies of advanced machinery and technical expertise. It meant in effect that there were continued shortages of certain types of advanced equipment and as a result attempts were made to develop high-cost substitutes. Moreover, the rigidity of foreign trade management, under the state trading monopolies, did little to ease matters. Imports of key products rarely occurred in the quantity and quality desired, while slack delivery dates led to bottlenecks. The Soviet Union, the one country in a position to assist its lesser developed neighbours, was more interested at this stage in exploiting them for her own benefit. In addition, the virtual absence of any coordination among member countries in their planning severely limited the prospects of gain from inter-country specialization and inevitably led to the duplication of high-cost production facilities especially in the heavy industries. Spulber (1966) goes as far as to suggest that the duplication of similar facilities in each country was greater than under pre-war protectionist policies.

The apparent lack of cooperation among the socialist countries in this period is perhaps surprising, given that soon after the war a move was made in this direction. In 1949, the CMEA (or Comecon) was established for the purpose of achieving closer relations and more integrated development among the countries of the socialist camp. It seems to have achieved little of substance in its early years, possibly because each country was trying, in slavish imitation of the earlier Soviet model, to become as self-sufficient as possible. But of greater importance at this particular time was the fact that relations were soured by the uncompromising Soviet policy on reparations and its hardline attitude towards deviationists and political disturbances within the socialist bloc, for example in Poland and Hungary.

During the latter half of the 1950s, external relations generally, both within the eastern bloc and with the west, took a turn for the better. The first step was made towards obtaining greater unity within the socialist camp by the coordination of national plans through the CMEA, leading to the 1962 agreement on basic principles for the international socialist division of labour. It was recognized that future growth would depend increasingly on greater mutual cooperation and specialization in industry and technology in place of the autarchic policies hitherto pursued. Thus instead of launching their plans separately and independently of each other, most countries began to initiate their plans simultaneously and for the first time attempted to coordinate them to some degree on the basis of international specialization. Although the degree of coordination attained should not be exaggerated, the new policy did presuppose that foreign trade and exchange would come to play a greater role in subsequent development. The reforms in management and pricing systems in the 1960s, which strengthened the incentives for the more efficient allocation of resources, also opened up greater opportunities for international trade. At the same time, the rigid control over trading activities was relaxed and bilateral trade agreements were operated in a more flexible manner. Furthermore, instead of subordinating foreign trade to the plan as was formerly the case, the plans were drawn up to take account of the requirements of foreign trade. Bilateral trade balancing among member countries was not abandoned completely, but there was a noticeable increase in multilateralism, through credit and clearing arrangements, a process encouraged by the establishment of the Bank for International Economic Cooperation in 1964. The policy of closer integration within the eastern bloc continued under the aegis of the CMEA during the latter half of the 1960s and early 1970s.

Relations with the west also improved from the later 1950s onwards as the political climate became more favourable. At this stage, most of the dealings remained on a bilateral basis, but during the 1960s trade between east and west was increasingly liberalized and several long-term contracts were concluded. The process of relaxation was facilitated by the work of various international associations or organizations including the EEC and GATT, several of the eastern countries being members of the latter by the early 1970s. Even so, the socialist countries still retained restrictions on trade with western countries, especially on goods that eastern Europe believed it could readily provide. Conversely, western countries were forced from time to time to raise barriers against 'dumped goods' from eastern Europe.

Despite the impediments to intercourse in the early years, the trade of the eastern bloc grew rapidly through the period up to 1970, though it began from a low base. On average it increased by about 10 per cent per annum, a rate faster than the growth of national income, and slightly in excess of world trade. The share of world trade of the eight socialist countries increased steadily from 5 per cent in 1948 to about 10–11 per cent by the later 1960s, compared with around 6.5 per cent in 1938. Moreover, if anything, the trade of these countries with non-socialist countries increased more rapidly than intra-eastern trade. The most active sector was trade in manufactured products, reflecting the increasing industrialization of these countries.

The rate of trade expansion was rapid both in per capita terms and in relation to national income. The share of trade in national income in some countries doubled between the early 1950s and the late 1960s. Moreover, imports more than kept pace with national income growth, which suggests that economic development was not seriously impeded by a restriction on imports, though initially import ratios were well below the pre-war level. However, trade levels, in per capita or national income terms, were still low by western standards. Surprisingly, perhaps, the economic reforms and liberalization of trade in the 1960s do not appear to have led to any marked acceleration in foreign trade growth. This in part may be explained by the fact that high rates of expansion were recorded in the later 1950s after the low levels at the peak of the Cold War earlier in the decade.

Assessment

However impressive the growth in eastern Europe during the post-war period there is no gainsaying that it was not based on secure foundations. As we shall see in due course, the later history of the region demonstrates this all too clearly (see Chapter 11). Much of the expansion in this period involved extensive growth (additions to factor inputs or growth at any price), while too little attention was paid to efficiency and factor productivity growth, which deteriorated over time. By the 1980s, a significant proportion of manufacturing industry was operating at negative value-added. One estimate for the Soviet Union suggests that in its country's entire history total factor productivity was only positive between 1957 and 1965, the era of Krushchev's reforms (Swain 1998, 203–5). Thus far from catching up with the west, the eastern block was slipping further behind in efficiency and technical credibility.

The reasons why this was so are not difficult to discern. In a desperate attempt to drive their economies forward, the authorities focused on extensive growth in the heavy sectors of industry and neglected consumer goods, agriculture and services. They also paid lip service to efficiency and technical development. This was probably an inevitable outcome of the rigid and inflexible planning system, which could not readily adjust to changed conditions and which lacked the requisite price signals to provide the incentive for change in the first place. In addition, the limited consumer market provided little incentive to improve the design and quality of retail products. The grotesque structure and design of the typical Russian car is proof of this lacking. Furthermore, the limited exposure to foreign intercourse, especially with the west, meant that the demonstration effect of design and technology was largely absent. The contrast here with Japan is instructive, a country only too ready to imitate western methods.

In short, however well-intentioned the advocates of central planning may have been, in the long term, it just did not work. The rigidity and inflexibility of centralized planning, recognized to a limited extent in the partial reforms of the 1960s, and its top-heavy hierarchical structure, lacked the facility to respond to change, which in time would have enabled these countries to overcome their legacy of historical backwardness. In consequence, the pressures and tensions within the system steadily accumulated in subsequent years and eventually exploded after 1989 (see Chapter 11).

Questions for discussion

1   Examine some of the main structural changes in the economies of eastern Europe after 1950.
2   How efficient was the extensive growth phase of the socialist economies of eastern Europe?
3   Evaluate the gains made by the consumer in eastern Europe.
4   What did the economic reforms of the 1960s achieve?
5   What part did foreign trade play in the socialist economies?

9 Western capitalism in the 1970s

Introduction

The first half of the 1970s will probably come to be regarded as a watershed in the development of western capitalist economies. Effectively, the period marked the end of the 'super-growth' phase of the post-war period, which culminated in the feverish and speculative boom of the early 1970s. From that time, according to Samuel Brittan (*Financial Times*, 14 February 1980), 'everything seems to have gone sour and we have had slower growth, rising unemployment, faster inflation, creeping trade restrictions and all the symptoms of stagflation'. Indeed, compared with the relatively placid and successful decades of the 1950s and 1960s, that of the 1970s was an extremely turbulent period, reminiscent in some respects of the inter-war years, though parallels between the two periods can easily be pushed too far.

Europeans might be forgiven if they believed in the later 1960s or even in the early 1970s, as their American counterparts undoubtedly did in the later 1920s, that they had entered an era of perpetual prosperity. Certainly, at that time, there were signs, for example on the price front, that difficulties were accumulating, but few people probably suspected that such problems were more than temporary in nature, and few would have envisaged that the leading economies would soon be faced with a severe recession together with a host of other problems, many of which were unfamiliar to a post-war generation of young people who had experienced sustained and fairly stable real income growth, low unemployment and gently rising prices throughout their lifetime.

The recession following the boom of 1972–73 was in itself a shock, because for the first time in the post-war period output actually contracted sharply in most countries, though certainly not to the same extent as in the slump of 1929–32. The recessionary phases before this time had been both shorter and milder, involving for the most part a deceleration in the rate of growth rather than an absolute decline in economic activity. Moreover, the recession of 1974–75 was accompanied not only by rising unemployment on a scale not previously experienced since the inter-war years, but also by strong inflationary pressures. The latter were exacerbated by resource problems, particularly in the energy sector, which became more or less a permanent feature of the whole decade, and these in turn led to severe balance-of-payments difficulties and exchange crises in a number of countries.

Given the convergence of so many unfavourable factors, it is perhaps not surprising that the strength of the subsequent recovery was less pronounced than that from other recessions of the post-war period, or that policy-makers began to question the practicality of using traditional demand-management tools to stimulate economic activity. After a brief spurt in 1976, the growth in output remained weak and hesitant in the later 1970s, being constrained at times by inflation, resource bottlenecks (particularly in energy), and policy factors. As a consequence, the direction of government policy shifted away from the traditional priorities of full employment and growth towards the more urgent ones of controlling inflation, maintaining balance-of-payments stability and securing an adequate supply of resources. At the same time, there was perhaps an ever-increasing awareness that some of the problems of the 1970s, notably the continued pressure on energy resources, might be of a more long-term nature, and that the real forces of growth were entering a phase of weakness as the technological opportunities of the post-war period became partly exhausted.

One of the main questions to be considered, therefore, is why things went so wrong for the market economies of the western world in the 1970s, and also why governments were able to do so little to restore the *status quo*. In turn, this entails a recapitulation of some of the factors that were responsible for the high and sustained growth experience of the period before the early 1970s. First, however, it is useful to gain some perspective from a brief review of the performance of the western economies during the decade in question.

Growth and instability in the 1970s

Although the major events of the 1970s are no doubt familiar, the main economic trends are less well known. The data in Tables 9.1 and 9.2 illustrate clearly that growth was less vigorous in the 1970s than in the previous decade or for that matter than in the 1950s. The average rate of growth of gross domestic product for the European countries (EU15) fell from 4.8 to 3.0 per cent, while in the case of industrial production the decline was even greater, from 5.4 to 2.6 per cent. All countries experienced a marked deceleration in economic activity, in some cases by more than 50 per cent on the previous decade. Another notable feature was the greater dispersion of growth rates, especially in industrial production, compared with previously. For industrial production, they ranged from nil in the case of Luxembourg to 6.5 per cent in Portugal and 7.0 per cent in Greece, whereas in the 1960s, most countries had fallen in the band of between 5–7 per cent.

Not only was economic growth slower than in the two decades before the early 1970s (though, it should be added, it was still respectable when set against the long-term trend) but it was also less stable than previously. Rates of activity varied significantly from year to year, and during 1974–75, there were absolute contractions in most countries, an unusual feature by post-war standards because recessionary phases had normally been characterized by decelerations in rates of growth rather than by absolute declines.

Table 9.1 Growth rates of gross domestic product (per cent per annum) 1961–80

	1961–70	1971–80	1970	1971	1972	1973	1974	1975	1976	1977	1978	1979	1980
Austria	4.7	3.6	7.1	5.1	6.2	4.9	3.9	−0.4	4.6	4.7	−0.4	5.5	2.3
Belgium	4.9	3.4	6.2	3.8	5.3	6.1	4.2	−1.3	5.7	0.6	2.8	2.3	4.4
Denmark	4.5	2.2	2.0	2.7	5.3	3.6	−0.9	−0.7	6.5	1.6	1.5	3.5	−0.4
West Germany	4.4	2.7	5.0	3.1	4.3	4.8	0.2	−1.3	5.3	2.8	3.0	4.2	1.0
Greece	8.5	4.6	8.9	7.8	10.2	8.1	−6.4	6.4	6.9	2.9	7.2	3.3	0.7
Spain	7.3	3.5	4.2	4.6	8.1	7.8	5.6	0.5	3.3	2.8	1.5	0.0	1.3
France	5.6	3.3	5.7	4.8	4.4	5.4	3.1	−0.3	4.2	3.2	3.4	3.2	1.6
Ireland	4.2	4.7	2.7	3.5	6.5	4.7	4.3	5.7	1.3	8.1	7.1	3.1	3.1
Italy	5.7	3.6	5.3	1.9	2.9	6.5	4.7	−2.1	6.5	2.9	3.7	5.7	3.5
Luxembourg	3.5	2.6	1.7	2.7	6.6	8.3	4.2	−6.6	2.5	1.6	4.1	2.3	0.8
Netherlands	5.1	3.0	5.8	4.5	3.1	5.0	4.1	0.2	4.8	2.3	2.4	2.2	1.2
Portugal	6.4	4.7	7.6	6.6	8.0	11.2	1.1	−4.3	6.9	5.5	2.8	5.6	4.6
Finland	4.8	3.4	7.5	2.1	7.6	6.7	3.0	1.2	−0.4	0.2	2.1	7.0	5.3
Sweden	4.6	2.0	6.5	0.9	2.3	4.0	3.2	2.6	1.1	−1.6	1.8	3.8	1.7
UK	2.9	1.9	2.4	2.0	3.6	7.3	−1.7	−0.7	2.8	2.4	3.4	2.8	−2.2
EU15	4.8	3.0	4.9	3.3	4.4	6.0	1.9	−0.6	4.5	2.7	3.0	3.6	1.3
US	4.2	3.2	0.1	3.4	5.6	5.9	−0.6	−0.4	5.5	4.7	5.5	2.9	−0.3
Japan	10.1	4.4	10.3	4.4	8.4	8.0	−1.2	3.1	4.0	4.4	5.3	5.5	2.8

Source: European Commission *European Economy*, No. 68, 1999, Table 10, 118–19.

Table 9.2 Growth rates of industrial production (excluding construction) (per cent per annum) 1961–80

	1961–70	1971–80	1970	1971	1972	1973	1974	1975	1976	1977	1978	1979	1980
Austria	5.6	4.0	8.9	6.2	7.7	4.9	5.0	-6.2	6.3	4.0	2.5	7.3	2.8
Belgium	5.0	2.3	3.0	1.7	7.5	6.1	4.7	-9.8	7.7	0.5	2.4	4.5	-1.3
Denmark	6.2	1.9	2.6	2.3	4.4	3.3	-0.7	-6.0	9.7	0.8	2.2	3.7	0.2
West Germany	5.3	1.9	5.8	1.0	3.6	6.4	-1.7	-6.2	6.8	2.7	1.9	5.1	0.0
Greece	* 10.0	7.0	10.2	11.4	14.1	15.4	-1.6	4.3	10.6	2.1	7.5	6.1	1.0
Spain	† 10.4	5.1	7.4	6.5	16.3	11.1	7.4	-3.2	4.4	5.4	2.8	0.4	0.7
France	5.1	3.2	5.7	6.5	5.5	6.7	2.4	-7.2	8.8	1.4	2.5	4.4	2.2
Ireland	6.8	4.5	3.3	4.0	4.4	10.8	-0.5	-3.8	8.7	8.0	7.8	7.9	-1.3
Italy	7.0	3.3	6.6	-0.6	4.9	9.7	4.0	-8.9	11.7	0.0	2.0	6.7	5.2
Luxembourg	2.4	0.0	0.4	-1.3	4.2	12.0	3.4	-21.8	3.7	0.6	3.1	3.4	-3.5
Netherlands	7.2	2.9	9.2	6.0	4.8	7.2	5.0	-4.8	8.0	0.0	1.0	3.6	-0.8
Portugal	5.0	6.5	6.4	7.8	13.1	11.8	2.6	-4.9	3.4	13.3	6.7	7.2	5.5
Finland	7.3	4.6	12.1	4.8	8.7	7.1	4.8	-3.9	0.8	0.5	5.2	10.6	7.9
Sweden	6.1	1.0	6.0	1.1	2.2	6.5	4.3	-2.1	-0.6	-5.5	-1.9	6.0	0.0
UK	2.4	1.0	0.5	-0.5	1.8	9.0	-2.0	-5.4	3.2	5.3	2.8	3.8	-6.5
EU15	5.4	2.6	5.1	2.1	4.9	7.8	1.4	-6.3	6.9	2.3	2.3	4.8	0.3
US	4.9	3.1	-3.4	1.5	9.6	8.0	-1.4	-8.8	9.2	8.1	5.8	3.4	-2.8
Japan	13.6	4.1	13.6	2.7	7.4	14.9	-4.0	-11.0	11.1	4.1	6.4	7.3	4.7

Source: European Commission European Economy, No. 68, 1999, Table 12, 122–23.

Notes: * 1963–70; † 1962–70.

The recession of 1974–75 can be regarded in part as an automatic reaction to the very vigorous boom of 1972–73, when activity in the major industrial countries synchronized rather more closely than in previous cyclical upswings. Rates of expansion were also running well above trend, especially in 1973; in that year, industrial production grew at a rate close to 50 per cent above the average for the 1960s, and in the case of the UK, it was some three times the post-war average. Such high rates of growth were clearly not sustainable for long because capacity constraints soon began to bite, in some cases in the form of balance-of-payments disequilibria. But at the same time, there were several unfavourable factors, notably accelerating inflation and the disturbances in the oil market, which did much to erode business confidence. By 1974, expansion was grinding to a halt and in the following year many countries experienced a decline in economic activity. Experience varied considerably from country to country: the largest economies, and especially those dependent on imported oil, tended to be the hardest hit, whereas some of the smaller countries, including Greece, Ireland and Norway, maintained a reasonably creditable performance. For the EU countries as a whole, industrial production declined by 6.3 per cent in 1975, while even greater falls were recorded outside Europe, notably in the United States and Japan. Such steep declines in production had never been experienced in the post-war years and they were reminiscent, though by no means as severe, as those recorded in the early 1930s (Capie and Collins 1977). The first year of recovery, 1976, witnessed equally steep rises in activity, with industrial production especially growing above trend again. Thereafter growth wilted once more, and in the latter half of the 1970s, it was well below the post-war trend line. By the turn of the decade it was grinding to a halt again.

Thus throughout most of the 1970s, but more especially in the latter half of the decade, growth in the European economies, as well as in many non-European ones, fell below full capacity potential. Not surprisingly, this shortfall was reflected in rising unemployment levels and underutilized capacity. In the later 1970s, unemployment in the EU15 was on average roughly twice that of the 1960s and early 1970s, at around 5 per cent, while current output was running at between 5 and 15 per cent below full capacity. At the same time, export and productivity growth slackened markedly, though the downward shift was not so severe as that in industrial production.

Probably the most notable feature of the 1970s, and one that was largely responsible for the subsequent policy constraints, was the pervasive nature of inflation. Though experience varied a great deal among the various countries, it can be readily seen from Table 9.3 that the rate of increase in consumer prices was on average two to three times that of the 1960s. Inflationary pressures had in fact been building up in the later 1960s and early 1970s, but the really big upsurge occurred in the middle of the 1970s, when most countries recorded rates well into double figures. After 1975, there was a noticeable moderation in inflationary pressures, though by the end of the decade inflation rates were once again creeping upwards and they were still much higher than in the post-war years.

In fact, it is the high and sustained level of inflation that really makes the 1970s unique, the nearest parallel being the European experience of the early 1920s. In

Table 9.3 Consumer prices (annual percentage changes seasonally adjusted) 1961–80

	1961–70	1971–80	1970	1971	1972	1973	1974	1975	1976	1977	1978	1979	1980
Austria	3.5	6.2	3.9	5.0	6.5	6.6	10.0	7.9	6.5	5.7	4.0	4.3	6.1
Belgium	3.1	7.1	2.6	5.3	5.6	5.9	12.7	12.5	7.8	7.2	4.3	3.9	6.7
Denmark	5.8	10.4	6.6	8.3	8.2	11.7	15.0	9.9	9.9	10.6	9.2	10.4	10.7
West Germany	2.8	5.2	3.9	5.6	5.6	6.7	7.5	6.0	4.2	3.4	2.7	4.2	5.8
Greece	2.4	13.9	3.4	2.9	4.4	16.1	24.9	12.8	14.8	12.8	13.2	16.2	22.9
Spain	5.8	15.0	6.1	7.7	7.7	11.3	17.7	15.5	16.4	23.7	19.1	16.5	15.7
France	4.2	9.8	5.0	6.0	6.3	7.4	14.8	11.8	9.9	9.4	9.1	10.7	13.3
Ireland	5.1	14.0	12.4	9.4	9.7	11.6	15.7	18.0	20.1	14.2	8.2	15.1	18.6
Italy	3.8	14.6	5.0	5.5	6.2	14.2	21.2	16.2	17.7	16.7	12.8	15.5	20.6
Luxembourg	2.5	6.5	4.3	4.7	5.1	4.9	10.0	10.2	9.3	5.7	3.4	4.9	7.5
Netherlands	4.1	7.6	4.4	7.7	8.0	9.4	9.5	10.0	9.0	6.1	4.4	4.9	6.8
Portugal	2.8	17.3	3.2	7.0	6.3	8.9	23.5	16.0	18.1	27.3	21.3	25.2	21.6
Finland	4.7	11.5	1.7	6.8	8.4	12.2	19.6	16.6	13.3	11.7	8.0	8.2	11.0
Sweden	4.1	9.6	5.0	7.6	6.4	7.6	10.3	10.9	11.0	10.8	11.6	7.9	12.4
UK	3.9	13.3	6.0	8.7	6.5	8.5	17.1	23.3	15.8	14.7	9.4	13.7	16.1
EU15	3.8	10.7	4.9	6.6	6.4	9.2	14.9	13.6	11.7	11.6	9.1	10.7	13.2
US	2.4	7.1	4.7	4.5	3.5	5.4	10.1	8.1	5.7	6.6	7.3	9.0	10.9
Japan	5.6	8.8	7.2	6.9	5.9	11.1	21.0	11.3	9.8	7.5	4.6	3.6	7.5

Source: European Commission *European Economy*, No. 68, 1999, Table 25, 266–67.

longer-term perspective, the growth of western economies during the 1970s was respectable and it is only against the background of the sustained boom of the 1950s and 1960s that it appears mediocre. Furthermore, compared with the desultory performance of the inter-war years, the record of the 1970s, in terms of both output and employment, was infinitely better. One could argue, therefore, that it was the high growth rates of the post-war years that were abnormal, and that the downward shift in the 1970s represented a move back towards the more sustainable long-term rates of development. Of course, this assertion raises important implications not only about the determinants of growth in the 1970s and beyond, but also from the point of view of the type of policy strategy required to deal with the problems of the period.

Before dealing with the policy dilemmas facing governments in this decade, we need to look more closely at the main factors responsible for the weaker economic performance in this period. It would be all too easy to see the difficulties of the decade as a response to cyclical disturbances and/or specific shocks such as the energy crisis and inflation, and the constricting effects these had on growth and policy formation. On the other hand, it could also be argued that the shift to a lower growth profile in the 1970s was partly an inevitable consequence of longer-term forces involving a partial reversal of the growth-promoting factors of the post-war years. In effect, this would imply some weakening of real growth force in the 1970s, which were in turn aggravated by specific problems and policy factors.

Of course, the several factors mentioned above are not mutually exclusive. However, because the problems of the 1970s have been readily identified in terms of the specific shocks imparted by energy and inflation, it is essential to begin by examining the implications of these two factors before analysing the extent to which the secular growth forces of the post-war boom years had waned in strength over the course of time.

Energy and commodity problems

Energy, and oil in particular, is the key element in this sector, and the reader should need no reminding of why this is so. Raw materials and food also posed intermittent problems during the 1970s, but on a lesser scale than energy.

An important factor in the remarkable rise in output and real incomes during the 1950s and 1960s must undoubtedly be the favourable terms of trade experienced by industrial countries. After the sharp rise in commodity prices during the Korean War boom (1950–51), the costs of energy, food and raw materials declined and remained low relative to those of industrial products until the early 1970s. Even by the later 1960s, when upward pressure on commodity prices was becoming apparent, the price of food, raw materials and energy was on average lower than in the early 1950s, whereas manufactured prices had risen slightly during this period. This resulted in a significant gain in the terms of trade for industrial Europe to the consequent benefit of real incomes and growth.

An important aspect of the favourable position with regard to the supply and price of energy and raw materials in the post-war decades was that it led to the rapid development of energy-intensive sectors, not only in terms of the most obvious mass penetration of cars, consumer durables and chemical products throughout the income ranges, but also in terms of the intensive use of petroleum as a fuel and source of heat in industry and for domestic purposes. This response was scarcely surprising given the relative cheapness and abundance of energy supplies, but it did render the industrial world vulnerable to any sudden distortion in supplies and prices, such as the one that occurred in 1973–74. Primary product prices rose on average by 160 per cent during this period and then oscillated at the enhanced level over the next few years. Fuel prices, on the other hand, under the impact of the new OPEC crude prices announced late in 1973, rose by 300 per cent or more. Subsequently, the pressure on oil prices abated until the later 1970s, when there was a renewed upward thrust, though less severe than that of the earlier period.

A sudden uplift in commodity prices of this order of magnitude could scarcely fail to have an adverse impact on the major industrial countries, more especially because they had been accustomed for some time to gently falling or fairly stable commodity prices. Manufactured goods prices reacted more slowly to the price upsurge and hence the terms of trade of the advanced industrial countries deteriorated sharply. Britain, for example, suffered a 27 per cent deterioration in her terms of trade within a period of two years, and even by 1978, a unit of imports still absorbed 17 per cent more exports than in 1972 (Rostow 1979).

The global price explosion of the early 1970s was partly engendered by the strong and heavily synchronized boom in industrial countries at this time and by supply deficiencies in some commodities, and it must also be remembered that it took place against the background of accumulating inflationary pressures extending back to the later 1960s (see below). But it was the oil price shock of 1973 and the continuing tenuous nature of the sources of supply that were to wreak the most havoc on the industrial west. While the oil price increase was not the proximate cause of the initial price upsurge or the only factor contributing to the subsequent recession in economic activity, it certainly aggravated both tendencies and had both inflationary and deflationary implications for the main industrial countries. On the one hand, while the oil price rise put direct pressure on costs and thereby intensified the inflationary process and squeezed industrial profit margins, on the other hand, it had at least two important deflationary implications. First, it checked the growth of energy-intensive sectors, which had underpinned the post-war boom, and second, it transferred a large block of purchasing power to OPEC countries, which took time to recycle given their fairly low capacity to absorb industrial imports. The real income effects were partly reflected in large balance-of-payments deficits in some of the major oil-importing countries as the oil producers amassed substantial current account surpluses. These peaked at about $60 billion in 1974 and thereafter fell to about one-half that level during 1975–77. By the latter half of 1978, when the accumulations had dwindled to small proportions and had ceased to have significant effects on the trade and activity of industrial countries, a new wave of oil price increases and supply difficulties threatened to start the process off once again. However, at least to the turn of the decade, the pressures were less severe than those experienced in the first round of price changes.

Largely as a result of the oil price increases, OECD countries taken as a whole swung from surplus into deficit on external account in 1973–74 and continued to remain in overall deficit for the next three years. However, the impact varied a great deal from country to country. Britain, Italy and France, together with some of the smaller, less industrialized European countries, were badly hit and they were forced to take severe deflationary action in order to try to reduce their large external deficits and at the same time stabilize their weak exchange rates. By contrast, Germany, the United States and Japan were able to absorb the oil deficits without too much difficulty thanks to a strong upsurge in exports, particularly to OPEC countries. For a time, these three countries were able to accumulate surpluses on their current accounts, though these began to disappear towards the end of the decade under the impact of further oil price rises and a weakening dollar.

It is difficult to estimate with any great precision the full economic impact of the oil pressures of the 1970s, because there are so many indirect repercussions that cannot be quantified accurately, apart from the fact that the energy problem was only one of several that adversely affected economic activity in this period. Estimates by OECD suggest that the real income loss stemming from the oil price shock of the early 1970s may have been of the order of 2 per cent of OECD area GNP, with a similar magnitude for the second oil shock (see Chapter 10). Rostow (1979) maintains that the OECD area suffered declines in total output in 1974–75 of about twice the level that could be directly attributed to the rise in oil prices. The size of the price effects was probably of a similar order of magnitude. However, although the overall impact on the industrial west should not be overdramatized, it may be noted that such estimates do not allow for the many indirect effects, for example the deterioration in business confidence and domestic investment as a result of continued cost pressures, nor do they take account of the adverse impact on economic activity of restrictive government policy to deal with external deficits and inflation. Moreover, a large part of the OPEC oil balances were initially placed on deposit in the leading banks of the western nations, which helped to augment liquidity and gave a further boost to the inflationary spiral.

Inflationary pressures

Though the leap in oil prices in the first half of the 1970s added a further twist to the inflationary spiral, it cannot be regarded as the initial cause of the acceleration of inflation nor even the main contributor to the continued high level of inflation throughout the 1970s. For one thing, inflation had been a persistent feature of the whole post-war period, though the relatively moderate and creeping inflation after the Korean War has generally been regarded as beneficial on balance, even if at times it caused some degree of concern. Second, inflation began to accelerate noticeably in the later 1960s and was already approaching double figures in a number of countries before the oil price explosion of late 1973. Moreover, in the later 1970s, when the pressure on oil prices eased, the rate of inflation, though much reduced from the peak level of 1974, remained much higher than in the 1950s and first half of the 1960s.

Because inflation was one of the overriding issues of the decade, its causes and implications require close inspection. It is not an easy task to unravel precisely the proximate causes of the price inflation of the 1970s because several interrelated factors were at work. For example, although it is clear that there were special forces at work in the sharp price upsurge in the early 1970s, it is also evident that longer-term forces were operating to push up the underlying rate of inflation. Thus, a secular upward trend in inflation from the mid-1960s had superimposed on it a cyclically or partly cyclically generated price boom in the early 1970s; hence the high rates of inflation in these years. The subsequent fallback from those high rates may be regarded as a reaction to the cyclical downturn and also to policy effects, but the inflation rate remained obstinately high throughout the rest of the decade partly because the underlying long-term pressures had not been removed and partly because of certain ratchet effects that prevented a rapid reversal to previous inflation levels.

An important element in the price explosion in the early part of the decade was of course the strong and synchronized upswing in economic activity among the major industrial countries in 1972–73. In these years, output was growing well above trend, which put pressure on commodity prices and led to shortages and speculation. Two other factors compounded the situation: first, since the middle of the 1960s, there had been growing tension in some commodity markets, notably grain, as a result of declining reserve stocks in America and poor harvests in Asia and Russia; by 1974, US grain reserves had been reduced to about one-third the level of the early 1960s. Second, at the end of 1973, came the dramatic hike in oil prices.

However, it must be noted that the strong industrial boom of 1972–73 was in part engendered by policy action and that it took place against a background of substantial growth in international liquidity. As a result of slack conditions and stubbornly high unemployment at the beginning of the 1970s, attempts were made in several countries to stimulate economic activity. These erred on the side of generosity, partly because an abundance of international monetary reserves made it possible for governments to pursue highly expansionary policies. World exchange reserves, which had grown only slowly in the previous two decades at between 2 and 3 per cent per annum, shot up into double figures in 1970, and between 1969 and 1973, total international reserves rose by some 136 per cent. This explosion was occasioned primarily by the enormous outpouring of American dollars as a result of the policy of benign neglect on the part of the US authorities with regard to the country's heavy external deficits. In turn, these dollars were absorbed into the European banking system (in 1971 alone non-US monetary authorities added more dollars to their official reserves than in all of human history up to that date) and were used as a basis for domestic monetary expansion. It is an ironic fact that the Bretton Woods fixed exchange rate system, which formerly had been a source of maintaining international monetary stability, became, in its final years, a destabilizing element and a source of inflation as central banks outside the United States sought to prevent the collapse of the system and the depreciation of the dollar, and forestall the appreciation of their own currencies. Eventually, of course, the strains imposed upon the system proved to be too large to be absorbed. The dollar was devalued and Britain, partly for domestic and political reasons, adopted a floating rate in 1972. This ushered in a period of floating exchange rates, tempered periodically by attempts among several European countries to circumscribe the range of the floating.

In most countries, therefore, the price explosion was preceded or accompanied by reflationary measures and monetary expansion. The combined growth of the nominal money supply (M1) in eleven major industrial countries almost doubled between 1970 and 1972, from 7.5 to 14.0 per cent a year, whereas in the case of the EEC countries it rose from 9.9 to 18.3 per cent per annum. The highest rates were recorded in Italy, averaging 23 per cent a year between 1970 and 1973, and Japan, where it peaked at 30 per cent in 1971. Even in Germany, the high architect of monetary probity, the rate of expansion doubled between 1970 and 1972 (7.1 to 14.5 per cent), though it fell back sharply thereafter. After 1972, rates of monetary expansion tended to slacken off in most countries, though they still remained substantially above those of the 1960s. However, it should be noted that monetary expansion was tending to rise on balance during the course of the 1960s.

If the immediate causes of the price upsurge of the early 1970s are apparent, the continued high level of inflation throughout the remainder of the decade is less readily so. It is true that inflation rates eased off markedly after 1975 under the influence of tighter monetary control, including a shift to monetary targeting, fiscal restraint and various forms of prices and incomes policies as well as some moderation in commodity prices. Nevertheless, it was not possible to revert to the modest levels of inflation of the 1950s and early 1960s, and this presented governments with an important policy dilemma with respect to growth versus inflation (see below).

Several possible reasons can be put forward to explain the continuing unfavourable situation on the price front. For one thing, monetary growth still remained excessive compared with past standards. In fact, throughout most of the decade, the rate of monetary growth in many countries was inconsistent with exchange stability and price inflation of the German order of magnitude of around 5 per cent. This situation partly reflected the large public sector deficits and borrowing requirements of governments as they attempted to fulfil commitments in terms of collective goods and welfare payments at a time when the budgetary revenue base was weakening. Of course, the share of government spending had been rising steadily since the war, putting increasing strain on available resources, and at the same time, possibly influencing the nature of wage claims and the allocation of resources.

During the course of the 1970s, wage claims were increasingly based upon past price changes and expected inflation rates, which created a built-in rigidity in the cost system. Moreover, with increasing union power and the disappearance of the traditional trade-off between unemployment and wage demands, high claims were more readily conceded and validated in monetary terms than was the case in the past. This tendency was most apparent in Britain, despite periodic declarations of intent about monetary control, and hence wage pressures became the main stumbling block to regaining price stability. At the same time, the wage problem may be seen as part of an accumulating long-term pressure arising from the government's increasing demands on incomes during the post-war period. A study by Thornton (1979) showed that over the period 1952–75, the income retention ratio of the average manufacturing worker in Britain (that is, after deductions of income tax, national insurance contributions, etc.) declined from 96.8 to 77 per cent, with the major part of the fall occurring in the 1960s and the first half of the 1970s. What is particularly important is that the increasing deductions encouraged unions to bargain on the basis of the growth of net real earnings, thus necessitating higher demands in terms of gross earnings, while price variables had an increasingly stronger influence on these demands over time.

Intermittent pressure on resources, mainly raw materials and oil again later in the 1970s, coupled with renewed doubts about fuel supply prospects, did little to ease the situation. At the same time, slower economic growth and lower productivity growth meant a reduced rate of offset to cost pressures. Some countries were affected particularly severely by specific problems. For instance between 1973 and 1976, both Britain and Italy experienced a sharp wage-price exchange rate spiral arising largely from excessive monetary creation, while in the later 1970s the dollar was subject to excessive weakness. In some countries, large government deficits posed a problem. This was especially true of Britain, where, in the later 1970s, these were being funded at high nominal interest rates into the twenty-first century. This made it problematic to reduce inflation rapidly, because it would erode the tax revenue base for servicing the high-cost debt.

Of course, it is difficult to eradicate inflation quickly, even though technically not impossible. It would require a sharp tightening of monetary and fiscal policy, which would have serious implications for the real economy and unemployment. It is doubtful whether in most countries there was sufficient political consensus as to the priority for such drastic action. This could have been because the reduced inflation rates of the later 1970s were more acceptable to the majority of people than further increases in unemployment, at least until the money illusion effects finally wore off.

Nevertheless, governments for most of the 1970s regarded inflation control as the number one priority and to all intents and purposes policy shifted in the direction of dealing with this problem. Of course, this raised a serious policy dilemma, in that emphasis given to checking inflation made governments reluctant to stimulate activity even at a time of underused resources and high unemployment. Thus, in a sense the loss of output growth in the 1970s may be regarded as a result of inflation in so far as policy measures were directed towards price restraint, apart from the fact that business confidence was eroded by the difficulties of coping with cost pressures and weakened markets. On the other hand, it may well be the case that the underlying growth potential was less strong than in the 1950s and 1960s, and that the real forces of growth were insufficient to regain the growth momentum of the super-boom years. If this assumption is correct, it follows that any attempt to regain the former growth trajectory by stimulatory measures would simply have produced more inflation. For the long term, therefore, the main problem would be how to absorb additional resources, particularly labour, without running up against the constraint of inflation. These policy implications are explored more fully in the last section.

How strong were real growth forces?

Energy problems and inflation may be regarded as two important constraints on growth pertaining specifically to the 1970s. In effect, they lowered the equilibrium growth rate of the major industrial nations, an equilibrium growth rate being defined as a sustainable rate of growth consistent with balance-of-payments equilibrium and price stability.[1] These constraints were likely to remain operative for some time. However, whether the sluggish growth performance of the major economies after 1973 can be wholly attributed to such special factors is more debatable. Certainly, they had important depressive effects on activity but at the same time there is reason to believe that this period also experienced a secular decline in the growth generators of the post-war boom. If these forces provided a once-and-for-all thrust to growth in the 1950s and 1960s, then the shift to a lower growth profile would not be unexpected and would largely represent a return to the more sustainable historical growth trend.

In some respects, this hypothesis has affinity with views expressed by several writers as to the role of real forces in growth, for example, Rostow's leading sectors, Schumpeter's clustering of innovational activity and Hansen's dearth of investment opportunities. Basically, such theses tend to stress the apparent lumpiness of investment as a derivative of the strength of innovational opportunities. In turn, they can be linked to the structural transformation theses of the type postulated by Svennilson for the inter-war years and by Cornwall for the post-war period, the latter arguing the case for manufacturing as the engine of growth. The concept of 'deindustrialization' and the size of the public sector are also relevant to the events of the 1970s.

As a starting point to the discussion, it may be convenient to identify again the main forces of growth relevant to the boom years of the 1950s and 1960s. Apart from relatively cheap and plentiful supplies of raw materials and energy, low rates of inflation and monetary stability, which we have already dealt with, the following factors may be enumerated: (1) rapid diffusion of technical backlogs in Europe to catch up with American standards, associated in particular with leading manufacturing sectors; (2) elastic supplies of labour, resource reallocation and the favourable effects on productivity growth; (3) high rates of investment; and (4) high levels of demand bolstered by demand-management policies. Of course, it is important to recognize that these factors are closely interrelated. While the strength of these forces may have diminished over time, they were also in turn adversely affected by the specific difficulties of the 1970s. Moreover, the growth of the public sector and signs of deindustrialization may in part be regarded as a reflection of the weakening of the above forces of growth, and which may at the same time have had an adverse effect on growth potential.

At the end of the war, or perhaps more appropriately in 1950, when the main reconstruction phase was complete, it is clear that European countries had a unique opportunity to grow rapidly given favourable international conditions, because at that time, European income and productivity levels were well below those of America. Such conditions were largely met in the period through to the early 1970s, in that there was no serious pressure on the supply and price of commodities, inflation rates were modest, monetary disturbances were few and mild in nature, and the progressive dismantling of trade barriers gave ample opportunities to exploit the gains from international trade. Thus, by the middle of the 1970s, average productivity levels in many European countries were 80 per cent or more of those of America as against an average of 50 per cent in 1950 (Maddison 1979). In other words, during this period, European countries were able to close the gap significantly, and by the later date, the scope for substantial gains from moving towards best practice techniques was diminishing.

The process of catching up involved a significant structural transformation based on key sectors of activity. Manufacturing was the really dynamic sector, and within this branch of activity, there was a rapid diffusion of techniques in energy-intensive industries, including automobiles, consumer durable goods, electronics and chemicals. This stimulated high levels of investment in these sectors, and at the same time, it led to a substantial shift of resources, especially labour, from low productivity agriculture to the high-growth, high-productivity areas in manufacturing. The high and sustained level of demand, maintained in part by post-war demand-management policies, provided a favourable climate for investment, which, in turn, enabled the backlog of opportunities to be exploited.

There is no doubt that the basis of the post-war super-growth was severely dented in the 1970s. Energy-intensive sectors were badly hit by the pressure on oil supplies, while the income transfer effects reduced demand in the oil-importing countries. This, coupled with severe inflation, obviously created an uncertain and less attractive climate for investment. Not surprisingly, therefore, the revival of investment from the recession of 1974–75 was noticeably weaker than during similar phases of previous post-war cycles. However, although the adverse shocks and cyclical influences on investment were undoubtedly important, there are grounds for arguing that the underlying growth forces were weakening at this time.

This argument is based upon several premises. First, as already noted, the scope for further large gains from the catching-up process was limited by the 1970s, and the opportunities for further rapid expansion in the high-growth, energy-intensive sectors were less apparent as markets became saturated. Second, by the early 1970s the scope for large productivity gains from shifting labour from agriculture to industry was diminished. As a result of two decades or so of structural transformation, agricultural employment was less than 10 per cent of the labour force in six of the twelve countries analysed by Cornwall, compared with two at the beginning of the 1950s, and only three countries (Austria, Italy and Japan) still had large labour reserves in this sector. Indeed, in several countries, the rate of growth of the industrial labour force tended to decline or stagnate from the later 1960s, with adverse effects on productivity growth. For a time, the reduced supply of labour to this sector may have acted as a supply constraint, though it is difficult to invoke this argument for the later 1970s, given the high level of unemployment generally (cf. Knox 1979). But perhaps more important, though the scope for resource real-location was dwindling, as time went on, the shift of labour took on a more complex pattern involving a proportionate increase in the share of the service trades and the public sector at the expense of both agriculture and industry. If, as is frequently argued, productivity levels and growth rates are lower in these sectors, this tends further to depress growth potential.

The change in the pattern of labour deployment is important because it involved the stagnation or even decline of manufacturing employment in some countries: hence the term 'deindustrialization'. The trend was most apparent in Britain, though there is evidence that other major industrial countries were beginning to experience similar tendencies by the early 1970s (Cornwall 1977). In the British case, a forceful argument was put forward to the effect that manufacturing had been subject to a 'crowding out' effect as a result of the growth of non-marketable services, primarily public sector services (Bacon and Eltis 1976). Of course, the growth of the latter reflected shifts in tastes and patterns of demand that required a greater provision of public services in terms of education, medical and welfare care and housing, as well as private services such as tourism and leisure pursuits.

Most countries in the west experienced a rapid expansion of these sectors from the middle of the 1960s, and an OECD report (1978) on *Public Expenditure Trends* argued that 'beyond a certain point too rapid an increase in public expenditure can reduce productive potential by increasing the likelihood of inefficient allocation of resources and by lowering incentives to work and invest'. An increasing public sector share could also have important financial, balance-of-payments and productivity implications. On the other hand, while such repercussions may be important, it is not altogether convincing to argue that the erosion of the manufacturing base can be attributed to supply constraints (capital and labour) as a result of diversion of resources to the expanding service and public sectors.

Of course, it is true that the public sector may entice resources away from manufacturing because its market signals for labour and capital are more attractive. For example, in the case of labour, the public sector may offer higher rates of pay and cleaner and more secure jobs than in manufacturing, while one must not forget the status attraction of white-collar employment. Similarly, high interest rates offered on government stock at a time of reduced margins in manufacturing may have lured capital away from the latter sector. Furthermore, the indirect implications of higher government spending in terms of deficit financing, money supply and inflation may also be important for determining the climate of expectations for private enterprise. However, there is no firm evidence to suggest that manufacturing was starved of resources in these years, and in terms of labour recruitment, at least, the stagnation in manufacturing employment may have reflected a combination of greater productivity gains and/or diminished opportunities for expansion. In any case, high unemployment levels also provided plenty of slack in the labour market.

This last point seems a more plausible proposition given the massive application of new and known technologies in the post-war years and the rate at which the technology and productivity gap between Europe and America was being closed during this period. The dynamics of the post-war boom in manufacturing began to diminish as markets in the leading sectors became increasingly saturated and diminishing returns to existing technologies set in (Rostow 1979; Giarini and Loubergé 1978). Whether innovational opportunities are subject to some long-wave movement, as several writers suggest, is still a matter for debate, but it does seem possible that the weakening of manufacturing performance during the 1970s may partly have reflected the relative lack of large new fields of endeavour.

The sluggishness of manufacturing investment in the later 1970s may also be attributed to the cumulative effects of the long-term deterioration in profit shares and rates of return, and the concomitant rise in the wage-income share that had been taking place since the war. Cross-country comparisons of rates of return are fraught with difficulty because of definitional problems and differences in accounting practices among countries. Even studies within individual countries can often throw up conflicting results. By and large, however, most analyses appear to indicate that economic enterprise experienced a secular downward shift in rates of return in the post-war period, though the magnitude of the decline varied from country to country. One of the comparative studies sponsored by the OECD (Hill 1979) concluded that the trend towards declining profit shares and rates of return in the major European countries had been unmistakable, though, apart from Canada, the same could not be said of the non-European countries analysed, that is, Japan, Australia and the United States. The decline was most noticeable in Germany and the UK, where the share of net profits in net value added fell from 37 to 16 per cent and 30 to 7 per cent, respectively, over the period 1955–76. During the same time, net rates of return in manufacturing declined from 31 to 11 per cent in Germany and from 20 to 3 per cent in the UK. These are indeed remarkable falls and, as Hill points out, the extent of the deterioration was not fully appreciated by many observers, largely because it was obscured by the continuing practice of calculating profits and rates of return on the basis of historic costs. The distortion created by using historic cost-accounting principles is particularly serious in times of strong inflation of the type experienced in the 1970s.

Variations in trend rates of return among countries have little significance, in the short term at least, in terms of explaining inter-country differences in economic performance. This point is readily demonstrated from the obvious lack of correlation between the two variables in three major countries, namely the United States, the UK and Germany. But from the point of view of the long-term growth potential of the major economies, the trends in these variables are disturbing, as are those for wage-income shares, which, by virtue of their essentially reciprocal quality, tend to substantiate the above data. In contrast to the stability of the wage share in total income before 1939, the post-war period saw a dramatic rise in wage shares in all countries, amounting on average to some 20 percentage points for OECD countries as a whole during the period 1948–75 (Paldam 1979). Almost one-third of this change represented a genuine fall in the share of capital, about one-half of which took place in the years 1970–75, more especially in the last two. It is interesting to note the contrasting reactions of the shares during the two price shocks of 1950–51 (Korean War) and 1974–75. In the former case, wage earners bore the brunt of the loss, with a consequent rise in the share going to capital, whereas in the latter price upsurge, it was capital that suffered the loss as wage earners sought successfully to insulate themselves, thereby pushing up the wage/income ratio. At the same time, the steady advance in the wage/income share was probably aggravated by the declining proportion of gross earnings retained by the average worker after state deductions.

The implications of these trends were disquieting, to say the least. The genesis of the growth crisis of the 1970s can be seen partly in terms of a long-run deterioration in the income share of capital, which markedly accelerated in the 1970s as the strengthening bargaining power of labour operated to push up the wage/income share. During this later period, the critical point may have been reached in several countries in which the share of capital declined to around 15 per cent or less, that is, to a level insufficient to sustain long-run full employment growth rates, which Paldam puts at between 3 and 4 per cent per annum, but which may have been even higher in some cases. In other words, if the critical level of distributional shares between labour and capital had been reached or was fast approaching, the main problem would be to restrain any further rise in the wage/income ratio before it suffocated the share of capital. Again, this posed an awkward policy issue, because any attempt to stimulate economic activity could have pushed up the wage/income share, which, after two decades or more of Keynesian demand-management policies, had shown a consistent tendency to move in an upward direction. To the policy problems of the 1970s we now turn.

Macroeconomic management under stagflation

The events of the 1970s presented governments with a more difficult task, in terms of economic management, compared with that of the 1950s and 1960s. They were faced with a whole host of problems, many of them occurring simultaneously, namely inflation, rising unemployment, stagnating output, balance-of-payments difficulties, rising public sector deficits, currency disorders, not to mention specific supply problems. Although their severity and incidence varied from one country to another, most countries experienced several, if not all, of these unfavourable forces during the course of the decade. Not since the inter-war period, and even then prices and unemployment had not risen together, had there been a period in peacetime when so many adverse influences converged at one and the same time.

Inevitably, the extent and magnitude of the problems led to a significant shift in the balance of policy objectives and instruments of control from those that had been in use hitherto. During the 1950s and 1960s, the art of economic management had been primarily concerned with trying to achieve a stable economic framework, and this entailed governments juggling with a series of basically incompatible objectives, that is, growth, full employment, external equilibrium and price stability. Few countries, apart from perhaps Germany, were able to achieve all four goals simultaneously. Thus, though in practice priority was generally given to maintaining growth and full employment, it was frequently necessary to temper these ideals when considerations with regard to price stability and balance-of-payments equilibrium became pressing. Fortunately, pressures with regard to the latter rarely became acute enough, the UK excepted, to jeopardize the advancement of growth and full employment for any length of time. Hence reliance on demand-management policies, involving a combination of fiscal and monetary policies with varying degrees of emphasis, while never regarded as ideal, was not seriously brought into question. Occasionally, resort was made to other policies (changes in exchange rates, incomes policies, etc.), but these never became permanent policy weapons, while very little serious attention was given to supply considerations.

Though critics have sometimes argued that such policies were as much a cause of instability as a cure for it, on the surface at least, demand-management policies seemed to work well in so far as it is difficult to deny that the first two post-war decades were the most successful in terms of economic growth and stability in all human history. Not that one can credit governments with much of the honour for the economic growth success of this period because, according to Knox, 'Apart from national and international measures to maintain the level of total demand, the influence of government policy in the acceleration of overall economic growth in the non-Communist countries has been negligible' (Knox 1976). Indeed, it may in fact be argued that it was the underlying strength of the major economies and the relative absence of fundamental disequilibrium that made for successful management, rather than the other way round. Given strong real growth forces and consequently a shift of the supply schedule to the right, it was perfectly possible to sustain high equilibrium growth rates without, in most cases, running into serious balance of payments or price problems, a situation helped in part by some trade-off between wages and unemployment.

Once these good conditions evaporated, as they did progressively during the 1970s, the practicality of using traditional demand-management tools to achieve former objectives became less meaningful. During this period, priority had to be increasingly given to controlling inflation and dealing with external imbalances in preference to encouraging growth and maintaining full employment. These now became residual objectives, if that, because under conditions of high inflation and diminished growth potential, it was believed that any attempt to stimulate activity and employment, by fiscal or other means, would simply set off the inflationary spiral again. In line with this reasoning, the tools of economic management underwent a re-evaluation. The delicate combination of fiscal and monetary 'fine-tuning' gave way initially to direct policies in the form of income and price controls, but subsequently attention was shifted towards a more vigorous control of monetary aggregates, including monetary targeting. The new approach to management, though conditioned by immediate events, had, like its Keynesian counterpart, a respectable intellectual lineage stemming back to the 1950s under the pervasive influence of Milton Friedman.

Though the explosive inflation of the first half of the 1970s caused many countries to turn at first to direct price and income controls, it soon became clear that these not only caused distortions to market economies but also were regarded, for the most part, as temporary expedients that merely held back movements in wages and prices until the time when they were lifted or relaxed. Given their anticipated temporary nature, they could do little to provide a long-term solution to the underlying causes of inflation, though in some cases they formed an important adjunct to the introduction of monetary targeting. In the UK, for example, the government did not begin to use monetary targets until it had managed, against a background of incomes policy, to stabilize the growth of the money supply at around 10 per cent.

In many respects, it was logical that governments should turn attention to more rigorous control of monetary aggregates as an intermediary policy objective. It was not simply that the conditions of the time demanded a new initiative or that monetarism had suddenly become more respectable, though both factors played a part. It was rather the more pragmatic response to earlier events that exerted the crucial influence. The shift to monetary weapons focused attention on areas that had been allowed to get out of control in the early 1970s, namely excessive monetary growth associated in part with the willingness of governments to run exceptionally large budgetary deficits and resort to financing these through the banking system. Thus the increasing respectability of monetary policies reflected the lessons of past mistakes. The timing and nature of the move to more rigorous monetary control, involving basically the setting of targets or projections for the growth in the money supply or domestic credit aggregates, varied substantially from country to country, as did the instruments of control to achieve these targets (see McClam 1978). But most major countries in the later 1970s adopted some form of control of monetary aggregates, together with fiscal policies designed to stabilize or lower public sector deficits.

The more rigorous approach to monetary policy coupled with fiscal restraint was not overwhelmingly successful in terms of inflation control and, of course, there were important side-effects for the real economy. Most countries did achieve some success in reducing the rate of monetary growth from the high levels experienced earlier in the decade, while the pace of inflation was moderated considerably through to 1978. But the process was a slow and uneven one; inflation remained at a high level compared with post-war standards before the 1970s, and it began to accelerate again in 1979. There are several reasons why the policies achieved only partial success. To have secured a quick and complete check to inflation would have required more drastic monetary and fiscal action, which, given the implications in terms of the real economy, would not have been politically feasible. The second best option of moderate restraint was bound to take time given the lags inherent in policy action and the residual cost pressures still in the system. Second, the monetary targets were by no means firmly adhered to, with the result that monetary growth was allowed to deviate from the target path, often in a procyclical manner. This laxity in control derived in part from the accommodation of cost pressures, as for example in Italy between 1975 and 1976, when substantial overshooting of the total credit target occurred as a result of the wages explosion of 1975 being validated in monetary terms. The British authorities were confronted with similar pressures in 1979–80, which led to the spectacle of high public sector wage claims being validated in monetary terms despite the new Conservative government's determination to bring monetary expansion under control. Corresponding awards in the private sector were made possible by the high volume of bank lending to the corporate sector, but with serious implications for company liquidity. A further difficulty arose from the technical problems associated with monetary control. Generally speaking, the authorities found it difficult to get a firm grip on the monetary base because of the development of intermediary finance and the effects of international capital flows, while the problems associated with the financing of large public sector deficits caused short-term fluctuations in the money supply. The latter problem became almost a permanent feature in the UK from 1975, reflecting, according to one authority, the fact that 'official sales of gilt-edged tend to be rather tidal, periods of very large sales alternating with periods of very small sales. The institutional structure of the UK is such that when sales are deficient, the government's residual financing tends to be supplied by the banking system, usually in the form of Treasury bills, increasing both the money stock and the banks' reserve assets' (McClam 1978).

In the last resort, of course, the degree of monetary restraint can only go as far as the political consensus allows. Rostow (1979) has neatly summarized the political and social constraints involved in this context: 'Taxes, public expenditure, interest rates, and the supply of money are not determined antiseptically by men free to move economies along a Phillips curve to an optimum trade-off between the rate of unemployment and the rate of inflation. Fiscal and monetary policy are, inevitably, living parts of the democratic political process.' This clearly tempered the rigour with which the authorities pushed the new policies given the cost implications that they entailed in terms of output and employment, even though policies erred on the side of restraint. What this meant in practice is that the authorities for the most part supplied the amount of inflation demanded by the public and it appears that over time the upper bound to what were regarded as tolerable levels of inflation rose, making it more difficult to bring it fully under control.

In purely technical terms, it is fairly easy to prescribe the right policies to eradicate inflation, but because the economic and social implications of these would, in the short term at least, be so horrendous, it is not surprising that governments were reluctant to contemplate them. Consequently, while the control of inflation was generally regarded as the number one priority, there was also some attempt to 'minimise macroeconomic misery' in conditions of stagflation (see Perkins 1980). Inevitably, this meant an awkward policy compromise in an effort to resolve the dilemma of high unemployment and rapid inflation. Some would argue, however, that the policies of restraint designed to reduce inflation were pushed too far, to the consequent detriment of the real economy. It is certainly true that output growth in most countries was well below capacity potential for some time, and because this resulted in higher unit costs and lower productivity growth, it exacerbated the inflationary problem. Moreover, in so far as policy restraint led to income destruction, it diminished the tax revenue base of governments and thereby made it more difficult for the authorities to reduce budgetary deficits, which were regarded as a source of inflation. If a solution to the budgetary problem is sought through higher taxes, this adds a further cost-push element to inflation.

As far as policy is concerned the authorities faced something of a dilemma in the 1970s and in trying to solve it they became 'boxed in' by their own exertions. In an ideal world, a short sharp shock treatment was the obvious way out of the inflationary spiral, but politically this was not a viable solution at the time. Hence governments were forced to adopt an uneasy compromise mix of policies in an attempt to gain some trade-off between inflation, employment and growth. The problem with this approach was that it failed to eradicate inflation and left a residue of unemployment and slow growth. In the process, the authorities became confused as to the objectives and specification of different policy weapons.

In an inflationary climate, there is clearly a need for a consistent monetary policy, that is, one in which monetary expansion is compatible with the underlying growth potential of the economy and an acceptable rate of inflation. Indeed, any worthwhile attempt to deal with the price problem must involve the use of monetary weapons and the control of monetary aggregates. While it may not be essential to adhere to a rigid target for monetary expansion, it is important that the authorities adopt a figure that is consistent with the growth potential of the economy and the target for inflation. The specification of a monetary target is important for several reasons: it provides the monetary authorities with a firm yardstick with which to operate and should thereby prevent undue laxity in monetary control; at the same time, it can act as a useful public information signal, provided the authorities advertise the fact sufficiently, which in time will serve to impress upon the nation the need for restraint; and, finally, it should ensure that nominal interest rates move closer to their natural level. The latter aspect, as Perkins has recognized, is important, because in the past the refusal to allow nominal interest rates to rise sufficiently has had adverse effects on both inflation and output. When in times of high inflation interest rates are artificially depressed, the returns on financial assets become unattractive and this leads to a process of portfolio readjustment from financial to real assets, including goods and commodities, which raises the price of the latter. Moreover, in their efforts to hold down nominal interest rates below the natural level, the authorities may be forced to allow a faster growth of the money supply than would otherwise be the case. Then if any attempt is made to restrain demand and prices by resort to higher taxes, as some governments did between 1974 and 1976, this would add a further cost-push element to the system. Of course, these influences will serve to dampen real activity, but low real interest rates in themselves may have a similar effect through consumption. If returns on financial assets become negative in real terms, the propensity to save may rise, as was the case in the mid-1970s despite rapid inflation, as people attempted to restore their stock of savings in real terms. This in turn tended to depress consumption and outweighed any advantage in terms of investment derived from artificially low interest rates.

If monetary policy had been directed consistently towards achieving price stability, it would have been possible to follow a more constructive fiscal policy. For the reasons stated earlier, it may have been too much to expect a return to the high growth rates of earlier years, but given the degree of underutilized capacity, some moderate fiscal stimulus would not have been out of place, provided that it was financed in a non-inflationary manner. Unfortunately, the authorities became constrained in their actions by an obsessive fear of the inflationary implications of any fiscal relaxation. This was primarily a result of their failure to adhere to a firm monetary policy, a misconception about the role of fiscal policy, and a neglect of supply variables. What was required was not the traditional consumption-based tax remissions, but fiscal incentives that boosted investment and encouraged structural transformation, especially because the energy shocks had rendered obsolete part of the former capital stock. Yet this was the very time when public investment, especially in infrastructure, was being pruned. Second, in conjunction with a constructive fiscal policy, more attention needed to be devoted to the supply side, or the microeconomic foundations of growth, including improved resource allocation, the sponsoring of new technologies, the retraining and redeployment of labour, and the removal of restraints on trade and economic activity to improve the competitive environment, rather than the defensive strategies of the later 1970s, which had as their main objective the propping up of declining sectors of activity and the preservation of jobs. As the OECD warned in 1979 (*The Case for Positive Adjustment Policies*), without such new initiatives there was a danger of western capitalism becoming locked into 'a vicious circle whereby slow growth generates behaviour and policies which impair productivity and accentuate inflation; this prompts governments to adopt more cautious demand management policies and hence leads, directly or indirectly, to even slower growth'.

In other words, while priority should have been given to combating inflation by tight monetary control, it was also crucial that an effort be made to break out of the vicious circle of stagflation by shifting progressively away from the defensive policies adopted following the recession of 1974–75. The implications of the failure to solve the policy dilemma are explored further in the following chapter.

Questions for discussion

1   How did the oil-price shocks of the 1970s affect western Europe?
2   What were the main causes of the slowdown in growth?
3   Why was inflation so severe in the 1970s?
4   What changes occurred in economic policy during the 1970s?
5   Did real growth forces weaken in the 1970s?

10 Western Europe in the 1980s
The search for stability

Since the Second World War, European nations experienced two distinct periods of economic change. First, there was the long period of high and sustained growth from the late 1940s through to the early 1970s, which narrowed significantly the gap between American and west European levels of productivity that had existed at the start of the period. By the late 1960s, rapid growth and structural change seemed to be the natural order of things and the old trade cycle depressions a thing of the past.

Yet within a few years, this golden age scenario was all but at an end. Rising inflation, wage explosions, student unrest and political disturbances at the turn of the decade were the initial manifestations of a long period of chequered growth and economic gloom. Problems and shocks appeared with almost regular monotony. Commodity shortages, exchange disturbances following the break-up of the Bretton Woods system, oil shocks as a result of the machinations of the OPEC oil cartel, and strong labour resistance to economic adversity combined to produce recession or sluggish growth, high inflation, rising unemployment, and balance of payments and budgetary difficulties. The convergence of favourable factors that had characterized the post-war boom had been transformed into an equally strong convergence of disincentives to high and sustained growth.

As we saw in the previous chapter, western Europe was slowly struggling to extricate itself from these problems when the second oil shock undermined her fragile recuperation. This time, there was little cause for optimism that the disturbance could be accommodated without serious consequences. Because of a host of unresolved problems stemming from earlier shocks (for example inflation, budgetary deficits and wage pressures), governments could no longer afford to contemplate accommodating this new external shock as they had done previously. Thus, macroeconomic policy almost everywhere turned restrictive and hence recessionary forces were thereby compounded.

The 1980s therefore opened on an inauspicious note. Governments no longer dreamed of trying to restore the golden age and even their citizens were slowly acclimatizing themselves to a less favourable economic outlook. The main task now became one of searching for a new equilibrium, if need be at a lower level of activity and employment, that was consistent with low inflation, reduced budgetary deficits and external equilibrium. The rise in unemployment that this inevitably entailed was the price to be paid for failure to adjust fully to the distur-bances of the previous decade. Unfortunately, the higher levels of unemployment proved to be far from transitory. In the process of tackling the other issues, high unemployment became a permanent feature of most western nations. Even by the end of the decade, after several years of strong growth, unemployment remained as intractable as ever, so much so that it began to be questioned whether it was more of a structural or micro problem than a consequence of macroeconomic forces. By this time, however, the cycle of events was again moving adversely, prompting governments once more to revert to a cautionary policy stance. So by the turn of the decade, western nations were again teetering on the brink of recession, the duration and severity of which seemed likely to match that of the previous cyclical downturn.

General trends

A reaction to the vigorous boom of 1972–73 was only to be expected, but few people would have anticipated that the last quarter of the twentieth century would be one of chequered economic performance, when much of the world economy operated below full potential, with rates of growth only around half those of the golden age of the post-war period. A glance at Tables 10.1 and 10.2 reveals that economic growth in Europe slowed down markedly after 1973, while there was very little expansion in employment. The 1980s proved to be even weaker than the 1970s, with growth averaging barely half that of the super-boom years. Apart from Southeast Asia and China, growth was slower everywhere than in the previous decade, and much weaker than in the post-war years. World output (GDP) rose by just over 30 per cent in the 1980s compared with 45 per cent in the 1970s, while in per capita terms, this represented a rise of only about 1 per cent a year as a consequence of the increase in world population. The developed market economies did better because their population growth was modest. Even so, real per capita income growth was only about 2 per cent a year. Meanwhile, unemployment climbed sharply and approached double figures, that is over four times the average level in the 1960s.

Slower growth was accompanied by a greater degree of convergence in rates of performance among the major nations compared with previously. No doubt, this partly reflected the closer integration of western European nations during the course of the 1980s (see Table 10.2). In addition, there was a noticeable trend improvement in most economic indicators during the latter half of the decade. At the start of the period, most economic variables were highly unfavourable, with stagnant or falling output, rising inflation, negative investment, large government deficits, current account imbalances, and high unemployment. By the end of the decade, the picture had improved somewhat. On average, price inflation had been halved, the growth of GDP was running at around 3 per cent a year, investment was strongly positive and in most cases external deficits had been eliminated and budgetary positions had been consolidated. Only the unemployment scene remained as black as it had been ten years earlier (Table 10.3, Table 10.5).

Table 10.1 Growth rates of gross domestic product (per cent per annum) 1960–95

| | Real GDP | | | | | Real GDP per capita | | | | |
	60–73	73–79	79–89	89–95	60–95	60–73	73–79	79–89	89–95	60–95
EU15	4.7	2.5	2.2	1.5	3.1	4.0	2.1	2.0	1.1	2.6
OECD Europe	4.8	2.5	2.3	1.6	3.1	3.8	2.0	1.8	1.0	2.4
OECD less Europe	5.6	2.9	2.7	1.7	3.6	4.4	2.0	1.9	0.9	2.7
OECD	4.9	2.8	2.6	1.8	3.4	3.7	1.9	1.7	0.9	2.3

Source: OECD *Historical Statistics 1960–95*, Tables 3.1 and 3.2, 50–51.

Table 10.2 Growth rates of gross domestic product and industrial production (per cent per annum) 1961–90

	1961–70		1971–80		1981–90	
	GDP	Ind Prod	GDP	Ind Prod	GDP	Ind Prod
Austria	4.7	5.6	3.6	4.0	2.3	2.8
Belgium	4.9	5.0	3.4	2.3	1.9	2.0
Denmark	4.5	6.2	2.2	1.9	2.0	2.7
West Germany	4.4	5.3	2.7	1.9	2.2	1.9
Greece	8.5	* 10.0	4.6	7.0	0.7	1.0
Spain	7.3	† 10.4	3.5	5.1	3.0	1.9
France	5.6	5.1	3.3	3.2	2.4	1.1
Ireland	4.2	6.8	4.7	4.5	3.6	6.3
Italy	5.7	7.0	3.6	3.3	2.2	1.3
Luxembourg	3.5	2.4	2.6	0.0	4.5	3.7
Netherlands	5.1	7.2	3.0	2.9	2.2	1.4
Portugal	6.4	5.0	4.7	6.5	3.2	4.8
Finland	4.8	7.3	3.4	4.6	3.1	2.9
Sweden	4.6	6.1	2.0	1.0	2.0	1.9
UK	2.9	2.4	1.9	1.0	2.7	2.1
EU15	4.8	5.4	3.0	2.6	2.4	1.8
US	4.2	4.9	3.2	3.1	2.9	2.2
Japan	10.1	13.6	4.4	4.1	4.0	4.0

Source: European Commission *European Economy*, No. 68, 1999, Tables 10 and 12.

Notes: * 1963–70; † 1962–70.

The data in Table 10.3 illustrate clearly the marked difference between the first and second half of the decade. Performance everywhere was stronger in the later 1980s than in the first half of the period. In fact, in some areas, notably inflation, investment and current account balances, many European countries by the later 1980s had regained the levels achieved before the onset of the first oil crisis. Whether this marked the start of a new equilibrium, as some observers

Table 10.3 Key indicators of economic performance: Europe 12 (per cent per annum)

	1973/1960	1980/1973	1985/1980	1990/1985
Real GDP	4.8	2.2	0.5	3.1
Employment	0.3	0.1	−0.4	1.2
Investment	5.6	0.3	−0.6	5.7
Prices	4.6	12.4	8.8	4.1
Annual average % of GDP				
Current account balance	0.5	−0.5	−0.2	0.6
General government net borrowing/ lending	−0.6	−3.5	−5.3	−3.7

Source: Commission of the European Communities, *European Economy* 42, 1989, 111.

suggested at the time, is open to doubt. Commenting on the long recovery from 1982, the United Nations in their *World Economic Survey for 1990* were encouraged to believe that western nations 'are now on a track where, barring domestic and external shocks, they can look forward to continuing moderate expansion interrupted by no more than, at worst, moderate cyclical downturns. If so, the world economy could be more stable and dynamic in the 1990s than it was in the 1980s'. Yet, ironically, as these words were being written, recession was about to strike again, and it soon became apparent that many of the old problems had not been laid to rest. As the data in Table 10.1 indicate, rates of growth of GDP, both in absolute and in per capita terms, fell yet again, and in the early 1990s they were averaging only one-quarter to one-third those achieved in the 1960s and early 1970s.

Impact of the second oil shock

The second oil crisis at the end of the 1970s had a broadly similar impact to that of the first, accounting for some 2 per cent of OECD's GDP and with similar price and recessionary effects. But the cyclical experience after the two shocks was not identical by any means. The cyclical swings during OPEC 1 were sharper than those accompanying the second crisis. In 1973, before the first shock, there had been a strong boom in activity, with pronounced synchronization among the major industrial countries, whereas in the later 1970s, the upswing was weaker and less heavily synchronized, with the United States lagging western Europe. Moreover, whereas in 1975 there was a sharp drop in activity in most countries followed by an equally sharp rebound the following year, the later cyclical experience was more attenuated. Many countries experienced falls in output, but these were spread over three years, while on average growth was maintained, albeit at low rates. Nor was there any sharp rebound similar to that of 1976. This may be explained partly by the fact that following the erratic recovery after 1975, the underlying economic position was weaker by the early 1980s, while the contrasting policy stance of the major countries compared with earlier also had relevance in this context (see below).

Price changes were of a similar order of magnitude at the consumer level despite the fact that non-oil commodity prices were less buoyant than in the earlier period. On the other hand, several indicators, notably budgetary deficits, unemployment and external accounts, visibly deteriorated. By contrast, the volume of international trade held up rather better than previously.

The policy reaction of governments to the second oil crisis differed from that following the first. There was both a greater degree of policy convergence and more continuity in policy-making among the western nations. There was no repetition of the accommodating policies to offset real income losses of the oil price hike, as happened in the 1970s. This time, both fiscal and monetary policies were tightened progressively in most countries, the main exception being France between 1981 and 1982, which undertook a short-lived expansion programme. Thus, on balance, macroeconomic policy reinforced the recessionary effects of the

Table 10.4 Estimates of main forces on OECD output, 1978–81 (percentage contribution to change in real GDP)

	1978	1979	1980	1981
Oil	0.0	−0.5	−2.25	−0.5
Fiscal policy	0.5	−0.5	−0.5	−1.5
Monetary policy	0.0	0.0	0.0	−0.75
Change in GNP	4.0	3.0	1.25	1.5

Source: J. Llewellyn, 'Resource prices and macroeconomic policies: lessons from two oil price shocks', *OECD Economic Studies* 1, 1983, 207.

oil shock. The impact was reflected in the sharp rise in real interest rates, negative in the later 1970s, but turning strongly positive, with real rates averaging around 5 per cent by 1982 and 1983. Estimates in Table 10.4 suggest that by 1981, the negative impact of policy was substantially greater than that of oil, and in the following year it was probably even stronger.

This period marks the final break with conventional post-war policy thinking. Recessionary impulses would normally have signalled a move towards expansionary policies as in the past, and as occurred initially after the first oil shock. Arguably, however, there were strong pragmatic reasons why this was no longer appropriate in the conditions of the early 1980s despite the perception that a change in policy stance would aggravate recessionary forces and raise unemployment. First, the rise in oil prices was equivalent to an external tax for the oil-importing nations and it could be offset only at the expense of adverse repercussions elsewhere in the economies that bore the brunt of it. By the second oil crisis, it was realized that real income losses had to be borne by the oil importers in one form or another because they represented a process of income redistribution among nations. Far better, it was thought, that these losses should be incurred directly and without the inflationary consequences that accompanied the first oil shock. Governments were clearly anxious this time to avoid a repetition of the previous wage-price spiral and the ensuing currency depreciation. Moreover, there was also the possibility that the oil market might remain difficult for some time to come, in which case slower growth would help to conserve energy use.

Most governments were also concerned about their budgetary positions at this time. Large deficits had accumulated during the 1970s, and for several years efforts had been made, albeit with not a great deal of success, to reduce or stabilize them. Renewed recession weakened these efforts for a time because automatic stabilizers put renewed upward pressure on public spending at a time when the revenue base was shrinking. Thus, there was obviously no ardent desire to add to the problems by expansionary fiscal policies. In any case, fiscal laxness was regarded as a sign of financial weakness, which would have repercussions on exchange rates and inflation and help to undermine general confidence. In this regard, lessons were drawn from the German and Japanese experience following the first oil crisis. These two countries had adopted a stringent policy stance, which appeared to have met with considerable success in the later 1970s in terms of growth, inflation, exchange rates and current account balances. Italy, France and Britain, on the other hand, had rather the reverse experience.

Two other factors constrained expansionary policy initiatives. First, there was the increasingly popular belief that strong real wage resistance and the re-emergence of the real wage gap (see below), together with structural rigidities in labour markets and elsewhere, would tend to nullify the effects of any demand stimuli, which would therefore show up principally in higher inflation rather than increased output and employment. Second, there was the conviction that countries could not unilaterally stimulate their economies because of the adverse effects this would have on their exchange rates and balance of payments. This was vividly demonstrated in 1981–82, when France attempted a unilateral policy of expansion that soon had to be reversed for these very reasons. In some countries, Germany in particular, policy-makers also believed that renewed expansion would occur only through export-led growth as a result of rising world demand. Because Germany was the key economy in Europe with a strong currency, this clearly made it difficult for other nations to act independently.

Given the greater stringency of policy in the early 1980s and the unfavourable trends in several key indicators, it is perhaps surprising that economic activity remained as resilient as it did, and more robust than in 1974–75. A combination of high real interest rates, adverse terms of trade, high unit labour costs, a significant decline in factor productivity and weak final demand drove down rates of return on capital to their lowest levels of the post-war period. The profitability of business by the early 1980s averaged only two-thirds that of the 1960s and early 1970s. In some countries, notably Italy and the UK, rates of return on industrial capital dropped below the real interest rate for the first time in history (Figure 10.1).

In addition, there was growing competition from Asian countries, deepening debt crises in the developing nations, and creeping trade restrictions, mainly of the non-tariff variety. Furthermore, there were thought to be worrying problems on the supply side relating not only to the flexibility of factor markets and structural impediments to growth, but also regarding the rate at which western nations were taking up modern technology. The climate was therefore not conducive to business investment, and this is reflected in the marked slowdown in the growth of the capital stock and the decline in investment ratios.

Yet apart from one or two countries, notably the UK, where a combination of policy factors and an oil-induced rise in the exchange rate resulted in a sharp contraction in economic activity, few countries suffered significant falls in GDP, though industrial production setbacks were common in 1981. On balance, there was greater resilience than in the previous crisis, even though recovery took longer to materialize. Boltho (1984, 17) suggests that the resilience in consumer spending, partly through a decline in the propensity to save, was an important factor in explaining the avoidance of a major recession. In fact, however, real consumer spending was weaker than in 1974–75, as was public consumption. He also points to the better performance in investment, but again the data for western Europe through to 1983 do not appear to bear out this assertion either. Rather, the main factor seems to have been the relative buoyancy of exports, which continued to

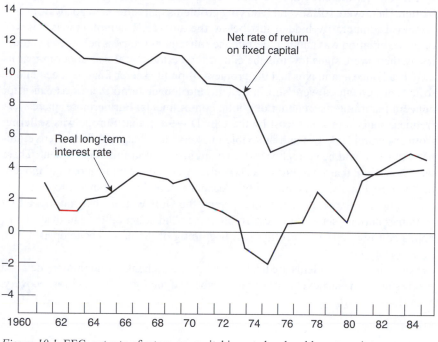

Figure 10.1 EEC: net rate of return on capital invested and real long-term interest rate
(per cent)

Source: OECD 1987.

expand, albeit at a reduced rate, throughout the recession, whereas there was a fall
in volume of some 4 per cent in 1975.

The long recovery

Despite the poor outlook for economic growth in the recessionary conditions
of the early 1980s, nevertheless western Europe subsequently experienced
nearly a decade of unbroken growth, weak at first in 1982–83, but averaging
around 2.5 per cent (GDP) a year over 1984–87 and then rising to 3 per cent
or more in the latter years of the 1980s. Inflation dropped sharply to levels comparable with those of the later 1960s, while wage pressures moderated and there
was some advance in productivity. These improvements helped to restore profitability and so investment rose strongly in the latter half of the decade. At the
same time, the European Community's external position returned to equilibrium
following the large deficits occasioned by the second oil price hike, while there
was a measure of consolidation in public finances. From the middle of the decade,
there was even some net employment creation, unemployment levels generally
peaking in 1984.

Yet whether the basis had been laid for sound and lasting growth is another matter. There were still several worrying problems that refused to go away, or that remained temporarily hidden just below the surface. Unemployment was one of these. Inflation was another; despite the substantial progress achieved in reducing it, there were signs towards the end of the period that it was about to rear its ugly head once again. Nor had the problem of public sector finances been laid to rest; many countries were still in deficit, and longer term, there was cause for concern regarding the funding of public commitments. Furthermore, there were frequent suggestions, not least by the OECD (1987), that Europe was suffering from structural rigidities and inflexible markets, and that until these were eliminated, there could be no real basis for sound growth and full employment. There was even a hint that some European countries were not keeping abreast of modern technology. Finally, at the turn of the decade, external disturbances, for example the political collapse of eastern Europe and the Gulf War, once again looked set to impart another setback to western progress. And so an all too familiar pattern appeared to be repeating itself, as the beginning of the new decade opened on a recessionary note.

Some of these problems are taken up later in the chapter, after a more detailed discussion of the achievements of the decade and the forces making for recovery.

Disinflation

One of the most notable achievements of the 1980s was the abatement of inflation. For much of the 1970s and early 1980s, inflation in western Europe had been both high and volatile, often running into double figures. For the years 1979–82, it averaged well over 10 per cent a year, though with marked variations between countries. Italy, Ireland and the UK had the highest rates (around 20 per cent at the peak), whereas at the other extreme, Germany and Switzerland experienced moderate inflation. A conscious decision was taken early on by the authorities in most countries not to tolerate the persistence of the high inflation rates of the past, which, by distorting the price mechanism, shortening time horizons and generally undermining confidence, were thought to have been responsible for the sluggish economic performance. Accordingly, monetary policy became increasingly restrictive and it was backed up by fiscal restraint, with the result that the recessionary impulses were intensified or prolonged. Two other factors also weighed heavily in the balance. First, the concern over the state of public finances and the growing burden of interest payments prompted governments to take action to consolidate their finances. Second, macroeconomic policy was strongly influenced by the course of events in the United States. Monetary restraint and growing fiscal deficits in the latter case led to high real interest rates and a strong appreciation of the dollar, so that European countries were forced to maintain a restrictive monetary stance and high real interest rates in order to defend their currencies against the dollar. Yet, while American policy certainly put pressure on Europe in this respect, the Federal deficit probably helped to sustain growth elsewhere through rising American imports, even though in time the fiscal problem of the United States became a matter of increasing concern both at home and abroad (Schafer 1988).

The tight policy stance coupled with the declared intention not to repeat the experience of the 1970s certainly helped to reduce inflationary expectations. Non-accommodating monetary policy, rather than fiscal restraint, probably made the major contribution to disinflation. In general, fiscal restraint tended to be rather less widespread, important in Germany, the UK and Japan, expansionary for a time in France and Italy, and broadly stable in the smaller European countries. Taking the OECD as a whole, there was little significant change in structural budget balances between 1980 and 1983, because increases in debt service payments and transfers tended to offset action to reduce budget deficits in many cases.

The disinflationary process was greatly assisted by the more favourable trend in commodity prices. Oil prices collapsed dramatically once the OPEC pricing cartel ceased to be effective; from a peak of $36 a barrel early in 1981, they fell to $26 in late 1985 and to a low of $11 early in 1986, before rising gently to around $16 a barrel. Raw material prices also fell back sharply until 1987 as a result of substantial additions to capacity, the slow recovery in world industrial activity and the development of substitutes. Thus between 1980 and 1988 the real price of non-fuel commodity exports from developing countries declined by some 40 per cent. Fluctuations in exchange rates, especially the sharp appreciation of the dollar in the first half of the 1980s, complicated the position somewhat, because it tended to offset part of the gain from falling commodity prices in so far as European imports were denominated in dollar terms. This position was reversed in the second half of the decade, however, when the dollar depreciated.

The third main factor bearing favourably on inflation was the shift in wage-setting behaviour, though in turn it should be stressed that the latter was considerably influenced by the first two factors. During the 1970s, a significant influence sustaining the inflationary momentum had been the tendency for wages to rise not only in response to price changes but also in anticipation of future changes. Wage earners, long accustomed to steady annual increases in real incomes, were not prepared to forgo these when the economy could no longer deliver them because of external shocks and declining productivity. Hence, they bargained for high nominal wage awards which for the most part were accommodated by monetary expansion, and so wage gains outstripped those warranted by changes in productivity and the terms of trade, leading to the emergence of a real wage gap. Wage-setting behaviour in this period was also adversely affected by the increasing inflexibility of labour markets through protective labour legislation and structural problems.

From 1982, there was a distinct improvement in the functioning of labour markets. Real wage resistance declined under the influence of recession and policy factors, helped also by the downward trend in commodity prices. Weak markets made it difficult for manufacturers to pass on cost increases and therefore stiffened their resistance to unjustified wage demands. Hence, real earnings growth abated and the real wage gap became favourable to an improvement in profitability. Moderation may also have been assisted by a greater degree of flexibility in labour markets through more part-time work, the reduction in union participation and a shift away from highly unionized staple industries, and also in some cases, the UK in particular, by legislation affecting industrial relations and wage bargaining.

By the middle of the 1980s, the disinflationary process had more or less run its course. Consumer price inflation in western Europe averaged around 2.5 per cent in 1986–87, which was better than that of the 1960s. Whether the problem had really been exorcized is another matter, however. It is noticeable that inflation began to creep up again in the later 1980s as the easing of the policy regime made way for an expansion in activity. The danger of expansionary policies being dispersed mainly in higher wages and prices rather than in real output may have lessened, but it had by no means been extinguished, a fact amply demonstrated by the sharp rise in UK inflation in 1989–90, largely as a consequence of overexuberant policy relaxation. However, few other countries were prepared to jeopardize the gains already made by injudicious action because the costs of disinflation had been heavy. What the experience of the past two decades had brought home, above all, was that 'it is less costly to maintain low inflation through non-accommodation of shocks as they occur, rather than to allow what might appear *ex ante* to be discrete, perhaps innocuous, increases in inflation to cumulate to levels that become economically and politically intolerable. This is the most important lesson from the disinflation of the 1980s' (Coe *et al*. 1988, 114).

Consumer spending and saving

The improvement in the inflationary situation encouraged a more confident stance on the part of consumers. Consumer spending was flat in the recession of the early 1980s, while savings were at record levels as households attempted to restore their real savings balances during a period of high inflation. But consumption began to pick up slowly after 1982, and from 1985 onwards, it was averaging more than 3 per cent per annum, being especially buoyant between 1986 and 1988. The rise in consumption was more stable and better sustained than in the previous cyclical recovery for several reasons. First, there was a general decline in household savings from the peak levels reached at the beginning of the decade. The decline in savings was especially marked in France, Britain and Italy. This can be attributed to the gradual erosion of the real balance effect on savings because of the fall in inflation, a high rate of family formation (which gave rise to a strong demand for housing and consumer durables), and a wealth effect as house prices and stock market values rose faster than incomes, thereby encouraging households to increase borrowing and spending and reduce savings. The strong rise in residential property values encouraged borrowing on the basis of enhanced asset values, as did the liberalization and innovations in financial markets. In fact, much of the fall in the savings ratio in the latter half of the decade, in the UK at least, was caused by a surge in borrowing induced by a lax monetary policy and the ease with which new credit could be secured under a more liberal financial regime. Two other factors further strengthened the forces of spending:

the continued weakness in commodity prices and a widespread shift in fiscal policy towards lower taxation in the latter part of the decade, both of which helped to sustain real income growth.

The effect of these combined forces was to make households feel considerably better off than before. Falling inflation and rapidly rising asset prices resulted in an improved wealth position, while rising real incomes through the improvement in economic activity, declining taxes and a favourable trend in the terms of trade improved the current income stream. This proved a potent and dangerous concoction, which sparked off a spending and borrowing spree, rising real debt levels and the erosion of savings.

Fixed investment

The rate of gross domestic capital formation also began to pick up significantly in most countries from 1984 onwards, after falls in 1981 and 1982 and a modest increase in 1983. By the latter half of the decade, investment was rising strongly and at a rate not seen since the early 1970s. The rate of growth of the capital stock began to increase once again, as did investment ratios, though the latter still remained a few percentage points below the levels reached in the early 1970s: 22 as against 26 per cent for the twelve Community countries.

One of the major factors in the revival of investment was, of course, the recovery in profitability. By the early 1980s, rates of return in some countries had sunk to low levels, and on average the profitability of business was down on the 1960s by over 30 per cent. The main influence behind the decline, apart from the sluggish rate of activity, was the trend deterioration in the relationship between wages and productivity growth, so that real unit labour costs rose at a time of weak final output prices. In addition, the unit costs of raw materials also rose sharply following the second oil crisis. At the same time, capital productivity had deteriorated sharply through the 1970s and early 1980s, because of lower rates of capital formation, lower capacity utilization, possibly some slowing down of technical advance and impediments to efficient capital use caused by structural factors and increasing government regulations. The result was that total factor productivity declined markedly, to only about one-quarter that of the 1960s.

The steady unwinding of these adverse trends during the 1980s led to a general improvement in profitability. Wage moderation was undoubtedly a major factor in the process. Real labour costs, which had previously been rising faster than productivity, were reversed after the early 1980s so that between 1981 and 1990 real unit labour costs fell on average by about 8 per cent. The growth in the productivity of labour remained well below the level of the 1960s, but at least the adverse gap between wages and productivity had been closed. Capital productivity also improved in the later 1980s, partly as a result of better capacity utilization and an increase in capital formation, as did total factor productivity, though still at rates one-half those of the 1960s. Profits were also boosted by more favourable terms of trade, leading to lower input costs, and by a strengthening of final output prices.

Though profitability levels undoubtedly improved, they still remained below those of the 1960s. Nevertheless, the recovery was sufficient to encourage a revival of investment. The latter was also stimulated by considerable rationalization and modernization of capacity and investment in new technology following a long period of sluggish investment. What is even more significant is that in the latter half of the decade, investment was becoming more employment creating, whereas previously, because of the configuration of relative factor prices, it had been primarily labour saving. Thus, in the years 1984–90, net employment creation in the European Community was of the order of 8 million persons. Of course, this had only a modest impact on the level of unemployment because other adverse influences were at work (see below).

International trade

One area that remained relatively buoyant in the recession of the early 1980s was international trade. The volume of exports of goods and services from western Europe, though well down on the level of the later 1970s, continued to expand on average at around 2 per cent per annum, which was a better performance than in the case of most other key economic indicators – and this despite serious balance-of-payments difficulties in many countries due to the oil shock (the major exception being the UK because of North Sea oil coming on stream), serious debt crises in the Third World, and a growing protectionist sentiment, reflected mainly in the proliferation of non-tariff barriers. Fortunately, however, unlike the 1930s, the major trading nations avoided a lurch into stringent policy protection, which did so much damage to trade and activity in the earlier period.

From 1983, trade once again became something of an engine of growth, though less strongly than in the boom years after the war. Total exports grew more rapidly than output, at around 5 per cent or more in western Europe through to 1990, with manufactured exports rising even faster. Closer integration among western nations, the liberalization of international capital movements, the stabilization of exchange rates, and the maintenance of a liberal trading environment, all helped to promote the recovery in trade. But perhaps of more significance as far as the initial upsurge was concerned was the strong demand generated for imports from the United States as a result of that country's domestic boom and the appreciation of the dollar. Thus, between 1983 and 1985, total US demand outpaced the growth of domestic output, whereas in most other countries except the UK and Italy the reverse occurred. This led to a sharp rise in American imports and an increasing trade deficit, the counterpart of which was equally large trade surpluses in Germany and Japan. By contrast, later in the decade, the position was partly reversed. Though the United States still recorded large external deficits, total domestic demand grew more slowly than output and the dollar depreciated so that increased exports helped to take up the slack. Japanese exports, on the other hand, slowed down as a result of the appreciation of the yen, whereas those of the European Community remained fairly buoyant.

Budget deficits and policy formation

Given the overriding problems of inflation and budgetary deficits, it was scarcely to be expected that government policy would play a crucial role in recovery from the recession. Indeed, as already noted, macroeconomic policy for a good part of the time concentrated on squeezing inflation out of the system, and it was only later in the decade that some modest relaxation was allowed.

An equally, if not more important, factor influencing the conduct of policy was the need to consolidate public finances. During the 1970s and early 1980s, most countries saw the emergence of large and growing budgetary deficits (5–10 per cent of GDP) and rapidly rising public debt/GDP ratios. The marked deterioration in budgetary positions was due to an explosion of public expenditure unmatched by revenue, largely resulting from the reallocation of resources arising from the two oil shocks, the slowing down of growth and the rise in unemployment, together with the inflexibility of expenditure commitments incurred in the good years of the 1960s. By the early 1980s, the problem had become sufficiently serious to prompt a fundamental reassessment of budgetary practices. Several considerations influenced the shift towards corrective action. First, large public sector deficits were thought to undermine confidence, especially in financial markets, because they were often associated with inflation. Second, there was serious concern about the future sustainability of such deficits and their financing, given the increasing inflexibility in expenditures and the rising burden of interest payments and transfer benefits. A third factor was the conviction that large public sectors *per se* had adverse effects on growth and employment, principally through the crowding out of private sector activity and the alleged adverse effects of transfer payments and high taxation on savings and investment. The evidence on this matter is mixed and conflicting (Katz *et al.* 1983; Friedlander and Sanders 1985), and policy response was often dictated more by ideological and political conviction than by sound economic reasoning, though concern about the size of budget deficits was genuine enough. In addition, there was a growing belief that even a balanced expansion of revenue and expenditure might be bad for growth because the rising tax burden could put pressure on wage costs, which would adversely affect profitability.

Despite firm resolve to deal with the problem, achieving fiscal correction was another matter. Because of the effects of the recession, the early years of the decade saw upward pressure on public spending at a time when revenues were far from buoyant. It was not until near the middle of the decade therefore that government attempts to rein back spending began to have some impact on the share of public spending in GDP, so that initially tax revenues bore the brunt of the adjustment process. Even in the latter part of the decade, when firmer control over spending was attained, increased tax revenues, as a result of the upswing in economic activity, were more important than the containment of spending in restoring public finances. Even so, fiscal consolidation was far from complete by the end of the period. No fewer than thirteen OECD countries were still in deficit, four of which recorded deficits of more than 5 per cent of GDP, while the size of the public sector was on average still greater than at the previous cyclical peak. In 1990, government spending as a share of GDP in the OECD area averaged more than 3 percentage points above that of 1979 (Oxley and Martin 1991, 175).

The experience of the 1980s demonstrates the difficulty of correcting public finances. There is an upward limit to taxation levels, beyond which they have an adverse impact on activity, while spending, once committed, is difficult to reverse. Many of the spending cuts were either cosmetic or marginal, being concentrated on public investment (the most detrimental as far as future growth is concerned), subsidies and wage bills, the last of these partly as a result of wage moderation and the containment of public sector employment growth. Moreover, the longer-term outlook was not encouraging because spending pressures were likely to increase in the future because of increasing dependence ratios, the restoration of public investment (especially on infrastructure facilities), the demand for more resources for health, education and pensions, and the relaxation of wage restraint in the public sector. In time, as the OECD recognized in one of its reports (1987), this might force governments to consider making fundamental changes in the way in which collective goods and services are financed. Alternatively, improvements in revenue collection and tax enforcement could be another possibility. Tax evasion was a growing problem everywhere, no more so than in Italy, where it had long been a problem of serious magnitude. It has been estimated that the tax revenue lost through evasion would have been sufficient to eliminate the whole of the Italian budgetary deficit in 1984 (Sassoon 1990, 119).

On balance, therefore, there was little scope for significant leverage to economic activity coming from macroeconomic policy. Both fiscal and monetary policy remained tight throughout the first half of the 1980s. In the later 1980s, there was some relaxation in monetary policy through a fall in interest rates and an expansion of the money supply, while in some countries tax reductions were implemented. The sudden stock market collapse of October 1987 prompted some easing of monetary policy, but the timing may have been inappropriate from the point of view of the real economy, given the strength of the recovery and the speculative asset situation. In the UK, for example, an overexpansionary monetary policy helped to fuel a housing boom and consumer spending spree, which had to be capped late in 1988. Thus, relaxation tended to be short-lived and the turn of the decade saw a shift towards policy tightening as the fear of old problems resurfaced.

The unemployment problem

One problem that refused to go away in the 1980s was unemployment. In fact, until the middle of the decade, unemployment was on an upward trend, rising into double figures in several countries. Even the sustained growth of the later 1980s failed to make much impact on the levels, despite some net employment creation. Unemployment percentages remained close to double figures in some of the larger countries. However, there was considerable divergence in rates of unemployment among countries, in contrast to the situation with respect to inflation and output

Table 10.5 Unemployment in Europe, 1960–90 (per cent)

	1960–68	*1969–73*	*1974–79*	*1980–85*	*1986–90*
Belgium	2.3	2.4	6.3	11.3	9.5
Denmark	2.0	1.4	5.5	9.3	8.6
France	1.7	2.6	4.5	8.3	9.8
West Germany	0.7	0.8	3.2	6.0	5.9
Ireland	5.0	5.6	7.6	12.6	16.2
Italy	3.8	4.2	4.6	6.4	7.7
Netherlands	1.2	2.0	5.1	10.1	8.8
Spain	2.4	2.7	5.3	16.6	18.7
UK	2.6	3.4	5.1	10.5	8.8
Austria	1.6	1.1	1.5	3.0	3.4
Finland	1.8	2.3	4.4	5.1	4.3
Norway	2.0	1.7	1.8	2.6	3.5
Sweden	1.3	1.8	1.5	2.4	1.7
Switzerland	0.1	0.0	1.0	1.7	1.9
United States	4.7	4.9	6.7	8.0	5.8
Japan	1.4	1.2	1.9	2.4	2.5

Source: R. Layard, S. Nickell and R. Jackman, *Unemployment: Macroeconomic Performance and the Labour Market*, Oxford: Oxford University Press, 1991, 398.

growth. Germany's unemployment remained consistently below that of many of her Community partners, while several of the smaller countries, notably Austria, Norway, Sweden and Switzerland, had an even better record, with rates not too far removed from those of the 1960s. The relative position of the United States also improved in the latter half of the decade, while Japan's record was exceptional throughout the period. The differences and the contrasts with earlier periods are shown in Table 10.5.

Not since the 1930s had such high levels of unemployment been seen. As then, some of the characteristics of the unemployment problem were familiar: the large regional differences, the sustained rise in the number of long-term unemployed, and the disproportionate incidence of unemployment among certain groups: the young and older workers, unskilled and the handicapped. However, one major difference with the earlier period was that changes in the level of economic activity seemed to have less impact on reducing the numbers of unemployed.

In fact, what is most noticeable is how limited the employment impact of growth was over the longer term, even back to the 1960s. Between 1960 and 1973, GDP growth in the European Community averaged 4.8 per cent a year, whereas employment expanded by only 0.2–0.3 per cent per annum. A growth rate of 2.4 per cent in the years 1973–79 had virtually no effect on employment, while in subsequent years through to 1986 employment growth was either negative or flat. Thus for the whole of the period 1973–87, some three-quarters of the rise in the available labour force was reflected in higher unemployment because the net growth in numbers employed was negligible. By contrast, the United States and Japan, and some of the smaller European countries, managed to generate substantial new employment, with the result that their unemployment rates were not much higher than in the early 1970s.

Jobless growth therefore seems to have been a peculiar feature of the major western European nations. Estimates suggest that a rate of growth of at least 2–2.5 per cent a year was required before employment responds positively (Commission of the European Communities 1989, 119). Thus, on the basis of a continuation of growth rates of around 3 per cent a year, as experienced in the later 1980s, and a labour force growth of 0.4 per cent a year, unemployment levels would continue to remain high, around 6 per cent, through to the mid-1990s, unless the employment/growth ratio changed for the better. In other words, a return to the former low levels of unemployment of the post-war years would have required higher rates of economic growth than those recorded in the later 1980s.

Attempts to explain the unemployment conundrum have taken several forms. They include the Keynesian aggregate demand version, the neoclassical real wage effect, the influence of structural rigidities in labour markets, and the impact of hysteresis. There are also the long-term changes in the growth of the labour supply to take into account. No one factor can explain the persistence of unemployment or differences between countries.

A higher level of aggregate demand and output would no doubt have eased the unemployment situation through greater employment creation had the authorities been disposed to impart a significant fiscal boost to their economies. Given the concern over inflation and budgetary deficits, this line of action was never seriously contemplated. Moreover, if, as was suspected, demand stimuli were more likely to feed through to prices than to output and employment, then there would be little point in taking such action. Indeed, if the relationship between output and employment growth of the 1960s and early 1970s had continued to prevail, then raising the rate of growth would not have had a marked impact on unemployment. However, one should also bear in mind that at a time when economic growth was sluggish, labour force growth was actually accelerating. Because of demographic factors that led to an increase in the proportion of the population of working age, together with an increase in female participation, the active labour force was growing more rapidly in the 1970s and 1980s than it had done previously. As the data in Table 10.6 show, it was growing at a rate of between 0.6 and 0.8 per cent per annum in these years, compared with only 0.2 per cent in the 1960s. Because employment growth, apart from the later 1980s, remained fairly constant at low levels (0.2 per cent), it was inevitable that most of the increase in the labour force would be translated into unemployment. And had the relationships between employment and output growth of the 1960s continued to hold in the later 1980s, the unemployment situation would have been worse than it actually was.

Clearly, then, forces on the labour supply side largely unconnected with the state of economic activity would have put considerable pressure on the labour market whatever the rate of growth. However, this does not mean that we have fully solved the paradox of high unemployment in the major European Community countries. The fact is that unemployment was a good deal higher than in many of the smaller countries and than in Japan and the United States. Moreover, labour

Table 10.6 Population, active population and employment in the Europe 12, 1970–90

	Percentage change per annum					
	1970/ 1960	1980/ 1970	1990/ 1980	1984/ 1980	1988/ 1984	1990/ 1988
Population	0.8	0.5	0.3	0.3	0.3	0.3
Active population	0.2	0.6	0.8	0.8	0.8	0.6
Employment	0.2	0.2	0.3	−0.6	0.9	1.2
	1960	1970	1980	1984	1988	1990
Unemployment	2.0	2.5	6.4	10.81	0.0	8.7

Source: Commission of the European Communities, *European Economy* 42, 1989, 120.

force growth was even more rapid in the latter countries, though only in the case of the smaller countries did it accelerate compared with the 1960s (OECD 1991).

Essentially, then, what we have to explain is why the larger European countries had an inferior employment record than the other countries. In seeking clarification of the differences, frequent recourse has been made to supply-side considerations. In broad terms, the main contention here is that European labour markets, for one reason or another, worked less efficiently than those elsewhere. This could be because of stronger real wage resistance, structural rigidities in labour markets, and the effect of hysteresis (lagged response to past events). The consequence would be to raise the non-accelerating inflation rate of unemployment (NAIRU), which would make it difficult to reduce unemployment without aggravating inflation.

There is some substance in all these points. Wages were less responsive to changes in unemployment, productivity and to a lesser extent prices in several of the major European countries than they were in the United States and Japan. Within Europe, Germany, Austria and Switzerland had a more flexible wage pattern than most other countries (Coe 1985, 117–19; OECD 1987, 132–34). This is consistent with their better unemployment record. The corollary would be that in other countries labour was too expensive, with wages rising faster than productivity and leading to a real wage gap, which dampened labour recruitment. This gap certainly appeared in the major countries during the 1970s and early 1980s, but thereafter it was eliminated as real wages moderated and profits were allowed to recover. This seems to imply that excessive real wages were not a potent force in constraining employment growth after the early 1980s. However, NAIRU estimates remained high for much of the decade, which indicates that factors other than real wage rigidity may have been a hindrance to employment creation. Incidentally, the fact that the NAIRU rates tended to be lower than actual rates of unemployment by the mid-1980s suggests that there may have been some leeway for modest fiscal expansion.

Structural factors can partly explain the increasing rigidities of European labour markets, which reduced their flexibility and efficiency in allocating labour among competing uses. These include impediments that reduce labour mobility among firms, industries, regions and occupations and into and out of unemployment, thereby resulting in a rise of the unemployment/vacancies ratio (the Beveridge curve). This in turn accounts for regional differences in unemployment and the disproportionate incidence of unemployment among different groups of workers.

The increasing rigidity of European labour markets was a consequence of two main factors: administrative regulations and the pattern of collective bargaining and wage determination. During the later 1960s and 1970s, various legislative enactments served to impede the microeconomic functioning of labour markets. These included minimum wage legislation, employment protection laws and generous benefit systems, some of which were only partly liberalized in the following decade. Second, restrictive work practices and inefficient methods of labour utilization were perpetuated by unsatisfactory bargaining systems, which hindered both the internal and the external mobility of labour and reinforced the protective employment regulations.

It is significant that labour market outcomes were consistently poorer in countries such as the UK, France, Belgium and Italy, where collective bargaining systems were neither subject to the direct constraints of decentralized bargaining at the enterprise level and competitive labour markets as in the United States and Japan, nor influenced by a recognition of national responsibility as occurred under the more coordinated and centralized negotiating procedures in the Nordic countries, Austria and Germany. Instead, 'the setting of wages and of the conditions of employment have typically functioned through a multiplicity of overlapping and competing levels, fragmenting employer solidarity and encouraging inflationary spirals of bargaining around long established pay relativities; and where the legal framework for bargaining has been poorly spelt out in terms of the rights and duties of the parties to collective agreements' (OECD 1987, 41).

Such fragmented systems of bargaining reduced the flexibility of labour markets both in terms of the allocative force of the price mechanism, for example through a narrowing of pay differentials between regions, occupations, skilled and unskilled workers, and through restrictive covenants that limited choice and protected 'insiders' (those in employment). They may also have affected the level of skill formation in so far as pay relativities favoured the unskilled and untrained, notably in Britain. Effectively what happened is that labour markets became more segmented principally between the 'insiders', that is, those with jobs who benefitted through higher wages and greater job security by virtue of restrictions on competition in the labour market, and the 'outsiders', or those unemployed who were excluded from effective participation in the labour market and who ultimately bore the cost of the system.

This combination of forces set the pattern whereby unemployment could feed upon itself through a process known as hysteresis. What might start out as a short-term demand problem transformed itself into a long-term supply phenomenon as the unemployed increasingly became a ghetto group marginalized out of the labour market through demoralization, loss of skill, age disability and lack of training. They therefore ceased to be an effective competitive force in the labour market and hence their influence on wage determination was reduced. This in turn reinforced rigidities and restrictive practices by 'insiders', who sought to safeguard the position of the majority even at the expense of more unemployment through early retirement, part-time working, reduced recruitment of young workers and the like. In this way, high unemployment could create the conditions for its own perpetuation (Lawrence and Schultz 1987, 45).

In their detailed cross-section study of unemployment patterns in nineteen OECD countries over three decades, Layard *et al*. (1991) argued that, while in the short term demand is a powerful determinant of unemployment, in the long run it is the supply side that dominates. Their supply-oriented model takes as a starting point the recent supply-side shocks to the system and then traces the relationships between prices, wages and unemployment within the framework of different institutional settings. Once equilibrium is disturbed and unemployment rises, it is difficult to return to the *status quo* because of inflexible labour markets and institutional constraints. These imperfections distort the efficient working of the labour market and thereby prevent unemployment, or the level of employment, being determined by optimal allocation processes. The most important impediments to efficient labour markets were found to be the system of wage determination and unemployment benefit provisions, both of which served to stiffen real wage resistance and restrictive practices in times of difficulty, with adverse effects on employment.

Variations in levels of unemployment among countries can therefore be attributed, in part at least, to differences in bargaining structures and institutional settings. Economies adapt better to external shocks when benefit systems discourage long-term unemployment (short-duration benefits) and when union densities are low, labour markets are competitive and there is a high degree of enterprise bargaining, as in the United States, Canada, Switzerland and Japan. Conversely, highly unionized labour markets may also perform satisfactorily provided that bargaining is coordinated and centralized (a relatively small number of agreements with broad coverage) and unemployment compensation schemes are restricted, and preferably where there are active labour market policies. The Scandinavian countries, Germany and Austria fall into this category. The worst scenario is one in which bargaining procedures are loosely coordinated, fragmented and decentralized, and benefit systems are generous. This generates conditions that encourage voluntary unemployment, structural rigidities in labour markets and mismatch unemployment. Several European countries fell into this category, including Britain, France, Italy, Spain and to a lesser extent the Netherlands.

There would therefore appear to be a sufficiently strong association between labour market characteristics and levels of unemployment (see Table 10.5) to suggest that supply-side factors were important in determining variations in unemployment across countries. In the major European countries, labour markets tended to function less efficiently than elsewhere. Haberler, quoting Marris (Haberler 1986, 67–68), stresses the basic structural impediments in European labour markets that rendered them less flexible than the American labour market and hence weaker employment generators. Europe as a whole therefore experienced higher unemployment, while at the same time the scope for effective macroeconomic policy action to deal with the problem was more limited.

Structural rigidities, innovation and competitiveness

It may be, as some writers have suggested, that the slowdown in Europe's growth since the mid-1970s was not a sign of deep-rooted economic problems but simply an inevitable return to more sustainable rates of growth following the exhaustion or partial exhaustion of many of the favourable factors that had powered the post-war boom. Some of these had clearly passed their peak, for example the effects of catch-up, the gains from trade liberalization and labour force reallocation, the diffusion of new technologies and favourable terms of trade. In this case, therefore, one would have expected some slowing down of growth at some stage irrespective of the influence of random shocks and government policies. Nevertheless, one should also bear in mind that the supply shocks severely undermined the energy-intensive basis of post-war growth, while the slowness and ineptitude with which governments adjusted to the supply shocks served to aggravate the deceleration in economic activity.

Notwithstanding these events, however, there were also some worrying signs that European countries were losing their former dynamism and experiencing perhaps a touch of sclerosis that comes with old age. The signs may be seen in increasing structural rigidities and the response to new technology.

The structural issue has been well aired in recent years. The OECD published a weighty tome on this subject in 1987, *Structural Adjustment and Economic Performance*, arguing that a return to sustainable growth in the longer term was dependent on a broad range of reforms of its microeconomic foundations in order to rejuvenate the efficiency with which economic systems worked. They claimed that 'experience has shown time and again that expansions cannot be maintained, and the cost of ensuing recessions is greatest, when the structural components of economies are functioning poorly' (1987, 49). The report dwelt upon virtually every conceivable supply-side aspect of economics, including education and skill formation, research, labour markets and industrial relations, financial markets, agriculture, industrial adjustment, trade, social policies and the public sector.

What was perhaps most remarkable was the extent of the problem: 'the range of areas in which policy reform is needed is so great' (OECD 1987, 49). Some obvious candidates, of course, were agriculture, labour markets, social policies and industrial adjustment policies, in which structural reform or the removal of inefficient subsidies and disincentives were urgently required. In other cases, for example education and training, the need was more for a reform of the structure and pattern of skill formation to cater for the requirements of new transferable skill technologies. Increasing the forces of competition both in trade and production was also deemed to be important, and here it should be noted that the European Community does not always live up to its declared intentions. If anything, it may be a source of structural rigidities and regulatory impediments in its own right.

Throughout the 1980s, governments tended to favour greater liberalization in markets and a certain degree of structural reform. This was reflected in measures taken to liberalize financial and transport markets, labour market reforms, modifications to minimum wage legislation, the tightening up of transfer payments and the privatization of state enterprises. The extent of the reforms varied from country to country, but in few cases did they make a really significant contribution to the more efficient working of markets. Governments also attempted to stabilize their budgetary finances and reduce the size of the public sector component, though with limited and mixed results (see above). This was in accord with the growing conviction, widespread among economists and policy-makers, that government spending, taxes, deficits and debt might be harmful to economic growth. Unfortunately, there was little agreement as to the nature, size and scope of the relationships.

Nevertheless, there was probably some justification for the growing concern about the size of the public sector. It had grown inexorably over the past three decades, so that by the mid-1980s, government outlays averaged some 50 per cent of GDP as against 32 per cent in 1960, creating problems of financing, eroding incentives, distorting choice and reducing resource efficiency. Moreover, because a large part of budgetary revenue (up to 40 per cent or more) consisted of revenue 'churning', that is, revenue returned to the original taxpayers mainly through transfers and subsidies, the cynically minded could justifiably feel that its main function was to keep an army of bureaucrats in jobs! That apart, there was reason to believe that the costs of financing programmes at the margin could be steep at high levels of expenditure and taxation, 'so that the costs of increasing the size of the public sector, as well as the gains from reducing it, are significantly larger than the average economic cost of public sector spending' (OECD 1987, 47).

Unfortunately, with public sector spending, as with structural issues, it is easy to point to anomalies, distortions, disincentives and impediments, but difficult to quantify their significance. Moreover, many of the relevant matters give rise to strong emotional, ideological or sectional feelings, which make analytical logic difficult to swallow. But as more recent events have clearly demonstrated, sooner or later most countries have to face up to some difficult decisions on these issues, especially with respect to the size, structure and financing of the public sector (see above and Chapter 13).

The other area that could be the cause for some concern is Europe's competitive position within the high technology field. There is some evidence, admittedly scrappy, that in the 1970s and 1980s, technical progress and innovation slowed down, more especially in the older energy-intensive sectors affected adversely by the oil shocks. This is consistent with the decline in effectiveness of research and development spending in such sectors, especially in terms of productivity growth, although aggregate research and development expenditure as a share of output held up well. This may therefore simply represent a hiatus as economies transform from one technological scenario to another, for example from energy-intensive sectors to information technology and electronic systems. However, rather more disturbing is the possibility that some of the major European countries may have

Table 10.7 Comparative changes in world export shares of technology-intensive products[a]

	1965	1975	1984
United States	27.5	24.5	25.2
Japan	7.3	11.6	20.2
France	7.3	8.4	7.7
Germany	16.9	16.8	14.5
UK	12.0	9.6	8.5
Italy			3.6

Source: F. Duchene and G. Shepherd (eds), *Managing Industrial Change in Western Europe*, London: Pinter, 1987, 36.

Note: [a]Technology-intensive products are defined as those for which research and development expenditures exceed 2.36 per cent of value added.

been losing ground in the high technology race. Data in Table 10.7 on comparative export shares in technology-intensive products do suggest that Europe may have been losing out to more dynamic Far Eastern competitors. This point can be amplified by reference to world trade in electronic products, in which Japan and the four 'little tigers' (Hong Kong, Taiwan, Singapore and South Korea) were coming to dominate the scene, with large positive trade balances as against growing deficits in European Community countries. This was a worrying trend because high technology skill-intensive fields of endeavour were one of the few comparative advantages left to high-income countries in world markets.

According to the OECD (1987, 214), European countries tended to lose out in international specialization because they increased their competitive advantage in sectors of activity with a low intensity of research and development, while losing ground in medium and high research and development sectors, especially the latter, in which their position worsened rapidly after the 1970s. This could be attributed mainly to 'slower and less judicious technological adjustment' than in other competitor countries, with the result that Europe's share of world trade in manufactures declined after the mid-1970s, while the shares of the United States and Japan remained fairly constant and non-OECD members increased their shares. Technological progress in Europe was impeded by structural rigidities and impediments in product and factor markets. These covered a wide area, including fragmentation of markets, insufficient competition (especially in sectors regulated by governments), slow adaptation of the industrial fabric and its related infrastructure, bottlenecks in skill formation, imperfections in capital markets, price and tax distortions inhibiting efficient resource allocation and technological diffusion, and severe labour market rigidities. The last of these was seen as one of the major impediments to progress on which the OECD (1987, 258) dilated at some length in forceful terms:

By reducing job mobility, labour market rigidities inhibit technological development and dissemination. By retarding organisational innovation, they slow down the process of application of new technologies, and by distorting relative factor price movements, they set the process in the wrong direction by placing excessive emphasis on the defensive strategies for controlling costs through capital/labour substitution. In doing so, they are likely to prevent a virtuous circle of technical progress, qualitatively balanced growth of investment, enhancing of the stock of human capital and net creation of jobs, from forming or operating fully. They may even help to create a vicious circle in which technological backwardness, investment centred on rationalization, depreciation of the stock of human capital, and a net decrease in job opportunities, reinforce one another.

Lasting stability?

By the end of the decade, official organizations were expressing guarded optimism about the future of the western economic system, the implication being that it had achieved a measure of stability whence sound growth could proceed. However, the equilibrium may have been more apparent than real, possibly no more robust than that perceived to obtain in the late 1920s. It is true that steady progress had been made during the 1980s in controlling inflation, stabilizing exchange rates and, to a lesser extent, consolidating budgetary accounts. There was also a greater degree of convergence in economic matters among European economies. However, it is far from clear that all the problems had been solved, and economies were by no means immune to the impact of disturbances. In other words, there was little ground for supposing that European nations were in a strong enough position to return to the high growth and full employment of the post-war years.

It may be unrealistic anyway to anticipate a resumption of a past performance because the long boom of 1948–73 can be regarded as something of an aberration. The high growth rates of that period were far out of line with long-term trend values and it is difficult to conceive of a repetition of so many favourable factors converging in time and space again. Again, low unemployment is not a pervasive phenomenon through time, nor is the absence of depressions. Historical record suggests that neither is the natural order of things.

Alternatively, it can be argued that sustained high growth and low unemployment could not be recaptured until full adjustment had been made to the supply shocks of the past. This is true in so far as the problems arising from those shocks such as inflation, wage determination, structural rigidities and budgetary problems had not been completely solved by the turn of the decade. On the surface, progress in the latter half of the 1980s looked solid enough, yet there are grounds for suspecting that all was not well underneath. It is significant, for example, that inflationary pressures soon began to reassert themselves once activity picked up, while labour market rigidities and other structural problems continued to prevail, which partly accounts for the stickiness of unemployment. Budgetary problems, too, were far from over. Consolidation was at best partial, and given the inflexibility of expenditures and the longer-term commitments envisaged, it was becoming clear that they could become more serious in the future. This fact alone acted as a serious constraint on the use of the fiscal weapon as a means of raising growth and employment. In any case, there were increasing doubts as to whether fiscal policies of the type traditionally used by governments would secure a permanent and viable increase in the level of employment, given the structural rigidities and weak real growth forces then prevalent in most western economies. Indeed, it was believed that such policies might exacerbate existing problems while doing little to restore the competitive strength of the economies in question. Modern economic management was, in short, becoming ever more complex and past conventional wisdom with regard to policymaking was fast losing its credibility.

Another possibility is that western Europe was becoming more sclerotic and therefore less adaptable to changing economic circumstances. As noted earlier, there is certainly some evidence of increasing structural rigidity and loss of technological dynamism, which weakened Europe's international competitiveness. In their *Annual Economic Report for 1988–89* the Commission of the European Communities recognized the need for more flexibility:

> The potential for non-inflationary growth can be strengthened by making European economies even more adaptable. Greater flexibility of markets and their positive effect on the behaviour and initiative of entrepreneurs is in itself a source of progress.

Yet ironically, the European Community itself may well have contributed to the problem in so far as its plethora of regulations and directives on the activities of economic agents circumscribed their freedom of operation and reduced the scope for greater flexibility and adaptation to change. The possible adverse impact of the European Community's, and subsequently the European Union's, activities has yet to be explored in depth.

Finally, it is important to recall that western Europe was becoming more dependent and at the same time more constrained by what happened in a number of key economies, namely those of the United States, Germany and Japan. The 'follow my leader' principle was readily apparent with respect to the shadowing of movements in key exchange rates and the reaction to US deficits. These countries, it seemed, would continue to set the standard in the future.

The inauspicious note on which the early 1990s opened partly overshadowed these more deep-seated underlying problems. The elements were similar, though not so strong, as those at the beginning of the previous decade: one or two disturbances, for example the collapse of the socialist regimes of eastern Europe and the prospect of German reunification, along with the Iraq–Kuwait conflict, increasing inflation, the drift into recession, plus a cautionary policy stance for good measure. One could perhaps be forgiven a feeling of *déjà vu*.

Questions for discussion

1   How did governments tackle inflation in the 1980s?
2   Why was unemployment so high and persistent in the 1980s and early 1990s?
3   Why did budgetary deficits become a problem from the mid-1970s?
4   To what extent did Europe suffer from structural rigidity in the 1980s?
5   Explain the forces making for recovery in the 1980s.

11 Eastern Europe in transition, 1970–90

If the period 1970–90 was a chequered one for western Europe, its problems paled into insignificance compared with the parallel traumas experienced by eastern Europe. Even the most pessimistic forecasters would have been hard pressed to predict the course of events. In the early 1970s, there seemed every indication that the impressive growth rates of the 1960s would continue. The Soviet Union began the period confidently, expecting to sustain communist rule both within and outwith its borders. Yet by its end, communism had withered and died in East Germany, Poland, Czechoslovakia, Bulgaria and Hungary, while it was also out of favour in countries that had pursued an independent line from Moscow (Romania and Yugoslavia). In Europe, outside the Soviet Union, communism held on by the skin of its teeth only in Albania. Moreover, the very survival of communism as the governing system of the Soviet Union was being seriously questioned, with several republics demanding their independence.

Although the 1989 revolutions in eastern Europe matched the French revolution of two centuries earlier for drama, it would be a mistake simply to review immediate causes. Rather, their spring roots also demand consideration, not least the failure of socialist economies to provide tolerable living standards for the mass of the population. The question also needs to be asked: why did the Soviet Union, which entered the 1970s as a recognized superpower, lose its grip? Then, too, there is the failure of the Soviet economy to respond to *perestroika*. Elsewhere, efforts to introduce economic and social reforms to uphold existing socialist systems proved equally unsuccessful.

Borrowing for growth

At the start, the 1970s were mapped out to continue reforms dating from the mid to late 1960s. Outside the Soviet Union, their extent was limited by the so-called Brezhnev doctrine. Too radical reform on western lines, which was contrary to Moscow's political, strategic and economic interests, could activate Soviet military intervention and occupation as it did in Czechoslovakia in 1968, when the 'Prague Spring' was snuffed out. The intention was thus to make existing centrally planned systems more efficient as a means of sustaining growth. Common threads linking the various Five-Year Plans that unfolded in 1970 included the need to delegate greater power to factory managers, the need to increase incentives for them and their workforces, and a greater freedom for enterprises to trade in foreign markets without undue state interference.

Another common ingredient was the desire to raise living standards. The East German Five-Year Plan, for instance, had as its 'primary task' the improvement of the 'material and cultural living standard' of the population. There was an acute housing shortage which needed to be tackled; 500,000 new apartment units were planned by 1975. That year, Romania's dictator Nicolae Ceausescu claimed, spuriously, that his reforms were 'creating a new type of life that guarantees its people well-being and happiness' (see below). In some countries, the emphasis on socialist consumerism was more evident than elsewhere. This reflected the varying stages of economic development and the amount of exposure to higher living standards in western Europe, as in East Germany, Yugoslavia, Hungary and Czechoslovakia. During the 1970s, many East Europeans acquired their first televisions, washing machines, fridges and, to a lesser extent, cars. Foreign holidays became the norm in several countries. By the middle of the decade, thirty-four times as many Hungarians were going abroad compared with 1960. Such was the demand for high-quality consumer goods in Yugoslavia that regular shopping trips were made to proximate western countries.

The emphasis on better living standards was not surprising. Success in this crucial area held out the prospect of political stability and improved labour productivity, a necessary condition for further growth as the working population fell in size and the number of peasants shrank, draining the reservoir of land workers that industry had previously drawn on. In the Soviet Union, for example, by 1971, the proportion of the population engaged in agriculture had declined to 26 per cent and by 1980, it stood at 14 per cent. This compared with a western average of 6 per cent. In less developed Bulgaria and Romania, the contraction was less pronounced.

Migration to the towns provided a means of upward mobility to former peasants. But by the 1970s, with the mass exodus nearing completion, the new urban dwellers expected to improve their quality of life. This, in turn, brought pressure on city jobs and accommodation. At the end of 1970, former Polish land workers provoked riots in Gdansk. The immediate cause was an increase in food prices (soon reversed), but there was also frustration at the lack of consumer goods. Such scarcity was endemic throughout the eastern bloc but again variations were evident; Romanians, for instance, were very much in the Polish boat whereas Hungarians had less cause for grievance.

The start of the 1970s saw the thawing of the Cold War through *détente*, opening up the prospect of more intimate east–west economic ties. Relations between the two Germanies improved, with their volume of trade more than doubling between 1974 and 1985, when it reached DM 16.5 billion a year. Over the period, although intra-German trade still remained only a tiny percentage of West Germany's total foreign transactions, for East Germany, its neighbour had assumed the status of most important trading partner after the Soviet Union. The basis of the economic relationship was West Germany's provision of large quantities of semi-finished goods and production materials, with East Germany supplying consumer goods, such as clothing, porcelain and electric motors. West Germany, with an eye to possible future reunification, gave generous loans and credits and had normal European Community tariffs waived.

It was generally recognized in eastern Europe that a high-tech phase of growth had dawned, for which it was ill prepared. Large quantities of western technology were deemed essential to bridge the gap with the west. Hungary, Yugoslavia, Poland and Romania, in particular, embraced a strategy of import-led growth, which found its most comprehensive form in Poland. The idea was to use western machinery and equipment to develop more sophisticated and competitive home industries. These would then export high-quality goods to the west, correcting the temporary imbalance between exports and imports and providing hard currency to repay western credits. That, at least, was the theory, though in practice things were to turn out differently (see below).

One impact of this policy was to reduce the volume of intra-CMEA trade as the more efficient sectors of each member economy diverted their best products to the west. The CMEA nonetheless continued to play an important role within the eastern bloc, as Table 11.1 indicates. In 1971, the 'Complex Programme' was agreed, which called for greater regional integration and introduced joint investment projects, almost all of them in the Soviet Union. Many of these concerned raw materials, such as oil and iron ore, for which the contribution of other CMEA members towards extraction costs was to increase. By 1976, these investments in the Soviet Union involved 1.4 billion roubles.

With the exception of Romania, the CMEA was almost totally dependent on the Soviet Union for supplies of oil, natural gas and other raw materials. Fortunately, in return for machinery and equipment, the Soviet Union adopted a special CMEA pricing formula, with charges much below world market prices. At the height of *détente*, in the mid-1970s (see Table 11.2) the Soviet Union continued to provide the CMEA with greater amounts of machines and equipment together with fuel and raw materials than the west did. The Soviet Union also imported more machines and equipment and consumer goods from CMEA sources, notwithstanding their inferior quality *vis-à-vis* western producers. Though not a member of the CMEA, Yugoslavia was compelled by European Community tariffs to redirect

Table 11.1 Inter-CMEA trade as a percentage of total
        trade, 1971–75

Bulgaria	70
Czechoslovakia	64
Poland	50
East Germany	65
Romania	39
Hungary	65
Soviet Union	46

Source: G. Graziani, 'Dependency structures in COMECON', *Review of Radical Political Economy* 13, 1981, 71.

Table 11.2 Composition of Soviet foreign trade in 1976 (per cent)

	Global	CMEA
Total exports	100.0	100.0
Machines and equipment	18.7	22.5
Fuels and other basic products	57.8	61.6
Consumer goods	3.1	2.8
Foodstuffs and others	20.4	13.1
Total imports	100.0	100.0
Machines and equipment	33.9	45.4
Fuels and other basic products	24.8	14.7
Consumer goods	13.0	19.1
Foodstuffs and others	28.3	20.8

Source: Graziani, 'Dependency structures in COMECON', *Review of Radical Political Economy* 13, 1981, 71.

much of its exports to the organization, the proportion rising from 32.3 to 41.9 per cent over 1973–78. But it remained dangerously dependent on western Europe for industrial goods, thereby creating balance-of-payments difficulties.

As Table 11.3 demonstrates, until the mid-1970s, most CMEA countries had at least respectable industrial growth rates as measured in net material product. Indeed, several exceeded plan targets. Poland's and Romania's spectacularly rising figures reflected their greater reliance on large doses of western credit, while the less addicted Bulgarian, Czech, East German and Hungarian economies returned more even results. The Soviet Union's performance was sluggish, highlighting inefficiency and the fact that, for political reasons, it preferred to give priority to CMEA trade even though it could have obtained better prices from the west for its raw materials.

Impact of the oil shocks

The effect of OPEC's oil price hike of 1973 was not as great on eastern Europe as on the west. Where the European Community needed to import almost 60 per cent of its energy requirements from third countries by 1975, the CMEA was autarkic in energy provision. Indeed, that year, the organization could afford the luxury of a net export of 100 million tons Standard Coal Equivalent (SCE): about one-third of West German consumption. Its relatively favourable position enabled eastern Europe to continue the movement from coal to oil burning without much hesitation. Yugoslavia was an exception. More exposed to the first oil shock, belatedly it began to develop indigenous coal and hydroelectric resources, though to little effect.

As net exporters of energy, the Soviet Union, Romania and Poland benefited, to differing degrees, from the global explosion in world energy prices. The Soviet Union, the world's largest producer and exporter of oil, did best. It registered an improvement in its overall net barter terms of trade, which averaged more than 30 per cent a year over 1971–85. The ratio of import to export volumes improved

Table 11.3 Net material product in eastern Europe (annual percentage change)

	1970	1971	1972	1973	1974	1975	1976	1977	1978	1979	1980	1981	1982	1983	1984	1985	1986	1987	1988	1989	1990
Bulgaria	7.1	6.9	7.7	8.1	7.6	8.8	6.5	6.3	5.6	6.6	5.7	5.0	4.2	3.0	4.6	1.8	5.3	5.0	2.4	-0.4	-13.6
Czechoslovakia	5.7	5.5	5.7	5.2	5.9	6.2	4.1	4.2	4.1	3.1	2.9	-0.1	0.2	2.3	3.5	3.0	2.6	2.1	2.4	1.3	-3.1
German Democratic Republic	5.6	4.4	5.7	5.6	6.5	4.9	3.5	5.1	3.7	4.0	4.4	4.8	2.6	4.6	5.5	5.2	4.3	3.3	2.8	2.1	-19.5
Hungary	4.9	5.9	6.2	7.0	5.9	6.1	3.0	7.1	4.0	1.2	-0.9	2.5	2.6	0.3	2.5	-1.4	0.9	4.1	-0.5	-1.1	-5.5
Poland	5.2	8.1	10.6	10.8	10.5	9.0	6.8	5.0	3.0	-2.3	-6.0	-12.0	-5.5	6.0	5.6	3.4	4.9	1.9	4.9	-0.2	-13.0
Romania	6.8	13.5	9.8	10.7	12.3	9.8	11.3	8.7	7.2	6.5	4.2	-0.4	4.0	6.0	6.5	-1.1	3.0	0.7	-2.0	-7.9	-10.5
Eastern Europe	5.7	7.3	8.0	8.3	8.6	7.6	6.1	5.8	4.2	2.0	0.3	-2.3	0.3	4.3	5.1	2.7	3.7	3.2	3.1	0.5	-12.0
Soviet Union	9.0	5.6	3.9	8.9	5.5	4.4	5.9	4.5	5.1	2.2	3.9	3.3	3.9	4.2	2.9	1.6	2.3	1.6	4.4	2.4	-4.0
Eastern Europe and the Soviet Union	8.0	6.1	5.1	8.7	6.5	5.4	5.9	4.9	4.9	2.1	2.7	1.7	2.8	4.1	3.6	2.2	3.0	2.1	4.0	1.8	-6.3

Source: United Nations, *Economic Survey of Europe in 1990–1991*, 1991, Appendix.

in equal measure without incurring trade deficits. Romania expanded its oil-refining capacity and failed to curb energy-guzzling industries, but with its oil reserves nearing exhaustion, this was a misguided policy. By 1980, oil production was reduced to only 250,000 barrels per day compared with a daily refining capacity of 700,000 barrels. The difference had to be imported, exposing the economy to price rises in crude oil and oil products (see below). Coal being its principal export, Poland profited from the increased demand for this alternative energy source.

In 1975, the Soviet Union, taking advantage of its improved bargaining position, embarked on a policy of narrowing the gap between Soviet and world oil prices. Immediately, Soviet CMEA prices increased by 30 per cent. An important change in the new CMEA Five-Year Plan (1976–80) was to allow for annual price changes rather than, as before, for them to be held for the duration. The effect was to reduce the time lag for price rises to make themselves felt. CMEA members therefore faced extra costs, a situation that worsened after the second oil price shock of 1979. Some were more affected than others. Romania, which became a net oil importer that same year, paid the highest price. Having lost favourable contracts with Iran after the Shah's fall, Romania was exposed through its hostility towards the Soviet Union. In 1980, the latter would only supply 1.4 million tons of crude oil, for which it charged world market prices. One estimate suggests that the cost of Romania's denial of substantial quantities of Soviet oil at normal CMEA prices was at least $1 billion (Drewnowki 1982, 117). East Germany, too, was hard hit, with the price of its imported Soviet oil rising by 17.6 per cent in 1979. Perhaps worst affected was Yugoslavia, which bore the full brunt of the rise in world oil prices. The dictates of energy conservation prompted not only petrol rationing but also passing on the full cost to the consumer, fuelling inflation, which rose from around 20 per cent in mid-1979 to 45 per cent two years later.

The position of the Soviet Union was not as favourable as it appeared. After three decades of uninterrupted growth, energy production slowed in the 1970s. Oil output peaked at 600 million tons in 1980. With the drying up of older wells, extraction and distribution costs escalated as new wells were sunk in western Siberia. To some extent, there was compensation from the exploitation of the world's largest gas field in the same location. In 1981, a $15 billion agreement was concluded with a West German–East European consortium to bring cheap gas to western Europe by pipeline. Siberia was also being exploited for its coal deposits. But it was far from being an ideal site. Siberia's remoteness demanded the construction of major feeder railways and special high-voltage power lines. The extreme climate (causing permafrost) required the use of specialist machinery, much of which was obtainable only from western sources. Reflecting these difficulties, marginal oil extraction costs increased tenfold over 1974–82. Several key industries, such as petrochemicals, located themselves in the region to compensate, only to find that the difficulty of recruiting and retaining labour compelled them to pay wages as much as 75 per cent above the Soviet norm.

The combination of relatively cheap Soviet raw materials and increased western credits deflected their recipients from addressing underlying economic problems, thereby exacerbating them. Insulated from the impact of the first oil shock, east European states, not least Poland and Romania, continued their import-led growth policies. Only with the second oil shock did it finally become apparent that this approach could not succeed. The resulting recession in western Europe reduced demand for imports from eastern Europe and by raising interest rates worsened the latter's mounting debt.

But even without the second oil shock, it is doubtful whether the import-led growth strategy could have succeeded. For example, western bankers calculated that even if Poland had achieved its annual growth rate targets of 3–4 per cent, not until the mid-1990s could its external debt have been reduced to a manageable size. In the event, eastern Europe simply lacked the trained personnel and economic infrastructure to absorb western technology properly and thereby produce competitive products. A great amount of western loans was misspent and wasted. Most east European governments elected to invest in energy-intensive sectors. Consumption of energy per unit of GNP within CMEA was around twice that in the west. Worse still, while under the impact of the first oil shock western Europe reduced its unit of consumption, in eastern Europe this continued to rise. The latter was about to be brought to account for its erroneous ways.

Slowdown and the need for reform

The ill-considered Soviet invasion of Afghanistan in December 1979 ended the cosy climate engendered by *détente*. By the early 1980s, western economists were pinpointing eastern Europe's mountain of debts as a major problem. It was feared that the east would be unable to repay its debt, or even to service it. Socialist governments stood accused of wasting the money. Western banks were also in the dock, their crime being to lend huge sums to totalitarian regimes that were deemed incapable of sound economic management. In perspective, however, the total east European debt was dwarfed compared with Latin America's colossal bill, which was twelve times as great.

Nevertheless, the debt problem was serious, and in the 1980s, to a greater or lesser degree, east European countries were to be afflicted by what became known as 'the Polish disease'. Briefly, this may be defined as an inability to bridge the technological gap with the west through imports. The result was a worsening balance-of-payments situation, with exports failing dismally to match imports. The scale of the accumulated foreign debt then acted as a decelerator and a drag on future growth. As Table 11.4 indicates, imports then had to be cut back in order to improve the balance-of-payments position. Over the period 1979–89, almost every east European country registered at least one year of negative growth (see Table 11.3). East Germany bucked the trend but 'only with a harsh austerity programme and significant economic assistance from West Germany' (Dawisha 1990, 170). So did the Soviet Union, but its industrial growth was considerably below target (see below).

By 1980–81, Poland was in crisis. An illegal trade union, Solidarity, sprang up, initially to protect living standards, though ultimately it assumed political

Table 11.4 Eastern Europe and the Soviet Union: balance of payments in convertible currencies (billion US dollars)

	1970	1971	1972	1973	1974	1975	1976	1977	1978	1979	1980	1981	1982	1983	1984	1985	1986	1987	1988	1989	1990
Bulgaria																					
Merchandise export	-0.5	0.5	0.5	0.7	0.9	1.0	1.1	1.2	-1.5	2.4	-3.3	3.4	-3.1	2.7	3.3	3.3	2.7	3.3	3.5	3.1	2.5
Merchandise import	0.5	0.5	-0.6	0.8	1.1	1.8	1.5	1.5	1.5	1.8	2.5	3.1	2.6	-2.7	-3.0	3.7	3.5	4.2	4.5	4.3	3.3
Balance	–	–	–	-0.1	-0.2	-0.8	-0.4	-0.3	0.1	0.5	0.8	-0.3	0.5	0.1	0.3	-0.4	-0.8	-1.0	-1.0	-1.2	-0.8
Invisibles	–	-0.1	–	-0.1	–	-0.1	–	0.1	–	-0.1	0.1	0.3	0.3	0.2	0.4	0.3	0.1	0.2	0.1	-0.1	-0.3
Current account	–	–	–	-0.1	-0.2	-0.9	-0.4	-0.3	0.1	0.6	0.9	0.6	0.8	0.3	0.7	-0.1	-0.7	-0.8	-0.8	-1.3	-1.1
Czechoslovakia																					
Merchandise export	0.8	1.0	1.2	-1.6	2.2	2.1	2.1	2.5	2.9	3.5	4.4	4.2	-4.1	-4.0	4.0	3.9	4.3	4.5	5.0	5.4	5.9
Merchandise import	0.9	1.0	-1.2	1.7	2.4	2.5	2.8	3.1	3.3	4.1	4.4	3.9	3.4	3.2	3.1	3.2	4.1	4.7	5.1	5.0	6.1
Balance	-0.1	-0.1	–	-0.2	-0.2	-0.4	-0.7	-0.6	-0.4	-0.5	–	-0.3	0.7	0.8	-0.9	-0.7	-0.2	-0.1	-0.1	0.4	-0.2
Invisibles	0.1	0.1	0.1	0.2	0.1	0.1	0.2	–	–	–	-0.3	-0.3	-0.1	0.1	0.2	0.1	0.2	0.2	0.2	-0.1	–
Current account	–	–	0.1	–	-0.1	-0.3	-0.6	-0.6	-0.4	-0.6	-0.3	–	0.4	0.9	1.1	0.7	0.4	0.1	0.1	0.3	-0.2
German Democratic Republic																					
Merchandise export	1.3	1.4	1.6	2.2	3.0	2.9	3.5	3.4	3.7	4.3	5.7	7.1	8.3	9.0	-9.1	10.6	-9.0	8.8	8.9	9.6	—
Merchandise import	1.5	1.6	2.1	2.9	4.0	4.0	5.1	4.8	4.7	6.1	7.4	7.1	6.8	7.7	8.1	7.9	8.2	9.1	9.9	10.5	—
Balance	-0.3	-0.2	-0.4	-0.7	-1.0	-1.0	-1.5	-1.4	-1.0	-1.8	-1.7	–	-1.5	1.3	1.0	2.7	0.8	-0.4	-1.1	-0.9	—
Invisibles	0.2	0.2	0.2	0.3	0.1	0.2	0.3	0.3	0.3	0.5	0.1	-0.4	-0.3	-0.1	–	–	0.3	0.6	0.5	0.2	—
Current account	-0.1	–	-0.2	-0.5	-0.9	-0.8	-1.3	-1.1	-0.7	-1.3	-1.6	-0.4	1.1	1.2	0.9	2.8	1.1	0.2	-0.6	-0.8	—
Hungary																					
Merchandise export	0.6	0.6	0.9	1.5	2.1	2.2	2.3	2.7	3.2	4.1	4.9	4.9	4.8	4.8	4.9	4.2	4.2	5.0	5.5	6.4	6.3
Merchandise import	0.7	0.8	0.9	1.4	2.5	2.5	2.5	3.0	4.0	4.2	4.6	4.4	4.2	4.1	4.0	4.1	4.7	5.0	5.0	5.9	6.0
Balance	-0.1	-0.2	-0.1	0.1	-0.4	-0.3	-0.2	-0.4	-0.8	-0.2	0.3	0.4	0.7	0.8	0.9	0.1	-0.5	–	0.5	0.5	0.3
Invisibles	–	–	–	-0.1	-0.1	-0.2	-0.2	-0.4	-0.5	-0.7	-0.6	-1.2	-1.0	-0.7	-0.8	-1.0	-1.0	-0.9	-1.3	-2.0	-0.2
Current account	-0.1	-0.3	-0.1	–	-0.5	-0.5	-0.4	-0.8	-1.2	-0.8	-0.4	-0.7	-0.3	0.1	0.1	-0.8	-1.5	-0.9	-0.8	-1.4	0.1
Poland																					
Merchandise export	-1.1	1.3	1.6	2.3	3.5	4.1	4.3	4.7	5.3	5.9	7.2	5.5	5.0	5.4	5.8	5.8	6.2	6.9	7.9	8.1	10.9
Merchandise import	1.0	1.1	1.8	3.6	5.6	6.9	7.0	6.6	7.4	8.0	8.1	6.2	4.6	4.3	4.4	4.6	5.1	5.9	7.0	8.0	8.6

(continued)

Table 11.4 (continued)

	1970	1971	1972	1973	1974	1975	1976	1977	1978	1979	1980	1981	1982	1983	1984	1985	1986	1987	1988	1989	1990
Balance	0.1	0.2	-0.2	-1.3	-2.1	-2.8	-2.7	-1.9	-2.1	-2.1	-0.9	-0.8	0.4	1.1	1.5	1.2	1.1	1.0	0.9	0.1	2.2
Invisibles	0.1	0.1	0.2	0.2	—	-0.2	-0.1	-0.3	0.4	-1.0	-1.7	-2.4	-2.6	-2.3	-2.2	-1.7	-1.7	-1.4	-1.5	-2.0	-1.5
Current account	0.1	-0.3	—	-1.1	-2.1	-3.0	-2.8	-2.1	-2.4	-3.1	-2.7	-3.1	-2.2	-1.2	-0.7	-0.5	-0.6	-0.4	-0.6	-1.9	0.7
Romania																					
Merchandise export	0.7	0.8	1.1	1.7	2.6	2.8	3.4	3.7	4.0	5.4	6.5	7.2	6.2	6.2	6.9	6.3	5.1	5.9	6.5	6.0	3.5
Merchandise import	0.8	0.9	1.1	1.7	2.9	2.9	3.3	3.8	4.6	6.5	8.0	7.0	4.7	4.6	4.7	4.8	3.2	3.4	2.9	3.5	5.1
Balance	-0.1	-0.1	-0.1	-0.1	-0.3	-0.1	0.1	-0.1	-0.6	-1.2	-1.5	0.2	1.5	1.7	2.2	1.4	1.9	2.4	3.6	2.6	-1.6
Invisibles	-0.1	-0.1	-0.1	-0.1	-0.2	-0.1	-0.1	-0.2	-0.2	-0.5	-0.9	-1.0	-0.9	-0.8	-0.6	-0.5	-0.4	-0.2	—	-0.3	0.1
Current account	-0.2	-0.1	-0.2	-0.2	-0.5	-0.3	-0.1	-0.3	-0.8	-1.7	-2.4	-0.8	0.7	0.9	1.5	0.9	1.5	2.2	-3.6	2.9	-1.5
Eastern Europe																					
Merchandise export	5.0	5.6	7.0	9.8	14.2	15.2	16.7	18.2	20.6	25.6	31.9	32.8	31.5	32.2	34.0	34.0	31.5	34.4	37.3	38.7	29.1
Merchandise import	5.4	6.0	7.7	12.1	18.4	20.7	22.2	22.8	25.4	30.7	35.0	31.7	26.3	26.5	27.3	28.2	28.7	32.4	34.5	37.3	29.1
Balance	-0.4	-0.4	-0.8	-2.3	-4.2	-5.4	-5.5	-4.6	-4.8	-5.2	-3.1	0.5	5.1	5.7	6.7	5.8	2.7	2.1	2.9	1.5	—
Invisibles	0.1	0.3	0.4	0.5	—	-0.3	—	-0.5	-0.7	-1.7	-3.3	-5.0	-4.5	-3.5	-3.0	-2.8	-2.4	-1.6	-1.9	-3.7	-2.0
Current account	-0.3	-0.1	-0.3	-1.8	-4.2	-5.7	-5.5	-5.2	-5.5	-6.9	-6.4	-4.5	0.7	2.2	3.7	3.0	0.3	0.5	0.9	-2.2	-2.1
Soviet Union																					
Merchandise export	-4.8	5.1	5.7	9.5	13.6	14.2	16.6	20.7	22.8	30.9	38.2	39.1	43.4	44.2	43.3	36.9	34.6	40.8	42.7	45.1	48.8
Merchandise import	4.3	4.6	6.2	9.0	12.0	18.7	19.3	18.8	21.8	26.7	34.8	39.9	39.1	38.0	36.6	36.2	33.3	32.7	39.2	47.4	50.2
Balance	0.4	0.5	-0.4	0.5	1.6	-4.5	-2.7	1.9	0.9	4.2	3.4	-0.7	4.3	6.2	6.7	0.7	1.4	8.1	3.5	-2.3	-1.4
Invisibles	0.5	0.3	0.3	-0.6	-0.7	0.3	0.1	—	—	0.1	-0.4	-0.9	-0.7	-0.4	—	-0.7	-0.9	-1.0	-1.2	-1.7	-3.1
Current account	0.9	-0.8	-0.2	1.1	2.4	-4.2	-2.6	1.9	1.0	4.3	3.0	-1.6	3.6	5.8	6.7	0.1	0.4	7.1	2.3	-4.0	-4.3
Eastern Europe and the Soviet Union																					
Merchandise export	-9.7	10.7	12.7	19.3	27.8	29.4	33.3	38.9	43.4	56.5	70.2	71.4	74.9	76.4	77.4	70.9	66.1	75.2	80.0	83.9	77.8
Merchandise import	9.8	10.6	13.9	21.0	30.4	39.3	41.4	41.7	47.3	57.5	69.8	71.6	65.4	64.5	64.0	64.4	62.0	65.0	73.7	84.7	79.3
Balance	—	0.1	-1.2	-1.8	-2.6	-9.9	-8.1	-2.8	-3.9	-0.9	-0.3	-0.2	9.4	11.9	13.4	6.5	4.1	10.2	6.3	-0.8	-1.5
Invisibles	0.6	0.6	0.7	1.1	0.7	—	0.1	-0.5	-0.6	-1.6	-3.7	-5.9	-5.2	-3.9	-3.0	-3.4	-3.4	-2.6	-3.2	-5.4	-5.1
Current account	0.6	0.7	-0.5	-0.7	-1.9	-9.9	-8.1	-3.3	-4.5	-2.6	-3.4	-6.1	4.2	8.0	10.4	3.1	0.8	7.6	3.2	-6.1	-6.6

Source: United Nations, *Economic Survey of Europe in 1990–1991*, 1991, Appendix.

ambitions. A cohesion of urban and rural workers, it soon boasted 10 million members and was a force to be reckoned with. After a wave of strikes in the summer of 1980, the government was forced to recognize Solidarity and to sack the Communist Party's leader since 1970, Edward Gierek, who was held responsible for the failed import-led growth strategy.

But the foreign debt legacy could not be removed so easily. In 1971, Poland's net external debt was a manageable $1.2 billion, but by 1979, it had risen to $20.5 billion (excluding short-term loans), reflecting the persistent inability of exports to overtake imports after 1972. Debt service (amortization and interest) rose twentyfold over the 1970s, and by 1980, it was absorbing 81.8 per cent of export earnings. Many investment projects, started in the early 1970s, had to be halted, either reducing export capacity or denying the population consumer goods. As economic growth slowed down from the mid-1970s (see Table 11.3), consumer demand could not be satisfied. In March 1979, the Ministry of Internal Trade admitted that this was the case with 280 products. Soon essential consumer articles were being rationed.

Open inflation infiltrated the system, with even the official cost-of-living index admitting a rise from 3 to 8.5 per cent over 1975–80. Farmers, tired of being offered worthless money by state purchasing agencies, withheld food supplies. Poland stopped making scheduled payments on its debts at the end of 1980. One year later, the import and export sectors collapsed as Poland struggled, in vain, to raise $500 million to cover interest due on its debts as the consequence of a rescheduling agreement (April 1981). With the economy in crisis and chaos reigning in the streets, the ruling Communist Party imposed martial law on 13 December 1981, when the ironically titled Military Council for National Salvation under a Polish general, Wojciech Jaruzelski, took over. This alternative was preferable to Soviet military intervention, but although Solidarity was temporarily curbed, the price was the imposition of American-led western sanctions. They would not be lifted until 1983 after martial law ended.

The Polish experience was a portent of what was to come later in the decade. At the time, Solidarity's gallant revolt did no more than attract limited support from workers' groups in the Soviet Union. That it failed to set off widespread discontent in the eastern bloc was partly due to the belief that living standards generally had risen in the 1970s. Imports of high-quality western consumer goods contributed to this illusion. So too did supplies of western grain, which enhanced meat production.

The truth was that across eastern Europe agricultural productivity had failed miserably to rise to the needs of more advanced industrial development (Table 11.5). Although there was some bad luck (Poland, for one, suffered an unusual run of above-average frost, snow, floods and other natural disasters, which impaired food supply), policy mistakes amplified the problems. Generally, there were too many inefficient state farms and not enough private farms or cooperatives. A key weakness was the failure to improve the poor agricultural labour productivity. In East Germany, despite heavy investment, this factor improved by only 45 per cent between 1970 and 1984, whereas for West Germany it was as much as 98 per cent.

Table 11.5 Gross agricultural output in eastern Europe (annual percentage change)

	1970	1971	1972	1973	1974	1975	1976	1977	1978	1979	1980	1981	1982	1983	1984	1985	1986	1987	1988	1989	1990
Bulgaria																					
Total	-3.9	1.9	-5.6	-1.3	-1.5	-7.5	-4.1	-4.7	-4.3	-6.1	-4.6	-5.9	-5.2	-7.2	-7.0	-12.3	11.7	-5.1	-0.1	0.4	-8.8
Crop	2.3	-0.3	8.5	0.2	-7.5	7.8	5.6	-9.5	4.5	5.6	-8.7	10.2	7.9	-17.4	14.4	-22.5	22.7	-8.8	-0.3	4.1	-14.0
Animal	6.9	6.1	1.4	3.1	7.4	7.3	2.0	2.0	4.0	6.5	0.3	2.2	2.6	3.0	1.1	-2.9	-3.7	-1.9	0.4	-2.6	-3.7
Czechoslovakia																					
Total	1.3	2.0	-4.3	-3.8	-2.2	-1.0	-3.2	9.4	-2.1	-3.3	-4.8	-2.5	4.4	-4.2	4.4	-1.6	0.6	-0.9	-2.9	-1.8	-3.7
Crop	-4.5	-0.4	4.5	4.0	1.5	-2.6	-8.2	16.8	1.7	-7.2	6.2	-5.3	13.9	2.8	6.1	-4.1	-2.5	1.8	4.0	1.7	-5.2
Animal	6.3	3.3	4.1	3.6	2.7	0.2	0.5	-4.3	2.4	-0.3	3.9	-0.5	-2.0	5.4	3.1	0.4	2.9	0.3	2.1	2.0	-2.6
German Democratic Republic																					
Total	3.8	-0.3	-9.3	-0.3	-7.2	-2.0	-5.0	6.2	-1.1	-3.0	1.3	-1.5	-4.1	-3.9	6.6	3.9	—	-0.3	-2.1	-1.6	—
Crop	-10.8	-5.9	18.3	-7.8	8.8	-9.6	12.5	20.9	—	5.3	-3.2	2.3	1.5	0.9	11.5	-5.3	-3.7	-0.3	-6.6	1.4	—
Animal	—	4.0	4.4	5.3	6.1	2.2	-0.6	-0.1	1.7	1.8	3.8	1.5	-7.0	5.5	4.1	3.1	2.2	-0.3	0.3	1.7	—
Hungary																					
Total	-5.7	-7.6	2.6	-6.3	-3.2	-3.7	-2.7	10.9	-1.1	-1.5	4.6	2.0	-7.3	-2.7	2.9	-5.5	-2.4	-2.0	-4.3	-1.3	-6.5
Crop	-16.4	9.5	5.8	7.8	0.5	4.7	-7.1	12.3	-1.5	-3.2	-7.6	-1.6	9.4	-7.5	4.9	-5.4	3.7	-5.5	7.5	0.1	-10.5
Animal	10.4	5.5	-1.0	4.5	6.4	2.5	2.7	-9.6	3.7	0.1	1.9	2.4	5.3	2.2	1.0	-5.6	1.1	1.5	1.5	-2.7	-2.0
Poland																					
Total	-2.2	-3.6	8.4	-7.3	1.6	-2.1	-1.1	1.4	-4.1	-1.5	-10.7	-3.8	-2.8	-3.3	5.7	0.7	-5.0	-2.3	1.2	1.5	-1.4
Crop	4.3	1.1	7.8	6.5	-0.7	-3.0	5.0	-7.2	5.4	-3.7	-15.2	18.9	-2.5	5.9	7.4	-2.0	6.3	-2.0	-0.3	-2.7	—
Animal	-1.1	6.6	-9.0	8.2	4.2	-1.0	-8.7	13.7	2.6	1.3	-5.6	-8.9	-3.2	0.4	3.7	4.0	3.2	-2.7	3.2	-0.1	-3.2
Romania																					
Total	-4.9	18.9	9.7	-1.0	-1.1	-2.9	17.3	-0.8	-1.2	-5.7	-5.0	-0.4	6.9	—	13.3	-0.7	-5.5	-8.9	-5.7	-5.1	-3.0
Crop	-11.8	26.3	-7.6	-3.2	0.6	0.6	21.5	-5.0	-4.3	6.5	-6.1	-1.0	15.2	-3.5	19.1	1.1	-8.8	-14.0	8.4	-1.7	—
Animal	5.4	8.9	12.5	7.7	1.5	6.7	11.5	5.6	2.7	3.7	-3.1	-0.6	-3.7	5.0	6.2	0.5	-1.4	-2.6	3.0	-8.9	—
Eastern Europe																					
Total	0.5	-5.1	-7.3	-4.1	-2.3	0.2	1.2	-3.2	2.1	0.8	-3.7	-1.9	1.5	1.2	6.8	-0.9	-1.8	-2.9	-1.9	—	—
Crop	-1.1	3.9	8.7	2.0	0.7	-1.8	1.8	1.4	-1.5	-0.4	-5.9	6.5	5.3	-0.7	10.0	-2.5	1.4	4.2	1.5	1.4	—
Animal	2.8	5.9	6.4	6.3	4.4	1.9	-0.8	7.4	2.7	1.9	-1.3	-2.3	-2.2	3.1	3.6	0.9	1.9	-1.4	2.1	-1.8	—

Soviet Union

Total	−10.3	1.1	−4.1	16.1	−2.7	−5.3	6.5	4.0	2.7	−3.1	−1.9	−1.0	−5.5	−6.2	−0.1	0.1	−5.3	−0.6	1.7	−0.8	−2.3
Crop	11.8	−1.3	−7.7	27.1	−10.0	−10.5	18.4	−1.8	−5.0	−5.9	−2.3	−2.4	9.2	6.0	−1.9	−1.0	6.1	−2.7	−1.4	1.0	−4.3
Animal	8.7	3.5	−0.6	−6.1	5.2	−2.5	−2.4	9.4	0.8	−0.7	−1.6	0.1	2.6	6.3	1.4	1.0	4.7	1.2	4.1	1.6	−0.8
Eastern Europe and the Soviet Union																					
Total	−7.0	2.4	−0.4	12.0	−1.1	−3.5	4.6	3.7	−2.5	−1.8	−2.5	−0.1	−4.1	−4.5	−2.1	−0.2	−4.1	−1.4	1.8	−0.5	—
Crop	7.6	−0.3	−2.5	18.3	−6.7	−7.6	12.7	−0.8	3.9	−4.2	−3.5	0.4	7.9	3.8	1.8	−1.5	4.5	−3.2	−0.4	1.1	—
Animal	6.7	4.3	1.7	−6.2	4.9	−0.9	−1.8	8.7	1.5	0.3	−1.5	−0.8	0.9	5.2	2.1	1.0	3.7	0.4	3.4	0.5	—

Source: United Nations, *Economic Survey of Europe in 1990–1991*, 1991, Appendix.

he start of the 1970s, Erich Honecker, General Secretary of the ruling Socialist ty Party, declared that his country must become self-sufficient in foodstuffs. As it turned out, this aim was not to be achieved. Across eastern Europe, agricultural output trends were disastrous, often resulting in food shortages and necessitating rationing, which inevitably engendered discontent. It was as if a stabilizing rug had been pulled from under the leaderships of eastern Europe. No matter how hard they tried, they could not find their feet again. Poland was a classic case. There, per capita food consumption fell by as much as 15 per cent over 1981–83, just at the time when the Jaruzelski regime was seeking legitimacy and support for economic reform. The knock-on effect of food shortages was to impair labour productivity and to undermine official blandishments seeking to portray an improving situation.

Lamentable agricultural performance was a common east European problem, but in the Soviet Union it was, if anything, even more of an Achilles heel. It had been hoped to attain self-sufficiency in grain by 1980. But that year, imports amounted to 27.8 million tonnes, and they remained at that level or higher throughout the 1980s. Its import dependency would have been even costlier had it not coincided with a glutted world market. As it was, grain imports accounted for over one-fifth of the total Soviet import bill, proving a drain on hard currency reserves. This was a price that had to be paid in 1980–81, after the second poorest home harvest since the 1960s, when food shortages in Soviet cities precipitated several unofficial strikes.

By the early 1980s, it was apparent that the Soviet economy was in deep trouble. Leonid Brezhnev's final years in office from the early 1970s to 1982 came to be called *zastoi* (stagnation) (Table 11.6). All major economic indicators turned unfavourable from the mid-1970s, creating increasing concern among the leadership. There was a recognition that economic weakness could mean losing the renewed arms race with the United States, begun in 1980 by the newly elected American president, former actor Ronald Reagan, who denigrated the Soviet Union as 'the evil empire'. Two years later, the American leader considered the Soviet economy to be in a 'desperate situation'. One of his spokesmen went as far as to call it a 'basket case'.

Certainly, there was no lack of Soviet commitment in the arms field. Indeed, western experts suspected that as much as 10–15 per cent of GNP was devoted to the military-industrial sector. But huge expenditure alone was not enough. There was also a technological dimension. Wherever Soviet weaponry came up against

Table 11.6 Soviet economic growth, 1966–85 (per cent per annum)

	1966–70	*1971–5*	*1976–80*	*1981–5*
National income	7.1	5.1	3.8	3.1
Industrial output	8.5	7.4	4.5	3.7
Agricultural output	3.9	2.4	1.7	1.1

Source: I. Derbyshire, *The Politics in the Soviet Union*, London: Chambers, 1987, 91.

American (as in the Syrian–Israeli clashes), the former's inadequacies were exposed. In 1987, Mikhael Gorbachev bemoaned that 'the most worrying [feature] is that we have started lagging behind in scientific-technical development'. Another manifestation of this was in the field of microcomputers. By 1987, there were only around 200,000 of them in the whole of the Soviet Union against over 25 million in the United States, which were of much greater sophistication. The military commitment helped depress production through siphoning off high-quality resources (absorbing about a third of machinery output in the 1970s).

The enormous effort devoted to armaments (conventional and nuclear) helps to explain why the share of services actually fell from 29.5 to 20.3 per cent in the period 1950–80, the reverse expectation for an advanced industrialized nation. Again, while the share of total investment in industry rose significantly in the 1970s, it was not used effectively. For instance, a new blast furnace technique developed in the Soviet Union was employed by only 11 per cent of its steel industry compared with 75 per cent of Japan's. Nor was there sufficient replacement investment, with the result that up to 40 per cent of available machine tool capacity was engaged on equipment repair. Much Soviet investment focused on energy and agriculture, though in the latter case, it did not result in the transformation and efficiency of that sector. By contrast, housing and transportation systems were badly neglected, laying the seeds for future unrest. Finally, management and organization left much to be desired. Neither managers nor workers were seen as being sufficiently motivated. A leaked government document dating from 1983 (the Novosibirsk Report) was scathing about the labour force. The Soviet worker's productivity was too low, he lacked discipline and motivation, often being involved in 'pilfering, various shady dealings at state expense, the development of illicit business, "backhander" payments and official remuneration irrespective of the results of work' (Aage 1984, 19). Here, was an early recognition of the emergence across eastern Europe of the 'underground economy', which was to become ever more significant as living standards declined.

Perestroika: impetus for reform

It is little realized that one of Gorbachev's immediate predecessors as General Secretary of the Communist Party of the Soviet Union, Yuri Andropov (1982–84), initiated the process of reform. He began to address the perceived problems of labour discipline, low agricultural output and poor scientific diffusion in industry. But the so-called 'Andropov effect' was no more than a quickly dissolved ripple, aided by exceptionally mild winters, which reduced the strain on the creaking railway system and contained demand for fuel. Andropov confessed he 'felt the need to be very cautious in dealing with an economy on such a scale and of such complexity' as the Soviet Union's and in the final analysis was only tinkering with the system. Much bolder reform initiatives were needed.

They were provided by Gorbachev. Assuming office in March 1985, he was consumed by the need to cure the economy's ills. His policy of *uskorenie* (acceleration) similarly focused on the symptoms of deceleration: inefficiency, poor-quality products and technological backwardness. Gorbachev appeared like a breath of fresh air compared with his recent predecessors. Comparatively young (he had not fought in the Second World War), vigorous and outspoken, he was even prepared to go on the streets and engage in dialogue with ordinary citizens. These characteristics, combined with his optimistic and idealistic oratory, were reminiscent of President Kennedy. Gorbachev's slogans, enunciated whenever he encountered criticism, were *'perestroika'* (restructuring) and *'glasnost'* (openness). Ultimately, Gorbachev failed to resurrect the economy, though his revisionism unleashed forces that brought down communism across eastern Europe.

Gorbachev embarked on a series of campaigns intended to revitalize the ailing Soviet economy. The twelfth Five-Year Plan sought to increase the proportion of investment for the modernization and retooling of existing factories from 38.5 to 50.5 per cent over the years 1986–90. The underlying concept was the notion that such intensive re-equipment would raise the average level of technology, resulting in increased efficiency and quality. Success would wean the Soviet Union from its dependence on imported manufactures and provide the bedrock for the growth of the neglected consumer sector by the end of the century. A related campaign saw the establishment of a new independent agency, Gospriemka, in 1986, charged with enforcing new quality standards. The aim was for 95 per cent of Soviet machines to be compatible with the best world standards by 1991–93.

A further series of measures attacked the 'human factor'. *Glasnost* was initially directed against corrupt and inefficient state officials, from the Politburo to factory management. Meeting workers on factory visits, Gorbachev encountered heated resentment towards bureaucrats and their special privileges: shops stocking goods unavailable to the general population, dachas, hospitals, limousines with reserved lanes on highways. Whereas Stalin used terror to achieve his ends, Gorbachev sought to make officials more accountable and exposed them to public criticism. Most important, they no longer held their positions for life. By February 1986, a new generation of technocrat specialists had replaced state ministers in charge of such key industries as oil, petrochemicals, iron and steel, and transport. To stream-line planning, a number of super-ministries were created, through merging minor ministries. There was, too, an anti-alcohol campaign, which recalled American Prohibition. Vodka was one of the few commodities in plentiful supply, but its increased consumption fostered absenteeism from work and low industrial productivity. Alcohol production was cut, prices were raised to punitive levels, the number of selling outlets was reduced and their opening hours were restricted, the minimum drinking age went up, and fines were levied for drunkenness. Finally, there was an attempt to control the mushrooming underground economy. This campaign aimed to eradicate speculation, embezzlement, bribery and the employment of state facilities for private gain.

In none of these areas was much success attained. Acute bottlenecks soon manifested themselves in machine-building, and by 1989, production was way off target. Initially, Gospriemka's overzealous pursuit of its mission saw around 6 billion roubles' worth of output rejected in 1987. This said much about the appalling quality of Soviet manufactures. It was also a level of rejection that could not be tolerated. Gospriemka accordingly lost its teeth and, once more, quantity, the god of centrally planned economies, ruled the roost. The anti-alcohol campaign became a victim of its own success. Restricting opening hours and officially available alcohol only created queues, which increased the time that addicted workers took off. The policy stimulated a vast moonshining industry, inflating the size of the black market. What the government failed to recognize was vodka's appeal as a means for the population to escape the drab reality of communism. Soft drinks, the officially preferred alternative, just did not compare in this crucial respect. Gorbachev, derided by drinkers as 'the Mineral Water Secretary', lost some of his initial popularity.

Other east European states either watched developments in the Soviet Union as interested and sympathetic onlookers or were determined not to be diverted from their own chosen paths. In the latter category fell East Germany and Romania. To the Honecker regime, any suggestion of 'market forces' was heresy. The industrial structure must be determined in advance. There could be nothing accidental about it. The East German government also wanted to see how *perestroika* worked itself out. This view-from-the-sidelines approach reflected the official view that there was nothing fundamentally wrong with the economy. The Honecker regime was already well into an austerity programme and a campaign to improve labour productivity. New combines (Kombinates) incorporated research and development with production under one roof in an effort to reduce the time taken to introduce new technology into manufacturing processes. There were around 130 Kombinates at national level, with an average of 25,000 workers each. They produced components of a particular product and operated as a monopoly. A limited number of private and collective enterprises were also introduced into the service sector in an effort to satiate consumer demand. There was the recognition that *perestroika* carried with it dangerous political implications via its sister concept, *glasnost*. When a minister spoke in favour of *glasnost*, he was despatched to a mental clinic!

In Romania, Ceausescu's path to modernism involved Stalinist methods that were anathema to Gorbachev. In March 1988, the increasingly despised dictator began 'systemization'. Intended to achieve urbanization by the year 2000, the policy involved the destruction of half of the country's 13,000 villages. Its brutality was exemplified by the bulldozing of a cluster of villages around Bucharest with just 48 hours' notice. Ceausescu's attitude towards *perestroika* was also determined by his previous announcement, in December 1982, that Romania would pay off its foreign debt by 1990. This goal entailed cutting back drastically on western food imports, with the result that widespread rationing was in place from 1983. The authoritarian regime was totally insensitive towards even the most basic requirements of the population. In consequence, living standards were the lowest in Europe except for Albania, the continent's poorest country. Ceausescu's extensive family controlled all key positions: his brothers oversaw the armed forces, counterintelligence and agriculture, his wife Elena's brother managed the trade unions, and their son headed the Young Communist League. Together they enjoyed a lavish lifestyle reminiscent of the most decadent Roman emperors.

In Romania, the only concession to private enterprise was the tolerated existence of the black market, not least because it benefited corrupt government officials.

Bulgaria and Czechoslovakia were less overtly hostile to *perestroika*, but in practice pursued only superficial reforms. In July 1987, the Bulgarian leadership announced sweeping political and economic reforms, which seemingly went much deeper than the Soviet role model. Only subsequently did it emerge that there was little substance beneath the rhetoric, merely a desire to keep on good terms with Moscow. The Czech economy remained dominated by heavy industry, with the official private sector employing only 0.6 per cent of the working population as late as 1988. Hungary, too, pursued only minor reforms despite being afflicted by the lowest growth rate in eastern Europe when Gorbachev came to power and having failed to shake off its foreign debt, which by 1989 was the highest both per capita and per unit of GNP. In Yugoslavia, *glasnost* struck a chord, symbolized by a growing public debate on the country's future. As for Poland, Jaruzelski's government was sympathetic towards Soviet reforms, not least because Solidarity remained a potent force. In 1987, it went as far as to hold a referendum on proposed political and economic reforms. Even so, the military dictator nevertheless went ahead with a modified programme of reforms, despite failing to win sufficient support.

The shortage economy

By the late 1980s, the 'shortage economy' had become the norm for eastern Europe, sowing the seeds for revolution. A shortfall of public revenue was endemic throughout the region. In 1988, the Soviet Union admitted that its internal budget had been in deficit since 1976. In 1985 the shortfall was about 2.5 per cent of GDP, by 1987 almost 8.5 per cent. Subsequently, Gorbachev conceded, 'We lost control over the financial situation. . . . This was our most serious mistake in the years of *perestroika*.'

Gorbachev called the deficit 'the worst heritage from the past', but in many ways the actions of his regime served only to worsen the shortfall in revenue. Most important of all, it failed to reverse the slowdown in economic growth. The anti-alcohol campaign (see above), an own goal if ever there was one, deprived the state of an estimated 6.2 billion roubles in turnover tax in 1985–86, aggravating the budget deficit. Although there was some cutback in military expenditure as relations with the west improved, the defence sector continued to absorb vast amounts, which are impossible to quantify given that only a small proportion was disclosed in published figures. The occupation of Afghanistan was believed to have cost five billion roubles annually. This Soviet 'Vietnam' was not finally unhitched until 1988, when the occupying troops at last began to be withdrawn. In seeking mitigating factors, Gorbachev was undoubtedly unlucky to have been burdened with the financial consequences of two major disasters. First, on 26 April 1986, the world's worst recorded nuclear accident occurred at the Chernobyl nuclear power complex in the Ukraine. The official death toll was put at 31, but was almost certainly higher. A radioactive cloud, which was eventually to affect northwestern Europe, contaminated surrounding farmland. The loss of 4 million kilowatts of electricity necessitated power cuts in the winter of 1986–87. Second, Armenia suffered from an earthquake on 7 December 1988, necessitating an emergency aid programme.

The effort to keep the external Soviet account in balance took several forms. Exports, especially of fuels and raw materials, to the non-socialist countries were increased, while imports were reduced. Gold exports were also raised substantially. But several forces conspired to defeat the objective. The cost of the campaigns, including machinery imports, increased extraction costs for oil, the fall in world oil prices (the value of petroleum export sales fell from 30.9 to 20.7 billion roubles in 1984–88) and poor grain harvests in 1988 and 1989 ate into hard currency reserves.

Another price to pay was increasing discontent among the population. Imported consumer goods were cut back in 1986–89 (affecting sales tax revenue) because of the need for western machine tools to service heavy industry. As the size of the budget deficit increased, so money printing presses worked overtime. Only the control of basic goods prices in state shops suppressed inflation, but other prices began to rise. Gorbachev hoped for some relief from cooperatives and private farms, but they were so hidebound with regulations that they failed to increase the supply and range of goods available. By June 1989, there were only 133,000 cooperatives throughout the Soviet Union compared with 90 million in China. Again, the private farm initiative was no more than a laboratory experiment, with only 20,000 existing in April 1989. Both sectors responded to long queues by increasing their prices, bringing discredit on themselves (some farms fell victim to arsonists). Soviet television, no longer the propaganda vehicle of old, carried interviews with women angry with Gorbachev at the queues they faced. Driven by the twin fears of a future fall in the value of the rouble and no goods to buy, citizens resorted to hoarding. The buyers' panic ensured that Soviet stores, at various times, were emptied of such basic stocks as milk, sausages, meat and salt. A further impact of the lack of goods was to push up savings, with the growth rate of households' financial assets rising substantially from the mid-1980s, reaching 14.9 per cent in 1989.

It was a similar story in Poland. Too much money was chasing too few goods, leading to rationing and mass queuing on a first-come, first-served basis. In one instance, it took a fortnight for a family to take it in turns to queue for a washing machine. The housing situation was even more absurd. No one could join the Cooperative Housing Association accommodation list until they were 18. By 1987, the waiting list was 57 years, which meant, given a life expectancy of 67 years, that applicants could expect to be eight years dead by the time they succeeded! For some, the answer to the shortages was the black market. Trading in American dollars gave the beleaguered Jaruzelski regime a means to reduce the mountain of money in circulation, not least because of the zloty's rapidly depreciating value.

It should be noted that budget deficits and inflation were symptoms of the efforts to reform centrally planned economies. Once this process got under way it became more difficult to direct monetary flows so that government revenues matched expenditures. Printing money to finance the deficit was the line of least resistance, but was no panacea, because it brought inflation. More open government in the Soviet Union forced the admission of a budget deficit. The public was no longer fooled by reassuring statistics that did not correspond to reality. As the head of the Soviet statistical office, *Goskomstat*, remarked, there was no longer any point to efforts 'to attempt to save the "honour of the uniform" by claiming that in spite of occasional shortcomings, which are being overcome, the situation on the whole and in general is not bad'. Elsewhere, socialist pride dictated that the figures were massaged to conceal the true picture. Not until 1989–90, after revolutions had swept away the old guard (see below), did revised figures become available. They revealed, for instance, that Bulgaria's fiscal deficit was as much as one-tenth of net material product by 1988, Hungary's budget deficit was 55 billion forints by 1989, while East Germany's domestic debt was put at 130 billion marks, almost half of its national income.

The shortage economy was exemplified in Romania by energy. Epitomizing the waste and inefficiency was the aluminium plant at Slatinia that consumed as much electricity as the entire consumer sector. Electricity and gas tariffs were raised to damp down demand and restrictions on consumption were introduced. The average household was allowed only enough electricity to power one light bulb per room for two to three hours a day. There was, too, a shortage of light bulbs and lighting equipment. Further exacerbating the situation were periodic failures of the national grid. As for gas, apartments could be heated only to very low temperatures. The lack of electricity meant that around a quarter of the land area intended for irrigation was neglected. This contributed to food scarcity (see above).

In East Germany, another variant of the shortage economy was on display: labour. In December 1979, Honecker alluded to 'the new situation' created by the retirement of a large percentage of the workforce. There were not enough foreign workers willing and able to fill the gaps. The shortfall was worsened by the tendency in centrally planned economies to hoard workers when target deadlines approached and through the use of antiquated machinery and equipment. By 1989, a staggering 17 per cent of employees in manufacturing and energy provision (280,000 workers) devoted their time to machine repair. The shortage of labour produced a statistical mirage: because there was no labour reserve, it appeared as if East German labour productivity was outpacing West German labour productivity. Pride and propaganda led the Honecker regime to insist that all was well. What it could not hide was the fact that on the other side of the Berlin Wall, West Germans enjoyed a more attractive lifestyle, romanticized in glossy television programmes that could be picked up in East Germany.

Revolution in Eastern Europe

By 1989, the economies of eastern Europe were in a morass, sinking ever deeper into difficulties, no matter what palliatives were tried. Sharply declining living standards and rising nationalism proved the death knell for the one-party communist state. It was no longer possible to shirk the fact that socialist economies could not compete with western technology or consumerism. But because most of the countries of eastern Europe had embarked on some form of market reform, an inherent contradiction became apparent. The simple fact was that it was not possible to superimpose a free market economy onto a centrally planned one. The coexistence of the two systems meant that the market economy was continually held back and rendered ineffective. State controls, for instance, dictated that not all prices reflected scarcity (except on the black market). Suffocating restrictions ensured that no budding class of entrepreneurs emerged. The army of meddling bureaucrats created by central planning was naturally hostile to the birth pangs of private enterprise, which was seen as job threatening. Ultimately, only political revolution could resolve the contradiction.

The Soviet Union demonstrated all these shortcomings and more. The 1988 Enterprise Law had the intention of shifting decision-making gradually from the centre to the enterprises themselves. State orders were to decrease as a proportion of output each year (though they would remain by far the greater part). Managers could dispose of any target surplus at the best price they could negotiate. The theory was that the anticipated profits would replace state subsidies, thus easing the budget deficit.

The half-baked measure was doomed to failure. It patently failed to promote a move to the market system or reduce the role of planners and ministries. With no wholesalers to sell the surplus to, most managers preferred, as before, to deal with the ministries. These, in turn, were pleased to accept, not least because the business justified their continued existence. In many ways, the Enterprise Law worsened the situation. Free to select product mix, managers increased the proportion of expensive goods, squeezing out cheaper items. Elected by the workforce, managers responded easily to demands for higher wages, thereby increasing overall demand. Only belatedly, in June 1990, did Gorbachev act to remove the workers' right to select their managers.

These examples could be multiplied. Suffice it to say that by 1989, *perestroika* had failed to produce a fundamental restructuring of the Soviet economy. In contrast, *glasnost* had taken deeper root. Even though Gorbachev had not dared to expose himself to popular election, democratization at lower levels and the introduction of a parliament in June 1989 made him appear increasingly conservative compared with more radical reformers, such as Boris Yeltsin. *Glasnost*, with its open criticism of the Soviet past, had another unwanted ramification for Gorbachev: it encouraged the three Baltic states, Latvia, Lithuania and Estonia, incorporated into the Soviet Union by Stalin in 1940, to seek their independence. Nor were they the only trouble spots. In 1988, inter-ethnic conflict erupted between the republics of Azerbaijan and Armenia over the disputed enclave of Nagorno-Karabakh. The same year Georgians called for their independence. There were nationalist stirrings too in Russia, the Ukraine, Byelorussia and Moldavia.

The economic consequences of rising nationalism were profound. The Baltic states, better supplied than many other parts, attracted non-residents in search of provisions. The Baltic authorities responded by banning the sale of selected products to outsiders. Soon this phenomenon spread throughout the Soviet Union. After Moscow insisted that only residents could buy its produce, eight surrounding regions retaliated by banning deliveries of milk to the Soviet capital. The Azeri blockade of Armenia prevented goods from coming in or out. Central planners had boasted that they did not need to duplicate supplies. But the dispute cut off a Vladimir tractor factory from its only source of tyres, with the result that many machines were supplied to rural areas without tyres. Again, as most cigarette paper was produced in Armenia, national shortages resulted.

In the past, strikers were either imprisoned or committed to mental institutions. *Glasnost* changed all this and the strike became a weapon of ethnic and worker unrest. Heavy industry workers went on strike not for more wages but for more consumer goods on which to spend their money. During July 1989, over half a million workers in Siberia and the Ukraine came out over poor food supplies and provisions such as soap. Because these regions were vital to the economy, the government was forced to import more, adding to its debt problem. The first mass miners' strike took place a month after the Congress of the People's Deputies opening session, inspired by its unprecedented criticisms of the government.

Karl Marx had predicted that capitalism would explode. In the event, it was communism that imploded. The Soviet Union's internal problems placed it in no position, even if it had desired, to prevent other east European countries from renouncing communism. Gorbachev's wish to reduce the huge nuclear weapons stockpile through *détente* with the west showed his recognition that its technological and financial assistance was vital. By comparison, the Soviet Union's economic ties within the CMEA were increasingly seen as a burden. From 1986, the Soviet Union's exports to other CMEA members declined dramatically, reflecting a shift of trade towards the west and declining oil prices. Such was the turnaround that by 1989, both Hungary and Czechoslovakia had built up trade surpluses with the Soviet Union of the order of 1 billion transferable roubles. Envious of the European Community, in July 1988, Gorbachev tried, and failed, to convert the CMEA into a genuine common market. While Hungary and Poland supported the idea, Bulgaria and Czechoslovakia were lukewarm, East Germany had reservations, with Romania definitely opposed. A similar division was apparent over the proposed introduction of a convertible currency, the necessary precondition of a common market. In January 1989, the CMEA celebrated its fortieth anniversary, but by then it was looking increasingly like a spent force. A sharp fall in intra-CMEA trade started in 1989, accelerating in 1990, when it fell by as much as one-fifth in volume.

Events were now to move rapidly, as communism was swept away in eastern Europe in a domino-like way. The process was facilitated by instant communications via television and radio, with news of one revolution spreading quickly and causing another. The underlying reason was the pent-up frustration and resentment of populations at their governments' failure to provide them with decent living standards. Most important was the Soviet Union's benevolent attitude to change. In March 1989, Gorbachev approved the new Hungarian multi-party system and accepted the round-table negotiations between Solidarity and the Polish government, which produced free elections in which the Communist Party was roundly beaten. Increasingly, Soviet spokesmen suggested that the Brezhnev doctrine was no longer sacrosanct. In a famous remark, one said that it was now 'the Sinatra doctrine': allowing other countries to 'do it their way'. Gorbachev himself reaffirmed this in speeches of June and July 1989, when he said that each state had the right to build socialism as it saw fit.

The new mood soon manifested itself in East Germany. Hungary was one of the few places where the population was allowed to travel abroad. Now that communism had collapsed there, it became a magnet for East Germans seeking a new life in the west. West German television reported that Hungary had opened its frontier with Austria, which became an escape route into West Germany. Hundreds, and then thousands made the bid for freedom. On 7 October 1989, East Germany celebrated its fortieth anniversary, with Gorbachev and Honecker standing side by side at the anniversary parade. A nearby demonstration rang out with the cry, 'Gorby, help us!' Soon mass protests had broken out in the major cities. Honecker was forced to resign on 18 October 1989, but this palliative was not enough. More demonstrations followed, with yet more people leaving when Czechoslovakia opened its frontier on 3 November. Conceding defeat, the ruling Politburo resigned and the opposition New Forum was legalized. By now the exodus totalled 200,000 (1 per cent of the population). On 9 November, the unthinkable happened: East Germany opened its frontiers, including the Berlin Wall, the dismantlement of which was begun by jubilant citizens hacking at its hated concrete structure.

The next day, the longest-serving leader in eastern Europe, Todor Zhivkov, was toppled from power in Bulgaria by party colleagues. His misguided efforts to 'Bulgarianize' the country's Muslim community prompted a mass exodus into Turkey and severely damaged the economy. Attention then switched to Czechoslovakia, where demonstrations in Prague quickly spread and led the government to resign early in December. Finally, the hated Nicolae Ceausescu was removed from power in Romania. Increasingly, he and his extended family, which was prepared to let the population inhabit a Dark Ages environment while they wallowed in luxury, were regarded as an anachronism. With the armed forces refusing to act against demonstrators, Ceausescu and his wife attempted to flee. Caught, after a summary trial reminiscent of the French revolution, they were executed on Christmas Day.

Yugoslavia, the first communist regime established outside the Soviet Union following the Second World War, looked destined to survive the upheavals. In reality, the Balkan question, which had lain virtually undisturbed since 1918, was about to raise its ugly head again. Already, efforts towards further economic reform had foundered on differences between the republics of Croatia, Slovenia and Serbia on how they should be implemented. Politically, only Serbia wished to preserve the federation; the other republics wanted either a looser arrangement or outright independence. Increasingly, it looked as if only civil war could resolve the situation.

The outlook for change

It is one thing to bring down a regime overnight, quite another to restructure and revitalize an economy. A number of common problems were faced by the new regimes: first, the need to convert the currency, which required a price shock, or shocks, to adjust to world market prices; second, the abolition of central planning; last, the privatization of state enterprises and the creation of legal and financial infrastructures to stimulate private industry. There were also problems unique to a particular country, the most obvious being German reunification in the case of East Germany, where the original owners of property confiscated by the state in 1949–89 were entitled to compensation. Nothing could be done with a commercial building until they were traced. Sometimes, multiple owners appeared. Intending property developers had to compensate them before going ahead. In Romania, the new regime wisely reversed Ceausescu's barbaric policies: foodstuffs geared for export were redirected to the consumer market, 'systematization' was ended, large and expensive construction projects were halted, domestic restrictions on the use of electricity and gas were lifted, and energy and thermal-heat were redirected from industry to the municipal and private sectors. The result of this proconsumer approach, predictably enough, was to place a severe strain on the balance of payments, with imports from the convertible currency area increasing by 54.3 per cent in the first three-quarters of 1990.

Because no country had yet successfully jumped across the enormous chasm separating communism from capitalism, there was no consensus on the correct sequencing. The danger with excessive devaluation, as adopted by Poland in January 1990, was that it brought cost-push inflation. On the other hand, it could be argued that such a move would encourage many firms to export. In 1990, Polish exports rose by 15 per cent in volume, while the rest of eastern Europe's (excluding those of Yugoslavia) contracted by some 10 per cent. Hungary and Romania preferred a more gradualist approach, but this assumed the continuance of a stable political base.

The signs were that the new regimes would find it difficult to create order from the chaos they inherited, not least because external conditions were not always favourable. The world economic slowdown, the collapse of CMEA trade, the brief, but stinging, oil price shock resulting from the Iraqi invasion of Kuwait: all these factors represented further hurdles over a long course. Gorbachev had once spoken of a 'Common European Home' and many east European governments cherished the hope that the two halves of Europe could converge and become one big happy family under the umbrella of the European Community.

That ambition could only be a distant dream, the immediate task being the modernization of the economies. As in the 1970s, western aid was sorely needed. The new Romanian regime went cap in hand to the IMF, coming away with credits of over $1 billion. Not a member of the IMF, the Soviet Union, now seen as a credit risk by western banks concerned at the uncertain political situation and what they considered wasted expenditure, could obtain $17 billion of new credits in 1990 only through their being underwritten by western governments.

The wheel had turned full circle, but unlike the 1970s, the west was not prepared to lend without influence. There was no prospect of another Marshall Plan. In 1990, the Group of 24 (G24) advanced industrial nations agreed to back reforms in eastern Europe, providing greater access to their markets, technical assistance and limited financial support. The same year, the G24 and international financial institutions met the urgent balance-of-payments problems of Hungary and Poland with new credits. The latter country's payments were rescheduled to give its reforms greater time to work. The European Community also began negotiations with Czechoslovakia, Hungary and Poland, with a view to creating an industrial free trade system.

While the west also looked to bolster Soviet reforms, close study suggested that the Soviet economy was so inefficiently run that any major aid would be wasted. In December 1990, the Houston Four Report recommended that assistance be restricted to three areas: food, technical aid and selected projects (especially energy). By that time, the big question was how much longer Gorbachev could survive. Public support for him had plunged to 20 per cent by July 1990 (from a high of 90 per cent in his early days). The economic revival he had promised now seemed a pipedream and he was blamed for bringing the Soviet Union to the brink of economic collapse. Even the official Soviet statistical agency conceded that GNP fell by 2 per cent in 1990, the first fall since 1945. Taking inflation into account, it was probably of the order of 8–10 per cent. By 1990, parliaments in all fifteen Soviet republics had passed resolutions demanding their own sovereignty. Some major cities began to take the initiative towards market reform without reference to the centre. His authority diminished, Gorbachev offered to change the country's name to the Union of Sovereign Soviet Republics. Cynics suggested that the UFFR was a better title: the Union of Fewer and Fewer Republics. Soon, the Goliath of communism was to be toppled from its pedestal by nationalist stones coming from all directions, along with innumerable statues of the once revered Lenin.

Eastern Europe's dramatic transformation from communist states to fledgling democracies over the period under review stemmed from the failure to match the growth levels achieved in the 1960s. Extensive western credits and, for most countries, insulation from the worst effects of the oil shocks provided the means to avoid addressing fundamental economic and social problems in the 1970s. But by the following decade, less favourable circumstances compelled socialist governments to introduce limited reforms, which invariably promised much but delivered little. The one reform that might have made all the difference (the introduction of a true free market economy) was consciously avoided, essentially because it would have turned communism on its head. Even as late as April 1990, Gorbachev bemoaned: 'They say, "Let's have free enterprise and give the green light to all forms of private ownership". . . . But I cannot accept such ideas. . . . They are impossible ideas.' The result of introducing only limited private ventures into the morass of a centrally planned economy was inevitably that their green shoots failed to take root.

Eastern Europe's communist regimes, by and large, continued to structure their economies in favour of sector A (heavy, construction and defence industries) to the detriment of sector B (light, consumer industries). *Perestroika*, wherever it appeared, merely tinkered with the existing system; it patently failed to transform it. What had sustained growth in the 1960s (high inputs of capital investment, labour and raw materials) was no longer available in the required dosages. With these inputs becoming scarce, planners sought to increase productivity through imports of western technology, but the opportunity was wasted. By the late 1980s, demonstrators were calling not just for political freedom but also for comprehensive market reforms. The revolutions of 1989 provided the platform for reforms on western lines, but also brought the prospect of high unemployment.

Questions for discussion

1   What was the significance of the 1970s to the eventual collapse of the east European command economies?
2   Why did the Soviet economy become relatively backward?
3   Did *perestroika* have any more than a marginal effect on the economic development of the Soviet bloc economies?
4   What were the immediate background economic factors in the political revolutions of 1989?
5   Why did technological progress in eastern Europe fall behind that of the west?

12 Towards a united Europe, 1990–2000

In the final decade of the twentieth century, the Continent of Europe was no longer the epicentre of the Cold War, which finally ended with the collapse of the Soviet Union in December 1991. Great cities like Prague and Warsaw, previously shut off by the 'Iron Curtain', suddenly became as accessible to westerners as Paris and London. As the political divisions melted away, so the prospects of economic convergence between the western and eastern parts of Europe were never brighter. A major fulcrum for this was the European Union (EU). It faced a wave of applications to join its ranks from former Soviet satellites anxious to cement their democratic free market credentials and sought to bind the majority of its existing members closer together and enhance economic performance through the much-vaunted single market and single currency projects. At the same time, Europe was confronted with a panoply of problems, not least the persistence of high unemployment, escalating welfare costs, overregulation in some countries and a dismal start for the euro, which, by the time the new millennium dawned, had significantly depreciated against other major currencies.

European competitiveness

The European Economic Community (EEC), founded by the Treaty of Rome in March 1957, had become the European Community (EC) by 1967, following the merger of the EEC with the European Atomic Energy Community and the European Coal and Steel Community. The original members (France, West Germany, Italy and the three Benelux countries) enjoyed a surge of economic growth that persuaded Britain, Denmark and Ireland to join in 1973 (the second wave). In the event, this proved an inauspicious entry point, coinciding as it did with the end of the Long Boom. Nevertheless, the EC continued to be a magnet for democratic European countries, not least because of the generous subsidies it extended to poorer regions and to agriculture via the Common Agricultural Policy (CAP), and during the 1980s, Greece (1981), Portugal and Spain (both 1986) (the so-called 'Mediterranean Club') boosted the overall membership to twelve.

Whereas the American and Japanese economies had recovered from the oil shocks by the early 1980s, the EC continued to be afflicted by high unemployment, declining productivity and struggled to penetrate overseas markets. It became increasingly apparent that the EC's problems had less to do with the after-effects of the stagflation of the 1970s than with its own overbureaucratic and overprotective structure, which stifled innovation and competition. The term 'Eurosclerosis' was invented by Herbert Giersch to encapsulate the problem. 'Eurosclerosis' came to embrace a range of Europe-specific impediments to global competitiveness: from an overextended welfare system, which, its proponents argued, encouraged the unemployed to remain idle rather than actively seek work, to heavily subsidized state industries and a surfeit of red tape. The Ball-Albert report of 1983 highlighted the costs of 'non-Europe', an umbrella term for the general ineffectiveness of intergovernmental collaboration within the EC and the absence of genuine trade integration. There was the daily example of lorry drivers being needlessly delayed for hours on end at EC borders because of the need to fill in customs forms and comply with national regulations. Indeed, the bureaucracy generated an estimated 80 million forms annually! There was, too, the alarming statistic that, by 1982, whereas the United States and Japan had contained their public sector expenditure (as a percentage of GDP) to around 35 per cent, for the EC as a whole it had shot up from 32 per cent in 1960 to 50 per cent by 1982. The authors considered that the EC economy had been balkanized and that without the introduction of a truly common market, as envisaged by the authors of the Treaty of Rome, the EC could not reassert itself as a major player in the world economy.

With EC unemployment standing at 12 million by 1983, the Ball-Albert report found a receptive audience, leading the European Parliament to instigate a report, which confirmed and reinforced its findings. At the Fontainebleau summit of heads of government in the summer of 1984, a number of impediments to increased integration were resolved, including the long-running dispute over Britain's annual contribution to the EC budget, which led to the Dooge Committee being established. Its report, published in March 1985, advocated a 'homogeneous internal economic space'.

To general enthusiasm, Jacques Delors, the then President of the European Commission (the EC's permanent bureaucracy) pushed forward the concept of a single European market (SEM) to create a truly integrated trading area without internal borders in which the original aims of the Treaty of Rome (the free movement of labour, goods, capital and services) was finally achieved. To remove the stifling bureaucracy and red tape would, a White Paper of 1985 indicated, require more than 300 measures. The European Council gave its blessing to the legislative programme at the Milan summit of June 1985, the prelude to the Single European Act, which was ratified on 1 July 1987. By this, a Europe 'without frontiers' would come into effect on 1 January 1993, with the intention of removing non-tariff trade barriers. Qualified majority voting in the European Council of Ministers was introduced to try to ensure that, unlike in the past, individual member states did not exercise their veto to block unpalatable proposals backed by a majority.

The SEM was expected to benefit consumers by levelling the economic playing field and, through more intense competition and economies of scale, bring down prices and lead to greater choice. Within the global economy, it was anticipated that the SEM would markedly improve European competitiveness. As Margaret

Thatcher enthused in her Bruges speech of September 1988: 'By getting rid of barriers, by making it possible for companies to operate on a Europe-wide scale, we can best compete effectively with the United States, Japan and other new economic powers emerging in Asia and elsewhere.' Indeed, the Cecchini Report of the same year predicted that up to five million new jobs would be created and that the Community's GDP would be boosted by between 3 and 6 per cent.

A raft of preliminary measures, which helped to foster a boom in the later 1980s, preceded the SEM. In fact, the SEM legislative programme (referred to as '1992') was far from complete when the SEM officially opened to the fanfare of bonfires across participant countries at the start of 1993. At that time, it encompassed twelve states and 344 million consumers, accounting for some 25 per cent of world economic output. The SEM's reach was further unfurled in January 1995, when Austria, Finland and Sweden were included to form the 'European Economic Area'. Following this third enlargement, the EU encompassed the world's largest trading area, one-third greater than the United States market and ahead of its rival NAFTA (United States, Canada and Mexico) in terms of population, GDP and share of world trade.

There was no overnight revolution (in fact, the initial opening period was dogged by a recession and rising unemployment) and some governments were laboriously slow in placing SEM legislation on the statute book. For instance, by 1996, only three members had pushed through public procurement directives. The assiduous British complained: 'We practise European unity, the others just talk about it' (Strange 1998, 109). Moreover, there was a distinction between principle and practice. In theory, the SEM liberalized air transport: in actuality, national carriers still often enjoyed a privileged position (such as the retention of cherished landing slots). The recent arrival of low-cost budget operators on selected routes has made some difference (forcing British Airways to introduce its own version, Go, for example), but the fact was that on standard flights the cost of travel generally remained excessive compared with longer haul tariffs. The short haul journey from London to Marseilles, for example, was the most expensive trip per air mile in Europe. Dublin-based Ryanair was the largest of the budget operators, and the European low fares travel market rose from a value of $0.45 billion in 1996 to $1.5 billion in 2000. But until low-cost operators covered a wider range of destinations, budget travel would be the exception rather than the rule. Again, the SEM did not produce the anticipated general fall in prices, leading the European Commission to instigate a study in 1998 as to why substantial price differentials remained across the EU and why American prices were significantly lower for a majority of key products.

The SEM was not a truly common market in the same way as the United States. It lacked a common language and culture. There were no common tax rates (VAT varied considerably), which could mean, for example, that a lorry driver or motorist paid widely different prices for fuel. Again, alcohol and tobacco products varied widely in price because of different tax regimes, and the resulting discrepancy in after-tax prices in Britain stimulated a cross-Channel black market that took advantage of cheaper Continental tariffs. Again, there was not a

European-wide law that governed firms, leading to a lack of standards in accounting, acquisitions and mergers and other areas. The controversy over 'mad cow disease' in Britain demonstrated the continued power of national governments to ban products. Further, the lack of a European transport authority (actually proposed in the 1950s) was a continued weakness, which periodic French lorry drivers' strikes exploited to bring about expensive cross-Channel traffic standstills.

On the positive side, there is some evidence that the SEM galvanized north–south trade to the benefit of the southern economies, which also benefited from the increase in intra-industry trade from 35 to 42 per cent of total trade between 1985 and 1994. Certainly, the SEM stimulated acquisitions and mergers, with Europe's share rising from 9.5 per cent of the world total during 1985–87 to 28.8 per cent over 1991–93. The destruction of trade barriers had the greatest impact on the bigger economies, such as Britain, France and Germany. Moreover, the easier crossing of borders considerably speeded up delivery times, thereby stimulating cross-border trade. Indeed, following the adhesion of most of the EFTA countries in January 1995, internal trade constituted some 63 per cent of total trade for the EU fifteen. There were signs by the turn of the century that the SEM was having a positive impact on job creation, which the OECD (1999) attributed to 'the implementation of more comprehensive labour and product market reforms in an increasingly large number of countries'. It warned, nonetheless, that the process was by no means uniform, that much still needed to be done, and ideally wanted to see the speeding up of changes.

The quest for a single currency

As the SEM failed to reap the expected dividends, the feeling grew that it could only be truly complete and effective with a single common currency. This would avert exchange costs and stimulate cross-border trade. The antecedents of a single currency stretch way back into history. In 1807, Napoleon remarked that 'I want the whole of Europe to have one currency'. The little emperor's ultimate failure to conquer the Continent left the project stillborn until the EEC came into being. Even then the founding members were perfectly content to operate their individual currencies within the dollar-dominated Bretton Woods system until it ran into difficulties in the late 1960s, presaging its collapse between 1971 and 1973. This crisis concentrated minds and led to the short-lived 'snake in the tunnel' system, initiated in 1972 in an attempt to restrict fluctuations between member currencies. In the volatile economic conditions of the 1970s, it was doomed to failure, but served only to postpone efforts towards closer economic and monetary union.

In December 1978, the Brussels summit of the EC authorized the creation of the European Monetary System, whose intention was to bring down inflation rates across the community as a platform for growth. Within it, the Exchange Rate Mechanism (ERM), based on the snake, restricted member currencies to a maximum fluctuation each side of the rate of 2.25 per cent. However, in March 1979, Italy was permitted a more generous 6 per cent, setting a dangerous precedent that Spain, Britain and Portugal subsequently emulated. To this weakness was added another: growing inflexibility. So where there had been frequent realignments between 1979 and 1987, with the powerful Deutschmark revalued six times and weaker ERM currencies devalued, once the ERM became a vehicle for the single currency, its adaptability went out of the window and a crisis loomed.

In June 1988, the Committee for the Study of Economic and Monetary Union (EMU) was established by the European Council to determine whether a single currency would benefit the SEM. The resulting Delors Report of 1989 answered in the affirmative and proposed a three-stage approach to the implementation of a single currency. In Stage One (1 July 1990 to 31 December 1993), capital controls would be removed, inflation and interest rate differentials reduced and intra-European exchange rates stabilized. In Stage Two (1 January 1994 to 31 December 1998), national economic policies would converge further, with ERM members pegging their currencies and the European Monetary Institute (EMI) would plan the final transition. Finally, in Stage Three (from 1 January 1999), the EMI would be supplanted by a European Central Bank (ECB) and the exchange rates of qualifying members would be immutably fixed before a single currency, which was later christened the euro, was introduced.

Once Stage One commenced, overnight the maintenance of ERM currency parities became a benchmark of EMU credibility. This timing was unfortunate, to say the least. Britain joined the ERM in October 1990 largely to benefit from the Bundesbank's revered anti-inflation policy. But, as the enormous costs deriving from unification with the former East Germany became apparent, the German central bank began to raise its rates, which, unofficially, were the benchmark for ERM members to follow. By September 1992, Britain had come to within a quarter of a percentage point of the German base rate, but the Bundesbank resolutely refused to move downwards. Speculators then made a killing, which forced sterling and the Italian lira out of the ERM. A further crisis in July 1993 led to the widening of the normal fluctuation bands to parameters of plus or minus 15 per cent, except for the Deutschmark and the Dutch guilder, which remained within the narrower band. The experience had a traumatic effect on the already sceptical British, who negotiated an 'opt out' at the Maastricht summit of December 1991.

That summit, which led to the 1992 Treaty on European Union (the Maastricht Treaty), established five basic entry criteria for the single currency. These were price stability, exchange rate stability, interest rate stability, sound public finances, and a satisfactory ratio of public debt to GDP. Meeting the convergence criteria did not prove an easy task, and several wheezes were applied to qualify. The French raided the France Telecom pension fund to reduce their deficit; Italy resorted to a special euro tax and dipped into the severance pay fund of public companies about to be privatized; Belgium sold off public buildings and some of its gold reserves. Whether ingenious or deceitful, such measures had nothing to do with economic performance and obviated the financial discipline that the Maastricht entry conditions were designed to provide. Even a stability pact, intro-duced in December 1996 at German insistence, made little difference. France and Germany, the axis of the EU and driving forces of EMU, differed fundamentally on the aims of the single currency. The French preferred a 'soft' euro and saw its

Table 12.1 Qualified success on convergence criteria

	Budget deficit/GDP 3%	Debt/WP 60%	Price inflation 2.7%
EMU Hopefuls			
Austria	2.5	66.1	1.2
Belgium	2.1	122.2	1.5
Finland	0.9	55.8	1.2
France	3.0	58.0	1.2
Germany	2.7	61.3	1.5
Ireland	−0.9	67.0	1.2
Italy	2.7	61.3	1.5
Luxembourg	−1.7	6.7	1.4
Netherlands	1.7	70.4	1.9
Portugal	2.5	62.0	1.9
Spain	2.6	68.3	1.9
Refuseniks			
Britain	1.9	53.4	1.9
Sweden	0.4	76.6	1.9
Denmark	−0.9	55.8	1.2
Rejected			
Greece	−4.0	108.0	5.9

Source: *The European*, 2–8 March 1998, 1.

primary role as to generate employment and growth. The Germans wanted a 'hard' euro, which would maintain its value against the dollar, contain inflation and underpin sustained growth. As usual, the outcome was political fudge. At French insistence, the stability pact was not as tough as the Germans wanted, while the first president of the ECB, a Dutchman (Wim Duisenberg) with the requisite anti-inflationary credentials to please Bonn, stepped down after four years of a pro-spective eight-year term in favour of a Frenchman.

On a strict reading of the Maastricht criteria, only tiny Luxembourg would have qualified. Apart from price inflation, for which eleven countries easily met the entry conditions, there were problems (see Table 12.1). Belgium, for example, was lumbered with a debt ratio more than twice the permitted limit but squeezed in on a technicality: the generous view that it was falling sufficiently to warrant admis-sion. Indeed, of the twelve applicants, Greece alone, which remained the EU's poorest member, was denied entry in the first wave. Eleven economies formed the euro-zone when the single currency was launched at the start of 1999. However, the euro itself, in the form of notes and coins, was not due to be introduced into circulation until 2002. In the interim, individual currencies continued to operate.

The performance of the euro

One year after its launch, the euro resembled the Italian lira far more than the Deutschmark, which its supporters hoped it would supplant as a bedrock for economic strength and suppressing inflation. Over its first twelve months, the euro depreciated by 15 per cent against the dollar, 12 per cent against sterling and over 20 per cent against the yen. This decline was of a similar magnitude to that of sterling before it was forced out of the ERM.

In its first year of operation, the euro struggled to establish itself as a major currency against the dollar and yen, at one point even falling below parity with the greenback. A lack of confidence in the euro became apparent. Throughout 1999, European investors tended to move out of euros into overseas markets. By February 2000, the ECB was becoming concerned at the impact of the continued weakness of the euro on price stability and sought to address this by increasing the key refinancing rate. The inherent problem of the impossibility of arriving at an interest rate to suit all eleven euro-zone members soon manifested itself. In April 1999, the ECB cut its base rate to accommodate German calls to stimulate their struggling economy, only to face accusations from prospering countries of ignoring their requirements. By October 1999, the ECB had changed tack and began raising interest rates with a view to strengthening the euro.

At the same time, there were some more positive indicators over the medium to longer term. The European corporate bond market was a barometer of confidence, where multinational companies, who previously favoured borrowing in dollars and yen, moved much of their debt into euros. This reflected the fact that they perceived the advantages of trading within the euro-zone without the traditional currency risks. Although sterling fell against the dollar, it remained strong against the euro, making British goods uncompetitive on the Continent and influencing BMW to sell off its loss-making Rover operation at Longbridge. Proponents of British entry into the single currency were given ammunition to argue that non-membership was damaging competitiveness. By spring 2000, the persistent weakness of the euro (effectively amounting to a competitive devaluation) had given a mild uplift to growth and inflation across the euro-zone. The OECD (1999) noted that the fragile currency stimulated export orders in France, Germany and Italy. Although the booming Irish economy faced rising import costs, which threatened to stoke up inflation, it was an exception to the rule, because only around 10 per cent of demand in the euro-zone was fed by imports.

It took the Federal Reserve over a quarter of a century to embed the dollar as a single currency across the United States and itself as the American system's central bank and it will require at least a full economic cycle to make an informed judgement about the success or failure of the euro. But it was already apparent that there were flaws in its management that, sooner rather than later, would have to be addressed. These include the notorious secrecy of the ECB and the associated lack of confidence in its decisions; transfer mechanisms between the poor and rich member states; and the coordination of fiscal and monetary policies. Over time, some appreciation of the euro was probable, especially when the American boom finally ended and its Achilles heel of a substantial and ever-worsening external current account deficit finally rang alarm bells with currency holders. By contrast, the euro-zone enjoyed a significant balance-of-payments surplus on current account, which, when other confidence factors became favourable, would result in a rising euro. This expectation came to pass but had the effect of shrouding the flaws in the single currency project, which came back to haunt decision-makers (see Chapter 14).

The post-revolutionary economies: the transition to the market

The close of the twentieth century required eastern European economies to undergo momentous shifts in terms of economic structures, trade orientation, attitudes and values, as they moved from centrally planned systems to market-based models. Moreover, by the new millennium not only were the transition economies endeavouring to stabilize themselves in an unfamiliar capitalist environment, they were also seeking to meet basic entry-level requirements to join the EU. The situation faced by the post-communist countries has been called the 'simultaneity problem': making the adjustment to democracy at the same time as moving to become free-market economies.

The ingredients required for the transition were immense. The goals were low inflation, stable employment and a higher standard of living to sustain democracy. To reach the El Dorado demanded some painful adjustments as economies moved away from a reliance on heavy industry and agriculture towards manufacturing and services. Table 12.2 indicates the significant differences between centrally planned and free-market economies at the start of the transition process. It will be seen, for example, that the agricultural sectors of the former were significantly larger than the latter, whereas the opposite was true of financial services. In the interim, significant levels of unemployment were inevitable as state-subsidized jobs contracted and before the embryonic capitalist economy gathered momentum. There were, too, legacies from the past to be dealt with, such as pollution and the privatization of land (agricultural and industrial) formerly under state control. The framework to foster a successful transition also needed to be put in place, including major infrastructure development, a legal system, currency adjustment to world market conditions, the establishment of private banking and finance, new office blocks and pollution treatment plants to deal with heavy industrial effluent.

Given the sheer scale of the transformation task, it was inevitable that some countries forged ahead faster than others would. The early leaders were Poland, Hungary and the Czech Republic (created in 1993, when the sluggish Slovakia conveniently insisted on its independence). Slovenia joined them after a brief part (one week) in the Yugoslav Civil War, and by 1999, could boast almost 90 per cent of households with a fixed telephone line and 11 per cent of personal computers connected to the Internet, which was high by eastern European standards. The 'shock-therapy' and 'big bang' approach of the leaders demanded some brave decisions. In early 1991, the Czech Republic (then part of Czechoslovakia) began an extensive stabilization programme incorporating price and trade liberalization, a massive devaluation (50 per cent) of the currency, and two successive waves of mass privatization of state enterprises, propelled by a voucher scheme. This strategy had paid off by the mid-1990s, when inflation and unemployment were under

Table 12.2 Structure of employment (%) in 1989

Sector	Bulgaria	Czech Republic	Hungary	Poland	Romania	Slovakia	France	Germany	Canada	South OECD	North OECD
Agriculture	19.0	11.7	16.6	26.8	27.9	13.8	6.4	3.8	4.3	10.7	4.1
Mining	2.6	3.6	2.0	3.4	2.3	1.0	0.4	0.7	1.4	0.4	1.0
Manufacturing	34.9	34.0	28.6	24.5	33.0	32.1	21.4	31.6	17.0	22.0	26.3
Electricity, gas, water	0.8	1.4	2.6	1.1	1.2	1.6	1.0	0.9	1.0	0.9	1.1
Construction	7.8	7.3	7.0	7.8	7.0	11.63	7.3	6.6	6.1	8.1	6.4
Trade	9.2	11.5	11.3	8.9	5.9	11.1	17.2	16.3	23.4	19.3	17.4
Transportation	6.8	6.5	7.7	7.2	6.9	6.4	6.5	5.9	6.6	6.0	6.0
Finance	0.6	0.5	0.8	1.0	0.3	0.4	9.7	8.0	11.2	6.1	8.6
Community services	18.4	23.5	23.4	19.3	15.3	22.0	30.2	26.3	28.9	26.5	28.7

Source: R. Jackman, 'Do reform and unemployment go hand in hand? The prospect for Eastern Europe', *CentrePiece*, 2, summer 1997, 4.

control and GDP growth was in the range of 3 to 6 per cent. Although this performance was not sustained thereafter, indicating that the transformation process needs
to go even further (such as the need to ensure efficiency gains from privatization
and the protection of small shareholders), the republic's westernization process
was well under way.

Hungary was best placed to make the transition to the market, having introduced the most far-reaching economic reforms of the Soviet bloc in its final
days. These gave it a head start in that it already had *in situ* a rudimentary legal
and institutional structure to support a free-market economy. Accordingly, it pursued a middle course between 'big bang' and slow adjustment. Nonetheless, the
process was still a painful one, bringing recession between 1990 and 1993, when
GDP fell by 17 per cent, at the end of which period the current account deficit
registered 10 per cent of GDP. Against this background, the government elected
to introduce a more far-reaching stabilization programme in March 1995, aimed
at producing sustainable low-inflationary growth. Wages were contained in the
public sector, the currency was further devalued and expenditure cut. This paid
off, leading to a declining government deficit that (not including privatization
revenues) had fallen to 3.5 per cent of GDP by 1996 compared with 8.4 per cent
in 1994. By 1998, GDP was growing at 5.1 per cent and inflation was at 14.3 per
cent, almost half the figure for 1995 (28 per cent) and continued to fall. Privatization
was virtually completed, giving the private sector over 80 per cent of GDP by
1999 and employment figures representing over two-thirds of the labour force.
In turn, foreign direct investment (FDI) was encouraged, reaching $16 billion
cumulatively by late 1998 (aside from inter-company loans), equivalent to one-
third of GDP.

The laggards were led by Bulgaria, Romania and the Slovak Republic, which
reflected their deeper embroilment in the excesses of communism and corresponding reluctance to shed quickly its vestiges. Bulgaria, for example, proved loath to
relinquish state control over productive resources. It took a severe economic crisis
in 1996, when GDP shrank by 10 per cent, currency reserves plummeted to one
month of imports and inflation roared away (peaking at a monthly rate of 243 per
cent in February 1997) that the state was at last galvanized into serious action.
Long-postponed structural reforms were initiated, the IMF supported a currency
board to impose financial discipline, faltering privatization was accelerated and
more controlled prices were liberalized. Similarly, Romania only launched a
belated reform programme (February 1997) after several years of dismal economic performance and registering higher poverty rates than was usual for the
region. However, continued political instability impeded the pace of reform.
Again, the laggards proved most reluctant to release state-owned banks into the
private sector unlike the fast-track reform economies, such as Estonia, Hungary
and Poland. Only in 1999, a full decade after the revolutions did the laggards,
such as Croatia, Bulgaria and Romania, see the error of their ways and begin
to privatize the banking sector. Domestic banks by themselves could not make
much difference. By 1998, total bank assets in central and eastern Europe stood at
66 per cent of GDP, considerably below that of its westernized neighbours Austria

(266 per cent) and Germany (173 per cent). Foreign penetration was required and here the signs were encouraging, with foreign banks' share of the banking market in the region leaping from 20 per cent to 32 per cent during 1998 and continuing to rise thereafter.

The leaders proved more willing to accept the western prescription of macro-economic stabilization in combination with rapid liberalization. Reflecting on ten years of transition, a World Bank representative suggested: 'Market-oriented reforms, combined with social reforms and institutional strengthening have worked to turn former socialist, centrally-planned economies around and can put them on a sustainable path of economic growth and social inclusion' (Wolf 1999). Poland, one of those to grasp the nettle, witnessed a compound annual rate of economic growth between 1993 and 1998 of 5.6 per cent and by the latter date its real GDP stood 17 per cent above the level when transition began.

There can be general benefits in being a latecomer, not least in being able to embrace the latest technology and leapfrog outdated equipment. This is particularly true in the telecommunications field, in which the Czech Republic became the first former communist state to fully liberalize the market. In 1987, the EC recognized the significance of mobile communications and elected to introduce common standards. This led to GSM (Global System for Mobile communications) which by the 1990s was unofficially embraced as the world standard for second-generation digital telephony. This opened up eastern Europe to state-of-the-art telecommunications technology largely provided by western European manufacturers and systems providers. Indeed, it was in this area that FDI was most telling and widespread. Here, too, the telecommunications sell-off was at the forefront of the region's privatization initiatives. Indeed, in this sector, above all, there was a replication of the global trend for spectacular subscriber growth for mobile phone networks, attracting billions of dollars of investment. Deutsche Telecom led the way and by 1999 had the most extensive coverage, with interests stretching from central Europe to the Balkans and Russia. In the emerging markets of eastern Europe, where the majority existed on cash rather than credit transactions, pre-paid cards were favoured. By 1999, Slovenians were making around 40 per cent of their calls utilizing the GSM network, while even Romania, one of the poorer economies, boasted a high rate of mobile telephone use, reflecting the fact that mobiles were cheaper to purchase than a fixed line.

In the transition process, major financial aid and advice was being afforded by an array of western institutions: the PHARE (Poland and Hungary Assistance for Restructuring the Economy) programme, the European Bank for Reconstruction and Development (EBRD), established in 1991 with the specific intention of facilitating economic progress in former communist states, the IMF, the EU's European Investment Bank (EIB) and the World Bank Group. The World Bank, for example, began to provide systematic country economic memoranda, starting with the more advanced economies, such as Poland and Estonia, to assist them to meet the entrance criteria to join the EU (see below) through financing structural 'pre-accession' measures. In October 1997, the European Commission established a joint working group with the World Bank, the EBRD and EIB to see how best to coordinate their development programmes and attract private international financial institutions such as investment banks and financial corporations. International intervention generally had a positive impact, allowing governments to 'blame' the IMF and other institutions for the medicine of painful economic reform.

With the notable exception of Slovenia, the constituent parts of Yugoslavia did not benefit from the post-communist economic transformation process, because they descended into a bitter inter-ethnic conflict, known as the Yugoslav Civil War (1991–95). Moreover, Serbia later became embroiled in a no-win situation with the west over Kosovo, which resulted in the devastation of much of its economic infrastructure. This was unfortunate, to say the least, because Yugoslavia, an early outcast from the Soviet bloc, already straddled its trade between east and west and was well placed to deepen its links with the latter. The Serb-orchestrated civil war put paid to that and Serbia became an international pariah, subject to western economic sanctions. Apart from a brief period when its role in ending the civil war brought Serbia some external economic relief, it remained an outcast unable to access loans from the IMF and other international lending institutions. Unlike the rest of the Balkans, the international community was not prepared to assist with Serbia's economic development until its long-standing president, Slobodan Milošević, fell from power. As Chris Patten, the member of the European Commission responsible for External Relations, told the Southeastern Europe Regional Funding Conference on 29 March 2000: 'while Milošević is in power, the serious [aid] money stays in the vault'. Serbia was isolated economically while the west sought to nurture neighbouring countries, such as Macedonia and Croatia. In March 2000, Macedonia was the first nation from the old Yugoslavia to conclude a stabilization and association agreement with the EU. This held out some hope for the future yet the fact remained that Macedonia's economy traditionally relied heavily on trade with Serbia. Similarly, Montenegro, formally part of the new Yugoslavia with Serbia, attempted to westernize its economy. But its common border limited the extent to which it could break with its more powerful neighbour, Serbia, which normally supplied 60 per cent of its food requirements. When Montenegro opened its frontier with Albania Serbia responded by blocking imports through imposing police checkpoints on the routes between Serbia and Montenegro. In view of this situation, the west cautioned Montenegro not to declare independence lest it trigger a Serb invasion. Milošević's hold onto power could be explained by his ruthlessness, as expressed by his loyal security forces, the divided opposition and the fact that he deliberately nurtured the domestic black economy to engender some loyalty from those who profited from it. Finally, Milošević went too far and provoked NATO's military intervention over Kosovo in 1999, which led to his fall from power, opening the way for Serbia to be embraced by the EU once it had stabilized and recovered from the ethnic struggles of recent years.

A negative economic legacy of NATO's war against Serbia over Kosovo was a blocked river Danube because bridges were destroyed by air strikes. The river rises in Germany, whence it flows through Austria, Slovakia, Hungary, Slovenia,

Croatia, Serbia, Romania, Bulgaria, Moldova and Ukraine. Once a nodal trade artery between central and eastern Europe, traffic on the Danube reached a peak of 100 million tons in 1987, but had fallen back dramatically to 19 million tons by 1994. The emerging economies then began to reverse the trend, especially Bulgaria, Romania and Slovakia, all of whom relied on river transport to ship bulky low-value goods. The blockage meant that Bulgaria and Romania could not move agricultural and raw material products upstream, and the region's expanding tourist industry was affected. Cruises through Serbia, Romania and Bulgaria became impractical and voyages had to stop at Bucharest. All this led the Bucharest-based Danube Commission, comprised of ten countries with direct interests in the river, to seek international aid to remove the obstructions and rebuild the bridges. Clearing and bridge rebuilding began with EU financial assistance.

Europe in the global economy

In the final part of the twentieth century, the United States reasserted itself as the dominant global player. By January 2000, its economy had experienced 107 consecutive months of growth, the longest period of prosperity since the 1860s. Ronald Reagan's assumption of the presidency in January 1981 began the renaissance. 'Reaganomics' drove growth through tax concessions and a renewed, technology-driven Cold War arms race, which helped to consign the Soviet Empire to oblivion. The spin-offs from the latter did much to usher in the cyber-age, e-commerce and the Internet, which dramatically reduced business costs. Leading the field was Microsoft, which became the world's largest company and its founder, Bill Gates, the world's richest man. With the end of the Cold War, the process accelerated and information technology (IT) stocks led to record surges on the Wall Street stock market driven by the NASDAQ index, a trend which also moved to Europe, especially London. Analysts believed that the American economy was experiencing an upward phase of the S-curve, in which technological innovations improve productivity by leaps and bounds. A related view was that where the oil shocks of the 1970s produced slower growth and enhanced inflation, the IT 'shock' had the reverse effect. Arising from this, a sustainable American annual growth rate of 5 per cent was regarded by optimists as not beyond the realm of possibility.

Some of the American trends were evident in the European economy, but here growth was more sluggish than spectacular. Germany led the way, with 19.5 million Internet users by 1999 and 47.8 million projected by 2003. Again, Germany led Europe in online advertising revenue, which reached $92 million in 1999, representing 3 per cent of the worldwide online total. Over 25 per cent of the 80 million strong German population owned personal computers by 1999, with 10 per cent of them accessing the Internet. Britain was second to Germany, boasting five million subscribers online by 1999, but the rest of Europe was some way behind. European businesspeople generally were perceived to be too conservative when compared to their risk-taking American counterparts, who were more willing to face bankruptcy, which did not carry the same stigma.

European leaders recognized this shortcoming at the Lisbon summit of March 2000, when their chairman declared the EU's new ambition to become the 'most competitive and dynamic knowledge-based economy in the world' (Norman 2000). It was yet to be seen whether Europe would produce equivalent e-commerce businesses to the enormously successful Yahoo!, Hotmail and Priceline.com in the United States. Similarly, there was a fundamental difference in the American and European approaches to Internet access. American consumers paid for Internet access rather than for phone calls, whereas in Britain and the Continent ISPs (Internet Service Providers) were free but variable tariffs were charged for time on the World Wide Web (WWW). Accordingly, peak time daytime Internet access could be prohibitively expensive and served as a deterrent to wider Internet use. The Blair government, in particular, recognized this and sought to emulate the American system and lead Europe by example. But until Europe replicated the American IT infrastructure of broadband access, it would remain one step behind. Indeed, cynics dubbed the WWW, the 'world wide wait', for once America woke up, the speed of Internet access was considerably slowed as the European Internet gateways become overloaded. Within a few years, however, these impediments had been overcome as IT companies across Europe, with government encouragement, undertook major investments in Internet infrastructure.

Certainly, the instantaneous nature of global communications brought by cyber-space, with e-mails being sent to anywhere on Earth at the touch of a button and lengthy documents attached to them or quickly faxed down telephone lines, speeded up business activity enormously. In March 2000, Tony Blair, the then British Prime Minister, spoke of a 'new industrial revolution' founded on e-commerce and the Internet. Reflecting this, commentators made a distinction between the 'old economy' of long-established 'blue chip' companies and the 'new economy' centred on IT, which created overnight 'dot.com millionaires' in Britain. In March 2000, several 'new economy' performers with surging technology stocks displaced some long-established names from the FTSE 100 (the leading companies on the London Stock Exchange). There was undoubtedly immense potential in the new economy, especially in driving down distribution and staffing costs, some of which had already been realized, but equally evidence that many of the high-tech companies were a long way from even realizing a profit. The virtual worldwide electronic marketplace had its attractions (for example, for consumers living in remote rural areas), but equally there were competing drawbacks. A reluctance to disclose credit card details (in Germany, in any event, only one in seven consumers had a credit card!), the desire to shop personally and inspect goods at first hand, added costs of delivery and the frequent stipulation to spend minimum amounts, all acted as deterrents. In fact, e-tailing has been compared with mail order, which also came to Europe from across the Atlantic. It too created instant millionaires but ultimately failed to achieve a dominant market position. In Britain during 1999, mail order represented only around 5 per cent of the retail market. The real transformation would come when the majority of the population in the industrialized world could access the Internet via interactive televisions rather than through a computer. Then, as with mobile phones, which were transformed from a luxury to a household item in a matter of a few years, the IT revolution will consume the general population. By the second decade of the twenty-first century, these trends were apparent as Internet shopping took hold, offering a greater range of goods, competitive prices and the convenience of home delivery at a time when rising fuel costs made consumers more reluctant to make long journeys in their cars to out-of-town superstores.

Globalization brought the liberalization of trade barriers, deregulation of markets, the spread of multinationals, the freer movement of capital and a trend towards free trade promoted by the General Agreement on Tariffs and Trade (GATT) and its successor the World Trade Organization (WTO). Under the impact of globalization, the EU as a whole sought to improve its export performance while at the same time maintaining a degree of protection for sensitive industries. In the motor car industry, for example, Voluntary Export Restraints were deployed to restrict outside competition, especially from Japan. The bicycle industry faced being swamped by cheap Chinese makes between 1989 and 1991, which persuaded Brussels to apply a massive 34.4 per cent anti-dumping duty to counter the threat. Similarly, in 1998, suppliers of unbleached cotton were faced with anti-dumping duties, leading India to bring the issue before the WTO.

The EU's stance smacked of trying to have it both ways. Indeed, Susan Strange (1998, 107) considered that 'the trade policies of Europe are an inconsistent mix of openness and protection'. The protectionist inclinations of the EU received a jolt when the WTO, with greater clout than the GATT, was established in January 1995. This caused further ructions between the EU and the United States, which wanted the Europeans to minimize or remove their protectionist measures. The 'banana war' was a case in point. The EU's complex set of quotas, tariffs and licences for bananas reflected the historical trading links with its members' former colonies. The arrangements discriminated against Central American banana producers and their largely American distributors. The issue came before the WTO in 1998, which deemed the arrangements illegal. However, the EU's response did not satisfy the United States. Another ongoing dispute concerned growth hormones in meat, as used in American cattle, which the EU banned on health grounds. Although the WTO found against the EU, it allowed it to submit scientific evidence to substantiate its case. In an effort to pressurize the EU, the United States imposed limited sanctions. Finally, the United States applied pressure on the EU to 'open up' to imports of steel and other manufactured goods from struggling economies, such as Russia, but the European Commission steadfastly resisted.

The EU was not alone, of course, in instigating trade protection measures, and as well as benefiting from them could suffer in equal measure. It estimated, for example, that India's import restrictions denied an annual increase in exports to the world's biggest democracy of potentially one billion euros. Again, the European Commission (1999) calculated that the American tax treatment of foreign corporations gave American firms an annual export subsidy of around two billion euros, a state of affairs that it sought to change through the WTO. Then, too, Chile and South Korea's discriminatory taxes on alcoholic drinks had a negative impact on the EU, the world's biggest producer and exporter of spirits.

The commission used trade for political purposes. The EU had a vested interest in ensuring a stable eastern Mediterranean, not least because of the oil factor. To this end, it instigated a customs union agreement with Turkey, which sought to strengthen its links to the west. Coming into force in January 1996, the accord mutually removed tariffs on industrial products and Turkey embraced the EU's Common External Tariff, leading to a significant fall in her average tariff level. This agreement was preceded in November 1995 by the European-Mediterranean Partnership, which was concluded in Barcelona between the EU and Algeria, Cyprus, Egypt, Israel, Jordan, Lebanon, Malta, the Palestinian Authority, Syria, Tunisia and Turkey, to facilitate political, economic and social dialogue. In general terms, the partnership sought to provide the framework for a common area of peace and stability, collaboration in the problem areas of immigration and drug smuggling, the extension of EU economic assistance and, by the year 2010, the possibility of a free trade area in industrial products. Turkey, which applied for full EU membership in 1987, was denied candidate status until December 1999 because of its human rights record. It now has to meet the Copenhagen criteria (see below). By dangling before the Turks the long-cherished possibility of full membership, the EU hoped to promote reconciliation with Turkey's historic enemy, Greece, over territorial disputes in the Aegean and the long-running Cyprus dispute. In similar vein, the EU concluded partnership and cooperation agreements with Russia, Belarus, the Ukraine and several other states from the former Soviet Union. Again, these sought to enhance trade and to provide a measure of economic stability to entrench democratic tendencies (see Chapter 13).

The oil shocks derailed the global economy in the 1970s. Indeed, prices increased sixfold between 1971 and 1973, with a further gallop at the end of the decade. Thereafter, aside from the brief period at the start of the Gulf Crisis, arising from Iraq's invasion of Kuwait in August 1990, prices fell, reaching a low of $10 a barrel by the late 1990s, which was lower in real terms than the 1960s. There were three main reasons for this decline in prices. First, demand fell as the economies in Europe, Southeast Asia and North America slowed down at various points and energy conservation strategies were implemented. Second, oil sources outside the Arab-dominated oil cartel, OPEC (Organization of Petroleum Exporting Countries), came on stream, for example from the North Sea. Third, disunities within OPEC, especially between Iran, Iraq and Saudi Arabia, rendered it difficult to agree production targets. By the turn of the century, however, there were clear signs of a changing climate, which threatened sustained economic growth. The economies in Europe and Asia were in a recovery phase, while the United States continued its spectacular growth, all of which combined to push up demand for oil. The new oil producers of the 1980s no longer had considerable stocks, leading Saudi Arabia, Kuwait and the United Arab Emirates to reassert their former dominance of the market. The fall in oil prices, although it did not entirely dispel the divisions within OPEC, did serve to persuade its members to reduce oil production in 1999 and to restrict the enlargement of output below American desires in March 2000.

Constraints on growth

During the 1990s, the lightly regulated American economy returned unemployment figures that were virtually half those of the EU. Unemployment became a problem for Europe in the 1970s, as traditional industries declined, and it refused to go away. By 1998, the number out of work across the EU stood at 18 million. Europe's persistently high unemployment since the 1970s generated a debate over its causes and potential solutions. Some critics associated the jobless figures with the 'Continental model': excessive state spending ratios, overregulated labour markets and high tax rates. Aldcroft (1993, 288) identified a key disparity: 'In most EC countries the labour force was growing at a faster rate than previously at a time when the state of economic activity was considerably lower'. Then, too, there was the problem of a relative lack of export success in world markets, which has limited job creation.

The focus of the debate over the reasons for high EU unemployment shifted to supply-side rigidities. The OECD (1994), in particular, identified these as a fundamental cause. It was suggested that although the SEM may have removed many obstacles in the markets for goods and services, labour market impediments remained. On the employers' side, they were penalized for taking on extra workers through increased taxes and were not free to 'hire and fire' according to demand, which acted as a disincentive to add to the workforce. On the employees' side, relatively high taxes on low incomes persuaded many low-skilled workers to remain on the dole.

As Table 12.3 indicates, all EU countries experienced low unemployment rates from 1961–73 when, with the end of the 'Golden Age', the jobless figures rocketed upwards. Since 1990, the figures became more variable, reflecting different rates of economic growth. With Ireland, for instance, where the economy was boosted by massive injections of EU aid, the fastest rate of economic growth (around 11.9 per cent) was achieved through the 1990s. Unemployment tumbled in unison, from a high of 15.5 per cent in the late 1980s to 4.7 per cent in 2000. Similarly, Britain, the Netherlands, Luxembourg and Portugal achieved respectable growth rates and their rates of unemployment also diminished. The two driving engines of EU growth, Germany and France, experienced unacceptably high rates of unemployment in the final decade of the twentieth century, which helps to explain the relatively poor economic performance of the EU as a whole. As well as structural impediments, Germany faced the unique burden of absorbing the backward economy of the former East Germany and its largely unskilled workforce. By American standards, the EU's unemployment returns were excessive, with only Austria, the Netherlands and Luxembourg achieving unemployment rates below that of the United States.

A major difference between the United States and the EU was in job creation. Over the period 1991–95, total employment rose by 1.3 per cent per annum, whereas in the EU it fell by 0.5 per cent a year. Luxembourg and Ireland were exceptional in equalling or exceeding the American expansion in employment. Later in the decade, the EU began to improve its employment figures, recording a

Table 12.3 Annual average rates of unemployment (% of the civilian labour force)

	1961–1973	1974–1985	1986–1990	1991–1995	1996	1997	1998 Estimate
Austria	1.4	2.5	3.4	3.7	4.3	4.4	4.4
Belgium	2.0	7.7	8.7	8.5	9.7	9.2	8.8
Denmark	0.9	6.4	6.4	8.6	6.8	5.6	5.1
Finland	2.3	4.8	4.2	13.5	14.8	12.7	11.4
France	2.2	6.4	9.7	11.1	12.4	12.4	11.9
Germany	0.7	4.2	5.9	7.3	8.9	9.9	9.4
Greece	4.2	3.8	6.6	8.3	9.6	9.6	9.6
Ireland	5.7	10.6	15.5	14.5	11.6	9.8	7.8
Italy	5.2	7.0	9.6	10.3	12.0	12.1	12.2
Luxembourg	0.0	1.7	2.1	2.5	3.0	2.8	2.8
Netherlands	1.3	7.1	7.4	6.4	6.3	5.2	4.0
Portugal	2.5	6.9	6.1	5.6	7.3	6.8	4.9
Spain	2.8	11.3	18.9	20.9	22.2	20.8	18.8
Sweden	2.0	2.4	2.0	7.2	9.6	9.9	8.2
UK	2.0	6.9	9.0	9.5	8.2	7.0	6.3
EUR 11	2.5	6.6	9.4	10.4	11.8	11.8	10.9
EUR 15	2.4	6.4	8.9	10.0	10.9	10.6	10.0

Source: European Commission, *Spring Economic Forecasts*, Brussels: European Commission, 30 March 1999.

rise in employment of 1.1 per cent in 1998, a figure comparable with the American return (1.5 per cent).

The late 1990s saw unemployment in Britain and the Netherlands fall to well below the EU average. In both instances, employment creation throughout the decade was impressive, with job creation in the Netherlands increasing in the order of 15–20 per cent by its close. Cynics pointed out that the measurement of unemployment had changed, leading to people who previously would have been recorded as out-of-work moving to non-employment categories, especially disability and early retirement. The French President, Jacques Chirac, commented that 'if unemployment is lower in Britain than France, it owes no thanks to the virtues of economic liberalism but because the English fiddle their figures' (Nickell and Van Ours 2000, 7). There was some truth in this. By 1998, some 32 per cent of the 55 to 64 age group among Dutch males were on disability benefit, with a corresponding figure for Britain of 20 per cent. This represented a seismic shift since the early 1970s, when in both nations the percentages were less than 10 per cent. Nickell and Van Ours (2000, 31) suggested that the increase was not due to a greater level of disability *per se*, but rather to the two governments making it easier to claim this form of benefit, which 'tend to be higher and more secure than unemployment benefit, since there is little pressure to take up work'. Moreover, pressure from central government on benefit offices to reduce the politically sensitive headline unemployment rate often led their staff to encourage the unemployed who struggle to find work onto disability benefits. With employment buoyant, the New Labour government in Britain, which took office in May 1997, began to tighten up the regulations, not least because of the escalating cost of incapacity benefits. But a political backlash led it to backtrack and impose the new rules only on future rather than existing claimants. For the able unemployed, both Britain and the Netherlands imposed a tightening of the benefits regime, with the Netherlands, via its 'active labour market policy', leading the way in applying sanctions to the unemployed who persistently refused work. Both countries also devoted increasing attention to labour training schemes to help the unemployed into work. All this occurred against a background of weakening trade union power in Britain and the Netherlands which dates from the early 1980s, leading to union representation becoming far less prevalent in the expanding private sector, a fact that encouraged job creation.

The generally high level of EU unemployment led the Essen European Council summit in December 1994 to identify five key areas to help alleviate the problem. These were investing in vocational training to improve employment opportunities, increasing the employment-intensiveness of growth, cutting non-wage labour costs, improving labour market policies and providing better help to groups that are particularly prone to unemployment. Later, the Treaty of Amsterdam of October 1997, which amended the Treaty of Rome, enshrined employment creation as a definite policy objective. The treaty also established an advisory Employment Committee to monitor member states' employment and labour market strategies and to provide advice. In March 2000, at the Lisbon summit, the EU unveiled a strategy for bolstering employment and competitiveness, two themes that would continue to galvanize attention.

In 1900, the typical American life span was 47 years; by the end of the century it was 76. The increase in average longevity is a global phenomenon (see Table 12.4), which created mounting pressures on state-funded pension schemes. For example, the Italian funding of pensions was consuming 15 per cent of GDP by 1997, reflecting the fact that the population in Italy had the highest life expectancy in Europe. Again, Germany's policy was to pay 70 per cent of a retired person's former salary as a state pension, a level of generosity that is unsustainable in the long term. Indeed, a 'pension time bomb' is ticking whereby, with birth rates falling and unemployment generally higher than before, the prospect looms of there being more pensioners than workers. The Thatcher government in Britain recognized the problem to a degree when it controversially severed the link between state pensions and average earnings. But its attempt dramatically to slash central government spending ultimately failed: by 1997 the figure, as a proportion of GDP, was similar to that when the Conservatives took office after a period of 'tax and spend' Labour. The inexorable rise in welfare spending was a European-wide phenomenon, which burdened and constrained central government. The French social security deficit, for example, stood at FF244 billion by 1997. France was criticized as 'one of the most state-dominated nations in the EU, with a costly welfare state (obligatory social charges are around 45 per cent of GDP, compared with about 35 per cent in America), a large public sector and a generous provision of public services' (Andrews 1999, 45). An interim solution to the funding of

Table 12.4 The world's oldest populations

Country	Percentage of Population over 60
Sweden	17.3
Italy	16.0
Greece	15.9
Norway	15.9
Belgium	15.8
United Kingdom	15.2
Denmark	15.2
Germany	15.2
France	14.9
Spain	14.9

Source: World Health Organization, 1998.

public pensions would be to lift the age of retirement (the United States did so in 1983 when it went up from 65 to 69), but this carried political implications. The issue of funding state pensions and other welfare benefits will not go away, but the political consequences of reform acts as a powerful disincentive for governments to embrace radical change.

Europe's expanding frontiers

The redrawing of the map of Europe has been a constant feature of the past millennium. Its driving force was war and rampant nationalism, with the continent being responsible for over two-thirds of the twentieth century's 110 million war-related deaths. The great majority of these occurred before 1946, and the end of the Second World War marked a turning point. Thereafter, nationalism, except in isolated instances, such as the Yugoslav Civil War, Northern Ireland, the Basque province of Spain and Cyprus, has not led to conflict. Indeed, the EU, which sought to downplay nationalist tendencies, became the great propellant of change. The question of 'What is Europe?' became ever more pertinent. Once Mont Blanc was its highest mountain, but after the collapse of the Soviet Union, it was to be found in the Caucasus. Europe's expanding geographical area reflected the momentous political changes that followed the end of the Cold War. After the accession of Finland and Sweden, the EU gained a 13,000-kilometre border with the Russian Federation. The latter, with its 'Wild West' style economy, where tax evasion, fraud, unpaid wages and the Russian Mafia were the order of the day, was likely to remain the eastern edge of the EU. To the south, however, the EU was poised to expand further its Mediterranean dimension by incorporating Cyprus, whilst trade agreements further afield with the likes of Israel and Malta through the 'EU-Mediterranean Agreement' may presage the eventual extension of membership around the 'Inland Sea'.

It proved easier for the leading economies of eastern Europe (Hungary, Poland and the Czech Republic) to procure NATO membership than to gain entry into the

EU. Although the EU Edinburgh summit of 1992 recognized that an expansion of membership eastwards was possible, no timetable was laid down. In the meantime, only associate membership was accorded to former Soviet bloc economies, which merely afforded limited trade concessions, while EU protection remained in sensitive areas, such as agriculture and textiles. This led to resentment, a feeling among the region's government that the Community wanted to prise open their markets while protecting its own. The European Council laid down conditions for full membership at Copenhagen in June 1993, which included stable democracy and a market economy that could withstand the considerable pressures of membership. There, the position remained until July 1997 when 'Agenda 2000' was launched by the European Commission, an ambitious programme to expand the EU in the early part of the new century.

At this point, the Commission regarded Poland, the Czech Republic, Hungary, Slovenia, Cyprus and Estonia as most likely to meet the Copenhagen criteria first. These became earmarked as 'first-wave' applicants. The 'second-wave' countries (Bulgaria, Latvia, Lithuania, Romania and Slovakia) were expected to join later. In October 1999, the rules of entry were altered when the European Commission promised that the quicker a country underwent reforms, the faster it could expect to join the EU. With the Balkans still unstable and signs of a reversion to a milder form of socialism in parts of central and eastern Europe, this move was suffused with political as well as economic calculations. 'For the first time since the fall of the Roman Empire', remarked Romani Prodi, the Commission's president, 'we have the opportunity to unite Europe – and this time it will not be by force of arms but on the basis of shared ideals and agreed common rules' (Fletcher 1999).

By December 1999, thirteen candidates were on the official list for eventual membership with the first expected to be admitted in 2004. There were enormous implications attached to enlargement of this magnitude. The threat of political paralysis in decision-making saw the extension of qualified majority voting in the Amsterdam Treaty. This process needed to go further still, but there were differences among members over the areas to be encapsulated. To allow in so many new members under existing rules threatened to bankrupt the EU, not least because of their relative backwardness. Already over the period 1994–99, the Structural Funds, the financial component of regional development policy, were consuming one-third of total EU spending. The European Commission therefore proposed capping total spending on the backward regions to 0.46 per cent of EU GNP and to restrict the funding for any one member to 4 per cent of its GDP. The 'Objective One' regions, wherein GDP per capita represented less than 75 per cent of the EU average, comprised one-quarter of the community's population in 1997. Established by the Treaty of European Union, the Objective One regions were seen to suffer from a multitude of handicaps, including poor infrastructure (transport, energy and telecommunications), weak industrial structures with outmoded production methods, backward agricultural techniques and doggedly high unemployment, especially among the young, unskilled and older workers. The main beneficiaries of Cohesion Funding were Ireland and the Mediterranean Club. All of Greece (often portrayed as the 'black sheep' of the EU) qualified for Objective

One funding, and by 1998, EU funding to modernize its infrastructure amounted to 3 per cent of its GNP. Unusually, Greeks were more likely to use public transport than to own private cars. After Athens lost the bid to stage the centennial Olympic Games, the EU ploughed in seven billion ecus to transform the capital's infrastructure, including a new international airport, a metamorphosis that persuaded the Olympic Committee to award the 2004 Games to Greece. The Mediterranean members were naturally concerned as to whether they would continue to receive such favourable attention once the eastern enlargement occurred. Already, as from March 1998, tighter spending limits eliminated some of Britain's poorer regions from qualifying for 'Objective One' status. New objectives were defined for the Structural Funds over the period 2000–2006, which reflected a further tightening of eligibility criteria. The new Objective One was restricted to regions where GDP per capita was below 75 per cent of the EU average, consuming two-thirds of the Structural Funds budget. The new Objective Two would cover the economic and social rehabilitation of regions outside the scope of Objective One that were experiencing structural adjustment problems. The new Objective Three would coordinate the development of human resources beyond the regions that fell within Objective One eligibility.

Similarly, the CAP, the largest component of the EU budget, would need adjustment in view of the substantial farming communities in many of the prospective new entrant economies. When it was introduced, the CAP resolved the EEC's food self-sufficiency problem but its guaranteed farm prices (well above world market prices) proved costly. The ensuing controversies surrounding 'butter mountains' and 'wine lakes' were symptomatic of the overproduction problems surrounding the CAP, the generosity of which did not discriminate between efficient and inefficient producers. As the recipient of the largest slice of farm subsidies, France was most resistant to change. Serious reform began only in 1992, following which the organization of the markets in arable crops, beef, veal, milk and wine was changed. Intervention prices were set to fall while farmers were compensated with increased aid with a view to improving global competitiveness. Agriculture in the accession countries would be assisted with prior funding to assist in the adjustment process. At the same time, EU membership was liable to create great hardship among the small-scale farmers of candidate countries, especially in Poland, where 26 per cent of the working population was engaged in agriculture in 1999. Indeed, the Polish Peasants' Party estimated that just 200,000 of the country's two million farms would remain after the joining process was complete.

Europe at the turn of the new millennium

By January 2000, the American economic boom had created 20 million jobs, reducing unemployment to a 30-year low. Britain, which traditionally had followed the American rather than the European economic cycle, was experiencing a more modest boom, achieving an annual average growth rate of 2.9 per cent over the period 1995–99, below the American performance (3.9 per cent), but considerably better than the euro-zone economies (2.1 per cent). After British unemployment touched almost three million in the 1990–92 recession, by the start of the new century it had fallen to below 1.4 million, the best figure for two decades, and two million extra jobs were generated. In the EU generally, following a recession in 1992–93, recovery began, haltingly at first, in 1994, stuttering in the mid-1990s, but strengthening from 1996. Because the EU, like the United States, to a large extent traded with itself, its economic recovery was not adversely affected by the financial and economic shocks in the Far East, Russia and Latin America. Indeed, by 1998 exports represented only 9.7 per cent of the GDP of the EU membership and 13.7 per cent of the eleven euro-zone members. That year the EU inflation rate fell to 1.6 per cent, reflecting the slowest rate of price increase for forty years. The factors driving the recovery included the favourable inflationary environment, increasing profits stimulating investment, a modest (by recent standards) rate of nominal wage growth and improving labour productivity. Over the course of 1998, EU unemployment fell from 10.6 to 10 per cent, a welcome improvement, and by 1999, 16.3 million (9.2 per cent) were out of work, with the figures continuing to fall. In the spring of 2000, the European Commission forecast that four million new jobs would be created by the close of 2001, which, if borne out, would reduce unemployment to 14.4 million. Nevertheless, the proportion of out-of-work remained both historically high and considerably in excess of the United States and Japan. Moreover, the headline EU rate disguised above-average returns among certain member states (for example, Spain, Italy, France and Finland).

Globalization was also driving the process of borderless capitalism and it became increasingly difficult to speak of 'the European model'. Even the French embarked on the privatization road, which embraced leading names such as French Telecom and the motor car manufacturer Renault. By the turn of the century hostile takeovers were more liable to succeed than fail. Vodafone took over its German rival Mannesmann in February 2000 following on recently successful takeovers in British and French banking and energy and Italian insurance and telecoms. Shareholders, big and small, could not resist the rewards stemming from a takeover, with Vodafone's bid a prime example. Furthermore, rationalization was a logical progression from the more cut-throat competition stemming from globalization, deregulation, the single market and the single currency zone. Reflecting this, cross-border mergers rose from less than one-third of European mergers by volume between 1990 and 1998 to almost half by 1999.

Europe was experiencing both widening and deepening: widening through taking on board a tranche of new members; deepening through the single currency and other mechanisms that spread the influence of Brussels and may lead in time, inexorably, to the creation of a European 'super-state' to rival the United States. Gorbachev's desire to see a 'common European home' embracing the states of the former Soviet Union now looked a more distant prospect than it did, following the optimism that accompanied the lowering of the hammer and sickle from the Kremlin in December 1991. Although the Cold War was over, there remained a perceptible division in Europe between the EU and the Commonwealth of Independent States. This divide, although not having the ideological overtones and military posturing of the Cold War, seemed liable to remain an enduring feature of the New World Order. So too did the trend towards a two-tier Europe within the EU, already reflected by the single currency and liable to be accentuated by the incorporation of new members from central and eastern Europe and beyond.

At the start of the twentieth century, Europe held a dominant position in the world economy led by Britain and Germany, challenged only by the distant United States and emerging Japan. However, it lost that dominance with the outbreak of the First World War, a process that was completed by the Second World War and its aftermath. It was to avert the possibility of a third conflagration that the European Economic Community was founded, which, by binding its member economies together, would make a further repeat unthinkable. In this aim it succeeded, and Europe, generally, has experienced an unprecedented period of peace since 1945 on which to embed economic prosperity and rising living standards. The exception was the Balkans, where Greece (1946–49) and Yugoslavia (1991–95) were engulfed in civil war, Romania (1989), which was unique in experiencing a bloody revolution when the Soviet bloc collapsed, and Kosovo (1999), which prompted NATO intervention to restore the outcast Albanian refugees to their homes. Southeastern Europe remained the most unstable region of the Continent, as it was a century before when two Balkan wars (1912–13) formed the prelude to the outbreak of global conflict. One outcome of the rekindled inter-ethnic hatreds was an exodus of refugees, who sought political asylum elsewhere in Europe, rather like the Jews who fled from Nazi persecution. In recognition of the dangers posed, the EU formed a stability pact for the region, with the intention of spending twelve billion euros over the period 2000–2006, half of which would go to Bulgaria and Romania. 'Those efforts', Chris Patten warned, 'must be matched by equal determination on the part of the countries of the region to deliver on reform'.

The Maastricht Treaty sought 'an ever closer union between the peoples of Europe'. Seven years later, the European Commission president considered that: 'Now, as never before, we have the chance to create a Europe in which all the peoples of this continent can live together in peace, security, freedom, justice and equality' (Fletcher 1999). As the new century loomed, some fundamental questions raised themselves: whether an EU of 28 or more members could function as effectively as one with fifteen; whether the single market and single currency would make the difference; whether the Balkans could be brought into the European mainstream; whether the economy of the Russian Federation could become truly westernized and integrated with the rest of Europe; whether the general prosperity prevailing would be undermined by rising oil prices, as in the 1970s; whether public expenditure was kept in check or got out of control; whether Europe could cure structural unemployment blackspots in an ultra-competitive age of globalization; whether the 'pensions time bomb' could be defused; whether Europe embraced the IT revolution as resolutely as the United States, the world's leading economy.

The OECD (1999) warned that an improved budgetary position could lead to a relaxed fiscal stance, thereby repeating 'the policy mistakes made in the late 1980s and early 1990s which led to a rapid deterioration in fiscal positions'. What seemed certain was that Europe would not recover the dominant position it enjoyed in 1900, but was likely to remain a middleweight performer in the global economy, which constantly looks to punch above its weight in heady rhetoric but never quite delivers the knockout blow.

Questions for discussion

1   Why did the European Community adopt the single European market and with what initial results?
2   What factors led to the introduction of a single currency?
3   Why was the post-communist economic performance of the transition economies so variable?
4   What were the implications of an enlarged European Union?
5   What were the major problems facing the European economy as it entered the twenty-first century?

13   The new millennium

Into the new millennium

As the new millennium opened to a fanfare of celebrations across the Continent, there seemed every reason to be sanguine about the prospects facing the European economy and especially for the engine of its growth, the European Union. In January 2002, the euro became legal tender as six billion new banknotes and 37 billion new coins came into circulation, with optimists predicting it would deepen integration and usher in a new upward growth trajectory. The European Central Bank pronounced that the single currency heralded the 'dawn of a new age'. Yet in retrospect it is evident that in this period of heady optimism, the seeds were sown for a severe global economic downturn originating in the flagging United States before the end of the first decade of the twenty-first century. Globalization, the interconnectedness of the world banking system and loosened financial regulations lay at the heart of this crisis, which engulfed European economies to different degrees. Between 2002 and 2008, there was a worldwide surge in cheap and irresponsible lending that formed the prelude to a severe downturn in the mature economies, which first afflicted the American economy and quickly spread to Europe.

The opening years of the new millennium were dominated by political shocks emanating from the United States: the attacks by Al Qaeda in September 2001 on the World Trade Center and the Pentagon and the associated American-led invasions of Afghanistan and Iraq under the auspices of the 'War on Terror'. Economically, these cataclysmic events exacerbated existing American weaknesses: a ballooning national debt, which kept rising remorselessly, overdependence on oil imports not least from the Middle East (still the most unstable region in the world) and a loss of manufacturing competitiveness, which slowed economic growth to a crawl in the world's biggest economy and sucked in imports. Against this backdrop, the performance of the euro-zone seemed relatively bright. Ironically, Germany, the traditional powerhouse of the European economy, proved the laggard, still absorbing the costs of assimilating the poorer eastern half inherited from the collapsed Soviet bloc, so that between 1996 and 2001, annual growth measured in GDP averaged 1.6 per cent against 2.8 per cent returned across the euro-zone. German difficulties made a huge difference, because as the largest Continental economy, Germany was responsible for one-third of euro-zone output. German dependence on manufactured exports was not helped by the rising euro as the new currency took hold, strengthening against a weakening dollar.

Whereas the matured industrialized economies could return only sluggish growth rates, the emerging economies, led by Brazil, China, India, Indonesia, Russia and Turkey, surged at record speed, with thirteen newly industrializing countries growing by 7 per cent or more per annum for a quarter of a century. In 2002, the term BRICs (Brazil, Russia, India, China) was coined by Goldman Sachs to distinguish the leading players. By 2011, the emerging economies were responsible for generating over three-quarters of global growth. Indeed, the impetus was barely curtailed by the financial crisis of 2007–8. Booming conditions continued, leading the IMF to predict that by 2013, emerging markets could account for over half of global output, as defined by purchasing-power parity. The Chinese alone generated a fifth of the world's manufactured goods, with China usurping Japan as the second largest economy after the United States. Shanghai, with a population of 23 million, was the fastest growing city in the world, one of eleven Chinese cities with populations exceeding six million, which stood in stark contrast to eleven members of the European Union with populations below this figure. China became the world's leading exporter and second largest importer. The Chinese, having for years been associated with cheap mass-produced products, also entered the higher end of the market, while also eclipsing the Americans in 2009 as the world's largest motor car market. Indeed, there was huge irony in China buying into American debt, becoming the United States' biggest foreign creditor ('America's credit card'), fuelling its huge appetite for Chinese manufactured exports. Commentators began suggesting that it was only a matter of time before the ultimate role reversal occurred and China became the world's leading economy. At the same time, in some respects, China was still trailing the industrialized world in key economic indicators. For example, the average salary there was less than the average unemployment benefits in the European Union. Again, India spawned an affluent middle class and developed a space programme yet the masses still lived in poverty, attracting overseas aid from Britain, which kept India as the leading recipient of its overseas aid programme because of the deprivation of the masses and in the hope of facilitating lucrative trade contracts. Moreover, the massive populations of the leading emerging economies (China and India having one billion plus populations) means that they have to keep generating more jobs than in rival matured economies, while incipient inflationary pressures were also a growing concern, threatening to erode the real value of their trade surpluses. China also could not escape from the European problem of a rising elderly population, which will exceed the numbers in work within a generation.

In contrast with previous historical epochs, the emerging economies have blurred the distinction between them and mature industrialized economies by moving into areas such as the manufacture of semi-conductors, pharmaceuticals and information technology services, which hitherto were the preserve of the latter. Thus, in the United States, between 1990 and 2008, only 600,000 new jobs were created in the manufacturing sector, with the government and healthcare industry by far the largest employers. Another key area where the rising powers adversely affected the mature economies was the energy field. China imported half its oil requirements and India an even bigger proportion, much of it from the Middle East. These Asian powers' huge and growing appetites for finite supplies of 'black gold' meant that even when the western powers went into recession, the price of oil per barrel remained abnormally high, helping to prevent a sustained recovery in the industrialized world. Thus, the price of oil largely remained around $100 a barrel, which in monetary terms equated to the cost following the oil shocks of the 1970s. Figures from the International Energy Agency suggest global oil consumption averaged 89 million barrels a day in 2011 against 88.3 million in 2010 and 76.6 million in 2000, representing a rise of 16 per cent over the first decade of the new millennium. The only blip occurred in 2008, when the price per barrel of oil fell from around $150 to $40, which owed as much to speculators as to underlying demand and supply. During 2011, notwithstanding sluggish economic growth in many areas, including Europe, world oil use still rose by 1 per cent, with crude averaging $111 a barrel. Much of the upsurge came from Asia, where Chinese demand was growing by 7–8 per cent per annum, making China the second biggest consumer of oil after the United States. This new phenomenon dictates that unlike in previous downturns, when crude oil prices fell and reduced fuel costs then helped to stimulate a recovery through a self-correction mechanism, the albatross of high energy bills will remain a constraint. Moreover, per-capita oil use across most of Asia is well below the west and nowhere near an optimum level, so the trend is bound to worsen over time as vehicle ownership mushrooms in the east. Already, the International Energy Agency predicts that global oil average consumption will reach 95 million barrels by 2015, equating to a 25 per cent increase in consumption over sixteen years.

Again breaking the normal trend, many of the emerging economies enjoyed surplus capital in abundance, some of which they invested in western economies, such as government bonds. China held more reserves in dollars and euros than any other country, accumulating over $3 trillion. One economist even spoke of the creation of a 'Southern Silk Road', an economic area forged by an emerging trade area across Asia, Latin America, Africa and the Middle East, which does not need either America or Europe. Moreover, emerging economy firms, searching for new markets, actively invested in western economies, such as Britain, through making acquisitions and thereby gaining a foothold in overseas territories. The Indian firm Tata took over Corus, an Anglo-Dutch steel company, in 2007 and a year later acquired Jaguar Land Rover, with its Halewood plant, shipping some cars in kit form to India for assembly to avoid import duties. Such activity was also beneficial to the host country through job creation, revitalizing otherwise moribund sectors. Moreover, emerging economies began taking on infrastructure projects to ensure that important trading partners remained in step with developments in transport. For instance, Dubai was providing the capital and engineering expertise to construct a new London dock on the River Thames, while the Chinese were engaged in modernizing Liverpool's dock facilities and providing the steel for the new Forth road bridge. By 2011, Jaguar Land Rover had been transformed from a loss-making motor car manufacturer to a marquee earning profits of £1 billion.

The following year its profits reached £1.5 million, selling 314,433 cars, with China representing the biggest growth area, where sales leapt by 71 per cent to exceed 50,000 units. Rolls Royce too saw its fortunes metamorphose as the burgeoning Chinese middle class eagerly bought luxury cars to symbolize their elevated status. Indeed, over the period under review, China spawned a million millionaires, and by 2011, was registering more patents than Germany. For China, Europe became its biggest export market (trade between the two was worth €1 billion a day by 2011), whereas the United States, having sent over a quarter of its exports to Europe in 1999, witnessed a contraction to 18 per cent by 2011 (albeit trade still worth $400 billion).

The emerging markets encroached on the French and Italian consumer goods exports, leading Italy to inherit the title of 'sick man of Europe' from Germany. When the billionaire media mogul Silvio Berlusconi came to power in 1994, after forming his own party, Forza Italia (Go Italy), named after a football chant, the expectation was that he would reinvigorate the moribund Italian economy. He lasted less than a year, returning in May 2001 and again in April 2008, as leader of a new centre-right party, People of Freedom, becoming Italy's longest serving post-war Prime Minister. Even when he enjoyed a comfortable majority, Berlusconi demonstrated that his promised economic liberalism was a facade. Entrenched corruption persisted and no serious effort was made to introduce meaningful reforms. The cheque was always in the post and nothing fundamental changed. Economic competitiveness continued to decline, corruption remained pervasive and private interests prevailed over public interests, not least Berlusconi's efforts to protect his business empire and evade prosecution for malpractices. Reminiscent of the posturing Mussolini, Berlusconi cut an equally absurd figure abroad, quickly losing credibility with fellow European leaders, leading him to seek solace on the fringes with the comical dictator of Libya, Muammer Gaddafi (with whom he concluded a treaty of eternal friendship in 2008) or Vladimir Putin, the semi-autocratic leader of Russia. Attending his final European summit meeting, Berlusconi fell asleep during the deliberations and when awake underlined the absurdity of his leadership through his insistence that nothing was wrong with the Italian economy because the beaches and hotels were still busy!

By 2005, several strong performances were evident within the euro-zone, nurtured by the European Central Bank's low interest rates policy, especially in Ireland, Spain and Greece, which took full advantage. Outside the currency union, the ten new European Union members returned strong growth figures as they played catch-up with the more prosperous and mature members in the west, benefiting from much lower labour costs, which attracted inward investment. Some 40 per cent of Chinese foreign direct investment, for example, was in southern and eastern Europe.

Germany transformed its fortunes to become the world's second largest exporter after China, leading it to buck the trend in western Europe and the United States by managing to reduce unemployment, which declined from 8.5 per cent of the workforce in 2007 to 7.1 per cent by 2011, leaving less than three million out of jobs, a situation last seen in 1992. Much of this success can be attributed to the

Schröder government's Agenda 2010 initiative, a reform programme that began in 2005. It attacked the escalating welfare budget by slashing unemployment benefits to incentivize work, cut red tape for businesses and forged a deal with the labour unions whereby they agreed to stabilize wages in return for the government enhancing job security. The latter was achieved through a 'short work' scheme. To avert layoffs, workers' hours were reduced, the government stepping in to meet the resultant shortfall in wages. By the programme's peak in May 2009, 1.5 million workers were involved at a cost of 4.6 billion euros per annum. Subsequently, the OECD estimated that the programme prevented 500,000 job losses during the economic downturn of 2008–9.

Alongside government action, initiatives in the private sector bolstered exports. The *Mittelstand,* comprising the numerous small and medium-size manufacturing companies, which were generally family-owned, found niche markets through concentrating on producing sophisticated goods that the emerging economies struggled to compete with. Because of their German identity, these firms placed greater emphasis than multinationals on employing native workers and again differed in not chasing short-term profits but looked more to the long term. One manufacturing sector, in which the *Mittelstand* figured heavily, was upmarket machine tools, which found ready markets in the emerging economies. Another key German manufacturing sector was the automobile industry, which bristled with high-quality marquees such as Audi, BMW, Daimler and Porsche. The opening of the emerging markets provided a welcome surge in demand, with China contributing a quarter of BMW's global profits. Volume manufacturers also excelled through penetrating emerging markets, leading Volkswagen to overtake Toyota as the world's leading motor car manufacturer in 2011. The United States remained the largest market for German marquees and remained ahead of China in this period. Finally, German exports were given an enormous boost by adhesion to the euro, which helped to keep down the prices of manufactured goods, enhancing the superior competitiveness of German labour against other euro-zone members, with around 80 per cent of Germany's trade surplus deriving from trade with the remainder of the European Union.

The expansion of the European Union

To join the ranks of the European Union, a state needed to fulfil the political and economic criteria laid down by the Copenhagen criteria (1993), which demanded a stable democratic government with a fully functioning judiciary that upheld the rule of law and had associated institutions in place. There was unprecedented expansion during the first decade of the new millennium, yet certain unspoken parameters existed. The European Union might, for example, eventually embrace some of the bigger players in the former Soviet Union like Ukraine but is unlikely ever to contemplate incorporating the Russian Federation, which, under Putin, reverted to a semi-autocratic style of leadership with the semblance but not the reality of democratic government. Nor, despite lip service to the contrary, is it foreseeable that Turkey will ever join because of certain ever-present impediments (see below). The actual process leading to membership could be protracted or relatively brief, depending on the circumstances in each case, application being followed by a pre-accession agreement as a prelude to the ratification of the final accession treaty, which every member state needed to approve.

By 2010, the European Union boasted a total population of over 500 million people (three-quarters of whom lived in urban areas), representing 7.3 per cent of the global population, covered 4.4 million square kilometres, with a nominal GDP, measured in purchasing power parity, of one-fifth of the world economy. There were two waves of expansion at the start of the millennium. In 2004, a swathe of new members were added (Cyprus, the Czech Republic, Estonia, Hungary, Latvia, Lithuania, Malta, Poland, Slovakia and Slovenia) in the largest enlargement to date. Three years later, in January 2007, Bulgaria and Romania joined the ranks. Alongside this, the euro-zone expanded to encompass seventeen members with Slovenia (2007), Cyprus and Malta (2008), Slovakia (2009) and Estonia (2011) adopting the single currency. Entry into the euro-zone was a natural progression provided the Maastricht convergence criteria were met and no opt-out was negotiated. The fresh entrants were not without their problems, leading the new Balkan members and Hungary to be warned about their transgressions.

The sheer size of the European enterprise generated some outwardly impressive statistics. The European Union is the largest economy in the world, the largest exporter, the biggest importer of goods and services and the best trading partner of several key economic actors (China, India and the United States, for example) in the developed and developing world. Again, by 2010, 161 of the top 500 largest corporations in the world based their headquarters within the European Union. Taken in aggregate terms, the economic performance of the European Union was respectable for much of the period under review. In May 2007, for instance, unemployment stood at 7 per cent, inflation at 2.2 per cent and the public deficit at –0.9 per cent of GDP. However, average economic indicators can be misleading and tend to disguise the fact that there were hugely varying individual performances and the worst performers began to threaten to bring down the edifice.

Growth figures for the members of the European Union were relatively bright in the period 2000–06, but the crisis emanating from the United States sent shock waves reverberating through the European financial system. Governments became weighed down with increasing debt burdens and there was a downward trend, with several economies recording negative growth figures.

Turkey became an increasingly important economic force in the period under review, coinciding with the premiership of Recep Tayyip Erdogan, leader of the conservative Justice and Development Party, which won successive elections in 2002, 2007 and 2011, enjoying an increasing share of the vote, which rose from 34 to 49 per cent. With a popular mandate, the government set about transforming Turkey's negative image as a country of political instability and military coups, eventually feeling confident enough to oust the generals associated with political interference. Erdogan continued the reforms begun in 1983 to open up the economy and orientate it towards a market-based model with an increasing role for the private sector. Through cutting government controls on foreign trade and

Table 13.1 Real GDP growth rate: volume percentage change on previous year

	2000	2001	2002	2003	2004	2005	2006	2007	2008	2009	2010	2011
EU 27	3.9	2.2	1.3	1.4	2.5	2.0	3.3	3.2	0.3	-4.3	2.0	1.5f
Eurozone	3.8	2.0	0.9	0.7	2.2	1.7	3.3	3.0	0.4	-4.3	1.9	1.4f
Belgium	3.7	0.8	1.4	0.8	3.3	1.7	2.7	2.9	1.0	-2.8	2.3	1.9f
Bulgaria	5.7	4.2	4.7	5.5	6.7	6.4	6.5	6.4	6.2	-5.5	0.2	1.8f
Czech Republic	4.2	3.1	2.1	3.8	4.7	6.8	7.0	5.7	3.1	-4.7	2.7	1.7f
Denmark	3.5	0.7	0.5	0.4	2.3	2.4	3.4	1.6	-0.8	-5.8	1.3	1.0
Germany	3.1	1.5	0.0	-0.4	1.2	0.7	3.7	3.3	1.1	-5.1	3.7	3.0
Estonia	14.0	6.3	6.6	7.8	6.3	8.9	10.1	7.5	-3.7	-14.3	2.3	7.5f
Ireland	9.3p	4.8p	5.9p	4.2p	4.5p	5.3p	5.3p	5.2p	-3.0p	-7.0p	-0.4p	0.9p
Greece	3.5p	4.2p	3.4p	5.9p	4.4p	2.3b	5.95p	3.0p	2.3b	-3.3p	-3.5p	-6.8f
Spain	5.0	3.7	2.7	3.1	3.3	3.6	4.1	3.5	0.9	-3.7	-0.1	0.7
France	3.7	1.8	0.9	0.9	2.5	1.8	2.5	2.3	-0.1	-2.7	1.5	1.7f
Italy	3.7	1.9	0.5	0.0	1.7	0.9	2.2	1.7	-1.2	-5.1	1.5	0.2f
Cyprus	5.0	4.0	2.1	1.9	4.2	3.9	4.1	5.1	3.6	-1.9	1.1	0.5f
Latvia	6.1	7.3	7.2	7.6	8.9	10.1	11.2	9.6	-3.3	-17.7	-0.3	5.3f
Lithuania	12.3	6.7	6.8	10.3	7.4	7.8	7.8	9.8	2.9	-14.8	1.4	5.9
Luxembourg	8.4	2.5	4.1	1.5	4.4	5.4	5.0	6.6	0.8	-5.3	2.7	1.1f
Hungary	4.2	3.7	4.5	3.9	4.8	4.0	3.9	0.1	0.9	-6.8	1.3	1.7f
Malta		-1.5	2.8	0.1	-0.5	3.7	2.8	4.3	4.3	-2.6	2.9	2.1f
Netherlands	3.9	1.9	0.1	0.3	2.2	2.0	3.4	3.9	1.8	-3.5	1.7	1.2f
Austria	3.7	0.9	1.7	0.9	2.6	2.4	3.7	3.7	1.4	-3.8	2.3	3.1f
Poland	4.3	1.2	1.4	3.9	5.3	3.6	6.2	6.8	5.1	1.6	3.9	4.3f
Romania	2.4	5.7	5.1	5.2	8.5	4.2	7.9	6.3	7.3	-6.6	= 1.6	2.5f
Slovenia	4.3	2.9	3.8	2.9	4.4	4.0	5.8	6.9	3.6	-8.0	1.4	-0.2
Slovakia	1.4	3.5	4.6	4.8	5.1	6.7	8.3	10.5	5.9	-4.9	4.2	3.3f

Finland	5.3	2.3	1.8	2.0	4.1	2.9	4.4	5.3	0.3	-8.4	3.7	2.9
Sweden	4.5	1.3	2.5	2.3	4.2	3.2	4.3	3.3	-0.6	-5.0	6.1	3.9
United Kingdom	4.5	3.2	2.7	3.5	3.0	2.1	2.6	3.5	-1.1	-4.4	2.1	0.8
Iceland	4.3	3.9	0.1	2.4	7.8	7.2	4.7	6.0	1.3	-6.7	-4.0	2.1f
Norway	3.3	2.0	1.5	1.0	4.0	2.6	2.5	2.7	0.0	-1.7	0.7	1.6
Switzerland	3.6	1.2	0.4	-0.2	2.5	2.6	3.6	3.6	2.1	-1.9	2.7	1.9
Montenegro	:	1.1	1.9	2.4	4.4	14.7	8.6	10.6	6.9	-5.7	2.5	2.7
Croatia	3.8	3.7	4.9	5.4	4.1	4.3	4.9	5.1	2.2p	-6.0p	-1.2p	0.6f
FYR of Macedonia	4.5	-4.5	0.9	2.8	4.6	4.4	5.0	6.1	5.0	-0.9	1.8f	3.0f
Turkey	6.8	-5.7	6.2	5.3	9.4	8.4	6.9	4.7	0.7	-4.8	9.0	7.5f
USA	4.1	1.1	1.8	2.5	3.5	3.1	2.7	1.9	-0.3	-3.5	3.0	1.7
Japan	2.3	0.4	0.3	1.7	2.4	1.3	1.7	2.2	-1.0	-5.5	4.4	-0.9

Key: : = not available; b = break in series; f = forecast; p = provisional value.

Source: Eurostat.

investment and privatizing public sectors together with the introduction of a new currency, the Turkish new lira, in January 2005 (becoming the Turkish lira in January 2009), to help curb inflation, spectacular GDP growth averaging 7 per cent was achieved from 2002 and 2007. Although there was then a slowdown because of the global financial crisis, strong growth resumed in 2010 and continued to set Turkey apart from members of the European Union. Turkey became a favoured holiday destination for many, attracting 31 million visitors by 2008. The automotive industry too expanded by leaps and bounds, becoming the sixth largest producer in Europe by 2008, overtaking Italy, ranking fifteenth overall in world motor vehicle production. Turkish shipbuilding was another success story, rated fourth in the world by 2007. Turkish Airlines mirrored leading growth sectors, expanding its routes globally and enhancing its marketability through becoming the official carrier of some of Europe's most renowned football clubs like FC Barcelona and Manchester United, whose players appeared in television advertisements. The European Union became Turkey's largest trading partner, taking 59 per cent of exports and accounting for 52 per cent of imports by 2005. This reflected Turkish membership of a customs union with the European Union from 1995, which served to augment manufacturing output for exports and encouraged foreign direct investment from Europe. In turn, Turkey invested extensively in Bulgaria and Romania, its Black Sea neighbours, and Russia, construction and contracting companies leading the way.

Notwithstanding the transformation of Turkey's image abroad to some extent, membership of the European Union remained a distant prospect. Turkey became an associate member of the European Economic Community in 1963, applying for full membership in 1987, commencing formal accession negotiations in 2005. Five years earlier Greece dropped its previous staunch opposition to its traditional antagonist, taking the view that it was better to deal with Turkey inside the European Union framework. However, tremendous obstacles still remained. Despite the remarkable transformation of the economy, agriculture still constituted 9 per cent of GDP in 2010 (against 26 per cent for the industrial sector and 65 per cent for the services sector), employing 24.7 per cent of the workforce, and if the Common Agricultural Policy were extended to Turkish farming, this would threaten to overwhelm it. More insuperable obstacles were Turkey's human rights record and the ongoing problem of Cyprus. Discrimination against the substantial Kurdish minority and Turkey's failure to acknowledge that there was an Armenian genocide during the First World War were held against it, especially by Austria, France and Germany, the leading objectors to Turkish entry. Indeed, the French and Germans argued that Turkey should be extended a privileged partnership because granting full membership to a country with a predominantly Muslim population was too problematic. The continued occupation of northern Cyprus, invaded in 1974, remained a thorny issue of contention. Turkey continued to be the only country to recognize the Turkish Cypriot state, declared in 1983, which was sustained only because of Ankara's support through a large standing garrison, economic aid and tourism. Ironically, the Turkish Cypriot north supported reunification in a referendum in 2004, only for the Greek Cypriot south to vote against in the secure knowledge that the European Union would accept the latter as a new member regardless. The enmity between the two sides was reignited when up to eight trillion tonnes of gas was discovered off Cyprus's eastern coast. Turkey attempted to stop the exploration, but Russian involvement helped ensure that this came to nothing. After being rebuffed in laying claim to a share of the profits, Turkish Cypriots commenced their own undersea explorations.

For the foreseeable future, therefore, Turkey will remain outside in the cold politically, although economically it has become so intertwined with the European Union that it cannot escape the impact of any contractions therein. Before the global financial crisis, Turkish exports to the monolith stood at 56 per cent, falling back to 47 per cent by 2011 as the sovereign debt crisis hit home. Again, this trend was reflected in external finance, on which Turkey depended. Foreign direct investment mushroomed from $571 million in 2002 to $19.1 billion by 2007, falling back to $6.3 billion in 2010. Ironically, Turkish economic growth was carried along on the momentum of the tantalizing prospect of European Union membership, and several obstacles were swept aside in the quest to attain this. As it became clear that Turkey remained so near yet so far, opinion polls reflected a drop in support for accession and the leadership pronounced that with or without it their objective was to join the ranks of the top ten global players by 2023. Moreover, developments within the Middle East, the old stamping ground of the Ottoman Empire, were opening up an alternative scenario, so Turkey could look east as well as west. The anti-Americanism across the region in the wake of the controversial invasion of Iraq in 2003, the Arab Spring of 2011, the lack of Arab leadership and the European Union's fractured foreign policy created business opportunities, which Turkey was best placed to take advantage of.

In the period under review, there were also several countries aspiring to join the European Union and others wanting to adopt the euro. Of the former, Croatia was closest to entry, signing an accession treaty on 9 December 2011 and, subject to a favourable referendum result, was set to become the twenty-eighth member in 2013. Iceland, Macedonia, Montenegro and Turkey are candidate countries, whilst Bosnia and Herzegovina together with Serbia are expected to join them in the near future now that they have become stable democracies after the pandemonium stemming from the Yugoslav civil wars in the 1990s. Given these special circumstances for countries of the western Balkans, the Stabilization and Association Process was created to deal with their applications. In addition, the four remaining members of the European Free Trade Area (Iceland, Liechtenstein, Norway and Switzerland) are part of the single market through the European Economic Area, with all bar Iceland liable to restrict their association to a trading relationship for the foreseeable future.

The Eastern Partnership, unveiled in Prague in May 2009, comprised Armenia, Azerbaijan, Belarus, Georgia, Moldavia and Ukraine, all former Soviet republics with aspirations to join the European Union but no immediate prospects of achieving their ambition. The intention was to improve political and economic relations via Association Agreements, the establishment of a new free trade area and freedom of movement for the 76 million populations of the six countries through visa-free travel. Poland, a great enthusiast of the project, paved the way by reaching an agreement with Ukraine in July 2009 over supplanting permits with visas. Russia greatly objected to this development, accusing the European Union of trying to carve out a new sphere of influence and seeking alternate energy sources, to which Sweden, the co-author of the partnership alongside Poland, responded that all members joined freely. Belarus, a recognized dictatorship, attracted particular criticism but the European Union justified its inclusion by arguing that Russian influence was thereby lessened and in the hope that a democratic government might emerge. During 2011, efforts to improve communications and to modernize the transport links of the six were instigated by the European Union, leading to the establishment of the Eastern Partnership Transport Panel.

Russia becomes an energy superpower

Under the ruthless presidency of Vladimar Putin (2000–2008), a former head of the Federal Security Service, the successor to the KGB, who regarded the collapse of the Soviet Union as 'the greatest geostrategic catastrophe of the twentieth century', Russia returned to an authoritarian style of leadership (ironically styled 'managed democracy' in the manner of Gorbachev's 'market socialism', a contradiction in terms), which sought to reassert regional dominance predominantly through exploiting its energy resources in an era of increasing demand. The heavy presence of the emerging economies in the global marketplace ensured a ready market for food, energy and raw materials, which was reflected in rising world commodity prices. As a net exporter of commodities, Russia became a major beneficiary of this trend, which allowed it to recover from the crash of 1998 when it defaulted on its domestic and foreign debt and devalued the rouble. Customs duties and taxes from the energy sector were responsible for almost half of federal budget revenues. The state coffers were also filled by rising gold, platinum, nickel and copper prices. Indeed, Russia boasted the world's third-largest foreign currency reserves of £200 billion by 2011.

The Russian Federation covered an area of 17.1 million kilometres, four times the size of the European Union. During the Putin presidency, the Russian Federation went from being the twenty-second to the eleventh largest economy in the world, averaging growth of 7 per cent per annum. The consumerism evident in the large cities like Moscow and St Petersburg reflected the rise of an affluent middle class, which increased sevenfold from eight million to 55 million between 2000 and 2006. Indeed, Moscow overtook New York in having more billionaires than anywhere in the world. At the other extreme, the number of people living below the poverty line remained high at 14 per cent by 2008 (albeit a fall of 16 per cent since 2000), which partly reflected a considerable upswing in prices. Pensioners and unskilled workers made up a substantial part of the poor. Poverty and unhealthy lifestyles meant the Russian Federation experienced a falling population and much reduced life expectancy compared with the European Union. The Russian Federation was home to 141.9 million inhabitants by 2009, some three-and-a-half times less than the European Union (501.1 million in 2010), which also had a greater population density of 116 citizens per kilometre against 8.3 citizens per kilometre in the former, wherein there were vast swathes of remote and inhospitable terrain.

To a certain extent, the Russian Federation's economy was similar to the Soviet Union's, which also became heavily dependent on generating hard currency earnings from oil and gas exports. However, there was a key difference: where the Soviets never fully exploited these resources because of communist dogma, inefficiencies and lack of western expertise and investment the post-Soviet era rectified these impediments, making the Russian Federation the world's largest oil producer and the second-largest exporter after Saudi Arabia. In November 1992, President Yeltsin privatized the oil industry, creating three vertically integrated companies (Lukoil, Surgut and Yukos), which replicated western models and incorporated exploration, production, refining and marketing underneath one umbrella, also embracing leading-edge western extractive equipment and recruiting experts from the west, including personnel from BP, ExxonMobil and Shell. In 1999, before coming to power, Putin published an article on 'Mineral Natural Resources' which envisioned Russia's oil and gas reserves as fundamental to economic recovery and ultimately making Russia 'a great economic power'. Slowly but surely, after the Russian energy sector began to deliver, Putin began clawing back some control for the state, and it soon became clear that he would brook no challengers. Igor Sechin, a key economic advisor, was put in charge of Rosneft, the state-run major oil company, which, with another state-controlled enterprise (Gazprom), emerged from the breakup of Yukos, whose oligarch, Mikhail Khordorkorkovsky, was imprisoned. Amid threats, Gazprom went on to acquire a stake in Shell's £10 billion Sakhalin II oil and gas offshore project, followed by the takeover of BP's massive Kovykta gas field in Siberia during June 2011. A year later, BP elected to sell its share in the joint venture, TNK-BP, which had begun nine years before and made it the strongest foreign player in the Russian oil industry, after encountering increasing difficulties operating within Russia such as the blocking of a proposal to explore the Russian Arctic with Rosneft. The changed business environment reflected the fact that in the 1990s, when Russia was in a weak position politically and economically, contracts signed with foreign energy companies were highly favourable to them.

The remoteness of the gas and oil fields dictated that a network of pipelines needed to be constructed. During the Soviet period, these shifted oil within the USSR and its satellites, beginning to develop export potential to western Europe from the 1980s. The Russian Federation inherited 46,000 kilometres of crude oil pipelines, 15,000 kilometres of petroleum product pipelines and 152,000 kilometres of natural gas pipelines. Compared with the United States, which, despite being only 55 per cent the size of the Russian Federation, boasted four times as many oil pipelines and double the number of natural gas pipelines, these statistics were not impressive. The disparity could be partly explained by the fact that most of the American network was in private hands. The privatization drive in the Russian Federation of the 1990s added impetus to the need for upgrading the existing network and adding capacity. Gas pipelines delivered to the European Union via Ukraine, Belarus and the Baltic Sea. Germany was the biggest customer, by 2009 taking almost 30 per cent of the Russian natural gas exported to the European Union, followed by Italy, with 17 per cent. Four European Union members, perhaps suspicious of the Russian Federation's propensity to play politics with energy supplies in its backyard, refrained from taking any of their natural gas supplies from the Russian Federation.

At 4000 kilometres, the Druzhba oil pipeline, inherited from the Soviet period, was the longest in the world, running from the eastern part of European Russia through Ukraine, Belarus, Poland, Hungary, Slovakia, the Czech Republic and ending in Germany, utilizing twenty pumping stations en route. Its name means 'friendship', but there was nothing fraternal about the Russian Federation's attitude. In retaliation for increasing the prices of its energy from the Russian Federation, Ukraine responded by raising the transit fees and demanding to be paid in euros rather than roubles. After a tense standoff, in which the Russians threatened to cut off supplies to the Czech Republic, Hungary and Slovakia, Ukraine's terms were broadly accepted, although the net effect was to reduce the supplies to these customers from 17.1 million tonnes in 2008 to 15 million tonnes in 2010.

Geopolitics was fundamental to the west's decision to rehabilitate the supply of oil from Baku, capital of Azerbaijan, which used to be one of the main energy hubs of the USSR. A secular country, Azerbaijan became a key American ally in the post-Cold War era. The Caspian Sea, the largest landlocked body of water in the world, lay above some of the largest oil and gas fields in the world. During the Soviet period, all energy routes emanating from the Caspian Sea ran through Russia. Once the USSR collapsed, the prospect of non-Russian routes opened up. A proposal for a pipeline running from Baku via Tbilisi, capital of Georgia, to Ceyhan, a port on the Mediterranean coast of Turkey (known as the BCP pipeline) originated from Ankara in 1992, just after the fall of the Soviet Union. The more direct route was through Armenia, but because Armenia remained in dispute with Azerbaijan over the status of Nagorno-Karabakh, Georgia was preferred as a route provider. The Ankara Declaration of 29 October 1998, signed by Azerbaijan, Georgia, Kazakhstan and Turkey at the behest of the United States, gave impetus to the project, which was formalized by an intergovernmental agreement the following year and the establishment of the Baki-Tbilisi-Ceyhan Pipeline Company in August 2002, a consortium of eleven energy companies led by BP. Construction of the 1768-kilometre-long pipeline commenced in April 2003 and was completed in May 2005. Capable of carrying a million barrels of oil per day at a speed of 2.2 metres per second aided by eight pumping stations, the $3.9 billion project was designed to last for forty years. Some 70 per cent of the funding came from third parties, including the European Bank for Reconstruction and Development, the World Bank, seven export credit agencies and a syndicate of fifteen commercial banks. The main sources of the pipeline's oil were the Azeri-Chirag-Guneshli oilfield in the Caspian Sea belonging to Azerbaijan and Aktau in Kazakhstan. The latter wanted to commence a trans-Caspian oil pipeline from Aktau to Baku but desisted after Iran and Russia voiced their objections, instead sending oil in tankers to the Sangachal Terminal. The Russians resented creeping western influence in the South Caucasus, traditionally a region where they held sway, fearing that the west could use the security of the pipeline as a pretext to station armed forces there. This seems unlikely (the 2008 Russian military intervention in Georgia over a territorial dispute failed to elicit outside help and the latter remained outside NATO, despite wanting to join). The hope that the BTC pipeline would lessen western dependence on Middle East oil was a key reason why it materialized, but initially only 1 per cent of global demand was being met from this source.

Through its heavy reliance on energy revenues, the Russian Federation was putting all its eggs in one basket and modernization of the economy was not being driven as relentlessly as might have been the case in different circumstances. The prospect of exploiting offshore energy resources, especially in the Arctic region, only tended to put off reforms, as did the continually high price of energy in the world economy, which the Russian Federation, unlike its predecessor, was in a position to exploit fully. For the Russian Federation to maintain its leading ranking as the world's top producer of crude oil, a position accorded by the International Energy Agency in 2010, prices must remain buoyant, foreign markets stay constant and ideally expand, modernization continue and new fields open up. As in the former Soviet Union, corruption was rife, and there is a falling population at a rate of 800,000 a year, reflecting the persistence of poverty in rural areas (albeit there was a fall in the percentage of Russians classed as poverty-stricken from 25 to 12 per cent between 2002 and 2010), a high number of abortions and unhealthy lifestyles, with alcoholism still a problem. Indeed, some estimates suggest the population could fall from 140 million to just over 100 million half-way through the new century.

In seeking to reestablish the fear in which the old Soviet Union was regarded at the height of the Cold War, the Russian Federation increasingly acted the role of the awkward member of the international community, for example by vetoing efforts by the United Nations to bring the repressive Assad regime in Syria to heel. This reflected the fact that Syria, an old ally of the Soviet Union, represented the Russian Federation's last surviving foothold in the Middle East (the Syrian port of Tartus was the Russian navy's only port outside Russian territory) and a trading partner that was a fervent purchaser of Russian weapons because its other sources were cut off by international sanctions. Indeed, Russian arms sales increased exponentially to the point at which they ranked second only to the United States. Putin challenged the idea of a 'unipolar' world dominated by the United States, commissioning new aircraft, nuclear submarines and missiles, selling a £500 million all-weather missile-defence system to Iran and £1.5 billion of armaments to Venezuela, two nations that defied American will. During the lead-up to the war with Georgia, the Russian Federation banned imports of its wine and increased the price of gas in an effort to make the Georgian government bend to their will. As a consequence, Georgian wine is now a rarity within the Russian Federation. Other neighbours (Belarus, Lithuania and Ukraine) also faced threats to their natural gas supplies.

The Russian Federation pursued a dual policy of strengthening ties with Europe while at the same time developing economic relations with China, Japan and the Asian 'tigers' as an insurance policy. The European policy has not been judged a success, as reflected by the fact that European partners began to seek alternative energy sources, thereby accentuating the second strand. Moreover, the euro crisis underlined the fact that Asia offered better business opportunities. This led, in 2012, to the establishment of a Minister for the Development of the Far East of the Russian Federation. Siberia, traditionally a source of raw materials, is earmarked to become a critical modernized sector of the economy and there is talk of creating a third economic capital beyond the Urals (Moscow being the political capital and St Petersburg the cultural capital) with Ekaterinburg, Krasnoyarsk and Khaborovsk vying for the honour. The shift away from a western policy drew impetus from the European Union's efforts to persuade the Russian Federation to embrace western political models, which were regarded as arrogant, whereas the Asians happily do business without preconditions.

Putin returned to the presidency in May 2012, when Dmitry Medvedev stepped down from the role he assumed from Putin in 2008 after he became Prime Minister, the latter pulling the strings behind the scenes. At the same time, the presidential term increased from four to six years, prompting comparisons with Leonid Brezhnev, who ruled the Soviet Union for eighteen years (1964–82). Should Putin run again in 2018 and serve a further two terms, he would reach his seventies in office. Brezhnev was 75 when he died of a heart attack, his failing health symptomatic of the stagnant state of the Soviet economy by that time. The parallels were not lost on the regime. 'Brezhnev wasn't a minus for the history of our country, he was a huge plus' a Putin spokesman lectured a Russian television network. 'He laid the foundations of the economy, agriculture etc.' In autumn 2011, Putin visualized the creation of a 'Eurasian Union', 'an unbreakable union of free republics', which gathered together the old Soviet republics and created an economic bloc between the European Union and Asia. This vision contained echoes of the former Soviet bloc.

That Putin would win the 2012 election was not in doubt, even though his allure was beginning to wane with the electorate, as reflected in anti-Putin jokes and the dismissal of his United Russia as the 'party of thieves and swindlers' after the tainted parliamentary election of December 2011. The rising affluent middle class, centred on the big cities, became increasingly less willing to support Putin, who nevertheless still enjoyed substantial support from the masses, who admired his belligerent spirit and willingness to assert himself on the international stage. In March 2012, Putin predictably won a third term as president. Despite allegations of ballot rigging, Putin clearly attracted the most votes, although his popularity was in decline, not least because of the absence of serious opposition (the communists coming in a good way second). To ensure victory and appeal to his base of support outside the cities (state workers, elderly people and rural dwellers), Putin promised higher wages and pensions, expanding the popular 'baby bonus' payments to cover a third child, as well as increased military spending, which followed a doubling of salaries for personnel in the one-million-strong army in

January 2012. Indeed, military expenditure rose by a quarter in 2011 to reach £16.2 billion, and a new £94.5 billion rearmament programme was announced, intended to replace half of existing military equipment by 2015. These measures were dependent for funding on a continued high oil price; Citigroup estimated that the ideal would be $150 a barrel based on a calculation that for additional government spending equivalent to a 1 per cent increase in Russian GDP demanded a rise of $10 per barrel on global markets. Otherwise, without the cushioning effect of high oil prices, there was the danger of building up a large government deficit that could become a drag on economic growth.

The crash

Whilst the United States remained far and away the world's hegemon, there were signs of cracking in the edifice of the most powerful country the world has ever known. Since the Second World War, as the leading light of the 'free' world and liberal capitalism, America wielded its financial muscle to support nations willing to resist extremism and, where it perceived its vital interests to be at stake, as in Korea, Vietnam, Kuwait, Afghanistan and Iraq, did not hesitate to intervene militarily. This propensity for intervention persisted despite the fact that economic productivity and wealth creation became misaligned with ever-rising military expenditure as the cost of high-tech weaponry escalated. Moreover, projecting influence directly or indirectly through military campaigns, covert operations and the several 'special relationships' the United States enjoyed with Israel, Egypt, Pakistan, Saudi Arabia and other nations, which receive huge payouts to keep them on side, escalated out of all proportion. Thus, despite its share of world GDP shrinking to 20 per cent, the United States still accounted for 50 per cent of the world's military expenditure to maintain its superiority. The conundrum has meant that for years expenditure far exceeded revenues, so that the gap must be covered through selling Treasury bonds (of five, ten and thirty years' duration), which are bought mainly by foreigners, chiefly oil-rich states like Saudi Arabia or Asian governments and banks.

The saying that 'when America sneezes the rest of the world catches a cold', so apposite to the Great Depression period, was still relevant in the new century and contributed to its first major economic downturn, which reverberated around the globe. The origins lay in the Reagan and Thatcher revolutions of the 1980s, which gave greater prominence to free markets, introducing banking deregulation, a trend that was accentuated with the collapse of communism in eastern Europe and the advent of capitalism in China, where the new leader Deng Xioping famously said, 'It doesn't matter what colour the cat is as long as it catches the mouse' and 'To be rich is glorious'. By the mid-1990s, finance companies and investment houses were keen to indulge in riskier areas. This was encouraged by the repeal in 1999 of the Glass-Steagal Act of 1933, which separated investment from commercial banking in the United States. In the new financial environment of light-touch regulation, investors developed a gold-rush mentality. When dot-com companies went through boom and bust, investors moved out of equities and into real estate, taking advantage of a trend whereby home owners, seeking higher living standards, borrowed against the value of their property. At a time of rising house prices (during the bubble period 2000–2008 the average price of an American home doubled from $300,000 to $600,000), this seemed a surefire bet. The chairman of the US Federal Reserve, Alan Greenspan, took a relaxed view towards bubbling property prices, rashly assuming that the financial system was self-stabilizing and in the belief that the central bank need not question asset prices. If anything, he fanned the flames by cutting interest rates, helping to sustain the credit boom and taking a relaxed view towards new financial instruments called derivatives. Middle-income households facing falling wages and typically having credit card debt of $20,000 to $30,000 at exorbitant rates of interest, visualized rising house prices as a means to pay bills off and maintain their lifestyle. Eventually, this philosophy embraced the lower strata of society, which were just as keen to share in the American Dream. Mortgage securities, originating in the 1980s, became the mechanism whereby speculators could exploit the situation. Rather than wait for the term of the mortgage to mature as with a traditional housing loan, mortgage securities were utilized to sell on into the capital markets as CDOs (Capital Debt Obligations). Later, these became renowned as toxic assets: they were sold on in the American and global financial markets, paying yields. Because these were triple A, double A and single A rated by American credit agencies, their attraction increased when in fact they were hugely risky investments, the majority of loans sold on to Wall Street being refinance loans. Yet borrowers were not required to disclose their income. Indeed, lenders fell over themselves to encourage home owners to take out loans, not least because of massive personal bonuses (many finance managers received over $1 million a year for garnering business). No attention was paid as to whether the loans were affordable in the knowledge that the CDOs could be sold on to Wall Street investment banks and beyond. High fees were charged up front, which were so exorbitant that it was not uncommon for a household to take out several refinance loans in short order.

The unravelling process began in the autumn of 2006, when the stock market fell and the real estate bubble started to burst because many borrowers were failing to meet their monthly mortgage payments, foreclosures increased and the debt returned to the originator. A trigger was the abrupt lower credit ratings meted out to subprime mortgage structured securities, the downgrade puncturing the previous optimism and bringing the realization that other securities were at risk. A whirlpool effect was created as subprime losses in 2007 fed into a credit boom and speculative equity investing, which began to come unstuck at the same time. Sharp increases in oil and food prices accentuated the developing crisis. The price of a barrel of oil exceeded $100 for the first time in January 2008, peaking at $147.30 in July 2008. On 15 September 2008, Lehman Brothers went bankrupt, spreading panic on the interbank loan market. Its collapse was preceded by large-scale withdrawals by its creditors as banks, hedge funds and other investors abandoned ship, setting off a wider market crisis. The global recession that resulted produced falling international trade, rising unemployment and collapsing commodity prices. Indeed, the noted economist Paul Krugman even spoke of the start of 'a second Great Depression'.

Several European banks were sucked into the American subprime bond market, whereby poor people were targeted to take out home mortgages who had no prospect of ever repaying the loan. Yet because these investments, incredulously, were triple A rated, they attracted reputable investors, including the German IKB bank, which subsequently lost $15 billion on its subprime bonds. The illusion that there was a riskless asset especially appealed to normally cautious German bankers, who failed to see beneath the hype of glib American salesmen from Wall Street. Belgium's biggest banking group, Dexia, boasted a substantial portfolio of subprime loans. It was rescued by the French and Belgian governments, which poured billions of euros into it, and received the largest amount of loans from the Federal Reserve at a discount. Icelandic banks were not so lucky and all three major commercial lenders collapsed as interbank lending suddenly dried up, their government earning the enmity of foreign powers and investors through refusing to take responsibility. In late September 2008, there came a sudden announcement that the Glitnir bank would be nationalized. Soon afterwards, the Lansbanki and Glitnir as well as Kaupthing, Iceland's biggest bank, went into receivership under the auspices of the Financial Supervisory Authority. The debt of the Icelandic banks was six times the size of their country's GDP. The British government employed anti-terrorist legislation to freeze Icelandic assets in the United Kingdom in an effort to protect the investments of around 300,000 citizens, which the Reykjavik government described as an unfriendly act, bringing about the worst relations between the two countries since the fishing dispute of the 1970s. Iceland's banks had gone on an irresponsible spending spree since 2003, fuelled by borrowing from international lenders. Because Iceland's population was tiny, mass unemployment did not follow financial collapse and bucked the trend.

Among the major European Union members, Britain suffered most because of the exposure of its financial services sector to the contagion. In quick succession, the Brown government, fearing alienating core Labour voters, came to the rescue of Northern Rock (which suffered the first run on a British bank for 150 years), followed by Bradford and Bingley through nationalization and facilitated rescue packages for other imperilled institutions such as Alliance and Leicester, HBOS and Lloyds TSB. These interventions in themselves were not sufficient to prevent the continued collapse in banking share prices. To calm down the markets, inject liquidity and protect investors, the Labour government unveiled a £400 billion bailout package in October 2008, while the Bank of England slashed interest rates until they reached a historic low of 0.5 per cent, where they would remain for the rest of the decade and beyond.

The biggest casualty of the crisis was Royal Bank of Scotland (RBS). Its story provides a salutary lesson in banking mismanagement. Originally, RBS was Scotland's largest bank, with a distinct Scottish identity, which made prudent investments and observed the golden banking rule of being able to balance the books from cash reserves and loans from other banks at the close of each day's trading. The management came to the view that, like the Bank of Scotland, they wished to transform RBS into an international banking force. To this end the bank recruited, in 1998, Fred Goodwin, originally a chartered accountant, who rose to the top at Clydesdale Bank before he reached the age of forty. A rising star, Goodwin was tough and determined, possessing extreme self-confidence in his own infallibility. His haughty persona dissipated the collegiate atmosphere that existed at RBS before his appointment. Hitherto, morning meetings served to thrash out issues in a friendly spirit, but under his watch, they became known internally as 'morning beatings', as he tore into an unfortunate executive for some perceived misdemeanour, telling them to 'suck it up'. He became known as 'Fred the Shred' and even senior management became loath to question his risk-laden decision making. As chief executive, Goodwin launched an audacious hostile takeover bid for NatWest bank, twice the size of RBS, representing the biggest takeover attempt in British banking history. Because the City was not enamoured with the management of NatWest, it encouraged the bid, which succeeded, and for a time, RBS acquired a faithful following in the City, which boosted the share price and encouraged Goodwin to embark on further acquisitions. Gaining access to NatWest savings and deposits gave him the wherewithal to do so and he set about the task with characteristic gusto. RBS began adding assorted businesses to its investment portfolio, including Dixon Car Sales, Edinburgh Airport, Gibraltar General Hospital, Tesco Pet Insurance and Ulster Bank. Goodwin was knighted in 2004 for his seeming managerial brilliance in generating healthy profits for RBS. On 14 September 2005, the Queen opened a new purpose-built headquarters in Edinburgh, located next to the airport, where private jets were on standby to whisk RBS executives around the globe.

Goodwin turned his attention to the United States, where RBS enjoyed a foothold through Citizens, a Rhode Island bank that focussed on serving the local community and avoided making unsecured loans. Under pressure from the RBS management to expand, Citizens ventured beyond its normal remit, first acquiring several small banks in New England and then entering the larger Philadelphia market, taking over Mellon Financial for $2.6 billion. Moving even further afield, Citizens went on to absorb Charter One, thereby gaining access to the vast Chicago market, which Sir Fred characterized as 'a very logical geographical extension to our acquisitions in the United States'. The move made RBS the seventh largest bank in the United States, but at a cost of £10.5 billion. Soon afterwards, a £1 billion stake was taken in the Bank of China.

By 2005, RBS had acquired over twenty-five assorted companies, spending almost £30 billion in the process. In retrospect, this marked the high watermark of Goodwin's reign. The City was beginning to have doubts about his management strategy, questioning the exorbitant price paid for Charter One, with the disquiet spreading to investors. At a shareholders' meeting, Sir Fred stood accused of being a megalomaniac intent on putting size before share value. 'I really don't think it stands a lot of scrutiny' was his curt reply. Faced with this sea change, Goodwin changed tack, shifting focus to corporate and investment banking through RBS Greenwich Capital based in Connecticut. It delved into the prime and subprime mortgage markets, becoming a leading player on Wall Street, dealing in complex bundles of loans that were sold on for huge gains. By 2005, RBS's profits were up by 22 per cent but almost two-thirds were generated by Greenwich Capital. This trend continued, with RBS profits rising by 15 per cent to over £4.6 billion in the first six months of 2006, 50 per cent deriving from Greenwich Capital. Then in late 2006, the American property bubble burst. At the start of 2007, HSBC admitted that losses on its portfolio of subprime mortgages were greater than previously thought. This shone the City's spotlight on other banks, but when its gaze fell on RBS Goodwin was in denial: 'The fact we don't become involved in subprime lending has been another land mine we've kept away from.' He failed to recognize that the whole banking system was infected, given the element of subprime lending within the complex financial bundles that had been tossed around Wall Street chasing profits.

Had Sir Fred stopped there, he might conceivably have been able to rescue the position. Instead he now made a fatal mistake, which more than doubled RBS's balance sheet to nearly £2 trillion. The Dutch bank ABN-AMRO was one of the largest in Europe, with an international reach extending to over fifty countries, including an American bank, a Brazilian bank and others located elsewhere, including Holland, Italy and India. Barclays Bank first expressed an interest in ABN-AMRO, which galvanized the fiercely competitive Goodwin to put together a consortium for a hostile takeover. The RBS share would include the investment bank and Lesalle, a Chicago bank with access to the lucrative American corporate market. In an effort to thwart RBS, ABN-AMRO sold off Lesalle but despite the fact that the investment bank was not an attractive proposition, Goodwin persisted. Compounding his folly, he announced that ABN-AMRO's books need not be scrutinized because of Barclays' interest and the fact that it was subject to financial regulation in several countries where it operated. Sir Fred and the RBS board, which was unanimous in authorizing the bid, convinced themselves that they were about to repeat their previous success with NatWest. They were also under pressure from ABN-AMRO and Santander to complete the deal. The RBS part of the bid amounted to €27 billion, most of which was paid in cash from reserves, an unusual move that converted a strong liquidity position into a precarious one.

The biggest takeover in global banking history briefly saw RBS occupy the position of the world's leading bank, as measured by assets, achieving Goodwin's ambition. But it was a false dawn. In December 2007, RBS finally conceded that it had suffered substantially from subprime losses, leading Sir Fred to announce that £1.5 billion was being written off. Worse still was the discovery that ABN-AMRO had been involved in hundreds of millions of dollars worth of subprime-related investments, which were now toxic. By April 2008, the RBS losses had reached £6 billion, with no end in sight, compelling the board to ask shareholders to stump up £12 billion in an effort to tide the bank over for at least a year. In August 2008, RBS announced pre-tax losses of £69.1 million. Despite developments, Goodwin's penchant for making incredulous statements continued, insisting 'we do have a business which is strong and resilient'. However, by

October, RBS shares were in free fall and there were no private financial institutions able or willing to bail out the bank. In fact, RBS came within two hours of running out of money. At this point, the Labour Prime Minister, Gordon Brown, rode to the rescue, while making his feelings apparent: 'Yes, I'm angry at RBS and what happened. Almost all the losses are in the subprime market of America and related to the acquisition of ABN-AMRO.' The government extended a £20 billion rescue package with strings attached, the most important being Goodwin's removal from the board. During his tenure, RBS shares reached new highs but, by the end of his reign, had lost 90 per cent of their value, reflecting total losses of £24.1 billion. Taking RBS under its wing cost the British government £45 billion, and losses continued as unprofitable acquisitions were offloaded, a contraction that had cost £38 billion by January 2012. Goodwin became a hate figure, a symbol of corporate greed, finding his house in Edinburgh vandalized, and eventually he suffered the indignity of being stripped of his knighthood.

Emergency responses were called for from individual countries and from international institutions, with the European Union, the IMF and the G20 members each playing prominent roles. The European Commission came up with a European Economic Recovery Plan, which was approved by the European Council in December 2008. The European stimulus plan involving €200 billion (1.5 per cent of European Union GDP) sought to restrict the impact of the global economic slowdown. It included short-term measures designed to bolster demand and sustain jobs combined with long-term measures to promote growth, such as investing in research and development. Significantly the European Commission gave carte blanche for euro-zone members to breach the Stability and Growth Pact, urged the European Central Bank to lower interest rates and proposed that governments should temporarily increase unemployment benefits, reduce taxes on low incomes and provide credit guarantees or subsidized loans to companies. The Commission President José Manuel Barroso described the plan as 'timely, temporary and targeted', beseeching member states to act together at a time of 'exceptional crisis'. The Commission's aim to persuade member states to contribute €170 billion of the €200 billion in the expectation that this would save millions of European jobs was fanciful. In practice, the proposals were not mandatory, and each member state had their own preferences over how best to stimulate recovery. Britain was unique in temporarily reducing the standard VAT rate to stimulate demand; Germany preferred to lower employer contributions; France increased the minimum wage and provided tax incentives to the housing sector; Spain introduced a social housing building programme; Italy gave tax rebates to households and companies; the Netherlands increased social benefits and public expenditure. The German Chancellor, Angela Merkel, poured cold water on the scheme, informing the Bundestag, the lower house of parliament, that Germany was not entering 'into the race for billions' and was already doing enough to stimulate recovery. 'We should walk a measured path and keep to the middle ground', she insisted, 'which is made-to-measure for the situation in Germany'. In the end, the European Central Bank pursued a circumspect route to ease the situation. Loath to cut its interest rate below 1 per cent or buy government bonds directly, instead commercial banks could access unlimited loans from the European Central Bank for up to a year in exchange for a wide range of collateral. In June 2009, €442 billion was injected into the financial system through this route, which banks used to purchase government bonds. The effect was to push down long-term interest rates and drive down short-term interest rates towards the American and British levels, their governments having embarked on a policy of quantitative easing (putting extra money into circulation and buying government bonds with central bank funds) and cutting the main bank base lending rate below 1 per cent.

The American-led banking crisis was not the only one to afflict the Continent. In 2004, the world economy returned its best rate of growth for thirty years as globalization, reflected by the interdependence of financial markets and the imprint of multinationals in more countries, aligned to low interest rates and deregulation, gathered pace. Yet beneath the outwardly impressive sheen all was not well. Within the euro-zone the 'one size fits all' mentality was storing up problems for the future. The low interest rate policy of the European Central Bank was intended to assist the slower growing members, not least Germany. In this aim it was effective. Between 2000 and 2008, Germany experienced an export boom, generating 66 per cent of its growth. At the same time, however, the euro-zone as a whole lost 10 per cent of its competitiveness. Indeed, with the appreciation of the euro until October 2009, the currency union suffered a loss in export market share, which was especially keenly felt in the peripheral economies. Led by Greece and Ireland, they found themselves able to borrow at low interest rates as if they were as failsafe performers as Germany and did so with the enthusiasm of a child opening their Christmas presents. But in this period, while Germany kept a lid on wages, unit labour costs in Greece, Italy, Ireland and Spain rose to 25 per cent or more above the German figure, leading the southern European nations to lose a quarter of their export share in global markets. Declining competitiveness allied to increasing debt was a recipe for disaster.

Ireland, one of the worst culprits, underwent a property boom starting in 1995, which peaked in 2007 at a valuation of £450 million. Three years earlier *The Economist* declared that Ireland had become the best place to live in the world because of its low tax environment, spectacular economic growth, high-quality education and idyllic scenery. Ireland was hailed as the Singapore of Europe and the Celtic Tiger. High-tech manufacturers from abroad were attracted and the resultant job creation saw immigrants exceed emigrants. Indeed, the number of foreign workers, who previously constituted only 1 per cent of the working population, rose above 12 per cent, a proportion last witnessed before the potato famine. The seeming Irish economic miracle was built on the traditional base of cheap labour, Greenwich Mean Time and the English language, to which were added tax cuts (especially on corporation duty) and reduced import duties, which preceded entry into the euro. This added fuel to the fire through low interest rates determined by the European Central Bank, enhanced investment from the European Union and accessing a much wider capital market. With Irish banks promoting low interest mortgages requiring no deposit by lenders and opening their doors to property developers, the building sector boomed. The results were stupendous: between 1987 and 2003, GDP per capita climbed from 70 per cent of the EU average to 136 per cent, unemployment plummeted from 17 to 4 per cent, while GDP growth attained 10 per cent per annum for most years, triple the EU average. From being one of the poorest countries in western Europe, Ireland was transformed into the fourth-richest country in the OECD, leapfrogging Britain and the United States. The term 'Irich' was coined. Surging tax revenues encouraged Irish governments to throw caution to the wind and increase spending dramatically, confident they could maintain a fiscal surplus. Average house prices rose by 330 per cent (and even higher in Dublin) as first-time buyers were tempted by 100 per cent mortgages and existing home owners increased their mortgages to extend their properties or construct another dwelling at home or overseas. Massive government tax breaks incentivizing new building and a lax attitude towards planning by local authorities stoked the property bubble. Over 700,000 new homes were built during the Celtic Tiger years, equating to one for every six of the 4.6 million citizens, a much greater proportion than England notwithstanding its far greater population. By 2007, the construction industry employed 20 per cent of the workforce.

Rising house prices outstripped incomes by five to one and household debt as a percentage of GDP went from 60 per cent to nearly 200 per cent, the highest in the developed world. This mattered a great deal because where in Britain the property sector represented less than 10 per cent of GDP, in Ireland it was 25 per cent. But the false optimism of the Celtic Tiger years led ministers to reject proposals to raise taxes to curb housing demand. In fact, in 2006, when the economy slowed, they did the opposite, slashing taxes to continue the illusion of an economic miracle. In September 2008, the banks ran out of luck and ceased lending overnight, the property bubble burst and Ireland became the first euro-zone member to go into recession. The Anglo-Irish Bank, with €72 billion of loans (half of Ireland's GDP) had to be nationalized and an €85 billion bailout from the European Union and IMF was required (the United Kingdom contributed £7 billion because Ireland was such an important trading partner). By 2011, property prices had fallen steeply, as much as 70 per cent in some cases, with around 40 per cent of home owners in negative equity. The construction industry contracted massively, leaving over 2,000 'ghost estates' across the country, which were either left incomplete or else only a fraction of their dwellings were owner occupied. Ireland now had the dubious distinction of boasting the largest mortgage debt per head in the world.

What had been taking place was a shift from west to east, which showed no signs of abating and looks set to accelerate in the next decade as western economies, encumbered by debt, uncompetitive wages, high unemployment and expensive welfare support networks, struggle to compete. Indeed, the Chinese joke was that unless Europe's decision-makers got their act together, the European Union would become a museum for Asians and Latins to visit. In 2001, world output stood at around $32 trillion, reaching $50 trillion by the time Lehman Brothers collapsed. By 2011, the figure had reached $70 trillion, but much of the growth derived from outside the western economies. Indeed, there is clearly now a two-speed world

Table 13.2 World Economic League top ten 2011

Position	Country	Previous Year's Position
1	United States	1
2	China	2
3	Japan	3
4	Germany	4
5	France	5
6	Brazil	7
7	United Kingdom	6
8	Italy	8
9	Russia	10
10	India	9

Source: Centre for Economic and Business Research Annual
World Economic League Table.

economy featuring slow-growing advanced economies (predominantly the United States, Europe and Japan) and fast-growing developing economies. Difficult economic conditions in the former should ensure that interest rates remain low. Over the first decade of the new century, an intermingling transpired to the extent that there was no longer a division between the top performers in mature and emerging economies.

It will be observed from Table 13.2 that the top five places remained unchanged but Brazil swapped places with Britain. The largest country in South America, with a population of 203 million people, Brazil had benefited hugely from the boom in commodities, extracting gold, silver, oil and minerals, mostly derived from the Amazon basin. As a stable democracy since 1985, Brazil attracted substantial outside investment, including from Europe. All of the BRIC countries were in the top ten and seem likely to remain there for the foreseeable future. This reflects a role reversal where debt has become more a developed than a developing country problem.

With the arrival of the new millennium, the European Union shared in the celebrations but it was not long before problems began to emerge. These were centred on banks that made risky investments that did not pay off and culminated in implosions that, because of their implications for wider financial viability, prompted interventions from governments to salvage the situation, which in turn increased the size of the national debt, especially in the British case. No sooner had these problems manifested themselves than a sovereign debt crisis, involving the peripheral members of the euro-zone, began to manifest itself, which threw into doubt the viability of the single currency project.

Issues for discussion

1. What were the main trends in the world economy between 2000 and 2011 and how did Europe fare in terms of growth and competitiveness?

2. Should the further enlargement of the European Union over the period be considered more in a positive than a negative light?
3. Why has Russia managed to prosper in the Putin era?
4. Evaluate the main causes of the global financial and economic downturn of 2007–9 and how the European economies were affected.

14 The euro-zone crisis

Emerging problems within the euro-zone

Compounding the economic downturn of 2008–9 was a lingering crisis that commenced in 2010 afflicting the so-called PIIGs (Portugal, Ireland, Italy and Greece) centred round sovereign debt problems, ushering in austerity measures by the afflicted euro-zone members at the behest of the European Union, European Central Bank and the IMF. Debt levels generally rose across the Continent, reflecting more sluggish growth. A resurgent Germany proved the exception, paradoxically reasserting its dominance in some ways yet reluctant to act as the leading European creditor. The dire situation rekindled the debates over the future direction of the European Union and brought the longevity of the single currency into doubt. By 2011, the resolution of the sovereign debt crisis was an all-consuming issue, leading to the collapse of several governments unable to cope, threatening an even greater banking crisis, with the reverberations seen as likely to tip much of the world economy again into recession. Indeed, having begun its life in benign economic conditions, the future of the euro-zone came under threat from a debt storm that refused to sweep through as politicians struggled to find a resolution that could reassure the unforgiving financial markets, which sensed blood. Crisis followed crisis as more troubled economies emerged, while those receiving aid struggled to implement contingent austerity measures, which created a political backlash from their people, bringing protestors on to the streets and condemning the politicians associated with them to defeat at the next election. Failure to find a resolution produced periodic outbursts of near panic and dire predictions, followed by calmer conditions until further developments fanned the flames once again. For instance, Jacques Delors, President of the European Commission from 1985 to 1995, was quoted by *Le Soir* in August 2011, warning that 'Europe is on the edge of the abyss'.

The creation of the single currency for a raft of European Union member states flew in the face of J.M. Keynes' dictum: 'Who controls the currency controls the government.' Such was the political momentum for a euro-zone that no serious consideration was given to problems that might arise when members got into serious economic difficulties. The assumption was made that there would be increasing convergence between member states who joined, despite their disparate economic performances, which proved to be a monumental miscalculation. The exuberance surrounding the arrival of the euro-zone ignored the lessons of history, which showed that currency unions between countries collapse sooner or later. The introduction of the euro in relatively benign economic conditions tended to blind decision-makers towards the dangers ahead. During its first few years, the euro appreciated against the dollar, reaching a high of $1.2185 in June 2004 as the Enron and WorldCom corporate accounting scandals weakened the dollar. The trend continued to 15 July 2008, when the rate reached $1.6038 as the United States became mired in recession. However, once the euro-zone encountered its own debt problems, this adversely affected the value of the euro. Only the strength of the German economy and other northern members prevented it from experiencing a catastrophic decline. Even so, by the end of 2011, the euro was trading at record lows against the dollar and the Japanese yen; the currency continued to struggle to hold its value in 2012 as the crisis refused to go away.

The French were the greatest proponents of the single currency project and it took some persuading for the Germans, especially the Bundesbank, to be convinced. Ever cautious, they were unique in retaining their old notes and coins as a precaution. The Bundesbank insisted that the European Central Bank could not act as a lender of last resort and that Eurobonds must be ruled out. For Berlin the attraction of the single currency was that it would overcome the problem of a strong Deutschmark, allowing German exporters to sell their output at artificially low prices. A further benefit to Germany was that its competitors within the euro-zone could not devalue their currency to restore competitiveness, as had frequently happened with Italy to benefit motor car marquees like Fiat. The Germans deluded themselves that the financial discipline required to qualify for membership would be maintained. In fact, once the entrants got beyond the gates, all restraint went out of the window, not least because there was no exit mechanism for errant members. At the time, William Hague, then leader of the British Conservative Party, was mocked for referring to the euro-zone as 'a burning building with no exits', but he was later vindicated. American and British economists critical of the project warned that a single central bank and currency without a unified state, as in the United States' monetary system, could not work. Jacques Delors, whose report instigated the single currency project, subsequently claimed to have in mind common economic policies to harmonize taxation, employment and welfare programmes, but his proposal was swept aside. Nor was any attention paid to the need for constant vigilance by the Council of Ministers to ensure that member states complied with the criteria for economic convergence. The euro was designed to prevent financial markets from distinguishing between countries on the basis of exchange rates. Instead markets discriminated on the basis of bond rates and many private investors were tempted by the more attractive rates offered by the peripheral members, which, within the new single currency framework, appeared to offer a safe investment and better returns.

The low interest rates arising from the requirements of the core economies centred on Germany encouraged irresponsible lending by governments and financial institutions in the Mediterranean members and Ireland. The core northern economies were destined to perform best within the new currency framework, whereas the peripheral southern economies struggled while taking on more and more debt, creating a time bomb that was soon set to explode. The temptation to borrow cheaply (in effect being treated as akin to Germany) proved too great and the latter indulged their fantasies, whereas the Germans, ever mindful of the hyperinflation of the 1920s and the Great Depression, which brought their nemesis Hitler to power, resisted; there was consequently no German credit boom, no explosion in wages and property prices remained stable across Germany, while the government stayed fiscally prudent, knowing that to act otherwise would be unacceptable to the electorate. German banks were the exception in helping to fund foreign lenders, delving into the American subprime market, hedge funds, credit default swaps, the Irish property boom, Icelandic banks and Greek government bonds. They would come to regret their decision.

Little consideration was given to addressing asymmetric shocks in the euro-zone. Economists recommended setting aside 2 to 3 per cent of GDP to meet this contingency, but the Franco-German axis of Helmut Kohl and Frances Mitterand overrode the idea. Again, the European Commission mooted a common Treasury, quietly dropping the proposal when opposition emerged. In June 1997, the Growth and Stability Pact, a German initiative, emerged from the Amsterdam summit, which sought to prevent members of the monetary union from letting their deficits get out of control, imposing a ceiling of 3 per cent of GDP. 'The rationale for the Stability Pact', wrote Eichengreen and Park (2004, 422), 'is that deficits today may imply deficits tomorrow, and that chronic deficits are problematic because they may lead to problems of debt sustainability that force the central bank to provide an inflationary debt bail-out.' However, large members proved resistant to being constrained, rebuffing the efforts of the European Commission and smaller members to impose collective discipline. Ironically, in view of later events, it was the Germans, struggling with the costs of reunification, that first breached the rules in 2003, followed by France, with a majority of finance ministers voting not to fine them, thereby setting a precedent that encouraged further misdemeanours. Of the large economies, Italy proved the worst offender. Admitted into the euro-zone notwithstanding the fact it failed to meet the Maastricht criteria, Italy was always likely to create difficulties. For political reasons, as a founding member of the European Economic Community, Italy could not be left out and the then German Chancellor, Gerhard Schröder, also mindful of the Italian propensity to devalue, insisted it must join the euro-zone, whereas the French, fearful that competing farmers whose countries stayed out could gain a competitive edge, were anxious that southern members, including Italy, must be incorporated. So a wheeze was created, whereby entrants no longer needed national debt below 60 per cent of their GDP but were required only to demonstrate that the trend was in that direction, which Rome could do. This proved to be wishful thinking. In July 2005, European Union finance ministers elected not to punish Italy for allowing its budget deficit to surge towards 5 per cent of GDP, considerably above the 3 per cent limit, while its overall debt was nearing 108 per cent of GDP, instead giving

Rome two years to retrench, notwithstanding that its government was embarking on ill-advised tax cuts. Spain was the solitary big player not to breach the annual borrowing limit between 1999 and 2007, but was swept off course thereafter in the wake of the 2008 financial crisis and the bursting of its property bubble.

Greece was always going to be the weakest link in the euro-zone. It failed to qualify for euro entry at the first attempt, when its public debt was 106 per cent of GDP, succeeding at the second try in January 2001 only because of fraudulent statistics. The deceit was aided by Goldman Sachs. A Greek employee in its London office, Addy Loudiadis, found a loophole in European Union accounting regulations that helped the Greek government to create the illusion of a falling national debt. A currency swap allowed Greece to hide €1 billion of debt and military expenditure was emasculated. In fact, the Greek economy never stayed within the 3 per cent target. By October 2011, the disparity in the economic performance of the strongest and weakest members was reflected by the fact that Germany could issue ten-year bonds on a yield of 1.74 per cent, whereas for Greece it was 23.89 per cent. Following its independence in 1830, Greece became hugely indebted to the Great Powers, leading to defaults on its debts in 1843, 1860, 1893 and 1932. Indeed, Greece has the unenviable record of being in default to its creditors more often than any other European country. Within Europe, it also scored highest in the record for missing repayments (half of the period since 1800). Greece has been called the 'richest country in the world which doesn't make anything'. The Greek economy was dependent on tourism, agriculture and the mercantile marine to generate income. In 1981 the left-wing Panhellenic Socialist Movement (PASOK) party came to power under Andreas Papandreou, which bloated the public sector, creating jobs in return for votes. This social contract between government and people ensured that the PASOK went on winning elections while peddling a Greek myth that all was well, but, in living beyond its means, an implosion was bound to come sooner or later. The situation was compounded by continued high defence spending because of rivalry with Turkey concerning control of the Aegean Sea, tension arising from the prospect of exploiting minerals found there and provocative Turkish overflights of Greek airspace.

Greece was admitted into the European Community in 1981 for political reasons, with the decision-makers in Brussels at the time hoping that eventually Greece's economic productivity would improve but, despite continual injections of aid money, no fundamental transformation occurred. The Greek nation celebrated entry into the euro-zone and the Prime Minister promised greater stability and new horizons. This delusory euphoria was accentuated by Greece becoming host to the 2004 Olympic Games. With the eyes of the world upon it (sceptics anticipating a disastrous staging), the Greek authorities spared no effort in constructing the site and modernizing transport links, including the lavish Athens metro underground system and the German-designed new international airport. Although the games passed off successfully the cost of hosting them (€12 billion) pushed up the deficit, which began to spiral out of control. At the same time, there was no structural transformation of the Greek economy. Rather than modernize, socialist governments continued to expand the public sector, which was highly inefficient, to create jobs and court votes. Moreover, several small-scale industries, such as clothing, shoes and handbags, which had thrived under the drachma through finding a market niche in between top-quality French and Italian manufacturers and the mass-produced ware from the developing world, were wiped out by the strong euro. Tourism also suffered because holidaymakers shifted their allegiance from Greece (and Italy, Portugal and Spain) towards cheaper Mediterranean destinations in Tunisia, Turkey and elsewhere.

Compounding Greek structural weaknesses were government largesse and wide-scale tax avoidance. Far too much Greek economic activity took place 'in the black', leaving no record. Examples abound. Owners of luxury motor yachts avoided VAT by getting their Filipino servants to pose as tourists hiring the boats because chartered vessels were zero-rated and received a generous allowance on diesel fuel, meaning a saving of €230,000 on a yacht worth €1 million. Some 800 retired politicians were given €80 million in 'transition grants'; civil servants received bonuses for washing their hands; university professors accessed European Union research funds to acquire motor cars and houses; farmers procured Mercedes and luxury private apartments through European Union grants intended to improve agricultural productivity. Not only was the state extremely generous to those at the top, it also sweetened the workers. Thus Members of Parliament were paid 16 monthly salaries a year, while civil servants and public workers received two monthly bonuses at Christmas and Easter. Several state enterprises rewarded workers with a five-day break each year at a luxury hotel of their choice; civil servants could earn bonuses for punctuality and even for using a Xerox machine. On the metro in Athens, train drivers received €60,000 salaries, while commuters were given the option to pay because there were no entry barriers; predictably many elected to travel free. The Greek system represented the economics of the madhouse, which created an entitlement culture.

Greek governments clearly bore the main share of the blame for what went on, but they also reflect the mentality ingrained in the people. Even tax inspectors were corrupt and open to bribery. A subsequent investigation discovered that 70 officials possessed properties worth between €800,000 and €3 million, despite officially earning only €51,000 per annum. Theodoros Pangalos, the Deputy Prime Minister and grandson of a 1920s dictator, reflected: 'We ate the money together.' Nevertheless, the cries of protestors in Syntagma Square in Athens, who began congregating there to denounce politicians as 'traitors and thieves', had a ring of truth to them: the main parties claimed €10 annually for every vote cast for them (against an equivalent of 70 centimes in Germany), while politicians used their salaries as collateral to procure bank loans, leaving them owing Greek banks €260 million. The political corruption endemic among the Greek political elite in turn engendered an attitude among the people, especially the professional classes, of tax avoidance, because any taxes collected were perceived as being wasted. By 2011, the Treasury was being deprived of an estimated €30 billion euros in taxes. This mattered a great deal when, according to the IMF, 75 per cent of Greek public spending was consumed by public sector pay and pensions.

The euro-zone sovereign debt crisis

In November 2009, George Papandreou was elected Greek prime minister of a new PASOK government in a landslide victory, over the centre-right party New Democracy, which had ruled Greece since 2004, promising a €3 billion stimulus package to court voters and to revive the economy. Once in office, having seen the books, he scrapped this commitment and equated the situation to being on board the *Titanic*. Eurostat, the European Union's statistics agency, began investigating Greece's finances, reporting in November 2010 that in 2009 it estimated that the government deficit reached 15.4 per cent of GDP and public debt amounted to 126.8 per cent of GDP, the highest in the euro-zone. By spring 2010, Papandreou was pleading for affordable interest rates but not getting them from the financial markets, leading him to request 'European support so we can borrow money under reasonable conditions'. A European Union summit (24–25 March 2010), the first of many on euro-zone debt problems, considered the Greek case. Although bail-outs were specifically ruled out by the Maastricht Treaty this impediment was sidestepped through recourse to Articles intended to deal with earthquakes and floods. This produced a €110 billion bail-out deal in May 2010, whereby the European Union contributed €80 billion and the IMF the remainder. It was designed to prevent Greece from defaulting on its debt and contingent on Greece implementing austerity measures. The Greek Finance Minister, George Papaconstantinou, stated that Greece had been asked to make a 'basic choice between collapse or salvation'. The Germans proved most reluctant to assist the Greeks. Chancellor Angela Merkel was sceptical, describing Greek austerity plans as 'very ambitious'. She saw the conditional bail-out as a warning to other endangered members of the euro-zone to avert the same fate.

However, within a short period, Greece had been joined by Portugal, Ireland and Spain. A year later, in May 2011, a €78 billion bail-out was agreed for Portugal, which was charged with reducing its budget deficit from 9.1 to 3 per cent of GDP by 2013. The deal followed the collapse of the Portuguese government in March 2011 after parliament rejected proposed austerity measures. Portugal had experienced the lowest growth rate of euro-zone members. Its industries found themselves priced out of markets through increased competition from Asia and eastern Europe. Although a privatization programme was under way, this was not vigorous; often former politicians rather than dynamic businessmen were put in charge, a form of 'soft corruption'. Rigid labour laws including employment protection contributed to Portugal's growing difficulties.

It was illusory for Europe's politicians to imagine that they had resolved the Greek problem. In fact, the austerity programme imposed on Greece only deepened recession, with the economy shrinking by 10 per cent between 2009 and mid-2011; unemployment remained stubbornly high; Greek public finances actually worsened as tax revenues fell even further. Far from being welcomed, external intervention was resented (the Greek finance minister protested that his country was being 'blackmailed and humiliated'), and there were echoes of the past, with swastikas emblazoned across the European Union flag by protestors.

The European Union, European Central Bank, and the IMF were not hailed as saviours but denounced as the 'troika'. The Papandreou government made a start in combating corruption, but faced an uphill battle against an unsympathetic electorate. It announced a reform of the state pension scheme, which had allowed some Greeks to retire in their forties, and decreed that all pension recipients must attend a bank once a year in person to substantiate that they were still living to address the ridiculous situation of children of deceased Greeks receiving their parents' pension for years, even decades. A former counterterrorism officer was appointed to enforce the collection of taxes owed to the state. Satellite imagery revealed to tax inspectors that there were 16,974 unregistered swimming pools in Athens. Spot-checks outside the capital's nightclubs discovered 6,000 people claiming incomes of only €10,000 per annum who owned cars valued at over €100,000.

However, there was no transformation of attitude either from the tax avoiders or the government, which paid lip service to the troika's requirements while seeking to avoid administering the more painful medicine. *Aúpio* (tomorrow) was a favourite word of the Greek language. By summer 2011, the Greek government was chasing €500 million from luxury yacht owners but managed to collect only €2.5 million. The extravagant special retirement regimes costing the state billions every year remained untouched, as did the 'closed shop' system that afflicted sectors of the economy. For example, in the pharmaceutical industry, chemists received €35 for every €100 worth of prescription drugs sold to customers, whereas in Germany the equivalent was €3.80, thereby costing the Greek state around €1.5 billion per annum. The government's promise to raise €50 billion through privatizing state assets, including banks, utilities and ports, was illusory. Papandreou's fanciful offer to include some Greek islands blithely ignored the fact that Greece lacked a land registry and the ownership of many prized plots was disputed. Even were this hurdle overcome, others would remain: eight ministers must sanctify an island's sale, non-European Union buyers require clearance from the Defence Ministry and 2,500 official licences and permits must be completed. By the time of the second bail-out (see below), no privatization had transpired, confirming a World Bank study of 2010 that ranked Greece 96th as a place to invest. Many of the government's gestures were contradictory. Imposing a 2 per cent tax on property holdings worth over €4 million, for instance, could act only as a disincentive to private investors when state land came onto the market. Again the PASOK government, with its wafer-thin majority, made no move to instigate reforms to the political system, which enraged the man on the street. The political parties offered expatriate Greeks free air tickets so that they could return home to vote. One reason why Olympus Airways went bankrupt was because the parties failed to meet the bills. Ordinary people were following their example and refusing to pay utility bills. Corruption remained rife in Greek society from top to bottom. Transparency International calculated that one in six of the population was involved in 'small envelopes' (*fakelaki*) to grease the palms of government officials, bribery worth at least €1 billion per year. Indeed, tax evasion actually worsened as the crisis deepened. In 2011, of five million taxpayers, only 33 admitted an income exceeding €750,000 and less than 300 conceded that their earnings lay between €400,000 and €750,000.

The widening debt crisis

Between them, Greece, Ireland and Portugal constituted 17 per cent of the GDP of the euro-zone. Their problems appeared to be containable. The danger was of contagion to bigger players. Spain and Italy now came under the spotlight. Spain had seemed like one of the success stories of the euro-zone, creating over half of the new jobs in the European Union between 2000 and 2005, generally returning a level of growth of over 3 per cent from 1997–2007. However, much of this was dependent on a real-estate boom that started in 1997 and ended in 2007, during which time five million new dwellings were built and the number of households increased by a quarter. The property-building mania generated 16 per cent of GDP and 12 per cent of employment at its peak. Property prices rocketed during this period, leading new home owners to take on excessive levels of debt as Spanish banks offered cheap loans. In 2008, the property bubble burst and unemployment, having stood at 7.6 per cent in October 2006, soared to stand at 20.33 per cent by December 2010. In January 2010, Spain began introducing austerity measures, which were intensified four months later. Spain's economy was fragile, but it managed to stay afloat through its banks, which by September 2011 held €142 billion of Spanish national bonds. Indeed, Spain's largest bank, Santander, had contributed to the British government's bail-out of its banking sector.

Italy too was not reliant on foreign investors to service its bonds (most of which were held domestically) but was facing debts nearing €1,900 billion, equivalent to 120 per cent of GDP, the second largest of the euro-zone after Greece. From the 1980s, Italian governments went on uncontrolled spending sprees. Aside from a brief period of surplus around entry into the euro, a high public deficit was the norm. At the same time, the north–south divide continued (between 2000 and 2006, depressed parts of the rural south elicited €27.4 billion in aid from the European Development Fund), corruption was corrosive, including the ever-present Mafia, and insufficient attention was paid to infrastructure development, market reforms and research investment. As a result, the country, notwithstanding its membership of the G8, had the fewest multinationals of the advanced economies. Small and medium-sized businesses predominated in the industrial north, which focused on high-quality exports to niche markets as a means to avert the fierce competition from emerging economies.

As the third-largest euro-zone member, Italy was regarded as 'too big to bail'. The Italian position was not aided by the tendency to announce draconian austerity measures to placate the markets, only then to withdraw them. This reluctance to act reflected the fear that austerity would accelerate the economic slowdown, while much-needed liberalization measures threatened the privileged positions of large corporations and the professional classes. Moreover, the rioting occasioned by threatened austerity measures elsewhere acted as a further disincentive to come to grips with the problem.

Table 14.1 Euro-zone debt as a percentage of
GDP, selected countries, 2010

Country	GDP (%)
Italy	118.4
Belgium	96.2
Ireland	94.9
Portugal	93.3
Germany	83.2
France	82.3
Austria	71.8
Netherlands	62.9
Spain	61.0
Finland	48.3
Eurozone average	85.4
United States	94.4

Source: Eurostat.

A key moment occurred at Deauville in October 2010, when European leaders decreed that bondholders must take losses as an integral part of future bail-outs. This decision injected credit risk into the euro-zone sovereign debt market and investors began dumping their bonds, seeking safe havens for their money (primarily German bunds or American Treasury stock).

The decision-makers took the view that there was a clear need to keep the Greek patient on the life support machine for two reasons. First, to write off all Greek debts would set a dangerous precedent, which other ailing euro-zone members might demand to follow. Second, European banks that were exposed to Greek debt would be severely weakened and in some instances in danger of collapse. If one failed the cascading effect risked setting off another Lehman Brothers style scenario. The Armageddon worst-case scenario would see a euro-zone country default, triggering a loss of confidence in the markets concerning other nations' debts, leading to an *en masse* withdrawal of liquidity from private sector banks, whose survival would be in grave doubt. The contagion could spread beyond the euro-zone as panicked investors withdrew their funds and sold shares in other banks, crippling the world's financial system. The best-case scenario would see politicians find a way to burden share between creditor and debtor nations, injecting liquidity into threatened banks and giving the European Financial Stability Facility (EFSF) (see below) more firepower to put out the flames before a wildfire developed that got out of control.

By the summer of 2011, it was apparent that the bail-out to Greece would not deliver the results anticipated. Without a second rescue package, Greece was heading for a default on its debt mountain. Behind closed doors at an emergency summit in Brussels, Merkel and the then French President Nicolas Sarkozy hatched a scheme to tide Greece over for the short term whilst seeking simultaneously to prevent contagion affecting other afflicted euro-zone members, thereby hoping to restore the confidence of the markets. The three elements that emerged were the reduction of interest rates to Greece, Ireland and Portugal, some losses to private investors to bring down Greece's debt and a conversion of the euro-zone's temporary bail-out fund into a more substantive and flexible financial instrument. The new €159 billion financing package created a new European Financial Stability Fund (EFSB) with powers to buy the debt of countries in difficulties and to fund bank rescues. Germany, as the euro-zone's biggest economy, would contribute 27 per cent of its war chest. Sarkozy equated it to a European monetary fund. The German *quid pro quo* for this was the insistence that private financial institutions must pay a price in the form of lower interest rates and deferred maturity on their Greek bond holdings amounting to €16 billion or over 21 per cent of the burden. Interest rates on Greece's emergency loans were reduced from 5.5 to 3.5 per cent, with the repayment period extended from seven to at least fifteen years, with a maximum term of thirty years. While the markets initially greeted news of the second bail-out with euphoria, this reflected the fact that the previous rescue attempts were so evidently flawed and wanting. Once the dust had settled and the fine detail or lack of it was examined, second thoughts were evident and reflected in renewed market turbulence. In effect, this was a barely disguised form of partial default, with private creditors being asked for partial debt forgiveness, an unprecedented step for a developed country since the Second World War.

Subsequently, the assumptions underpinning the agreement began to unravel as the world economy slowed down, the positions of other afflicted euro-zone members with sovereign debt problems worsened, and Greece's internal situation deteriorated as the populace rebelled against the austerity measures required by the troika. The fundamental flaw was that Greece was still left with more debt than it could possibly repay. To this point, not one public sector worker had been made redundant as the PASOK government sought to satisfy the troika enough to continue receiving tranches of money from the first bail-out agreement while at the same time not alienating supporters and imperilling its political survival.

If the euro was to have a long-term future, then the logical further steps would be fiscal union, the issuance of euro-zone–wide bonds bearing the same rate of interest and repayment periods, the creation of a European Monetary Fund and the transfer of funds from the richer north to the poorer south. Sarkozy intimated as much when he hailed the deal as 'a historic moment'. 'Our ambition', he admitted, 'is to seize the Greek crisis to make a quantum leap in euro-zone government.' However, French enthusiasm was dampened by German scepticism, borne of the realization that German taxpayers would carry the main burden. Jens Weidmann, the President of the Bundesbank, sounded a note of caution, issuing a statement that suggested that the principles underpinning the second bail-out carried dangerous connotations.

> By transferring sizeable additional risks to aid granting countries and their taxpayers, the euro area made a big step toward a collectivization of risks in cases of unsolid public finances and economic mistakes. That's weakening the foundations of a monetary union founded on fiscal self-responsibility.

In future, it will be even more difficult to maintain incentives for solid fiscal policies.

Efforts to harmonize fiscal governance are liable to meet the opposition of public opinion. In Germany, the widespread view was taken that Greeks were lazy and German taxpayers should not be asked to bail out profligate economies again and again without result. The contrasting retirement ages for public workers in Greece and Germany (55 against 67) was trumpeted as epitomizing the perceived contrast between the work ethics of the two countries.

What was apparent was that the fiscal imbalances of the smaller euro-zone economies (Greece, Ireland and Portugal) were containable and sufficient resources existed, given the political will to deploy them, to rescue this triumvirate from financial oblivion. Should the contagion spread to engulf Italy and Spain, however, then the resulting crisis could become unmanageable and the future of the euro itself might be at stake. Greece, for example, constituted only 2 per cent of the euro-zone GDP, whereas Spain and Italy combined accounted for 24 per cent, seemingly too big to be bailed out without capsizing the euro project. Italy was estimated to require £500 billion by the end of 2013, and if borrowing costs hit Greek levels of interest, then it would struggle to remain solvent.

The British decision to retain sterling and stay outside the euro-zone (which Margaret Thatcher famously called 'cloud cuckoo land') appeared vindicated. The exposure of British banks to Greek debt was only €2 billion, a quarter of their French and German counterparts. At the same time, Britain could not be completely disinterested in the fate of the single currency because half of its exports went to the European Union and much of the euro-zone's financial activity was transacted in the City of London. Moreover, because Ireland was a key trading partner the Conservative–Liberal coalition government elected to lend substantial sums to Dublin to ease its woes and by summer 2011 had assumed liabilities of £12.5 billion to assist Greece, Ireland and Portugal. As an IMF member, Britain paid a proportion of the funding devoted to addressing the euro-zone crisis.

Greece became the benchmark against which indebted countries measured the severity of their situation, an extreme to be avoided or against which their problems almost paled into insignificance. President Barack Obama, looking towards winning a second term in 2012, insisted that the United States was not Greece and the downgrading of America's credit rating from AAA to AA+ reflected the political malaise surrounding raising the borrowing ceiling on 12 August 2011 by two trillion dollars rather than any doubts that US Treasury bonds would not be repaid. Although the Chinese had, helpfully, invested some of their largesse in the euro-zone, there is no market beyond the United States that can absorb their surplus capital, meaning that Washington can continue to incur rising debt without fear that its largest creditor will take fright. Again, the prospect that Britain might become another Greece seemed far-fetched. To begin with, the scale of government debt did not bear comparison: whereas in 2011, the OECD estimated the net financial liabilities of Greece equated to 114.2 per cent of GDP, those of the United Kingdom were just under half that figure (56.3 per cent). Then again, when Greece

Table 14.2 The cost of rescuing the euro-zone

Country	GDP in 2011	Size of Bail-out	Source(s)	Date(s)
Greece	€215 billion	€247 billion	Bilateral loans, EFSF, IMF	May 2010 and February 2012
Ireland	€156 billion	€67.5 billion	Bilateral loans, EFSF, EU, IMF	November 2010
Portugal	€171 billion	€78 billion	EFSF, EU, IMF	May 2011
Spain	€1.1 trillion	€100 billion	EFSF or ESM	June 2012

Source: *Financial Times*, 11 June 2012.

was seeking to borrow on the capital markets, it was facing crippling interest rates in double digits, whereas Britain could borrow at a real rate of only 0.3 per cent, which was below most predictions of future growth, promising that tax revenues will grow faster than accumulated debt. This was of course to assume that interest rates would remain historically low. To avert a Greek-style crisis, the Bank of England had recourse to quantitative easing (printing money) to purchase government bonds, promote bank liquidity and encourage lending to businesses, a monetary easing not available to Greece because it belonged to a currency union. If this was overdone, then it risked stoking inflation, but used prudently, pumping extra notes into the financial system boosted the purchase of Treasury stock, whose attraction was compounded by Britain's continued AAA credit rating, the low interest rates on savings and the fluctuations of the stock market. By early 2012, the Bank of England had injected €325 billion into the economy.

The attitude of Germany (the spider in the web) was critical to the survival of the euro in its present form. One of Henry Ford's famous dictums is: 'The secret of success is to understand the point of view of others.' The German position softened to some extent as the crisis deepened (in 2010, Chancellor Merkel declared: 'We have a treaty under which there is no possibility of paying to bail out states'), although underlying Berlin's stance was an aversion to extreme solutions and a desire to instigate containing measures to prevent any debt default, which carried implications for the exposed German banking sector. There were four centres of power in Berlin (the Chancellery, the Finance Ministry, the Bundesbank and the Constitutional Court), which complicated the decision-making process. Cynics also suggested that the Germans had a vested interest in a struggling euro because it kept their exports competitive. Following an emergency summit in Paris between the French and German leaders on 16 August 2011, the outcome reflected German caution and Merkel's step-by-step approach. Although both pronounced themselves committed to further integration in the euro-zone (a 'real economic government'), Eurobonds were specifically ruled out for the moment because mutualizing debt whilst the seventeen members had such disparate fiscal and economic policies was illogical. 'We could imagine this', Sarkozy explained, 'but at the end of the process of integration of the euro-zone, not at the beginning.' 'Germany and France feel absolutely determined to strengthen the euro as our common currency and further develop it', declared Chancellor Merkel.

Many analysts were predicting that Greece was bound to default at some stage. By autumn 2011, with the troika holding back on extending a further tranche of the original bail-out, the Athens government admitted it would not be able to meet its borrowing targets in 2011. The question being asked was whether this was a consequence of a deepening recession or whether the authorities had failed to act vigorously enough to reduce borrowing. The troika took the latter view. Carlo Cottarelli, the IMF's leading fiscal affairs official, maintained the toughening approach latterly adopted towards Athens: 'Greece has shown that it is taking this programme seriously, obviously what was done is not enough, further adjustment is necessary. We have a team in Athens to assess which measures must be taken'. The Greek government naturally inclined towards the former view, wishing to avert yet more austerity measures. Although there was an element of truth in both explanations, the continued failure to collect tax revenue remained a major concern. To June 2011, the government had generated only 56.8 per cent of anticipated net tax revenues for the whole year. At the same time, public spending, at 69 per cent by the autumn, was moving ahead of budget. The Greek authorities resorted to a new property tax, with non-payers having their electricity supplies terminated through its administration via electricity bills. This tax, greater than any previously demanded, was to be applied to all property owners regardless of their circumstances. It was based on square metres, the age of the building and the average value of a neighbourhood, without taking income into account. The measure helped to convince European finance ministers to release the latest tranche of aid from the first bail-out in late November 2011, but was beginning to founder by the close of the year. The government announced that non-payers would not have their electricity cut off before their circumstances were reviewed; union workers occupied the power company's billing centre to prevent bills from being distributed; and an illicit group of electricians threatened to reconnect anyone whose power was disconnected. At the end of the year, tax collectors themselves went on strike, disgruntled at the prospect of losing their privileges. By then, too, the PASOK government had fallen after stepping out of line and threatening to call a referendum on the latest austerity measures.

In Italy, too, there was a change at the head of government, when Mario Monti became prime minister on 12 November 2011. Known as *Il Professore*, he was an economist with previous experience as a European commissioner, a technocrat without political affiliations, who could promote austerity measures designed to restore market confidence in the Italian economy, thereby lowering the cost of borrowing. Monti introduced an emergency austerity programme, which envisaged tax increases, pension reform and measures to combat tax evasion and which successfully passed both houses of parliament by 22 December. Further reforms, this time targeting the labour market, were unveiled on 20 January 2012, including proposals to open up certain privileged professions to greater competition, ending minimum tariffs for their services, and to reform Article 18 of the labour code to make it easier for employers to hire and fire workers. These provoked public demonstrations, which resulted in some watering down of the measures to get them through parliament. Monti's tenure was dependent on the continued political support of the main parties, which for the moment preferred him to administer the medicine. Trade unions were also strong in the public sector and deeply resistant to austerity measures. Indeed, in its 2012 report on the Italian economy, the European Commission criticized Monti's non-party government's performance. For example, its efforts to identify and restore unpaid taxes were deemed 'still insufficient' and remained a 'key challenge'. In May 2012, Monti instigated a spending review intended to find €4.2 billion in cuts, which Professor Francesco Giavazzi, one of Monti's harshest critics, likened to 'a timid mouse' because it would target only one-tenth of government spending. The OECD was also critical, projecting that the Italian economy would attain an annual average growth of only 0.5 per cent between 2012 and 2017, representing the poorest rate for the 41 countries in its survey.

The European banking sector, the largest in the world, was perilously exposed to a Greek default, especially French and German banks. Already, in October 2011, the Belgian banking group Dexia, the biggest in Belgium, was teetering on collapse through its exposure (€20.9 billion) to the sovereign debt from the troubled members of the euro-zone. Having been bailed out in 2008, when the French and Belgian governments became major shareholders, Dexia again verged on bankruptcy, becoming heavily reliant on short-term borrowing, while mostly lending long term. Ironically, Dexia had passed a round of stress tests for European banks three months before, which evidently were not severe enough and aimed primarily at satisfying the markets (only two banks emerged as problematic). Commercial banks stopped lending to Dexia and, following a 42 per cent plunge in its stock price, trading in its shares was halted. On 9 October 2011 (a Sunday), a rescue package was announced, whereby Belgium nationalized the consumer bank and the French municipal financing arm merged with the French state bank Caisse des Dépôts and Banque Postale, the banking arm of the French postal service. Dexia planned to create a 'bad bank' to absorb its bad assets, including Greek, Italian, Portuguese and Irish debt.

This example raised the wider question of how to shore up vulnerable banks in anticipation of a further worsening of the economic environment. The French wished to utilize the EFSF to support their banks, seeing this as a means to avert a downgrading of their triple A credit rating, a sensitive issue for Sarkozy, with presidential elections looming. However, the Germans wanted member states to first exhaust their own funding, fearing that to allow France to access the EFSF for this purpose would set a dangerous precedent that other struggling members would clamour to follow. The IMF estimated that the European banks might need €300 billion in additional capital should the debt crisis widen.

Europe's rescue plan found wanting

France and Germany were colluding to produce what Brussels officials called a 'Grand Bargain' to rescue the euro. The Germans demanded that there must be total oversight over the budgets of member states, with discipline enforced by stiff penalties on wrongdoers. For Berlin, this provided a way around authorizing the mass bail-out of profligate members by the European Central Bank, which would alienate German voters and probably be ruled illegal by the German constitutional court. Merkel extolled the virtues of a 'fiscal union' in a speech on 2 December 2011. In February 2012, 25 of the 27 European Union member states (Britain and the Czech Republic were the exceptions) agreed to back a new fiscal treaty to ensure that in future no country's budget deficit exceeded 3 per cent of GDP. This amounted to a return to the same rule enshrined in the Maastricht Treaty, except that that this time around, Berlin envisaged stiff penalties for errant members. Berlin was determined to introduce the vetting of national budgets to ensure compliance. Because all participants needed their parliaments or referenda to approve the new legislation, the fiscal treaty would take some time to come into effect. 'This is all about avoiding the next crisis', bemoaned Martin van Vliet, senior economist at ING Bank in Amsterdam. 'It has little effect on this one.'

At the final European summit of 2011, which fell just before Christmas (the fifteenth meeting to try to come to grips with the sovereign debt crisis), British Prime Minister David Cameron exercised Britain's veto for the first time to block a European Union-wide treaty because he wanted to protect the City of London against a transaction tax, which he feared could lead to an exodus of investment institutions to other financial centres where it is not applied. The London financial services industry, referred to internationally as 'the City', contained more banks and insurance companies than anywhere else in the world, competing with Wall Street in trades of stocks and shares. Other trades included gold and precious metals, futures, derivatives, shipping and energy. Easily Europe's biggest financial centre, considerably larger than the Paris Bourse and several times greater than Frankfurt, the City of London made an essential contribution to the British economy: 10 per cent of GDP, with the top-earning 1 per cent of earners contributing 27.7 per cent of all income taxes (from 2 per cent in 2000), generating £47 billion in 2011, which was greater than Treasury tax receipts from companies and sufficient to fund a third of the welfare state. Half of the elite of 308,000 people (equivalent to Coventry's population) resided in London and the southeast. Were these entrepreneurs to be alienated and leave the country, the financial implications for the government would be serious.

Towards the end of 2011, it was apparent that the leaders of the euro-zone had failed to get to grips with the sovereign debt crisis and that if anything their interventions made the situation worse, not better. Delors condemned them for acting 'too little too late'. The German and French leaders were more reactive than proactive, always two steps behind the markets. On numerous occasions, Merkel and Sarkozy pronounced they had reached a groundbreaking deal to save the euro-zone, bringing brief euphoria to the markets before dissection revealed the smoke and mirrors behind the latest conjuring trick. The European Central Bank's capacity to ease the situation was severely limited. Not only could it not act as a lender of last resort to debtor nations but it could purchase bonds only in the secondary markets. Since mid-2011, American investment houses, alarmed by the disarray in the euro-zone, had choked off access to short-term dollar funds, while interbank lending was also grinding to a halt.

What was looming was the nightmare scenario of a run on the banks, which could ripple through European and overseas markets on a scale that would make the Lehman Brothers crisis seem like small fry. Greece was already starting to experience a flight of capital from its banks, losing €14 billion in deposits between August and October 2011. Indeed, deposits in Greek banks had by then fallen by a quarter compared with their peak in 2007. No wonder that Sir Mervyn King, the Governor of the Bank of England, warned British banks to prepare to face an 'exceptionally threatening environment'. Indeed, in December 2011, King spoke of the prospect of a bigger contraction even than the Great Depression. In an effort to ward off the impending storm, the Bank of England, the US Federal Reserve and the Bank of Japan led an intervention by six central banks to cut the interest rate on emergency loans of dollars to struggling banks that were finding it increasingly difficult to access funds from American banks fearful of a euro-zone collapse. The move also reflected the fact that American banks and money market funds had already lent extensively to Europe and would be exposed if there was a contagious run on European banks. To guard against the worst-case scenario, Barclays Bank cut its debt exposure to Portugal, Italy, Ireland, Greece and Spain by 31 per cent between June and September 2011, while Prudential reduced its exposure to debt tied up in the most troubled economies to £49 million. Banks are not required to declare the size of their hedge funds, so the extent of any seismic shocks was an unknown quantity.

On 8 December 2011, the European Central Bank finally rode to the rescue, announcing that it would make available funds to commercial banks at its main interest rate (which was reduced to 1 per cent) at two auctions. The first elicited bids of €489 billion, and there were early signs of a similar effect to the action in June 2009. The second, in February 2012, released €500 billion amid evidence that Italian and Spanish banks, who accounted for 60 per cent of the take-up, were using the money to purchase government bonds, attracted by their higher yield. In the summer of 2012, the European Stability Mechanism, a permanent bail-out fund agreed in February 2011, was set to replace the EFSF, though whether it would have sufficient firepower to deal with all contingencies seemed doubtful. The idea was also mooted of the European Central Bank lending money to the IMF to lend on to euro-zone members in difficulties. Collectively, these measures bought time and avoided a widespread credit crunch. Indeed, there was some evidence that the European Central Bank's intervention had bolstered confidence to the extent that key investors (French mutual funds and German insurers) stopped selling peripheral government bonds and began to buy government stocks again.

The American credit ratings agencies, having been so remiss in anticipating the subprime crisis in the United States, became more proactive and judgemental towards the euro-zone crisis. Their pronouncements mattered because negative ratings increased perceived risk and thereby the cost of borrowing in bond markets. In January 2012, Standard & Poor's condemned austerity as self-defeating in that the associated measures only deepened the financial crisis, announcing a raft of downgrades which it justified as 'primarily driven by insufficient policy measures by EU leaders to fully address systematic stresses'. Portugal and Cyprus were relegated to junk status, while France and Austria both lost their coveted triple A status, leaving Germany as the sole remaining major economy within the euro-zone retaining a top rating, which meant that the bail-out funding became much more expensive. Fitch quickly followed, downgrading Belgium, Cyprus, Italy, Slovenia and Spain, while conferring junk status on Portugal. The following month, Moody's downgraded Italy, Portugal, Slovakia, Slovenia and Spain; at the same time placing Austria, Britain and France on 'negative' watch.

The 'Greece problem' became an epic that refused to go away. There were signs of a changing mood in Brussels orchestrated by Berlin that demanded guarantees that the required austerity measures would be adhered to. Equally, there was a determination among the Greek people not to bend to Germany's will. In the early hours of 13 February 2012, the Greek parliament approved a raft of cuts that were demanded by the troika to release money from the second bail-out fund. Otherwise, with €14.4 billion of loan repayments to private lenders falling due on 20 March 2012, Greece would default on its debts. The coalition government, formed in November 2011 led by Lucas Papademos, a former vice-president of the European Central Bank, had delayed acceding to the troika's demands until the eleventh hour, finally relenting when economic catastrophe appeared to be the alternative. Caught between a rock and a hard place, the coalition managed to retain cherished holiday bonuses but otherwise felt compelled to concede all along the line. The measures approved by parliament, with over 80,000 protesters outside the building, included a 22 per cent reduction in the minimum wage to €750 a month, slashing €1.1 billion from the health sector and €600 million in equal measure from defence and pensions. In addition, 150,000 redundancies in the public sector were envisaged by 2013. Greece had entered its fifth year of recession and yet privatization of the bloated public sector was barely evident, the Deutsche Telekom purchase of a 40 per cent stake in Greek telecommunications representing the solitary example over the last two years of austerity. In an editorial of 13 February 2012, *The Times* captured the absurdity of the Greek position and called for Greece to be allowed to default:

> The national average retirement age is 61. Vast numbers are eligible for early retirement, due to employment in what the government deems to be dangerous industries, which include hairdressers, masseurs, and trombonists. Greece needs to grow up. It cannot have a state that pays the public to retire early but does not collect taxes.

Equally, the expectation of the troika that austerity measures alone, which thus far had hit the private sector hardest, could engineer a position whereby Greece could begin to pay its own way was similarly deluded. Indeed, the uncertainty surrounding the future put off outside investors, worried that a devalued drachma might soon emerge from the chaos and confusion. Whilst the troika could decide to continue to bail out the Greeks indefinitely, growing political problems and economic difficulties elsewhere, creating competing demands for finite resources, seem likely to result sooner or later in an orderly default, once so-called 'back stops' are in place. German newspapers were already equating Greece to a failed state, a view echoed by its government, which wanted a European Union Commissioner to exercise veto powers over Greek taxes and spending, a leaked proposal that was immediately denounced by the proud Greeks as a breach of their sovereignty.

On 21 February 2012, following tortuous negotiations, euro-zone leaders approved the second bail-out for Greece, worth €130 billion, which Greek Finance Minister Evangelos Venizelos pronounced had averted a 'nightmare scenario', hailing the rescue package as 'maybe the most important deal in Greece's post-war history'. The accord reduced Greek debt by around 30 per cent, with banks, pension funds, insurers and assorted private creditors being asked to take a 'haircut' of 53.5 per cent on €206 billion of bonds, representing a 74 per cent write-down given protracted maturities. On Friday 9 March 2012, holders of €172 billion of Greek bonds accepted the largest debt restructuring in history, involving some 83.5 per cent of eligible bonds, a participation that subsequently rose to 95.7 per cent after the Greek government, with the approval of euro-zone finance ministers, invoked retrospective 'collective action clauses' compelling the

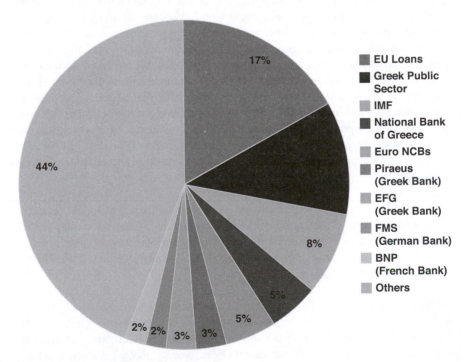

Figure 14.1 Largest Greek creditors

Source: Barclays Capital, Bank of Greece, EU, IMF

dissenters to comply. The action led the International Swaps and Derivative Association to class the deal as a 'credit event', thereby triggering insurance payments. The fact that the great majority had demurred ensured that the impact of this was limited. In essence, most private investors fell into line because the stark alternative was receiving nothing. With this hurdle surmounted, the troika agreed to release the funding required to avert a Greek default.

In theory, the package would reduce Greek debt to 120 per cent of GDP by 2020 (deemed as the maximum viable by the IMF) and Athens could return to the financial markets in 2015. However, following the previous pattern, doubts quickly surfaced. For Greece to meet this target demanded years of austerity and contraction to achieve an internal devaluation, recent history suggesting that the measures required would not deliver and be difficult to implement in the face of a hostile electorate. Indeed, a leaked European Union document concluded: 'Even under the most optimistic scenario, the austerity measures being imposed on Athens risk a recession so deep that Greece will not be able to climb out of the debt hole.' Under an 'alternative scenario', the Greek economy failed to recover, leaving debt at an unsustainable 160 per cent of GDP by 2020, clearly raising the prospect of the need for further bail-outs. Given that the German Finance Minister had already referred to aiding Greece as akin to throwing money into 'a bottomless pit', the political support for yet more aid was questionable, opening up the prospect of a formal Greek default in the near future. Already, with the two bail-outs, almost the equivalent of €10,000 per Greek had been extended by the troika, an enormous amount for a small country. The leading credit agencies (Moody's, Standard & Poor's and Fitch) downgraded Greece into 'restricted default'.

Key economic indicators for Greece tend to support the pessimists. In 2011, the European Union projected that Greek GDP would fall by 6.1 per cent, but by the end of the year the figure was 7 per cent, making the forecast of minus 4.8 per cent for 2012 appear unattainable. Again, unemployment, in a country of 11 million people, increased to 126,000 during November 2011 (20.9 per cent) and this was bound to worsen as the government cut the public sector in line with the troika's requirements. Indeed, by 2012, the Greek economy had shrunk by 16 per cent, the largest contraction of any developed country since the Great Depression. To a lesser extent, Portugal, Italy and Spain too illustrated the problem of restoring lost competitiveness within a fixed exchange system when a country suffers from a high debt stock, an argument that was enunciated by Irving Fisher in *Debt Deflation Causes of Great Depressions* (1933). 'The deflationary bias of current policy', decried *The Times* in its leader of 22 February 2012, 'carries an unmistakable whiff of the downturn of the 1930s, when a monetary dogma took precedence over policies for growth. Then it was the gold standard; now it is a currency union that has locked together widely differing economies while providing no means of escape.' This view was echoed by the financier George Soros (2012a, 17), who warned that 'there's a real danger that the euro will undermine the political cohesion of the European Union'. Indeed, while understanding Berlin's position, he decried its approach as self-defeating:

Germany aggravated the situation by imposing draconian conditions and insisting that Greece should pay penalty rates on the loans in the rescue package that Germany and other states provided. The Greek economy collapsed, capital fled, and Greece repeatedly failed to meet the conditions of the rescue package. Eventually Greece became patently insolvent. Germany then further destabilized the situation by insisting on private sector participation in the rescue. This pushed the risk premiums on Italian and Spanish bonds through the roof and endangered the solvency of the banking system. The authorities then ordered the European banking system to be recapitalized. This was the coup de grace. It created a powerful incentive for the banks to shrink their balance sheets by calling in loans and getting rid of risky government bonds, rather than selling shares at a discount (Soros 2012b, 18).

The effect was to shift the onus for carrying odious government debt onto the European Central Bank, which became the largest holder of Greek bonds, a buying policy that brought its Italian head, Mario Draghi, into disfavour with the Germans and is probably unsustainable. Moreover, the technocratic governments in Greece and Italy, effectively imposed at the behest of Berlin, could survive only until the next election and their successors are likely to challenge the severity of austerity measures.

Towards a 'Grexit'?

The likelihood of a Greek exit ('Grexit') from the euro-zone increased exponentially when the Greek general election of May 2012 produced political paralysis, with no party winning an outright majority. Notwithstanding discussions between the Greek president and party leaders, a coalition could not be produced, leading to the announcement of a further election on 17 June. What alarmed European leaders, especially Chancellor Merkel, was the emergence of a left-wing party, Syriza, which promised to renounce 'the memorandum' (as the document attached to the second bail-out deal was called) and its detested austerity conditions. Syriza came second to New Democracy, with the discredited PASOK party's support collapsing. Early opinion polls began suggesting that Syriza, the champion of wage labour and the afflicted middle class, might win outright next time, raising the spectre of Greece becoming the first member to exit the euro-zone. Its charismatic young leader, Alexis Tsipras, promised to square the circle: to ditch the austerity measures and yet still retain the euro. The troika had stipulated that Greece identify €11.5 billion of public spending cuts in 2013–14. Merkel warned the Greeks that the next election would, in effect, be a referendum on whether Greece wished to remain in the euro-zone. In turn, Christine Lagarde, Managing Director of the IMF, publicly informed Greece that the conditions attached to the bail-out were not renegotiable but were an integral part of the package, in effect warning that further tranches of funding would not be forthcoming, thereby forcing Greece into a default on its debt mountain. To emphasize that they meant business, the troika withheld €1 billion of a €5.4 billion tranche due in May. In an ill-considered interview, Lagarde suggested that Greeks should help themselves by starting to pay their taxes, which angered the target audience, with Syriza pointing to her €400,000-a-year tax-free salary. At the same time, in another auspicious move, Eurocrats in Brussels announced they were making contingency plans for a Greek exit while, across the English Channel, the Bank of England admitted that it was drawing up its own scheme as a precaution. Ironically, opinion polls suggested that a clear majority of Greeks wanted to retain the euro as their currency, but others also indicated that many did not wish to pay the price imposed by the troika. In the event, New Democracy narrowly won the June election, as older voters rallied to its cause, but it too hoped to negotiate an easing of the austerity conditions that had produced political and economic turmoil. By not renouncing the memorandum of understanding, Greece sealed its immediate future in the euro-zone, but at the G20 summit in Los Cabos, Mexico, which followed the election, Chancellor Merkel gave no indication that she was willing to relent. 'The Greek government', she pronounced, 'will and must naturally follow through on the commitments that were made. There can be no loosening of the reform steps.' New Democracy wanted an extra two years (to 2016 rather than 2014) to meet the requirement to achieve a budget surplus (excluding debt service charges) of 4.5 per cent of GDP, turning round a deficit of 5 per cent of GDP in 2011.

As the sanctity of the second Greek bail-out came into question, the 'Merkozy' partnership, which had sought to guide the European Union through the crisis, ended when Sarkozy lost the French presidential election to his socialist rival, François Hollande, who came to office having threatened to renegotiate the fiscal pact and insisting that growth measures must take precedence over austerity. Like his predecessor, who liked to pretend that he was the equal of his German counterpart when he was clearly always playing second fiddle, Hollande went to Berlin with high expectations, but arrived in the German capital much the worse for wear, drenched by a heavy downpour, diminished to looking like a drowned rat desperately seeking shelter. Merkel refused to shift her ground, and their differences were apparent when Hollande reignited the question of Eurobonds as a way forward. His looser attitude towards fiscal rectitude was epitomized by his pledge to reverse Sarkozy's lifting of the French pension age from 60 to 62 and to raise the minimum wage, populist measures that helped propel him into office and win a parliamentary majority in June, but a trend that might, if persisted with, push France into the problem camp. Already the IMF was predicting that the French budget deficit would reach 3.9 per cent of GDP in 2013, confounding Hollande's projection that a reduction to 3 per cent of GDP was achievable. Indeed, a European Commission economic report issued in late May 2012 considered France's deficit too high and warned that additional measures were necessary to prevent it from ballooning out of control. Its concerns were aired against a background of declining French competitiveness, as reflected by a fall in exports of nearly 20 per cent as a share of global trade between 2005 and 2010.

Compounding the Greek problem was a developing Spanish crisis deriving from its collapsed property sector, which helped to foster the highest level of unemployment in the world and more houses for sale than in the United States. In total, Spanish households, firms and government accumulated foreign debts of nearly €1 trillion, over 90 per cent of GDP. Spain's banking sector became perilously exposed because of all the bad debts on its books and struggled to access foreign capital. The government, too, struggled to borrow, with yields on ten-year sovereign bonds hitting 6.6 per cent on 30 May 2012, close to the tipping point at which Greece, Ireland and Portugal were compelled to seek bail-outs. The government of Mariano Rajoy insisted that it could avert a bail-out, but the markets remained deeply skeptical, not least because its own efforts to deal with the situation were found wanting. Bankia, an imperilled savings bank and the fourth biggest lender, was nationalized, but this was contingent on the government finding €19 billion it did not have, which failed to satisfy the European Commission. Most of the government's efforts, orchestrated by Eurocrats in Brussels, were directed towards reducing the budget deficit from 8.9 per cent of GDP in 2011 to 3 per cent by 2013. In a June 2012 report on the health of European economies, the European Commission conceded that Spain was being asked to make too fast an adjustment and was now willing to give a year's grace provided the government tackled the banking crisis, stuck to a responsible budget and extended discipline to the troubled regions (in June 2012, Fitch put eight of their indebted regional governments on negative outlook). It was doubtful whether the Spanish government alone could meet the costs involved in eradicating bad assets from the banks and recapitalizing the survivors. By the early summer of 2012, as Spain struggled to raise funds, the signs were that it wanted a direct injection of cash into the banks but not a bail-out, because this would come with strings attached. With the Greek elections looming, pressure was applied from Brussels to resolve the situation before what could be a further retrograde step in the crisis. The Spanish government was persuaded to seek up to €100 billion to shore up its banks. Because Spain was already implementing austerity measures, no fiscal conditions were attached, allowing Mariano Rajoy to represent this as a 'line of credit'. The bail-out also differed from previous ones in being confined to the banking sector. The markets registered their displeasure, seeing this move as admittance that Spain could soon be shut out of bond markets and in the expectation that if all the money was taken, the extra debt would add around 10 per cent to the national debt burden, which could be unsustainable without outside financial aid. Reflecting this view, Moody's, on 13 June 2012, downgraded Spanish bonds to a notch above junk status. Ultimately, bail-outs covering the troubled Spanish regions and government debt are likely to be required, but if the latter were granted this would turn the market's spotlight onto Italy, which would most likely be a step too far for the available rescue funds.

The political paralysis surrounding the crisis led a frustrated Mario Draghi, President of the European Central Bank, to warn in May 2012 that the European Central Bank could not fill the vacuum created by the lack of decisive action by member states that rendered the euro-zone 'unsustainable' and on the verge of 'disintegration'. Olli Rehn, the European Union's leading economic official, also called for urgent action to avoid collapse. Mario Monti warned of the 'huge possibilities of contagion' as capital flight from Greece and Spain reflected the view that they were the epicentre of the crisis. Cyprus was sucked into the vortex because of its huge exposure to Greece, having come through the past two years because of Russian aid, which was no longer sufficient because of growing defaults in Greece. Known as the 'Iceland' of the South, Cyprus had a banking system nine times the size of GDP, with assets of €157 billion. Unless Russia rode to the rescue again, it too was likely to need a bail-out in the near future.

The extent to which euro-zone economies had diverged rather than converged, as the optimists advocating a single currency envisaged, was evident from bond yields. By May 2012, Germany, regarded as a safe haven for investors, was able to issue two-year bonds carrying zero interest, while yields on its ten-year bonds were also at a record low. Conversely, Greece, the weakest member of the euro-zone, was shut out of the bond markets, while Ireland, Portugal, Spain and Italy struggled to find buyers for their bonds, notwithstanding more attractive yields, because investors were not convinced that their money was safe and would be repaid at the end of the term. This was in stark contrast to the optimistic years of the euro-zone, when any country's sovereign bonds were regarded as a safe bet, an illusion that helped to create the crisis. It also owed much to the cultural differences between member states. The efficient, hard-working and thrifty Germans were prepared to make the necessary sacrifices to get through the difficult period engendered by absorbing the costs of reunification. By contrast, southern members' populations had ingrained attitudes that were the polar opposite to Germans and their governments elected to gamble and invest unwisely, shirking the opportunity to instigate structural reforms to modernize and come up to the Teutonic level, an expectation that in any event was probably beyond them.

What no rescue package (often derided as 'sticking plasters') could deliver was a solution to what George Osborne, the British Chancellor, has called 'the structural vulnerabilities underlying the EMU'. The absence of financial discipline, poor levels of productivity and lack of competitiveness in some euro-zone states, the factors that congealed to produce the crisis, remained ever present. Although financial rescues provided 'sticking plasters', these fundamental problems lingered despite the proverbial can being kicked further down the road.

The G20 summit (18-19 June 2012) brought into sharp relief the wrangling among world leaders over the delicate balance of the global economy, with even China and India experiencing slower growth in the first part of 2012. European leaders, especially Chancellor Merkel, came under intense pressure to stem the escalating euro-zone crisis. It was clear that Spain and Italy were endangered because their borrowing costs were at or near unsustainable levels. As a consequence, it was agreed that the two European rescue funds (the EFSF and the European Stability Mechanism) could purchase their bonds directly on the financial markets, thereby getting round the need to offer bail-outs with conditions attached. The assumption underlying this intervention was that, through demonstrating the euro-zone's resolve to stand by its beleaguered members, the cost of borrowing would be driven down. President Hollande referred to 'mechanisms that allow us to fight speculation'. This was seen as a move towards low interest

Eurobonds. There was also a hint that a more integrated European banking system, mirroring the US Federal Deposit Insurance Corporation, which guaranteed deposits in the event of failing banks, would emerge. More broadly, the EU leaders wanted the IMF to increase its emergency funding to $456 billion. Significantly, the leading emerging economies (China, India and Russia) proved willing to contribute, but the United States refused. This produced an impassioned retort from José Manuel Barroso, President of the European Commission, when a Canadian journalist asked him why North America should pay for Europe's folly.

> Frankly, we are not here to receive lessons in terms of democracy or in terms of how to handle the economy. This crisis was not originated in Europe. . . . [it] originated in North America, and much of our financial sector was contaminated by, how can I put it, unorthodox practices from . . . the financial market.

Such an attitude ignored the malpractices of European bankers, citizens, businessmen, property developers, governments and the European Union in originating and exacerbating the euro-zone crisis. It also reflected the view beyond Europe that the resources exist within the Continent to resolve the situation if only the politicians grasp the nettle. President Obama conceded that the summit had failed to produce 'a silver bullet', while adding, hopefully, that 'the sense of urgency among the leaders is clear'. In this respect, the American leader sought to lead by example through citing his stimulus programme, which had kickstarted the US economy back into life. Some commentators sensed the beginnings of a shift in the German position. Chancellor Merkel, although ruling out a stimulus programme, hinted at further action when she told a press conference: 'From the side of the European Union, we argued unanimously and collectively that we are determined to solve the crisis, and to do it in a mix of fiscal consolidation, growth initiatives, and deepening of European co-operation. That reached very attentive ears here.'

On 29 June 2012, the nineteenth European summit concerning the euro-zone crisis took place in Brussels. Expectations were low and the usual fudge was expected. In the event, the outcome was more consequential than usual because Italy and Spain, supported by France, pressurized Germany into making concessions to produce a stabilization of the current situation. There were a number of breakthroughs. Euro-zone rescue funds could now make direct cash injections to recapitalize troubled banks and purchase sovereign bonds. The immediate impact was aimed at rescuing Spanish banks without adding to Spain's national debt, which had troubled the Spanish government and the markets, with the further prospect of buying Italian bonds to ease Rome's borrowing costs. Ireland also came into the picture, because it was acknowledged that the austerity terms of its bail-out might be revised. A key concession to reassure the markets was the stipulation that loans to Spanish banks would not be accorded seniority status in repayments, thereby not discouraging private bondholders. A €120 billion growth pact was also announced (although this derived from existing funds).

All these measures represented a defeat for the German approach and *Der Spiegel* under the headline 'The night Merkel lost' accused her of leading Germany into a 'debt union'. Rajoy pronounced that: 'This is a triumph of the euro. We want this currency to go on. We want more integration, more budgetary integration, more monetary integration. The European project is today stronger and more credible than yesterday.' Hollande was similarly euphoric: 'We agreed to fully use tools without additional requirements for these countries.' In reality, the crisis was still far from over and no overarching solution was in sight. As a quid pro quo, Merkel demanded and got agreement for the supervision of banks by the European Central Bank as a move towards a full banking union. She stuck to her guns over Eurobonds (having dismissed them outright: 'Not as long as I am alive'), insisted that the deal represented a compromise and, with the details still to be worked out, suggested there had been no violation of the German philosophy of 'no reward without performance'. Moreover, full fiscal, economic and political union, as in the successful American model, remained a distant prospect. The European Council president, Herman von Rompoy, revealed that officials would produce a plan for 'genuine economic and monetary union. The aim is to make the euro an irreversible project'. But many possibly insuperable political hurdles lay ahead.

Problems and prospects

As Gordon Brown (2010, 191) reflected, 'despite initial successes, the euro, tested in its first crisis, has found it difficult to overcome the challenge it has faced. And today, with forecasts for annual European growth now much less than 2 per cent for years to come, Europe is finding it difficult to agree on how to cope with the challenge of rebuilding European growth without a prolonged crisis.' To utilize American jargon, growth below this level is equated to 'stall speed', whereby an aircraft goes into freefall, and economies again become mired in recession. Indeed, what was striking about the aftermath of the 2008–9 Great Recession was the general lack of a pronounced recovery in the major industrial economies. The first quarter of 2011 saw European Union members return mixed economic performances. Germany managed a growth rate that bettered the peak achieved in 2008. This trend continued and German exports were at record levels by the end of 2011, with €888 billion sold that year, giving a trade surplus of €132 billion. The recovery of the British economy remained fragile, as the coalition government sought to rein in the public sector, recklessly expanded under Labour, in the hope that the private sector could compensate. This rebalancing act was fraught with difficulties, not least higher transitional unemployment, while increasing inflationary pressures pointed to rising interest rates, with all the dangers they entailed. Indeed, far from shrinking, the national debt actually increased, passing the £1 trillion mark for the first time by January 2012. As an insurance against a recurrence of the recent banking crisis, the separation of retail and investment banking was required, but not easy to implement. Again, reducing the massive welfare bill was proving difficult to achieve in practice, especially at a time of rising unemployment.

For the European Union, containing the sovereign debt crisis remains a pressing concern. It is no exaggeration to state that success or failure will determine the future of the euro-zone. What should be emphasized is the distinction between short-term fixes and long-term remedies. These are not mutually exclusive, because should the former fail, then the latter will become immaterial. Liquidity solutions can only prop up the system and will not address the fundamental issue of a lack of competitiveness and overspending on welfare among the sluggish economies. Some element of sovereign default is likely even if it is dressed up as something else, such as rescheduling or reprofiling. What cannot be disguised is the fact that the peripheral economies became trapped in a vicious cycle: an unproductive economy exacerbated budget deficits, leading governments to cut spending and increase taxes, which further contracted growth. Heavily dependent on external funding, access to commercial financing was choked off by extortionate interest rates, reflecting the level of risk from investing in government bonds. Assistance from the European Union, European Central Bank and the IMF came with strings attached, which alienated voters and endangered the longevity of the governments seeking to implement required cuts. Some commentators began referring to 'the lost decade', considering that the years 2012–20 will be dominated by efforts to cure the debt overhang, Chancellor Merkel envisaging that at least ten years are required before steady and upward growth can resume in the euro-zone. As the largest contributor to bail-out funds, Germany was the conductor of the orchestra. In a speech to the Bundestag on 2 December 2011, Chancellor Merkel reiterated the German position on the sovereign debt crisis. 'There are no quick and easy answers', she insisted. The Chancellor distinguished the European Central Bank from the Bank of England and Federal Reserve, which had a 'different task'. She again ruled out resort to Eurobonds as a solution: 'A joint liability for others' debts is not acceptable.' Yet, although the European Stability Mechanism, replacing the ESFB, came into effect in July 2012, with funding of €1 trillion, this in itself is unlikely to be sufficient to manage the continuing euro crisis. Should Italy require help then, as the third-largest debtor country in the world after Japan and the United States, it would make the previous recipients of bail-outs pale into insignificance: servicing €2 trillion of debt requires €35 billion a month.

Germany needed to invest almost €1.5 trillion to bring its formerly communist eastern half on a par with the western half. It was clear that the salvation of the euro-zone lay largely in German hands (fiscal union, Eurobonds and full deployment of the European Central Bank) but equally apparent that it would take a seismic shift in the crisis to move Berlin. German decision-makers naturally feared that too many bail-outs and pay-outs would begin to threaten its own top credit rating, which in turn would undermine the rescue packages that were predicated on Germany's cheap borrowing costs and esteemed position in the markets. The culminating point of the euro crisis was yet to come. Whenever it arrives, Berlin will have the deciding voice. Conscious of the high expectations resting on Germany, Merkel sought to play these down in a speech to the Bundesbank on 13 June 2012. 'We do not create policies for the markets, but for the future of our people. Germany's strength is not infinite', she insisted. 'Germany's powers, too, are not unlimited. Consequently, our special responsibility as the leading economy in Europe means we must be able to realistically size up our powers, so we can use them for Germany and Europe with full force.' The problem with the German approach remained that it was projecting medium-term to long-term solutions, requiring treaty changes for a crisis that kept escalating and with each incremental step increasingly threatened to bring the euro project down altogether. Ironically, the best-selling book in Germany was *Europe Doesn't Need the Euro* by Thilo Sarrazin, a former member of the executive board of the Bundesbank. On 9 June 2012 *Die Welt*, a populist newspaper, ran a two-page article under the headline: 'Return of the D-Mark. Would it Work?'

The obsession with addressing the sovereign debt issue meant that comparatively little attention or funding was devoted to addressing a concomitant aspect of the crisis, rising and persistent unemployment, which afflicted the strugglers most of all. Indeed, George Soros warned at the Davos summit in 2012 that unless the European Union engineered a growth strategy, it risked falling into a 'deflationary debt spiral'. At the start of the millennium, just below 20 million people were out of work across the EU-27, just short of 9 per cent of the total labour force. From then until mid-2005, the figure fluctuated between 19 and 21 million, falling steadily thereafter to reach a low of 16 million (6.7 per cent) in the first quarter of 2008 before the financial shocks sent it spiralling in the opposite direction. The steepest rise occurred in 2008–9, when the rate went up by 1.9 percentage points (albeit less than in the United States, where the rise was 3.5 percentage points). The increase from 2008–10 was of such magnitude that it completely wiped out the fall achieved from 2005–7. The only exceptions to the trend were Austria, Germany, Malta and Luxembourg. Belgium, France, Finland, Romania, Sweden and the United Kingdom managed to contain the increase to below 0.5 per cent over 2009–10. Unsurprisingly, the countries with the most extreme sovereign debt problems fared worst: Greece saw its unemployment rise from 13.9 per cent to 19.2 per cent between October 2010 and October 2011; Spain went from 20.4 per cent in 2010 to 22.9 per cent in 2011. Some economists estimated that the latter figure was an overestimate and the true figure stood at around 19 per cent because of the black economy (in Madrid, for instance, vans illicitly pick up workers who are on unemployment benefit).

Persistent unemployment was a feature in all but a few countries. Some 3.8 per cent of the labour force in 2010 for the EU27 was recorded as out of work for over a year, with nearly half lacking a job for over two years. This reflected a lack of job creation to some extent but also a culture of welfare dependency, whereby increasing numbers regarded living off state benefits as a way of life. The attitude of claimants was that they would be worse off in work, a stance that was especially prevalent in Britain. By 2012, the coalition government was seeking to cap the total income payable in benefits to £26,000 per annum, which was still above the minimum wage. Disability benefits under the Labour governments (1997–2010) had rocketed, because recipients did not have to actively seek work. As with Labour's policy of getting fifty per cent of youngsters into universities, the facility served to massage the unemployment statistics to make them appear less bad than the reality. When the Liberal Democrat Conservative coalition came to power, it found that an alarming proportion of disability benefit recipients could do some form of work as it initiated a more rigorous reassessment process. Some claimants on income support had no intention of finding employment, while others made do with state hand-outs and work that went unrecorded in the black economy. Youth unemployment (those aged between 15 and 24) rates also shot up sharply from 2008. Indeed, the rate was almost twice as great as that for the total workforce for most of the past decade (2000 to early 2008), after which the two rates converged. There was also a differential between male and female unemployment at the start of the millennium, but in 2009 the rate for women fell below that of men for the first time, a trend that continued into 2010, when male unemployment was greater in 14 of the 27 member states. That same year more were out of work who left school without going on to further education (14.2 per cent across the European Union), with those possessing a tertiary education qualification finding it easier to gain employment (4.9 per cent were unemployed) with some exceptions. In Britain, where gaining a degree was no longer exceptional because of the numbers involved, many graduates struggled to find work, often having to take poorly remunerated menial jobs for which they were overqualified. The European Commission's Europe 2020 strategy, which embraced an agenda for new skills and jobs and a 'Youth on the Move' initiative at least recognized the problem. Unveiled by the European Commission on 3 March 2010, it sought to improve the employment rate of the working population aged 20–64 to at least 75 per cent, thereby taking 20 million people out of poverty. Such targets were laudable but almost certainly unattainable, given strong competition from outside the European Union.

The future of the European Union itself was now a live issue again. Critics, especially on the left, maintain that the institution is imperfect because economic and monetary union has not gone far enough, with economic union and fiscal harmonization yet to happen. For these to be achieved, a 'political Europe' is required, but its nature has yet to be determined: the options being a confederation of nation states, wherein members can still put their national interests first; or a federal union that subsumes national identities within a super-state, a United States of Europe. In practice, neither is likely to emerge in the foreseeable future. More probable, perhaps, is a European Finance Ministry as a better alternative to seventeen members of the euro-zone with divergent fiscal policies. The persistent problem has been that economically the solutions to the euro-zone crisis are obvious but the political will to embrace them has been lacking as member states put their national interests first. Further afield, the ambiguity over whether the leadership of the world economy is in a transition period creates its own uncertainties, with the United States, albeit still the largest single contributor to the IMF and World Bank, no longer fit for purpose as a lender of last resort or the progenitor of a new Marshall Aid style grandiose rescue plan, which is now beyond its resources and willpower. The American dollar remains the global reserve currency, but the greenback has long since lost its sheen, and the Chinese and Russians have begun calling for a replacement without one being in sight, the euro having become tainted by the sovereign debt crisis. China might eventually step up to the plate, but as a bastion of communism rather than democracy can never truly fill America's shoes. Further, should the Chinese economic boom begin to stall, perhaps because of rising inflation or falling world demand for its exports, then this scenario too would carry adverse ramifications for the global economy, including Europe.

After a confident beginning, therefore, the new millennium entered its second decade with growth projections downgraded for most of the industrialized European economies, as well as the United States, reflecting uncertainty over the immediate economic future, which was blighted by the debt overhang largely incurred during a period of heady optimism that engendered foolish risk taking that came back to haunt decision-makers. On 14 November 2011, Chancellor Merkel referred to the greatest crisis facing Europe since World War Two. What remained to be determined was whether this enormous hurdle can be surmounted as a prelude to legislating financial discipline to ensure that there would be no repeat. Jean Monnet, the founding father of the European Union, liked to say that when Europe experienced a crisis it emerged stronger from the experience. On 29 January 2012, President Sarkozy opined that 'Europe is no longer on the edge of the abyss', a comment that ironically followed the loss of France's triple A credit rating and joined a plethora of optimistic assessments from the French leader that turned out to be premature. Again, in March 2012, after the finalization of the second Greek bail-out, he declared that the problem was 'solved'. Whether he genuinely believed this or was electioneering remains to be seen when the French government records are opened. The resurgence of the crisis soon afterwards, repeating the pattern since the euro crisis began, suggests in fact that it is a systemic crisis that still has some way to run and that the future of European Monetary Union remains uncertain.

Issues for discussion

1. Why was the single currency project flawed?
2. Discuss the sovereign debt crisis and the reasons why it was not resolved quickly and grew worse.
3. What were the circumstances in which Greece became heavily indebted?
4. Why have the solutions put forward to manage the Greek debt problem failed to put Greece onto the road to recovery?
5. Why did the sovereign debt crisis spread beyond Greece and with what effect?
6. Is there more cause to be pessimistic than optimistic about the future of the euro-zone?

Notes

1 The end of the old order, 1914–21

1 The main one was of course the Treaty of Versailles, concluded with Germany on 28 June 1919, after the Paris Peace Conference in the first half of that year. Most of the new territorial arrangements were mapped out at this conference. Subsequently treaties were concluded with Austria (St Germain, 10 September 1919), with Bulgaria (Neuilly, 27 November 1919), with Hungary (Trianon, 4 June 1920) and with Turkey (Sèvres, 10 August 1920, superseded in 1923 by the Treaty of Lausanne).

2 More precisely, the Saar coalmines went to France but the Saar itself was put under League trusteeship.

3 Not all scholars would agree with this interpretation.; see in particular the works of Boyce and Steiner.

2 Post-war reconstruction and instability problems in the 1920s

1 The countries included in the following discussion are Austria, Czechoslovakia, Bulgaria, Hungary, Poland, Romania, Yugoslavia and the Soviet Union. The German post-war reconstruction phase is dealt with separately below since her position was different from the countries listed.

2 The Locarno Pact, signed by Britain, France, Germany and Italy, guaranteed the existing Franco-German border.

3 The Germany inflation is covered in more detail below.

4 It is perhaps worth noting that Zara Steiner sees the 1920s as a decade in its own right rather than a prelude to the 1930s and the later global conflict. Contrary to the position adopted in this volume, she rejects the notion that the peace treaty settlement, despite all its shortcomings, was a precursor of that conflict.

5 The battle for Europe 1939–45

1 It should be noted that there has been a long and controversial debate among scholars regarding Hitler's war aims and strategies, which cannot be entered into here. Readers should refer to the sources listed for this chapter for further information.

2 After the German annexation of Austria, Neville Chamberlain gave up any notion of trying to save Czechoslovakia or assisting France to do so. In fact, the French followed suit soon after, albeit less readily. Chamberlain was more concerned about defending British territories overseas and preserving vital lines of communication and was not averse to seeing some peaceful changes in Europe relating to Austria, Danzig and Czechoslovakia. So why Britain should have been more concerned about the fate of Poland, the most unloved country in Europe, and been prepared to go to war on her behalf is something of a mystery, especially as Germany's

conquest of the country would have provided a stronger defence against Bolshevik Russia.

3 This was a remarkable achievement given that it took some 5000 Germans to control two million Norwegians, whereas Denmark's population was twice that. In fact, the Norwegian conquest in total was a very costly exercise because for much of the war Norway was garrisoned by some 12 German divisions involving no fewer than 350,000 troops. However, it did not absolve Denmark from contributing large amounts of agricultural produce to Germany, while around 30,000 Danes worked in northern Germany.

4 The saga of the Channel Islands is a curious one. Hitler was fanatical about fortifying the islands to make sure that Britain did not reclaim them, yet they never played any significant part in Hitler's strategy. By mid-1942, the Germans stationed on the islands had risen to 37,000, which was a higher concentration of armed forces per square mile than in Germany itself. After evacuation, the population of the islands was just over 60,000, so there was more than one German for every two islanders, whereas in Guernsey the ratio was one to one. In the course of the occupation, the islands became a heavily armed fortress, with some 16,000 slave workers being drafted in to construct massive concrete fortifications including underground tunnels and hospitals, which resulted in the Channel Islands being better fortified than the land behind the Atlantic Wall built against an Allied invasion. It was a relatively peaceful occupation with little overt resistance and a large part of the inhabitants worked for the Germans, either directly or indirectly. The islands had a military government, which contained few Nazis and no Gestapo, and the island governments were allowed a measure of autonomy until the end of the war (unlike Denmark). See Bunting 1995 for full details of the occupation.

5 The Baltic states were something of an anomaly. They were included in the eastern sector administration along with Byelorussia (see below), but in July 1940, Hitler had decided that they should be annexed to the Reich at some future date, presumably after ethnic cleansing, Germanization and resettlement had been carried out. This followed their forced incorporation into the Soviet Union in June 1940 as Stalin became alarmed at the fall of France, having anticipated a repeat performance of the Western Front stalemate of the First World War.

6 The deliveries were by no means inconsiderable. During the first year of the agreements, the Soviet Union delivered to Germany one million tons of cereals, half a million tons of wheat, 900,000 tons of oil, 500,000 tons of phosphates and 100,000 tons of cotton along with smaller amounts of other commodities. The scale of the deliveries increased in the following year and continued right up until Germany invaded the Soviet Union on 22 June 1941. In return the Soviet Union received from Germany various items of machinery and equipment as well as technical assistance. Altogether between September 1939 and June 1941, total deliveries amounted to some 4541 thousand tons of foodstuffs and materials, over 80 per cent of which consisted of grains, timber and oil (see Bullock 1962, 573, 646).

7 A large part of the conquered Russian territory remained under military government throughout the war. This comprised the region south of Leningrad and much of the territory east of the river Dnieper.

8 But not Galicia, which Hitler intended to annex to the Reich in due course and which was placed temporarily under the governor general of occupied Poland.

9 This nullified the impact of Germany's 'wonder weapon', the jet fighter bomber, which was either grounded or could take to the air only for a matter of minutes.

10 The Maginot Line project (named after André Maginot, French defence minister 1929–32) was designed to fortify France's northeastern frontier with Germany. It was constructed between 1930 and 1935 and consisted of a series of concrete forts at three-mile intervals with anti-tank obstacles, barbed wire and mines to protect them. The line extended from Luxembourg to the Swiss and Belgian borders but it did

not cover the Belgian border itself. It was a formidable defensive system but suffered from two serious defects. It did not have any anti-aircraft defences, which meant that the *Luftwaffe* had little difficulty in overflying it with impunity. The second, and key, weakness was that it ended at the Belgian border so that German forces could sweep into France through the Ardennes forest, wrongly thought to be impenetrable to armour, in May 1940. Ironically, the fortifications served their original purpose in resisting attack and few forts were breached. However, had Krupps been able to perfect their monster 80-cm gun in time, it would have been possible to crush the Maginot Line because it was designed to cope with shells of only up to 42-cm calibre. (See Kemp 1981).

11 Neville Chamberlain once observed that the French 'could not keep a secret for more than half an hour or a government for more than six months'.

12 In so doing, he breached his own golden rule of not engaging in a war on two fronts. Had he instead focused on unseating the British in the eastern Mediterranean and begun constructing the Atlantic Wall much earlier, Germany would have been difficult to defeat.

13 The obsession with the eastern campaign diverted Hitler's attention from the importance of other theatres of war, especially the Mediterranean, which Rommel warned him about, but which he regarded rather as a sideshow. Rommel was never given sufficient manpower and equipment to sustain a full and effective offensive against Britain's control of the sea lanes in the Mediterranean. Only three per cent of German military forces were committed to this theatre by 1942, the bulk of Germany's military power being devoted to campaigns in the Balkans and Russia. The German Naval High Command had pressed for a stronger Mediterranean strategy against Britain but Hitler was not interested. Theoretically, Germany's chief ally, Italy, should have been able to secure the Mediterranean and North Africa but she was too weak for the task. So, by the summer of 1943, almost all Axis activity in the southern theatre of war had come to an end and the opportunity of taking control of Egypt and Suez had gone for ever (Rich 1973, 178). Hitler envisaged giving priority to the Mediterranean only *after* the conquest of Russia.

9 Western capitalism in the 1970s

1 For this purpose, price stability is defined as a non-accelerating or gently decelerating rate of inflation. In the short term, the equilibrium growth rate with policies to effect a sharp reduction in inflation may be negative. Under these conditions, employment is a residual.

Further reading

Inevitably, the size of the reading list has grown with each new edition of this volume. Students should not be deterred by its length, however. It is designed to provide a wide and varied list of sources such that readers can find additional material on any topic that they wish to investigate in greater depth.

General works

Aldcroft, D. H. and Morewood, S. *Economic Change in Eastern Europe since 1918*, Aldershot: Edward Elgar, 1995.

Aldcroft, D. H. and Oliver, M. J. *Exchange Rate Regimes in the Twentieth Century*, Cheltenham: Edward Elgar, 1998.

Aldcroft, D. H. and Sutcliffe, A. (eds) *Europe in the International Economy 1500 to 2000*, Cheltenham: Edward Elgar, 1998.

Bairoch, P. 'Europe's gross national product: 1800–1975', *Journal of European Economic History*, 5, Fall 1976.

Berend, I. T. and Ranki, G. *Economic Development in East Central Europe in the 19th and 20th Centuries*, New York: Columbia University Press, 1974.

Bideleux, R. and Jeffries, I. *A History of Eastern Europe: Crisis and Change*, second edition, London: Routledge, 2007.

Boyce, R. *The Great Interwar Crisis and the Collapse of Globalization*, Basingstoke: Palgrave Macmillan, 2009.

Cipolla, C. M. (ed.) *The Fontana Economic History of Europe*, Vol. 5, *The Twentieth Century* (Parts 1 and 2), and Vol. 6, *Contemporary Economies* (Parts 1 and 2), London: Collins/Fontana, 1976.

Crampton, R. J. *Eastern Europe in the Twentieth Century*, London: Routledge, 1994.

Crampton, R. and Crampton, B. *Atlas of Eastern Europe in the Twentieth Century*, London: Routledge, 1996.

El-Agraa, Ali M. *The European Union. Economics and Policies*, ninth edition, Cambridge: Cambridge University Press, 2011.

Emmott, W. *Good Italy Bad Italy: Why Italy Must Conquer its Demons to Face the Future*, New Haven, CT: Yale University Press, 2012.

Good, D. F. 'Economic growth in Europe's third world: central and eastern Europe, 1870–1989', in D. H. Aldcroft and R. Catterall (eds) *Rich Nations – Poor Nations: the Long-run Perspective*, Cheltenham: Edward Elgar, 1996.

Hobsbawm, E. *The Age of Extremes: The Short Twentieth Century*, London: Michael Joseph, 1994.

Judd, A. *Postwar: A History of Europe Since 1945,* hmdm: Penguin/Allen Lane, 2005.

Landes, D. S. *The Unbound Prometheus: Technological Change and Industrial Development in Western Europe from 1750 to the Present,* Cambridge: Cambridge University Press, 1969.

Lundberg, E. *Instability and Economic Growth,* New Haven, CT: Yale University Press, 1968.

Maddison, A. *Economic Policy and Performance in Europe, 1913–1970,* London: Collins/Fontana, 1973.

— *The World Economy in the 20th Century,* Paris: OECD, 1989.

— *Monitoring the World Economy 1820–1992,* Paris: OECD, 1995.

Marks, S. *The Ebbing of European Ascendancy: An International History of the World 1914–1945,* London: Hodder Arnold, 2002.

Marwick, A. *War and Social Change in the Twentieth Century,* London: Macmillan, 1974.

Mazower, M. *Dark Continent: Europe's Twentieth Century,* London: Penguin, 1999.

Nolan, M. *The TransAtlantic Century. Europe and the United States, 1890–2010,* Cambridge; Cambridge University Press, 2012.

Oliver, M. and Aldcroft, D. H. (eds) *Economic Disasters of the Twentieth Century,* Cheltenham: Edward Elgar, 2007.

Parker, R. A. C. *Europe 1914–45,* London: Weidenfeld and Nicolson, 1969.

Svennilson, I. *Growth and Stagnation in the European Economy,* Geneva: United Nations, 1954.

Tipton, F. B. and Aldrich, R. *An Economic and Social History of Europe, 1890–1939,* Basingstoke: Macmillan, 1987.

— *An Economic and Social History of Europe, from 1939 to the Present,* Basingstoke: Macmillan, 1987.

Warleigh-Lack, A. *European Union. The Basics,* second edition, London: Routledge, 2009.

Chapter 1 The end of the old order, 1914–21

Aldcroft, D. H. *From Versailles to Wall Street: The International Economy, 1919–1929,* London: Penguin, 1977.

— *Studies in the Interwar European Economy,* Aldershot: Ashgate, 1997.

— 'The Versailles legacy', *History Review,* 29, Dec. 1997.

Alpert, P. 'The impact of World War I on the European economy', in W. C. Scoville and C. J. La Force (eds) *The Economic Development of Western Europe from 1914 to the Present,* Lexington, MA: D. C. Heath, 1969.

Berend, I. T. and Ranki, G. 'The economic problems of the Danube region at the break-up of the Austro-Hungarian monarchy', *Journal of Contemporary History,* 4, 1969.

Bowley, A. L. *Some Economic Consequences of the Great War,* London: Thornton Butterworth, 1930.

Boyce, R. *The Great Interwar Crisis and the Collapse of Globalization,* Basingstoke: Palgrave Macmillan, 2009.

Broadberry, S. and Harrison, M. (eds) *The Economics of World War I,* Cambridge: Cambridge University Press, 2005.

Dockrill, M. L. and Gould, J. D. *Peace without Promise: Britain and the Peace Conferences, 1919–23,* London: Batsford, 1981.

Ferguson, N. *The Pity of War,* London: Allen Lane/Penguin Press, 1998.

Hardach, G. *The First World War 1914–1918,* London: Penguin, 1977.

Henig, R. *Versailles and After 1919–1933*, London: Routledge, 1995.

Hill, M. *The Economic and Financial Organization of the League of Nations: A Survey of Twenty-Five Years' Experience*, Washington, DC: Carnegie Endowment for International Peace, 1946.

Hogan, M. J. 'The United States and the problem of international economic control: American attitudes toward European reconstruction, 1918–20', *Pacific Historical Review,* 44, 1975.

Keynes, J. M. *The Economic Consequences of the Peace*, London: Macmillan, 1919, and *A Revision of the Treaty*, London: Macmillan, 1922.

Lampe, J. R. 'Unifying the Yugoslav economy 1918–21: misery and early misunderstandings', in D. Djordjevic (ed.) *The Creation of Yugoslavia, 1914–18*, Santa Barbara, CA: Clio Books, 1980.

League of Nations *Agricultural Production in Continental Europe during the 1914–18 War and the Reconstruction Period*, Geneva: League of Nations, 1943a.

— *Europe's Overseas Needs 1919–1920 and How They Were Met*, Geneva: League of Nations, 1943b.

— *Relief Deliveries and Relief Loans 1919–1923*, Geneva: League of Nations, 1943c.

MacMillan, M. *Peacemakers: Six Months That Changed the World: The Paris Peace Conference of 1919 and Its Attempt to End War,* London: John Murray, 2003.

Mantoux, E. *The Carthaginian Peace or the Economic Consequences of Mr. Keynes*, London: Oxford University Press, 1946.

Marks, S. *The Illusion of Peace: International Relations in Europe 1918–1933*, London: Macmillan, 1976.

Marwick, A. *The Deluge*, London: Bodley Head, 1965.

Mazower, M. *Hitler's Empire: Nazi Rule in Occupied Europe,* London: Penguin Books, 2009.

Mendershausen, H. *The Economics of War*, New York: Prentice Hall, 1941.

Milward, A. S. *The Economic Effects of the World Wars on Britain*, London: Macmillan, 1970.

Mitrany, D. *The Effect of the War in South-Eastern Europe*, New Haven, CT: Yale University Press, 1936.

Newman, W. J. *The Balance of Power in the Interwar Years 1919–1939,* New York: Random House, 1968.

Orde, A. *British Policy and European Reconstruction after the First World War*, Cambridge: Cambridge University Press, 1990.

Overy, R. J. *Why the Allies Won*, London: Jonathan Cape, 1995.

Ross, G. *The Great Powers and the Decline of the European States System 1914–1945*, London: Longman, 1983.

Schulz, G. *Revolutions and Peace Treaties 1917–1920*, London: Methuen, 1972.

Sharp, A. *The Versailles Settlement: Peacemaking in Paris, 1919*, Basingstoke: Macmillan, 1991.

Silverman, D. P. *Reconstructing Europe after the Great War*, Cambridge, MA: Harvard University Press, 1982.

Singleton, J. 'Destruction . . . and misery: the First World War', in M. J. Oliver and D. H. Aldcroft (eds), *Economic Disasters in the Twentieth Century,* Cheltenham: Edward Elgar, 2007.

Stearns, P. N. *European Society in Upheaval*, London: Macmillan, 1967.

Steiner, Z. *The Lights That Failed: European International History 1919–1933*, Oxford: Oxford University Press, 2005.

Trachtenberg, M. 'Reparations at the Paris Peace Conference', *Journal of Modern History,* 1979.

Weinberg, G. L. 'The defeat of Germany in 1918 and the European balance of power', *Central European History*, 2, 1969.

Chapter 2 Post-war reconstruction and instability problems in the 1920s

Aldcroft, D. H. *From Versailles to Wall Street: The International Economy, 1919–29,* London: Penguin, 1977.

— 'Destabilising influences in the European economy in the 1920s', in C. Holmes and A. Booth (eds) *Economy and Society: European Industrialisation and Its Social Consequences: Essays Presented to Sidney Pollard,* Leicester: Leicester University Press, 1991.

— 'The twentieth century debt problem in historical perspective', *Journal of European Economic History,* 30, 2001.

— 'Currency stabilization in the 1920s: success or failure?', *Economic Issues*, 7, 2002.

— *Europe's Third World: The European Periphery in the Interwar Years*, Aldershot: Ashgate, 2006.

Aldcroft, D. H. and Morewood, S. *Economic Change in Eastern Europe since 1918,* Aldershot: Edward Elgar, 1995.

Aldcroft, D. H. and Oliver, M. J. *Exchange Rate Regimes in the Twentieth Century,* Cheltenham: Edward Elgar, 1998.

Balderston, T. 'Links between inflation and depression: German capital and labour markets 1924–31', in G. D. Feldman and E. Müller-Luckner (eds) *Die Nachwirkungen der Inflation auf die Deutsche Geschichte 1924–1933,* Munich: R. Oldenbourg, 1985.

— 'The origins of economic instability in Germany 1924–30: market forces versus economic policy', *Vierteljahrshrift für Sozial- und Wirtschaftsgeschichte*, 69, 1982.

Barkai, H. 'Productivity patterns, exchange rates and the gold standard restoration debate of the 1920s', *History of Political Economy*, 25, 1993.

Berend, I. T. and Ranki, G. *The Hungarian Economy in the Twentieth Century*, London: Croom Helm, 1985.

Born, K. E. 'The German inflation after the first world war', *Journal of European Economic History*, 6, 1977.

Boross, E. A. *Inflation and Industry in Hungary, 1918–1929*, Berlin: Haude & Spener, 1994.

Braun, H.-J. *The German Economy in the Twentieth Century*, London: Routledge, 1990.

Bresciani-Turroni, C. *The Economics of Inflation: A Study of Currency Depreciation in Postwar Germany*, London: Allen & Unwin, 1937.

Brown, W. A. *The International Gold Standard Reinterpreted 1914–1934*, 2 vols, New York: National Bureau of Economic Research, 1940.

Cagan, P. 'The monetary dynamics of hyperinflation', in M. Friedman (ed.) *Studies in the Quantity Theory of Money*, Chicago, IL: University of Chicago Press, 1956.

Clarke, S. V. O. *Central Bank Cooperation, 1924–31*, New York: Federal Reserve Bank, 1967.

Clavin, P. and Wessels, J-C. 'Transnationalism and the League of Nations: understanding the work of its economic and financial organisation', *Contemporary Economic History*, 14, 2005.

Costigliola, F. 'The United States and the reconstruction of Germany in the 1920s', *Business History Review*, 50, 1976.

Davis, J. S. *The World Between the Wars 1919–39: An Economist's View*, Baltimore, MD: Johns Hopkins University Press, 1969.

Dulles, E. L. *The French Franc 1914–1928: The Facts and Their Interpretation*, London: Macmillan, 1929.

Falkus, M. E. 'The German business cycle in the 1920s', *Economic History Review*, 28, 1975.

Feinstein, C. H. (ed.) *Banking, Currency, and Finance in Europe Between the Wars*, Oxford: Oxford University Press, 1995.

Feldman, G. D. *The Great Disorder: Politics, Economics and Society in the German Inflation, 1914–1924*, Oxford: Oxford University Press, 1993.

Ferguson, N. *Paper and Iron: Hamburg Business and German Politics in the Era of Inflation, 1897–1927*, Cambridge: Cambridge University Press, 1995.

Freris, A. F. *The Greek Economy in the Twentieth Century*, London: Croom Helm, 1986.

Graham, F. D. *Exchange, Prices and Production in Hyperinflation Germany, 1920–23*, Princeton: Princeton University Press, 1930.

Grossman, G. *The Industrialization of Russia and the Soviet Union*, London: Collins/ Fontana, 1971.

Harris, C. R. *Germany's Foreign Indebtedness*, London: Oxford University Press, 1935.

Harrison, J. *The Spanish Economy in the Twentieth Century*, London: Croom Helm, 1985.

Hodne, F. *The Norwegian Economy 1920–1980*, London: Croom Helm, 1983.

Holtfrerich, C.-L. *The German Inflation 1919–1923*, Berlin: Walter de Gruyter, 1986.

Jack, D. T. *The Restoration of European Currencies*, London: P. S. King, 1927.

Johansen, H. C. *The Danish Economy in the Twentieth Century*, London: Croom Helm, 1987.

Kemp, T. *The French Economy, 1919–1939: The History of a Decline*, Harlow: Longman, 1972.

Kent, B. *The Spoils of War: The Politics, Economics and Diplomacy of Reparations, 1918–1932*, Oxford: Clarendon Press, 1989.

Kirk, D. *Europe's Population in the Interwar Years*, Geneva: League of Nations, 1946.

Lampe, J. R. *The Bulgarian Economy in the Twentieth Century*, London: Croom Helm, 1986.

Laursen, K. and Pedersen, J. *The German Inflation, 1918–1923*, Amsterdam: North Holland Publishing Company, 1964.

League of Nations *International Currency Experience: Lessons of the Interwar Period*, Geneva: League of Nations, 1944.

— *The Course and Control of Inflation: A Review of Monetary Experience in Europe after World War I*, Geneva: League of Nations, 1946.

Lewis, W. A. *Economic Survey 1919–1939*, London: Allen & Unwin, 1949.

Marks, S. *The Illusion of Peace: International Relations in Europe 1918–1933*, London: Macmillan, 1976.

Meyer, R. H. *Bankers' Diplomacy: Monetary Stabilisation in the Twenties*, New York: Columbia University Press, 1970.

Mommen, A. *The Belgian Economy in the Twentieth Century*, London: Routledge, 1994.

Moulton, H. G. and Pasvolsky, L. *War Debts and World Prosperity*, Washington, DC: Brookings Institution, 1932.

Munting, R. *The Economic History of the USSR*, London: Croom Helm, 1982.

Newman, W. J. *The Balance of Power in the Interwar Years 1919–1939,* New York: Random House, 1968.

North, D. C. 'International capital movements in historical perspective', in R. F. Mikesell (ed.) *U.S. Private and Government Investment Abroad,* Eugene: University of Oregon Books, 1962.

Nove, A. *An Economic History of the USSR,* London: Penguin, 1969.

Palyi, M. *The Twilight of Gold 1914–1936: Myths and Realities,* Chicago, IL: Henry Regnery, 1972.

Pasvolsky, L. *Economic Nationalism of the Danubian States,* London: Allen & Unwin, 1928.

Pollard, S. and Holmes, C. (eds) *Documents on European Economic History,* Vol. 3, *The End of Old Europe 1914–1939,* London: Edward Arnold, 1973.

Rogers, J. H. *The Process of Inflation in France, 1914–1927,* New York: Columbia University Press, 1929.

Royal Institute of International Affairs *The Balkan States: A Review of the Economic and Financial Developments of Albania, Bulgaria, Greece, Roumania and Yugoslavia since 1919,* London: Oxford University Press, 1936.

— *The Problem of International Investment,* London: Oxford University Press, 1937.

Schuker, S. A. *American Reparations to Germany 1919–33: Implications for the Third World Debt Crisis,* Princeton, NJ: Princeton University Press, 1988.

Shepherd, H. L. *The Monetary Experience of Belgium 1914–1936,* Princeton, NJ: Princeton University Press, 1936.

Steiner, Z. *The Lights That Failed: European International History 1919–1933,* Oxford: Oxford University Press, 2005.

Taylor, J. *The Economic Development of Poland, 1919–1950,* New York: Cornell University Press, 1952.

Tracy, M. *Agriculture in Western Europe: Crisis and Adaptation since 1880,* London: Cape, 1964.

van Zanden, J. L. *The Economic History of the Netherlands,* London: Routledge, 1988.

von Rauch, G. *The Baltic States: The Years of Independence 1917–1940,* London: G. Hurst and Company, 1974.

Voth, H.-J. 'Wages, investment and the fate of the Weimar Republic: a long-term perspective', *German History,* 11, 1993.

— 'Did high wages or high interest rates bring down the Weimar Republic: a cointegration model of investment in Germany, 1925–30', *Journal of Economic History,* 55, 1995.

Webb, S. *Hyperinflation and Stabilization in Weimar Germany,* Oxford: Oxford University Press, 1989.

Wicker, E. 'Terminating hyperinflation in the dismembered Habsburg Monarchy', *American Economic Review,* 76, 1986.

Wolf, H. C. 'Inflation and stabilization in Latvia 1918–22', *Economic Systems,* 25, 2001.

Chapter 3 Economic crisis and recovery, 1929–39

Aldcroft, D. H. 'The development of the managed economy before 1939', *Journal of Contemporary History* 4, 1969.

— 'The disintegration of Europe 1918–45', in D. H. Aldcroft and A. Sutcliffe (eds), *Europe in the International Economy 1500 to 2000,* Cheltenham: Edward Elgar, 1999.

Aldcroft, D. H. and Oliver, M. J. *Exchange Rate Regimes in the Twentieth Century,* Cheltenham: Edward Elgar, 1998.

Arndt, H. W. *The Economic Lessons of the Nineteen-Thirties*, London: Cass, reprinted 1963.

— *The Origins and Course of the German Economic Crisis, November 1923 to May 1932*, Berlin: Haude & Spener, 1933.

Balderston, T. 'The banks and the gold standard in the German financial crisis of 1931', *Financial History*, 1, 1994.

Bernanke, B. and James, H. 'The gold standard, deflation and financial crises in the great depression: an international comparison', in R. G. Hubbard (ed.) *Financial Markets and Financial Crises*, Chicago: University of Chicago Press, 1991.

Bernanke, B. S. 'Nonmonetary effects of the financial crisis in the propagation of the great depression', *American Economic Review*, 73, 1983.

Booth, A. 'Britain in the 1930s: a managed economy?' *Economic History Review*, 40, 1987.

Boyce, R. *The Great Interwar Crisis and the Collapse of Globalization*, Basingstoke: Palgrave Macmillan, 2009.

Calomiris, C. W. 'Financial factors in the great depression', *Journal of Economic Perspectives*, 7, 1993.

Carroll, B. A. *Design for Total War: Arms and Economics in the Third Reich*, Paris: Mouton, 1969.

Choudhri, E. V. and Kochin, L. A. 'The exchange rate and the international transmission of business cycle disturbances: some evidence from the great depression', *Journal of Money, Credit and Banking*, 12, 1980.

Eichengreen, B. *Golden Fetters; The Gold Standard and the Great Depression, 1919–1939*, Oxford: Oxford University Press, 1992.

— 'The origins and nature of the great slump revisited', *Economic History Review*, 45, 1992.

Eichengreen, B. and Hatton, T. J. (eds) *Interwar Unemployment in International Perspective*, Dordrecht: Kluwer Academic Publishers, 1988.

Eichengreen, B. and Irwin, D. A. 'Trade blocs, currency blocs and the reorientation of world trade in the 1930s', *Journal of International Economics,* 38, 1995.

Eichengreen, B. and Portes, R. 'The anatomy of financial crises', in R. Portes and A. K. Swoboda (eds) *Threats to International Financial Stability*, Cambridge: Cambridge University Press, 1987.

Eichengreen, B. and Portes, R. 'Debt and default in the 1930s: causes and consequences', *European Economic Review,* 30, 1986.

Eichengreen, B. and Sachs, J. 'Exchange rates and economic recovery in the 1930s', *Journal of Economic History,* 45, 1985.

Einzig, P. *World Finance 1935–1939*, London: Kegan Paul, Trench Trubner, 1937.

Evans, R. J. *The Third Reich in Power 1933–1939*, London: Allen Lane/Penguin, 2005.

Feinstein, C. H., Temin, P. and Toniolo, G, *The European Economy between the Wars*, Oxford: Oxford University Press, 1997.

Fleisig, H. W. *Long-term Capital Flows and the Great Depression: The Role of the United States, 1927–1933*, New York: Arno Press, 1975.

Forbes, N. *Doing Business with the Nazis: Britain's Economic and Financial Relations with Germany, 1931–1939*, London: Frank Cass, 2000.

Foreman-Peck, J., Hallett, A. G. and Ma, Y. 'Optimum international policies for the world depression 1919–33', *Economies et Sociétés*, 22, 1996.

Fremdling, G. M. 'Did the United States transmit the great depression to the rest of the world'? *American Economic Review*, 75, 1985.

Friedman, P. *Impact of Trade Destruction on National Incomes: A Study of Europe, 1924–1938*, Gainesville: University Presses of Florida, 1974.

Galbraith, J. K. *The Great Crash*, Harmondsworth: Penguin, 1961.

Garside, W. R. (ed) *Capitalism in Crisis: International Responses to the Great Depression*, London: Pinter, 1993.

Garside, W. R. 'The great depression 1929–33', in M. Oliver and D. H. Aldcroft (eds) *Economic Disasters of the Twentieth Century*, Cheltenham: Edward Elgar, 2007.

Grytten, O. H. 'Why was the great depression not so great in the Nordic countries? Economic policy and unemployment', *Journal of European Economic History*, 37, 2008.

Gilbert, M. *Currency Depreciation*, Philadelphia, PA: University of Pennsylvania Press, 1939.

Hamilton, J. D. 'Monetary factors in the great depression', *Journal of Monetary Economics*, 19, 1987.

— 'The role of the international gold standard in propagating the great depression', *Contemporary Policy Issues*, 6, 1988.

Harris, S. E. *Exchange Depreciation: Its Theory and History with some Consideration of Related Domestic Policies*, Cambridge, MA: Harvard University Press, 1936.

Hedberg, P. 'Bilateralism and bargaining power. Belligerent Germany and the small country of Sweden during the 1930's', *Journal of European Economic History*, 38, Winter 2009.

Hodson, H. V. *Slump and Recovery, 1929–37*, London: Oxford University Press, 1938.

Hogg, R. L. *Structural Rigidities and Policy Inertia in Interwar Belgium*, Brussels: AWLSK, 1986.

— 'The causes of the German banking crisis of 1931', *Economic History Review*, 37, 1984.

— *The German Slump: Politics and Economics 1924–1936*, Oxford: Clarendon Press, 1986.

James, H. 'Financial flows across frontiers during the interwar depression', *Economic History Review*, 45, 1992.

— 'Innovation and conservatism in economic recovery: the alleged Nazi recovery of the 1930s', in W. R.Garside (ed.) *Capitalism in Crisis: International Responses to the Great Depression*, London: Pinter Publishers, 1993.

Johnson, H. C. *Gold, France and the Great Depression, 1919–1932*, New Haven: Yale University Press, 1997.

Kindleberger, C. P. *The World in Depression, 1929–1939*, London: Penguin, 1973.

Klein, B. H. *Germany's Economic Preparations for War*, Cambridge, MA: Harvard University Press, 1959.

Klemann, H. and Kudryashov, S. *Occupied Economies: An Economic History of Nazi-occupied Europe, 1939–1945*, London: Berg, 2012.

Knauerhase, R. *An Introduction to National Socialism 1920–1939*, Columbus, OH: C. E. Merrill, 1972.

League of Nations *The Course and Phases of the World Economic Depression*, Geneva: League of Nations, 1931.

Meltzer, A. H. 'Monetary and other explanations of the start of the great depression', *Journal of Monetary Economics*, 2, 1976.

Middleton, R. *Towards the Managed Economy: Keynes, the Treasury and the Fiscal Policy Debate of the 1930s*, London: Methuen, 1985.

Montgomery, G. A. *How Sweden Overcame the Depression, 1930–33*, Stockholm: Benniers, 1938.

Olsson, S-O. *Managing Crises and De-globalisation: Nordic Foreign Trade and Exchange*

1919–1939, London: Routledge, 2010.

— 'Transportation and rearmament in the Third Reich', *Historical Journal*, 16, 1973.

Overy, R. J. 'Cars, roads and economic recovery in Germany, 1932–38', *Economic History Review*, 28, 1975.

— *The Nazi Economic Recovery, 1932–1938*, London: Macmillan, 1982.

— *The Inter-war Crisis*, London: Longman, 1994.

— *War and Economy in the Third Reich*, Oxford; Oxford University Press, 1994.

Parker, R. E. *The Economics of the Great Depression: A Twenty-First Century Look Back at the Economics of the Interwar Era*, Cheltenham: Edward Elgar, 2007.

Rees, G. *The Great Slump: Capitalism in Crisis, 1929–33*, London: Weidenfeld & Nicolson, 1970.

Richardson, H. W. *Economic Recovery in Britain, 1932–9*, London: Weidenfeld & Nicolson, 1967.

Robbins, L. *The Great Depression*, London: Macmillan, 1934.

Sarti, R. *Fascism and the Industrial Leadership in Italy, 1919–1940*, Berkeley, CA: University of California Press, 1971.

Schubert, A. *The Credit-Anstalt Crisis of 1931*, Cambridge: Cambridge University Press, 1991.

Steiner, Z. *The Triumph of the Dark: European International History 1933–1939*, Oxford: Oxford University Press, 2011.

Svennilson, I. *Growth and Stagnation in the European Economy*, Geneva: United Nations, 1954.

Temin, P. 'The beginning of the depression in Germany', *Economic History Review*, 24, 1971.

— *Did Monetary Forces Cause the Great Depression?* New York: W. W. Norton, 1976.

Thomas, B. *Monetary Policy and Crisis: A Study of Swedish Experience*, London: Routledge, 1936.

Thomas, M. 'Rearmament and economic recovery in the late 1930s', *Economic History Review*, 36, 1983.

Timoshenko, V. P. *World Agriculture and the Depression*, Ann Arbor, MI: University of Michigan Business Studies, vol. 5, 1933.

Topp, N.-H. 'Influence of the public sector on activity in Denmark 1919–39', *Scandinavian Economic History Review*, 43, 1985.

Tortella, G. 'Patterns of economic retardation and recovery in south-western Europe in the nineteenth and twentieth centuries', *Economic History Review*, 47, 1994.

United Nations, *International Capital Movements During the Interwar Period*, New York: United Nations, 1949.

van der Wee, H. (ed.) *The Great Depression Revisited: Essays on the Economics of the Thirties*, The Hague: Nijhoff, 1972.

Welk, W. G. *Fascist Economic Policy*, Cambridge, MA: Harvard University Press, 1938.

Williams, D. 'The 1931 financial crisis', *Yorkshire Bulletin of Economic and Social Research*, 15, 1963.

Yeager, L. B. *International Monetary Relations: Theory, History and Policy*, New York: Harper & Row, 1966.

Chapter 4 Eastern Europe and the periphery in the 1930s

Aldcroft, D. H. 'Depression and recovery: the Eastern European experience', in W. R.

Garside (ed.) *Capitalism in Crisis: International Responses to the Great Depression*, London: Pinter, 1993.

— *Europe's Third World: The European Periphery in the Interwar Years*, Aldershot: Ashgate, 2006.

Aldcroft, D. H. and Morewood, S. *Economic Change in Eastern Europe since 1918*, Aldershot: Edward Elgar, 1995.

Batou, J. and David, T. *Uneven Development in Europe 1918–1939*, Geneva: Droz, 1998.

Berend, I. T. *Decades of Crisis: Central and Eastern Europe before World War II*, Berkeley, CA University of California Press, 1998.

Crampton, R. J. *Eastern Europe in the Twentieth Century*, London: Routledge, 1994.

Crampton, R. and Crampton, B. *Atlas of Eastern Europe in the Twentieth Century*, London: Routledge, 1996.

Davies, R. W., Harrison, M. and Wheatcroft, S. G. *The Economic Transformation of the Soviet Union, 1913–1945*, Cambridge: Cambridge University Press, 1994.

Emmott, W. *Good Italy, Bad Italy: Why Italy Must Conquer its Demons to Face the Future*, New Haven, CT: Yale University Press, 2012.

Ellis, H. S. 'Exchange Control in Austria and Hungary', *Quarterly Journal of Economics*, 54, 1939.

— *Exchange Control in Central Europe*, Cambridge, MA: Harvard University Press, 1941.

Grenzebach, W. S. *Germany's Informal Empire in East-Central Europe: German Economic Policy toward Yugoslavia and Rumania, 1933–1939*, Stuttgart: Franz Steiner Verlag, 1988.

Harrison, M. and Davies, R. W. 'The Soviet military-economic effort during the second five-year plan', *Europe-Asia Studies*, 49, 1997.

Herschlag, Z. Y. 'Turkey: achievements and failures in the policy of economic development (during the inter-war period 1919–39)', *Kyklos*, 7, 1954.

Hertz, F. *The Economic Problem of the Danubian States. A Study in Economic Nationalism*, London: Gollancz, 1947.

Hocevar, T. 'The Albanian economy 1912–44: a survey', *Journal of European Economic History*, 3, 1987.

Hoptner, J. B. *Yugoslavia in Crisis, 1934–1941*, New York: Columbia University Press, 1962.

Jackson, M. R. and Lampe, J. R. 'The evidence of industrial growth in South Eastern Europe before the second world war', *East European Quarterly*, 16, 1983.

Jelavich, B. *History of the Balkans*. Vol. 2 *Twentieth Century*, Cambridge: Cambridge University Press, 1983.

Kaiser, D. E. *Economic Diplomacy and the Origins of the Second World War: Germany, Britain, France and Eastern Europe, 1930–1939*, Princeton: Princeton University Press, 1980.

Kaser, M. C. and Radice, E. A. (eds) *The Economic History of Eastern Europe 1919–1975*, Vol. I *Economic Structure and Performance Between the Wars*, Oxford: Oxford University Press, 1985.

— *The Economic History of Eastern Europe 1919–1975*, Vol. II *Interwar Policy, the War and Reconstruction*, Oxford: Oxford University Press, 1986.

Keyder, C. *The Definition of a Peripheral Economy: Turkey 1923–29*, Cambridge: Cambridge University Press, 1981.

Kofman, J. *Economic Nationalism and Development: Central and Eastern Europe Between the Two World Wars*, Oxford: Westview Press, 1997.

Lee, S. J. *The European Dictatorships 1918–1945*, London: Methuen, 1987.

Leitz, C. *Economic Relations between Nazi Germany and Franco's Spain 1936–1945*, Oxford: Oxford University Press, 1996.

— 'Arms as levers: material and raw materials in Germany's trade with Romania in the 1930s', *International History Review*, 19, 1997.

Littlefield, F. C. *Germany and Yugoslavia, 1933–1941. The German Conquest of Yugoslavia*, New York: Columbia University Press, 1988.

Lungu, D. B. *Romania and the Great Powers, 1933–1940*, Durham: Duke University Press, 1989.

Maier, G. S. 'The economics of Fascism and Nazism' in C. S. Maier (ed.) *In Search of Political Stability: Explanations in Historical Political Economy,* Cambridge: Cambridge University Press, 1987.

Mazower, M. *Greece and the Interwar Economic Crisis*, Oxford: Oxford University Press, 1991.

Milward, A. S. 'The Reichsmark bloc and the international economy', in H. W. Koch (ed.) *Aspects of the Third Reich*, London: Macmillan, 1985.

Momtchiloff, N. *Ten Years of Controlled Trade in South-eastern Europe*, Cambridge: Cambridge University Press, 1944.

Neal, L. 'The economics and finance of bilateral clearing agreements: Germany, 1934–38', *Economic Review*, 32, 1979.

Pearton, M. *Oil and the Romanian State*, Oxford: Oxford University Press, 1971.

Political and Economic Planning *Economic Development in South-East Europe*, London: PEP, 1945.

Polonsky, A. *The Little Dictators: The History of Eastern Europe since 1918*, London: Routledge & Kegan Paul, 1975.

Ranki, G. 'Problems of southern European economic development (1918–38)', in G. Arrighi (ed.) *Semiperipheral Development: the Politics of Southern Europe in the Twentieth Century*, Beverly Hills: Sage Publications, 1985.

Raupach, H. 'The impact of the great depression on Eastern Europe', in H. van der Wee (ed.) *The Great Depression Revisited. Essays on the Economics of the Thirties*, The Hague: Martinus Nijhoff, 1972.

Ritschl, A. O. 'Nazi economic imperialism and the exploitation of the small: evidence from Germany's secret foreign exchange balances, 1938–40', *Economic History Review*, 54, 2001.

Rothschild, J. *East Central Europe Between the Two World Wars*, Seattle: University of Washington Press, 1974.

Rothschild, K. W. *Austria's Economic Development Between the Two Wars*, London: Frederick Muller, 1947.

Royal Institute of International Affairs *The Balkan States: A Review of the Economic and Financial Developments of Albania, Bulgaria, Greece, Roumania and Yugoslavia since 1919*, London: Oxford University Press, 1936.

— *The Baltic States*, London: Oxford University Press, 1938.

— *South-Eastern Europe: A Political and Economic Survey*, London: Oxford University Press, 1939.

Seton-Watson, H. *Eastern Europe Between the Wars 1918–1941*, Cambridge: Cambridge University Press, 1945.

Stoakes, G. *Hitler and the Quest for World Dominion,* Leamington Spa: Berg Publishers, 1986.

van Roon, G. *Small States in Years of Depression: the Oslo Alliance, 1930–1940*, Assen: Van Gorcum, 1989.

von Rauch, G. *The Baltic States: The Years of Independence 1917–1940*, London: G. Hurst and Company, 1974.

Warriner, D. *Economics of Peasant Farming*, London: Oxford University Press, 1939.

Wessels, J. W. *Economic Policy and Microeconomic Performance in Inter-war Europe: the Case of Austria*, Wiesbaden: Franz Steiner, 2007.

Chapter 5 The battle for europe 1939–45

Beevor, A. *Stalingrad*, London: Penguin Books, 1999.

Bessel, R. *Nazism and War*, London: Weidenfeld and Nicolson, 2005.

Braun, H.-J. *The German Economy in the Twentieth Century*, London: Routledge, 1990.

Brown, A. J. *Applied Economics, Aspects of the World Economy in War and Peace*, London: Allen & Unwin, 1947.

Browning, C. R. *The Origins of the Final Solution: The Evolution of Nazi Jewish Policy September 1939-March 1942*, London: Arrow Books, 2005.

Bullock, A. *Hitler: A Study in Tyranny*, Harmondsworth: Penguin Books, 1962.

— *Hitler and Stalin: Parallel Lives*, London: Fontana Press, 1993.

Bunting, M. *The Model Occupation: the Channel Islands under German Rule, 1940–1945*, London: Harper Collins, 1995.

Burleigh, M. *The Third Reich: A New History*, London: Pan Books, 2001.

Child, C. J. 'The concept of the New Order', in A. Toynbee and V. M. Toynbee (eds) *Survey of International Affairs, 1939–1946*, London: Oxford University Press, 1954.

Dumett, R. 'Africa's strategic minerals during the second world war', *Journal of African History*, 261, 1985.

Edgerton, D. *Britain's War Machine: Weapons, Resources and Experts in the Second World War*, London: Allen Lane, 2011.

Einzig, P. 'Hitler's "New Order" in theory and practice', *Economic Journal*, 51, 1941.

Ericson, E. E. *Feeding the German Eagle: Soviet Economic Aid to Nazi Germany, 1933–1941*, Westport CT, 1999.

Evans, R. J. *The Third Reich at War: How the Nazi Led Germany from Conquest to Defeat*, London, Allen Lane/Penguin, 2008.

Ferguson, N. 'The Second World War as an economic disaster', in M. Oliver and D. H. Aldcroft (eds) *Economic Disasters of the Twentieth Century*, Cheltenham: Edward Elgar, 2007.

Freeman, M. *Atlas of Nazi Germany: A Political, Economic and Social Anatomy of the Third Reich*, London: Longman, 1995.

Frumkin, G. *Population Changes in Europe since 1929*, London: Allen & Unwin, 1951.

Giltner, P. *In the Friendliest Manner: German and Danish Economic Cooperation during the Nazi Occupation 1940–1945*, New York: Peter Lang, 1998.

Harrison, M. 'Resource mobilisation for World War II: the U.S.A., U.K., U.S.S.R., and Germany, 1938–45', *Economic History Review*, 41, 1988.

— *The Economics of World War II: Six Great Powers in International Comparison*, Cambridge: Cambridge University Press, 1998.

Harvey, P. 'Finance', in A. Toynbee and V. M. Toynbee (eds) *Survey of International Affairs, 1939–1946*, London: Oxford University Press, 1954.

— 'The planning of the New Order in Europe', in A. Toynbee and V. M. Toynbee (eds) *Survey of International Affairs, 1939–1946*, London: Oxford University Press, 1954.

Hauner, M. 'Did Hitler want world dominion?' *Journal of Contemporary History*, 13, 1978.

Hillgruber, A. 'England's place in Hitler's plans for world dominion', *Journal of Contemporary History*, 9, 1974.

Hillman, H. C. 'Comparative strength of the great powers', in A. Toynbee and F. T. Ashton-Gwatkin (eds) *Survey of the International Affairs 1939–1946: the World in March 1939*, London: Oxford University Press, 1952.

Höhne, H. *The Order of the Death's Head: The Story of Hitler's SS*, London: Secker & Warburg, 1969.

Homze, E. L. *Foreign Labor in Nazi Germany*, Princeton: Princeton University Press, 1967.

Jensen, W. G. 'The importance of energy in the first and second world wars', *Historical Journal*, 11, 1968.

Kaldor, N. 'The German war economy', *The Manchester School*, 14, 1946.

Kamenetsky, I. *Secret Nazi Plans for Eastern Europe*, New Haven, CT: College and University Press, 1961.

Kaser, M. C. and Radice, E. A. (eds) *The Economic History of Eastern Europe 1919–1975*, Vol. II *Interwar Policy, the War and Reconstruction*, Oxford: Oxford University Press, 1986.

Kemp, A. *The Maginot Line: Myth and Reality*, London: Frederick Warne, 1981.

Kershaw, I. *Hitler 1936–45: Nemesis*, London: Allen Lane/The Penguin Press, 2000.

Klein, B. H. *Germany's Economic Preparations for War*, Cambridge, MA: Harvard University Press, 1959.

Kulischer, E. M. *Europe on the Move: War and Population Changes, 1917–47*, New York: Columbia University Press, 1948.

Marwick, A. *War and Social Change in the Twentieth Century*, London: Macmillan, 1974.

Mason, T. *Nazism, Fascism and the Working Class*, Cambridge: Cambridge University Press, 1995.

Mazower, M. 'Hitler's New Order', *Diplomacy and Statecraft*, 7, 1996.

— *Dark Continent: Europe's Twentieth Century*, London: Penguin, 1999.

— *Hitler's Empire: Nazi Rule in Occupied Europe*, London: Penguin Books, 2009.

— *The German Economy at War*, London: Athlone Press, 1965.

— *The New Order and the French Economy*, London: Oxford University Press, 1970.

Milward, A. S. *The Fascist Economy in Norway*, London: Oxford University Press, 1972.

— *War, Economy and Society, 1939–1945*, Berkeley: University of California Press, 1979.

Overy, R. J. 'Hitler's War and the German economy: a reinterpretation,' *Economic History Review*, 35, 1982.

— *Goering: the 'Iron Man'*, London: Routledge & Kegan Paul, 1984.

— *The Road to War*, London: Routledge & Kegan Paul, 1989.

— *War and the Economy in the Third Reich*, Oxford: Oxford University Press, 1994.

— *Why the Allies Won*, London: Jonathan Cape, 1995.

— *The Penguin Historical Atlas of the Third Reich*, London: 1996.

— 'The Nazi economy: was it geared to war?' *Modern History Review*, September 1998.

— *The Dictators: Hitler's Germany and Stalin's Russia*, London: Allen Lane, 2004.

Rich, N. *Hitler's War Aims: Ideology, the Nazi State, and the Course of Expansion*, London: André Deutsch, 1973.

— *Hitler's War Aims: The Establishment of the New Order*, London: André Deutsch, 1974.

— *Hitler and Churchill: Secrets of Leadership*, London: Weidenfeld & Nicolson, 2003.

Roberts, A. *The Storm of War*, London: Penguin Books, 2010.

Rothschild, J. *Return to Diversity: A Political History of East Central Europe Since World War II*, Oxford: Oxford University Press, 1989.

Royal Institute of International Affairs *Occupied Europe: German Exploitation and its*

Postwar Consequences, London: RIIA, 1944.

Snyder, T. *Bloodlands: Europe between Hitler and Stalin*, London: Bodley Head, 2010.

Speer, A. *Inside the Third Reich*, London: Sphere Books, 1971.

Toland, J. *Adolf Hitler*, Hertfordshire: Wordsworth Editions Limited, 1997.

Toynbee, A. and Toynbee, V. M. (eds) *Hitler's Europe: Survey of International Affairs 1939–1946*, London: Oxford University Press, 1954.

Tooze, A. 'Hitler's gamble', *History Today*, 56, 2006.

— *Wages of Destruction. The Making and Breaking of the Nazi Economy*, Penguin/Allen Lane, 2006.

Trevor-Roper, H. R. *The Last Days of Hitler*, London: Pan Books, 1952.

Weinberg, G. L. *Germany, Hitler and World War II*, Cambridge: Cambridge University Press, 1995.

Wright, G. *The Ordeal of Total War 1939–1945*, New York: Harper & Row, 1968.

Zagoreff, S. D., Vegh, J. and Bilimovich, A. D. *The Agricultural Economy of the Danubian Countries 1935–45*, Stanford, CA: Stanford University Press, 1955.

Chapter 6 Europe's reconstruction

Barnett, C. *The Audit of War and the Illusion and Reality of Britain as a Great Nation*, London: Macmillan, 1986.

Birchard, R. E. 'Europe's critical food situation', *Economic Geography*, 24, 1948.

Caincross, A. K. *The Price of War: British Policy on German Reparations 1941–1949*, Oxford: Blackwell, 1986.

Eichengreen, B. (ed.) *Europe's Postwar Recovery*, Cambridge: Cambridge University Press, 1995.

Gillingham, J. *Coal, Steel and the Rebirth of Europe, 1945–1955*, Cambridge: Cambridge University Press, 1991.

Harper, I. *America and the Reconstruction of Italy, 1943–1948*, Cambridge: Cambridge University Press, 1986.

Hogan, M. J. *The Marshall Plan: America, Britain and the Reconstruction of Western Europe, 1947–1952*, Cambridge: Cambridge University Press, 1987.

Killick, J. *The United States and European Reconstruction 1945–1960*, Edinburgh: Keele University Press, 1997.

Kynaston, D. *Austerity in Britain 1945–51*, London: Bloomsbury, 2008.

Lowe, K. *Savage Continent: Europe in the Aftermath of World War II*, London: Viking, 2012.

Lynch, F. M. B. 'Resolving the paradox of the Monnet Plan; national and international planning in French reconstruction', *Economic History Review*, 37, 1984.

Makinen, G. A. 'The Greek hyperinflation and stabilization of 1943–46', *Journal of Economic History*, 46, 1986.

Mayer, H. C. *German Recovery and the Marshall Plan, 1948–1952*, Bonn: Edition Atlantic Forum, 1969.

Meimberg, R. *The Economic Development in West Berlin and in the Soviet Union*, Berlin: Berliner Zentralbank, 1951.

Mendershausen, H. *Two Postwar Recoveries of the German Economy*, Amsterdam: North-Holland, 1955.

Milward, A. S. *Reconstruction of Western Europe, 1945–51*, London: Methuen, 1984.

Reichlin, L. 'The Marshall Plan reconsidered', in B. Eichengreen (ed.) *Europe's Postwar Recovery*, Cambridge: Cambridge University Press, 1995.

Roskamp, K. W. *Capital Formation in West Germany*, Detroit, MI: Wayne State University Press, 1965.

Rothschild, J. *Return to Diversity: A Political History of East Central Europe Since World War II*, Oxford: Oxford University Press, 1989.

United Nations (Department of Economic Affairs) *Economic Report: Salient Features of the World Economic Situation 1945–47*, New York, January 1948.

— *Economic Surveys of Europe in 1948, 1949, 1950, 1951*, Geneva: United Nations, 1949, 1950, 1951, 1952.

United Nations (Economic Commission for Europe), *Economic Survey of Europe Since the War: A Reappraisal of Problems and Prospects*, Geneva: United Nations, 1953.

Wallich, H. C. *Mainsprings of the German Revival*, New Haven, CT: Yale University Press, 1955.

Chapter 7 The golden age of post-war economic growth

Abert, J. G. *Economic Policy and Planning in the Netherlands, 1950–1965*, New Haven, CT: Yale University Press, 1969.

Aerts, E. and Milward, A. S. (eds) *Economic Planning in the Postwar Period*, Leuven: Leuven University Press, 1990.

Alford, B. *British Economic Performance, 1945–75*, London: Macmillan, 1988.

Allen, K. and Stevenson, A. *An Introduction to the Italian Economy*, London: Martin Robertson, 1974.

Apel, E. *European Monetary Integration: 1958–2002*, London: Routledge, 1998.

Armstrong, P., Glyn, A. and Harrison, J. *Captialism Since 1945*, Oxford: Blackwell, 1991.

Balassa, B. (ed.) *European Economic Integration*, Amsterdam: North-Holland, 1975.

— 'Export composition and export performance in the industrial countries 1953–71', *Review of Economics and Statistics*, 61, 1979.

Barnouin, B. *The European Labour Movement and European Integration*, London: Pinter, 1986.

Bjerve, P. J. 'Trends in quantitative economic planning in Norway', *Economics of Planning*, 8, 1968.

Boltho, A. (ed.) *The European Economy: Growth and Crisis*, Oxford: Oxford University Press, 1982.

Bordo, M. and Eichengreen, B. (eds) *A Retrospective on the Bretton Woods System*, Chicago, IL: Chicago University Press, 1993.

Bremer, J. and Bradford, M. R. 'Incomes and labour market policies in Sweden, 1945–70', *IMF Staff Papers*, 31, 1974.

Bronfenbrenner, M. (ed.) *Is the Business Cycle Obsolete?* Chichester: Wiley, 1969.

Carré, J. J., Dubois, P. and Malinvaud, E. *French Economic Growth*, London: Oxford University Press, 1975.

Clout, H. D. (ed.) *Regional Development in Western Europe*, third edition, London: D. Fulton Publishers, 1989.

Cohen, C. D. *British Economic Policy, 1960–1969*, London: Butterworth, 1971.

Cohen, S. S. *Modern Capitalist Planning. The French Model*, London: Weidenfeld & Nicolson, 1969.

Crafts, N. and Toniolo, G. (eds) *Economic Growth in Europe since 1945*, Cambridge: Cambridge University Press, 1996.

Cripps, T. F. and Tarling, R. J. *Growth in Advanced Capitalist Economies, 1950–70*,

Cambridge: Cambridge University Press, 1973.

Denison, E. F. *Why Growth Rates Differ*, Washington, DC: Brookings Institution, 1967.

Denton, G. R., Forsyth, M. and Maclennan, M. *Economic Planning and Policies in Britain, France and Germany*, London: Allen & Unwin, 1968.

Dow, J. C. R. *The Management of the British Economy, 1945–1960*, Cambridge: Cambridge University Press, 1964.

Dowrick, S. and Nguyen, D. T. 'OECD comparative economic growth 1950–85: catch-up and convergence', *American Economic Review*, 79, 1989.

Dumke, R. H. 'Reassessing the Wirtschaftswunder: reconstruction and postwar growth in an international context', *Oxford Bulletin of Economics and Statistics*, 52, 1990.

Dyker, D. (ed.) *The National Economies of Europe*, London: Longman, 1992.

Eichengreen, B. *Reconstructing Europe's Trade and Payments*, Manchester: Manchester University Press, 1993.

Emery, R. F. 'The relation of exports and economic growth', *Kyklos*, 20, 1967.

Estrin, S. and Holmes, P. *French Planning in Theory and Practice*, London: Allen & Unwin, 1983.

Foley, B. (ed.) *European Economies Since the Second World War*, London: Macmillan, 1998.

Giersch, H., Paqué, K.-H. and Schmieding, H. *The Fading Miracle: Four Decades of Market Economy in Germany*, Cambridge: Cambridge University Press, 1992.

Graham, A. and Seldon, A. (eds) *Government and Economics in the Postwar World*, London: Routledge, 1990.

Griffiths, R. T. 'Macroeconomic planning in the Netherlands 1945–58', in E. Aerts and A. S. Milward (eds) *Economic Planning in the Postwar Period*, Leuven: Leuven University Press, 1990.

Hallett, G. *The Social Economy of West Germany*, London: Macmillan, 1973.

Hansen, B. *Fiscal Policy in Seven Countries, 1955–1965*, Paris: OECD, 1969.

Henig, S. *The Uniting of Europe: From Discord to Concord*, London: Routledge, 1997.

Hennessey, J., Lutz, V. and Scimone, G. *Economic Miracles: Studies in the Resurgence of the French, German and Italian Economies since the Second World War*, London: Andre Deutsch, 1964.

Hough, J. R. 'French economic policy', *National Westminster Bank Quarterly Review*, May 1976.

James, H. *International Monetary Cooperation Since Bretton Woods*, Oxford: Oxford University Press, 1996.

Jones, H. G. *Planning and Productivity in Sweden*, London: Croom Helm, 1977.

Keith, E. G. (ed.) *Foreign Tax Policies and Economic Growth*, New York: Columbia University Press, 1966.

Kiker, B. F. and Vasconcelles, A. S. 'The performance of the French economy, 1949–64', *Economics of Planning*, 8, 1968.

Kindleberger, C. P. *Europe's Postwar Growth: The Role of Labour Supply*, Cambridge, MA: Harvard University Press, 1967.

Krenzel, R. 'Some reasons for the rapid economic growth of the German Federal Republic', *Banca Nazionale del Lavoro Quarterly Review*, 64, 1963.

Landes, D. *The Wealth and Poverty of Nations: Why Some are Rich and Some are Poor*, London: Little Brown and Company, 1998.

Licari, J. A. and Gilbert, M. 'Is there a postwar growth cycle?', *Kyklos*, 27, 1974.

Lieberman, S. *The Growth of European Mixed Economies, 1945–1970: A Concise Study of the Evolution of Six Countries*, Cambridge, MA: Schenkman, 1977.

— *Growth and Crisis in the Spanish Economy 1940–93*, London: Routledge, 1995.

Lindbeck, A. *Swedish Economic Policy*, London: Macmillan, 1975.

Lubitz, R. 'Export-led growth in industrial economies', *Kyklos*, 27, 1973.

Lundberg, E. *Instability and Economic Growth*, New Haven, CT: Yale University Press, 1968.

Lutz, V. *Italy: A Study in Economic Development*, London: Oxford University Press, 1962.

— 'The postwar business cycle in Western Europe and the role of government policy', *Banca Nazionale del Lavoro Quarterly Review*, 13, 1960.

— *Economic Growth in the West*, London: Allen & Unwin, 1964.

Maddison, A. 'Explaining economic growth', *Banca Nazionale del Lavoro Quarterly Review*, 25, 1972.

— *The World Economy in the Twentieth Century*, Paris: OECD, 1989.

Marglin, S. A. and Schor, J. B. (eds) *The Golden Age of Capitalism: Reinterpreting the Postwar Experience*, Oxford: Clarendon Press, 1990.

Maynard, G. and van Ryckeghem, W. A. *A World of Inflation*, London: Batsford, 1976.

Michaely, M. *The Responsiveness of Demand Policies to Balance of Payments: Postwar Patterns*, New York: National Bureau of Economic Research, 1971.

Middleton, R. *The British Economy Since 1945: Engaging with the Debate*, Basingstoke: Macmillan, 2000.

OECD *The Growth of Output 1960–1980*, Paris: OECD, 1970.

Oulès, F. *Economic Planning and Democracy*, Harmondsworth: Penguin, 1966.

Podbielski, G. *Italy: Development and Crisis in the Postwar Economy*, London: Oxford University Press, 1974.

— *The Wasting of the British Economy: British Economic Policy 1945 to the Present*, London: Croom Helm, 1982.

Pollard, S. *The International Economy Since 1945*, London: Routledge, 1997.

Postan, M. M. *An Economic History of Western Europe, 1945–1964*, London: Methuen, 1967.

Rostow, W. 'The world economy since 1945', *Economic History Review*, 33, 1985.

Sandford, C. T., Bradbury, M. S. and Associates, *Economic Policy*, London: Macmillan, 1970.

Scammell, W. *The International Economy since 1945*, London: Macmillan, 1980.

Sheahan, J. *Promotion and Control of Industry in Postwar France*, Cambridge, MA: Harvard University Press, 1963.

— *Modern Capitalism: The Changing Balance of Public and Private Power*, London: Oxford University Press, 1965.

Shonfield, A. 'Stabilisation policies in the West: from demand to supply management', *Journal of Political Economy*, 75, 1967.

Sutcliffe, A. *An Economic and Social History of Western Europe Since 1945*, London: Longman, 1996.

Temin, P. 'The golden age of European growth: a review essay', *European Review of Economic History*, 1, 1997.

— 'The golden age of European economic growth reconsidered', *European Review of Economic History*, 4, 2002.

Tew, J. H. B. *The Evolution of the International Monetary System, 1945–88*, fourth edition, London: Hutchinson Education, 1988.

Toniolo, G. 'Europe's golden age, 1950–73: speculation from a long-run perspective', *Economic History Review*, 51, 1998.

United Nations (Economic Commission for Europe), *Economic Survey of Europe in 1961*,

Part 2, *Some Factors in Economic Growth in Europe During the 1950s*, Geneva: United Nations, 1964.

— *Economic Survey of Europe in 1971*, Part 1, *The European Economy from the 1950s to the 1970s*, New York: United Nations, 1972.

Van Ark, B. and Crafts, N. (eds) *Quantitative Aspects of Postwar European Economic Growth*, Cambridge: Cambridge University Press, 1996.

Van der Wee, H. *Prosperity and Upheaval in the World Economy 1945–1980*, London: Penguin, 1986.

Von Tunzelmann, N. 'The main trends of European economic history since the second world war', in D. Dyker (ed.) *The National Economies of Europe*, London: Longman, 1992.

Vonyó, T. 'Postwar reconstruction and the golden age of economic growth', *European Review of Economic History*, 12, 2008.

Whiting, A. 'An international comparison of the instability of economic growth', *The Three Banks Review*, March 1976.

Zweig, K. *Germany Through Inflation and Recession: An Object Lesson in Economic Management, 1973–1976*, London: Centre for Policy Studies, 1976.

Chapter 8 The socialist economies of Eastern Europe, 1950–70

Aldcroft, D. H. and Morewood, S. *Economic Change in Eastern Europe since 1918*, Aldershot: Edward Elgar, 1995.

Alton, T. P. 'Economic structure and growth in Eastern Europe', in Joint Committee of US Congress, *Economic Developments in Countries of Eastern Europe*, Washington, DC: US Government Printing Office, 1970.

Balassa, B. and Bertrand, T. J. 'Growth performance of eastern European economies and comparable western European countries', *American Economic Review*, May, 1970.

Berend, I. T. *Central and Eastern Europe 1944–1993: From the Periphery to the Periphery*, Cambridge: Cambridge University Press, 1996.

Bideleux, R. and Jefferies, I. *A History of Eastern Europe: Crisis and Change*, London: Routledge, 1998.

Ehrlich, E. 'Economic growth in Eastern Central Europe after World War II', in A. Szirmai, B. van Ark and D. Pilot (eds) *Explaining Economic Growth*, Amsterdam: North Holland, 1993.

Ernst, M. 'Postwar economic growth in eastern Europe (a comparison with western Europe)', in *New Directions in the Soviet Economy*, Part IV, *The World Outside*, Washington, DC: US Government Printing Office, 1966.

Goldman, J. 'Fluctuations and trend in the rate of economic growth in some socialist countries', *Economics of Planning*, 8, 1968.

Jeffries, I. (ed.) *Industrial Reform in Socialist Economies: From Restructuring to Revolution*, Aldershot: Edward Elgar, 1992.

Johnson, P. M. *Redesigning the Communist Economy: The Politics of Economic Reform in Eastern Europe*, Berkeley: University of California Press, 1989.

Kaser, M. C. (ed.) *The Economic History of Eastern Europe 1919–1975*, Vol. III, *Institutional Change within a Planned Economy*, Oxford: Oxford University Press, 1986.

Lavigne, M. *The Socialist Economies of the Soviet Union and Europe*, trans. T. G. Waywell,

London: Martin Robertson, 1974.

Lewis, P. G. *Central Europe since 1945*, London: Longman, 1994.

Litván, G. (ed.) *The Hungarian Revolution of 1956: Reform, Revolt and Repression 1953–1963*, London: Longman, 1996.

Myant, M. *The Czechoslovak Economy, 1948–88*, Cambridge: Cambridge University Press, 1989.

Nove, A. *An Economic History of the USSR*, Harmondsworth: Penguin, 1972.

Rothschild, J. *Return to Diversity: A Political History of East Central Europe since World War II*, Oxford: Oxford University Press, 1989.

Schenk, C. R. *The Decline of Sterling: Managing the Retreat of an International Currency, 1945–1992*, Cambridge: Cambridge University Press, 2010.

Smith, A. H. *The Planned Economies of Eastern Europe*, London: Macmillan, 1983.

Spulber, N. *The State and Economic Development in Eastern Europe*, New York: Random House, 1966.

Staller, G. J. 'Fluctuations in economic activity: planned and free-market economies, 1950–60', *American Economic Review*, 54, 1964.

Swain, G. and Swain, N. *Eastern Europe since 1945*, Basingstoke: Macmillan, 1993.

Swain, N. J. 'The Visegrad countries of Eastern Europe', in B. J. Foley (ed.) *European Economies Since the Second World War*, London: Macmillan, 1998.

Tampke, J. *The People's Republics of Eastern Europe*, London: Croom Helm, 1983.

United Nations (Economic Commission for Europe), *Economic Survey of Europe in 1961*, Part 2, *Some Factors in Economic Growth in Europe During the 1950s*, Geneva: United Nations, 1964.

—— *Economic Survey of Europe in 1971*, Part 1, *The European Economy from the 1950s to the 1970s*, New York: United Nations, 1972.

Vonyó, T. 'Socialist industrialization or post-war reconstruction? Understanding Hungarian economic growth, 1949–67', *Journal of European Economic History*, 39, 2010.

Wilczynski, J. *Socialist Economic Development and Reforms*, London: Macmillan, 1972.

—— *Industrial Progress in Poland, Czechoslovakia and East Germany 1937–1962*, London: Oxford University Press, 1964.

Zaubermann, A. 'Russia and Eastern Europe, 1920–70', in C. M. Cipolla (ed.) *The Fontana Economic History of Europe*, Vol. 6, *Contemporary Economies*, Part 2, London: Collins/Fontana, 1976.

Chapter 9 Western capitalism in the 1970s

Argy, V. 'Monetary stabilisation and the stabilisation of output in selected industrial countries', *Banca Nazionale del Lavoro Quarterly Review*, 129, 1979.

Bacon, R. and Eltis, W. *Britain's Economic Problem: Too Few Producers*, London: Macmillan, 1976.

Bilson, J. F. O. 'The "vicious circle" hypothesis', *IMF Staff Papers*, 26, 1979.

Capie, F. and Collins, M. 'The developed world in recession: an historical comparison', *The Banker*, 127, 1977.

Castles, F. and Dowrick, S. 'The impact of government spending levels on medium-term economic growth in the OECD, 1960–85', *Journal of Theoretical Politics*, 2, 1990.

Cobham, D. 'The politics of the economics of inflation', *Lloyds Bank Review*, 128, 1978.

Corkill, D. *The Development of the Portuguese Economy: A Case of Europeanization*, London: Routledge, 1999.

Cornwall, J. *Modern Capitalism*, Oxford: Martin Robertson, 1977.

Cuthbertson, K. *Macroeconomic Policy: The New Cambridge, Keynesian and Monetarist Controversies*, London: Macmillan, 1979.

Eckstein, O. *The Great Recession*, Amsterdam: North-Holland, 1978.

Eltis, W. 'The failure of Keynesian conventional wisdom', *Lloyds Bank Review*, 122, 1976.

Giarini, O. and Loubergé, H. *The Diminishing Returns of Technology: An Essay on the Crisis in Economic Growth*, London: Pergamon, 1978.

Haberler, G. *Economic Growth and Stability*, Los Angeles, CA: Nash, 1974.

Hansen, A. H. *Full Recovery or Stagnation ?*, London: A & C. Black, 1938.

— *Business Cycles and National Income*, New York: Norton, 1951.

Heller, H. R. 'International reserves and world-wide inflation', *IMF Staff Papers*, 23, 1976.

Hill, T. P. *Profits and Rates of Return*, Paris: OECD, 1979.

Jones, D. 'Output, employment and labour productivity in Europe since 1955', *National Institute Economic Review*, August, 1976.

Katz, C. J., Mahler, V. A. and Franz, M. G. 'The impact of taxes on growth and distribution in developed capitalist economies: a cross national study', *American Political Science Review*, 77, 1983.

Klein, P. A. *Business Cycles in the Postwar World*, Washington, DC: American Enterprise Institute for Public Policy Research, 1976.

Knox, F. *Governments and Growth*, London: Saxon House, 1976.

— *Labour Supply in Economic Development*, London: Saxon House, 1979.

Lieberman, S. *The Contemporary Spanish Economy: A Historical Perspective*, London: Allen & Unwin, 1982.

— 'Phases of capitalist development', *Banca Nazionale del Lavoro Quarterly Review*, 121, 1977.

Maddison, A. 'Long run dynamics of productivity growth', *Banca Nazionale del Lavoro Quarterly Review*, 128, 1979.

Mandel, E. *The Second Slump: A Marxist Analysis of Recession in the Seventies*, London: New Left Books, 1978.

McClam, W. D. 'Targets and techniques of monetary policy in western Europe', *Banca Nazionale del Lavoro Quarterly Review*, 124, 1978.

Meiselman, D. I. and Laffer, A. B. (eds) *The Phenomenon of Worldwide Inflation*, Washington, DC: American Enterprise Institute for Public Policy Research, 1975.

Mensch, G. *Stalemate in Technology*, Cambridge, MA: Ballinger, 1979.

— *Towards Full Employment and Price Stability*, Paris: OECD, 1977.

— *Public Expenditure Trends*, Paris: OECD, 1978.

OECD, *Facing the Future*, Paris: OECD, 1979.

— *Monetary Targets and Inflation Control*, Paris: OECD, 1979.

— *The Case for Positive Adjustment Policies*, Paris: OECD, 1979.

Oppenheimer, P. M. and Posner, M. V. 'World economic expansion amidst monetary turbulence', *Midland Bank Review*, Spring, 1979.

Paldam, M. 'Towards the wage-earner state: a comparative study of wage shares 1946–75', *International Journal of Social Economics*, 6, 1979.

Parkin, M. and Zis, G. (eds) *Inflation in the World Economy*, Manchester: Manchester University Press, 1976.

Peacock, A. T. and Shaw, G. K. 'Is fiscal policy dead?', *Banca Nazionale del Lavoro Quarterly Review*, 125, 1978.

Perkins, J. O. N. *The Macroeconomic Mix to Stop Inflation*, London: Macmillan, 1980.

— *The World Economy: History and Prospect*, London: Macmillan, 1978.

Rostow, W. W. *Getting from Here to There*, London: Macmillan, 1979.

Schumpeter, J. A. *Business Cycles*, 2 vols. New York: McGraw-Hill, 1939.

Shadow European Economic Policy Committee, 'Europe enters the eighties', *Banca Nazionale del Lavoro Quarterly Review*, 129, 1979.

Thirlwall, A. P. 'The balance of payments constraint as an explanation of international growth rate differences', *Banca Nazionale del Lavoro Quarterly Review*, 128, 1979.

Thornton, J. S. 'The wage/tax spiral in the UK', *The Business Economist*, 11, 1979.

Vaciago, G. 'Fiscal versus monetary rules', *Banca Nazionale del Lavoro Quarterly Review*, 124, 1978.

Worswick, G. D. N. 'The end of demand management', *Lloyds Bank Review*, 123, 1977.

Chapter 10 Western Europe in the 1980s: the search for stability

Abramovitz, M. 'Catching up, forging ahead, and falling behind', *Journal of Economic History*, 46, 1986.

— *Thinking About Growth*, Cambridge: Cambridge University Press, 1989.

Adams, W. J. *Restructuring the French Economy: Government and the Rise of Market Competition Since the War*, Washington, DC: Brookings Institution, 1989.

Atkinson, P. and Chouraqui, J. C. 'The origins of high real interest rates', *OECD Economic Studies*, 5, 1985.

Baker, L., Brittain, A. and Major, R. 'Macroeconomic policy in France and Britain', *National Institute Economic Review*, 110, 1984.

Barbone, L. and Poret, P. 'Structural conditions and macroeconomic responses to shocks: a sensitivity analysis for four European countries', *OECD Economic Studies*, 12, 1989.

Bean, C. R. 'European unemployment: a survey', *Journal of Economic Literature*, 32, 1994.

Boltho, A. 'Economic policy and performance in Europe since the second oil shock', in M. Emerson (ed.) *Europe's Stagflation*, Oxford: Oxford University Press, 1984.

Brett, E. A. *The World Economy Since the War: The Politics of Uneven Development*, London: Macmillan, 1985.

Britton, A., Eastwood, F. and Major, R. 'Macroeconomic policy in Britain and Italy', *National Institute Economic Review*, 118, 1986.

Chan-Lee, J. H. and Sutch, H. 'Profits and rates of return', *OECD Economic Studies*, 5, 1985.

Chan-Lee, J. H., Coe, D. T. and Prynes, M. 'Macroeconomic changes and macroeconomic wage disinflation in the 1980s', *OECD Economic Studies*, 8, 1987.

Coe, D. T. 'Nominal wages, the NAIRU and wage flexibility', *OECD Economic Studies*, 5, 1985.

Coe, D. T. and Holtham, G. 'Output responsiveness and inflation: an aggregate study', *OECD Economic Studies*, 1, 1985.

Coe, D. T., Durand, M. and Stiehler, U. 'The disinflation of the 1980s', *OECD Economic Studies*, 11, 1988.

Commission of the European Communities *European Economy* 42, 1989.

— *European Economy*, 46, 1990.

Corkill, D. R. *The Portuguese Economy since 1974*, Edinburgh: Edinburgh University Press, 1993.

Cornwall, J. *Modern Capitalism: the Growth and Transformation from the Golden Age to the Age of Decline*, Cheltenham: Edward Elgar, 2006.

Dean, A., Durand, M., Fallon, J. and Hoeller, P. 'Savings trends and behaviour in OECD countries', *OECD Economic Studies*, 14, 1990.

Duchene, F. and Shepherd, G. (eds) *Managing Industrial Change in Western Europe*, London: Pinter, 1987.

Elmeskov, J. and MacFarlan, M. 'Unemployment persistence', *OECD Economic Studies*, 21, 1993.

Emerson, M. (ed.) *Europe's Stagflation*, Oxford: Oxford University Press, 1984.

Englander, A. S. and Egabo, T. 'Adjustment under fixed exchange rates: application to the European Monetary Union', *OECD Economic Studies*, 20, 1993.

Englander, A. S. and Gurney, A. 'Medium-term determinants of OECD productivity', *OECD Economic Studies*, 22, 1994.

— 'OECD productivity growth: medium term trends', *OECD Economic Studies*, 22, 1994.

Englander, A. S. and Mittelstadt, A. 'Total factor productivity and structural aspects of the slowdown', *OECD Economic Studies*, 10, 1988.

Englander, A. S., Evenson, R. and Hanazaki, M. 'R & D, innovation and the total factor productivity slowdown', *OECD Economic Studies*, 11, 1988.

Fitoussi, J. and Phelps, E. S. *Slump in Europe*, Oxford: Blackwell, 1988.

Friedlander, R. and Sanders, J. 'The public economy and economic growth in western market economies', *American Sociological Review*, 50, 1985.

Gaffney, J. (ed.) *France and Modernisation*, Aldershot: Avebury, 1988.

Giono, C., Richardson, P., Roseveare, D. and van den Nord, P. 'Potential output, output gaps and structural budget balances', *OECD Economic Studies*, 24, 1995.

Graham, A. and Seldon, A. (eds) *Government and Economies in the Postwar World: Economic Policies and Comparative Performance 1945–85*, London: Routledge, 1990.

Haberler, G. 'The slowdown of the world economy and the problem of stagflation', in D. Lal and M. Wolf (eds) *Stagflation, Savings and the State*, New York: Oxford University Press, 1986.

Hoj, J., Kato, T. and Pilat, D. 'Deregulation and privatisation in the service sector', *OECD Economic Studies*, 25, 1995.

Katz, C. J., Mahler, V. A. and Franz, M. G. 'The impact of taxes on growth and distribution in developed capitalist economies: a cross national study', *American Political Science Review*, 77, 1983.

Lal, D. and Wolf, M. (eds) *Stagflation, Savings and the State*, New York: Oxford University Press, 1986.

Lawrence, R. Z. and Schultz, C. L. (eds) *Barriers to European Growth: A Transatlantic View*, Washington, DC: Brookings Institution, 1987.

Layard, R., Nickell, S. and Jackman, R. *Unemployment: Macroeconomic Performance and the Labour Market*, Oxford: Oxford University Press, 1991.

Lingberg, E. 'The rise and fall of the Swedish model', *Journal of Economic Literature*, 23, 1985.

Llewellyn, J. 'Resources, prices and macroeconomic policies: lessons from two oil price shocks', *OECD Economic Studies*, 1, 1983.

Lombard, M. 'A re-examination of the reasons for the failure of Keynesian expansionary policies in France 1981–83', *Cambridge Journal of Economics*, 19, 1995.

Maddison, A. 'Growth and slowdown in advanced capitalist economies: techniques of quantitative assessment', *Journal of Economic Literature*, 25, 1987.

— *The World Economy in the Twentieth Century*, Paris: OECD, 1989.

— *Dynamic Forces in Capitalist Development*, Oxford: Oxford University Press, 1991.

Marglin, S. and Schor, J. B. (eds) *The Golden Age of Capitalism: Reinterpreting the Postwar Experience*, Oxford: Clarendon Press, 1990.

Marris, S. 'Why Europe's recovery is lagging behind, with an unconventional view of what should be done about it', *Europe*, March–April, 1984.

McCormick, B. J. *The World Economy: Patterns of Growth and Change*, Oxford: Philip Allan, 1988.

— *Structural Adjustment and Economic Performance*, Paris: OECD, 1987.

OECD *Historical Statistics 1960–1990*, Paris: OECD, 1991.

Orr, A., Edey, M. and Kennedy, M. 'Real long-term interest rates: the evidence from pooled-time-series', *OECD Economic Studies*, 24, 1995.

Oxley, H. and Martin, J. P. 'Controlling spending and deficits: trends in the 1980s and prospects for the 1990s', *OECD Economic Studies*, 5, 1981.

Patat, J.-P. and Lutfalla, M. *A Monetary History of France in the Twentieth Century*, London: Macmillan, 1990.

Price, R. W. R. and Muller, P. 'Structural budget indicators and the interpretation of fiscal policy stance in OECD countries', *OECD Economic Studies*, 5, 1985.

Rowthorn, R. and Wells, J. *Deindustrialisation and Foreign Trade*, Cambridge: Cambridge University Press, 1987.

Sassoon, D. 'Italy', in A. Graham and A. Seldon (eds) *Government and Economies in the Postwar World: Economic Policies and Comparative Performance 1945–85*, London: Routledge, 1990.

Saunders, P. and Klau, F. 'The role of the public sector: causes and consequences of the growth of government', *OECD Economic Studies*, 4, 1985.

Schafer, J. R. 'What the U.S. current account deficit of the 1980s has meant for other OECD countries', *OECD Economic Studies*, 10, 1988.

Somers, F. (ed.) *European Economies: A Comparative Study*, London: Pitman, 1991.

Soskice, D. 'Wage determination: the changing role of institutions in advanced industrialised countries', *Oxford Review of Economic Policy*, 6, 1990.

Tsoukalis, L. *The New European Economy: The Politics and Economics of Integration*, Oxford: Oxford University Press, 1997.

— *World Economic Survey 1990*, New York: United Nations, 1990.

United Nations, *Economic Survey of Europe 1990–1991*, New York: United Nations, 1991.

Urwin, D. *Western Europe since the War*, London: Longman, 1989.

Chapter 11 Eastern Europe in transition, 1970–90

Aage, H. 'Economic problems and reforms: Andropov's 15 months', *Nordic Journal of Soviet and East European Studies (Sweden)*, 1 (2), 1984.

Aldcroft, D. H. and Morewood, S. *Economic Change in Eastern Europe since 1918*, Aldershot: Edward Elgar, 1995.

Almond, M. *The Rise and Fall of Nicolae and Elena Ceausescu*, London: Chapman and Hall, 1991.

Aslund, A. *Gorbachev's Struggle for Economic Reform*, London: Pinter, 1989.

Berend, I. *The Hungarian Economic Reforms 1953–1988*, Cambridge: Cambridge University Press, 1990.

Boeri, T. and Keese, M. 'Labour markets and the transition in central and eastern Europe', *OECD Economic Studies*, 18, 1992.

Bryson, P. J. and Melzer, M. *The End of the East German Economy*, London: Macmillan, 1991.

Carter, B. and Singleton, F. *The Economy of Yugoslavia*, London: Croom Helm, 1982.

Childs, D. *The GDR: Moscow's German Ally*, London: Allen & Unwin, 1983.

Clarke, R. A. (ed.) *Poland: The Economy in the 1980s*, London: Longman, 1990.

Commission of the European Communities, *European Economies Special Edition* No. 2, *The Path of Reform in Central and Eastern Europe*, Brussels: European Community, 1991.

Dawiska, K. *Eastern Europe, Gorbachev and Reform*, second edition, Cambridge: Cambridge University Press, 1990.

De Nevers, R. *The Soviet Union and Eastern Europe: The End of an Era*, London: Brasseys, 1990.

Derbyshire, I. *The Politics in the Soviet Union*, London: Chambers, 1987.

Dowson, A. H. *Planning in Eastern Europe*, London: Croom Helm, 1986.

Drewnowski, J. (ed.) *Crisis in the East European Economy*, London: Croom Helm, 1982.

Easterly, W. and Fischer, S. 'The Soviet economic decline', *World Bank Economic Review*, 9, 1995.

Federal Institute for Soviet and International Studies, *The Soviet Union, 1987–1989: Perestroika in Crisis?* London: Longman, 1990.

Gilberg, T. *Nationalism and Communism in Romania*, Oxford: Westview Press, 1990.

Gomulka, S. *Growth, Innovation and Reform in Eastern Europe*, Madison, WI: University of Wisconsin Press, 1986.

Goodman, M. I. *What Went Wrong With Perestroika?* New York: Norton, 1991.

Graziani, G. 'Dependency structures in Comecon', *Review of Radical Political Economy*, 13, 1981.

International Monetary Fund and others, *A Study of the Soviet Economy*, 3 vols., Paris: OECD, 1991.

Johnson, P. M. *Redesigning the Communist Economy*, New York: Boulder, 1981.

Kennedy, P. *The Rise and Fall of the Great Powers*, London: Unwin Hyman, 1988.

Korbonski, A. 'CMEA, economic integration and perestroika: 1949–89', *Studies in Comparative Communism*, 23, 1990.

Lane, D. *Soviet Society under Perestroika*, second edition, London: Routledge, 1992.

Mason, D. S. *Revolution and Transition in East-Central Europe*, Oxford: Westview Press, 1996.

McAuley, A. (ed.) *Soviet Federalism: Nationalism and Economic Decentralisation*, Leicester: Leicester University Press, 1991.

Myant, M. *The Czechoslovak Economy, 1948–88*, Cambridge: Cambridge University Press, 1989.

Narkiewicz, O. A. *Eastern Europe 1968–1984*, London: Croom Helm, 1986.

Nello, S. S. *The New Europe: Changing Economic Relations between East and West*, London: Harvester Wheatsheaf, 1991.

Nove, A., Hohmann, H. H. and Seidenstecher, G. *The East European Economies in the 1970s*, London: Butterworth, 1982.

Okey, R. *Crisis in Eastern Europe: Roots and Prospects*, London: Social Market Foundation, 1990.

Pockney, B. P. *Soviet Statistics since 1950*, Aldershot: Gower, 1991.

Schopflin, G. 'The end of communism in eastern Europe', *International Affairs*, 66, 1990.

Selbourne, D. *Death of the Dark Hero: Eastern Europe, 1987–90*, London: Cape, 1990.

Sleifer, J. *Planning Ahead and Falling Behind: the East German Economy in Comparison with West Germany, 1936–2002*, Berlin: Akademie Verlag, 2006.

Spulber, N. *Restructuring the Soviet Economy*, Ann Arbor, MI: University of Michigan Press, 1991.

Summerscale, P. *The East European Predicament*, Aldershot: Gower, 1982.
Sword, K. (ed.) *The Times Guide to Eastern Europe*, London: Times Books, 1990.
United Nations, *Economic Survey of Europe in 1981*, New York: United Nations, 1982.
— *Economic Survey of Europe in 1989–1990*, New York: United Nations, 1990.
— *Economic Survey of Europe in 1990–1991*, New York: United Nations, 1991.
Van Brabant, J. M. *Remaking Eastern Europe – On the Political Economy of Transition*, London: Kluwer, 1990.
Wadekin, K. E. (ed.) *Communist Agriculture: Farming in the Soviet Union and Eastern Europe*, London: Routledge, 1990.
Winiecki, J. *The Distorted World of Soviet-type Economies*, London: Routledge, 1988.
Zwass, A. *The Economies of Eastern Europe in a Time of Change*, London: Macmillan, 1984.

Chapter 12 Towards a united Europe, 1990–2000

Aldcroft, D. H. 'Why unemployment has remained so high in Europe', *Current Politics and Economics of Europe*, 3, 1993.
Aldcroft, D. H. and Morewood, S. *Economic Change in Eastern Europe since 1918*, Aldershot: Edward Elgar, 1995.
Andrews, J. 'The quiet French Revolution', in *The World in 2000*, London: The Economist Group, 1999.
Artis, M. J. 'The unemployment problem', *Oxford Review of Economic Policy*, 14, 1998.
Ball, R. J. and Albert, M. *Towards European Economic Recovery in the 1980s*, Brussels: European Parliament, 1983.
Bank of England, *Practical Issues Arising from the Euro*, December 1999.
Barnes, I. *The European Union and World Trade*, Hull: Hidcote Press, 1996.
BBC 2 Television 'Money Programme', feature on e-tailing, 9 April 2000.
Benoit, B. 'Land of laptops and lederhosen', *Financial Times*, 17 February, 17, 2000.
Bideleux, R. and Jeffries, I. *A History of Eastern Europe: Crisis and Change*, second edition, London: Routledge, 2007.
—*The Balkans: A Post-Communist History*, London: Routledge, 2007.
Boltho, A. and Toniolo, G. 'The assessment: the twentieth century – achievements, failures, lessons', *Oxford Review of Economic Policy*, 14, 1998.
Castle, S. 'Revival hopes are dashed by Milošević', *The Independent on Sunday*, 19 March 2000, 24.
Cecchini, P. *The European Challenge: 1992 – the Benefits of a Single Market*, Aldershot: Wildwood House, 1988.
Cottrell, R. 'Europe's worksheet', in *The World in 2000*, London: The Economist Group, 1999.
Danopoulos, C. P. and Ianeva, E. 'Poverty in the Balkans and the issue of reconstruction: Bulgaria and Yugoslavia compared', *Journal of Southern Europe and the Balkans*, 1, 1999.
Davidson, I. *Jobs and the Rhineland Model*, London: Federal Trust, 1997.
Delors Committee *Report on Economic and Monetary Union in the European Community*, Luxembourg: Office for Official Publications of the EC, 1988.
Dyker, D. (ed.) *The European Economy*, second edition, London: Longman, 1999.
The Economist 'The European Union decides it might one day talk Turkey', 18 December 1999, 35.

— 'What is Europe?', 12 February 2000, 13–14.

— 'Europe's new capitalism', 12 February 2000, 97–100.

Eichengreen, B. 'European monetary unification: a *tour d'horizon*', *Oxford Review of Economic Policy*, 14,1998.

European Commission, '*Agenda 2000*', Brussels: European Commission, 1997.

— *The Mediterranean Society: A Challenge for Islam, Judaism and Christianity*, London: Kogan Page, 1998.

— *Towards a More Global Economic Order*, London: Kogan Page, 1998.

— *Shaping Actors, and Shaping Factors in Russia's Future*, London: Kogan Page, 1998.

— *The European Union and World Trade*, Luxembourg: Office for Official Publications of the European Communities, 1999.

Feinstein, C. 'Structural change in the developed countries during the twentieth century', *Oxford Review of Economic Policy*, 14, 1998.

Fletcher, M. 'Prodi urges EU to back entry for 12 new states', *The Times*, 14 October 1999, 3.

Foley, B. J. 'France: A case of Eurosclerosis?', in B. J. Foley (ed.) *European Economies since the Second World War*, London: Macmillan, 1998.

George, V. and Taylor, P. *European Welfare Policy: Squaring the Circle*, London: Macmillan, 1996.

Gillespie, R. (ed.) *The Euro-Mediterranean Partnership: Political and Economic Perspectives*, London: Frank Cass, 1997.

Grimwade, N. 'Developments in the economies of the European Union', *Journal of Common Market Studies*, 37, 1999.

Jackman, R. 'Do reform and unemployment go hand in hand? The prospect for Eastern Europe', *CentrePiece*, 2, Summer, 1997.

Jobbins, D. 'Eye witness: blocked Danube endangers trade expansion', *The Times Higher Educational Supplement*, 14 May 1999, 11.

Jones, E., Frieden, J. and Torres, F. (eds) *Joining Europe's Monetary Club: The Challenges for Smaller Member States*, London: Macmillan, 1998.

Jovanovic, M. N. *International Economic Integration: Limits and Prospects*, second edition, London: Routledge, 1998.

Keegan, W. 'Swings and roundabouts for the euro', *The Observer*, Business Section, 4, December 1994.

Lampe, J. R. *Yugoslavia as History: Twice there was a Country*, second edition, Cambridge: Cambridge University Press, 2000.

Larres, K. (ed.) *Germany since Unification: The Domestic and External Consequences*, London: Macmillan, 1998.

Laurent, P.-H. and Marescueau, M. (eds) *The State of the European Union Vol. IV: Deepening and Widening*, Colorado: Lynne Rienner, 1998.

Leader article, 'Oil spill. The most important OPEC decision for at least a decade', *The Times*, 27 March 2000, 19.

Maitland, A. 'Throw the rule-book out of the window', *Financial Times*, 8 February 2000.

May, A. *Britain and Europe since 1945*, Harlow: Addison Wesley Longman, 1998.

Mayhew, A. *Recreating Europe: The European Union's Policy Towards Central and Eastern Europe*, Cambridge: Cambridge University Press, 1998.

McRae, H. 'The new-economy bicycle has some serious wobbles built in', *The Independent*, 7 April 2000, 21.

Monti, M. *The Single Market and Tomorrow's Europe*, London: Kogan Page, 1996.

Morewood, S. 'Europe at the crossroads 1974–2000', in D. H. Aldcroft and A. Sutcliffe (eds) *Europe in the International Economy 1500 to 2000*, Cheltenham: Edward Elgar, 1999.

Nicholl, W. and Schoenberg, R. (eds) *Europe beyond 2000: The Enlargement of the European Union towards the East*, London: Whurr, 1998.

Nickell, S. and Van Ours, J. 'Mirage or miracle? Labour market performance in Britain and the Netherlands', *CentrePiece*, 5, Spring 2000.

Norman, P. 'Joint push towards the new economy', *Financial Times*, 27 March 2000, 21.

— 'Brussels says EU to grow at fastest rate since 1989', *Financial Times*, 12 April 2000, 6.

OECD, *The OECD Jobs Study: Evidence and Explanation*, Paris: OECD, 1994.

— *Economic Outlook*, No. 66, November 1999.

— *Germany, France and the Integration of Europe: A Realistic Interpretation*, London: Cassell, 1998.

Paterson, T. 'Polish farmers declare war over EU membership', *Guardian*, 18 April 2000, 17.

PM Communications, 'Turkey: On the road to Europe', *Sunday Telegraph*, special supplement, 13 February 2000.

— 'Central and Eastern Europe. The telecoms revolution', *Sunday Telegraph*, special supplement, 12 March 2000.

Puga, D. 'Recipe for reform: regional policy for an enlarging European Union', *CentrePiece*, 2, Autumn 1997.

Redmond, J. and Rosenthal, G. G. (eds) *The Expanding European Union: Past, Present and Future*, London: Lynne Rienner, 1998.

Reece, D. 'Rise and rise of the budget airlines', *Sunday Telegraph*, 23 April 2000, B9.

Rhodes, C. (ed.) *The European Union in the World Community*, London: Lynne Rienner, 1998.

Robertson, B. A. *The Middle East and Europe: The Power of Deficit*, London: Routledge, 1998.

Smith, D. 'Euro showdown', *Sunday Times*, 5 December 1999, 1, 13.

— 'Can Britain ride the technology shock wave?', *Sunday Times*, 6 February 2000, 3, 4.

Smith, D. and Rhodes, T. 'Up up and away: But how long can the West's greatest boom last?', *Sunday Times*, 16 January 2000, 1:14.

Smith, K. E. *The Making of EU Foreign Policy: The Case of Eastern Europe*, London: Macmillan, 1998.

Strange, S. 'Who are EU? Ambiguities in the concept of competitiveness', *Journal of Common Market Studies*, 36, 1998.

Swain, N. J. 'The Visegrad countries of Eastern Europe', in B. J. Foley (ed.) *European Economies Since the Second World War*, London: Macmillan, 1998.

Tracy, M. *Agricultural Policy in the European Union and other Market Economies*, second edition, Brussels: Agricultural Policy Studies, 1997.

Wolf, M. 'Transition proves long and hard', *Financial Times*, Central and Eastern Europe Survey, II, 10 November 1999.

Wood, A. *North–South Trade, Employment and Inequality: Changing Fortunes in a Skills-driven World*, Oxford: Clarendon Press, 1994.

Young, A. R. 'The adaptation of European foreign economic policy: from Rome to Seattle', *Journal of Common Market Studies*, 38, 2000.

13 The new millennium

Aalto, P. (ed.) *Russia's Energy Policies. National, Interregional and Global Levels*, Cheltenham: Edward Elgar, 2012.

Arvanitopoulos, C. (ed.) *Turkey's Accession to the European Union: An Unusual Candidacy*, London: Springer, 2010.

Baldwin, R. and Wyplosz, C. *The Economics of European Integration*, third edition, London: McGraw-Hill Education, 2009.

Bootle, R. *The Trouble with Markets: Saving Capitalism from Itself*, new edition, London: Nicholas Brealey Publishing, 2011.

Bonner, W. and Wiggin, A. *The New Empire of Debt. The Rise and Fall of An Epic Financial Bubble*, second edition, New Jersey: John Wiley & Sons, 2011.

Brummer, A. *The Crunch: How Greed and Incompetence Sparked the Credit Crisis*, London: Random House Business Books, 2009.

Cable, V. *The Storm: The World Economic Crisis and What It Means*, London: Atlantic Books, 2009.

Cooper, G. *The Origins of Financial Crises: Central Banks, Credit Bubbles and the Efficient Market Fallacy*, London: Harriman House Publishing, 2010.

Dabrowski, M. and Rostowski, J. (eds) *The Eastern Enlargement of the European Union*, London: Springer, 2005.

Darling, A. *Back from the Brink: 1000 Days at Number 11*, London: Atlantic, 2011.

Das, S. *Extreme Money: The Masters of the Universe and the Cult of Risk*, London: FT Press, 2011.

Davis, H. *The Financial Crisis. Who is to Blame?* London: Polity, 2010.

Dejuan, O and Febrero, E. (eds) *The First Recession of the 21st Century: Competing Explanations,* Cheltenham: Edward Elgar, 2011.

Dumas, C. and Choyleva, D. *The American Phoenix: And why China and Europe will Struggle after the Coming Slump*, London: Profile Books, 2011.

Eichengreen, B. and Park, B. (eds) *The World Economy after the Global Crisis: A New Economic Order for the 21st Century*, New York: World Scientific Books, 2012.

Eichengreen, B. and Yung, Y. C. 'Out-of-step policies threaten global growth', *Current History*, December 2004.

Farrell, R. *Chinese Investment in the World Economy*, Cheltenham: Edward Elgar, 2012.

Gamze, A. and Carkolu, A. (eds), *Turkey and the EU: Accession and Reform*, London: Routledge, 2012.

Gerhands, J. and Hans, S. 'Why not Turkey? Attitudes towards Turkish membership in the European Union among citizens in 27 countries', *Journal of Common Market Studies*, 49, 2011.

Hutchins, C. *Putin*, London: Matador, 2012.

Hutton, W. *The Writing on the Wall: China and the West in the 21st Century*, London: Abacus, 2008.

Kandiyoti, R. *Pipelines: Flowing Oil and Crude Politics*, London: I.B.Tauris, 2012.

Kates, S. *The Global Financial Crisis: What Have We Learnt?* Cheltenham: Edward Elgar, 2011.

Krugman, P. *The Return of Depression Economics and the Crisis of 2008*, London: Allen Lane, 2008.

Lanchester, J. *Whoops! Why Everyone Owes Everyone and No One Can Pay*, London: Penguin, 2010.

Legrain, P. *Aftershock. Reshaping the World Economy after the Crisis*, London: Little, Brown, 2010.

Lewis, M. *Boomerang. The Meltdown Tour*, London: Allen Lane, 2011.

Libman, A. and Vinokurov, E. 'Regional integration and economic convergence in the post-

Soviet space: experience of a decade of growth', *Journal of Common Market Studies*, 50, 2012.

Lucas, E. *The New Cold War: Putin's Russia and the Threat to the West*, London: Palgrave Macmillan, 2008.

Lybeck, J.A. *A Global History of the Financial Crash of 2007–10*, Cambridge: Cambridge University Press, 2010.

Mason, P. *Meltdown: The End of the Age of Greed*, London: Verso, 2010.

— *Why It's Kicking Off Everywhere: The New Global Revolutions*, London: Verso, 2012.

Mourlon-Druol, E. A. *A Europe Made of Money. The Emergence of the European Monetary Union*, Cornell, Cornell University Press, 2012.

Noord, P. van de and Szekely, I. (eds) *Economic Crisis in Europe: Causes, Consequences and Responses*, London: Routledge, 2011.

Orban, A. *Power, Energy and the New Russian Imperialism*, Washington, D.C.: Praeger, 2008.

Peston, R. *Who Runs Britain? And Who's To Blame for the Economic Mess We're In*, London: Hodder, 2008.

Rattner, S. 'The secret of Germany's success', *Foreign Affairs*, 90, 2011.

Roxburgh, A. *The Strongman. Vladimir Putin and the Struggle for Russia*, London: I.B.Tauris, 2011.

Smith, K.C. *Russian Energy Politics in the Baltics, Poland and the Ukraine: A New Stealth Imperialism?* Washington, D.C.: Center for Strategic and International Studies, 2004.

Soros, G. *The Crash of 2008 and What It Means: The New Paradigm for Financial Markets*, New York: Public Affairs, 2009.

Spence, M. 'The impact of Globalization on income and employment', *Foreign Affairs*, 90, 2011.

Stuermer, M. *Putin and the Rise of Russia: The Country That Came in From the Cold*, London: Phoenix, 2009.

Turner, G. *The Credit Crunch: Housing Bubbles, Globalisation and the Worldwide Economic Crisis*, London: Pluto, 2008.

— *No Way to Run an Economy: Why the System Failed and How to Put it Right*, London: Pluto, 2009.

Yergin, D. *The Quest. Energy, Security, and the Remaking of the Modern World*, London: Allen Lane, 2011.

Yueh, L. *The Economy of China*, Cheltenham: Edward Elgar, 2012.

14 The euro-zone crisis

Baldwin, R., Gros, D. and Laeven, L. (eds) *Completing the Eurozone Rescue: What More Needs to be Done?* London: Centre for Economic Policy Research, 2010.

Beblavý, M., Cobham, D. and Ŏdor, L. (eds) *The Euro Area and the Financial Crisis*, Cambridge: Cambridge University Press, 2011.

Brown, G. *Beyond the Crash. Overcoming the First Crisis of Globalisation*, London: Simon & Schuster, 2010.

Crowson, N.J. *Britain in Europe*, London: Routledge, 2011.

Eichengreen, B. 'When currencies collapse', *Foreign Affairs*, 91, January/February 2012.

European Commission http://ec.europa.eu/.

Featherstone, K. 'The Greek sovereign debt crisis and EMU: A failing state in a skewed regime', *Journal of Common Market Studies*, 49, 2011.

Feldstein, M. 'The failure of the Euro', *Foreign Affairs*, 91, January/February 2012.

Grauwe, P.De, *Economics of Monetary Union*, eighth edition, Oxford: Oxford University Press, 2009.

Gros, D. 'The misdiagnosed debt crisis', *Current History*, March 2012.

Haberras, J. *The Crisis of the European Union*, Cambridge: Polity, 2012.

Hess, F.L. 'Why austerity won't work in Greece', *Current History*, March 2012.

Hopkin, J. 'Can Italy's Monti save the Euro?' *Current History*, March 2012.

International Monetary Fund www.img.org/.

Jones, E. 'Europe's threatened solidarity', *Current History*, March 2012.

Krugman, P. *End this Depression Now!* New York: W.W. Norton & Co., 2012.

Lapavitsas, C. *Crisis in the Eurozone*, London: Verso, 2012.

Lynn, M. *Bust. Greece, the Euro, and the Sovereign Debt Crisis*, London: Bloomsberg, 2011.

Manolopoulos, J. *Greece's 'Odious' Debt: The Looting of the Hellenic Republic by the Euro, the Political Elite and the Investment Community*, London: Anthem Press, 2011.

Marsh, D. *The Euro: The Battle for the New Global Currency*, new edition, New Haven: Yale University Press, 2011.

Organisation for Economic Co-operation and Development, www.oecd.org/.

Pryce, V. *Greekonomics: The Euro Crisis and Why Politicians Don't Get It*, London: Biteback Publishing, 2012.

— 'How to save the Euro', *New York Review of Books*, LIX, February 23 – March 7 2012a.

Soros, G. *Financial Turmoil in Europe and the United States*, New York: Public Affairs, 2012b.

Van den Noord, P. and Szekely, I. *Economic Crisis in Europe: Causes, Consequences and Responses*, London: Routledge, 2011.

Van Overtveldt, J. *The End of the Euro: The Uneasy Future of the European Union*, London: Agate Publishing, 2011.

Van Rie, T. and Mark, J. 'The European Union at work? The European Employment Strategy from crisis to crisis', *Journal of Common Market Studies*, 50, 2012.

Index

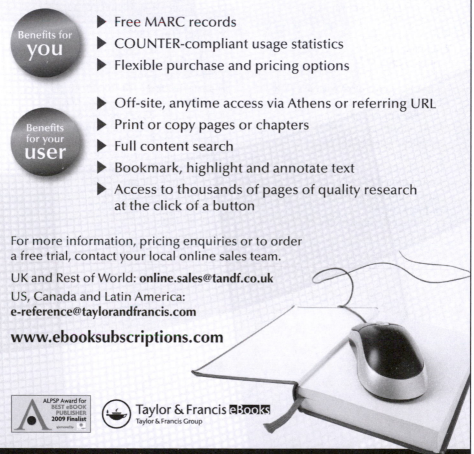